The Playbill® Broadway Yearbook

Second Annual Edition
2005–2006

Robert Viagas
Editor

Amy Asch
Assistant Editor

Kesler Thibert
Book Designer

Aubrey Reuben   Ben Strothmann
Photographers

David Gewirtzman
Production Assistant

Melissa Merlo
Editorial Assistant

PLAYBILL® BOOKS

The Playbill Broadway Yearbook: Second Annual Edition, June 1, 2005–May 31, 2006
Robert Viagas, Editor

ISBN-13: 978-1-5578-3718-9
ISBN-10: 1-55783-718-X
ISSN-1932-1945

Published by PLAYBILL® BOOKS
525 Seventh Avenue, Suite 1801
New York, NY 10018
Email: yearbook@playbill.com
Internet: www.playbill.com

Printed by WALSWORTH PUBLISHING COMPANY
Commercial Book Group
389 Piedmont Street
Waterbury, CT 06706

Exclusively distributed by APPLAUSE THEATRE & CINEMA BOOKS/Hal Leonard Corporation.

Applause Theatre & Cinema Books
19 West 21st Street, Suite 201
New York, NY 10010
Phone: (212) 575-9265
Fax: (212) 575-9270

SALES AND DISTRIBUTION

North America:

Hal Leonard Corp.
7777 West Bluemound Road
P. O. Box 13819
Milwaukee, WI 53213
Phone: (414) 774-3630
Fax: (414) 774-3259
Email: halinfo@halleonard.com
Internet: www.halleonard.com

Europe:

Roundhouse Publishing Ltd.
Millstone, Limers Lane
Northam, North Devon EX 39 2RG
Phone: (0) 1237-474-474
Fax: (0) 1237-474-774
Email: roundhouse.group@ukgateway.net

Special Thanks

Special thanks to Amy Asch, Pam Karr, Morgan Allen, Aubrey Reuben, Ben Strothmann, Melissa Merlo, David Gewirtzman, Philip Birsh, Alex Near, Natasha Williams, Alex Corporato, Jim Ayala, Andrew Ku, Pat Cusanelli, Robert Simonson, Kenneth Jones, Phil DiChiara, Jenny Shoemaker, Pam Smith, the staff at Sardi's, Bill Blackstock and other stage doormen, Courtney Merlo, Catherine Ryan, Nicholas Viagas and Lillian Viagas whose help, advice and guidance made this project possible.

And the Second Edition Yearbook Correspondents who shared their stories with such wit and insight:

William Barnes (twice), Steven Beckler, David Bonnano, Todd Buonopane, Donna Lynne Champlin, Michael Clarkston, Jennifer Cody, Richard Costabile, James Corden, Eugenio Derbez, Jenny Dewar, Erin Dilly (for the second year), Diane DiVita, Saidah Arrika Ekulona, Allison Fischer, Jack Gianino, Laurie Goldfeder, Jane Grey, James Harker, Roy Harris, Michael E. Harrod, Mylinda Hull, Meredith Inglesby, Marcus Paul James, Travis Kelley, Madeleine Kelly, Christopher Kenney, The Kids of *The Color Purple*, Sid King, Eddie Korbich, Stephen Kunken, Neil Krasnow (twice), Chad Kimball, Nichole Larson, Leslie C. Lyter, Elizabeth Marvel, Judy McLane, Charles Means, Elizabeth Moloney, Cass Morgan, Rick Najera, Kris Koop Ouellette (for the second year), Jill Paice, Valerie A. Peterson, Pete Sanders, Angie Schworer, Tim Semon, Christopher Sieber, Greg Smith, Jamie Lee Smith, Jennifer Smith, Suzanne Somers, Judine Somerville, Rachel Stern, Barclay Stiff, Richard Topol, David Turner, Jason Viarengo and James Yaegashi.

Also the Broadway press agents who helped set up interviews and photo sessions: especially Chris Boneau, Adrian Bryan-Brown, John Barlow, Michael Hartman, Pete Sanders, Richard Kornberg, Bob Fennell, Philip Rinaldi and their staffs.

Plus Joan Marcus, Paul Kolnik, Carol Rosegg and all the photographers whose work appears on these pages.

And, most of all, thanks to the great show people of Broadway who got into the spirit of the Yearbook and took time out of their busy days to pose for our cameras. There's no people like them.

Preface

Curtain going up on the second annual edition of *The Playbill Broadway Yearbook*!

For theatre lovers just joining us, you're in for a royal tour of Broadway's backstages.

Those returning for a second time will find this new edition has more of all the features they liked last year. Between June 1, 2005 and May 31, 2006 seventy-one shows played on Broadway, up six from last season. Each one has a chapter, from *Absurd Person Singular* to *Woman in White*. To those we've added longer Scrapbook sections, a timeline of the year's headlines, more insider Events like the Broadway Bowling League championships, and more Faculty groups like Hudson Scenic and the team that brings you the Tony Awards. The result is a book that is eighty pages larger than last year's.

Once again we've set a goal of getting photos of every person working on Broadway—not just the actors and writers, but every stagehand, usher, dresser and stage doorman. If a face is missing, it's only because they or their company manager passed, or because they missed not only the official in-theatre photo session, but the last-chance make-up session at Sardi's. The second edition contains more than 4000 photos that depict more than 7000 of the great people who make Broadway happen.

Highlights

One of the great pleasures of working on the *Yearbook* is interacting with the Correspondents from each show. Each show chooses its own correspondent, often an actor, but sometimes another member of the crew. We have a standing list of questions for them to answer about the likes, dislikes and anecdotes of each show's company.

In addition to playing herself in *Blonde in the Thunderbird*, Suzanne Somers also reported on life backstage at that short-lived show. Kris Koop Ouellette of *Phantom of the Opera* wrote a detailed account of the night that show became the longest-running in Broadway history. *The Color Purple* chose four of the children in the cast, and they gave a kids'-eye-view of that big musical.

Jen Cody, who has become a fixture at BC/EFA events reprising her *Urinetown* role as Little Sally, wisecracked her way through the backstage of *The Pajama Game*. Angie Schworer, the enthusiastic Ulla from *The Producers* whose face is on every poster and who acts as goodwill ambassador from the show at many Broadway events, reports from backstage at the St. James.

Some Correspondents followed our stand-

It made him feel like he was back on Broadway again.

ing list of questions exactly; some added a few categories of their own; some tossed out the questions entirely and told their stories in their own unique way. Christopher Sieber, who stops *Spamalot* every night as Sir Dennis Galahad, gave us a highly Pythonesque recollection of famous (and infamous) quotes from the creation of that show. *Chicago* just sent interesting stats on their show, which celebrated its ninth anniversary.

We loved them all, and thank them all for their work as irreverent historians.

Explanations

The *Yearbook* tries to include everyone who works on a show during the course of a season. But many shows, especially the long running ones, experience considerable turnover among actors. Here is our system for including them in the yearbook.

Each show's chapter lists a date that can be found on the lower right-hand corner of the title page. This is usually the opening night, for new shows. For older shows the date is either the last week in September (chosen to mark the beginning of the fall season) or the week on which there was a major cast change. The entire chapter takes its cue from this date.

The cast list, crew list and the list of actor headshots are the ones used as of that date. Actors listed as "Alumni" are those who left the cast between June 1, 2005 and that date.

Actors listed as "Transfer Students" are those who joined the cast after that date.

The photos of stage crew, ushers, orchestra and theatre staff generally are taken within the first few weeks of the run. However, many shows prefer to wait until late spring to stand for their photos.

We try to photograph everyone working on a show. If a person is absent on *Yearbook* photo day, they may be listed as "not pictured" at the discretion of each show's management.

No show or employee is required to appear in the *Yearbook*. Cooperation with the yearbook staff is entirely voluntary. Some shows, groups and individuals opt not to pose for staff photos or to designate a Correspondent. But every Broadway show is invited to participate.

Reviews

When we began working on *The Playbill Broadway Yearbook* in 2004-05 we hoped it would be embraced by the professional theatrical community, but we were delighted to discover that it also struck a chord with regular theatregoers everywhere. We heard from teens dreaming of a career in show business who said they couldn't wait to join the people on these pages who seemed to be having so much fun. We heard from one avid Broadway lover who hasn't been able to attend any shows in recent years because he is caring for his elderly mother. He wrote that the *Yearbook* book made him feel like he was back on Broadway again.

We even got some thumbs-up reviews. Columnist Liz Smith called the *Yearbook* "wonderful." XM Radio's critic said, "I've been having trouble putting [it] down." And Robert Osborne of *The Hollywood Reporter* wrote, "It's such a magnificent idea and such a valuable one for theatre buffs.... Mark this down as a new essential for anyone who loves, and follows, today's theatre scene."

That's just what we were shooting for, and we hope we've topped it with the second edition you hold in your hands.

Robert Viagas
June 2006

TABLE OF CONTENTS

Timeline 2005-2006

Opening Nights, News Headlines and Other Significant Milestones of the Season

Broadway broke some records and said some significant hellos and goodbyes in the 2005-2006 season. Here are the headlines, day by day.

June 1, 2005—Elaine May returns to Broadway with her trio of short comedies, collectively titled *After the Night and the Music*, starring Jeannie Berlin, Jere Burns, J. Smith-Cameron, Brian Kerwin and Eddie Korbich.

June 5, 2005—The 59th annual Tony Awards ceremony is held at Radio City Music Hall and hosted by Hugh Jackman. *Monty Python's Spamalot* is named Best Musical, *Doubt* is named Best Play; and Best Revival awards go to *La Cage aux Folles* and *Glengarry Glen Ross*.

Summer 2005—Owners of the building at 1551 Broadway, which housed Times Square landmarks Howard Johnson's, the Gaiety male burlesque and the theatre where Off-Broadway's *The Perfect Crime* played for many years, evicted its tenants in advance of being torn down. The Gaiety space had been the Orpheum Dance Hall from 1917 to 1964 and served as one of the inspirations for the ambience of *Sweet Charity*.

June 9, 2005—Hal Holbrook brings his one-man show *Mark Twain Tonight!* to the Brooks Atkinson Theatre, giving 2005 audiences a chance to see a characterization he's been developing since the first Broadway production in 1966.

June 16, 2005—Lynn Redgrave, Kate Burton, Michael Cumpsty and John Dossett star in a revival of W. Somerset Maugham's *The Constant Wife*.

July 11, 2005—Antony Sher impersonates Italian chemist and Holocaust survivor Primo Levi in the National Theatre of Great Britain's production of *Primo*, based on Levi's memoir, "If This Is a Man."

July 17, 2005—Actress and pitchwoman Suzanne Somers tells her life story in the solo show *The Blonde in the Thunderbird*.

August 14, 2005—Director Don Scardino uses multiple actors to bring onetime Beatle John Lennon to life in the kaleidoscopic musical tribute, *Lennon*.

August 25, 2005—*Beauty and the Beast* wins the Broadway Show League softball championship in Central Park, beating three-time victors *The Producers* 13-3.

September 19, 2005—The June 2004 broadcast of the 58th Annual Tony Awards wins the Emmy Award for Outstanding Variety, Music or Comedy Special. Host Hugh Jackman will also win the Emmy Award for Outstanding Individual Performance in a Variety or Music Program.

September 20, 2005—Former Tony Awards host and *Taboo* producer Rosie O'Donnell officially takes over the role of Golde in *Fiddler on the Roof*.

Who is this celebrity producer and which show did she use her multimillion-dollar clout to champion? See December 1.

September 22, 2005—The Tony Awards Administration Committee establishes guidelines for a new category to be added at the 2006 awards: Actor or Actress for an Outstanding Performance in a Recreated Role.

October 2, 2005—Playwright August Wilson dies at age 60, just months after completing a cycle of ten dramas about African-American life in the 20th century, two of which, *Fences* and *The Piano Lesson*, won Pulitzer Prizes.

October 6, 2005—Jill Clayburgh and Richard Thomas play a cooking maven and distracted genius in Richard Greenberg's new comedy *A Naked Girl on the Appian Way*.

October 13, 2005—Onetime Cheech & Chong comedian Cheech Marin makes his Broadway directing debut with *Latinologues*, Rick Najera's collection of comic monologues about the Latino experience in America. Najera co-stars with Eugenio Derbez, Rene Lavan and Shirley A. Rumierk.

October 13, 2005—British playwright Harold Pinter wins the Nobel Prize for Literature.

October 16, 2005—Broadway's Virginia Theatre is renamed the August Wilson Theatre for the playwright who died two weeks earlier. It opened in 1925 as The Guild Theatre, home of The Theatre Guild.

October 20, 2005—Joseph Brooks serves as composer lyricist, librettist and director of *In My Life*, a musical about a romance between a composer with Tourette's Syndrome and the magazine writer who falls in love with him—all for the entertainment of God, who appears as a blue-collar worker wearing a baseball cap.

October 25, 2005—The 2005 Tony Honors for Excellence in Theatre are bestowed on Peter Neufeld and the Theatre Communications Group in a ceremony at Tavern on the Green.

October 27, 2005—Tony winners Nathan Lane and Matthew Broderick re-team for a revival of Neil Simon's *The Odd Couple*, which promptly sells out virtually its entire six-month scheduled run. The run is later extended.

October 28, 2005—Jordan Roth, the young Broadway producer and son of well-established producer Daryl Roth, is named resident producer of Jujamcyn Theaters, the third-largest landlord of Broadway theatres and one active in producing.

November 3, 2005—Michael Cerveris and Patti LuPone star in an unusual revival of Stephen Sondheim's *Sweeney Todd*. Under the direction of John Doyle the ten cast members also serve as the orchestra, doubling on musical instruments when they are not performing in a scene. Tony winner LuPone delights audiences with her capable tuba playing.

November 6, 2005—The close harmonies and personal dramas of the doo-wop group Frankie Valli and The Four Seasons are turned into a crowd-pleasing songbook musical *Jersey Boys*.

Early November 2005—The top price for Broadway tickets rises to $110. Tony winner *Monty Python's Spamalot* leads the way, with several other big musicals soon following suit.

November 10, 2005—Tony winner Judy Kaye moves her sold-out Off-Broadway hit *Souvenir* to the Lyceum Theatre. She embodies eccentric socialite Florence Foster Jenkins, who pursued a classical singing career despite being completely tone-deaf.

Mid November 2005—Two leading ladies of big musicals prove to be old-fashioned troupers when confronted with health problems. Maria Friedman leaves previews of *The Woman in White* to have surgery for breast cancer, but will return in time for the opening night. Sutton Foster breaks her wrist during the out-of-town tryout for *The Drowsy Chaperone*, but goes on with her arm in a cast.

November 17, 2005—Friedman recreates her London performance in the leading role of the gothic musical *The Woman in White*, with a score by Andrew Lloyd Webber and David Zippel.

November 21, 2005—Giant talking lizards emerge from the ocean to confront a human couple about keeping their minds open to all the great possibilities of life in a major revival of *Edward Albee's Seascape*, directed by Mark Lamos and featuring George Grizzard and Frances Sternhagen.

November 23, 2005—The film adaptation of Tony-winning musical *Rent* debuts, featuring most of the original Broadway cast.

Thanksgiving, 2005—Broadway's box offices

Photos by Aubrey Reuben

have a feast: The week ending November 27 proves to be the highest grossing Thanksgiving week in history, with $20.8 million worth of tickets sold, up 20 percent from 2004. Attendance is the fourth highest in history for that holiday week, with 259,948 seats filled.

December 1, 2005—After being talked up for weeks by talk show host Oprah Winfrey, who is one of the producers, the musical adaptation of Alice Walker's novel *The Color Purple* bows on Broadway, featuring LaChanze as Celie.

December 6, 2005—*Monty Python's Spamalot* earns top fundraising honors in the "17th Annual Gypsy of the Year" competition, raking in $367,084 toward a $2,972,721.15 total for the event, which benefits Broadway Cares/Equity Fights AIDS. For the second year in a row, the sculpted dancers of *The Lion King* impress the judges, winning the coveted award for best stage presentation, "I Remember He Said…."

December 7, 2005—Playwright Harold Pinter accepts the Nobel Prize for Literature, and makes international headlines when he uses his acceptance speech to rip into America's foreign policy, not only in Iraq, but throughout the world for the past half-century, saying, "The crimes of the United States have been systematic, constant, vicious, remorseless, but very few people have actually talked about them…. You have to hand it to America. It has exercised a quite clinical manipulation of power worldwide while masquerading as a force for universal good. It's a brilliant, even witty, highly successful act of hypnosis."

December 8, 2005—Irish-American tavern owner Gabriel Byrne tries to live up to a past that never was in Doug Hughes's revival of Eugene O'Neill's *A Touch of the Poet.*

December 11, 2005—Living legend Chita Rivera recounts her life story in dance in the musical, *Chita Rivera: The Dancer's Life*, direct-

ed by Graciela Daniele, and featuring a script by Terrence McNally and some new songs by Lynn Ahrens and Stephen Flaherty, along with familiar tunes from her many hits over the past five decades.

December 16, 2005—Film adaptation of Tony-winning musical *The Producers* opens, featuring Nathan Lane, Matthew Broderick and key members of the original cast from the Tony-winning original production—along with many familiar Broadway faces.

December 20-22, 2005—Transit workers go on strike, shutting down New York's subways and buses—but not theatres. Broadway actors are seen biking and roller-blading to work as the ting-ting-ting of busy pedicab bells is heard around Times Square. Author and ex-Pythonite Eric Idle ad-libs on the stage of *Monty Python's Spamalot* to the delight of audiences, as actors wend their way to the theatre.

December 31, 2005—The League of American Theatres and Producers, Inc. closes the books on 2005, reporting that Broadway grossed a record-breaking $825 million—the highest grossing calendar year in Broadway history. This figure is up 10.2 percent from the 2004 total of $749 million. Paid attendance for Broadway in 2005 reached 11.98 million, the highest calendar year paid attendance in the past two decades—a 5.7 percent increase from 11.33 million in 2004.

January 1, 2006—The League additionally reports that the week ending 1/1/2006 boasted the highest gross of any week in Broadway history, at $25.2 million, and the second highest audience capacity percentage in recorded history, at 93.9 percent. The gross is up 14.3 percent from the same week the previous season. The capacity is behind only the week of 12/30/01, which enjoyed a 95.5 percent capacity.

January 8, 2006—Actress Rita Moreno visits Chita Rivera backstage at her show, *Chita*

Goodbye old friend: See January 16.

Rivera: The Dancer's Life. They embrace, laying to rest the supposed feud between the two for Rita getting Chita's role of Anita in the film of *West Side Story*. Rita calls Chita, The Queen of Musical Theatre, according to columnist Liz Smith.

January 8, 2006—Also today, the Tony-nominated *Fiddler on the Roof* revival plays its last performance. At the farewell party Rosie O'Donnell helps co-star Harvey Fierstein shave off the beard he grew for the role of Tevye.

January 9, 2006—*The Phantom of the Opera* plays its 7,486th performance, surpassing *Cats* to become the longest-running show in Broadway history. Less than two weeks earlier, the show enjoyed the best box-office week in its history.

January 10, 2006—All three new cast members of the 2005 Tony-winning Best Play *Doubt*, Eileen Atkins, Ron Eldard and Jena Malone, miss their first performance in the show owing to a flu that's been sweeping backstages of many shows: The evening proves a bonanza for their understudies.

January 16, 2006—McHale's restaurant, the unofficial watering hole for Broadway's tech folk and their friends, closes after decades at the corner of 46th Street and Eighth Avenue.

January 24, 2006—Chita Rivera reunites with *Bye Bye Birdie* co-star Dick Van Dyke for four performances of her show, *Chita Rivera: The Dancer's Life.*

January 26, 2006—Sarah Jones embodies a crowd of immigrant comedians at a fictional open-mike night in Queens in her one-woman show, *Bridge and Tunnel.*

Police tape closes off the main entrance to the Times Square subway station. Why? See December 20.

Timeline 2005-2006

January 27, 2006—A theatrical tradition bites the dust. No more piles of opening night congratulatory telegrams, as Western Union announces it is discontinuing telegram and commercial messaging services after 145 years.

January 30, 2006—Tony- and Pulitzer-winning playwright Wendy Wasserstein (*The Heidi Chronicles*) dies at age 55 of lymphoma, just months after completing her final play, *Third*.

January 30, 2006—The Theater Hall of Fame celebrates its 35th anniversary by inducting director/choreographer Graciela Daniele, costume designer William Ivey Long, playwright William Gibson, set designer Ben Edwards, director Sir Peter Hall, and actors Sada Thompson, John Lithgow and Dorothy Loudon.

January 31, 2006—Frantic cell phone text messaging draws a crowd of more than one thousand people when word gets out that composer Stephen Sondheim has joined Patti LuPone and the cast of *Sweeney Todd* at the Eugene O'Neill Theatre, where they are autographing copies of the newly-released cast album.

January 31, 2006—Broadway theatres dim their lights at curtain time in Wendy Wasserstein's memory.

January 31, 2006—Beloved lunch spot Barrymore's Restaurant on 45th Street closes its doors after decades in business.

February 2006—Disney begins screening *High School Musical* on the Disney Channel. The story of a jock who tries out for the HSM becomes one of the top-rated TV movies ever, becomes Topic One for the tween set, makes instant stars of leads Zac Efron (as Troy), and Vanessa Hudgens (Gabriella), places seven of the top ten song downloads on iTunes, and is rebroadcast repeatedly on the cable channel. Key phrase: "We need to save our show from people who don't know the difference between a Tony Award and Tony Hawk!" Hawk is a professional skateboarder.

February 2, 2006—Cynthia Nixon and John Slattery play a devastated couple trying to deal with the death of their young son in David Lindsay-Abaire's drama, *Rabbit Hole*.

February 16, 2006—Patrick Wilson, Amanda Peet, Jill Clayburgh and Tony Roberts star in Scott Elliott's revival of Neil Simon's 1963 comedy about seemingly mismatched newlyweds, *Barefoot in the Park*.

February 23, 2006—Broadway's newest star proves to be Harry Connick, Jr.'s chest, as he wows critics by appearing shirtless during the curtain calls of Kathleen Marshall's high-energy revival of *The Pajama Game*, co-starring Kelli O'Hara.

March 5, 2006—Playwright Martin McDonagh receives the 2006 Academy Award for Best Live Action Short Film for his *Six Shooter*. He uses part of his acceptance speech to plug his upcoming Broadway production, *The Lieutenant of Inishmore*.

March 6, 2006—The League of American Theatres and Producers releases its annual report on demographics and finds that attendance by visitors from other countries has surpassed pre-9/11 levels, having fallen by more than half during the first year after the 2001 terrorist attacks.

March 12, 2006—Jarrod Emick leads the cast of *Ring of Fire*, a musical tribute to country singer Johnny Cash.

March 30, 2006—Lisa Kron opens *Well*, her meta-theatrical "solo with other people" about her health, her mom and herself.

April 9, 2006—The revelation of a family secret makes a shambles of a 60th birthday party in David Eldridge's *Festen*, starring Larry Bryggman, Michael Hayden, Ali MacGraw and Julianna Margulies.

April 17, 2006—Ben Gazzara and Zoë Wanamaker star in a revival of Clifford Odets's Depression-era classic, *Awake and Sing!*

April 17, 2006—Also today, the Pulitzer Prize committee opts to give no prize for drama this year.

April 19, 2006—Film star Julia Roberts makes her Broadway debut as one point of a love triangle in the Broadway premiere of Richard Greenberg's drama, *Three Days of Rain*.

April 20, 2006—Alan Cumming plays Macheath in Scott Elliott's revival of the Brecht-Weill classic musical, *The Threepenny Opera*, with a new translation by Wallace Shawn. Also featured in the cast: Cyndi Lauper, Jim Dale, Ana Gasteyer and Nellie McKay.

April 23, 2006—Nicholas Hytner imports his London hit, *The History Boys*, Alan Bennett's drama about conflicts at a British boys' school.

April 24-25, 2006—*Wicked* and *The Color Purple* take top honors in the 20th Annual BC/EFA "Easter Bonnet" Competition.

April 25, 2006—Anne Rice's best-selling "Vampire Chronicles" becomes the musical *Lestat*, with a score by Elton John and Bernie Taupin, starring Hugh Panaro and Carolee Carmello.

April 27, 2006—Stephen Lynch plays a two-bit crooner with his eye on a star in the musical *The Wedding Singer*, co-starring Laura Benanti.

April 29, 2006—*Rent* celebrates its 10th anniversary on Broadway with a reunion event at the Nederlander Theatre.

April 30, 2006—The music of R&B group Earth, Wind & Fire ignites the dance musical *Hot Feet*, directed and choreographed by Maurice Hines.

May 1, 2006—The TKTS discount ticket booth, a Times Square landmark since 1974, closes today to make way for a new booth promised to be built on the site over the next six months. Operations move temporarily to a kiosk at the Marriott Marquis Hotel.

May 1, 2006—A devoted fan takes audiences on a tour of his favorite musical-that-never-was in *The Drowsy Chaperone*, starring Sutton Foster as a leading lady who just can't seem to give up the stage.

May 3, 2006—Transfer of Martin McDonagh's Off-Broadway hit *The Lieutenant of Inishmore*, a bloody black comedy about a romance between two terrorists.

May 4, 2006—A footloose faith healer (Ralph Fiennes), his patient wife (Cherry Jones) and his loyal manager (Ian McDiarmid) see their lives change when something extraordinary happens during a healing, in a revival of Brian Friel's drama, *Faith Healer*.

May 7, 2006—It's David Schwimmer for the defense in Jerry Zaks's revival of *The Caine Mutiny Court-Martial*.

May 9, 2006—A man seeks professional help after he has close encounters with an entity he believes to be the ghost of his dead wife, in Conor McPherson's drama, *Shining City*.

May 10, 2006—Josh Strickland and Jenn Gambatese seem to fly through the African jungles in Disney's stage adaptation of its animated film musical, *Tarzan*, with a score by Phil Collins.

May 31, 2006—Broadway closes its books on its most bountiful season ever. A record 12 million seats were occupied, more than four-fifths of all that were available. A record $861.6 million worth of tickets were sold, 12 percent more than in 2004-05.

Robert Viagas

Who is this basketball player and how did he inspire a whole generation of future musical theatre fans? See February.

Photo courtesy The Disney Channel

Head of the Class

Trends, Extraordinary Achievements and Peculiar Coincidences of the Season

Most Tony Awards: *The History Boys* (6).

Most Cell Phone Rings at a Single Performance: *A Touch of the Poet* reported 10; *The Caine Mutiny Court-Martial* reported "9 or 12." Special mention to Richard Griffiths of *History Boys*, whose legendary willingness to stop the show and berate owners of ringing cell phones made his classes at the Broadhurst Theatre well-behaved indeed.

Most Roles Played by a Single Performer in a Single Show: Sarah Jones in *Bridge & Tunnel* (14).

Men Are Dogs (Shows That Featured Unfaithful and/or Abusive and/or Drunken Male Main Characters): *Barefoot in the Park, Blonde in the Thunderbird, The Color Purple, Chita Rivera: The Dancer's Life, The Constant Wife, Dirty Rotten Scoundrels, The Drowsy Chaperone, Faith Healer, Festen, The History Boys, Hot Feet, Jersey Boys, Lennon, The Lieutenant of Inishmore, The Pillowman, Ring of Fire, Shining City, A Streetcar Named Desire, Sweeney Todd, The Threepenny Opera, A Touch of the Poet, The Wedding Singer, Woman in White.*

Awards They Should Give: #1 Best New Showtune. Our nominees: "Show Off" from *The Drowsy Chaperone.* "Come Out of the Dumpster" from *The Wedding Singer.* "Ever More Without You" from *Woman in White.* "The Color Purple" from *The Color Purple.*

It's Not Easy Being Green (Shows in which significant characters were, at some point, green): *Wicked, Seascape, Avenue Q, Tarzan* and *The Pillowman.* Also: *The Wedding Singer* had a song titled "All About the Green."

The Colors of My Life: *The Color Purple, Woman in White.* Also: *Ring of Fire* contained a song "The Man in Black."

Pleasant Dreams: *The Drowsy Chaperone, Pajama Game, The Pillowman, After the Night and the Music, Awake and Sing!*

Awards They Should Give: #2 Best Special Effects. Our nominees: The opening sequence of *Tarzan.* The fire that consumes vampires in *Lestat.* The transformation of a dingy apartment into a glamorous 1920s townhouse in *The Drowsy Chaperone.* The ghost in *Shining City.*

Don't Call Us (Shows With Audition Scenes): *The Producers, Jersey Boys, Souvenir, Hairspray, The Color Purple, Phantom of the Opera, Chita Rivera: The Dancer's Life, Blonde in the Thunderbird, Lennon, In My Life. Hot Feet, Bridge & Tunnel, Drowsy Chaperone, The Wedding Singer.*

Bare Skin (On Stage or in Titles, or in Statues): Shug Avery in *The Color Purple.* The statue in *Light in the Piazza.* Princeton and

Kate Monster in *Avenue Q. A Naked Girl on the Appian Way.* The underwear scenes in *Barefoot in the Park, The Threepenny Opera* and *The History Boys.* Shirtlessness in *Hot Feet, Festen, Tarzan* and *The Pajama Game.*

Monkeys Monkeys Monkeys: *The Drowsy Chaperone, Tarzan, Wicked, The Lion King.*

Awards They Should Give: #3 Hottest Couple. Our nominees: Kelli O'Hara and Harry Connick, Jr. in *The Pajama Game.* Vivian Nixon and Michael Balderrama in *Hot Feet.* Danny Burstein and Beth Leavel in *The Drowsy Chaperone.* Stephen Lynch and Laura Benanti in *The Wedding Singer.* Josh Strickland and Jenn Gambatese in *Tarzan.* Alison Pill and David Wilmot in *The Lieutenant of Inishmore.* Eddie Korbich and J. Smith-Cameron in *After the Night and the Music.* Brian Charles Rooney and Alan Cumming in *The Threepenny Opera.*

Off-Site Hangout Most Frequently Named by Yearbook Correspondents: Angus McIndoe.

Awards They Should Give: #4 Best New Rendition of an Old Song in a Revival or Jukebox Musical. Our nominees: "My Eyes Adored You" in *Jersey Boys.* "Hernando's Hideaway" in *The Pajama Game.* "The Happy Life" in *The Threepenny Opera.* "The Worst Pies in London" in *Sweeney Todd.* "Give Peace a Chance" in *Lennon.* "All That Jazz" in *Chita Rivera: The Dancer's Life.*

Calling Dr. Scholl: *The Drowsy Chaperone* had a song "Cold Feets." The Hilton Theatre had a show called *Hot Feet* about a pair of magic shoes. *Spelling Bee* had the song "Magic Foot." And then, of course, there are the magic slippers in *Wicked.*

Actors From *Harry Potter* Film or Book Projects: Richard Griffiths ("Uncle Vernon" in *HP,* "Hector" in *The History Boys*), Ralph Fiennes ("Lord Voldemort" in *HP,* "Frank Hardy" in *Faith Healer*). Frances de la Tour ("Madame Olympe Maxime" in *HP,* "Mrs. Lintott" in *The History Boys*), Zoë Wanamaker ("Madame Hooch" in *HP,* "Bessie Berger" in *Awake and Sing!*), Jim Dale (voice of all characters in *HP* Books on Tape, "Mr. Peachum" in *The Threepenny Opera*).

"American Idol" Finalists on Broadway: Diana DeGarmo in *Hairspray,* Josh Strickland in *Tarzan,* Frenchie Davis in *Rent.*

Awards They Should Give: #5 Valiant Performances Under Adverse Conditions. Our nominees: Carolee Carmello in *Lestat.* David Turner in *In My Life.* Julia Murney in *Lennon.* Maria Friedman (cancer surgery during previews) in *Woman in White.* Sutton Foster (broken wrist during tryouts) in *The Drowsy Chaperone.*

The Ultimate Typecasting (Actors Who Played Themselves or Characters Based on Themselves): Chita Rivera in *Chita Rivera: The Dancer's Life,* Suzanne Somers in *Blonde in the Thunderbird,* Billy Crystal in *700 Sundays,* Lisa Kron in *Well,* Sarah Jones in *Bridge & Tunnel* and Bob Martin in *Drowsy Chaperone.*

Shows With Characters Based on Other Real People Who Are Still Alive: Gary Coleman in *Avenue Q.* The Four Seasons and Joe Pesce in *Jersey Boys.* Young Chita in *Chita Rivera.* Jayne Houdyshell playing Lisa Kron's mom in *Well.* The 1980s icon impersonators in *The Wedding Singer,* especially "Fake Cyndi Lauper," considering the real Cyndi Lauper was in *Threepenny Opera* just seven blocks uptown.

Awards They Should Give: #6 Best Showstopping Moment in a New Musical. Our nominees: The climactic train scene in *Woman in White.* Sutton Foster's encore after "Show Off" in *The Drowsy Chaperone.* The Four Seasons singing "Sherry Baby" for the first time in *Jersey Boys.* Rita Gardner using a well-timed vulgarism at the end of "Note From Grandma" in *The Wedding Singer.* Chita Rivera recreating the styles of the various choreographers she's worked with in *Chita Rivera: The Dancer's Life.*

Awards They Should Give: #7 Best Showstopping Moment in a New Play. Our nominees: The all-French scene in *The History Boys.* The final moment of *Shining City.* The erased-tape scene in *Rabbit Hole.* The bloody climax of *The Lieutenant of Inishmore.*

The Playbill Broadway Yearbook 2005 • 2006

Shows

Absurd Person Singular

First Preview: September 22, 2005. Opened: October 18, 2005.
Closed December 4, 2005 after 29 Previews and 56 Performances.

PLAYBILL®

BILTMORE THEATRE

MANHATTAN THEATRE CLUB

Artistic Director
LYNNE MEADOW

Executive Producer
BARRY GROVE

Presents

ABSURD PERSON SINGULAR

by
ALAN AYCKBOURN

with

**MIREILLE ENOS   CLEA LEWIS   SAM ROBARDS
ALAN RUCK   DEBORAH RUSH   PAXTON WHITEHEAD**

Scenic Design
JOHN LEE BEATTY

Costume Design
JANE GREENWOOD

Lighting Design
BRIAN MacDEVITT

Sound Design
BRUCE ELLMAN

Production Stage Manager
DIANE DiVITA

Directed by
JOHN TILLINGER

Casting
**NANCY PICCIONE/
DAVID CAPARELLIOTIS**

Director of Artistic Operations
MANDY GREENFIELD

Production Manager
RYAN McMAHON

Director of Development
JILL TURNER LLOYD

Director of Marketing
DEBRA A. WAXMAN

Press Representative
BONEAU/BRYAN-BROWN

General Manager
FLORIE SEERY

Director of
Artistic Development
PAIGE EVANS

Director of
Artistic Production
MICHAEL BUSH

Special funding for this production is provided by the Blanche and Irving Laurie Foundation.

Manhattan Theatre Club wishes to express its appreciation to
Theatre Development Fund for its support of this production.

10/18/05

CAST
(in order of appearance)

Jane ....CLEA LEWIS

Sidney ....ALAN RUCK

Ronald ....PAXTON WHITEHEAD

Marion ....DEBORAH RUSH

Eva ....MIREILLE ENOS

Geoffrey ....SAM ROBARDS

Stage Manager: NEIL KRASNOW

ACT I
Last Christmas. Sidney and Jane's kitchen.

ACT II
This Christmas. Geoffrey and Eva's kitchen.

ACT III
Next Christmas. Ronald and Marion's kitchen.

UNDERSTUDY
For Jane, Eva: CRISTA MOORE

Sam Robards and Mireille Enos.

Photo by Joan Marcus

Absurd Person Singular

Mireille Enos
Eva

Clea Lewis
Jane

Sam Robards
Geoffrey

Alan Ruck
Sidney

Deborah Rush
Marion

Paxton Whitehead
Ronald

Crista Moore
Understudy

Alan Ayckbourn
Playwright

John Tillinger
Director

John Lee Beatty
Scenic Designer

Jane Greenwood
Costume Design

Brian MacDevitt
Lighting Design

Bruce Ellman
Sound Designer

Lynne Meadow
Artistic Director,
Manhattan Theatre
Club, Inc.

Barry Grove
Executive Producer,
Manhattan Theatre
Club, Inc.

FSD SECURITY OFFICER
Olanrewaj Ayinde

CREW AND FRONT OF HOUSE STAFF

On Floor (L-R): Karen Diaz (Usherette), Valerie D. Simmons (Theatre Manager), Denise Cooper (Company Manager), Derek Moreno (Dresser).
Seated Around Table (L-R): Jeff Dodson (Master Electrician), Anne Michelson (Production Assistant), Johannah-Joy Magyawe (Assistant House Manager), Diane DiVita (Production Stage Manager), Aimee Halfpenny (Intern), Meghann Early (Usherette), David Dillon (Box Office Treasurer).
Third Row (L-R): Michael Growler (Wardrobe Supervisor), Marion M. Geist (Hair Supervisor), Daniel Kerrigan (Apprentice), Louis Shapiro (Sound Engineer), Sue Poulin (Apprentice), Timothy Walters (Head Propertyman), Neil Krasnow (Stage Manager), Wendy Wright (Usherette), Johanna Comanzo (Assistant Box Office Treasurer).
Back Row (L-R): Danita Johnson (Usherette), Bruce Dye (Usher), Edward Brashear (Usher), Don Maxwell (Flyman), Patrick Murray (Automation Operator), Catherine Burke (Usherette), Jackson Ero (Usher), Chris Wiggins (Head Carpenter), and Stephanie Valcarcel (Assistant Box Office Treasurer).

Photos by Ben Strothmann

Absurd Person Singular

MANHATTAN THEATRE CLUB STAFF

Artistic Director	**Lynne Meadow**
Executive Producer	**Barry Grove**
General Manager	**Florie Seery**
Director of Artistic Production	**Michael Bush**
Director of Artistic Development	**Paige Evans**

Director of Artistic Operations ......**Mandy Greenfield**
Artistic Associate/
Assistant to the Artistic Director ....Amy Gilkes Loe
Artistic Assistants ....Lisa Dozier, Kacy O'Brien
Director of Casting ....**Nancy Piccione**
Casting Director ....**David Caparelliotis**
Casting Assistant ....Jennifer McCool
Literary Manager ....**Emily Shooltz**
Play Development Associate/
Sloan Project Manager ....Aaron Leichter
Play Development Assistant ....Annie MacRae
Director of Musical Theatre ....**Clifford Lee Johnson III**
Director of Development ....**Jill Turner Lloyd**
Director, Corporate Relations ......Karen Zornow Leiding
Director, Individual Giving ....Casey Reitz
Director, Planning and Projects ....Blake West
Director, Foundation and
Government Relations.......................Josh Jacobson
Manager, Individual Giving ....Allison Goldstein
Development Associate/
Foundation & Gov't Relations ....Andrea Gorzell
Development Associate/Planning & Projects ...Liz Halakan
Development Database Coordinator ....Rey Pamatmat
Patrons' Liaison ....Antonello Di Benedetto
Director of Marketing ....**Debra A. Waxman**
Marketing Manager ....Dale Edwards
Marketing Associate/Website Manager ......Ryan M. Klink
Director of Finance ....**Jeffrey Bledsoe**
Business Manager ....Holly Kinney
HR/Payroll Manager ....Darren Robertson
Senior Business Associate
& HR Coordinator ....Denise L. Thomas
Business Assistant ....Thomas Casazzone
Manager of Systems Operations ....Avishai Cohen
Systems Analyst ....Andrew Dumawal
Associate General Manager ....**Seth Shepsle**
Company Manager/
New York City Center ....**Lindsey T. Brooks**
General Management Assistant ....Rebecca Sherman
Assistant to the Executive Producer ....Bonnie Pan
Director of Subscriber Services ....**Robert Allenberg**
Associate Subscriber Services Manager ......Andrew Taylor
Subscriber Services Representatives ....Mark Bowers,
Alva Chinn, Rebekah Dewald,
Matthew Praet, Rosanna Consalvo Sarto
Director of Telesales and Telefunding .....**George Tetlow**
Assistant Manager ....Terrence Burnett
Director of Education ....**David Shookhoff**
Asst. Director of Education/Coordinator,
Paul A. Kaplan Theatre Management Program ...Amy Harris
Education Assistants ....Kayla Cagan, Sarah McLellan
MTC Teaching Artists.....................Stephanie Alston,
David Auburn, Michael A. Bernard,
Carl Capotorto, Chris Ceraso,
Charlotte Colavin, Andy Goldberg,
Elise Hernandez, Jeffrey Joseph,
Lou Moreno, Michaela Murphy,
Melissa Murray, Angela Pietropinto,
Carmen Rivera, Judy Tate,

Candido Tirado, Joe White
Theatre Management Interns ....Marisa Alford,
Dottie Allen, Jill Amato,
Jennifer Bellusci, Katharine Boies,
Kari Foster, Aimee Halfpenny,
Stephanie Madonna, Kristin Miller,
Emily Plumb, Rebecca Rozin,
Sarah Ryndak, Sarah Schacter,
Christopher Taggart, Shayla Titley,
Christina Trivigno, Sage Young,
Romana Zajac

The Paul A. Kaplan Theatre Management Program, MTC's internship program, is designed to train the next generation of theatre leaders.

Randy Carrig Casting Intern ....Kristin Svenningsen
Reception/Studio Manager ....Lauren Snyder
Production Manager ....**Ryan McMahon**
Associate Production Manager ....Bridget Markov
Assistant Production Manager ....Ian McNaugher
Technical Director ....**William Mohney**
Associate Technical Director ....Adam Lang
Assistant Technical Director ....Peter Gilchrist
Shop Foreman ....Shayne Izatt
Assistant Shop Foreman ....Nicholas Morales
Carpenter ....Brian Corr
Scenic Painting Supervisor ....**Jenny Stanjeski**
Lights and Sound Supervisor ....**Matthew T. Gross**
Properties Supervisor ....**Scott Laule**
Assistant Properties Supervisor ....Dana Lewman
Props Carpenter ....Peter Grimes
Costume Supervisor ....**Erin Hennessy Dean**
Assistant Costume Supervisor ....Michelle Sesco

GENERAL PRESS REPRESENTATIVES
BONEAU/BRYAN-BROWN
Chris Boneau   Jim Byk
Aaron Meier

Script Readers......................Sadie Foster, Liz Jones,
Michelle Tattenbaum,
Mark von Sternberg, Kathryn Walat,
Ethan Youngerman
Musical Theatre Reader ....Emily King

SERVICES
Accountants ....ERE, LLP
Advertising..................................SpotCo/
Drew Hodges, Jim Edwards,
Tom McCann, Aaliytha Davis
Marketing Consultants.............The Marketing Group/
Tanya Grubich, Laura Matalon,
Trish Santini, Bob Bucci,
Erica Schwartz
Web Design ....Pilla Marketing Communications
Legal Counsel ....Paul, Weiss, Rifkind,
Wharton and Garrison LLP,
John Breglio, Deborah Hartnett
Real Estate Counsel ....Marcus Attorneys
Labor Counsel ....Harry H. Weintraub/
Glick and Weintraub, P.C.
Special Projects ....Elaine H. Hirsch
Insurance ....DeWitt Stern Group Inc/
Anthony Pittari

Maintenance ....Reliable Cleaning
Production Photographer ....Joan Marcus
Cover Illustration ....Steven Guarnaccia
Cover Design ....SpotCo
Theatre Displays ....King Display

GROUP SALES BOX OFFICE
(212) 398-8383 or (800) 223-7565

For more information visit
www.ManhattanTheatreClub.com

PRODUCTION STAFF FOR
ABSURD PERSON SINGULAR

Company Manager	**Denise Cooper**
Production Stage Manager	**Diane DiVita**
Stage Manager	Neil Krasnow
Assistant Director	Henry Wishcamper
Associate Scenic Designer	Eric Renschler
Assistant Scenic Designer	Andrew Lu
Assistant Costume Designer	Alixandra Englund
Assistant Lighting Designer	Rachel Eichorn
Assistant Sound Designer	Erin M. Ballantine
Fight Director	**Rick Sordelet**
Dialect Coach	**Charlotte Fleck**
Hair Supervisor	Marion M. Geist
Light Board Programmer	Marc Polimeni
Automation Operator	Patrick Murray
Flyman	Don Maxwell
Dresser	Margiann Flanagan
Production Assistant	Anne Michelson

MUSIC CREDITS
"Will You Still Love Me Tomorrow?" by Gerry Goffin and Carole King. Used by permission of Screen Gems-EMI Music Inc. All rights reserved

SPECIAL THANKS
Spode
Royal China

CREDITS
Lighting equipment by PRG Lighting. Sound equipment by Masque Sound. Automation by Hudson Scenic Studio. Natural herbal cough drops courtesy of Ricola USA.

MANHATTAN THEATRE CLUB/
BILTMORE THEATRE STAFF

Theatre Manager	**Valerie D. Simmons**
Assistant House Manager	Johannah-Joy Magyawe
Box Office Treasurer	**David Dillon**
Assistant Box Office Treasurers	Johanna Comanzo, Stephanie Valcarcel
Head Carpenter	Chris Wiggins
Head Propertyman	Timothy Walters
Sound Engineer	Louis Shapiro
Master Electrician	Jeff Dodson
Wardrobe Supervisor	Michael Growler
Apprentices	Daniel Kerrigan, Sue Poulin
Engineers	Deosarran/Richardo Deosarran
Security	OCS/Initial Security
Lobby Refreshments	Sweet Concessions

Absurd Person Singular
SCRAPBOOK

1. (L-R) Sam Robards, Mireille Enos, Paxton Whitehead, Deborah Rush, Clea Lewis and Alan Ruck arrive at the opening night party at The Supper Club.
2. Ruck with guest Walter Cronkite on opening night.

Yearbook Co-correspondents: Diane DiVita, PSM, and Neil Krasnow, Stage Manager.

Opening Night Gifts: Framed window cards, Christmas ornaments, gin & bitter lemon, English Christmas crackers, Tiffany pens, books, cards, candy, flowers, Champagne, New York Yankees paraphernalia and mechanical dogs. There were two offstage characters in the show, Dick & Lottie Potter. Wardrobe Supervisor Michael Growler, and Dresser Margiann Flanagan filled flower pots with delicious chocolate brownies and topped the pots with pictures depicting themselves as a hiking Dick & Lottie.

Celebrity Visitor and What He Said: Hal Prince came to an early preview and said, "I saw the original. It was very funny."

The Gypsy of the Year Sketch: We wanted to present "Three Minutes of Four Gestures with Sam Robards," but Standards & Practices considered it a tad too racy. As a side note, you haven't lived until you've heard Sam's rendition of "Hurry Back." (In the original key. Keys?)

Person Who Performed the Most Roles: All performing members of the company played only one role each. Two of our understudies covered two roles each. Stage Manager Neil Krasnow played as many as three roles during understudy rehearsals (including an especially memorable afternoon as Jane). By far, our production assistant, Anne Michelson, who often played Jane, Eva, Sidney and Geoffrey, performed the greatest number of roles. Special mention must be made of Production Stage Manager Diane DiVita who used to play all seven Von Trapp children in understudy rehearsals for *The Sound of Music*.

Person Who Has Done the Most Shows: According to the Internet Broadway Database, Paxton Whitehead has done 15 Broadway shows (13 as an actor and 2 with the credit "Book adapted by"). His understudy, John Christopher Jones has done 14 shows. Our director, John Tillinger, has done 24 shows (7 as an actor and the remainder as a director). Our Fight Director, Rick Sordelet, has done 28 shows. Our Lighting Designer, Brian MacDevitt, has done 39 shows and our Scenic Designer, John Lee Beatty, has done 76 shows, but the winner would have to be our Costume Designer, Jane Greenwood, who has done a whopping 110 Broadway shows to date! This was the Broadway debut of Mark H. Dold, Clea Lewis, and Anne Michelson.

Special Backstage Rituals: Prior to each performance, Clea "Comedy Shark" Lewis and Alan Ruck would make love (frottage) to the audience through the house curtain. Clea would then instruct Alan "Don't eat the nuts" in reference to an upcoming moment in Act I. During Act I, two bags of Walker's Crisps were opened onstage. As Act I came to a close, the stage right prop table became the place to be as we munched away on the now-dead props. Any crisps that weren't immediately devoured went into an "Eat Me" container and were gone by the end of the show.

As he got in place for the top of Act III, Paxton Whitehead would always say "radio" to stage management to remind himself to turn it off during the upcoming scene. During Act III, Mireille Enos had to prepare and eat a peanut butter and butter sandwich onstage. When she exited with the sandwich during the Act, the deck stage manager would be standing by to eat the half of the sandwich that she hadn't eaten onstage.

Favorite Moment During Each Performance (Onstage or Off): Onstage, the moment that consistently got the most fabulous audience response occurred during Act II. Mireille Enos as Eva spent the entire Act trying to kill herself by various methods including jumping from a window, knifing, gas, pills, hanging and electrocution. As Eva was next trying to get the cap off a container of poison, Deborah Rush as Marion entered, hitting her with the door and knocking her out cold. The audience always screamed in surprise and delight at this beautifully executed bit of stage business.

Offstage, twenty-five blocks offstage to be exact, our hands-down favorite moment by far would have to be Calvin, Sebastian and Stanley's superb staging of "The Circle of Life" (complete with post-show talkback).

Favorite In-Theatre Gathering Place: Without a doubt, that would be the stage management office (where the candy jar is kept). Amazingly, we squeezed as many as eight people at a time into a very small (approximately seven feet by eight feet) space.

Least Favorite In-Theatre Gathering Place: The "farting corners" upstage right and downstage left. Better there than onstage....

Favorite Off-Site Hangout: The Dakota.

Favorite Snack Food: Chocolate. The company of *Chitty Chitty Bang Bang* sent us a giant jar of truly scrumptious Hershey's chocolates. We went through it very quickly but kept refilling it throughout the run.

Absurd Person Singular
SCRAPBOOK

1. Deborah Rush arrives at the opening night party.
2. Marquee of the Biltmore Theatre.
3. Sam Robards with mom Lauren Bacall at The Supper Club.

Favorite Meal: Ruck's Homemade Gumbo. Delicious!!!

Sunday Brunch in the Greenroom: Deviled eggs, oatmeal, waffles, cheese, fruit, breakfast sausage, bacon, coffee cake, coffee, quiche, juice, donuts, bagels and cream cheese, rice pudding, black cat pudding, Little Debbie snack cakes, cupcakes, cookies, pizza, strawberry cheesecake, apple brown betty, hummus and a multitude of various breads and crackers.

Mascot: George the dog.

Favorite Therapy: Starbucks Chantico and the candy in the stage management office.

Most Memorable Ad-Lib: Our most notable ad-libs always seemed to involve the upstage left door in Act I. At one performance, the door got slammed so hard that it went past the doorjamb and got profoundly stuck. It wasn't truly an ad-lib because we'd decided how to deal with the problem ahead of the actual moment, but when we got to Clea Lewis's re-entrance through the door, Alan Ruck had to tell her character to "go around to the front." She then ran downstage right and entered from the living room.

A few weeks later, we had the reverse problem when the door just wouldn't stay closed. One of the major plot points of Act I involved the character of Jane (played by Clea Lewis) locking herself out of the house. At one performance, when Clea exited, the door bounced open behind her. It was then up to Alan Ruck to get it closed on his next entrance. When we got to the point where Clea re-enters and finds herself locked out, the door popped open on her, and she had to close it and magically re-lock herself out. The audience loved it. When Clea re-entered later in the scene, she changed the line "I locked myself out" to "I SORT OF locked myself out," and the audience howled their approval!

Also, since textually there was a party taking place offstage during most of Act I, we daily had a running series of both appropriate and inappropriate party ad-libs going on in the stage right wing.

Memorable Stage Door Fan Encounter: Memorable in a bad way was the freaky stalker from France who was in love with and wanted to marry one of our actresses.

Latest Audience Arrival: This would have to be the man who never made it to the show. After dropping off his wife outside the theatre, he proceeded to crash his car at a local parking garage. When he didn't show up, his poor wife was understandably hysterical in the lobby, and the police were involved in a search for him. He eventually made it to the theatre.

Busiest Day at the Box Office: Most of the box office activity on 47th street was across the street from us at the Brooks Atkinson (where *The Odd Couple* was playing).

Catchphrase: Bogie used to love….

Memorable Directorial Note: "Is it time for a moratorium on line notes?"

Most Embarrassing Moment: One female company member flashed another female company member just as a male member of Local One was walking around the corner. Needless to say, it made his day!

Silly Stuff: To help cast members remember their drinks glasses, we posted a big sign by the stage right entrance that read, "GLASS?" Throughout the run, this sign was continually modified to say such things as "LASS", "GAS", "GLA (Gay Liberation Army)" and "ASS". The day after a cast member neglected to bring a bowl onstage, a sign was posted that read "BOWL?" Within a few hours of being put-up the defacement began starting with "BOWEL", "BONER", etc. The things we do to pass the time… At one cast member's request, the next sign to go up queried "BRAIN? TONGUE?" to help him remember two things he felt he was forgetting to bring onstage.

For hygienic reasons, our props department covered all drinks glasses with protective lids (which happened to say "Radisson" on them). One day, Sam Robards discovered that these lids made excellent Frisbees. He was especially fond of flying them towards the stage manager. He loved to throw Altoids at us too.

Best Place for Holiday Shopping: The second Annual Holiday Arts & Craft Show held in the Biltmore wardrobe room.

Company Legend: Assistant Director Henry Wishcamper (#38756) who completed the New York City Marathon in 5:23:27.

Legendary Legends Who Attended the Show: Lauren Bacall (mother of Sam Robards) and Walter Cronkite (father-in-law of Deborah Rush).

Red Sox vs. Yankees: The Automation position upstage left was dubbed "Casa de Ruth" and a second gaff tape sign warned, "No Red Sox fans allowed." In spite of this, during playoffs, both Red Sox and Yankees fans visited between cues to watch the games on satellite TV. Dan Kerrigan, King of the Rally Caps!

Slogan (paraphrased from Amy Sedaris): "Manhattan Theatre Club. Sleeps 650."

Coolest Things About Being in This Show: The amazing Company, House Crew at The Biltmore and our lovely company manager, Denise Cooper.

After the Night and the Music

First Preview: April 28, 2005. Opened: June 1, 2005.
Closed July 3, 2005 after 39 Previews and 38 Performances.

PLAYBILL®

After the **NIGHT** *and the* **MUSIC**

CAST
(in order of appearance)

Curtain Raiser
Gloria	J. SMITH-CAMERON
Keith	EDDIE KORBICH
Brittany	DEIRDRE MADIGAN
Bartender	JERE BURNS
Another Man	BRIAN KERWIN
Another Woman	JOANNA GLUSHAK

Giving Up Smoking
Joanne	JEANNIE BERLIN
Sherman	JERE BURNS
Mel	BRIAN KERWIN
Kathleen	J. SMITH-CAMERON

Swing Time
Mitzi Grade	J. SMITH-CAMERON
Darryl Grade	JERE BURNS
Gail	JEANNIE BERLIN
Ron	BRIAN KERWIN

Stage Manager: DENISE YANEY

UNDERSTUDIES
For Keith: JOEL BLUM; for Brittany, Gail: JOANNA GLUSHAK; for Gloria, Joanne, Kathleen and Mitzi Grade: DEIRDRE MADIGAN; for Bartender, Another Man, Sherman, Mel, Darryl Grade and Ron: PETER MARX.

BILTMORE THEATRE

MANHATTAN THEATRE CLUB

Artistic Director
LYNNE MEADOW

Executive Producer
BARRY GROVE

Presents

After the **NIGHT** *and the* **MUSIC**

Three New Plays in Two Acts

by

ELAINE MAY

with

JEANNIE BERLIN   JERE BURNS   JOANNA GLUSHAK
BRIAN KERWIN   EDDIE KORBICH
DEIRDRE MADIGAN   J. SMITH-CAMERON

Scenic Design	*Costume Design*	*Lighting Design*
JOHN LEE BEATTY	MICHAEL KRASS	PETER KACZOROWSKI

Original Music and Sound Design	*Wig Design*
JOHN GROMADA	PAUL HUNTLEY

Choreography	*Production Stage Manager*
RANDY SKINNER	ROY HARRIS

Directed by

DANIEL SULLIVAN

Casting	*Director of Artistic Operations*	*Production Manager*
NANCY PICCIONE/ DAVID CAPARELLIOTIS	MANDY GREENFIELD	RYAN MCMAHON

Director of Marketing	*Press Representative*
DEBRA A. WAXMAN	BONEAU/BRYAN-BROWN

General Manager	*Director of Artistic Development*	*Director of Artistic Production*
FLORIE SEERY	PAIGE EVANS	MICHAEL BUSH

Produced by Special Arrangement with Julian Schlossberg and Roy Furman.

Manhattan Theatre Club wishes to express its appreciation to Theatre Development Fund for its support of this production.

6/1/05

Photo by Joan Marcus

(L-R) Brian Kerwin, J. Smith-Cameron, Jeannie Berlin and Jere Burns in *Swing Time*.

After the Night and the Music

Jeannie Berlin
Joanne, Gail

Jere Burns
Bartender, Sherman, Darryl Grade

Joanna Glushak
Another Woman

Brian Kerwin
Another Man, Mel, Ron

Eddie Korbich
Keith

Deirdre Madigan
Brittany

J. Smith-Cameron
Gloria, Kathleen, Mitzi Grade

Joel Blum
Understudy Keith

Peter Marx
Understudy Mel, Ron

Elaine May
Playwright

Daniel Sullivan
Director

John Lee Beatty
Scenic Design

Peter Kaczorowski
Lighting Design

John Gromada
Original Music and Sound Design

Randy Skinner
Choreographer

Paul Huntley
Wigs

Lynne Meadow
Artistic Director, Manhattan Theatre Club, Inc.

Barry Grove
Executive Producer, Manhattan Theatre Club, Inc.

Photo by Joan Marcus

(L-R): Jere Burns and J. Smith Cameron express nervousness about an extramarital encounter in *Swing Time*.

After the Night and the Music

Photos by Ben Strothmann

CREW
(L-R): Chris Kurtz (Electrician), Patrick Murray (Flyman), Chris Wiggins (Head Carpenter), Shanna Spinello (Production Assistant), Lou Shapiro (Sound Engineer), Denise Yaney (Stage Manager), Margiann Flanagan (Dresser), Tim Walters (Head Propertyman), Bree Wellwood (Local One Apprentice), Sue Poulin (Local One Apprentice) and Michael Growler (Wardrobe Supervisor).

FRONT OF HOUSE STAFF
(L-R): Ed Brashear, Antonio Lopez, Wendy Wright, Meghann Early, Renee Hicks, Bru Dye, Cathy Burke and Valerie Simmons (Theatre Manager).

After the Night and the Music

MANHATTAN THEATRE CLUB STAFF

Artistic Director ....**Lynne Meadow**
Executive Producer ....**Barry Grove**
General Manager ....**Florie Seery**
Director of Artistic Production ....**Michael Bush**
Director of Artistic Development ....**Paige Evans**
Director of Artistic Operations ......**Mandy Greenfield**
Artistic Associate/
Assistant to the Artistic Director ....Amy Gilkes Loe
Artistic Assistants ....Lisa Dozier, Kacy O'Brien
Director of Casting ....**Nancy Piccione**
Casting Director ....**David Caparelliotis**
Casting Assistant ....Jennifer McCool
Literary Manager ....**Emily Shooltz**
Play Development Associate/
Sloan Project Manager ....Aaron Leichter
Play Development Assistant ....Lara Mottolo
Director of
Musical Development ....**Clifford Lee Johnson III**
Design Associate ....**John Lee Beatty**
Director of Writers in Performance ....**Steve Lawson**
Director of Corporate Relations ....Karen Zornow Leiding
Director, Individual Giving ....Casey Reitz
Director, Planning and Projects ....Blake West
Director, Foundation and
Government Relations.........................Josh Jacobson
Manager, Individual Giving ....Allison Goldstein
Senior Associate, Corporate Relations...........Scott Pyne
Development Associate ....Belinda Batson
Development Associate/
Database Coordinator ....Rey Pamatmat
Patrons' Liaison ....Antonello Di Benedetto
Director of Marketing ....**Debra A. Waxman**
Marketing Manager ....Dale Edwards
Marketing Associate/Website Manager ......Ryan M. Klink
Director of Finance &
Administration ....**Michael P. Naumann**
Business Manager ....Holly Kinney
Business Associate ....Denise L. Thomas
Business Assistant ....Thomas Casazzone
Manager of Systems Operations ....Avishai Cohen
Systems Analyst ....Andrew Dumawal
Associate General Manager ....**Seth Shepsle**
Company Manager/NY City Center ..**Lindsey T. Brooks**
Assistant to the Executive Producer ....Erin Day
Director of
Subscriber Services ....Robert Allenberg
Associate Subscriber Services Manager ......Andrew Taylor
Subscriber Services Representatives ....Mark Bowers,
Alva Chinn, Rebekah Dewald,
Matthew Praet,
Rosanna Consalvo Sarto
Director of Telesales and Telefunding ...**George Tetlow**
Assistant Manager ....Terrence Burnett
Director of Education ....**David Shookhoff**
Assistant Director of Education/
Coordinator, Paul A. Kaplan Theatre
Management Program ....Amy Harris
Education Assistants ....Kayla Cagan, Jackie McDonnell
MTC Teaching Artists ....Stephanie Alston,
David Auburn, Carl Capotorto,
Chris Ceraso, Charlotte Colavin,
Andy Goldberg, Elise Hernandez,
Jeffrey Joseph, Lou Moreno,
Michaela Murphy, Melissa Murray, Angela
Pietropinto,Carmen Rivera,
Judy Tate, Candido Tirado, Joe White

Theatre Management Interns ....Caroline Alexander,
Marisa Alford, Courtney Brown,
Travis Garner, Andrea Gorzell,
Aimee Halfpenny, Jennifer Leeson,Stephanie Madonna,
Samantha Mascali, Rebecca Sherman, Christopher Taggart
Randy Carrig Casting Intern ....Daryl Eisenberg
Reception/Studio Manager ....Lauren Snyder
Production Manager ....**Ryan McMahon**
Associate Production Manager ....Bridget Markov
Assistant Production Manager ....Ian McNaugher
Technical Director ....**Bill Mohney**
Assistant Technical Director ....Adam Lang
Assistant Technical Director ....Benjamin Lampman
Carpenters .....Brian Corr, Shayne Izatt, Nicholas Morales
Scenic Painting Supervisor ....**Jenny Stanjeski**
Lights and Sound Supervisor ....**Willy Corpus**
Properties Supervisor ....**Scott Laule**
Assistant Properties Supervisor ....Arlene Marshall
Props Carpenter ....Peter Grimes
Costume Supervisor ....**Erin Hennessy Dean**
Assistant Costume Supervisor ....Michelle Sesco

GENERAL PRESS REPRESENTATIVES
BONEAU/BRYAN-BROWN

Chris Boneau	Jim Byk
Aaron Meier	Erika Creagh

Script Readers ....Rachel Axler, Liz Jones,
Sadie Foster, Michelle Tattenbaum,
Kathryn Walat, Ethan Youngerman
Musical Theatre Reader ....Emily King

SERVICES
Accountants ....ERE, LLP
Advertising ....SpotCo
Drew Hodges, Jim Edwards,
John Lanasa, Aaliytha Davis
Marketing Consultants ....The Marketing Group/
Tanya Grubich, Laura Matalon,
Trish Santini, Bob Bucci, Erica Schwartz
Corporate Sponsorship ....Amy Willstatter's
Bridge to Hollywood/Broadway, LLC
Market Research ....Audience Research and Analysis/
George Wachtel, Aline Chatmajian
Internet Services ....Artztek LLC
Legal Counsel ....Paul, Weiss, Rifkind,
Wharton and Garrison LLP,
John Breglio, Deborah Hartnett
Real Estate Counsel ....Marcus Attorneys
Labor Counsel ....Harry H. Weintraub/
Glick and Weintraub, P.C.
Special Projects ....Elaine H. Hirsch
Insurance ....DeWitt Stern Group Inc/Anthony Pittari
Maintenance ....Reliable Cleaning
Production Photographer ....Joan Marcus
Cover Photography ....Andrew French
Cover Design ....SpotCo
Theatre Displays ....King Display

GROUP SALES BOX OFFICE
(212) 398-8383
or
(800) 223-7565

For more information visit
www.ManhattanTheatreClub.com

PRODUCTION STAFF FOR
AFTER THE NIGHT AND THE MUSIC
Company Manager ....**Denise Cooper**
Production Stage Manager ....**Roy Harris**
Stage Manager ....Denise Yaney
Dance Arrangements ....Randy Skinner,
Brad Ross, Wayne Barker
Orchestration ....Michael Patterson
Fight Consultant ....Brent Langdon
Assistant Director ....Jeremy Lewit
Associate Scenic Designer ....Eric Renschler
Assistant Scenic Designer ....Yoshinori Tanokura
Assistant Costume Designer ....Tracy Christensen
Assistant Lighting Designer ....James Milkey
Assistant Sound Designer ....Jeremy Lee
Hair Supervisor ....Marion M. Geist
Assistant Choreographer ....Sara Brians
Automation Operator ....Stephen "Crash" Burns
Flymen.....................Alex Gutierrez, Patrick Murray
Dresser ....Margiann Flanagan
Production Assistant ....Shanna Spinello

SPECIAL THANKS
Faces and Names,
12th Street Bar and Grill

CREDITS
Lighting equipment by PRG Lighting. Sound equipment by
Masque Sound. Scenic elements by Great Lakes Scenic
Studios. Automation by PRG/Scenic Technologies. Natural
herbal cough drops courtesy of Ricola. Digital printing by
Backdrop Productions.

MUSIC CREDITS
"Over the Rainbow," "We're Off to See the Wizard,"
"Munchkinland" by Harold Arlen and E.Y. Harburg, ©EMI
Feist Catalog Inc. (ASCAP). "Riffin' at the Ritz" by Benny
Goodman, ©EMI Robbins Catalog (ASCAP). "Dancing in
the Dark," "Something to Remember You By," "You and the
Night and the Music" by Arthur Schwartz and Howard
Deitz, © Arthur Schwartz Music Publishing. All rights
reserved. Used by permission.

MANHATTAN THEATRE CLUB/
BILTMORE THEATRE STAFF

Theatre Manager ....**Valerie D. Simmons**
Assistant House Manager ....Johannah-Joy Magyawe
Box Office Treasurer ....**David Dillon**
Assistant Box Office Treasurers ....Steven Clopper,
Kim Warner
Head Carpenter ....Chris Wiggins
Head Propertyman ....Timothy Walters
Sound Engineer ....Louis Shapiro
Master Electrician ....Jeff Dodson
Wardrobe Supervisor ....Michael Growler
Apprentices.....................Sue Poulin, Bree Wellwood
Engineers ....Deosarran, Richardo Deosarran,
Mohd Alamgir Hossain, Ariel Muñoz
Security ....OCS Security
Lobby Refreshments ....Sweet Concessions

After the Night and the Music
SCRAPBOOK

1. (L-R): J. Smith-Cameron, Brian Kerwin, Eddie Korbich, Jeannie Berlin and Jere Burns at the opening night party at Copacabana.
2 Director Dan Sullivan (R) and wife/actress Mimi Lieber.
3. J. Smith-Cameron at "Stars in the Alley."
4. Playwright Elaine May and Stanley Donen at the opening night party.

Photos by Aubrey Reuben

Correspondent: Eddie Korbich, "Keith"

Opening Night Gifts: Elaine May sent us the hugest food gift basket ever, including chocolate cookies, macadamia cookies, chocolate truffles, chocolate pretzels and eight bottles of Bordeaux. It was just beautiful. We also got engraved crystal mugs with the name of the show and the opening date.

Celebrity Visitors: Guess who? Elaine's former partner, Mike Nichols. I was walking backstage when he stopped me and put his hand out and said, "Great, great job," and I think he was sincere. We also had Phil Donahue and Marlo Thomas. She was just lovely but Phil was a blast. He just grabbed me and shook my hand, and it was just a delightful, delightful evening.

Backstage Ritual: J. Smith-Cameron, Jere Burns and I do a thing where he kisses us at the bar where the play takes place. He plays the bartender and gives us both big kisses just before the curtain goes up.

Favorite Moment: I'm in the first section, and my play is only 15 minutes long. There's a moment when J. asks if I'm gay and I say, "No, I'm not attractive enough to be gay." It always gets a laugh. And then we dance.

In-Theatre Gathering Place: We have a Sunday brunch in the greenroom, and that's where we get together. Roy Harris makes us special things. He wrote a cookbook, "Recipes and Remembrances," with recipes from people he worked with.

Favorite Snack Food: Roy's sister's recipe for Caramel German Chocolate Cake, with Cool Whip/Heath Bar topping.

Mascot: Director Stanley Donen, Elaine's longtime pal, shows up all the time and we have fun conversations about *Singin' in the Rain* and all those great musicals he did. God, he is great.

Favorite Therapy: Tap class between shows on Wednesday. Sara Brians, the assistant choreographer, is teaching it.

Who Wore the Least: Brian Kerwin gets down to his man-thong in the third play.

Memorable Ad-Lib: Offstage, Brian yelled "Hey Growler [our dresser], my thong is torn!"

Heaviest/Hottest Costume: My fat suit.

Memorable Directorial Note: "This bad blocking will change." And then it didn't.

Nicknames: J. nicknamed me Eddie "The Brick" Korbich. I came from musicals and here I was with the big boys in straight drama. J. had never danced on stage before, so every time we'd do a step or two I'd give her a wink.

Sweethearts: It's a joke: J. did a show with Mary Testa once, and in every show she picks a boyfriend to have. So on this show J. chose Brian as her "show boyfriend."

Also: Jeannie Berlin used to say, "Every time I saw you doing the waltz hops section of your dance, I knew the end of your play was coming and that meant I was on next, and I'd get this feeling of utter terror." So now when I start to do my hops, I always send her good vibes.

All Shook Up

First Preview: February 20, 2005. Opened: March 24, 2005.
Closed September 25, 2005 after 33 Previews and 213 Performances.

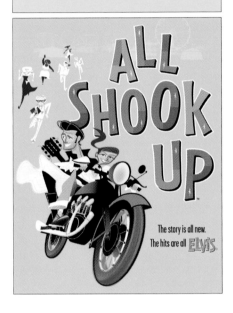

PLAYBILL

The story is all new.
The hits are all Elvis.

CAST
(in order of appearance)

Natalie Haller/Ed	JENN GAMBATESE
Jim Haller	JONATHAN HADARY
Dennis	MARK PRICE
Sylvia	SHARON WILKINS
Lorraine	NIKKI M. JAMES
Chad	CHEYENNE JACKSON
Mayor Matilda Hyde	ALIX KOREY
Dean Hyde	CURTIS HOLBROOK
Sheriff Earl	JOHN JELLISON
Miss Sandra	LEAH HOCKING

ENSEMBLE
BRAD ANDERSON, JUSTIN BOHON,
JUSTIN BRILL, PAUL CASTREE,
CARA COOPER, MICHAEL CUSUMANO,
FRANCESCA HARPER, TRISHA JEFFREY,
MICHELLE KITTRELL, ANIKA LARSEN,
MICHAEL X. MARTIN, KAREN MURPHY,
JOHN ERIC PARKER, JUSTIN PATTERSON,
MICHAEL JAMES SCOTT,
JENNY-LYNN SUCKLING,
VIRGINIA WOODRUFF

TIME
A 24-hour period, during the summer of 1955

PLACE
A small you-never-heard-of-it town
somewhere in the Midwest

Continued on next page

⇒N⇐ PALACE THEATRE
UNDER THE DIRECTION OF
STEWART F. LANE, JAMES M. NEDERLANDER AND JAMES L. NEDERLANDER

Jonathan Pollard   Bernie Kukoff
Clear Channel Entertainment   Harbor Entertainment   Miramax Films   Bob & Harvey Weinstein
Stanley Buchthal   Eric Falkenstein   Nina Essman/Nancy Nagel Gibbs   Jean Cheever   Margaret Cotter
in association with
Barney Rosenzweig   Meri Krassner   FGRW Investments   Karen Jason   Phil Ciasullo Conard
present

ALL SHOOK UP
Inspired by and featuring the songs of ELVIS PRESLEY®

Book by
Joe DiPietro

Starring

Jenn Gambatese   Jonathan Hadary   Leah Hocking   Curtis Holbrook   Cheyenne Jackson
Nikki M. James   John Jellison   Alix Korey   Mark Price   Sharon Wilkins

Featuring

Brad Anderson   Justin Bohon   Justin Brill   Paul Castree   Cara Cooper   Michael Cusumano   Randy A. Davis
Jennie Ford   Francesca Harper   Trisha Jeffrey   Michelle Kittrell   Anika Larsen   Michael X. Martin   Karen Murphy
John Eric Parker   Justin Patterson   Jenelle Lynn Randall   Michael James Scott   Jenny-Lynn Suckling   Virginia Woodruff

Set Design	Costume Design	Lighting Design	Sound Design	Wig & Hair Design
David Rockwell	**David C. Woolard**	**Donald Holder**	**Brian Ronan**	**David H. Lawrence**

Orchestrations	Dance Music Arrangements	Music Coordinator	Associate Director
Michael Gibson **Stephen Oremus**	**Zane Mark**	**Michael Keller**	**Daniel Goldstein**

Casting	Press Representative	Marketing	Associate Choreographers
Bernard Telsey Casting	**Barlow • Hartman**	**TMG** The Marketing Group	**Lorna Ventura** **JoAnn M. Hunter**

General Management	Production Stage Manager	Technical Supervisor	Associate Producers
Alan Wasser Associates **Allan Williams**	**Lois L. Griffing**	**Juniper Street Productions**	**Marcia Goldberg** **Greg Schaffert**

Music Supervision and Arrangements by
Stephen Oremus

Additional Choreography by
Sergio Trujillo

Choreographed by
Ken Roberson

Directed by
Christopher Ashley

Originally Produced for Goodspeed Musicals • Michael P. Price, Executive Producer • Sue Frost, Associate Producer
Original Cast Recording album from Sony BMG

All Shook Up and Elvis Presley are registered trademarks of Elvis Presley Enterprises, Inc.

LIVE BROADWAY

6/1/05

Cheyenne Jackson (center) leads the cast in singing "C'mon Everybody."

Photo by Joan Marcus

All Shook Up

MUSICAL NUMBERS

ACT I

"Love Me Tender"	Natalie, Dennis
"Heartbreak Hotel"	Barflies
"Roustabout"	Chad
"One Night With You"	Natalie
"C'mon Everybody"	Chad, Company
"Follow That Dream"	Chad, Natalie
"Teddy Bear/Hound Dog"	Chad, Sandra, Dennis, Natalie
"That's All Right"	Sylvia, Lorraine, Chad, Dennis, Barflies
"(You're the) Devil in Disguise"	Matilda, Ladies Church Council
"It's Now or Never"	Dean, Lorraine, Company
"Blue Suede Shoes"	Ed, Chad
"Don't Be Cruel"	Chad, Jim
"Let Yourself Go"	Sandra, Statues
"Can't Help Falling in Love"	Company

ACT II

"All Shook Up"	Company
"It Hurts Me"	Dennis, Company
"A Little Less Conversation"	Ed, Company
"The Power of My Love"	Chad, Jim, Sandra
"I Don't Want To"	Chad
"Jailhouse Rock"	Chad, Prisoners
"There's Always Me"	Sylvia
"If I Can Dream"	Chad, Lorraine, Dean, Company
"Can't Help Falling in Love" (Reprise)	Earl, Jim, Sylvia, Matilda
"Fools Fall in Love"	Natalie, Company
"Burning Love"	Chad, Natalie, Company

Dance Captains:
RANDY A. DAVIS,
JENNIE FORD

Assistant Dance Captain:
JENNY-LYNN SUCKLING

SWINGS
RANDY A. DAVIS, JENNIE FORD,
JENELLE LYNN RANDALL

UNDERSTUDIES
For Natalie Haller:
CARA COOPER, ANIKA LARSEN
For Jim Haller:
BRAD ANDERSON, MICHAEL X. MARTIN
For Dennis:
JUSTIN BRILL, PAUL CASTREE
For Sylvia:
FRANCESCA HARPER, VIRGINIA
WOODRUFF
For Lorraine:
TRISHA JEFFREY, JENELLE LYNN RANDALL
For Chad:
BRAD ANDERSON, JUSTIN PATTERSON
For Mayor Matilda Hyde:
KAREN MURPHY, JENNY-LYNN SUCKLING
For Dean Hyde:
JUSTIN BOHON, JUSTIN BRILL
For Sheriff Earl:
MICHAEL X. MARTIN, JUSTIN PATTERSON
For Miss Sandra:
MICHELLE KITTRELL, ANIKA LARSEN,
JENNY-LYNN SUCKLING

BAND
Conductor/Keyboard: Stephen Oremus
Associate Conductor: August Eriksmoen
Reeds: Charles Pillow, Tim Ries,
Andy Snitzer, Don McGeen
Lead Trumpet: Joe Giorgianni
Trumpets: Tino Gagliardi, Brian Pareschi
Trombone: Mike Davis
Organ/Keyboard 2: August Eriksmoen
Guitars: Ken Brescia, Chris Delis
Bass: Cary Potts
Drums: Steve Bartosik
Percussion: Joe Mowatt

Music Coordinator: Michael Keller
Music Copying: Kaye-Houston Music/
Anne Kaye & Doug Houston
Synthesizer Programmer: Andrew Barrett
for Lionella Productions, Ltd.
Guitars provided by Gibson Guitars, Inc.

Cheyenne Jackson (center)
and the Ensemble.

Photo by Joan Marcus

All Shook Up

Jenn Gambatese
Natalie Haller/Ed

Jonathan Hadary
Jim Haller

Leah Hocking
Miss Sandra

Curtis Holbrook
Dean Hyde

Cheyenne Jackson
Chad

Nikki M. James
Lorraine

John Jellison
Sheriff Earl

Alix Korey
Mayor Matilda Hyde

Mark Price
Dennis

Sharon Wilkins
Sylvia

Brad Anderson
Ensemble

Justin Bohon
Ensemble

Justin Brill
Ensemble

Paul Castree
Ensemble

Cara Cooper
Ensemble

Michael Cusumano
Ensemble

Randy A. Davis
Ensemble; Dance Captain

Jennie Ford
Ensemble; Dance Captain

Francesca Harper
Ensemble

Trisha Jeffrey
Ensemble

Michelle Kittrell
Ensemble

Anika Larsen
Ensemble

Michael X. Martin
Ensemble

Karen Murphy
Ensemble

John Eric Parker
Ensemble

Justin Patterson
Ensemble

Jenelle Lynn Randall
Ensemble

Michael James Scott
Ensemble

Jenny-Lynn Suckling
Ensemble; Assistant Dance Captain

Virginia Ann Woodruff
Ensemble

Joe DiPietro
Book

Christopher Ashley
Director

Ken Roberson
Choreographer

Sergio Trujillo
Additional Choreography

Stephen Oremus
Music Supervision/ Arrangements/ Orchestrations

All Shook Up

David Rockwell
Set Design

David C. Woolard
Costume Designer

Donald Holder
Lighting Design

Brian Ronan
Sound Design

David H. Lawrence
Hair Design

Michael Gibson
Orchestrations

Michael Keller
Music Coordinator

Juniper Street Productions/
Guy Kwan, John Paull, Hillary Blanken,
Kevin Broomell, Ana-Rose Greene
Technical Supervisor

Bernard Telsey
Casting, C.S.A.
Casting

Alan Wasser
Associates
General Manager

Jonathan Pollard
Producer

Nina Essman
Producer

Nancy Nagel Gibbs
Producer

Harvey Weinstein
Producer

Margaret Cotter
Producer

Aaron Harnick and David Broser
Harbor Entertainment
Producer

Eric Falkenstein
Producer

Marcia Goldberg
Associate Producer

TRANSFER STUDENTS 2005-2006

Renee Monique
Brown
Ensemble

Mike Cannon
Ensemble

Joseph Corella
Ensemble

Cicily Daniels
Ensemble

Ashley Amber Haase
Ensemble, Swing

April Nixon
Ensemble

Julie Reiber
*Ensemble, Natalie
Haller/Ed*

Brian Sears
*u/s Dean Hyde,
Dennis, Sheriff Earl*

All Shook Up

Photos by Ben Strothmann

CREW
Back Row (L-R): Aaron Straus, Mark Rampmeyer.
Center Row (L-R): David Grevengoed, Mike Bernstein, Carlos Martinez, Ian Michaud, Marvin Crosland, Bobby Kelly, Dave Brown.
Kneeling (L-R): Jack Anderson and Geoff Vaughn.

BOX OFFICE
(L-R): Bob Kitson, Cissy Caspare
and Pat Purpura.

STAGE MANAGEMENT
(L-R): Chris Zaccardi, Megan Schneid,
Lois L. Griffing and
Paul J. Smith.

All Shook Up

ORCHESTRA
(L-R): Tim Ries, Tino Gagliardi, Joe Giorgianni, Andy Snitzer, August Eriksmoen, Mike Davis, Don McGeen, Joe Mowatt, Chris Delis, Cary Potts and Steve Bartosik.

FRONT OF HOUSE
In Front: Rose Zangale. Second Row (L-R): Alyson Handleman, Helen Geanolaes, Patricia Marsh, Sandra Darbasie, Dixon Rosario, Jr., Desteny Bivona. Third Row (L-R): Gloria Hill, Paul Vanderlinen, Edie Sanabria, Jennifer Butt and Bill Mullen.

All Shook Up

STAFF FOR *ALL SHOOK UP*

GENERAL MANAGEMENT
ALAN WASSER ASSOCIATES
Alan Wasser   Allan Williams
Lane Marsh   Aaron Lustbader

GENERAL PRESS REPRESENTATION
BARLOW•HARTMAN
Michael Hartman   John Barlow
Wayne Wolfe   Andrew Snyder

CASTING BY
Bernard Telsey Casting
Bernard Telsey   Will Cantler   David Vaccari
Bethany Knox   Craig Burns   Tiffany Little Canfield
Christine Dall   Stephanie Yankwitt

COMPANY MANAGER
Mark Shacket

PRODUCTION MANAGEMENT
JUNIPER STREET PRODUCTIONS
Hillary Blanken   John Paull III
Kevin Broomell   Guy Kwan

PRODUCTION STAGE MANAGER ....
..........LOIS L. GRIFFING
Stage Manager ....Paul J. Smith
Assistant Stage Managers ....Megan Schneid,
Chris Zaccardi
Associate Company Manager ....Maria T. Mazza
General Management Associates ....Thom Mitchell,
Connie Yung
Associate Director ....Daniel Goldstein
Associate Choreographer ....Lorna Ventura
Music Coordinator ....Michael Keller
Rehearsal Pianist ....Jason DeBord
Dance Captains ....Randy A. Davis, Jennie Ford
Assistant Dance Captain ....Jenny-Lynn Suckling
Make-Up Designer ....Angelina Avallone
Associate Scenic Designer ....Robert Bissinger
Associate to Mr. Rockwell ....Barry Richards
Assistant Scenic Designers ....Ted LeFevre,
Dan Kuchar, Todd Ivins,
Michael Auszara, Ed Pisoni,
Rob Andrusko, Richard Jaris
Assistants to Mr. Rockwell ....Nikita Polyanski,
Corinne Merrill, Daniela Galli
Assistant to Mr. Harnick and Mr. Broser ....Lisa Lapan
Model Makers ....Rachel Janocko, Joanie
Schlafer,
Morgan Moore, Mike Dereskewicz
Associate Lighting Designer ....Jeanne Koenig
Associate Lighting Designer/
Automated Lighting ....Aland Henderson
Assistant Lighting Designer ....Michael P. Jones
Assistant to the Lighting Designer ....Jesse Belsky
Associate to Donald Holder ....Hilary Manners
Automated Lighting Programmer ....Richard Tyndall
Associate Sound Designer ....Mike Farfalla
Associate Costume Designer ....Kevin Brainerd
Assistant Costume Designers ....Daryl A. Stone,
E. Shura Pollatsek
Costume Buyer ....Rebecca Bentjen
Costume Assistant ....Matthew Pachtman
Costume Interns ....Angie Harner (Chicago),
Bretta Heilbut (NY)
Production Electrician ....Jimmy Maloney
Production Properties Supervisor ....Timothy Abel
Head Carpenter ....Jack Anderson
Assistant Carpenters ....Dave Brown, Matt Lynch,
Geoffrey Vaughn
Head Electrician ....Carlos Martinez
Assistant Electricians ....Kevin Barry, Michael
Taylor
Head Properties Supervisor ....Michael Bernstein
Assistant Properties Supervisor ....Marvin Crosland
Head Sound Engineer ....Aaron Straus
Assistant Sound Engineer ....TJ McEvoy
Production Wardrobe Supervisor ....Debbie Cheretun
Assistant Wardrobe Supervisor ....James Hall
Hair Supervisor ....Wanda Gregory
Assistant Hair Supervisor ....Mark Adam Rampmeyer
Hairstylist ....Charlene Belmond
Production Management Associates .....Ana-Rose Greene,
Emily Lawson
Production Assistants ....Robert M. Armitage,
Nellie Beavers, Dan Creviston,
Sara Gammage, Annie Leonhart,
Matthew Melchiorre,
Blake Merriman, Chris Zaccardi

Production Associate to Mr. Pollard ....Susan Vargo
Synthesizer Programmer ....Andrew Barrett,
Lionella Productions LTD
Music Dept. Production Assistants ....Justin A.
Malakhow,
Alan Schmuckler (Chi), Joshua Salzman
Copyists ....Kaye-Houston Music, Inc.
Legal Counsel ....Franklin, Weinrib, Rudell & Vasallo/
Elliot Brown, Daniel Wasser,
Jonathan Lonner
Insurance ....DeWitt Stern Group
Banking ....JP Morgan Chase & Co./
Richard Callian, Michele Gibbons
Accounting ....Rosenberg Neuwirth & Kuchner/
Chris Cacace, Patricia Pedersen
Audit ....Robert Fried, C.P.A.
Travel ....Road Rebel Entertainment Touring
Payroll Service ....Castellana Services Inc.
Advertising ....SpotCo/Drew Hodges, Jim Edwards,
Tom Greenwald, Jim Aquino,
Lauren Hunter
Marketing ....The Marketing Group/
Laura Matalon, Tanya Grubich,
Marti Wigder Grimminck,
Jenny Richardson,
Trish Santini, Jennifer Shultz
Merchandising ....SFX Theatrical Merchandising,
Larry Turk
Web Designer ....Simma Park
Theatre Displays ....King Displays, Inc.
Production Photographer ....Joan Marcus

Cover illustration by Jonas Bergstrand.
© Gladys Music 2004.
Elvis Presley is a trademark of Elvis Presley Enterprises, Inc.

CREDITS AND ACKNOWLEDGMENTS
Scenery and scenic effects built and electrified by ShowMotion, Inc., Norwalk, Connecticut and PRG Scenic Technologies, New Windsor, NY. Scenery painted by Scenic Art Studios, Cornwall, NY. Show control and scenic motion control featuring stage command systems® by PRG Scenic Technologies. Show control, fly automation and special effects using AC2 computerized motion control system by ShowMotion Inc. Softgoods built by I. Weiss and Sons, Inc., Long Island City, NY. Lighting equipment from PRG Lighting, North Bergen, NJ. Sound equipment from PRG Audio, Mt. Vernon, NY. Specialty props executed by The Spoon Group, Rahway, NJ; and Jauchem and Meeh, Brooklyn, NY. Additional hand props courtesy of George Fenmore, Inc. Acrylic drinkware by U.S. Acrylic, Inc. Costumes made by Barbara Matera Ltd, Parsons-Meares Ltd., Studio Rouge, Timberlake Studios Inc., Tricorne; uniforms by Park Coats; custom shirts by CEGO; custom leatherwear by Francis Hendy; custom gloves by Dorothy Gaspar; millinery by Arnold S. Levine, Inc., and Rodney Gordon, Inc.; uniform hats by Tanen Co.; custom sweaters by Maria Ficalora Knitwear Ltd.; shoes made by Capezio Dance-Theatre Professional Shop, JC Theatrical Shoes and LaDuca Shoes NYC; fabric dyeing/printing by Dye-Namix and Gene Mignola Inc. Leatherwear in part courtesy of SCHOTT NYC; men's undershirts courtesy of 2(x)ist. Study guide by Peter Royston/GUIDEWRITE. Special thanks to Goodspeed Musicals Costume Rentals. Custom wigs executed by D.H. Lawrence Enterprises, Inc. Interstate hauling by Clark Transfer, Inc. Natural herb cough drops courtesy of Ricola USA, Inc. Rehearsed at The New 42nd Street Studios. Special thanks to Fred Gallo.

SPECIAL THANKS
Susan Aberbach, Belinda Aberbach, David Beckwith, Jennifer Burgess, Carol Butler, Carolyn Christensen, Jennifer DeLange, Gibson Musical Instruments and Epiphone Guitars, Joanna Hagan, Alexander Hartnett, Gary Hovey, Debbie Johnson, Roberta Korus, Tom Levy, Richard Mincheff, Todd Morgan, Steven Rodner, Patrick Roy, Adina Schecter, Tim Schmidt, Abbie Schroeder, Jack Soden, Michael Sukin, Beth Williams, Scott Williams, Scott Yoselow

SONG CREDITS
"Love Me Tender" by Elvis Presley and Vera Matson; published by Elvis Presley Music (administered by Cherry River Music Co. and by Chrysalis Songs) (BMI). **"Roustabout"** by Bill Giant, Bernie Baum and Florence Kaye; published by Elvis Presley Music (administered by Cherry River Music Co. and by Chrysalis Songs) (BMI). **"Heartbreak Hotel"** written by Elvis Presley, Mae Boren Axton and Tommy Durden; published by Sony/ATV Songs LLC, dba Tree Publishing Co. (BMI). **"One Night"** written by Dave Bartholomew and Pearl King; published by Elvis Presley Music (administered by Cherry River Music Co. and by Chrysalis Songs) and by Sony/ATV Songs LLC (BMI). **"C'mon Everybody"** written by Joy Byers; published by Gladys Music (administered by Cherry Lane Music Publishing Company, Inc. and by Chrysalis Music) (ASCAP). **"Follow That Dream"** words by Fred Wise, music by Ben Weisman; published by Warner Chappell Music Inc. on behalf of Chappell & Co. Inc. (ASCAP) and by Spirit Two Music Inc. on behalf of Erika Publishing (ASCAP). **"Hound Dog"** written by Jerry Leiber and Mike Stoller; published by Gladys Music (administered by Cherry Lane Music Publishing Company, Inc. and by Chrysalis Music) and by Universal-MCA Music Publishing (ASCAP). **"Teddy Bear"** written by Kal Mann and Bernie Lowe; published by Gladys Music (administered by Cherry Lane Music Publishing Company, Inc. and Chrysalis Music) (ASCAP). **"That's All Right"** written by Arthur Crudup; published by Crudup Music and Unichapel Music, Inc. (BMI). **"Devil in Disguise"** written by Bill Giant, Bernie Baum and Florence Kaye; published by Elvis Presley Music (administered by Cherry River Music Co. and by Chrysalis Songs) (BMI). **"It's Now or Never"** written by Aaron Schroeder and Wally Gold Published by Rachel's Own Music [administered by A. Schroeder International Ltd,] and by Gladys Music [administered by Cherry Lane Music Publishing Company, Inc. and by Chrysalis Music] (ASCAP). **"Blue Suede Shoes"** written by Carl Perkins; published by Wren Music Co. Inc, on behalf of Carl Perkins Music, c/o MPL Communications, Inc. (BMI) **"Don't Be Cruel"** written by Otis Blackwell and Elvis Presley; published by Elvis Presley Music (administered by Cherry River Music Co. and by Chrysalis Songs) and by EMI Music Publishing (BMI). **"Let Yourself Go"** written by Joy Byers; published by Gladys Music (administered by Cherry Lane Music Publishing Company, Inc. and by Chrysalis Music) (ASCAP). **"Can't Help Falling in Love"** written by George David Weiss, Hugo Peretti and Luigi Creatore; published by Gladys Music (administered by Cherry Lane Music Publishing Company, Inc. and by Chrysalis Music) (ASCAP). **"All Shook Up"** written by Otis Blackwell and Elvis Presley; published by Elvis Presley Music (administered by Cherry River Music Co. and by Chrysalis Songs) and by EMI Music Publishing (BMI). **"It Hurts Me"** written by Joy Byers and Charles E. Daniels; published by Gladys Music (administered by Cherry Lane Music Publishing Company, Inc. and by Chrysalis Music) and by Warner/Chappell Music Inc. (ASCAP). **"A Little Less Conversation"** written by Mac Davis and Billy Strange; published by Elvis Presley Music (administered by Cherry River Music Co. and by Chrysalis Songs) (BMI). **"The Power of My Love"** written by Bill Giant, Bernie Baum and Florence Kaye; published by Elvis Presley Music (administered by Cherry River Music Co. and by Chrysalis Songs) (BMI). **"I Don't Want To"** words by Janice Torre, music by Fred Spielman; published by Gladys Music (administered by Cherry Lane Music Publishing Company, Inc. and by Chrysalis Music) (ASCAP). **"Jailhouse Rock"** written by Jerry Leiber and Mike Stoller; published by Jerry Leiber Music and Mike Stoller Music (ASCAP). **"There's Always Me"** written by Don Robertson; published by Don Robertson Music Corp. (ASCAP). **"If I Can Dream"** written by W. Earl Brown; published by Gladys Music (administered by Cherry Lane Music Publishing Company, Inc. and by Chrysalis Music) (ASCAP). **"Fools Fall in Love"** written by Jerry Leiber and Mike Stoller; published by Jerry Leiber Music and Mike Stoller Music (ASCAP). **"Burning Love"** written by Dennis Linde; published by Sony/ATV Songs LLC (BMI).

All Shook Up

Scrapbook

Photos by Aubrey Reuben

1. Members of the cast pose at a CD signing at the Virgin Megastore in Times Square (L-R): Mark Price, Curtis Holbrook, Cheyenne Jackson, Nikki M. James, Leah Hocking and Jenn Gambatese.
2. Gambatese at the opening day of the Broadway Softball League in Central Park.
3. The cast performs at the Virgin Megastore.
4. (L-R): Kelli Carpenter, comedienne Judy Gold, Gold's two sons, Gambatese (kneeling) and Jackson backstage at the Palace Theatre.
5. (L-R): Nikki M. James, Cheyenne Jackson and Curtis Holbrook at "Broadway on Broadway" in Times Square.

Avenue Q

First Preview: July 10, 2003. Opened: July 31, 2003.
Still running as of May 31, 2006.

PLAYBILL

CAST
(in order of appearance)

Princeton, Rod ....BARRETT FOA
Brian ....JORDAN GELBER
Kate Monster, Lucy
& others ....STEPHANIE D'ABRUZZO
Nicky, Trekkie Monster, Bear
& others ....CHRISTIAN ANDERSON
Christmas Eve.........................ANN HARADA
Gary Coleman ....NATALIE VENETIA BELCON
Mrs. T., Bear & others...JENNIFER BARNHART
Ensemble ....MATT SCHREIBER,
HOWIE MICHAEL SMITH

Place: an outerborough of New York City
Time: the present

UNDERSTUDIES

For Princeton/Rod – MATT SCHREIBER,
HOWIE MICHAEL SMITH; for Brian –
MATT SCHREIBER; for Kate Monster/Lucy –
BECCA AYERS, JENNIFER BARNHART;
for Nicky/Trekkie/Bear – MATT SCHREIBER,
HOWIE MICHAEL SMITH; for Mrs. T./Bear –
BECCA AYERS, MINGLIE CHEN,
CARMEN RUBY FLOYD, ANN SANDERS;
for Christmas Eve – MINGLIE CHEN,
ANN SANDERS; for Gary Coleman – CARMEN
RUBY FLOYD.

DANCE CAPTAIN: Natalie Venetia Belcon

AVENUE Q BAND
Keyboard/Conductor: Gary Adler
Keyboard/Associate Conductor: Dorothy Martin
Reeds: Patience Higgins; **Drums:** Scott Neumann
Bass: Maryann McSweeney
Guitars: Brian Koonin

⑧ GOLDEN THEATRE
A Shubert Organization Theatre
Gerald Schoenfeld, *Chairman*   Philip J. Smith, *President*

Robert E. Wankel, *Executive Vice President*

Kevin McCollum   Robyn Goodman   Jeffrey Seller
Vineyard Theatre   and   The New Group
present

Music and Lyrics by
Robert Lopez and Jeff Marx

Book by
Jeff Whitty

Based on an Original Concept by
Robert Lopez and Jeff Marx

with

**Christian Anderson, Jennifer Barnhart, Natalie Venetia Belcon,
Stephanie D'Abruzzo, Barrett Foa, Jordan Gelber, Ann Harada**

Puppets Conceived and Designed by
Rick Lyon

Set Design	Costume Design	Lighting Design	Sound Design
Anna Louizos	**Mirena Rada**	**Howell Binkley**	**Acme Sound Partners**

Animation Design	Music Director & Incidental Music	Music Coordinator	Casting
Robert Lopez	**Gary Adler**	**Michael Keller**	**Cindy Tolan**

General Manager	Technical Supervisor	Production Stage Manager
John Corker	**Brian Lynch**	**Robert Witherow**

Press Representative	Marketing	Associate Producers
Sam Rudy Media Relations	**TMG-The Marketing Group**	**Sonny Everett Walter Grossman Mort Swinsky**

Music Supervision, Arrangement
and Orchestrations by
Stephen Oremus

Choreographer
Ken Roberson

Directed by
Jason Moore

*Avenue Q was supported by a residency and public staged reading at the
2002 O'Neill Music Theatre Conference of the Eugene O'Neill Theater Center, Waterford, CT*

LIVE
BROADWAY

9/26/05

Jennifer Barnhart and
Christian Anderson
with
Trekkie Monster

Photo by Nick Reuchel

Avenue Q

Christian Anderson
Nicky, Trekkie Monster, Bad Idea Bear #1 & Others

Jennifer Barnhart
Mrs. T., Bear & Others

Natalie Venetia Belcon
Gary Coleman

Stephanie D'Abruzzo
Kate Monster, Lucy & Others

Barrett Foa
Princeton/Rod

Jordan Gelber
Brian

Ann Harada
Christmas Eve

Becca Ayers
Understudy for Kate Monster, Lucy, Mrs. T., Bear

Minglie Chen
Understudy for Christmas Eve, Mrs. T., Bear

Carmen Ruby Floyd
Understudy for Gary Coleman, Mrs. T., Bear

Ann Sanders
Ensemble

Matt Schreiber
Ensemble

Howie Michael Smith
Ensemble

Jeff Whitty
Book

Robert Lopez and Jeff Marx
Music and Lyrics, Original Concept

Jason Moore
Director

Ken Roberson
Choreography

Stephen Oremus
Music Supervision/ Arrangements/ Orchestrations

Rick Lyon
Puppet Design

Anna Louizos
Set Design

Mirena Rada
Costume Design

Howell Binkley
Lighting Design

Tom Clark, Mark Menard, and Nevin Steinberg,
Acme Sound Partners
Sound Design

Gary Adler
Musical Director/ Conductor/ Incidental Music

Michael Keller
Music Coordinator

John Corker
General Manager

Kevin McCollum
Producer

Robyn Goodman
Producer

Jeffrey Seller
Producer

Sonny Everett
Associate Producer

Mort Swinsky
Associate Producer

Avenue Q Alumni 2005-2006

Angela Ai
Understudy for Christmas Eve

Avenue Q

Leo Daignault
Ensemble

Aymee Garcia
*Understudy for
Christmas Eve,
Kate Monster, Lucy,
Mrs. T, Bear*

Peter Linz
Ensemble

Rick Lyon
*Nicky, Trekkie
Monster, Bear &
Others*

Mimosa
*Understudy for
Christmas Eve*

Jasmin Walker
*Understudy for
Gary Coleman*

Leo Daignault
Ensemble

Mary Faber
*Kate Monster, Lucy
& Others*

Aymee Garcia
*Understudy for
Christmas Eve,
Kate Monster, Lucy,
Mrs. T, Bear*

Evan Harrington
Brian

Sala Iwamatsu
Christmas Eve

Jasmin Walker
*Understudy for
Gary Coleman*

SCRAPBOOK

1. The cast celebrates the show's
1000th performance backstage.
2. Stephanie D'Abruzzo (L) and
Ann Harada at "Broadway on
Broadway."
3. "Avenue Q Swings" at Birdland.
Back Row (L-R): Christian
Anderson, Maryann McSweeney,
Laura Marie Duncan, Christine
Pedi, Barrett Foa, Giselle Jackson.
Front (L-R): Ann Harada and
Stephanie D'Abruzzo.

Avenue Q

Awake and Sing!

First Preview: March 23, 2006. Opened: April 17, 2006.
Still running as of May 31, 2006.

PLAYBILL

AWAKE AND SING!

CAST

(in order of speaking)

Ralph Berger ....PABLO SCHREIBER
Myron Berger................JONATHAN HADARY
Hennie Berger ....LAUREN AMBROSE
Jacob ....BEN GAZZARA
Bessie Berger ....ZOË WANAMAKER
Schlosser..............................PETER KYBART
Moe Axelrod ....MARK RUFFALO
Uncle Morty ....NED EISENBERG
Sam Feinschreiber ....RICHARD TOPOL

Time: The mid 1930s
Place: An apartment in the Bronx, New York City

Act I:
A winter evening
Intermission
Act II, Scene 1:
One year later, afternoon
Two-minute pause
Act II, Scene 2:
Later that night
Intermission
Act III:
A week later

Continued on next page

⑥ BELASCO THEATRE
111 West 44th Street
A Shubert Organization Theatre
Gerald Schoenfeld, *Chairman*   **Philip J. Smith,** *President*

Robert E. Wankel, *Executive Vice President*

LINCOLN CENTER THEATER
under the direction of
ANDRÉ BISHOP and **BERNARD GERSTEN**
presents

AWAKE AND SING!

by **CLIFFORD ODETS**

with (in alphabetical order)

LAUREN AMBROSE   NED EISENBERG   BEN GAZZARA

JONATHAN HADARY   PETER KYBART   MARK RUFFALO

PABLO SCHREIBER   RICHARD TOPOL   ZOË WANAMAKER

sets **MICHAEL YEARGAN**   costumes **CATHERINE ZUBER**   lighting **CHRISTOPHER AKERLIND**

sound **PETER JOHN STILL** and **MARC SALZBERG**   stage manager **ROBERT BENNETT**

casting **DANIEL SWEE**   general press agent **PHILIP RINALDI**

director of development **HATTIE K. JUTAGIR**   director of marketing **LINDA MASON ROSS**

general manager **ADAM SIEGEL**   production manager **JEFF HAMLIN**

directed by **BARTLETT SHER**

LCT gratefully acknowledges generous support in memory of Robert J. Blinken.
The Blanchette Hooker Rockefeller Fund has provided a major grant for this production.
Additional support is provided by the David Berg Foundation.
AWAKE AND SING! is supported by the Doris Duke Charitable Foundation Endowment Fund at LCT.
Special thanks to the New York City Department of Cultural Affairs and the Council of the City of New York.

American Airlines is the official airline of Lincoln Center Theater.
Merrill Lynch is a 2006 LCT season sponsor.

LCT wishes to express its appreciation to Theatre Development Fund for its support of this production.

Get your copy of the Lincoln Center Theater Review on AWAKE AND SING!
available at stands near the exit doors, featuring a rare interview with Clifford Odets.

4/17/06

(L-R): Jonathan Hadary, Mark Ruffalo, Ned Eisenberg and and Ben Gazzara.

Photo by Paul Kolnik

Awake and Sing!

Cast Continued

Assistant Stage Manager ....DENISE YANEY

UNDERSTUDIES
For Myron Berger and Uncle Morty:
TONY CAMPISI

For Jacob and Schlosser:
STAN LACHOW

For Hennie Berger:
ANNIE PURCELL

For Ralph Berger:
CHARLES SOCARIDES

For Moe Axelrod and Sam Feinschreiber:
ED VASSALLO

For Bessie Berger:
LORI WILNER

Photo by Paul Kolnik

(L-R): Pablo Schreiber
and Ben Gazzara.

Lauren Ambrose
Hennie Berger

Ned Eisenberg
Uncle Morty

Ben Gazzara
Jacob

Jonathan Hadary
Myron Berger

Peter Kybart
Schlosser

Mark Ruffalo
Moe Axelrod

Pablo Schreiber
Ralph Berger

Richard Topol
Sam Feinschreiber

Zoë Wanamaker
Bessie Berger

Tony Campisi
*Understudy for
Myron Berger and
Uncle Morty*

Stan Lachow
*Understudy for
Jacob and Schlosser*

Annie Purcell
*Understudy for
Hennie Berger*

Charles Socarides
*Understudy for
Ralph Berger*

Ed Vassallo
*Understudy for
Moe Axelrod and
Sam Feinschreiber*

Lori Wilner
*Understudy for
Bessie Berger*

Clifford Odets
Playwright

Bartlett Sher
Director

Michael Yeargan
Sets

Catherine Zuber
Costumes

Christopher Akerlind
Lighting

Awake and Sing!

Marc Salzberg
Sound

William Berloni
Animal Trainer

Robert Bennett
Stage Manager

Denise Yaney
*Assistant
Stage Manager*

André Bishop
*Artistic Director,
Lincoln Center
Theater*

Bernard Gersten
*Executive Producer,
Lincoln Center
Theater*

FRONT OF HOUSE STAFF
Front Row (L-R):
Dexter Luke and Eugenia Raines.

Second Row (L-R):
Gwendolyn Coley, Meaghan McElroy, Terry Lynch.

Third Row (L-R):
Elisabel Asencio, Kathleen Dunn, Daniel Rosario.

Back Row (L-R):
Tina Bashore and David Josephson.

Photos by Ben Strothmann

STAGE CREW
Front Row (L-R):
Susan Goulet (House Electrician),
Rodd Sovar (Dresser), Dylan Foley
(Properties), Heidi Brown
(House Properties), George Dummitt
(House Carpenter), Nichole Amburg
(Dresser).

Back Row (L-R):
Denise Yaney (Stage Manager),
Cyrille Blackburn (Production Assistant),
Neil B. McShane (Electrician),
Valerie Speadling (Sound Operator),
Paul Luddick (Dresser), Greg Husinko
(Electrician), Rob Cox (Animal Handler),
Patrick O'Connor (Properties),
John Weingart (Production Carpenter),
Al Toth (Deck Carpenter)
and Joseph Moritz (House Flyman).

Awake and Sing!

Photo by Ben Strothmann

BOX OFFICE
(L-R): Thomas (Tommy) Sheehan (Treasurer) and Jules Ochoa.

LINCOLN CENTER THEATER

ANDRÉ BISHOP	BERNARD GERSTEN
ARTISTIC DIRECTOR	EXECUTIVE PRODUCER

ADMINISTRATIVE STAFF
GENERAL MANAGER ....ADAM SIEGEL
Associate General Manager ....Melanie Weinraub
General Management Assistant ....Beth Dembrow
Facilities Manager ....Alex Mustelier
Assistant Facilities Manager ....Michael Assalone
GENERAL PRESS AGENT ....PHILIP RINALDI
Press Associate ....Barbara Carroll
PRODUCTION MANAGER ....JEFF HAMLIN
Associate Production Manager ....Paul Smithyman
DIRECTOR OF
DEVELOPMENT ....HATTIE K. JUTAGIR
Associate Director of Development ....Rachel Norton
Manager of Special Events and
Young Patron Program ....Karin Schall
Grants Writer ....Neal Brilliant
Coordinator, Patron Program ....Sheilaja Rao
Development Associate ....Chris Chrzanowski
Assistant to the
Director of Development ....Marsha Martinez
Development Assistant/
Special Events ....Nicole Lindenbaum
DIRECTOR OF FINANCE..........DAVID S. BROWN
Controller ....Susan Knox
Systems Manager................Stacy Valentine-Thomas
Finance Assistant ....Kellie Kroyer
DIRECTOR OF
MARKETING ....LINDA MASON ROSS
Marketing Associate ....Denis Guerin
Marketing Assistant ....Elizabeth Kandel
DIRECTOR OF EDUCATION ....KATI KOERNER
Associate Director of Education ....Dionne O'Dell
Assistant to the Executive Producer ...Barbara Hourigan
Office Assistant ....Kenneth Collins
Messenger ....Esau Burgess
Reception ....Andrew Elsesser, Daryl Watson

ARTISTIC STAFF
ASSOCIATE DIRECTORS ......GRACIELA DANIELE,
NICHOLAS HYTNER,
SUSAN STROMAN,
DANIEL SULLIVAN
DRAMATURG and DIRECTOR,
LCT DIRECTORS LAB ....ANNE CATTANEO
CASTING DIRECTOR ....DANIEL SWEE, CSA

MUSICAL THEATER
ASSOCIATE PRODUCER ....IRA WEITZMAN
Artistic Administrator ....Julia Judge
Casting Associate ....Camille Hickman

In Loving Memory of
GERALD GUTIERREZ
Associate Director 1991-2003

SPECIAL SERVICES
Advertising ....Serino-Coyne/Jim Russek
Christin Seidel
Principal Poster Artist ....James McMullan
Poster Art for *Awake and Sing!*............James McMullan
Counsel ....Peter L. Felcher, Esq.;
Charles H. Googe, Esq.;
and Rachel Hoover, Esq. of
Paul, Weiss, Rifkind, Wharton & Garrison
Immigration Counsel ....Theodore Ruthizer, Esq.;
Mark D. Koestler, Esq.
of Kramer, Levin, Naftalis & Frankel LLP
Auditor ....Douglas Burack, C.P.A.
Lutz & Carr, L.L.P.
Insurance ....Jennifer Brown of
DeWitt Stern Group
Photographer ....Paul Kolnik
Travel ....Tygon Tours
Consulting Architect ....Hugh
Hardy,
Hardy Holzman Pfeiffer Associates
Construction Manager ....Yorke Construction
Payroll Service ....Castellana Services, Inc.

STAFF FOR *AWAKE AND SING!*
COMPANY MANAGER.......MATTHEW MARKOFF
Assistant Director ....Sarna Lapine
Assistant Set Designer ....Mikiko Suzuki
Assistant Costume Designers ....David Newell,
Michael Zecker
Assistant Lighting Designer ....Ben Krall
Production Carpenter ....Bill Nagle
Production Flyman ....John Weingart
Production Propertyman ....Mark Dignam
Production Electrician ....Neil McShane
Production Sound Engineer ....Valerie Spradling
Moving Light Programmer ....Steve Garner
Props Coordinator ....Christopher Schneider
Dialect Coach....................................Ralph Zito
Wardrobe Supervisor......................James Wilcox
Dressers ....Nichole Amburg, Paul Ludick,
Rodd Sovar

Wig Designer ....Tom Watson
Ms. Wanamaker's Wig ....Campbell Young
Hair Supervisor ....Susan Schectar
Makeup Designer ....Angelina Avallone
Production Assistants ....Jason Hindelang,
Cyrille Blackburn
Animal Handled by ....Robert Cox

Technical Supervision by
Walter Murphy and Patrick Merryman

Animal Trained by
William Berloni Theatrical Animals, Inc.

CREDITS
Scenery constructed by PRG Scenic Technologies. Costumes by Angels, The Costumiers; John Cowles; Carelli Costumes; Eddie Dawson; and Brian Hemeseth. Sound by PRG Audio. Lighting by PRG Lighting. Shoes by LaDuca Shoes. Special thanks to Bra*Tenders for hosiery and undergarments. Telephone bellset courtesy of Boise Contemporary Theater. Natural herb cough drops courtesy of Ricola USA, Inc.

Awake and Sing!
SCRAPBOOK

1. (L-R): Sunrise Coigney, her husband Mark Ruffalo, Elke Gazzara and husband Ben Gazzara at the opening night party at the Marriott Marquis Hotel.
2. Zoë Wanamaker arrives at the party.
3. Jonathan Hadary.

Correspondent: Richard Topol, "Sam Feinschreiber"

Opening Night Gifts: Ned Eisenberg and Mark Ruffalo compete between themselves to see who can make the most noises during the play. Some are written into the script, such as when Ned constantly says "Quack quack." On opening night, Ned got everybody a dancing Easter duck toy, garishly yellow with a ribbon. When you push it, it quacks and dances. I guess you could call that the Most Frightening Opening Night Gift.

I took a photo of our theatre's marquee and framed it with the Playbill cast lists from our production, and from the original production, which played here at the Belasco 71 years ago. It's an historical document.

Celebrity Visitors: We've had plenty but the most exciting were Buck Henry, Mike Nichols and Diane Sawyer. Mike Nichols told me, "You know, I believed you were Jewish the whole time."

Hal Prince wrote to director Bartlett Sher, saying thanks for reminding him why he works in the theatre.

Most Shows: It's got to be Ben Gazzara, with Zoë Wanamaker chasing him down the alley.

Special Backstage Rituals: During Act I, I sleep. Ned does Tai Chi. Zoë warms up in her dressing room, then goes onto the stage and tunes herself up to the space.

Favorite Moment During Each Performance: During Act II, Zoë delivers the line, "You could buy a two-cent pickle in the Berlin market." Janeta and Mark and Lauren and I are sitting offstage left, and for about five minutes before and after that line we make up variations on it. Also, when everyone is gathering for the curtain call just before the end of Act III, there is a moment of beautiful

stillness onstage and in the audience when it starts to snow on Pablo. It's a moment frozen in time.

In-Theatre Gathering Places: Zoë's room has a couch, so when we have Champagne or something, we tend to sit in there. She's sort of our den mother. We also invade everybody's dressing room with a cake when it's a birthday.

Off-Site Hangout: Café Un Deux Trois. Jose, the manager, keeps it open late for us. Our opening night party was scheduled someplace else but, afterward, we all went back to Trois.

Favorite Snack Food: We has a brilliant rehearsal cookie jar, and we grew to expect food every day. But when we got to the Belasco, it didn't follow. It's a little depressing, actually, but we don't really miss it because we eat so much onstage as part of the show: Some of us have a meal in Act I and another in Act II. It's turkey and peas, but eight times a week (16 for some of us) it gets to taste like prison food.

Mascot: Barney, our dog. Robert Cox is his handler. He comes around and visits all the actors before every show.

Favorite Therapy: Vocal Zone.

Memorable Ad-Lib: Mark is supposed to deliver a line, "A guy who slips off a roof don't leave a note before he does it." One night he said, "A guy who jumps off…er, *slips* off a roof don't leave a note before he does it."

Cell Phone Rings: Not so many during Act I, but we don't have a reminder at this theatre, so it gets pretty bad in Act II and Act III as people come back from intermission and forget to turn them off.

Memorable Stage Door Fan Encounter: A 15-year-old girl from England wore a T-shirt that had a British flag and the words, "British Girls Love Mark Ruffalo." Actually, she was sweet and shy. And Mark Ruffalo is happily married.

Memorable Directorial Note: The best note was the one Bart gave us the first day. He said he wanted us to work on the play the way the Grateful Dead make music. It's an incredible ensemble. It's a jam, and everybody's integral to the process. Bart also told us that we should dedicate each performance to somebody very specific in our lives. It was a way of making us willing to be inspired differently at every performance.

Ghostly Encounters Backstage: Nobody has had a specific strong one, but everybody's aware of the ghosts in the theatre. We feel loved and protected by the ghosts. Maybe some of them are from the original production. I did *Julius Caesar* here last year and I can tell you it was a very different vibe.

Coolest Thing About Being in This Show: There are nine people in this cast who every show step up to the plate and swing for the fences. And nobody ever strikes out.

Barefoot in the Park

First Preview: January 24, 2006. Opened: February 16, 2006.
Closed May 21, 2006 after 26 Previews and 109 Performances.

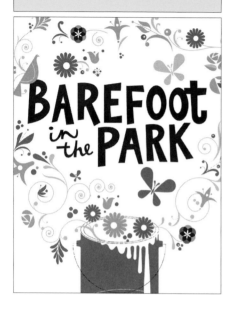

CAST
(in order of appearance)

Corie Bratter .... AMANDA PEET
Telephone Repairman .... ADAM SIETZ
Deliveryman .... SULLIVAN WALKER
Paul Bratter .... PATRICK WILSON
Corie's Mother, Mrs. Banks ...... JILL CLAYBURGH
Victor Velasco .... TONY ROBERTS

UNDERSTUDIES

For Paul, Telephone Repairman, Deliveryman:
BENIM FOSTER

For Corie:
ERIN FRITCH

For Mrs. Banks:
JENNIFER HARMON

For Victor Velasco:
SULLIVAN WALKER

---

⑤ CORT THEATRE
138 West 48th Street
A Shubert Organization Theatre

Gerald Schoenfeld, *Chairman*   Philip J. Smith, *President*

Robert E. Wankel, *Executive Vice President*

Robyn Goodman   Roy Gabay   Walt Grossman   Geoff Rich
Danzansky Partners   Ergo Entertainment   Ruth Hendel
in association with
Paramount Pictures

present

Amanda Peet   Patrick Wilson
Jill Clayburgh   Tony Roberts

in

Neil Simon's
BAREFOOT in the PARK

with
Adam Sietz and Sullivan Walker

Set Design	Costume Design	Lighting Design	Sound Design
Derek McLane	**Isaac Mizrahi**	**Jason Lyons**	**Ken Travis**

Production Stage Manager	Press Representative	Casting
Valerie A. Peterson	**Richard Kornberg & Associates**	**Judy Henderson**

Marketing	Props Coordinator	Production Manager
Margery Singer	**Kathy Fabian**	**Showman Fabricators**

General Manager
Roy Gabay

Associate Producers
Leah and Ed Frankel
Oliver Dow
CJ Entertainment/URL Productions
Stephen Kocis

Directed by
Scott Elliott

2/16/06

Tony Roberts, Jill Clayburgh and Amanda Peet chat over cocktails.

Photo by Carol Rosegg

Barefoot in the Park

Amanda Peet
Corie Bratter

Patrick Wilson
Paul Bratter

Jill Clayburgh
Mrs. Banks

Tony Roberts
Victor Velasco

Adam Sietz
Telephone Repairman

Sullivan Walker
Delivery Man

Benim Foster
Understudy for Paul, Telephone/ Deliveryman

Erin Fitch
Understudy for Corie

Jennifer Harmon
Understudy for Mrs. Banks

Neil Simon
Playwright

Scott Elliott
Director

Derek McLane
Set Design

Isaac Mizrahi
Costume Design

Jason Lyons
Lighting Design

Richard Kornberg & Associates
Press Representative

Robyn Goodman
Producer

Roy Gabay
Producer/ General Manager

Elie Landau, Yeeshai Gross, Donny Epstein
Ergo Entertainment
Producer

Ruth Hendel
Producer

Patrick Wilson and Amanda Peet try out their newly installed phone in Neil Simon's comedy.

Barefoot in the Park

BOX OFFICE
(L-R):
Diane Heatherington,
Chuck Loesche
and Jennifer Holze.

TICKET TAKERS
(L-R): Louie Palminteri,
Catherine Cosara
and Danielle Smith.

FRONT OF HOUSE STAFF
(L-R):
Front Row (L-R): Nicole McIntyre,
Danielle Smith, Jessica Hidalgo,
Jeanine Beckly.
Back Row (L-R): Marilyn Molina,
Robert De Jesus, Lea Leflen and
Brugman Auiles.

Photos by Ben Strothmann

Barefoot in the Park

Photo by Ben Strothmann

STAGE CREW
Back Row (L-R): Neil Krasnow, Valerie A. Peterson, Duane McKee, Natasha Steinhagen, Steve Loehle, Kim Prentice
Front Row (L-R): Scott DeVerna, Kay Grunder, Dylan Rafael (Standby) and Lonnie Gaddy

GENERAL MANAGEMENT
Roy Gabay Theatrical Production & Management
Cheryl Dennis, Daniel Kuney, Chris Aniello

COMPANY MANAGER
Cheryl Dennis

GENERAL PRESS REPRESENTATIVES
Richard Kornberg & Associates
Tom D'Ambrosio   Don Summa
Carrie Friedman   Laura Kaplow-Goldman

PRODUCTION SUPERVISION
Showman Fabricators, Inc.
Kai Brothers, Annie Jacobs

Production Stage Manager ....Valerie A. Peterson
Stage Manager ....Neil Krasnow
Assistant Director ....Marie Masters
Associate Set Designer ....Todd Potter
Assistant Costume Designer ....Courtney Logan
Associate Lighting Designer ....Rachel Eichorn
Associate Sound Designer ....Shannon Slaton
Wardrobe Supervisor ....Kay Grunder
Dresser ....Kim Prentice
Hair Supervisor..........................Natasha Stienhagan
Props Coordinator ....Kathy Fabian
Production Props ....Steve Loehle
Props Assistants ....Carrie Mossman, Carrie Hash
Production Carpenter...............................Frank Illo
Production Electrician ....Brian McGarity
Production Sound Supervisor ....Duane McKee
Production Assistant ....Sara Sahin
Press Assistant ....Alyssa Hart

Assistant to Ms. Goodman ....Josh Fiedler
Accountant ....Elliot Aronstam/
Robert Fried FK Partners
Banking ....JP Morgan Chase
Insurance ...........................D.R. Reiff & Associates
Legal ....John Silberman & Associates/
Karen Levinson
Payroll Services ....Castellana Services, Inc.
Car Service ...................I.B.A. Luxury Sedan Service/
Danny Ibanez
Advertising..SpotCo/
Drew Hodges, Jim Edwards,
John Lanasa, Kim Smarsh
Theatre Displays ....King Displays
Production Photographer ....Carol Rosegg
Marketing ....Margery Singer Company
Website ....David Risley, Pygmalion
Designs

CREDITS
Scenery supplied by Great Lakes Scenic Studios. Lighting equipment supplied by Hudson Sound & Light. Costumes constructed by Tricorne, Inc. Sound equipment provided by Sound Associates. Mr. Wilson's tailoring by Gilberto Designs. Wig construction by Paul Huntley. Makeup designed by Patrick Eichler for M*A*C Cosmetics. Emer'gen-C super energy booster provided by Alacer Corp. Ricola natural herb cough drops courtesy of Ricola USA, Inc.

SPECIAL THANKS
The production would like to thank Emanuel Azenberg, Ira Pittelman, Andrea Hein, Paul Blake, Stuart Rosenstein and Susan Vargo, Second Stage Theatre, Ann Guay, Mary

Wilson, Eliza Brown, Josh Escajeda, Aardvark Interiors, Jung Griffin, Passaic Metal and Building Company and Trey Gillen.

Barefootintheparkbroadway.com

 THE SHUBERT ORGANIZATION, INC.
Board of Directors

Gerald Schoenfeld	**Philip J. Smith**
Chairman	President
Wyche Fowler, Jr.	**John W. Kluge**
Lee J. Seidler	**Michael I. Sovern**

Stuart Subotnick

Robert E. Wankel
Executive Vice President

Peter Entin	**Elliot Greene**
Vice President -	Vice President -
Theatre Operations	Finance
David Andrews	**John Darby**
Vice President -	Vice President -
Shubert Ticketing Services	Facilities

CORT THEATRE
House Manager ....Joseph Traina

Barefoot in the Park
SCRAPBOOK

Yearbook Correspondents: Valerie A. Peterson (PSM) and Neil Krasnow (SM).

Opening Night Gifts: Bathrobes with the show logo, engraved martini shakers, flowers, Champagne, wine, Jack Daniel's, cookies, candy, cards, candles, leather portfolios with our initials embossed on the cover, Kiehl's products, Tiffany Champagne flutes.

Opening Night Party: The Boathouse in Central Park.

Person Who Performed the Most Roles: Benim Foster understudied three roles (Paul Bratter, Telephone Repairman & Delivery Man) and made his Broadway debut performing the role of Telephone Repairman on April 21, 2006. He also played the Delivery Man for one performance.

Person Who Has Done the Most Shows: The crew, of course, has done countless shows. In his thirteen years at the Cort alone, House Carpenter Eddie Diaz has done 18 shows (two of which, *Face Value* and *Bobbi Boland*, closed in previews/never officially opened). Tony Roberts has done 22 Broadway shows (including the original production of *Barefoot in the Park*). Producer/General Manager Roy Gabay has done 20 and counting. Jennifer Harmon has done 17. This was the Broadway debut of Amanda Peet, Adam Sietz, Benim Foster and Erin Fritch.

Special Backstage Rituals: At "places," stage management would give Amanda Peet the house count, tell her that "the needle's on the record player" and introduce Adam Sietz. Amanda and Adam Sietz always shared a moment where she would entreat him to hurry up and join her onstage so that she would have a scene partner and not be stuck onstage alone. Not knowing about this, when Erin Fritch (making her Broadway debut on March 28) went on for Amanda, she did the same thing, even using the exact same words, "Hurry up, and get out here!" During the final weeks, Amanda, Patrick, Adam and stage management also played a Pre-show "The Price Is Right"-style game to guess the house count.

As the play takes place in a fifth floor walk-up, various methods were used by the actors to prepare for their entrances including jumping up and down, jumping jacks, stepping up and down onto a chair, running, The Twist, attempted jump rope, trampoline and, when needing to enter drunk, spinning around and around and around until dizzy.

Prior to Act II, Jill Clayburgh and Amanda Peet would rinse their mouths with brandy (yes, real alcohol in the workplace) and Patrick Wilson would rinse his with Scotch (yes, more real alcohol in the workplace) to aid in the sensation of being drunk. Tony Roberts just acted. Adam Sietz threatened to drink the spit bucket but, fortunately, never did.

Sign-In: Patrick Wilson would always sign in using a different word. As the week progressed, the individual words would turn into complete thoughts that were often quite profound. Witness: "Spats aren't worn nearly enough, unlike dance belts."

The Smudging of The Cort: When, after repeated attention, the front door of the set continued to be temperamental and refused to close consistently, our lead producer Robyn Goodman requested some sage be burned. The next evening, Robyn and stage management smudged the theatre. That night, we had one of our rougher shows (angry spirits on their way out?), but after that, the door worked much better.

Ghost Story: Production Props Steve Loehle saw a ghost down in the basement. The ghost was sitting on the sofa (facing the TV) in the wardrobe area. When Steve looked at the sofa, he saw the depressed seat area lose its depression as if someone was getting up, but there was no one there.

The Curse of the Cort: Bullshit.

The Easter Bonnet: Through the dedicated efforts of the entire company (who signed and signed and signed), we raised a total of $76,694.45, winning the award for the most money raised by a Broadway play. In addition to money, some of the following items were found in our buckets: Orbit gum wrapper, Ricola wrapper, taxi receipt, Wollman Rink receipt, Bagel Boy receipt and the top from a rewetting drops container.

Nicknames: Hair Supervisor Natasha Stienhagen is known throughout the business as "Nabba."

House Prop man Lonnie Gaddy was sometimes called "Snowman." This was due to the fact that he sometimes got covered with snow during the second major shift.

The dishwasher in the basement was nicknamed Rosie, Jr. in honor of the Local One crew member it replaced.

Puzzles, Puzzles Puzzles: Tony Roberts is a whiz at *The New York Times* crossword puzzle (in ink of course). Neil Krasnow sometimes did the Monday or Tuesday puzzle but only in pencil (which Tony considers "amateur"). On the other hand, Neil successfully completed several fiendish and difficult Su-Doku puzzles that Tony, after hours of trying to solve, threw into the trash with great frustration.

Favorite Pre-Show Warm-Up: Amanda Peet singing and dancing the entire opening sequence from *A Chorus Line*.

Favorite Moments During Each Performance (Onstage or Off): Patrick Wilson drinking the

1. (L-R): Jill Clayburgh, Patrick Wilson, Amanda Peet, Tony Roberts at the opening night party at the Boathouse in Central Park 2. Producer Robyn Goodman and director Scott Elliott at the Cort Theatre on opening night. 3. Amanda Peet and Patrick Wilson at the Boathouse.

Photos by Aubrey Reuben

Barefoot in the Park
SCRAPBOOK

martini. Patrick Wilson shoving a huge piece of cake into his mouth. Dresser Kim Prentice dancing through the second scene change.

Favorite In-Theatre Gathering Place: The Cort is rather intimate so we were never far away from each other.

Favorite Off-Site Hangout: Even though we all enjoyed each other's company, we didn't spend much time together outside of the theatre. It was just a bunch of grown-ups, coming in, doing our jobs and going home. Except for the trip to Atlantic City!

Favorite Snack Food: The rehearsal hall and greenroom were always well stocked with such treats as candy, cookies, crackers, fruit, string cheese and beef jerky. Also, since there was a full cake needed in the second act and only one piece was consumed onstage, there was always an Entenmann's cake with chocolate Duncan Hines frosting (19.25 grams of trans fat per container) available to snack on in the basement.

Thursday Dinners: Every Thursday, following understudy rehearsals, the understudies would go out to dinner together.

Sunday Brunches: Insane amounts of food: bagels, cream cheese, lox, orange juice, apple juice, chicken wings, chicken fingers, deli, cole slaw, shrimp, fruit, vegetables, cheese, croissants and pastries & Danish, mini éclairs, black & white cookies, ruggelach, pecan tarts, pecan pie, Dunkin' Donuts, Krispy Kreme donuts, Entenmann's donuts, Munchkins, muffins, empanadas, salad, mini hot dogs, seafood salad, cupcakes, two-bite brownies, Quiche Lorraine, artichoke dip, guacamole & chips, caramel corn, sandwiches, deviled eggs, pretzels, potato chips, mini quiches, lemon squares, milanesa, Subway, salmon, scones, pie, pizza and post-show Champagne.

More Food: A highlight of the spring was a barbecue hosted by House Manager Joe Traina that took place in the East Alley following a Saturday matinee and featured his world-famous ribs.

Least Favorite Meal: Amanda Peet had to eat canned beef stew onstage at each performance. If that's not suffering for your art, we don't know what is.

Mascot: Wardrobe Supervisor Kay Grunder's baby, Dylan, who spent every Wednesday and Saturday matinee with us. Honorable mention: Sophie Sietz (who at the age of three can recreate, word perfect, the entire "Where's the bathtub" scene), Noah Sietz & Cordelia Foster who didn't visit as often, but when they did, always made us smile.

Mascot In-Utero: The child of Patrick Wilson and Dagmara Dominczyk.

Favorite Therapy: The laughter of the audience.

Memorable Ad Lib-less Moment: During one preview, Adam Sietz, as the Telephone Repairman, repaired the phone that was ripped out of the wall at the end of the previous scene, delivered Neil Simon's full-of-subtext speech

Curtain call on opening night.

about how sometimes phones break down, but can be fixed, turned to exit and tripped over the phone cord, ripping it out of the wall. There was nothing left to say or do but stuff the cord back into the wall and exit.

Memorable Ad-Lib: At another performance, while Adam was repairing the phone, a cell phone rang loudly in the audience. On the third ring, Adam picked up the prop phone to see if anyone was there. The audience howled! Patrick jumped right in and asked him whether anyone was there.

That was our most memorable ad-lib until the final performance when Patrick delivered his instantly legendary cake plate and fork into the briefcase maneuver.

Most Notable Understudy Rehearsal Moment: A tie between the looong kiss Velasco gave Mrs. Banks and the flood in the basement.

Most Cellphone Rings: We never had more than a few scattered rings here and there. One day during preset, one of the crew members left his cellphone onstage (just stage right of the skylight). As it was turned on, and there was absolutely no way to reach it until the curtain came in for the first scene change, we spent most of the first scene in fear that it would go off. Fortunately, it didn't.

Like a Musical: Theatre Manager Joe Traina, an accomplished musician who plays both clarinet and alto sax, could often be found playing during preset. Add to this, the fact that several of our cast members have starred in Broadway musicals and could be heard singing/vocalizing, and we'd often get the sense that we were backstage at a musical and not a straight play.

Busiest Day at the Box Office: The weekend Ben Brantley said we sucked, we sold out several performances. That Saturday night we even sold all twenty standing room slots.

Catchphrase: "Is the curtain up? The curtain's up, right? It's like a library out there."

Memorable Actor Question: "Is that too Old School?"

Memorable Directorial Note: "I like backs."

April 2, 2006: The day of THE LISP.

Tastiest Unused Back-Up Prop: Jelly beans.

Ah, Nostalgia… Next to the stage door, there was a phone list of Broadway theatres and other venues. It wasn't surprising to see the Schoenfeld and the Jacobs still listed as the Plymouth and the Royale, but it was nostalgic to see the Ritz (the Kerr number was handwritten in below), the Criterion Center and the Hellinger listed.

Mardi Gras: French-Quarter-born Jennifer Harmon made sure that everyone had masks and beads with which to celebrate!

Jeopardy: Question: "Lily Rabe, who starred in *Steel Magnolias*, is the daughter of Jill Clayburgh and this playwright." Contestant answer: "Who is Neil Simon?"

Warning: NEVER try to open liquid black shoe polish when wearing your Isaac Mizrahi costume.

Patrick Wilson's Day Job: Counter-person at Chipotle.

Blind Item: Which two Shubert employees had a $100 bet that the show would/would not run until the Tonys?

Most Generous: Scott Deverna.

Most Deserving of a Complete Tiffany Table Setting: Cheryl Dennis.

Rising Moons: During the final weekend, two of our actors decided to moon a third actor. When the third actor stepped off stage to deliver a line and saw the two moons, he promptly wet them both down with his water bottle. They then had to play the next scene with soggy bottoms. Classic!

Neil Simon on Broadway: This revival of *Barefoot in the Park* surpassed the Broadway runs of *Catch a Star*, *Little Me* (1982 revival), *Fools*, *45 Seconds from Broadway*, *Proposals* and *Little Me* (1998 revival).

Coolest Thing About Being in This Show: The remarkable company that made going to work each and every day a joyous experience (and a Production Contract is always nice, too).

Beauty and the Beast

First Preview: March 9, 1994. Opened: April 18, 1994.
Still running as of May 31, 2006.

PLAYBILL®

Disney's
BEAUTY AND THE BEAST

CAST
(in order of appearance)

Young Prince	BRIAN COLLIER
Enchantress	ELIZABETH POLITO
Beast	STEVE BLANCHARD
Belle	ASHLEY BROWN
Bookseller	GLENN RAINEY
Lefou	ALDRIN GONZALEZ
Gaston	GRANT NORMAN
Three Silly Girls	TRACY GENERALOVICH, MICHELLE LOOKADOO, TIA MARIE ZORNE
Maurice	JAMIE ROSS
Wolves	ANA MARIA ANDRICAIN, BRIAN COLLIER, CHRISTOPHER DeANGELIS, ELIZABETH POLITO
Cogsworth	JEFF BROOKS
Lumiere	PETER FLYNN
Babette	PAM KLINGER
Mrs. Potts	ALMA CUERVO
Chip	TREVOR BRAUN

(Wed. Eve., Fri., Sat. Mat., Sun. Eve.)
ALEXANDER SCHEITINGER
(Tues., Thurs., Sat. Eve., Sun. Mat.)

Madame de la Grande Bouche	MARY STOUT
Salt and Pepper	CHRISTOPHER DeANGELIS, BREK WILLIAMS
Doormat	BRIAN COLLIER
Cheesegrater	ROD ROBERTS
Monsieur D'Arque	GLENN RAINEY

Townspeople, Enchanted Objects
ANA MARIA ANDRICAIN, ANN ARVIA,
GINA CARLETTE, BRIAN COLLIER,
CHRISTOPHER DeANGELIS,
KEITH FORTNER,
TRACY GENERALOVICH,
DAVID E. LIDDELL,
MICHELLE LOOKADOO,
STEPHANIE LYNGE,
CHRISTOPHER MONTELEONE,

Continued on next page

LUNT–FONTANNE THEATRE
UNDER THE DIRECTION OF
JAMES M. NEDERLANDER AND JAMES L. NEDERLANDER

Disney Theatrical Productions
presents

STEVE BLANCHARD   ASHLEY BROWN
in

DISNEY's
BEAUTY AND THE BEAST

Music by	*Lyrics by*	*Book by*
ALAN MENKEN	HOWARD ASHMAN & TIM RICE	LINDA WOOLVERTON

with

GRANT NORMAN   JEFF BROOKS   ALMA CUERVO   PETER FLYNN   JAMIE ROSS

TREVOR BRAUN   ALDRIN GONZALEZ   PAM KLINGER
ALEXANDER SCHEITINGER   MARY STOUT

ANA MARIA ANDRICAIN   ANN ARVIA   GINA CARLETTE   BRIAN COLLIER
CHRISTOPHER DeANGELIS   KEITH FORTNER   TRACY GENERALOVICH   MICHELLE LOOKADOO
DAVID E. LIDDELL   STEPHANIE LYNGE   CHRISTOPHER MONTELEONE   BILL NABEL
BRIAN O'BRIEN   ELIZABETH POLITO   GLENN RAINEY   ROD ROBERTS
DARIA LYNN SCATTON   JENNIFER SHRADER   BREK WILLIAMS   TIA MARIE ZORNE

Scenic Design	*Costume Design*	*Lighting Design*
STANLEY A. MEYER	ANN HOULD-WARD	NATASHA KATZ

Sound Design	*Hair Design*	*Illusion Design*	*Prosthetics*
JONATHAN DEANS	DAVID H. LAWRENCE	JIM STEINMEYER JOHN GAUGHAN	JOHN DODS

Associate Producer/Company Manager	*Production Supervisor*	*Production Stage Manager*
MARK ROZZANO	HARRIS PRODUCTION SERVICES	JOHN BRIGLEB

Casting	*Associate Director*	*Associate Choreographer*	*Press Representative*
BINDER CASTING/ MARK BRANDON	KEITH BATTEN	KATE SWAN	BONEAU/ BRYAN-BROWN

Fight Direction	*Dance Arrangements*	*Music Coordinator*
RICK SORDELET	GLEN KELLY	JOHN MILLER

Orchestrations	*Musical Supervision & Vocal Arrangements*	*Music Direction & Incidental Music Arrangements*
DANNY TROOB	DAVID FRIEDMAN	MICHAEL KOSARIN

Choreography by
MATT WEST

Directed by
ROBERT JESS ROTH

DISNEY ON BROADWAY   ©Disney

10/1/05

Steve Blanchard
as the Beast and
Sarah Litzsinger
as Belle.

Photo by Joan Marcus

Beauty and the Beast

MUSICAL NUMBERS

ACT ONE

Overture
Prologue
"Belle" .... Belle, Gaston, Lefou, Silly Girls, Townspeople
"No Matter What"* .... Maurice, Belle
"No Matter What"* (Reprise) .... Maurice
"Me"* .... Gaston, Belle
"Belle" Reprise .... Belle
"Home"* .... Belle
"Home"* (Reprise) .... Mrs. Potts
"Gaston" .... Lefou, Gaston, Silly Girls, Tavern Patrons
"Gaston" (Reprise) .... Gaston, Lefou
"How Long Must This Go On?"* .... Beast
"Be Our Guest" .... Lumiere, Mrs. Potts, Cogsworth, Madame de la Grande Bouche,
Chip, Babette, Enchanted Objects
"If I Can't Love Her"* .... Beast

ACT TWO

Entr'acte/Wolf Chase
"Something There" .... Belle, Beast, Lumiere, Mrs. Potts, Cogsworth
"Human Again" .... Lumiere, Madame de la Grande Bouche, Cogsworth, Mrs. Potts,
Babette, Chip, Enchanted Objects
"Maison des Lunes"* .... Gaston, Lefou, Monsieur D'Arque
"Beauty and the Beast" .... Mrs. Potts
"If I Can't Love Her"* (Reprise) .... Beast
"A Change In Me"* .... Belle
"The Mob Song" .... Gaston, Lefou, Monsieur D'Arque, Townspeople
"The Battle" .... The Company
"Transformation"* .... Beast, Belle
"Beauty and the Beast" (Reprise) .... The Company

*Music by Alan Menken and lyrics by Tim Rice.
All other lyrics by Howard Ashman and music by Alan Menken.

ORCHESTRA

Conductor — MICHAEL KOSARIN
Associate Conductor — KATHY SOMMER
Assistant Conductor — JOSEPH PASSARO
Assistant Conductor — AMY DURAN

Concertmaster: Suzanne Ornstein
Violins: Lorra Aldridge, Evan Johnson, Roy Lewis,
Kristina Musser
Cellos: Caryl Paisner, Joseph Kimura
Bass: Jeffrey Carney
Flute: Kathy Fink
Oboe: Vicki Bodner
Clarinet/Flute: KeriAnn Kathryn DiBari
Flute/Clarinet: Tony Brackett
Bassoon, Contrabassoon: Charles McCracken
Trumpets: Neil Balm, James de la Garza
French Horns: Jeffrey Lang, Anthony Cecere
Robert Carlisle
Bass Trombone/Tuba: Paul Faulise
Drums: John Redsecker
Percussion: Joseph Passaro
Harp: Stacey Shames
Keyboards: Kathy Sommer, Madelyn Rubinstein

Music Coordinator - JOHN MILLER

Cast Continued

BILL NABEL, BRIAN O'BRIEN,
ELIZABETH POLITO, GLENN RAINEY,
ROD ROBERTS, DARIA LYNN SCATTON,
JENNIFER SHRADER,
BREK WILLIAMS, TIA MARIE ZORNE
Voice of Prologue Narrator .... DAVID OGDEN
STIERS

UNDERSTUDIES
Enchantress: GINA CARLETTE, DARIA LYNN
SCATTON

Young Prince: KEITH FORTNER, DAVID E.
LIDDELL

Beast: CHRISTOPHER MONTELEONE,
BRIAN O'BRIEN, BREK WILLIAMS

Belle: ANA MARIA ANDRICAIN, JENNIFER
SHRADER

Bookseller: KEITH FORTNER, DAVID E.
LIDDELL

Lefou: BRIAN COLLIER, KEITH FORTNER

Gaston: CHRISTOPHER MONTELEONE,
BRIAN O'BRIEN, BREK WILLIAMS

Silly Girls: GINA CARLETTE, DARIA LYNN
SCATTON

Wolves: GINA CARLETTE, KEITH FORTNER,
DAVID E. LIDDELL, DARIA LYNN SCATTON

Maurice: BILL NABEL, GLENN RAINEY

Cogsworth: BILL NABEL, GLENN RAINEY

Lumiere: CHRISTOPHER DEANGELIS, BILL
NABEL

Babette: TRACY GENERALOVICH, MICHELLE
LOOKADOO

Mrs. Potts: ANN ARVIA, STEPHANIE LYNGE

Madame de la Grande Bouche: ANN ARVIA,
STEPHANIE LYNGE

Salt and Pepper: KEITH FORTNER, DAVID E.
LIDDELL

Doormat: KEITH FORTNER, DAVID E.
LIDDELL

Cheesegrater: KEITH FORTNER, DAVID E.
LIDDELL

Monsieur D'Arque: BILL NABEL, BRIAN
O'BRIEN

SWINGS
Gina Carlette, Keith Fortner,
David E. Liddell, Daria Lynn Scatton

DANCE CAPTAIN
Daria Lynn Scatton

Ashley Brown as Belle.

Photo by Joan Marcus

Beauty and the Beast

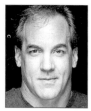
Steve Blanchard
Beast

Ashley Brown
Belle

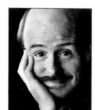
Grant Norman
Gaston

Jeff Brooks
Cogsworth

Alma Cuervo
Mrs. Potts

Peter Flynn
Lumiere

Jamie Ross
Maurice

Trevor Braun
Chip at certain performances

Aldrin Gonzalez
Lefou

Pam Klinger
Babette

Alexander Scheitinger
Chip at certain performances

Mary Stout
Madame de la Grande Bouche

Ana Maria Andricain
Ensemble

Ann Arvia
Ensemble

Gina Carlette
Ensemble/Swing

Brian Collier
Young Prince, Doormat, Ensemble

Christopher DeAngelis
Ensemble/Salt

Keith Fortner
Ensemble/Swing

Tracy Generalovich
Ensemble/Silly Girl

David E. Liddell
Fight Captain

Michelle Lookadoo
Silly Girl

Stephanie Lynge
Ensemble

Christopher Monteleone
Ensemble

Bill Nabel
Ensemble

Brian O'Brien
Ensemble

Elizabeth Polito
Enchantress/ Ensemble

Glenn Rainey
Ensemble/ Bookseller/ Monsieur D'Arque

Rod Roberts
Ensemble/ Cheesegrater

Daria Lynn Scatton
Ensemble/Swing

Jennifer Shrader
Ensemble

Brek Williams
Ensemble/Pepper

Tia Marie Zorne
Ensemble/Silly Girl

Alan Menken
Composer

Tim Rice
Lyrics

Linda Woolverton
Book

Beauty and the Beast

Robert Jess Roth
Director

Matt West
Choreographer

Stanley A. Meyer
Scenic Designer

Ann Hould-Ward
Costume Designer

Natasha Katz
Lighting Designer

Jonathan Deans
Sound Designer

David H. Lawrence
Hair Designer

Jim Steinmeyer
Illusions

John Dods
Prosthetics Designer

Jay Binder, CSA
Casting

Mark Brandon
Casting

Keith Batten
Associate Director

Kate Swan
*Associate
Choreographer*

Rick Sordelet
Fight Director

John Miller
Music Coordinator

Danny Troob
Orchestrator

David Friedman
*Music Supervision/
Vocal Arrangements*

Michael Kosarin
*Music Direction/
Incidental Music
Arrangements*

Thomas Schumacher
*Disney Theatrical
Productions*

DISNEY'S
BEAUTY AND THE BEAST
ALUMNI
2005-2006

Matthew Gumley
*Chip at certain
performances*

Patrick O'Neil Henney
*Chip at certain
performances*

Brynn O'Malley
Ensemble

Denny Paschall
*Cheesegrater/
Ensemble*

Brooke Tansley
Belle

Marguerite Willbanks
Ensemble

DISNEY'S
BEAUTY AND THE BEAST
TRANSFER STUDENTS
2005-2006

Christopher Duva
Cogsworth

Gina Ferrall
*Madame de la
Grande Bouche*

Meredith Inglesby
Babette

Jeanne Lehman
Mrs. Potts

Sarah Litzsinger
Belle

Garrett Miller
*Salt and Pepper/
Ensemble*

Beauty and the Beast

Mark Price
Lefou

Rob Sutton
Ensemble

Jacob Young
Lumiere

(L-R): David L. Bornstein (Head Propertyman), Peter Byrne (Assistant Electrician)

Photos by Ben Strothmann

STAGE MANAGEMENT
(L-R): Michael Biondi (Stage Manager), Gregory Covert (Stage Manager), Anglea Piccinni (Stage Manager)

WARDROBE
Seated (L-R):
Eric Rudy (Assistant Wardrobe Supervisor), Claire Verlaet (Dresser), Barbara Hladsky (Dresser), Joan Weiss (Dresser)

Second Row (L-R):
Ginny Hounsell (Star Dresser), Rose Keough (Dresser), Theresia Larsen (Dresser)

Third Row (L-R):
Karen Eifert (Dresser), James Cavanaugh (Dresser), Billy Hipkins (Dresser)

Fourth Row (L-R):
Rita Santi (Star Dresser),
Michael Piatkowski (Dresser), Matt Logan (Dresser), Suzanne Sponsler (Dresser)

BOX OFFICE
(L-R): Michael Kane, Joseph Olcese (Head Treasurer)

MERCHANDISE
(L-R): Ann Marie Rosano, Jeff Knizner (Retail Manager)

Beauty and the Beast

STAGE CREW
Back Row (L-R):
Edward Schultz and Ed Crimmins.

Middle Row (L-R):
Gerald Schultz (Asst. Electrician/
Vari*Lite Operator), Bill Horton
(Asst. Electrician/Special Effects Technician),
Peter Byrne (Asst. Electrician/Front Light),
James Travers.

Front Row (L-R):
David Brickman and Mitchell Christenson.

HAIR DEPARTMENT
(L-R):
Jackie Weiss (Wig Crew),
Thom Gonzalez (Hair Supervisor),
Mark Rampmeyer (Wig Crew),
Taurance Williams (Wig Crew), and
Valerie Gladstone (Wig Crew).

Photos by Ben Strothmann

FRONT OF HOUSE STAFF
Seated (L-R):
Carlo Mosarra, Honey Owen, Paul Campbell,
Carmela Cambio.

Second Row (L-R):
Sharon Grant, Angalic Cortes, Madeline Flores,
Evelyn Hynes, Marion Danton, Rosalind Joyce,
Tracey Malinowski (House Manager).

Third Row (L-R):
Omar Aguilar, Joey Cintron, Mildred Villano,
Christine Corrigan, Jessica Gonzalez.

Fourth Row (L-R):
Melody Rodriguez, Lauren Banyai,
Georgette Soto.

Back Row (L-R):
Barry Jenkins, Paul Perez, William Pacheco,
Dennis Cintron and Joe Smith.

Beauty and the Beast

STAFF FOR *BEAUTY AND THE BEAST*

Company Manager ....MARK ROZZANO
Assistant Company Manager ....Keith D. Cooper

Production Supervision ....Harris Production Services

General Press Representative ....Boneau/Bryan-Brown
Chris Boneau, Jim Byk,
Juliana Hannett

Production Stage Manager ....John Brigleb
Stage Manager .............................M.A. Howard
Stage Manager ....Michael Biondi
Stage Manager ....Michael Wilhoite
Dance Captain ....Daria Lynn Scatton
Fight Captain ....David E. Liddell

Puppet Design Consultant ....Michael Curry

Special Effects Consultant ....Jauchem & Meeh, NYC

Associate Production Supervisor ....Tom Bussey
Production Manager ....Elisa Cardone
Associate Scenic Designer ....Dennis W. Moyes
Principal Set Design Assistant ......Edmund A. LeFevre, Jr.
Set Design Assistants ....Stephen Carter,
Judy Gailen, Dana Kenn,
Sarah Lambert
Associate Lighting Designers ....Gregory Cohen,
Dan Walker
Assistant Lighting Designers ....Rob Cangemi,
Maura Sheridan
Automated Lighting Programmers ....Aland Henderson,
Richard W. Knight
Associate Sound Designer ....John Petrafesa, Jr.
Original Pyrotechnic Designer ....Tylor Wymer
Automated Lighting Tracker ....John Viesta
Projection Effects ....Wendall K. Harrington
Associate Costume Designer ....Tracy Christensen
Assistants to Ms. Hould-Ward ....David C. Paulin,
Markas Henry, Mark Musters,
Fabio Toblini
Assistant to Mr. Lawrence ....Linda Rice
Synthesizer Programming...................Dan Tramon,
Bruce Samuels

Production Carpenter ..........................B.B. Baker
Production Flyman ....Peter H. Jackson III
Production Electrician ....Todd Davis
Production Property Master ....Joseph P. Harris. Jr.
Production Sound Engineer ....Scott Anderson
Production Wardrobe Supervisor ....Sue Hamilton
Production Hair Supervisor ....Wanda Gregory,
Valerie Gladstone
Production Prosthetics Supervisor ....Angela Johnson

Head Carpenter ...............................B.B. Baker
Flyman ....Frank Frederico
Assistant Carpenter ....Mark Hallisey
Automation Carpenters ....Andrew D. Elman,
Hugh M. Hardyman
Head Electrician ....Tom Brouard
Assistant Electrician/Front Light ....Peter Byrne
Assistant Electrician/
Special Effects Technician ....William C. Horton, Sr.
Assistant Electrician/Vari*Lite Operator ....Gerald Schultz
Sound Effects Engineer ....Ned Hatton
Head Propertyman ....David L. Bornstein
Assistant Propertyman ....John Lofgren
Wardrobe Supervisor ....Julie Ratcliffe

Assistant Wardrobe Supervisor ....Eric Rudy
Ms. Brown's Dresser ....Ginny Hounsell
Mr. Blanchard's Dresser ....Rita Santi
Wardrobe Crew ....Suzanne Sponsler, Joseph Davis,
Dan Foss, Billy Hipkins,
Barbara Hladsky, Rose Keough,
Theresia Larsen, Matt Logan,
Michael Piatkowski,
Claire Verlaet, Joan Weiss
Makeup/Prosthetics Supervisor ....Vincent T. Schicchi
Hair Supervisor ....Thom Gonzalez
Assistant Hair Supervisor ....Paula Shaffer
Wig Crew ....George Fraggos, Anita Lausevic,
Kevin Phillips, Jackie Weiss,
Taurance Williams

Additional Orchestrations ....Michael Starobin,
Ned Ginsberg
Music Preparation Supervisor ....Peter R. Miller,
Miller Music Service
Assistant to Mr. Menken ....Rick Kunis
Assistant to Mr. Rice ....Eileen Heinink
Assistant to John Miller ....Matthew P. Ettinger
Rehearsal Pianists ....Glen
Kelly,
Madelyn Rubinstein, Amy Duran

Advertising ....Serino Coyne, Inc.
Press Associates ....Adrian Bryan-Brown,
Brandi Cornwell, Erika Creagh,
Adriana Douzos, Jackie Green,
Hector Hernandez, Jessica Johnson,
Kevin Jones, Eric Louie, Aaron Meier,
Joe Perrotta, Linnae Petruzzelli,
Matt Polk, Susanne Tighe
Casting Associates ....Jack Bowdan, C.S.A.,
Laura Stanczyk,
Sarah Prosser
Payroll Manager ....Cathy Guerra
Production Assistants ....Bari Kartowski,
Mika Hadani, Alison Miller
Production Photography ....Joan Marcus,
Marc Bryan-Brown
Production Travel ....Jill Citron
Children's Tutoring. ....On Location Education
Chaperone ....Jeff Statile
Theatre Displays ....King Displays
Safety & Health Consultants ....CHSH, Inc.,
New York City
Originally Produced by
Robert W. McTyre ....Producer
Don Frantz ....Associate Producer

Based on the Disney Film Disney's
BEAUTY AND THE BEAST,
directed by Kirk Wise and Gary Trousedale.
Produced by Don Hahn.
Special thanks to all the artists and staff at
Walt Disney Feature Animation.
Tom Child, Initial Conceptual Development. Anthony
Stimac/Musical Theatre Works, Inc.

CREDITS
Scenic & Transformation Effect
Motion Control Featuring
Stage Command Systems™
by Scenic Technologies.
Scenic construction, sculpting and scenic painting by Scenic
Technologies. Additional scenery by Variety Scenic Studios;
Hudson Scenic Studios, Inc.; Draperies by Showbiz

Enterprises and I. Weiss & Sons, Inc. Lighting equipment
by Four Star Lighting. Automated lighting by Vari-Lite, Inc.
Pani Projection by Production Arts Lighting Inc. Sound
furnished by Sound Associates Inc. Custom built props by
Seitzer and Associates. Table cloths by Decor Couture
Designs. Window treatments, hand and table linens by
O'Neil. Costumes executed by Barbara Matera Ltd. Foliage
by Modern Artificial. Costumes executed by Grace
Costumes, Inc. Dying, screening and painting by Fabric
Effects Incorporated. Surface designs and costume crafts by
Martin Izquierdo Studios. Prosthetics by John Dods Studio.
Millinery by Douglas James, Arnold S. Levine, Janet Linville
and Woody Shelp. Footwear by Capezio and J.C. Theatrical.
Vacuform costume sculptor by Costume Armour, Inc. Wigs
created by Bob Kelly Wig Creations, Inc. Opticals by
Fabulous Fanny's Myoptics. Gloves by LaCrasia Glamour
Gloves. Beast muscle system by Andrew Benepe Studio.
Costume harness and supports by J. Gerard. Additional
supports by Danforth Orthopedic. Special Adhesives by
Adhesive Technologies, Inc. Illusions by John Gaughan and
Associates. Invention and Magic Mirror by Tom Talmon
Studio. Pyrotechnical special effects materials supplied by
MP Associates, Inc. Pyrotechnical Equipment supplied by
LunaTech. All sound recording by Sound Designers Studio,
New York City. Emer'gen-C super energy booster provided
by Alacer Corp. Throat lozenges supplied by Ricola, Inc.

Cover Art Design © Disney

BEAUTY AND THE BEAST
originally premiered at
Theatre Under The Stars
Houston, Texas
December 2, 1993

Inquiries regarding the licensing of stock and amateur
productions of *Beauty and the Beast* or Elton John and Tim
Rice's *Aida* should be directed to Music Theatre
International, 421 W. 54th St., New York, NY 10019. Tel:
212-541-4684; www.MTIshows.com

NEDERLANDER

Chairman ....James M. Nederlander
President ....James L. Nederlander

Executive Vice President
Nick Scandalios

Vice President
Corporate Development
Charlene S. Nederlander

Senior Vice President
Labor Relations
Herschel Waxman

Vice President
Jim Boese

Chief Financial Officer
Freida Sawyer Belviso

STAFF FOR THE LUNT-FONTANNE
House Manager ....Tracey Malinowski
Treasurer ....Joe Olcese
Assistant Treasurer ....Gregg Collichio
House Carpenter ....Terry Taylor
House Electrician ....Dennis Boyle
House Propertyman ....Dennis Sabella
House Flyman ....Mike Walters
House Engineers ....Robert MacMahon,
Joseph Riccio III

Beauty and the Beast

DISNEY THEATRICAL PRODUCTIONS

President ....Thomas Schumacher
Senior Vice President & General Manager ....Alan Levey
Senior Vice President, Managing Director & CFO ....David Schrader

General Management

Vice President, International ....Ron Kollen
Vice President, Operations ....Dana Amendola
Vice President, Labor Relations ....Allan Frost
Director, Human Resources ....June Heindel
Director, Domestic Touring ....Michele Gold
Manager, Labor Relations ....Stephanie Cheek
Manager, Human Resources ....Cynthia Young
Manager, Information Systems ....Scott Benedict
Senior Computer Support Analyst ....Kevin McGuire

Production

Executive Music Producer ....Chris Montan
Senior Vice President, Creative Affairs ....Michele Steckler
Vice President, Creative Affairs ....Greg Gunter
Vice President, Physical Production ....John Tiggeloven
Purchasing Manager ....Joseph Doughney
Staff Associate Director ....Jeff Lee
Staff Associate Designer ....Dennis W. Moyes
Staff Associate Dramaturg ....Ken Cerniglia

Marketing

Vice President, Domestic Touring ....Jack Eldon
Director, New York ....Andrew Flatt
Manager, New York ....Michele Holland
Manager, New York ....Leslie Barrett
Manager ....Joel Hile

Sales

Vice President, Ticketing ....Jerome Kane
Manager, Group Sales ....Jacob Lloyd Kimbro
Assistant Manager, Group Sales ....Juil Kim
Group Sales Representative ....Jarrid Crespo

Business and Legal Affairs

Vice President ....Jonathan Olson
Vice President ....Robbin Kelley
Director ....Harry S. Gold
Attorney ....Seth Stuhl
Paralegal/Contract Administration ....Colleen Lober

Finance

Director ....Joe McClafferty
Manager, Finance ....Justin Gee
Manager, Production Accounting ....Bill Hussey
Senior Business Planner ....Jason Fletcher
Production Accountants ....Wilson Liu,
Barbara Toben
Analyst ....Ronnie Cooper

Controllership

Director, Accounting ....Leena Mathew
Manager, Accounting ....Erica McShane
Senior Analysts ....Stephanie Badie, Mila Danilevich, Adrineh Ghoukassian
Analyst ....Ken Herrell

Administrative Staff

Elliot Altman, Amy Andrews, Alice Baeza, Gregory Bonsignore, Craig Buckley, Karl Chmielewski, Dayna Clark, Matthew Cronin, Cristi Finn, Christina Fornaris, Dayle Gruet, Gregory Hanoian, Jonathan Hanson, Jay Hollenback, Connie Jasper, Kristine Lee, Janine McGuire, Jeff Parvin, Ryan Pears, Giovanna Primak, Roberta Risafi, Susan Rubio, Kisha Santiago, Lynne Scheurer

Disney Theatrical Productions • 1450 Broadway • New York, NY 10018
mail@disneytheatrical.com

BUENA VISTA THEATRICAL MERCHANDISE, L.L.C.

Vice President ....Steven Downing
Manager ....John F. Agati
Operations Manager ....Shawn Baker
Assistant Manager, Inventory ....Suzanne Jakel
Buyer ....Suzanne Araneo
Retail Supervisor ....Mark Nathman
Merchandising Assistant ....Ed Pisapia
On-site Retail Manager ....Jackie Velazquez
On-Site Assistant Retail Manager ....Anjie Maraj

The Company performs "Be Our Guest."

Photo by Joan Marcus

Beauty and the Beast
SCRAPBOOK

1. Backstage at the Lunt-Fontanne (L-R): Peter Flynn, Alex Scheitinger, Jeanne Lehman and Jeff Brooks.
2. (L-R): Alex Scheitinger, Alissa Zulvergold and Trevor Braun (in costume as Chip).
3. (L-R): Tracy Generalovich, Tia Marie Zorne and Michelle Lookadoo recoil from (front) Alex Scheitinger dressed as The Beast.

Correspondent: Meredith Inglesby, "Babette."

Special Backstage Rituals: There seems to be a lot of kissing. It is a very affectionate cast. There also seems to be a ritual of eating chocolate. I swear there are candy jars in every room backstage. Great for fitting into the Babette dress...NOT! At least it stretches.

Favorite Moment During Each Performance (On Stage or Off): When I get to change to a "human." Those feathers are heavy, man! Thanks to Kim in Physical Therapy my hips get help.

Favorite In-Theatre Gathering Place: The hair room is a good place to gather. There really isn't a very accessible greenroom in the Lunt (it is six flights up), so we gather stage left in the hair room or in the cross-under. Sundays after the show in the men's ensemble room is great. There is always something fruity and relaxing to drink.

Favorite Off-Site Hangout: Luxia, Thalia, Bar Central, Havana Central, Kevin St. James, and of course Vintage, thanks to my old college friend and ex-roomate Jeff Datillo. I really like a place called Bar Jamon down on 17th and Irving Place. It is a great Spanish wine and cheese bar in my 'hood.

Favorite Snack Foods: Wheat thins with hummus, fruit, Pringles (can't shake 'em), chocolate, wine.

Mascot: Scuttle.

Favorite Therapies: Yoga, massage, dinner with friends, Throat Coat Tea, neti pot, Grether's Pastilles (blackcurrant), Sabon carrot scrub.

"Carols for a Cure" Carol: "The Gift We Give."

"Gypsy of the Year" Skit: "Baby Mine" by Frank Churchill and Ned Washington.

"Easter Bonnet" Skit: "Les Disneyrable" by Christopher DeAngelis and Billy Hipkins.

Record Number of Cell Phone Rings During a Performance: We just hear a lot of babies talking full volume.

Memorable Stage Door Fan Encounter: Her name is Faith, and she is a die-hard *Beauty and the Beast* fan. More specifically, a Babette/Lumiere enthusiast. She always greets Peter Flynn and me with so much excitement that I can't help being moved.

Fastest Costume Change: When I turn into a human. The "chicken cutlets" alone take some time. I'd say Belle has the lightning fast changes, and her dresser is a great woman. Yay, Ginny!

Busiest Day at the Box Office: Lately every day, which is incredible for a show that has run for twelve years.

Who Wore the Heaviest/Hottest Costume: For heaviest, it is a tossup between Mary Stout as the Wardrobe and Jeff Brooks as Cogsworth. Hottest definitely goes to Steve Blanchard in the Beast costume. He keeps his dressing room cold and I don't blame him what with all the padding, prosthetics and not to mention all that HAIR.

Who Wore the Least: The Dinner Plates are pretty scantily clad. They are the Vegas showgirls of the cast.

Catchphrases Only the Company Would Recognize: "Time for the Dinner Dance," "Porcelain, porcelain, porcelain, porcelai-n...."

Memorable Directorial Note: "Be more of a Latin lover." And my favorite: "You haven't seen Lumiere as a human in 10 years...dust it off."

Embarrassing Moments: Falling during "Be Our Guest"/tango with Lumiere. I slipped on a feather and fell back, legs over head, feathers swirling, to land on my back center stage. Great moment for me on Broadway!

Also, when I left my Act II headpiece in the wig room and realized it a minute before my entrance. My dresser, Rose Keough, hated me that day. She did say she liked that I keep her in shape. Sorry Rose.

Company Legends: Mary Stout is a legend. I am amazed by her story of being hit by a hot-dog cart.

Tales From the Put-In: Simply that I felt shot out of a cannon.

Nicknames: Mere, Merf, Megadeth.

Coolest Thing About Being in This Show: First and foremost, the people with whom I work, from all the folks at Disney Theatricals, through Pyro Bill and everyone else in their respective departments, it is an honor to be associated with them. Secondly, performing my Broadway debut as a character from a story I embraced so dearly as a child. It was the culmination of girlish dreams come true. It keeps me lighthearted and appreciative.

The Blonde in the Thunderbird

First Preview: July 8, 2005. Opened: July 17, 2005.
Closed July 23, 2005 after 10 Previews and 8 Performances.

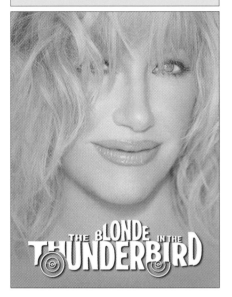

Suzanne Somers as
*The Blonde in the
Thunderbird*

Photo by Paul Parks

➤N➤ BROOKS ATKINSON THEATRE
UNDER THE DIRECTION OF JAMES M. NEDERLANDER AND JAMES L. NEDERLANDER

Alan Hamel

presents

Suzanne Somers

in

Written and Directed by
Mitzie and Ken Welch

Conceived by Suzanne Somers
Based on 'Keeping Secrets' and 'After the Fall'

Scenic and Lighting Design Roger Ball	Sound Design Robert Ludwig	Technical Supervisor Overlap Productions/ Tony Hauser
Music Direction/Orchestrations Doug Walter	Music Coordinator John Miller	Original Music and Lyrics Ken and Mitzie Welch
Production Stage Manager Robert Bennett	Press Representative The Publicity Office	General Manager The Sprecher Organization Ben Sprecher and Peter Bogyo

Special thanks to my friend Barry Manilow

7/17/05

Suzanne Somers
Performer

Ken & Mitzie Welch
Writers/Composers/Directors

Roger Ball
*Scenic and Lighting
Design*

John Miller
Music Coordinator

The Blonde in the Thunderbird

Peter Bogyo
General Manager

Ben Sprecher
General Manager

Alan Hamel
Producer

Photos by Melissa Merlo

BAND
Front Row (L-R): William Hayes (Percussion),
Doug Walter (Musical Direction/Orchestrations).
Back Row (L-R): Greg Dlugos (Keyboard/Associate Conductor),
Rich Mercurio (Drums) and Larry Saltzman (Guitar).

Not Pictured: Andy Erzin and Vincent Fay.

PROPS, WARDROBE AND HAIR
(L-R): Kelly Saxon (Wardrobe Supervisor), Mooney (Hair Design),
and Danny Paulos (House Props, sub).

Not Pictured: Joe Depaulo (House Props).

FRONT OF HOUSE STAFF
Front Row (L-R): Patricia Michaels (Usherette), Kathy Dib (Usherette), Brenda Brauer (Chief Usher),
Charlotte Brauer (Usherette), Barbara Carrellas (Theatre Manager).
Back Row (L-R): William Dillon (Ticket Taker), Robert Banyai (Usher), Brenden Imperato (Usher),
Roberto Rivera (Usher), Timothy Newsome (Usher) and Kimberlee Imperato (Usherette).

The Blonde in the Thunderbird

LIGHTING, SOUND AND VIDEO
Seated (L-R):
Robert Ludwig (Sound Mixer),
Chris Cronin (Sound Engineer).
Standing (L-R): Roger Ball
(Set and Lighting Designer/Production Supervisor),
Matthew S. Schechtman (Video Engineer),
Bill Staples (Follow Spot Operator),
Manny Becker (House Electrician)
and Joe Goldman (Cameraman).

Not Pictured:
Bennett Horowitz
(Assistant Lighting Designer/Programmer).

CARPENTRY and ELECTRICS
(L-R): Manny Becker (House Electrician),
and Joe Maher (Production Flyman).

Not Pictured:
Tom LaVaia (House Carpenter).

PRODUCTION AND COMPANY MANAGEMENT
(L-R): Robert Bennett (Production Stage Manager),
Maria Falcone (Assistant to the Authors),
Alan Hamel (Executive Producer),
Suzanne Somers (Performer/Star),
David van Zyll de Jong
(Apprentice Company Manager) and
Roger Ball (Set and Lighting Designer/Production
Supervisor).

Not Pictured:
Marsha Yanchuck
(Assistant to Mr. Hamel and Ms. Somers),
Cyrille Blackburn (Production Assistant).

Photos by Melissa Merlo

The Blonde in the Thunderbird

The Blonde in the Thunderbird
SCRAPBOOK

Photos by Aubrey Reuben

Correspondent: Suzanne Somers, "The Blonde in the Thunderbird"

Best Opening Night Telegram or Note: A memory book put together by my granddaughters.

Opening Night Gifts: My stagehand shirt. I was so flattered that these darling men gave me something so special.

Most Exciting Celebrity Visitor: John Ritter's son, Jason Ritter. It was touching and moving...and Jason looks just like his dad.

Special Backstage Rituals: One cup of strong, great coffee...fresh brewed about one hour before the show. Then chamomile tea while waiting in the wings, meditation in my quick-change booth for the final minutes. Then I flirt with the band.

Favorite Moment During Each Performance (Onstage or Off): Meeting with the crowds after the show at the stage door.

Favorite In-Theatre Gathering Place: My dressing room.

Favorite Snack Food: Does Chicken Francaise from the restaurant next door count as snack food?

Mascot: My cat Chrissy Snow, who waited dutifully at the hotel for me every day. She loves room service.

Favorite Therapy: Ricola lozenges and chamomile tea.

Memorable Ad-Lib: "I'm shedding," when my Chrissy Snow hairbands pulled a handful of hair out of my head.

Memorable Stage Door Fan Encounter: The woman who told me she had been at every single performance.

Memorable Directorial Note: Mitzie Welch, my director, said, "You're sitting on the crab." (There was no crab...it was all imaginary.) She was right. I was sitting on the imaginary crab, among many imaginary crabs on the floor. I corrected it the next performance.

Most Embarrassing Moment: When my bra came unhooked and I still had an hour of running back and forth across stage.

Coolest Thing About Being in This Show: It was the dream of my life. The greatest experience of my professional life.

Also: The band was surprised when I let them go three hours early on the first day of rehearsal. They were good and so was I. Why waste time?

1. Suzanne Somers arriving in style for her opening night.
2. Somers with husband Alan Hamel on opening night.
3. Somers and her son Bruce at the opening night party at Bolzano's.
4. Guest Frankie Avalon signs autographs at the party.
5. Somers (third from L) receives an award for her support of the uniformed services on stage after the June 9, 2005 performance.

Bridge & Tunnel

First Preview: January 13, 2006. Opened: January 26, 2006.
Still running as of May 31, 2006.

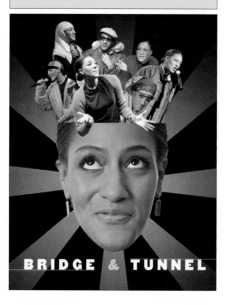

PLAYBILL

BRIDGE & TUNNEL

Sarah Jones as Lorraine Levine.

Photo by Brian Michael Thomas

THE HELEN HAYES THEATRE

MARTIN MARKINSON   DONALD TICK

Eric Falkenstein   Michael Alden   Boyett Ostar Productions
present

BRIDGE
&
TUNNEL

written and performed by
SARAH JONES

scenic design   lighting design   sound design
David Korins   **Howell Binkley**   **Christopher Cronin**

press representative   marketing
Pete Sanders Group   **Nancy Richards   Marcia Pendelton**

assistant director   production stage manager
Steve Colman   **Laurie Goldfeder**

technical supervision   general management   associate producer
Aurora Productions   **Richards/Climan, Inc.**   **Tom Wirtshafter**

directed by
Tony Taccone

Originally Produced at The Culture Project, NYC
Developed at Berkeley Repertory Theatre, Berkeley, CA

The producers wish to express their appreciation to the Theatre Development Fund
for its support of this production.

2/13/06

Sarah Jones
Playwright/Performer

Tony Taccone
*Director, and Artistic
Director, Berkeley
Repertory Theatre*

Steve Colman
Assistant Director

David Korins
Scenic Designer

Bridge & Tunnel

Howell Binkley
Lighting Design

Christopher Cronin
Sound Design

Asa Taccone
Music

Nancy Richards
Marketing

Eric Falkenstein
Producer

2005-2006 AWARD

TONY AWARD
Special Tony (Sarah Jones)

Michael Alden
Producer

Bob Boyett
Producer

Pat Flicker Addiss
Associate Producer

Marcia Roberts
Associate Producer

Elvera Roussel
Associate Producer

Robert Seymour (Doorman)

STAGE CREW
(L-R): Ron Mooney (House Carpenter), Roger Keller, Jr. (House Props), Laurie Goldfeder (Stage Manager), Robert Seymour (Stage Door), Bob Etter (Sound), Trevor McGinness (Wardrobe), Joe Beck (Electrician) and Chris Morey (Company Manager).

Bridge & Tunnel

Photo by Ben Strothmann

FRONT OF HOUSE STAFF
Back Row (L-R):
Matt Kuehl, Yuri Ivanov,
Alan Markinson (House Manager) and
John Biancamano (Head Usher).

Front Row (L-R):
Frank Biancamano, Berdine Vaval,
Linda Maley and Harry Joshi.

STAFF FOR *BRIDGE & TUNNEL*

GENERAL MANAGEMENT
Richards / Climan, Inc.
David R. Richards   Tamar Haimes
Leslie Anne Pinney

PRESS REPRESENTATIVE
The Pete Sanders Group
Pete Sanders   Shane Marshall Brown
Glenna Freedman

COMPANY MANAGER
Chris Morey

TECHNICAL SUPERVISION
Aurora Productions
Gene O'Donovan   W. Benjamin Heller II
Bethany Weinstein   Hilary Austin

PRODUCTION STAFF FOR *BRIDGE & TUNNEL*
Assistant Director ....Steve Colman
Associate Set Design ....Rod Lemmond
Assistant Set Design ....Lawrence Hutcheson
Associate Lighting Design ....Sarah E.C. Maines
Music ....DJ Rekha, Asa Taccone
Wardrobe Supervisor ....Trevor McGinness
Production Carpenter ....Ron Mooney
Production Electrician ....Joseph Beck
Production Props ....Roger Keller
Production Sound ....Robert Etter
Follow Spot Operator ....Douglas Purcell
Production Assistant ....Michelle Dunn
Assistant to the General Manager ...Amanda E. Berkowitz
Assistant to Sarah Jones ....Caitie Bradley
Advertising ....Serino Coyne, Inc./
Jim Russek, Christin Seidel, Jill Jefferson
Marketing ....Nancy Richards,
Marcia Pendelton
Audience Development ....Kojo Ade
Banking ....Commerce Bank/
Barbara Von Borstel, Ashley Elezi

Accounting ....FK Partners/
Robert Fried, Elliott Aronstam
Insurance ....DeWitt Stern Group/
Anthony Pittari, Peter Shoemaker
Legal Counsel ....Franklin, Weinrib,
Rudell & Vassallo P.C./
Jason Baruch
Payroll Service ....Castellana Services Inc.
Pre-production Photography ....Bob Handelman
Production Photography ....Paul Kolnik
Producer Associates ....Don McAlarnen, Ian Smith,
Megan Hart, Diane Murphy,
Theresa Pisanelli, Andrew Cleghorn,
Mark Marmer
Press Assistant ....Katie Kirby
Production Interns ....Mara Klein,
Brendan Wattenberg

Scenery by Center Line Studios
Lighting equipment by PRG Lighting
Sound equipment by One Dream Sound

Makeup Provided by
M*A*C

Sarah Jones would like to thank Meryl Streep, Michael Alden, Eric Falkenstein, the stellar *Bridge & Tunnel* Team, The Culture Project, Allan Buchman, Berkeley Rep, The Nuyorican Poets Café, Jayson Jackson, Caitie Bradley, Kori Wilson, National Immigration Forum, Frank Sharry, Karen Paul-Stern, Muzzafar Chishti, Margie McHugh, Judy Mark, Ford Foundation, Taryn Higashi, WK Kellogg Foundation, Terri Wright, Henri Treadwell, Frank Taylor, Equality Now, Gloria Steinem, Jessica Neuwirth, Taina Bien-Aime, Pam Shifman, Bryn Mawr College, The United Nations International School, Marjorie Nieuwenhuis, New York Civic Participation Project, SAKHI, Lois Smith, Ken Sunshine, (Frankfurt, Kurnit, Klein, and Selz), Lisa Davis, Mark Merriman, CAA, Kevin Huvane, George Lane, Jeffery Spiech, Olivier Sultan, Gloria Feliciano, Fiduciary Management Group, Ivan Thornton, Thomasina Thornton, John Howell, Rumzi Araj, Hala Araj, Emily Sklar, Breakthrough, Art Start, The Ghetto Film School, Joe Hall,

Sky Nellor, Bao Phi, Sadie Nash Leadership Project, Juan Jose Guttierez, Erica Portela, Kirk Nugent, CHIRLA, Michele Andrews, Wei Wah Chan, Mr. and Mrs. Mark Lii, Museum of Chinese in the Americas, Lev Ortenberg, Mr. Borsh, Nancy Hirsch, Leslie Farrington, Hannah Jones, The Farrington Family, The Jones Family, The Griggs Family, Penny Colman, Linda Hickson, Bob Colman, David Lewis-Colman, Crystal Lewis-Colman, Jonathan Colman, Katrin DeHaen, Renee Harris, Mariana Kirby, Naveed Alam, Bruce and Karolyn Gould, Bethann Hardison, David Skurnick, Felicia Noth.

SPECIAL THANKS
Meryl Streep
Cass Almendral, Dana Beck, Allan Buchman, Lisa K. Davis, Toni Hahn Davis, Robert Dragotta, David Drake, Chad Gracia, Johanna Haan, Megan Hart, Jayson Jackson, Sandra Johnson, William Johnson, Lori Machens, David Marcus, Mark Marmer, Scott Morfee, Marjorie Nieuwenhuis, Marcia Roberts, John G. Rubin, Elyse Singer, Tamara Lovatt Smith, Ken Sunshine, Tom Wirtshafter, Kori Wilson.

Natural herb cough drops supplied by
Ricola USA Inc.

Throat Coat provided by Traditional Medicinals.

THE HELEN HAYES THEATRE
owned and operated by
MARTIN MARKINSON and DONALD TICK
General Manager ....SUSAN S. MYERBERG
Associate General Manager ....Sharon Fallon

STAFF FOR THE HELEN HAYES THEATRE
HOUSE MANAGER ....ALAN R. MARKINSON
Treasurer.......................................David Heveran
Assistant Treasurers ....Michael A. Lynch,
Manuel Rivera
Engineer/Maintenance ....Hector Angulo
Head Usher ....John Biancamano
Stage Door ....Vincent Kwasnicki, Robert Seymour
Accountant ....Chen-Win Hsu, CPA., P.C.

Bridge & Tunnel

Correspondent: Laurie Goldfeder, Production Stage Manager

Opening Night Gifts: The borough of Queens declared opening day "Sarah Jones Day" and gave her a beautiful official certificate.

Most Exciting Celebrity Visitors: Harvey Keitel and Robert De Niro came together. That's enough excitement!

Most Roles: Sarah—she plays fourteen!

Favorite Snack Food: Sarah loves Baked Lays, chocolate chip granola bars and bananas. The crew loves anything that's free and full of sugar. I love anything considered fast food.

Favorite Therapies: Throat Coat Tea, Airborne.

Memorable Ad-Lib: A woman was talking out in the audience so Sarah as "Lorraine" said directly to her, "Honey, I'm talking right now."

Memorable Stage Door Fan Encounter: Someone actually asked me if I was Sarah Jones. (If you saw me you would realize why that's so funny.)

Sweethearts Within the Company: Steve Colman, Assistant Director, is married to Sarah.

Embarrassing Moments: Sarah's pants zipper was open for an entire show.

Sarah's big bright orange jacket is supposed to fly down from the grid. One night it got stuck on a light and she patiently waited as long as possible for it; thankfully it stayed there through the end of the show. I thought it might plop right on her head at any moment (and this costume weighs over ten pounds)!

1. Sarah Jones (L) arrives on opening night with supporter Meryl Streep.
2. Director Tony Taccone (L) with Jones at the opening night party at the United Nations' Delegates Dining Room.
3. The marquee of the Helen Hayes Theatre.
4. Jones with producer Eric Falkenstein.
5. Guests Randall Wreghitt and Anjali Bhimani at the opening night party.

Brooklyn: The Musical

First Preview: September 23, 2004. Opened: October 21, 2004.
Closed June 26, 2005 after 27 Previews and 284 Performances.

PLAYBILL

CAST
(in alphabetical order)

A City Weed/Taylor ....KEVIN ANDERSON
A City Weed/Streetsinger .CLEAVANT DERRICKS
A City Weed/Brooklyn ....EDEN ESPINOSA
A City Weed/Paradice ....RAMONA KELLER
A City Weed/Faith ....KAREN OLIVO

PLACE: A street corner under the Brooklyn Bridge.
TIME: Present.

VOCALISTS
LEE MORGAN, WILL SWENSON,
SHELLEY THOMAS, HANEEFAH WOOD

SWINGS
JULIE REIBER, HORACE V. ROGERS

UNDERSTUDIES
For Brooklyn:
JULIE REIBER, SHELLEY THOMAS
For Faith:
JULIE REIBER, SHELLEY THOMAS
For Paradice:
HANEEFAH WOOD, SHELLEY THOMAS
For Taylor:
LEE MORGAN, WILL SWENSON
For Streetsinger:
HORACE V. ROGERS, WILL SWENSON

DANCE CAPTAIN
JULIE REIBER

---

⑥ GERALD SCHOENFELD THEATRE
236 West 45th Street
A Shubert Organization Theatre
Gerald Schoenfeld, *Chairman*   Philip J. Smith, *President*

Robert E. Wankel, *Executive Vice President*

Producers Four   John McDaniel   Jeff Calhoun
Leiter/Levine & Scott Prisand   Jay & Cindy Gutterman Productions

In Association with
Transamerica, Robert G. Bartner, Dallas Summer Musicals Inc,
Rudy Durand, Danny Seraphine, Rick Wolkenberg and Sibling Entertainment

Present

BROOKLYN
The Musical

Book, Music and Lyrics by
Mark Schoenfeld & Barri McPherson

Starring
Kevin Anderson   Cleavant Derricks   Eden Espinosa   Ramona Keller   Karen Olivo

With
Lee Morgan   Julie Reiber   Horace V. Rogers   Will Swenson   Shelley Thomas   Haneefah Wood

Set Design	Costume Design	Lighting Design	Sound Design
Ray Klausen	Tobin Ost	Michael Gilliam	Jonathan Deans Peter Hylenski

Associate Director	Music Direction	Music Coordinator
Coy Middlebrook	James Sampliner	John Miller
Press Representative	Marketing	Casting
Boneau/Bryan-Brown	TMG - The Marketing Group	Dave Clemmons Casting
General Management	Production Stage Manager	Technical Supervisor
Ken Denison WWE	Kimberly Russell	TheaterSmith Inc. Smitty
Associate Producers	Coordinating Producer	Associate Producer
Feurring/Maffei/Pinsky	Lauren Doll	Ken Denison

Music Supervision, Arrangements & Orchestrations by
John McDaniel

Directed by
Jeff Calhoun

LIVE BROADWAY

6/1/05

Eden Espinosa (R) sings "Once Upon a Time."

Photo by Joan Marcus

Brooklyn: The Musical

MUSICAL NUMBERS

"Heart Behind These Hands" ....The City Weeds
"Christmas Makes Me Cry" ....Faith and Taylor
"Not A Sound" ....The City Weeds
"Brooklyn Grew Up" ....Brooklyn and the City Weeds
"Creating Once Upon A Time" ....Brooklyn and Faith
"Once Upon A Time" ....Brooklyn and the City Weeds
"Superlover" ....Paradice and the City Weeds
"Brooklyn In The Blood" ....Paradice, Brooklyn and the City Weeds
"Magic Man" ....Streetsinger and the City Weeds
"Love Was A Song" ....Taylor
"I Never Knew His Name" ....Brooklyn
"The Truth" ....Taylor, Brooklyn and the City Weeds
"Raven" ....Paradice
"Sometimes" ....Taylor and the City Weeds
"Love Me Where I Live" ....Paradice and the City Weeds
"Love Fell Like Rain" ....Brooklyn
"Streetsinger" ....Brooklyn, Streetsinger and the City Weeds
"Heart Behind These Hands" (Reprise) ....The City Weeds

ORCHESTRA

Conductor/Keyboard 1 — James Sampliner

Associate Conductor/Keyboard 2 — Daniel Weiss

Guitar 1 — John Putnam

Guitar 2 — Gary Sieger

Bass — Irio O'Farrill, Jr.

Drums — Shannon Ford

Reeds — Jack Bashkow

Percussion — Roger Squitero

Cello — Clay Ruede

Music Coordinator — John Miller

Emily Grishman Music Preparation:
Emily Grishman/Katharine Edmonds

Kevin Anderson
Taylor Collins

Cleavant Derricks
Streetsinger

Eden Espinosa
Brooklyn

Ramona Keller
Paradice

Karen Olivo
Faith

Lee Morgan
Vocalist

Julie Reiber
*Swing/
Dance Captain*

Horace V. Rogers
Swing

Will Swenson
Vocalist

Shelley Thomas
Vocalist

Haneefah Wood
Vocalist

Mark Schoenfeld and Barri McPherson
Book/Music/Lyrics

Jeff Calhoun
Producer/Director

Coy Middlebrook
Associate Director

John McDaniel
*Producer/
Music Supervisor/
Arranger/
Orchestrator*

Ray Klausen
Set Design

Tobin Ost
*Costume Design/
Associate Set Design*

Michael Gilliam
Lighting Design

Peter Hylenski
Sound Design

James Sampliner
*Conductor/
Music Direction*

Brooklyn: The Musical

John Miller
Music Coordinator

Dave Clemmons
Casting
Casting

Ken Denison WWE
*General Manager/
Associate Producer*

Christopher C. Smith,
Technical Director
Theatersmith, Inc.

Thom Gates
Stage Manager

Steven Leiter and Stan Levine
Producers

Gary Maffei
Associate Producer

Rick Wolkenberg
Co-Producer

Charlie Maffei
Associate Producer

Romelda T. Benjamin
Swing

Ramona Keller
(foreground) sings
"Love Me Where I Live"
while modeling one of
Tobin Ost's trash-based
costumes. Watching
her are (L-R)
Cleavant Derricks,
Eden Espinosa,
Kevin Anderson
and Karen Olivo.

Photo by Joan Marcus

Brooklyn: The Musical

Karen Olivo as Faith.

Photo by Joan Marcus

The Caine Mutiny Court-Martial

First Preview: April 14, 2006. Opened: May 7, 2006.
Closed May 21, 2006 after 27 Previews and 17 Performances.

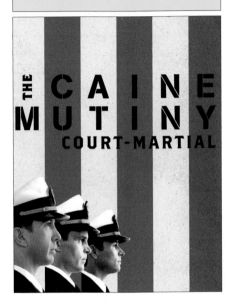

PLAYBILL®

CAST

Lt. Barney Greenwald ......DAVID SCHWIMMER
Lt. Stephen Maryk ....JOE SIKORA
Lt. Com. John Challee ....TIM DALY
Lt. Com.
    Philip Francis Queeg .... ŽELJKO IVANEK
Captain Blakely ....TERRY BEAVER
Lt. Thomas Keefer ....GEOFFREY NAUFFTS
Signalman Third Class
    Junius Urban ....PAUL DAVID STORY
Lt. (Jr. Grade) Willis Seward Keith ....BEN FOX
Capt. Randolph Southard ....MURPHY GUYER
Dr. Forrest Lundeen ....BRIAN REDDY
Dr. Bird.................................TOM NELIS
Stenographer ....TOM GOTTLIEB
Orderly ....ROBERT L. DEVANEY
Members of the Court ....PETER BRADBURY,
                            MICHAEL QUINLAN,
                            BRIAN RUSSELL,
                            DOUG STENDER
Party Guests ....DENIS BUTKUS,
                            GREG McFADDEN

TIME:
February, 1945

PLACE:
General Court-Martial Room of
the Twelfth Naval District, San Francisco

Continued on next page

236 West 45th Street
A Shubert Organization Theatre

Gerald Schoenfeld, *Chairman*   Philip J. Smith, *President*

Robert E. Wankel, *Executive Vice President*

JEFFREY RICHARDS   JERRY FRANKEL   DEBRA BLACK
ROGER BERLIND   RONALD FRANKEL
TERRY E. SCHNUCK   SHELDON STEIN   BARRY WEISBORD
in association with ROY FURMAN

present

DAVID   ŽELJKO   TIM
SCHWIMMER   IVANEK   DALY

in

THE **CAINE
MUTINY**
COURT-MARTIAL

by **HERMAN WOUK**

featuring
TERRY BEAVER   MURPHY GUYER   JOE SIKORA

with
ROBERT L. DEVANEY   SCOTT FERRARA   BEN FOX   GEOFFREY NAUFFTS
TOM NELIS   BRIAN REDDY   PAUL DAVID STORY

PETER BRADBURY   DENIS BUTKUS   TOM GOTTLIEB   GREG McFADDEN
MICHAEL QUINLAN   BRIAN RUSSELL   DOUG STENDER

Setting By	Costumes By	Lighting By
JOHN LEE BEATTY	WILLIAM IVEY LONG	PAUL GALLO

Sound By	Company Manager	Production Stage Manager
DAN MOSES SCHREIER	BRUCE KLINGER	STEVEN BECKLER

Casting By
STUART HOWARD, AMY SCHECTER & PAUL HARDT

Marketing
IRENE GANDY

General Management
ALBERT POLAND

Technical Supervisor
NEIL MAZZELLA

Directed by
JERRY ZAKS

LIVE BROADWAY

THE PRODUCERS WISH TO EXPRESS THEIR APPRECIATION TO THEATRE DEVELOPMENT FUND FOR ITS SUPPORT OF THIS PRODUCTION.

5/7/06

David Schwimmer (R) and Željko Ivanek (front).

Photo by Scott Landis

The Caine Mutiny Court-Martial

FROM THE *NAVY REGULATIONS*

Article 184. Unusual Circumstances

    It is conceivable that most unusual circumstances may arise in which the relief from duty of a commanding officer by a subordinate becomes necessary, either by placing him under arrest or on the sick list; but such action shall never be taken without the approval of appropriate higher authority, except when reference to such higher authority is undoubtedly impracticable because of the delay involved or for other clearly obvious reason.

Article 185. Conditions to Fulfill

    …the situation must admit of the single conclusion that the retention of command by such commanding officer will seriously prejudice the public interests. The subordinate officer must be thoroughly convinced that the conclusion to relieve his commanding officer is one which a reasonable, prudent, and experienced officer would regard as a necessary consequence from the facts thus determined to exist.

Article 186. Responsibility

    …An officer relieving his commanding officer must bear the legitimate responsibility for, and must be prepared to justify, such action.

AUTHOR'S NOTE by Herman Wouk

The Caine Mutiny Court-Martial is purely imaginary. No ship named *U.S.S. Caine* ever existed. The records show no instance of a U.S. Navy captain relieved at sea under Articles 184-186. The fictitious figure of the deposed captain was derived from a study of psychoneurotic case histories and is not a portrait of a real military person or a type; this statement is made because of the existing tendency to seek lampoons of living people in imaginary stories. The author served under two captains of the regular Navy aboard destroyer-minesweepers, both of whom were decorated for valor. One technical note: Court-martial regulations have been extensively revised since the second World War. This trial takes place according to instructions then in force. Certain minor omissions have been made for purposes of brevity; otherwise the play strictly follows procedures stipulated in *Naval Courts and Boards*.

Cast Continued

ACT ONE
The Prosecution

ACT TWO
Scene 1: The Defense
Scene 2: The Private Dining Room, the Fairmont Hotel, San Francisco

UNDERSTUDIES
For Orderly, Bird, Lundeen:
BRIAN RUSSELL
For Blakely, Southard:
MICHAEL QUINLAN
For Urban, Keith, Stenographer:
DENIS BUTKUS
For Maryk, Challee, Keefer:
ROBERT L. DEVANEY
For Queeg, Challee:
PETER BRADBURY
For Blakely, Southard, Lundeen:
DOUG STENDER
For Members of the Court, Keefer, Stenographer:
GREG McFADDEN
For Urban, Keith, Bird:
TOM GOTTLIEB

David Schwimmer
Lt. Barney Greenwald

Željko Ivanek
Lt. Com. Philip Francis Queeg

Tim Daly
Lt. Com. John Challee

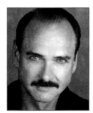

Terry Beaver
Captain Blakely

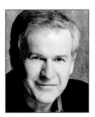

Murphy Guyer
Captain Randolph Southard

Joe Sikora
Lt. Stephen Maryk

Robert L. Devaney
Orderly

Ben Fox
Lt. J.G. Willis Seward Keith

Geoffrey Nauffts
Lt. Thomas Keefer

Tom Nelis
Dr. Bird

Brian Reddy
Dr. Forrest Lundeen

Paul David Story
Signalman Third Class Junius Urban

Peter Bradbury
Member of the Court

Denis Butkus
Party Guest

The Caine Mutiny Court-Martial

Tom Gottlieb
Stenographer

Greg McFadden
Party Guest

Michael Quinlan
Member of the Court

Brian Russell
Member of the Court

Doug Stender
Member of the Court

Herman Wouk
Playwright

Jerry Zaks
Director

John Lee Beatty
Scenic Design

William Ivey Long
Costume Designer

Paul Gallo
Lighting Designer

Dan Moses Schreier
Sound Designer

Jamibeth Margolis
Assistant Director

Neil A. Mazzella
*Technical
Supervision*

Albert Poland
General Manager

Jeffrey Richards
Producer

Jerry Frankel
Producer

Debra Black
Producer

Roger Berlind
Producer

Terry E. Schnuck
Producer

Roy Furman
Producer

STAGE CREW
Back Row (L-R):
Jimmy Lettis, Leslie Ann Kilian, Tim McWilliams,
Brien Brannigan, Jeff Koger, Phil Feller
Front Row (L-R):
Lisa Tucci, Tim Greer, Theresa Distasi,
Wendall Goings, Hilda Garcia-Suli

Photos by Ben Strothmann

STAGE MANAGEMENT
Steven Beckler and Lisa Dawn Cave

BOX OFFICE
(L-R): Katie Drury, Vigi Cadunz

The Caine Mutiny Court-Martial

DOORMEN
(Above) Lype O'Dell.
(Below) John Blake.

FRONT OF HOUSE STAFF
Front Row (L-R): Roz Nyman, Sandi Capasso, Cookie White, Raya Konyk.
Second Row (L-R): Kathleen Spock, Lisa Boyd, Michelle Moyna, Gillian Sheffler.
Third Row (L-R): Matt Blank, Alexandra Zavilowicz, Janet Kay, Michael Garro
Back Row: David Conte. Not Pictured: Francine Kramer.

STAFF FOR
THE CAINE MUTINY COURT-MARTIAL

GENERAL MANAGER
ALBERT POLAND
COMPANY MANAGER: BRUCE KLINGER

GENERAL PRESS REPRESENTATIVE
JEFFREY RICHARDS ASSOCIATES/IRENE GANDY
Adam Farabee   Alana Karpoff   Eric Sanders

MARKETING AND PROMOTIONS
BROTHERS AND SISTERS MARKETING
Irene Gandy

PRODUCTION
STAGE MANAGER .... STEVEN BECKLER
TECHNICAL SUPERVISOR .... NEIL MAZZELLA
Assistant Producer .... ALANA KARPOFF
Assistant Stage Manager .... Lisa Dawn Cave
Assistant Director .... Jamibeth Margolis
Assistant Set Designer .... Eric Renschler
Assistant Costume Designer .... Thomas Beall
Assistant Lighting Designer .... Philip Rosenberg, John Viesta
Assistant Sound Designers .... Phillip S. Peglow, Julie Pittman
Assistant to Mr. Poland .... Michael Gesele
Production Assistant .... Rachel Miller
Assistant to Mr. Berlind .... Jeffrey Hillock
Assistant to Ms. Black .... Betsy Montgomery
Production Carpenter .... Tim McWilliams
Production Electrician .... Jimmy Maloney

Head Electrician .... Jeff Koger
Production Properties .... Abe Morrison
Production Sound .... Brien Brannigan
Wardrobe Supervisor .... Lisa Tucci
Mr. Schwimmer's Dresser .... Tim Greer
Dressers .... Wendall Goings, Theresa Distasi, Hilda Garcia-Suli
Mr. Schwimmer's Photographer .... Davis Factor
Military Advisor .... Jack A. Green
Stenotype Instructor .... Carole Schwartz
Banking .... JPMorgan Chase
Accountant .... Rosenberg, Neuwirth & Kutchner/ Mark D'Ambrosi, Jana Jevnikar
Insurance .... DeWitt Stern Group/ Peter Shoemaker, Joe Bower, Stan Levine
Legal Counsel .... Nan Bases, Esq.
Advertising .... SpotCo/ Drew Hodges, Jim Edwards, Jim Aquino
Production Photographer .... Scott Landis
Payroll Services .... Castellana Services Inc.
Opening Night
Coordination .... Tobak Lawrence Company/ Suzanne Tobak
Company Mascots .... Lottie and Skye

CREDITS

Scenery constructed by Hudson Scenic Studio Inc. Lighting equipment from PRG Lighting. Sound equipment by Masque Sound & Recording. Costumes by Jennifer Love Costumes and Scafati Uniforms, Inc. U.S. Navy uniforms and accessories by Kaufman's Army & Navy, NYC. Courtroom furniture by Bergen Office Furniture and Men

of Steel. Built props by Craig Grigg, Jeremy Chernick and Rob Presley. Fabric props by Roy Rudin, Gerry McCarthy and Gene Mignola.

SPECIAL THANKS
Jack A. Green, Public Affairs Officer, Naval Historical Center, Washington, DC, for fielding the relentless bombardment of questions with grace and clarity; Douglas W. Gullickson, USMC, Ret.; Carl J. Tierney; Lincoln Center Theater.

THE SHUBERT ORGANIZATION, INC.
Board of Directors

Gerald Schoenfeld
Chairman

Philip J. Smith
President

Wyche Fowler, Jr.

John W. Kluge

Lee J. Seidler

Michael I. Sovern

Stuart Subotnick
Robert E. Wankel
Executive Vice President

Peter Entin
Vice President -
Theatre Operations

Elliot Greene
Vice President -
Finance

David Andrews
Vice President -
Shubert Ticketing Services

John Darby
Vice President -
Facilities

House Manager .... David M. Conte

The Caine Mutiny Court-Martial
SCRAPBOOK

Correspondent: Steven Beckler, Production Stage Manager.

Memorable Opening Night Fax: It has become an opening night tradition that people from the other shows all sign a page with their show's logo, then fax it to you with good wishes. Our walls backstage are lined with the logos of other shows. One cheeky young man from *History Boys* wrote that he's looking for a man in uniform between the ages of 20 and 50 and "seven inches, uncut."

Opening Night Gifts: We contributed to Broadway Cares/Equity Fights AIDS in each others' names and raised over $1,600. The producers gave us canvas tote bags with the show's logo. David Schwimmer gave everyone these extraordinary gourmet baskets from Dean & Deluca and everyone was eating out of them for days.

Most Exciting Celebrity Visitors and What They Said: Supreme Court Justice Anthony Kennedy came backstage and said he absolutely loved the show. Apparently he's also bitten by the bug because he told us he was involved with a production of *Hamlet* in Washington, DC. He and his wife could not have been nicer.

Special Backstage Ritual: Every evening at "places" the entire cast gathers on the stage, whether they're in the opening scene or not, and everyone wishes each other "Good show." It's a great group of people; one of the best casts and crews I've ever worked with.

Busiest Day at the Box Office: Sadly, we never had such a thing. Audience reaction was so strong during previews, I was sure it was going to translate into ticket sales…but it never did. It's something I'll never understand.

Favorite In-Theatre Gathering Place: Wardrobe. A lot of the actors who play the witnesses, and who only appear in Act I, spend Act II hanging out there.

Favorite Off-Site Hangout: I sure miss Barrymore's.

Favorite Snack Food: Wardrobe has jars of candy which they keep constantly refilled.

Mascots: Lottie and Skye.

Cell Phone Rings During a Performance: Tim Daly was giving his dramatic final speech to the court during one of our previews, and somebody's cell phone started ringing. It was a triple ring that went off, it must have been nine or twelve times. The person just refused to turn it off. I was appalled. Tim kept going because he's a pro. But there is a part of the audience that just doesn't understand how much craft goes into a live performance, and how difficult it is to do it while a cell phone is ringing.

Memorable Directorial Notes: This is my fifteenth show with Jerry Zaks, and I think he's one of the best directors around. Terry Beaver plays Captain Blakely, the judge, and there are two moments where Jerry Zaks helped him get laughs. One was the exchange where there is a Freudian reference. Jerry gave him a note, "Just lean in." It always got a laugh. Then there was another note: "Separate your laugh from the audience's laugh" so there would be two laughs in the same moment. I marvel at Jerry's eye for the intricacy of that kind of detail.

Coolest Thing About Being in This Show: This company and crew. There's just not a jerk in the group, and that's real unusual. It's great to come into the theatre on a nightly basis.

1. The cast applauds author Herman Wouk during curtain calls on opening night.
2. Director Jerry Zaks and David Schwimmer at the Sardi's cast party.
3. Actor Tim Daly (R) with aunt Glynis Daly (L) and sister Tyne Daly, at Sardi's.
4. Željko Ivanek (R) and Geoffrey Nauffts.
5. Producer Jeffrey Richards arrives at the Schoenfeld Theatre.

Chicago

First Preview: October 23, 1996. Opened: November 14, 1996.
Still running as of May 31, 2006.

PLAYBILL

CAST
(in order of appearance)

Velma Kelly	LUBA MASON
Roxie Hart	CHARLOTTE d'AMBOISE
Fred Casely	GREGORY BUTLER
Sergeant Fogarty	MATTHEW RISCH
Amos Hart	P.J. BENJAMIN
Liz	MICHELLE M. ROBINSON
Annie	SOLANGE SANDY
June	DONNA MARIE ASBURY
Hunyak	GABRIELA GARCIA
Mona	BRYN DOWLING
Matron "Mama" Morton	DEBRA MONK
Billy Flynn	HUEY LEWIS
Mary Sunshine	R. LOWE
Go-To-Hell Kitty	MICHELLE POTTERF
Harry	SHAWN EMAMJOMEH
Doctor	BERNARD DOTSON
Aaron	DENIS JONES
The Judge	BERNARD DOTSON
Bailiff	DENNY PASCHALL
Martin Harrison	STEVEN SOFIA
Court Clerk	DENNY PASCHALL
The Jury	SHAWN EMAMJOMEH

THE SCENE:

Chicago, Illinois. The late 1920s.

Continued on next page

⑤ AMBASSADOR THEATRE

A Shubert Organization Theatre
Gerald Schoenfeld, *Chairman*   Philip J. Smith, *President*

Robert E. Wankel, *Executive Vice President*

Barry & Fran Weissler
in association with
Kardana/Hart Sharp Entertainment
present

Charlotte d'Amboise   Luba Mason
Huey Lewis
P.J. Benjamin

in

CHICAGO

Lyrics by	Music By	Book by
Fred Ebb	**John Kander**	**Fred Ebb & Bob Fosse**

Original Production Directed and Choreographed by **Bob Fosse**

Based on the play by Maurine Dallas Watkins
also starring
Debra Monk   R. Lowe
with
**Donna Marie Asbury   Gregory Butler   Mindy Cooper   Bernard Dotson
Bryn Dowling   Shawn Emamjomeh   Gabriela Garcia   Denis Jones
Gary Kilmer   Dan LoBuono   Jeff Loeffelholz   Sharon Moore
Denny Paschall   Michelle Potterf   Matthew Risch
Michelle M. Robinson   Solange Sandy   Steven Sofia**

Supervising Music Director	Music Director
Rob Fisher	**Leslie Stifelman**

Scenic Design	Costume Design	Lighting Design
John Lee Beatty	**William Ivey Long**	**Ken Billington**

Sound Design	Orchestrations	Dance Music Arrangements
Scott Lehrer	**Ralph Burns**	**Peter Howard**

Script Adaptation	Musical Coordinator	Hair Design
David Thompson	**Seymour Red Press**	**David Brian Brown**

Casting	Original Casting
Howie Cherpakov C.S.A.	**Jay Binder**

Technical Supervisor	Production Stage Manager
Arthur Siccardi	**David Hyslop**

Associate Producer	Presented in association with
Alecia Parker	**Clear Channel Entertainment**

General Manager	Press Representative
B.J. Holt	**The Pete Sanders Group**

Based on the presentation by City Center's Encores!℠

Choreography by
Ann Reinking
in the style of Bob Fosse

Directed by
Walter Bobbie

Cast Recording on RCA Victor

LIVE BROADWAY

11/1/05

Huey Lewis as Billy Flynn

Photo by Richie Fahey

Chicago

MUSICAL NUMBERS

ACT I

ALL THAT JAZZ	Velma and Company
FUNNY HONEY	Roxie
CELL BLOCK TANGO	Velma and the Girls
WHEN YOU'RE GOOD TO MAMA	Matron
TAP DANCE	Roxie, Amos and Boys
ALL I CARE ABOUT	Billy and Girls
A LITTLE BIT OF GOOD	Mary Sunshine
WE BOTH REACHED FOR THE GUN	Billy, Roxie, Mary Sunshine and Company
ROXIE	Roxie and Boys
I CAN'T DO IT ALONE	Velma
MY OWN BEST FRIEND	Roxie and Velma

ACT II

ENTR'ACTE	The Band
I KNOW A GIRL	Velma
ME AND MY BABY	Roxie and Boys
MISTER CELLOPHANE	Amos
WHEN VELMA TAKES THE STAND	Velma and Boys
RAZZLE DAZZLE	Billy and Company
CLASS	Velma and Matron
NOWADAYS	Roxie and Velma
HOT HONEY RAG	Roxie and Velma
FINALE	Company

ORCHESTRA

Orchestra Conducted by LESLIE STIFELMAN
Associate Conductor: JEFFREY SAVER
Assistant Conductor: SCOTT CADY

Woodwinds:
SEYMOUR RED PRESS, JACK STUCKEY,
RICHARD CENTALONZA

Trumpets:
JOHN FROSK, DARRYL SHAW

Trombones:
DAVE BARGERON, BRUCE BONVISSUTO

Piano:
SCOTT CADY

Piano & Accordion:
JEFFREY SAVER

Banjo:
JAY BERLINER

Bass & Tuba:
RONALD RAFFIO

Violin:
MARSHALL COID

Drums & Percussion:
RONALD ZITO

Photo by Joan Marcus

Charlotte d'Amboise as Roxie Hart

Chicago

 Charlotte d'Amboise
Roxie Hart

 Luba Mason
Velma Kelly

 Huey Lewis
Billy Flynn

 P.J. Benjamin
Amos Hart

 Debra Monk
Matron "Mama" Morton

 R. Lowe
Mary Sunshine

 Donna Marie Asbury
June

 Gregory Butler
Fred Casely/ Dance Captain

 Mindy Cooper
Swing/ Dance Captain

 Bernard Dotson
Doctor/ The Judge/ Dance Captain

 Bryn Dowling
Mona

 Shawn Emamjomeh
Harry/The Jury

 Gabriela Garcia
Hunyak

 Denis Jones
Aaron

 Gary Kilmer
Swing

 Dan LoBuono
Swing

 Jeff Loeffelholz
Understudy Mary Sunshine

 Sharon Moore
Swing

 Denny Paschall
Bailiff/Court Clerk

 Michelle Potterf
Go-To-Hell Kitty

 Matthew Risch
Sergeant Fogarty

 Michelle M. Robinson
Liz

 Solange Sandy
Annie

 Steven Sofia
Martin Harrison

 John Kander and Fred Ebb
Music; Book/Lyrics

 Bob Fosse
Book

 Walter Bobbie
Director

 Ann Reinking
Choreographer

 John Lee Beatty
Set Design

 William Ivey Long
Costume Designer

 Ken Billington
Lighting Designer

 Ralph Burns
Orchestrations

 Rob Fisher
Supervising Music Director

 Peter Howard
Dance Music Arranger

 David Brian Brown
Wig/Hair Design

Chicago

Jay Binder,
Jay Binder C.S.A.
Original Casting

Arthur Siccardi,
Theatrical Services
Inc.
Technical Supervisor

Debra McWaters
*Assistant
Choreographer*

Barry and Fran
Weissler
Producers

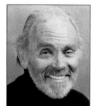

Morton Swinsky,
Kardana Productions
Producer

Shaun Amyot
*Bailiff/Count Clerk/
Dance Captain/Tap
Dance Specialty*

Brent Barrett
Billy Flynn

Brenda Braxton
Velma Kelly

Belle Calaway
*Standby Roxie Hart
and Matron "Mama"
Morton*

Michelle DeJean
Mona

Christopher McDonald
Billy Flynn

Dana Moore
Hunyak

James Patric Moran
*Doctor/Tap Dance
Specialty/
The Judge*

Clarke Peters
Billy Flynn

Josh Rhodes
*Martin Harrison/
Me and My Baby
Specialty*

D. Sabella-Mills
*Understudy
Mary Sunshine*

Brooke Shields
Roxie Hart

Mark Anthony Taylor
*Aaron/Harry/
Sereant Fogarty/
The Jury*

Mary Testa
*Matron "Mama"
Morton*

Tonya Wathen
Mona

Carol Woods
*Matron "Mama"
Morton*

Eric Jordan Young
*Doctor/Martin
Harrison/Me and My
Baby & Tap Dance
Specialty/The Judge*

Obba Babatundé
Billy Flynn

Eddie Bennett
Understudy

Raymond Bokhour
Amos Hart

Brenda Braxton
Velma Kelly

Roxane Carrasco
June

Kevin Chamberlin
Amos Hart

Michelle DeJean
Roxie Hart

Robin Givens
Roxie Hart

Mary Ann Lamb
Go-To-Hell Kitty

Chicago

Kevin Neil McCready
Fred Casely

John O'Hurley
Billy Flynn

Angel Reda
Annie

Josh Rhodes
*Martin Harrison/
Me and My Baby
Specialty*

D. Sabella-Mills
Mary Sunshine

Tracy Shayne
Roxie Hart

Mark Anthony Taylor
*Understudy/
Fred Casely and
Me and My Baby*

Jennifer West
Hunyak/Mona

Lillias White
*Matron "Mama"
Morton*

Bruce Winant
Amos Hart

Amra-Faye Wright
Velma Kelly

Eric Jordan Young
*Martin Harrison/
Me and My Baby
Specialty*

DOORMAN
Pat Green

HAIR & WARDROBE DEPARTMENT
Front Row (L-R): Paula Davis, Kevin Woodworth.
Back Row (L-R): Jo-Ann Bethell and Justen Brosnan.

BOX OFFICE
(L-R): Jim Gates, Tom McNulty and Tom Sheehan.

STAGE MANAGEMENT
(L-R): David Hyslop (Production Stage Manager), Terry Witter (Stage Manager) and Mindy Farbrother (Stage Manager).

Chicago

STAGE CREW
Front Row (L-R):
Luciana Fusco, Dennis Smalls,
Eileen MacDonald, Vince Jacobi,
Jimmy Werner, Charlie Grieco.

Second Row (L-R):
Joe Mooneyham (Standing), Bob Hale,
Lizard, Mike Guggino

Top:
William Nye.

FRONT OF HOUSE STAFF
First Row (L-R):
Charlene Collins (Usher),
Michael Kinsey (Theatre Refreshment),
Gerry Belitses (Usher),
Bill Daniels (Theatre Refreshments),
David Gamboa (Dewynters)

Second Row (L-R):
Lottie Dennis (Usher), Carol Bokun (Usher),
Jorge Velasquez (Usher)

Third Row (L-R):
Yunus Caskun (Usher), Jason Parris
(Usher), Dorothea Bentley (Directress)

Fourth Row (L-R):
Bobbi Parker (Usher), Danielle Banyai
(Usher) and David Loomis (Dewynters).

Not Pictured: Samuel A. Morris
(Education).

ORCHESTRA
Front Row (L-R):
Bruce Bonvissuto, Dave Bargeron,
John Johnson, Jay Berliner.

Second Row (L-R):
Ann Leathers, Mort Silver, Leslie Stifelman
(Conductor), Ron Raffio.

Back Row (L-R):
Stu Satalof, John Frosk, Scott Cady,
Ron Zito, Jack Stuckey
and Rick Centalonza.

Chicago

Chicago
Scrapbook

Correspondent: Pete Sanders, Publicist
• *Chicago* celebrated its ninth anniversary on Broadway November 14, 2005.
• *Chicago* has played more than 15,000 performances worldwide.
• An estimated 17 million people around the world have seen *Chicago*.
• *Chicago* has been performed in English, Dutch, German, Swedish, Spanish, Portuguese, Russian, Italian and French.
• The many stars who have headlined the Broadway company of *Chicago* include Bebe Neuwirth, Ann Reinking, James Naughton, Joel Grey, Marcia Lewis, Jasmine Guy, Charlotte d'Amboise, Sharon Lawrence, Marilu Henner, Sandy Duncan, Michael C. Hall, Wayne Brady, Melanie Griffith, Paige Davis, Jennifer Holliday, Robert Urich, Alan Thicke, Angie Stone, Louis Gossett, Jr., Taye Diggs, Vicki Lewis, Nana Visitor, Brent Barrett, Tom Wopat, Brooke Shields, Kevin Richardson, Huey Lewis, Robin Givens and John O'Hurley.
• *Chicago* has given the opportunity for the stars of foreign productions to make their Broadway debuts including Bianca Marroquin (Mexico), Denise Van Outen (U.K.), Terra C. Macleod (France and Canada), Petra Nielson (Sweden), Ute Lemper (U.K. and Germany), Ruthie Henshall (U.K.), Anna Montanaro (Germany and Austria), Pia Dowes (Holland), Marti Pellow (U.K.), Caroline O'Connor (Australia).
• This production of *Chicago* received 6 Tony Awards (including Best Musical Revival), 5 Drama Desk Awards, 5 Outer Critics' Circle Awards, 1 1998 Critics Circle Award, 1 Grammy Award (for Original Cast Recording), 2 Astaire Awards, 1 Drama League Award, 2 Bay Area Theatre Critics Circle Awards, 2 L.A. Drama Critics Circle Awards, 2 L.A. Ovation Awards, 1 Helen Hayes Award, 1 Black Theatre Alliance Award, 7 E.W. Awards, 2 Joseph Jefferson Awards and 1 Elliott Norton Award for the Broadway and National Touring companies.
• *Chicago* has played worldwide since its opening in 1996 in the following countries: England, Belgium, The Netherlands, Austria, Germany, Ireland, Scotland, Switzerland, Italy, France, Portugal, Greece, Israel, Russia, South Africa, China, Japan, South Korea, Canada, Mexico, Argentina, Brazil, Australia, Singapore.
As a result, *Chicago* had received 1 Olivier Award (Best Musical Production), 3 ACE Awards, 3 El Heraldo Awards, 3 Asociacion Mexicana de Criticos de Teatro Awards, 2 Helpman Awards, 4 Guldmasken Awards, and 2 Premio Qualidade Brasil Awards for its international productions.
• *Chicago* is scheduled to open in Dubai next year.
"Carols for a Cure: Carol: "Angels We Have Heard on High."
"Gypsy of the Year" Skit: "The Heart of Rock 'n' Roll" created by The Company, music by Huey Lewis.

1. The cast welcomes Brooke Shields (center) to the role of Roxie at a party at Bond 45.
2. Chicago's "merry murderesses" get a backstage visit from actor Shonn Wiley (L) and composer-lyricist Stephen Dolginoff whose Off-Broadway musical *Thrill Me* is set in 1924 Chicago.
3. (L-R): Kathleen Marshall and Rob Fisher clown for the camera at Shields' welcome party.
4. Liza Minnelli (front) visits the cast.
5. (L-R): Debra Monk and Bryn Dowling.

Chita Rivera: The Dancer's Life

First Preview: November 23, 2005. Opened: December 11, 2005.
Closed February 19, 2006 after 20 Previews and 72 Performances.

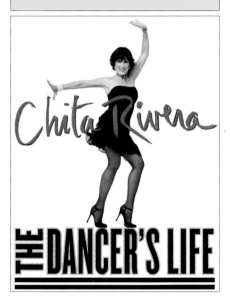

PLAYBILL®

CAST

Chita Rivera ....CHITA RIVERA
Little Chita Rivera/Lisa ....LIANA ORTIZ

THE ENSEMBLE

RICHARD AMARO, LLOYD CULBREATH,
MALINDA FARRINGTON,
EDGARD GALLARDO, DEIDRE GOODWIN,
RICHARD MONTOYA,
LAINIE SAKAKURA, ALEX SANCHEZ,
ALLYSON TUCKER

SWINGS

CLEVE ASBURY, MADELEINE KELLY

UNDERSTUDIES

For Little Chita Rivera/Lisa:
JASMINE PERRI
For Chita's Father/Tango Partner:
EDGARD GALLARDO
For Chita's *West Side Story* Partner:
RICHARD AMARO
For Camille:
MALINDA FARRINGTON, LAINIE SAKAKURA
For Colette:
MALINDA FARRINGTON, LAINIE SAKAKURA
For Big Spender Shadow:
ALLYSON TUCKER

DANCE CAPTAIN

MADELEINE KELLY

⑤ GERALD SCHOENFELD THEATRE

236 West 45th Street
A Shubert Organization Theatre

Gerald Schoenfeld, *Chairman*   **Philip J. Smith,** *President*

Robert E. Wankel, *Executive Vice President*

Marty Bell Aldo Scrofani Martin Richards Chase Mishkin
Bernard Abrams/Michael Speyer Tracy Aron Joe McGinnis
in association with Stefany Bergson Scott Prisand/Jennifer Maloney G. Marlyne Sexton
Judith Ann Abrams/Jamie deRoy Addiss/Rittereiser/Carragher

Present

CHITA RIVERA

in

Written by

TERRENCE McNALLY

Original Songs by
LYNN AHRENS   STEPHEN FLAHERTY

Featuring
RICHARD AMARO   CLEVE ASBURY   LLOYD CULBREATH   MALINDA FARRINGTON
EDGARD GALLARDO   DEIDRE GOODWIN   MADELEINE KELLY   RICHARD MONTOYA
LIANA ORTIZ   JASMINE PERRI   LAINIE SAKAKURA   ALEX SANCHEZ   ALLYSON TUCKER

Scenic Design by	Costume Design by	Lighting Design by
LOY ARCENAS	TONI-LESLIE JAMES	JULES FISHER & PEGGY EISENHAUER

Sound Design by	Hair Design by	Jerome Robbins Choreography Reproduced by	Bob Fosse Choreography Reproduced by
SCOTT LEHRER	DAVID BRIAN BROWN	ALAN JOHNSON	TONY STEVENS

Biographical Research by	Production Stage Manager	Associate Choreographer	Production Manager
PATRICK PACHECO	ARTURO E. PORAZZI	MADELEINE KELLY	AURORA PRODUCTIONS

Press Representative	Marketing Services	Music Coordinator	Casting by
BARLOW•HARTMAN	TMG-THE MARKETING GROUP	MICHAEL KELLER	MARK SIMON, CSA

Executive Producers	Associate Producers	General Management
MARTY BELL/ALDO SCROFANI	DAN GALLAGHER/MICHAEL MILTON	ALAN WASSER ASSOCIATES

Orchestrations by
DANNY TROOB

Musical Concepts, Arrangements & Direction by
MARK HUMMEL

Directed and Choreographed by
GRACIELA DANIELE

WORLD PREMIERE AT THE OLD GLOBE THEATRE SAN DIEGO, CALIFORNIA.
ARTISTIC DIRECTOR: JACK O'BRIEN / EXECUTIVE DIRECTOR: LOUIS G. SPISTO
The producers wish to express their appreciation to Theatre Development Fund for its support of this production.

LIVE BROADWAY

12/11/05

Chita Rivera (C), flanked by
dancers Edgard Gallardo
and Alex Sanchez.

Photo by Paul Kolnik

Chita Rivera: The Dancer's Life

MUSICAL NUMBERS

ACT I

PROLOGUE
"Perfidia" ....with Liana Ortiz, Richard Amaro

THE WHITE HOUSE
"Secret o' Life"

MI FAMILIA LOCA
"Dancing on the Kitchen Table"* ....with Richard Montoya, Edgard Gallardo,
Allyson Tucker, Lainie Sakakura,
Malinda Farrington, Richard Amaro

BALLET CLASS ....with Malinda Farrington, Deirdre Goodwin,
Lainie Sakakura, Allyson Tucker, Liana Ortiz

THE GYPSY LIFE
"Something to Dance About" (*Call Me Madam*) ....with Richard Montoya
"I'm Available" (*Mr. Wonderful*)
"Camille, Colette, Fifi" (*Seventh Heaven*) ....with Allyson Tucker, Deidre
Goodwin
"Garbage" (*The Shoestring Review*)
"Can-Can" (*Can-Can*) ....with Allyson Tucker, Malinda
Farrington,
Lainie Sakakura, Deidre Goodwin
"Mr. Wonderful" (*Mr. Wonderful*)

WEST SIDE STORY
"A Boy Like That"
"Dance at the Gym" (*Mambo*) ....Edgard Gallardo as Chita's Partner
with Ensemble
"Somewhere" ....with Ensemble

CO-STARS
"Put on a Happy Face" (*Bye Bye Birdie*) ....with Lloyd Culbreath
"Rosie" (*Bye Bye Birdie*) ....with Lloyd Culbreath
"Don't 'Ah Ma' Me" (*The Rink*)
"Big Spender" (*Sweet Charity*) ....with Deidre Goodwin
"Nowadays" (*Chicago*)

ACT II

ENTR'ACTE

THE AUDITION ....Lloyd Culbreath as The Choreographer
with Ensemble

THE MEN
Tangos: "Adios Noñino," "Detresse," "Calambre" ....with Richard Amaro, Liana Ortiz
"More Than You Know" ....with Ensemble

CHOREOGRAPHERS ....with Ensemble

THE SHOWS
"A Woman the World Has Never Seen"*
"Class" (*Chicago*)
"Chief Cook & Bottlewasher" (*The Rink*)
"Kiss of the Spider Woman" (*Kiss of the Spider Woman*)
"Where You Are" (*Kiss of the Spider Woman*) ....with Ensemble Men

THE WHITE HOUSE
"All That Jazz" (*Chicago*) ....with Liana Ortiz, Ensemble

*Original songs by Lynn Ahrens and Stephen Flaherty

ORCHESTRA
Conductor:
MARK HUMMEL
Associate Conductor:
GARY ADLER
Piano:
MARK HUMMEL
Keyboard 2:
GARY ADLER
Violin:
ENTCHO TODOROV
Cello:
WOLFRAM KOESSEL
Reeds:
TED NASH, MARK PHANEUF
Lead Trumpet:
JEFF KIEVIT
Trumpet:
JOHN CHUDOBA
Trombones/Tuba:
RANDY ANDOS
Bass:
JIM DONICA
Drums:
MICHAEL CROITER
Percussion:
BILL HAYES

Music Coordinator:
MICHAEL KELLER
Additional Orchestrations:
LARRY HOCHMAN
Synthesizer Programmer:
ANDREW BARRETT
Music Copying:
KAYE-HOUSTON MUSIC/
ANNE KAYE AND DOUG HOUSTON

Chita Rivera

Photo by Paul Kolnik

Chita Rivera: The Dancer's Life

Chita Rivera

Richard Amaro
*Ensemble/
Tango Dancer*

Cleve Asbury
*Assistant Dance
Captain/Swing*

Lloyd Culbreath
Ensemble

Malinda Farrington
Ensemble

Edgard Gallardo
Ensemble

Deidre Goodwin
Ensemble

Madeleine Kelly
*Dance Captain/
Swing/Associate
Choreographer*

Richard Montoya
Ensemble

Liana Ortiz
*Little Chita Rivera/
Lisa*

Jasmine Perri
*Understudy Little
Chita Rivera/ Lisa*

Lainie Sakakura
Ensemble

Alex Sanchez
Ensemble

Allyson Tucker
Ensemble

Terrence McNally
Playwright

Lynn Ahrens
Original Songs

Stephen Flaherty
Original Songs

Graciela Daniele
*Director,
Choreographer*

Mark Hummel
*Musical Concepts,
Arrangements &
Direction*

Danny Troob
Orchestrations

Jules Fisher and
Peggy Eisenhauer
Lighting Design

David Brian Brown
*Wig and Hair
Designer*

Tony Stevens
Fosse Choreography

Michael Keller
Music Coordinator

Alan Wasser
General Manager

Marty Bell
*Producer/
Executive Producer*

Aldo Scrofani
*Producer/
Executive Producer*

Chase Mishkin
Producer

Tracy Aron
Producer

Joe McGinnis
Producer

Scott Prisand
Co-Producer

Judith Ann Abrams
Co-Producer

Pat Flicker Addiss
Co-Producer

Jamie deRoy
Co-Producer

Chita Rivera: The Dancer's Life

Isabella DeVivo
*u/s Little Chita Rivera/
Lisa*

Dick Van Dyke
Special Guest

STAGE MANAGERS
(L-R): Gary Mickelson, Arturo E. Porazzi, David M. Beris.

Photos by Ben Strothmann

BOX OFFICE
Noreen Morgan and Barry Bond.

STAGE CREW
(L-R): Kenny McDonough, Leslie Ann Kilian, Peter Guernsey, Jim Kane, Brian Dawson, Tim McWilliams, Christopher Sloan, Andy Funk, Trish Simons and Greg Husinko.

Chita Rivera: The Dancer's Life

HAIR
Richard Orton

CONDUCTOR
Mark Hummel

Photos by Ben Strothmann

FRONT OF HOUSE STAFF
Front: Roz Nyman. Middle Row (L-R): Gwen Coley, Kathleen Spock, Sandy Capasso, David M. Conte, Laura Kay, Helen Lindberg, Michelle Moyna.
Back Row (L-R): John Hall, Greg Marlowe, Janet Kay, Desmond Boyle.
Not Pictured: Francine Kramer (Head Usher).

WARDROBE
(L-R): Francine Schwartz-Buryiak, Julianne Schubert-Blechman, Teri Pruitt, Dante Taylor

---

STAFF FOR *CHITA RIVERA: THE DANCER'S LIFE*

WEST EGG ENTERTAINMENT
Creative Director: Marty Bell
Managing Director: Aldo Scrofani
Director, Investor Relations: Tracy Aron
Creative Associate: Justine Lore
Directors: Marty Bell, Roger Lipitz
Gary McAvay, Tom Owens, Aldo Scrofani

GENERAL MANAGEMENT
ALAN WASSER ASSOCIATES
Alan Wasser   Allan Williams
Jim Brandeberry   Connie Yung

GENERAL PRESS REPRESENTATIVE
BARLOW•HARTMAN
Michael Hartman   John Barlow
Rick Miramontez   Jon Dimond

COMPANY MANAGER
Judi Wilfore

PRODUCTION MANAGEMENT
AURORA PRODUCTIONS, INC.
Gene O'Donovan   Ben Heller

Production Stage Manager .... **Arturo E. Porazzi**
Stage Manager .... Gary Mickelson
Assistant Stage Manager .... David M. Beris

Dance Captain .... Madeleine Kelly
Assistant Dance Captain .... Cleve Asbury
Ms. Rivera's Personal Assistant .... Rosie Bentinck
Makeup Designer and Stylist for Ms. Rivera ..... Kate Best
Makeup Design for Dancers .... Patrick Eichler/
                                        M•A•C Cosmetics
Associate Scenic Designer .... Christine Peters
Assistant Scenic Designer .... Matthew Myhrum

Associate Costume Designer .... Neno Russell
Assistant to Ms. James .... Lisa Renee Jordan
Assistant Lighting Designer .... Scott Davis
Moving Lights Programmer .... Thomas Celner
Associate Sound Designer .... Leon Rothenberg
Production Carpenter .... Donald Robertson
Assistant Carpenter/Flyman .... Paul Wimmer
Production Electrician .... Gregory Husinko
Moving Lights Tech .... Brian Dawson
Production Property .... Vera Pizzarelli
Production Sound .... Christopher Sloan
Wardrobe Supervisor .... Sharon Lewis
Dressers .... Janet Anderson, Jennifer Anderson,
                                Rob Bevenger, Kristen Sauter,
                                Francine Schwartz-Buryiak
Hair Supervisor .... Richard Orton
Ms. Rivera's Personal Publicist .... Merle Frimark

Director, New York Office of Joe McGinnis ..... Bart Kahn

Chita Rivera: The Dancer's Life

General Management Associates ....Thom Mitchell,
Aaron Lustbader

Production Management Associate ......Bethany Weinstein

Press Office Associates ...Dennis Crowley, Carol Fineman,
Bethany Larsen,
Wayne Wolfe, Leslie Baden,
Ryan Ratelle, Gerilyn Shur,
Andrew Snyder, Stephen J. Sosnowski

Production Assistant.............................Sarah Izzo

Dance Arranger for "Where You Are" ....David Krane

Synthesizer Programmer.....................Andrew Barrett
for Lionella Productions, Ltd.

Ms. Rivera's Physical Therapist ....Marika Molnar/
West Side Dance

Physical Therapist ....Jennifer Green/PhysioArts

Supervising Orthopedist ....Dr. David Weiss

Legal Counsel ....Frankfurt, Garbus, Klein & Selz/
S. Jean Ward

Music Rights Clearances ....Jane Halpern

Insurance ....DeWitt Stern Group/Peter Shoemaker

Banking ....City National Bank/Anne McSweeney

Accounting ....Rosenberg Neuwirth & Kuchner/
Chris Cacace

Travel ....Road Rebel Entertainment

Payroll Service ....Castellana Services Inc.

Rehearsal Studios ....New 42nd Street Studios,
Chelsea Studios

Advertising ....SpotCo/
Drew Hodges, Jim Edwards,
Jim Aquino, Lauren Hunter

Marketing ....Trish Santini, Ronni Seif,
Greg Ramos, Jennifer Shultz

Souvenir Merchandising ....LTS Enterprises,
Larry Turk and Max Merchandising

Web Designer ....Situation Marketing

Theatre Displays ....King Displays

Production Photographer.......................Paul Kolnik

Opening Night Coordinator ....Tobak Lawrence Company
Joanna B. Koondel, Suzanne Tobak

CREDITS

Scenery, show control and automated effects by Showmotion Inc. Norwalk, CT, using the AC2 computerized motion control system. Lighting equipment provided by PRG Lighting. Sound equipment provided by Masque Sound. Trucking by Clark Transfer. Local trucking by Prop Transport. Drumsticks provided by Pro-Mark Drumsticks and Mallets. Specialty props by Craig Grigg. Piano by Steinway and Sons. Ms. Rivera's dressing room designed by Matthew White and Frank Webb of White Webb, LLC. Women's costumes by Adrienne Wells and the Costume Shop of The Old Globe Theatre, Stacy Sutton costume shop supervisor. Men's clothing by Savoia Custom Men's Clothiers. Shoes by LaDuca Shoes. Ms. Rivera's shoes by T.O. Dey. Ballet shoes by Capezio. Can-Can hats by Lady Diane. Transportation provided by Lucariello Protection & Trans, Inc.

MUSIC CREDITS

"Perfidia" by Alberto Dominguez and Milton Leeds. Copyright Peer International Corporation. "Secret o' Life" by James Taylor. Country Road Music Inc. "Dancing on the Kitchen Table" by Lynn Ahrens and Stephen Flaherty. "A Quiet Thing" by John Kander and Fred Ebb. Used by permission of Alley Music Corp. and Trio Music. "Small Fry" by Hoagy Carmichael and Frank Loesser. Published by Famous Music Corporation (ASCAP). Used by permission. All rights reserved. "Make 'em Laugh" by Arthur Freed and Nacio Herb Brown. Published by EMI Robbins Catalog Inc. Used by permission. "You're Just in Love," "Something to Dance About," "It's a Lovely Day Today" (from *Call Me Madam*). Music and Lyrics by Irving Berlin. Used by special arrangement with the Rodgers and Hammerstein Organization on behalf of the Estate of Irving Berlin. "I'm Available," "Mr. Wonderful" (from *Mr. Wonderful*) by Jerrold Bock, Lawrence Holofcener and George David Weiss. Jerry Bock Enterprises. Copyright renewed 1995. Copyright 1956, renewed Abilene Music. Used by permission of Range Road Music, Inc., Alley Music Corp. "Guys and Dolls" by Frank Loesser. Used by permission of Frank Music Corp. "Camille, Colette, Fifi" (from *Seventh Heaven*) by Stella Unger and Victor Young. "Garbage" (from *The Shoestring Revue*). Music and lyrics by Sheldon Harnick. Used by special arrangement with R&H Music, on behalf of Mayerling Productions Ltd. All rights reserved. "Can-Can," "I Love Paris" (from *Can-Can*). Words and music by Cole Porter. Copyright 1952 (renewed), Chappell & Co., Inc. (ASCAP). Used by permission of the Cole Porter Musical and Literary Property Trusts. "A Boy Like That," "Dance at the Gym," "Somewhere," "Cool," "America" (from *West Side Story*). Based on a conception of Jerome Robbins. Book by Arthur Laurents. Music by Leonard Bernstein. Lyrics by Stephen Sondheim. Entire production directed and choreographed by Jerome Robbins. "My Man's Gone Now" (from *Porgy and Bess*) by George and Ira Gershwin. Copyright 1935 (renewed), George Gershwin Music (ASCAP), Ira Gershwin Music (ASCAP) and DuBose and Dorothy Heyward Memorial Fund Publishing (ASCAP). All rights administered by WB Music Corp. (ASCAP). All rights reserved. Used by permission. "Put on a Happy Face," "Rosie" (from *Bye Bye Birdie*). Copyright 1960 (renewed) by Charles Strouse and Lee Adams. Worldwide publishing by Charles Strouse Music (ASCAP). Helene Blue Musique Ltd., administrator. All rights reserved. "Put on a Happy Face" (from *Bye Bye Birdie*) is from the original cast recording, courtesy of Sony BMG Masterworks. "Big Spender," "If My Friends Could See Me Now," "There's Gotta Be Something Better Than This" (from *Sweet Charity*) by Cy Coleman and Dorothy Fields. Notable Music Co., Inc., Lida Enterprises Inc. "Folies Bergere" (from *Nine*). Words and music by Maury Yeston. Copyright 1982, Yeston Music Ltd. (BMI). Worldwide rights for Yeston Music Ltd. administered by Cherry River Music Co. (BMI). All rights reserved. "Only in the Movies," "Let's Make Love," "Kiss of the Spider Woman," "Where You Are" (from *Kiss of the Spider Woman*). Written by John Kander and Fred Ebb. Used by permission of Bro 'N Sis Music Inc., obo Kander and Ebb Inc. "Don't 'Ah Ma' Me," "Colored Lights," "Chief Cook and Bottle Washer" (from *The Rink*). Written by John Kander and Fred Ebb. Used by permission of Bro 'N Sis Music Inc., obo Kander & Ebb Inc. "Nowadays," "Class," "All That Jazz," "My Own Best Friend" (from *Chicago*) written by John Kander and Fred Ebb. Copyright 1975, Unichappell Music Inc. (BMI) and Kander and Ebb, Inc. (BMI). All rights administered by Unichappell Music Inc. All rights reserved. Used by permission. "Cuban Pete" by Jose Norman (aka Norman Henderson). Copyright 1936, J. Norris Music Publishing Co., Ltd. (PRS). All rights administered by WB Music Corp. All rights reserved. Used by permission. "Adios Noñino" by Astor Piazzolla. Editions Universelles. "Detresse" by Astor Piazzolla. Editions Universelles. "Calambre" by Astor Piazzolla. Editions Universelles. "More Than You Know" by Billy Rose, Edward Eliscu and Vincent Youmans. Copyright 1929 (renewed), WB Music Corp., Anne-Rachel Music Corp., Chappell & Co., LSQ Music Co. All rights reserved. Used by permission. "Steam Heat" (from *The Pajama Game*) by Richard Adler and Jerry Ross. Copyright 1954, renewed Lakshmi Puja Music and J&J Ross Music. Permission secured. All rights reserved. "Tradition" (from *Fiddler on the Roof*). Music by Jerry Bock. Lyrics by Sheldon Harnick. Jerry Bock Enterprises, copyright renewed 1992. These selections are used with special arrangement with R&H Music, on behalf of Mayerling Productions Ltd. All rights reserved. "A Woman the World Has Never Seen Before" by Lynn Ahrens and Stephen Flaherty.

---

www.thedancerslife.com

THE OLD GLOBE THEATRE STAFF

Artistic Director ....Jack O'Brien
Executive Director ....Louis G. Spisto
Artistic Director ....Craig Noel
General Manager ....Michael G. Murphy
Director of Production ....Robert Drake
Director of Marketing
and Communications ....Dave Henson
Director of Development ....Todd Schultz
Director of Finance ....Mark Somers
Technical Director ....Benjamin Thoron
Costume Director ....Stacy Sutton
Properties Director ....Neil A. Holmes

House Manager ....David Conte
House Electrician Supervisor ....Leslie Ann Kilian
House Prop Supervisor ....Patricia Simons
House Carpentry Supervisor ....Tim McWilliams

Chita Rivera: The Dancer's Life
SCRAPBOOK

Photos by Aubrey Reuben

Correspondent: Madeleine Kelly, Associate Choreographer, Dance Captain and Swing

Memorable Opening Night Notes: Chita Rivera and Graciela Daniele wrote personal notes to each member of the cast and crew. Almost every show on Broadway sent us a congratulatory fax and we taped them all to the wall.

Opening Night Gifts: Chita got us all sweatjackets with our names on the sleeve, and the show's logo on the back. The producers got us thick black robes that are just fabulous, and eight-by-tens of Chita singing "Nowadays" in the top hat. Graciela Daniele had glass figures of each of us made by Milon Townsend, and she gave Chita a ring that had belonged to her mom, who passed away.

Most Exciting Celebrity Visitors: Probably the most memorable is when Rita Moreno came, but we've had so, so many! Rita spoke to Edgard Gallardo in Spanish. A lot came from the original cast or film of *West Side Story*, like George Chakiris. We had Liza Minnelli, Rosie O'Donnell, Melanie Griffith and Ann-Margret. Tony Mordente put the whole Dick Van Dyke section together, assisted by Chita's daughter Lisa Mordente, which was kinda awesome.

Who Got the Gypsy Robe: Alex Sanchez, who was so surprised because had just won for *Chitty Chitty Bang Bang*.

Most Roles: Chita Rivera! Second is Edgard Gallardo. He's got the most costume changes, too.

Who's Done the Most Shows: Chita Rivera!

Special Backstage Rituals: The whole company (minus Chita) does a one-hour warmup in the balcony before each show—even on two-show days. Just before each performance, everyone says to Chita, "Melly Log." On the way to the stage, Chita gives everyone she sees two kisses, one on each cheek. Behind the curtain during the Entr'acte Chita plays Edgard's back like a drum. It's a show within a show.

Favorite Moments During Each Performance: The *West Side Story* section, "Nowadays" and "Tango." Also, when Dick Van Dyke joined the cast for a few days. I loved the magic of those two together on stage!

Company In-Joke: After Rita Moreno visited, we all said she'd be perfect as Chita's understudy.

Favorite In-Theatre Gathering Places: Chita Rivera's dressing room, and the quick-change booth in the basement.

1. The cast on the first day of rehearsal.
2. Rivera (R) at the lighting of the Times Square Christmas tree.
3. Guest Liza Minnelli on opening night.
4. Rivera's *Bye Bye Birdie* co-star Dick Van Dyke (L) brought roses for his onetime "Rosie" when he briefly joined the cast.

Chita Rivera: The Dancer's Life
SCRAPBOOK

Favorite Off-Site Hangouts: Barrymore's—until it closed. We also go to Bar Centrale at Joe Allen. Chita's favorite is the West Bank Café.

Favorite Snack Food: York Peppermint Patties. Edgard Gallarado, who is a fabulous cook, makes us this awesome peanut brittle. Also, an audience member who works for the Entenmann's bakery loved the show so much that he dropped off a week's worth of cookies, cake and doughnuts.

Mascot: Chita's dog, Casper.

Favorite Therapies: The producers gave us gift cards for Starbucks, where the company favorite is Tazo chai tea latte. We also use Ricolas, herbal tea, Emer'gen-C and Airborne, plus we get physical therapy twice a week. This company also loves acupuncture.

Memorable Ad-Libs: One night, Chita said "That's a misunderstanding," instead of "That's an understatement." Another night, during the eleven o'clock number, Chita inverted the lyrics. So she stopped and said to the audience, "This is live theatre," and they went nuts.

Fastest Costume Changes: Lloyd Culbreath out of "Tango" into "Choreographer's Wall." Edgard Gallardo out of "Choreographer's Wall" to bring Chita's chair out for the eleven o'clock number. Alex Sanchez out of "Where You Are" to playing the usher at the White House.

Heaviest/Hottest Costume: Chita has to wear two mike packs and I'm not even going to tell you where they are!

Catchphrases Only the Company Would Recognize: "Melly Log." "Put on a Sabu-Day."

Which Orchestra Member Played the Most Instruments: Bill Hayes, percussion.

Orchestra Member Who Played the Most Consecutive Performances Without A Sub: Michael Croiter.

Memorable Directorial Note: Graciela's speech after the gypsy run-through.

Embarrassing Moment: The second time we performed "America" after it was put into the show. It just didn't go well. Let's not say anything more about it.

Nicknames: Chita Rivera is "Cheety."

Sweethearts Within the Company: Alex Sanchez and Lainie Sakakura are married and have a little girl, Avelina.

Coolest Thing About Being in This Show: Working with Chita Rivera. Being onstage with a living legend, even if she hates being called a legend.

1. Rivera and the cast accept a standing ovation on opening night.
2. Rivera's daughter Lisa Mordente (R) arrives with dad (and Rivera's ex) Tony Mordente.
3. Guests Marin Mazzie and Terrence McNally arrive on opening night.
4. Rivera hugs her onstage alter-ego Liana Ortiz at the opening night party at Copacabana.
5. Guest Barbara Cook makes her entrance at the Schoenfeld Theatre.

Photos by Aubrey Reuben

Chitty Chitty Bang Bang

First Preview: March 29, 2005. Opened: April 28, 2005.
Closed December 31, 2005 after 34 Previews and 285 Performances.

PLAYBILL

IAN FLEMING'S "CHITTY CHITTY BANG BANG"

CAST

Caractacus Potts	RAÚL ESPARZA
Truly Scrumptious	ERIN DILLY
Grandpa Potts	PHILIP BOSCO
Baron Bomburst	KENNETH KANTOR
Baroness Bomburst	JAN MAXWELL
Goran	CHIP ZIEN
Boris	ROBERT SELLA
Childcatcher	KEVIN CAHOON
Toymaker	FRANK RAITER
Jeremy Potts	HENRY HODGES
Jemima Potts	ELLEN MARLOW
Coggins/Chicken Farmer	JB ADAMS
Phillips	DIRK LUMBARD
Lord Scrumptious	KURT VON SCHMITTOU
Sid	JEFF WILLIAMS
Violet	ROBYN HURDER
Vulgarian Flying Soldier	MATT LOEHR
Vulgarian Anthem Solo Dancer	SABRA LEWIS
Toby	MICHAEL HERWITZ
Inventors	JB ADAMS, ROBERT CREIGHTON, TIM FEDERLE, DIRK LUMBARD, WILLIAM RYALL, JEFF WILLIAMS

ENSEMBLE

JB ADAMS, TOLAN AMAN,
JULIE BARNES, TIMOTHY W. BISH,
TROY EDWARD BOWLES,
ROBERT CREIGHTON, ANTONIO D'AMATO,
STRUAN ERLENBORN, TIM FEDERLE,
ASHLEE FIFE, EMILY FLETCHER,
ROD HARRELSON, BEN HARTLEY,
MERRITT TYLER HAWKINS,
MICHAEL HERWITZ, ROBYN HURDER,
LIBBIE JACOBSON, SABRA LEWIS,
MATT LOEHR, DIRK LUMBARD,
GABRIELLA MALEK, MAYUMI MIGUEL,
MICHAEL MINDLIN, MALCOLM MORANO,
JACLYN NEIDENTHAL, HEATHER PARCELLS,

Continued on next page

HILTON THEATRE
A CLEAR CHANNEL THEATRE

DANA BROCCOLI, BARBARA BROCCOLI, MICHAEL G. WILSON,
FREDERICK ZOLLO, NICHOLAS PALEOLOGOS, JEFFREY SINE, HARVEY WEINSTEIN,
EAST OF DOHENY THEATRICALS and MICHAEL ROSE LIMITED
By Special Arrangement with MGM ON STAGE
present

RAÚL ESPARZA
ERIN DILLY   **PHILIP BOSCO**
in

IAN FLEMING'S
CHITTY CHITTY BANG BANG

Music and Lyrics by
RICHARD M. SHERMAN and ROBERT B. SHERMAN

Adapted for the stage by
JEREMY SAMS
Based on the MGM/United Artists Motion Picture

Also Starring
JAN MAXWELL   **KENNETH KANTOR**
CHIP ZIEN   **ROBERT SELLA**   **KEVIN CAHOON**
FRANK RAITER   **HENRY HODGES**   **ELLEN MARLOW**

Associate Director **PETER VON MAYRHAUSER**	Associate Choreographer **TARA YOUNG**	Production Stage Manager **MICHAEL J. PASSARO**	Fight Director **B.H. BARRY**
Casting by **JIM CARNAHAN, CSA**	Music Coordinator **SAM LUTFIYYA**	Additional Material by **IVAN MENCHELL**	Animal Trainer **WILLIAM BERLONI**
Associate Producer **FRANK GERO**	Production Managers **DAVID BENKEN JAKE BELL**	Press Representative **BARLOW • HARTMAN**	General Management **ALAN WASSER ASSOCIATES**

Orchestrations & Dance Arrangements by   Production Musical Supervisor   Musical Director
CHRIS WALKER   **ROBERT SCOTT**   **KRISTEN BLODGETTE**

Lighting Designed by   Sound Designed by
MARK HENDERSON   **ANDREW BRUCE**

Scenery & Costumes Designed by   Musical Staging & Choreography by
ANTHONY WARD   **GILLIAN LYNNE**

Directed by
ADRIAN NOBLE

LIVE BROADWAY

10/1/05

Raúl Esparza (center) performs "Me Ol' Bamboo" with the cast.

Photo by Joan Marcus

Chitty Chitty Bang Bang

MUSICAL NUMBERS

ACT I

The action takes place in England and Vulgaria.

Overture ....Orchestra
Prologue ....Company
You Two ....Caractacus, Jeremy and Jemima
Them Three ....Grandpa Potts
Toot Sweets ....Caractacus, Truly Scrumptious, Lord Scrumptious and Ensemble
Act English ....Boris and Goran
Hushabye Mountain..Caractacus
Come to the Fun Fair ....Company
Me Ol' Bamboo..Caractacus and Ensemble
Posh ....Grandpa Potts, Jeremy and Jemima
Chitty Chitty Bang Bang ....Caractacus, Truly, Jeremy and Jemima
Truly Scrumptious ....Jeremy, Jemima and Truly
Chitty Chitty Bang Bang (Nautical Reprise) ....Caractacus, Truly, Jeremy and Jemima
Chitty Takes Flight ....Company

ACT II

Entre'acte ....Orchestra
Vulgarian National Anthem ....Company
The Roses of Success...Grandpa Potts and Inventors
Kiddy-Widdy-Winkies ....Childcatcher
Teamwork ....Caractacus, Toymaker, Truly and Juvenile Ensemble
Chu-Chi Face ....Baron and Baroness
The Bombie Samba..Baroness, Baron and Ensemble
Doll on a Music Box/Truly Scrumptious (Reprise) ....Truly and Caractacus
Us Two/Chitty Prayer ....Jeremy and Jemima
Teamwork (Reprise)..Toymaker and Company
Chitty Flies Home (Finale) ....Company

Kevin Cahoon as The Childcatcher.

Photos by Joan Marcus

Philip Bosco (center) as Grandpa Potts.

Chitty Chitty Bang Bang

Raúl Esparza
Caractacus Potts

Erin Dilly
Truly Scrumptious

Philip Bosco
Grandpa Potts

Jan Maxwell
Baroness Bomburst

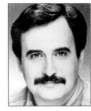
Kenneth Kantor
Baron Bomburst

Chip Zien
Goran

Robert Sella
Boris

Kevin Cahoon
Childcatcher

Frank Raiter
Toymaker

Henry Hodges
Jeremy

Ellen Marlow
Jemima

JB Adams
*Coggins/
Chicken Farmer/
Inventor/Ensemble*

Tolan Aman
Ensemble

Phillip Attmore
Swing

Julie Barnes
Ensemble

Timothy W. Bish
Ensemble

Troy Edward Bowles
Ensemble

Robert Creighton
Inventor/Ensemble

Antonio D'Amato
Ensemble

Struan Erlenborn
Ensemble

Tim Federle
Inventor/Ensemble

Ashlee Fife
Ensemble

Emily Fletcher
Ensemble

Rod Harrelson
Ensemble

Ben Hartley
Ensemble

Merritt Tyler Hawkins
Ensemble

Michael Herwitz
Toby/Ensemble

Rick Hilsabeck
Swing

Robyn Hurder
Violet/Ensemble

Libbie Jacobson
Ensemble

Sabra Lewis
*Vulgarian Anthem
Solo Dancer/
Ensemble*

Matt Loehr
*Vulgarian Flying
Soldier/Ensemble*

Dirk Lumbard
*Phillips/Inventor/
Ensemble*

Gabriella Malek
Ensemble

Joanne Manning
*Dance Captain/
Swing*

Chitty Chitty Bang Bang

Mayumi Miguel
Ensemble

Michael Mindlin
Ensemble

Malcolm Morano
Ensemble

Jaclyn Neidenthal
Ensemble

Heather Parcells
Ensemble

Lurie Poston
Ensemble

Craig Ramsay
Ensemble

William Ryall
Inventor/Ensemble

Bret Shuford
Ensemble

Jeff Siebert
*Dance Captain/
Fight Captain/Swing*

Julie Tolivar
Swing

Janelle Viscomi
Ensemble

Kurt Von Schmittou
*Lord Scrumptious/
Ensemble*

Mindy Franzese Wild
Swing

Jeff Williams
*Sid/Inventor/
Ensemble*

Ian Fleming
Original Author

Robert B. Sherman
and Richard M.
Sherman
Composers/Lyricists

Adrian Noble
Director

Gillian Lynne
*Musical Stager and
Choreographer*

Mark Henderson
Lighting Designer

Andrew Bruce
Sound Designer

Kristen Blodgette
Musical Director

Tara Young
*Associate
Choregrapher*

B. H. Barry
Fight Director

Jim Carnahan
Casting

William Berloni
Animal Trainer

David Benken
Production Manager

Alan Wasser,
Alan Wasser
Associates
General Manager

Harvey Weinstein
Producer

Bill Blackstock
Doorman

Gabriel Maysonette
Doorman

Chitty Chitty Bang Bang

 **Jeffrey Broadhurst**
Ensemble

 **Paul Canaan**
Ensemble

 **Rick Faugno**
*Ensemble/Inventor/
Understudy Goran*

 **Kearran Giovanni**
*Ensemble/Vulgarian
Anthem Solo Dancer*

 **Marc Kudisch**
Baron Bomburst

 **Alex Sanchez**
Ensemble

 **Emma Wahl**
Ensemble

 **Brynn Williams**
Ensemble

 **Jeffrey Broadhurst**
Ensemble

 **Paul Canaan**
Ensemble

 **Marc Kudisch**
Baron Bomburst

(L-R): Jan Maxwell and Marc Kudisch as Baroness and Baron Bomburst lead the chorus in "The Bombie Samba."

Photos by Joan Marcus

Chitty Chitty Bang Bang

Photo by Ben Strothmann

The *Chitty Chitty Bang Bang* Cast and Crew

1. Danielle Tiazio (Usher)
2. Tara Young
   (Associate Choreographer)
3. Seth Sklar-Heyn
   (Assistant Stage Manager)
4. Charlie Underhill
   (Stage Manager)
5. Fred (Dog)
6. Mayumi Miguel (Cast)
7. Michael Herwitz (Cast)
8. Troy Edward Bowles (Cast)
9. Gabby Malek (Cast)
10. Janelle Viscomi (Cast)
11. Jaclyn Neidenthal (Cast)
12. Lurie Poston (Cast)
13. Antonio D'Amato (cast)
14. Patches (Dog)
15. Henry Hodges (Cast)
16. Malcolm Morano (Cast)
17. Struan Erlenborn (Cast)
18. Bart (Dog)
19. Kenneth Kantor (Cast)
20. Kirsten Lake (Dog Wrangler)
21. Harriett (Dog)
22. Monica Shaffer (Dog Wrangler)
23. Argile (Dog)
24. Ken Fuller (Usher)
25. Robert Sella (Cast)
26. Rex Tucker-Moss (Makeup)
27. Caitley Symons (Wardrobe)

28. Michael Mindlin (Cast)
29. Kevin Cahoon (Cast)
30. Emily Fletcher (Cast)
31. Joanne Manning (Cast)
32. Libbie Jacobson (Cast)
33. Tolan Aman (Cast)
34. Timothy Bish (Cast)
35. John Santagata (Stagehand)
36. Christine Whitley (Usher)
37. Julia Wood (Usher)
38. Jeff Siebert (Cast)
39. Matt Loehr (Cast)
40. Sabra Lewis (Cast)
41. Tim Federle (Cast)
42. Vanessa Brown (Child Wrangler)
43. Jeffrey Broadhurst (Cast)
44. Dirk Lumbard (Cast)
45. Lady (Star Dog)
46. Chip Zien (Cast)
47. Jane Davis (Wardrobe)
48. Jason Heisey (Wardrobe)
49. Delilah Lloydd
    (Usher Shift Leader)
50. Nicole Ellingham (Usher)
51. Trisha Pfister (Usher)
52. Scott Scheidt (Sound)
53. Christina Foster (Dresser)
54. Stan Tucker (Music Director)
55. John R. Gibson (Head Sound)
56. Jennifer Barnes (Dresser)

57. Frank Raiter (Cast)
58. Julie Barnes (Cast)
59. Marc Kudisch (Cast)
60. Barney (Dog)
61. Franc Weinperl (Wardrobe)
62. Snickers (Dog)
63. Jenn Molloy (Wardrobe/Hair)
64. Carmel Vargyas (Hair)
65. Lois Griffing (Stage Manager)
66. Julie White (Usher)
67. Gillian Shafler (Usher)
68. Cherito Golding (Usher)
69. Lisa Lopez (Usher)
70. Elizabeth Reardon (Usher)
71. Laura Torrel (Usher)
72. Matt Blank (Usher)
73. Jeffrey Dobbins
    (House Manager)
74. Kirssy Toribio (Usher)
75. A. John Dancy (Usher)
76. Mike Chavez (Usher)
77. Mindy Wild (Cast)
78. Gary Kosloski (Orchestra)
79. Amber Adams (Stagehand)
80. Laura Ellington (Wardrobe)
81. Alice Bee (Wardrobe)
82. Jeff Williams (Cast)
83. Stu Satalof (Orchestra)
84. Adam Miller
    (Associate Company Manager)

85. Craig Ramsay (Cast)
86. Artie Friedlander (Head
    Electrician)
87. Jeff Wener (Electrician)
88. Semere Berhane (Usher)
89. Kenya Capers (Usher)
90. Errol Worthington (Usher)
91. Mariella Constanzi (Usher)
92. Sharon Hawkins (Usher)
93. John Mara (Child Wrangler)
94. Joe Caruso (Stagehand)
95. Mike Bernstein (Stagehand)
96. Chip White (Dresser)
97. Bob Kwiatkowski (Dresser)
98. Jeff Nelsen (Orchestra)
99. Thomas Schlenk
    (Company Manager)
100. Tom Augustine (Associate Hair
     and Wig Supervisor)
101. Rick Hilsabeck (Cast)
102. Kurt von Schmittou (Cast)
103. Jim Harris (Head Carpenter)
104. Danny Paul (Wardobe)
105. Kris C. Keene (Carpenter)
106. Kevin C. Keene
     (Sound Department)
107. Phillip Rolfe (Wardrobe)
108. J. Jared Jans (Hair)
109. Rod Harrelson (Cast)

Chitty Chitty Bang Bang

STAFF FOR
CHITTY CHITTY BANG BANG

GENERAL MANAGEMENT
ALAN WASSER ASSOCIATES

Alan Wasser	Allan Williams
Connie Yung	Robert Nolan

GENERAL PRESS REPRESENTATION
BARLOW•HARTMAN

Michael Hartman	John Barlow
Carol Fineman	Leslie Baden

COMPANY MANAGER
THOMAS SCHLENK

MARKETING
TMG – The Marketing Group

Stage Manager ....Charles Underhill
Assistant Stage Managers ....Seth Sklar-Heyn,
Jay McLeod
Associate Company Manager ....Adam J. Miller
Associate Director (UK) ....Johanne Davies
Associate Choreographer (UK) ....Frank Thompson
Dance Captain ....Joanne Manning
Dance Captain/Fight Captain ....Jeff Siebert

Associate Scenic Designer ....Paul Weimer
Assistant Scenic Designer ....Raul Abrego
Associate Costume Designer (UK) ......Christine Rowland
Associate Costume Designers (US) ....Patrick Chevillot,
Mitchell Bloom
Assistant Costume Designer ....Rick Kelly
Associate Lighting Designer ....Daniel Walker
Assistant Lighting Designer ....Kristina Kloss
Moving Lights Programmer ....Stuart Porter
Associate Sound Designer (UK) ....Simon Baker
Associate Sound Designer (US) ....Mark Menard

Production
Management ....Jake Bell Production Services, Ltd.
Production Technical Supervisor ....David Benken
Production Carpenter ....Stephen Detmer
Production Electrician ....Rick Baxter
Production Property ....Timothy Abel
Production Sound ....Scott Sanders
Production Wardrobe Supervisor ....Rick Kelly
Production Hair and Wig Coordinator ....Helen Gregor
Production Hair and Wig Supervisor ....Carmel Vargyas
Production Makeup &
Prosthetics Designer/Supervisor ....Angelina Avallone
Assistant Production Manager ....Ana M. Garcia
Production Management Assistant ....Jill Johnson

Head Carpenter ....Michael Kelly
Assistant Carpenter/Automation ....Michael Shepp
Head Electrician ....Joe "Fish" Cangelosi
Assistant Electrician ....Jason Wilkosz
Assistant Electrician/Pyrotechnician ....Norman Ballard
Head Property ....Robert Valli
Associate Wardrobe Supervisor ....Sarah Schaub
Wardrobe Staff ....Gilbert Aleman, Jennifer Barnes,
Alice Bee, Julienne Blechman,
Gary Biangone, Jane Davis,
Christina Foster, Jaymes Gill,
Robert Kwiatkowski, Laura Ellington,
Jenn Molloy, Ray Panelli, Danny Paul,
Phillip Rolfe, Caitley Symons,
Franc Weinperl, Chip White
Associate Hair and
Wig Supervisor ....Thomas Augustine
Hair and Wig Stylists ....Hazel Higgins,
Ryan McWilliams
Assistant Prosthetics Makeup ....Joshua Turi

Dialect Coach ....Deborah Hecht
Children's Guardians ....Bobby Wilson, Vanessa Brown
Tutoring ....On Location Education/
Teri Flemal, Kimberly Tobash
Animal Handlers ....Robert Cox, Kirsten Lake
Production Assistants ....Jay McLeod, Heather Banta
Assistants to Fight Director ....Brad Lemons,
Dan Renken
ZPI-Director of Development ....Jono Gero
General Management Associates ....Thom Mitchell,
Lane Marsh, Aaron Lustbader
General Management Office ....Jennifer Mudge,
Christopher Betz,
Jason Hewitt, Ethan Schwartz
UK General Management ....Michael Rose Limited/
Alex Halpern, Chloe Peel,
Janet Newman, David Morgan,
Michael Rose
Casting Associates ....Jeremy Rich, Carrie Gardner
Music Preparation (UK) ....Anne Barnard
Synthesizer
Programmer ....Music Art Technologies, Inc./
Brett Sommer

Legal Counsel ....Jay Harris, Esq.
Immigration Counsel ....Shannon Such, Esq.
Legal Counsel to EON Productions ......David Pope, Esq.
Insurance (US) ....Marsh USA, Inc./
Linda Badgett, Yasmine Ramos
Insurance (UK) ......Walton & Parkinson/Richard Walton
Banking ....JP Morgan Chase & Co.
Accounting ....Rosenberg Neuwirth & Kuchner/
Chris Cacace, Annemarie Aguanno
Payroll Service ....Castellana Services Inc.
Advertising (US) ....Serino Coyne/
Sandy Block, Angelo Desimini,
Victoria Cairl, Cara Christman
Advertising (UK) ....Dewynters UK
Merchandising ....Dewynters USA/James Decker
Logo Design and Graphics ....Dewynters UK
Production Photographer ....Joan Marcus
Publicity Photographer ....Andrew Eccles
Study Guide ....Peter Royston
Website Coordinator ....Jacob Hirzel

Theatre Displays ....King Displays, Inc.
Travel/
Transportation ....Road Rebel Entertainment Touring
Ground Transportation ....IBA-STAT Limo/
Danny Ibanez
Storage Facility for
Publicity Chitty ....Bridgehampton Motoring Club
Rehearsal Space ....New 42nd Street Studios
Opening Night Coordination ......Tobak-Dantchik Events
and Promotions/
Suzanne Tobak, Michael P. Lawrence

CREDITS AND ACKNOWLEDGEMENTS

Scenery fabricated, painted and automated by Hudson
Scenic Studio, Inc., Yonkers, NY. Chitty car, automation
and effects by Hudson Scenic Studio, Inc. Scenic elements
by Adirondack Scenic, Inc., Argyle, NY; F&D Scene
Changes Ltd., Calgary, Alberta. Scenic painting and soft
goods by Scenic Art Studios, New Windsor, NY. Scenic
elements provided by Beyond Imagination, Newburgh, NY.
Props provided by Proof Productions, Inc., Beyond
Imagination, John Creech Studios, The Spooon Group,
Jennie Marino of Moonboots Inc. for Toy Shop props.
Flying provided by Flying by Foy. Lighting by Fourth
Phase/PRG. Sound by Sound Associates. Pyro by Jauchem
& Meeh. Interstate hauling by Clark Transfer, Inc.
Costumes by Eric Winterling, Inc.; Euroco Costumes;
Carelli Costumes, Inc.; Barbara Matera, Ltd.; Seamless
Costumes; Werner Russold; By Barak; Jennifer Love
Costumes; Studio Rouge; Cego Custom Shirt; Douglas Earl
Costumes; and Sarah Persteins. Custom footwear by T.O.
Dey, Capezio Theatrical. Military uniform accessories
supplied by Kaufman's Army & Navy, NYC, Jan Finnell.
Hoisery and undergarments by Bra Tenders. Millinery by
Rodney Gordon, Inc.; Lynne Mackey Studio; Izquierdo
Studios, Ltd.; and FiTA Studios. Custom knitwear by C. C.
Wei. Custom medals by Carl W. Lemke Unique Jewelry.
Dying and silk screening by Gene Mignola, Inc. Fabric
painting by Jeffrey Fender, Robert Funk. Hair by Hugo
Royer International, Ltd. Throat lozenges provided by
Ricola. Emer'gen-C super energy booster provided by Alacer
Group. Original UK car automation and effects created by
Howard Eaton, Delstar and Stage Technologies.

The dogs in the show were adopted
from the following shelters:

Humane Society of New York; Ahisma Haven Rescue;
Humane Society of Central Delaware County, Inc.; Herding
Dog Rescue; ASPCA; Closter Animal Welfare Society, Inc.

There is a $.70 surcharge added to the price of each ticket
purchased, in support of the New 42nd Street's not-for-
profit projects on 42nd Street. An additional $.55 project
support surcharge is added to the price of each ticket by the
Hilton Theatre. Proceeds of the Hilton Theatre charge are
used for maintenance of the historic Hilton Theatre.

HILTON THEATRE STAFF

General Manager ....Micah Hollingworth
Assistant General Manager ....Jorelle Aronovitch
House Manager ....Jeffrey Dobbins
Facility Manager ....Jeff Nuzzo
Box Office Treasurer ....Peter Attanasio Jr.
Head Carpenter ....James C. Harris
Head Electrician ....Art J. Friedlander
Head of Properties ....Joseph P. Harris Jr.
Head of Sound ....John R. Gibson
Asst. Box Office Treasurer ....Spencer Taustine
Regional Accounting
Manager ....Patricia Busby O'Shaughnessy
Payroll Administrator ....Carmen Martinez
Shipping/Receiving.........................Dinara Ferreira
Administrative Assistant ....Jenny Kirlin

Chitty Chitty Bang Bang
SCRAPBOOK

Correspondent: Erin Dilly "Truly Scrumptious."

Memorable Note or Fan Letter: The best one I got was from Sally Ann Howes, who played my role in the film. She sent me a beautiful bouquet of flowers and a note saying, "I hope you have as much fun with Truly as I did."

Anniversary Parties and/or Gifts: We threw a celebration for our hundredth performance. The producers always angled the parties and the niceties toward the children in the cast, so the room was full of cupcakes.

Celebrity Visitors: Catherine Zeta-Jones and her kids came and we let them play on stage. Teri Hatcher came by with her daughter. Dakota Fanning came with her little sister.

"Carols for a Cure" Carol: "Let Them Go."

"Gypsy of the Year" Skit: "Chitty Chitty, Bye Bye" by Vanessa Brown, Brian Taylor and Bret Shuford.

Backstage Ritual: We always did a dance to the overture behind the closed curtain, but under master of ceremonies Rod Harrelson, it really became a whole detailed and complicated three-minute dance, in which Jan Maxwell was always front and center.

Favorite Moment During Each Performance (Onstage or Off): Onstage I always loved the first moment Chitty flew. But backstage there was a moment when Chip Zien and Robbie Sella exited and we had maybe a thirty-second pass. Just as we would pass the stage-right Stage Manager, we'd all enact a great work of art— "Madonna with Child" or "Sunday on La Grande Jatte" or or something by Matisse. Sometimes it was just obscene. I don't know why we did it, but I always looked forward to it.

Off-Site Hangout: The Hilton Bar.

Favorite Therapies: We had a wonderful PT woman twice a week because of the crazy rake of the stage. I also wound up doing lots of acupuncture owning to acid reflux from my pregnancy.

Memorable Ad-Lib: At the final performance, which I did six and a half months pregnant, Jemima says "Let's go on a picnic." I'm supposed to say, "I happened to have brought one," but then I added, "Oh wait, I ate it on the way over," and patted my big tummy.

Catchphrases: Eddie Bowles would do a performance called "Liza with a 'B'" whenever anybody really needed to laugh or blush.

Sweethearts Within the Company: Jan's dresser Laura Ellington and Robert Cox, our doggie wrangler, fell in love during the show.

In-House Parody Lyrics: As I got bigger, I'd call myself "Truly Plumptious."

Understudy Anecdote: In October I found out the hard way that my baby did not enjoy salmon. I had salmon between shows and by the middle of the evening show I had to leave. My understudy, Julie Tolivar, was throwing on my makeup and I was telling her "Have a good show!" between retches.

1. The kids' company celebrates the show's 100th performance with cupcakes backstage.
2. (L-R:) Jan Maxwell, Robert Sella, Kevin Cahoon, Philip Bosco, Raúl Esparza and Julie Barnes at the party.
3. (L-R:) Ellen Marlow, Henry Hodges and Erin Dilly perform at the 2005 "Stars in the Alley" event.

The Color Purple

First Preview: November 1, 2005. Opened: December 1, 2005.
Still running as of May 31, 2006.

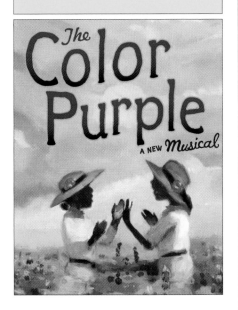

CAST

(in order of appearance)

Young Nettie, Mister Daughter,
Chief's Daughter ....CHANTYLLA JOHNSON
Young Celie, Mister Daughter, Young Olivia,
Henrietta ....ZIPPORAH G. GATLING
Church Soloist......................CAROL DENNIS
Church Lady/
Doris ....KIMBERLY ANN HARRIS
Church Lady/
Darlene.............VIRGINIA ANN WOODRUFF
Church Lady/
Jarene, Daisy ....MAIA NKENGE WILSON
Preacher, Prison Guard ....DOUG ESKEW
Pa................................JC MONTGOMERY
Nettie...............RENÉE ELISE GOLDSBERRY
Celie ....LaCHANZE
Mister ....KINGSLEY LEGGS
Young Harpo,
Young Adam ....LEON G. THOMAS III
Harpo ....BRANDON VICTOR DIXON
Sofia ....FELICIA P. FIELDS
Squeak ....KRISHA MARCANO
Shug Avery .....ELISABETH WITHERS-MENDES
Ol' Mister..................................LOU MYERS
Buster, Chief ....NATHANIEL STAMPLEY
Grady ....JC MONTGOMERY
Bobby ....JAMES BROWN III
Older Olivia.........BAHIYAH SAYYED GAINES
Older Adam ....GRASAN KINGSBERRY

Continued on next page

The Playbill Broadway Yearbook 2005-2006

⊛ **BROADWAY THEATRE**
1681 Broadway
A Shubert Organization Theatre
Gerald Schoenfeld, *Chairman*   Philip J. Smith, *President*
Robert E. Wankel, *Executive Vice President*

OPRAH WINFREY
SCOTT SANDERS   ROY FURMAN   QUINCY JONES
CREATIVE BATTERY   ANNA FANTACI & CHERYL LACHOWICZ   INDEPENDENT PRESENTERS NETWORK
DAVID LOWY   STEPHANIE P. McCLELLAND   GARY WINNICK   JAN KALLISH
NEDERLANDER PRESENTATIONS, INC.   BOB & HARVEY WEINSTEIN
ANDREW ASNES & ADAM ZOTOVICH   TODD JOHNSON

Present

Color Purple

BASED UPON THE NOVEL WRITTEN BY ALICE WALKER
AND THE WARNER BROS./AMBLIN ENTERTAINMENT MOTION PICTURE

Book by
MARSHA NORMAN

Music and Lyrics by
BRENDA   **ALLEE**   **STEPHEN**
RUSSELL   **WILLIS**   **BRAY**

Starring
LaCHANZE
ELISABETH WITHERS-MENDES   FELICIA P. FIELDS
BRANDON VICTOR DIXON   RENÉE ELISE GOLDSBERRY   KRISHA MARCANO
and KINGSLEY LEGGS

with KIMBERLY ANN HARRIS   MAIA NKENGE WILSON   VIRGINIA ANN WOODRUFF
LOU MYERS   CAROL DENNIS

JEANNETTE I. BAYARDELLE   JAMES BROWN III   ERIC L. CHRISTIAN   LaTRISA A. COLEMAN   BOBBY DAYE   ANIKA ELLIS
DOUG ESKEW   BAHIYAH SAYYED GAINES   ZIPPORAH G. GATLING   CHARLES GRAY   STEPHANIE GUILAND-BROWN
JAMES HARKNESS   FRANCESCA HARPER   CHANTYLLA JOHNSON   GRASAN KINGSBERRY   CORINNE McFARLANE
KENITA R. MILLER   JC MONTGOMERY   ANGELA ROBINSON   NATHANIEL STAMPLEY   JAMAL STORY   LEON G. THOMAS III

Scenic Design	Costume Design	Lighting Design	Sound Design
JOHN LEE BEATTY	PAUL TAZEWELL	BRIAN MacDEVITT	JON WESTON

Casting	Hair Design	Production Managers	Production Stage Manager
BERNARD TELSEY CASTING	CHARLES G. LaPOINTE	ARTHUR SICCARDI PATRICK SULLIVAN	KRISTEN HARRIS

Press Agent	Marketing	General Management
CAROL FINEMAN/BARLOW•HARTMAN	TMG - THE MARKETING GROUP	NLA/AMY JACOBS

Music Director	Dance Music Arrangements	Additional Arrangements	Music Coordinator
LINDA TWINE	DARYL WATERS	JOSEPH JOUBERT	SEYMOUR RED PRESS

Orchestrations	Music Supervisor & Incidental Music Arrangements
JONATHAN TUNICK	KEVIN STITES

Choreographed by
DONALD BYRD

Directed by
GARY GRIFFIN

World Premiere Produced by Alliance Theatre, Atlanta, GA
Susan V. Booth, Artistic Director   Thomas Pechar, Managing Director

12/1/05

Kimberly Ann Harris, Virginia Ann Woodruff and
Maia Nkenge Wilson as the Church Ladies.

Photo by Paul Kolnik

The Color Purple

MUSICAL NUMBERS

ACT ONE

Overture	Orchestra
Huckleberry Pie	Young Celie and Nettie
Mysterious Ways	Church Soloist, Church Ladies and Company
Somebody Gonna Love You	Celie
Our Prayer	Nettie, Celie, Mister
Big Dog	Mister and Field Hands
Hell No!	Sofia and Sisters
Brown Betty	Harpo and Men, Squeak
Shug Avery Comin' to Town	Mister, Celie and Company
Too Beautiful for Words	Shug Avery
Push Da Button	Shug Avery and Company
Uh Oh!	Church Ladies, Sofia, Squeak
What About Love?	Celie and Shug Avery

ACT TWO

African Homeland	Nettie, Celie, Olivia and Adam, Villagers
The Color Purple	Shug Avery
Mister's Song	Mister
Miss Celie's Pants	Celie, Shug Avery, Sofia and Women
Any Little Thing	Harpo and Sofia
I'm Here	Celie
The Color Purple (Reprise)	Celie, Nettie and Company

ORCHESTRA

CONDUCTOR: Linda Twine
ASSOCIATE CONDUCTOR: Joseph Joubert

TRUMPETS:
Barry Danielian, Brian O'Flaherty,
Kamau Adilifu
TROMBONES:
Larry Farrell, Jason Jackson
WOODWINDS:
Les Scott, Lawrence Feldman, Jay Brandford
KEYBOARDS:
Joseph Joubert, Shelton Becton
DRUMS/PERCUSSION:
Buddy Williams, Damien Bassman
GUITAR:
Steve Bargonetti
BASS:
Benjamin Franklin
VIOLINS:
Paul Woodiel, Mineko Yajima
VIOLA:
David Creswell
CELLO:
Clay Ruede

Music Coordinator: Seymour Red Press
Copyists: Emily Grishman Music Preparation
Katharine Edmonds/Emily Grishman
Synthesizer Programmer: Bruce Samuels

Photo by Paul Kolnik

(L-R): LaChanze and Elisabeth Withers-Mendes as Celie and Shug.

Cast Continued

ENSEMBLE

JAMES BROWN III, LaTRISA A. COLEMAN,
CAROL DENNIS, ANIKA ELLIS,
DOUG ESKEW,
BAHIYAH SAYYED GAINES,
ZIPPORAH G. GATLING,
CHARLES GRAY, JAMES HARKNESS,
FRANCESCA HARPER,
KIMBERLY ANN HARRIS,
CHANTYLLA JOHNSON,
GRASAN KINGSBERRY, JC MONTGOMERY,
LOU MYERS, ANGELA ROBINSON,
NATHANIEL STAMPLEY,
JAMAL STORY, LEON G. THOMAS III,
MAIA NKENGE WILSON,
VIRGINIA ANN WOODRUFF

SWINGS

JEANNETTE I. BAYARDELLE,
ERIC L. CHRISTIAN,
BOBBY DAYE,
STEPHANIE GUILAND-BROWN,
CORINNE McFARLANE

UNDERSTUDIES

For Celie:
JEANNETTE I. BAYARDELLE,
KENITA R. MILLER
For Shug Avery:
ANIKA ELLIS,
ANGELA ROBINSON
For Sofia:
CAROL DENNIS,
KIMBERLY ANN HARRIS
For Nettie:
JEANNETTE I. BAYARDELLE,
KENITA R. MILLER
For Mister:
CHARLES GRAY,
JC MONTGOMERY
For Harpo:
JAMES BROWN III,
NATHANIEL STAMPLEY
For Squeak:
FRANCESCA HARPER

Dance Captain:
STEPHANIE GUILAND-BROWN

Assistant Dance Captain:
JAMAL STORY

SETTING

The story takes place in Georgia
between 1909 and 1949.

The Color Purple

LaChanze
Celie

Felicia P. Fields
Sophia

Kingsley Leggs
Mister

Elisabeth
Withers-Mendes
Shug Avery

Brandon Victor Dixon
Harpo

Renée Elise Goldsberry
Nettie

Krisha Marcano
Squeak

Kimberly Ann Harris
*Church Lady/
Doris/Ensemble*

Maia Nkenge Wilson
*Church Lady/
Jarene/Daisy/
Ensemble*

Virginia Ann Woodruff
*Church Lady/
Darlene/Ensemble*

Lou Myers
Ol' Mister/Ensemble

Carol Dennis
*Church Soloist/
Ensemble*

Jeannette I. Bayardelle
Swing

James Brown III
Bobby/Ensemble

Eric L. Christian
Swing

LaTrisa A. Coleman
Ensemble

Bobby Daye
Swing

Anika Ellis
Ensemble

Doug Eskew
Preacher/Ensemble

Bahiyah Sayyed Gaines
Ensemble

Zipporah G. Gatling
*Mister Daughter/
Young Olivia/
Henrietta/Ensemble*

Charles Gray
Ensemble

Stephanie
Guiland-Brown
*Ensemble/
Dance Captain*

James Harkness
Ensemble

Francesca Harper
Ensemble

Chantylla Johnson
*Mister Daughter/
Chief's Daughter/
Ensemble*

Grasan Kingsberry
Ensemble

Corinne McFarlane
Swing

Kenita R. Miller
*Understudy
Celie/Nettie*

JC Montgomery
Pa/Grady/Ensemble

Angela Robinson
Ensemble

Nathaniel Stampley
Ensemble

Jamal Story
*Ensemble/
Assistant Dance
Captain*

Leon G. Thomas III
*Young Harpo/
Young Adam/
Ensemble*

Alice Walker
Original Author

The Color Purple

Marsha Norman
Bookwriter

Brenda Russell, Stephen Bray, Allee Willis
Composers/Lyricists

Gary Griffin
Director

Donald Byrd
Choreographer

John Lee Beatty
Set Design

Paul Tazewell
Costume Design

Brian MacDevitt
Lighting Design

Bernard Telsey,
Bernard Telsey
Casting, C.S.A.
Casting

Jonathan Tunick
Orchestrations

Linda Twine
Music Director

Angelina Avallone
Make-up Design

Joseph Joubert
*Additional
Arrangements*

Arthur Siccardi
*Production
Management*

Oprah Winfrey
Producer

Scott Sanders
Lead Producer

Roy Furman
Producer

Quincy Jones
Producer

Stephanie P.
McClelland
Producer

James L.
Nederlander,
Nederlander
Presentations, Inc.
Producer

Bob Weinstein
Producer

Harvey Weinstein
Producer

Adam Zotovich
Producer

Todd Johnson
Producer

Darlesia Cearcy
Nettie

LaTrisa A. Coleman
*Understudy for
Squeak*

Doug Eskew
*Understudy for
Ol' Mister*

Charles Gray
*Understudy for
Ol' Mister*

Gavin Gregory
Buster, Chief

Corinne McFarlane
*Understudy for
Young Harpo
Young Adam*

Kemba Shannon
Swing

Ricky Smith
*Young Harpo/
Young Adam*

The Color Purple

DOORPERSON
Billie Stewart

HEAD CARPENTER
Charlie Rasmussen

STAGE MANAGEMENT
Front Row (L-R): Neveen Mahmoud (Assistant
Stage Manager) and Doug Gaeta (Assistant
Company Manager).

Back Row (L-R): Kelly Stillwell (Assistant Stage
Manager), Kim Kelly (Company Manager),
Kristen Harris (Production Stage Manager) and
Glynn David Turner (Stage Manager).

BOX OFFICE TREASURER
Lenny Bonis

BOX OFFICE
Joe Wallace

PRODUCTION WARDROBE SUPERVISOR
Debbie Cheretun

Photos by Melissa Merlo

The Color Purple

STAGE CREW
Sitting (L-R): Valerie Frith (Star Dresser), Sonia Suzuki (Swing Dresser), Leah Loukas (Hair Dresser), Sakie Onozawa (Assistant Hair Supervisor), Juliete Silva (Makeup).

Second Row (L-R): Dora Suarez (Stitcher), Mia Neal (Hair Supervisor).

Third Row (L-R): Betty Gillispie (Star Dresser), Lizz Hirons (Dresser), Carin Ford (Production Sound), Bob Reiemers (Sound), Peter Becker (Sound Operator), Paulie DiVilla (Spotlight Operator), George Milney (House Electrician).

Back Row (L-R): Suzanne Delahunt (Dresser), Jay Woods (Dresser), Fred Castner (Dresser), Christina Dailey (Dresser), Ryan Essner (Carpenter), Jeff Lunsford (Carpenter), Charlie Heulitt (Production Carpenter), Mike Cornell (Production Electrician), Gary Marlin (Assistant Production Electrician), Rudolph Wood (Production Properties) and James Ernest (Props).

ORCHESTRA
Kneeling (L-R): Joseph Joubert, Steven Bargonetti, David Creswell

Standing (L-R): Buddy Williams, Les Scott, Mineko Yajima, Jay Brandford, Damien Bassman, Eddie Salkin (Sub), Benjamin Brown, Shelton Becton, Jim O'Connor (Sub)

Not Pictured: Lawrence Feldman, Larry Farrell, Barry Danelian, Brian O'Flaherty, Jason Jackson, Paul Woodiel, Clay Ruede and Kamau Adilifu.

Photos by Melissa Merlo

FRONT OF HOUSE STAFF
Front Row (L-R): Selina Nelson (Usher), Ulysses "Lou" Santiago (Security).

Middle Row (L-R): Michael Harris (House Manager), Vanessa Edenfield (Usher), Mattie Robinson (Usher), May Park (Usher), Lorie Bokun (Head Usher), Raufina Shayne (Usher), Melissa Klein (Bartender), Melissa Maniglia.

Back Row (L-R): John Cashman (Usher), Jorge Colon (Ticket Taker), Christian Borcan (Usher), Joe Amado (Usher), William Denson (Security), Patrick Joy (Bartender), Matt Wickert (Usher), Jerry Gallagher (Bar Manager), DeMond Nason (Bartender), Bill Daniels (Bartender) and Raylind Van Blake (Bartender).

The Color Purple

The African Homeland Dance Sequence

Photo by Paul Kolnik

The Color Purple
SCRAPBOOK

1. Alice Walker and Elisabeth Withers-Mendes take a curtain call on opening night.
2. Oprah Winfrey takes a bow on the stage of the Broadway Theatre on opening night.
3. Felicia P. Fields (L) surrounded by her family at the opening.
4. Derek Fordjour and LaChanze at the opening night party at the New York Public Library.

Correspondents: The Kids of *The Color Purple*: Zipporah G. Gatling, Chantylla Johnson, Corrine McFarlane and Ricky Smith.
Memorable Opening Night Fax: All the faxes from other Broadway shows.
Opening Night Gifts: Unanimous: Video iPods from Oprah!!
Most Exciting Celebrity Visitors: Meeting Oprah and Gayle, and being on Oprah's show.
Actor Who Performed the Most Roles In This Show: Jeannette Bayardelle.
Favorite Moment During Each Performance (On Stage Or Off): Being "bad kids" in the "Mister's Kids" scene.
Who Got the Gypsy Robe: JC Montgomery.
Favorite In-Theatre Gathering Place: Lower lobby when the whole cast gets together and we dance.
Favorite Off-Site Hangouts: Lazer-Tag, Mars 2112.
"Easter Bonnet" Skit: "Lillies in the Field" by the Men of *The Color Purple*. Named Best Presentation.
Favorite Snack Foods: Granola bars, cookies-n-cream yogurt, vanilla ice cream and Goobers.
Favorite Therapies: Ricola, and physical therapy with Alan.
Most Memorable Ad-Lib: One that made it in the show: Sofia to Harpo "Why don't you go to Memphis with your skinny little girlfriend too?!"

Memorable Stage Door Fan Encounter: Sinbad waiting outside with all the fans to make sure he told all the cast and company how great they were, and then going in to see the principals.
Fastest Costume Change: LaChanze.
Who Wore the Heaviest/Hottest Costume: Nate Stampley has a huge headdress in "Africa."
Who Wore the Least: Shug in the bathtub and all the female dancers in "Africa."
Coolest Thing About Being in This Show: Working with such cool people and meeting famous people. The opening night party was off the hook!

The Constant Wife

First Preview: May 27, 2005. Opened: June 16, 2005.
Closed August 21, 2005 after 23 Previews and 77 Performances.

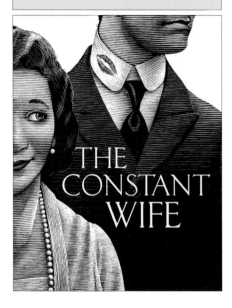

PLAYBILL

THE CONSTANT WIFE

CAST
(in order of appearance)

Mrs. Culver, Constance Middleton's
mother ....LYNN REDGRAVE
Bentley, the butler ....DENIS HOLMES
Martha, Constance's sister ....ENID GRAHAM
Barbara Fawcett, a friend .KATHLEEN McNENNY
Constance Middleton ....KATE BURTON
Marie-Louise, a friend ....KATHRYN MEISLE
John Middleton, F.R.C.S.,
Constance's husband ....MICHAEL CUMPSTY
Bernard Kersal, a friend ....JOHN DOSSETT
Mortimer Durham, Marie-Louise's
husband ....JOHN ELLISON CONLEE

TIME AND PLACE:

Act I: The Middleton's house in Harley Street,
London, 1926
Act II: Two weeks later
Act III: One year later

UNDERSTUDIES/STANDBYS

For Constance: KATHLEEN McNENNY;
for Martha, Marie-Louise: TARA FALK;
for Mrs. Culver, Barbara: LUCY MARTIN;
for John Middleton, Bernard Kersal:
TONY CARLIN; for Mortimer Durham, Bentley:
BOB ARI.

Production Stage Manager: LISA BUXBAUM
Stage Manager: LESLIE C. LYTER

AMERICAN AIRLINES THEATRE

ROUNDABOUT THEATRE COMPANY

TODD HAIMES, Artistic Director
ELLEN RICHARD, Managing Director
JULIA C. LEVY, Executive Director, External Affairs
Presents

Kate Burton
Michael Cumpsty   John Dossett
and
Lynn Redgrave
in

THE CONSTANT WIFE

by
W. Somerset Maugham

with

Kathryn Meisle   Enid Graham
John Ellison Conlee   Denis Holmes   Kathleen McNenny

Set Design Allen Moyer	*Costume Design* Michael Krass	*Lighting Design* Mary Louise Geiger	*Sound Design* David Van Tieghem *and* Jill BC Du Boff
Original Music by David Van Tieghem	*Hair and Wig Design* Paul Huntley	*Production Stage Manager* Lisa Buxbaum	*Dialect Coach* Deborah Hecht
Casting by Jim Carnahan, C.S.A. *and* Mele Nagler, C.S.A.	*Technical Supervisor* Steve Beers	*General Managers* Sydney Beers *and* Nichole Larson	*Founding Director* Gene Feist
Associate Artistic Director Scott Ellis	*Press Representative* Boneau/Bryan-Brown	*Director of Marketing* David B. Steffen	

Directed by
Mark Brokaw

Roundabout Theatre Company is a member of the League of Resident Theatres.
www.roundabouttheatre.org

6/16/05

(L-R) Kate Burton,
John Dossett
and Lynn Redgrave.

Photo by Joan Marcus

The Constant Wife

Kate Burton
Constance Middleton

Michael Cumpsty
John Middleton

John Dossett
Bernard Kersal

Lynn Redgrave
Mrs. Culver

Kathryn Meisle
Marie-Louise

Enid Graham
Martha

John Ellison Conlee
Mortimer Durham

Denis Holmes
Bentley

Kathleen McNenny
Barbara Fawcett

Bob Ari
Understudy Mortimer, Bentley

Tony Carlin
Understudy John Middleton, Bernard Kersal

Tara Falk
Understudy Marie-Louise, Martha

Lucy Martin
Understudy Mrs. Culver, Barbara Fawcett

William Somerset Maugham
Playwright

Mark Brokaw
Director

Allen Moyer
Set Design

Mary Louise Geiger
Lighting Design

Paul Huntley
Hair and Wig Design

Jonathan Solari
Costume Design Assistant

Jim Carnahan
Casting

Gene Feist
Founding Director Roundabout Theatre Company

Todd Haimes
Artistic Director, Roundabout Theatre Company

DOORMAN
Adolf Torres

BOX OFFICE
(L-R): Mead Margulies and Robert Morgan.

Not Pictured: Edward P. Osborne (Box Office Manager).

STAGE MANAGEMENT
(L-R): Lisa Buxbaum (Production Stage Manager) and Jonathan Donahue (Stage Manager).

Not Pictured: Leslie C. Lyter (Stage Manager).

Color photos by Ben Strothmann

The Constant Wife

Photos by Ben Strothmann

HAIR SUPERVISOR: Manuela LaPorte.

STAGE CREW
(L-R): Jill Anania, Dann Wojnar, Glenn Merwede
(Head Carpenter), Andrew Forste (Props),
Brian Maiuri (House Electrician)
and Nelson Vaughn.

WARDROBE
(L-R): Gosia Slota (Dresser), Susan J. Fallon
(Wardrobe Supervisor), Melissa Crawford
(Day Worker), Julie Hilimire (Dresser) and Patty
McKeever (Dresser).

FRONT OF HOUSE
Front Row (L-R): Edwin Camacho,
Jack Watanachaiyot, Zipporah Aguasvivas,
Jacklyn Rivera
Middle Row (L-R): Oscar Castillo, Ruth Conley,
Courtney Boddie
Back Row: Chucke Fernandez.

Not Pictured: Stephen Ryan (House Manager).

The Constant Wife

ROUNDABOUT THEATRE COMPANY STAFF

ARTISTIC DIRECTOR .... TODD HAIMES
MANAGING DIRECTOR .... HAROLD WOLPERT
EXECUTIVE DIRECTOR .... JULIA C. LEVY
ASSOCIATE
ARTISTIC DIRECTOR .... SCOTT ELLIS

ARTISTIC STAFF

DIRECTOR OF ARTISTIC DEVELOPMENT/
DIRECTOR OF CASTING .... **Jim Carnahan**
Artistic Consultant .... Robyn Goodman
Resident Director .... Michael Mayer
Associate Artists .... Scott Elliott, Bill Irwin,
Joe Mantello, Mark Brokaw
Consulting Dramaturg .... Jerry Patch
Artistic Assistant .... Jill Rafson
Casting Director .... Mele Nagler
Casting Associate .... Carrie Gardner
Casting Associate .... J.V. Mercanti
Casting Assistant .... Kate Schwabe
Casting Assistant .... Stephen Kopel
Artistic Intern .... Corinne Hayoun

EDUCATION STAFF

EDUCATION DIRECTOR .... **Megan Kirkpatrick**
Director of Instruction and
Curriculum Development .... Renee Flemings
Education Program Associate .... Lindsay Erb
Education Program Associate .... Stacey L. Morris
Education Assistant .... Cassidy Jones
Education Interns .... Monica Ammirati,
Catherine Taylor
Education Dramaturg .... Ted Sod
Teaching Artists .... Zakiyyah Alexander,
Phil Alexander, Cynthia Babak,
Victor Barbella, Brigitte Barnett-Loftis,
Caitlin Barton, Joe Basile, LaTonya Borsay,
Bonnie Brady, Mike Carnahan, Joe Clancy,
Melissa Denton, Stephen DiMenna, Joe Doran,
Tony Freeman, Shana Gold, Sheri Graubert,
Dennis Green, Susan Hamburger,
Karla Hendrick, Jim Jack, Alvin Keith,
Rebecca Lord, Erin McCready,
Andrew Ondrejcak, Laura Poe,
Nicole Press, Chris Rummel,
Drew Sachs, Anna Saggese, David Sinkus,
Vickie Tanner, Olivia Tsang,
Jennifer Varbalow, Leese Walker,
Eric Wallach, Diana Whitten,
Gail Winar, Kirche Zeile

ADMINISTRATIVE STAFF

GENERAL MANAGER .... **Sydney Beers**
Associate Managing Director .... Greg Backstrom
General Manager of the
Steinberg Center .... Don-Scott Cooper
General Counsel .... Nancy Hirschmann
Office Operations Manager .... Bonnie Berens
Human Resources Manager .... Stephen Deutsch
Network Systems Manager .... Jeff Goodman
Manager of Corporate and
Party Rentals .... Jetaun Dobbs
Facilities Manager .... Keith A. Smalls
Assistant to the General Manager .... Maggie Cantrick
Management Assistant .... Nicholas Caccavo
MIS Associate .... Lloyd Alvarez
MIS Assistant .... Anthony Foti
Receptionists .... Jennifer Decoteau,
Andre Fortson, Elisa Papa,
Nina Wheeler
Messenger .... Robert Weisser
Management Intern .... Tania Camargo

FINANCE STAFF

CONTROLLER .... **Susan Neiman**
Assistant Controller .... John LaBarbera
Accounts Payable Administrator .... Frank Surdi
Customer Service Coordinator .... Trina Cox
Business Office Associate .... David Solomon
Business Assistant .... Yonit Kafka
Business Intern .... Dana Harrington

DEVELOPMENT STAFF

DIRECTOR OF DEVELOPMENT ...... **Jeffory Lawson**
Director, Institutional Giving .... Julie K. D'Andrea
Director, Individual Giving .... Julia Lazarus
Director, Special Events .... Steve Schaeffer
Manager,
Donor Information Systems .... Tina Mae Bishko
Special Events Associate .... Elaina Grillo
Institutional Giving Associate .... Kristen Bolibruch
Development Assistant .... Stephenie L. Overton
Development Assistant .... Chelsea Glickfield
Assistant to the Executive Director ...... Robert Weinstein
Patrons Services Assistant .... Dawn Kusinski
Development Intern .... Lauren Hoshibata
Individual Giving Intern .... Dominic Yacobozzi

MARKETING STAFF

DIRECTOR OF MARKETING .... **David B. Steffen**
Marketing/Publications Manager .... Tim McCanna
Marketing Associate .... Sunil Ayyagari
Marketing Assistant .... Rebecca Ballon
Marketing Intern .... Thomas Channell
Website Consultant .... Keith Powell Beyland
DIRECTOR OF TELESALES
SPECIAL PROMOTIONS .... **Tony Baksa**
Telesales Manager .... Anton Borissov
Telesales Office Coordinator .... J.W. Griffin

TICKET SERVICES STAFF

DIRECTOR OF
SALES OPERATIONS .... **Jim Seggelink**
Ticket Services Manager .... Ellen Holt
Subscription Manager .... Charlie Garbowski
Box Office Managers .... Edward P. Osborne,
Jaime Perlman, Jessica Bowser
Group Sales Manager .... Jeff Monteith
Assistant Box Office Managers .... Paul Caspary,
Steve Howe, Robert Morgan
Assistant Ticket Services Managers .... Robert Kane,
David Meglino, Ethan Ubell
Ticket Services .... Solangel Bido,
Andrew Clements, Johanna Comanzo,
Thomas Dahl, Nisha Dhruna,
Adam Elsberry, Lindsay Ericson,
Scott Falkowski, Catherine Fitzpatrick,
Erin Frederick, Amanda Genovese,
Bill Klemm, Talia Krispel,
Alexander LaFrance, Krystin MacRitchie,
Mead Margulies, Chuck Migliaccio,
Carlos Morris, Nicole Nicholson,
Shannon Paige, Hillary Parker,
Thomas Protulipac, Amy Robinson,
Heather Siebert, Monté Smock,
Melissa Snyder, Lillian Soto,
Justin Sweeney, Greg Thorson,
Pamela Unger
Ticket Services Intern .... Jacki Rocha

SERVICES

Counsel .... Jeremy Nussbaum,
Cowan, Liebowitz & Latman, P.C.
Counsel .... Rosenberg & Estis
Counsel .... Rubin and Feldman, P.C.
Counsel .... Andrew Lance,
Gibson, Dunn, & Crutcher, LLP
Counsel .... Harry H. Weintraub,
Glick and Weintraub, P.C.
Immigration Counsel .... Mark D. Koestler and
Theodore Ruthizer
House Physicians .... Dr. Theodore Tyberg,
Dr. Lawrence Katz
House Dentist .... Neil Kanner, D.M.D.
Insurance .... Marsh USA Inc.
Accountant .... Brody, Weiss, Zucarelli &
Urbanek CPAs, P.C.
Advertising .... Eliran Murphy Group/Denise Ganjou
Events Photography .... Anita and Steve Shevett
Production Photographer .... Joan Marcus
Theatre Displays .... King Displays, Wayne Sapper

GENERAL PRESS REPRESENTATIVES

BONEAU/BRYAN-BROWN

Adrian Bryan-Brown   Matt Polk
Jessica Johnson   Joe Perrotta

Roundabout Theatre Company
231 West 39th Street, New York, NY 10018
(212) 719-9393.

CREDITS FOR THE CONSTANT WIFE

GENERAL MANAGERS .... Sydney Beers and
Nichole Larson
Company Manager .... Denys Baker
Production Stage Manager .... Lisa Buxbaum
Stage Manager .... Leslie C. Lyter
Technical Supervisor .... Steve Beers
Assistant Technical Supervisor .... Elisa R. Kuhar
Assistant Director .... Kip Fagan
Associate Set Designer .... Warren Karp
Associate Costume Designer .... Tracy Christensen
Assistant Costume Designer .... Dennis Ballard
Assistant to the Costume Designer .... Jonathan Solari
Assistant Lighting Designer .... Elizabeth Gaines
Head Carpenter .... Glenn Merwede
Head Electrician .... Brian Maiuri
Properties .... Andrew Forste
Wardrobe Supervisor .... Susan J. Fallon
Sound Engineer .... Dann Wojnar
Day Worker .... Melissa Crawford
Dressers .... Julie Hilimire, Patty McKeever,
Gosia Slota
Hair Supervisor .... Manuela LaPorte
Production Properties .... Alan Steiner
Production Assistant .... Joshua Pilote
Technical Apprentice .... Jill F. Anania
Scenery Constructed by .... Showman Fabricators, Inc.,
Long Island City, NY
Scenic Wallpaper
Provided by .... Ziska Childs Design, LLC
Lighting Equipment
Provided by .... PRG Lighting,
Production Resource Group
Construction of
Ladies Costumes by .... Barbara Matera, Ltd.
Construction of
Men's Costumes by .... Scafati, Paul Chang and
Virginia Johnson
Millinery by .... Arnold Levine
Custom Dyeing .... Gene Mignola
Wigs by .... Paul Huntley
Vintage Eye Wear by .... Fabulous Fanny's
Thanks to .... Fur and Furgery, Peter Fox,
Bra Tenders and La Crasia Gloves
Wallpaper Design Inspired by .... Wallpaper from
Nostell Priory, England,
owned by the National Trust
Piano Donated by .... Altenburg Piano House
Special Thanks to .... Frank Ventura
Special Thanks to .... Panteek.com

AMERICAN AIRLINES THEATRE STAFF

General Manager .... Sydney Beers
House Carpenter .... Glenn Merwede
House Electrician .... Brian Maiuri
Wardrobe Supervisor .... Susan J. Fallon
Box Office Manager .... Edward P. Osborne
House Manager .... Stephen Ryan
Associate House Manager .... Zipporah Aguasvivas
Head Usher .... Edwin Camacho
House Staff .... Courtney Boddie, Peter Breaden,
Oscar Castillo, Ilia Diaz, Anne Ezell,
Meghan Herbert, Elsie Jamin-Maguire,
Sherra Johnston, Rich McNanna,
Jacklyn Rivera
Security .... Julious Russell
Additional Security Provided by .... Gotham Security
Maintenance .... Chucke Fernandez, Ron
Henry,
Kenrick Johnson, Maggie Western
Lobby Refreshments .... Sweet Concessions

The Constant Wife
SCRAPBOOK

Photos by Aubrey Reuben

1. Kate Burton and Lynn Redgrave on opening night.
2. Michael Cumpsty and director Mark Brokaw at the opening night party at the Millennium Broadway Hotel.
3. John Dossett (R) arrives at the party with guest Ron Rifkin.
4. Kathryn Meisle at the party.
5. John Ellison Conlee on opening night.

Correspondent: Leslie C. Lyter, Stage Manager

Opening Night Gifts: Roundabout always takes a "Family Photo" of the cast and crew of each show, and gives it back, framed, on opening night. They're really fun and it's great to get them. Instead of giving each other presents, a lot of the cast made donations to Broadway Cares/Equity Fights AIDS and The Actors' Fund. Lynn Redgrave gave us each little individualized gifts. I got a journal. She put a lot of time into selecting these gifts, which meant a lot since she did it all just before opening night.

Most Exciting Celebrity Visitors: Vanessa Redgrave came to see Lynn, and we kept it top-secret until after the show. We get a lot of theatre-community types like Elaine Stritch and John Benjamin Hickey. It's a fun show for people who are real New York actors; a Somerset Maugham play is something most of them have never seen.

Who Has Done the Most Shows: Probably Denis Holmes, who has the most amazing resumé. He had worked with everybody in Kate Burton's family, except Kate herself. It had become a Burton family thing that he and Kate hadn't done a show together—and now were.

Special Backstage Rituals: The thing you always hear about American Airlines Theatre shows is that we do a famous Sunday brunch. Susan Fallon, who used to be a baker, always makes something great, master carpenter Glenn Merwede fries bacon, and tons of people run to the supermarket and back. We have people show up, even when they're no longer in the show, saying, "I'm in neighborhood, can I get some brunch?" A lot of people on this show have babies and young kids, and they all attend.

Favorite Moment During Each Performance: Just before we call places, the entire cast comes down to the stage whether or not they have an entrance at the top of show. Lynn starts the show on stage alone, but just before places, everyone takes a moment to hang together and joke around and play around.

Favorite In-Theatre Gathering Place: The trap room in our basement. It's where we have our brunches.

Favorite Off-Site Hangout: Café Un Deux Trois is usually a favorite for this theatre, but this is a cast with a lot of babies, so there's not a lot of hanging out afterward.

Favorite Snack Food: Fallon cake! You always pray your birthday will fall during the run, because she makes one of her great cakes. People anticipate getting one for weeks.

Favorite Therapy: We have no special therapy—but there seems to be a special obsession with cinnamon Altoids. We go through a lot of them.

Cell Phone Rings During a Performance: Rarely. We've been very lucky.

Memorable Audience Outburst: There is a huge laugh when Constance divulges a big secret about a character named John. One night, the laugh went on and on and just when it was starting to fade, a woman in the audience shouted, "How do you like that, John?" And the place just roared. It was all we could do to keep it together.

Memorable Stage Door Fan Encounter: There's no stage door, so no fan buildup.

Latest Audience Arrival: We've had a lot. Most are subway-related things, but fifteen minutes into the show, you often see thirty or more people streaming in.

Heaviest/Hottest Costume: Lynn Redgrave wears the biggest and most sweeping costume.

Memorable Directorial Note: Mark Brokaw's "Play through the positive."

Coolest Thing About Being in This Show: It's a fun bunch and everybody loves coming into work each day. What a fun experience we're all having—memorably fun and good.

Dirty Rotten Scoundrels

First Preview: January 31, 2005. Opened: March 3, 2005.
Still running as of May 31, 2006.

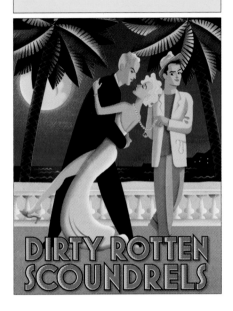

PLAYBILL

CAST

(in order of appearance)

Andre Thibault	GREGORY JBARA
Lawrence Jameson	JONATHAN PRYCE
Lenore	RACHEL DE BENEDET
Sophia	LAURA MARIE DUNCAN
Muriel Eubanks	JOANNA GLEASON
Conductor	TIMOTHY J. ALEX
Renee	RACHEL DE BENEDET
Freddy Benson	NORBERT LEO BUTZ
Jolene Oakes	MYLINDA HULL
Hotel Manager	TOM GALANTICH
Christine Colgate	RACHEL YORK
Nikos	TOM GALANTICH

THE ENSEMBLE

TIMOTHY J. ALEX, ROXANE BARLOW,
JACQUELINE BAYNE,
STEPHEN CAMPANELLA, JOE CASSIDY,
RACHEL DE BENEDET,
LAURA MARIE DUNCAN, SALLY MAE DUNN,
TOM GALANTICH, JASON GILLMAN,
AMY HEGGINS, RACHELLE RAK,
CHUCK SACULLA, DENNIS STOWE,
MATT WALL

Standby for Lawrence Jameson:
DENNIS PARLATO

Continued on next page

⑥ IMPERIAL THEATRE
249 West 45th Street
A Shubert Organization Theatre

Gerald Schoenfeld, *Chairman*   **Philip J. Smith,** *President*

Robert E. Wankel, *Executive Vice President*

THE DIRTY ROTTEN PRODUCERS
MARTY BELL   DAVID BROWN   ALDO SCROFANI   ROY FURMAN   DEDE HARRIS
AMANDA LIPITZ   GREG SMITH   RUTH HENDEL   CHASE MISHKIN   BARRY AND SUSAN TATELMAN
DEBRA BLACK   SHARON KARMAZIN   JOYCE SCHWEICKERT   BERNIE ABRAMS/MICHAEL SPEYER   DAVID BELASCO
BARBARA WHITMAN   WEISSBERGER THEATER GROUP/JAY HARRIS   CHERYL WIESENFELD/JEAN CHEEVER   FLORENZ ZIEGFELD
CLEAR CHANNEL ENTERTAINMENT *and* HARVEY WEINSTEIN
in association with
MGM ON STAGE/DARCIE DENKERT & DEAN STOLBER
and
THE ENTIRE PRUSSIAN ARMY
present

JONATHAN PRYCE   NORBERT LEO BUTZ

RACHEL YORK

JOANNA GLEASON   *in*   GREGORY JBARA

DIRTY ROTTEN SCOUNDRELS
Book by   *Music and Lyrics by*
JEFFREY LANE   DAVID YAZBEK

BASED ON THE FILM "DIRTY ROTTEN SCOUNDRELS"
WRITTEN BY DALE LAUNER AND STANLEY SHAPIRO & PAUL HENNING

Also Starring
MYLINDA HULL

TIMOTHY J. ALEX   ROXANE BARLOW   JACQUELINE BAYNE   CHRISTINE BOKHOUR   STEPHEN CAMPANELLA
JOE CASSIDY   JULIE CONNORS   JEREMY DAVIS   RACHEL DE BENEDET   LAURA MARIE DUNCAN
SALLY MAE DUNN   JENIFER FOOTE   TOM GALANTICH   JASON GILLMAN   GREG GRAHAM
AMY HEGGINS   RACHELLE RAK   CHUCK SACULLA   DENNIS STOWE   MATT WALL

Scenic Design	*Costume Design*	*Lighting Design*
DAVID ROCKWELL	GREGG BARNES	KENNETH POSNER

Sound Design	*Casting By*	*Associate Choreographer*
ACME SOUND PARTNERS	BERNARD TELSEY CASTING	DENIS JONES

Orchestrations	*Vocal Music Arrangements*	*Dance Music Arrangements*
HAROLD WHEELER	TED SPERLING	ZANE MARK
	DAVID YAZBEK	

Conductor	*Music Coordinator*	*Technical Supervisor*	*Production Stage Manager*
FRED LASSEN	HOWARD JOINES	CHRISTOPHER SMITH	MICHAEL BRUNNER

Press Representative	*Marketing*	*General Management*
BARLOW•HARTMAN	MARGERY SINGER COMPANY	THE CHARLOTTE WILCOX COMPANY

Executive Producer
MARTY BELL / ALDO SCROFANI

Music Direction and Incidental Music Arrangements by
TED SPERLING

Choreographed by
JERRY MITCHELL

Directed by
JACK O'BRIEN

JEWELRY BY QVC

WORLD PREMIERE AT THE OLD GLOBE THEATRE SAN DIEGO, CALIFORNIA.
ARTISTIC DIRECTOR: JACK O'BRIEN / EXECUTIVE DIRECTOR: LOUIS G. SPISTO

2/6/06

Jonathan Pryce (C) and the chorus sing "Give Them What They Want."

Photo by Carol Rosegg

Dirty Rotten Scoundrels

MUSICAL NUMBERS

ACT I

Overture	Orchestra, Ensemble
Give Them What They Want	Lawrence, Andre, Ensemble
What Was a Woman To Do?	Muriel, Women
Great Big Stuff	Freddy, Ensemble
Chimp in a Suit	Andre
Oklahoma?	Jolene, Lawrence, Ensemble
All About Ruprecht	Lawrence, Ruprecht, Jolene
What Was a Woman To Do? (Reprise)	Muriel
Here I Am	Christine, Ensemble
Nothing Is Too Wonderful To Be True	Christine, Freddy
The Miracle (Act I Finale)	Company

ACT II

Entr'acte	Orchestra, Ensemble
Rüffhousin' mit Shüffhausen	Freddy, Christine, Dr. Shüffhausen
Like Zis/Like Zat	Andre, Muriel
The More We Dance	Lawrence, Christine, Ensemble
Love Is My Legs	Freddy, Christine, Ensemble
Love Sneaks In	Lawrence
Son of Great Big Stuff	Freddy, Christine
The Reckoning	Lawrence, Freddy, Andre
Dirty Rotten Number	Lawrence, Freddy
Finale	Company

(L-R): Jonathan Pryce, Rachel York and Norbert Leo Butz sing "Dirty Rotten Number."

Photo by Carol Rosegg

Cast Continued

SWINGS
CHRISTINE BOKHOUR, JULIE CONNORS,
JEREMY DAVIS,
JENIFER FOOTE, GREG GRAHAM

UNDERSTUDIES
For Andre Thibault:
JOE CASSIDY,
DENNIS PARLATO
For Lawrence Jameson:
TOM GALANTICH
For Muriel Eubanks:
RACHEL DE BENEDET,
LAURA MARIE DUNCAN
For Freddy Benson:
JOE CASSIDY,
JASON GILLMAN
For Jolene Oakes:
JULIE CONNORS,
RACHELLE RAK
For Christine Colgate:
JULIE CONNORS,
LAURA MARIE DUNCAN

Dance Captain: GREG GRAHAM

*Jonathan Pryce is appearing with the
permission of Actors' Equity Association
pursuant to an exchange program
between American Equity and U.K. Equity.*

ORCHESTRA
Conductor: Fred Lassen
Associate Conductor: Jan Rosenberg
Assistant Conductor: Howard Joines
Concertmaster: Antoine Silverman
Violins: Michael Nicholas, Claire Chan
Cello: Anja Wood
Woodwinds: Andrew Sterman, Dan Willis,
Mark Thrasher
Trumpets: Hollis (Bud) Burridge, John Reid
Trombone: Mike Boschen
Horn: Theresa MacDonnell
Keyboards: Dan Lipton, Jan Rosenberg
Guitar: Erik DellaPenna
Bass: Mike DuClos
Drums: Dean Sharenow
Percussion: Howard Joines

Music Coordinator: Howard Joines
Music Copying: Emily Grishman Music Preparation/
Emily Grishman, Katharine Edmonds

Dirty Rotten Scoundrels

Jonathan Pryce
Lawrence Jameson

Norbert Leo Butz
Freddy Benson

Rachel York
Christine Colgate

Joanna Gleason
Muriel Eubanks

Gregory Jbara
Andre Thibault

Mylinda Hull
Jolene Oakes

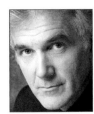
Dennis Parlato
*Standby for
Lawrence Jameson*

Timothy J. Alex
Conductor; Ensemble

Roxane Barlow
Ensemble

Jacqueline Bayne
Ensemble

Christine Bokhour
Swing

Stephen Campanella
Ensemble

Joe Cassidy
Ensemble

Julie Connors
Swing

Jeremy Davis
Swing

Rachel de Benedet
*Lenore; Renee;
Ensemble*

Laura Marie Duncan
Sophia; Ensemble

Sally Mae Dunn
Ensemble

Jenifer Foote
Swing

Tom Galantich
*Hotel Manager;
Nikos; Ensemble*

Jason Gillman
Ensemble

Greg Graham
*Dance Captain;
Swing*

Amy Heggins
Ensemble

Rachelle Rak
Ensemble

Chuck Saculla
Ensemble

Dennis Stowe
Ensemble

Matt Wall
Ensemble

Jeffrey Lane
Book

David Yazbek
Composer/Lyricist

Jack O'Brien
Director

Jerry Mitchell
Choreographer

Ted Sperling
*Music Director;
Incidental Music
Arranger;
Co-Vocal Arranger*

David Rockwell
Scenic Design

Gregg Barnes
Costume Design

Kenneth Posner
Lighting Design

Dirty Rotten Scoundrels

Tom Clark, Mark Menard and Nevin Steinberg, Acme Sound Partners
Sound Design

Bernard Telsey Casting, C.S.A.
Casting

Harold Wheeler
Orchestrations

Fred Lassen
Conductor

Howard Joines
Music Coordinator

Christopher C. Smith, Theatersmith, Inc.
Production Manager

Jorge Vargas
Makeup Designer

Margery Singer Company
Marketing

Charlotte Wilcox Company
General Manager

Michael Brunner
Production Stage Manager

Daniel S. Rosokoff
Assistant Stage Manager

Dana Williams
Assistant Stage Manager

Marty Bell
Producer/ Executive Producer

David Brown
Producer

Aldo Scrofani
Producer/ Executive Producer

Roy Furman
Producer

Dede Harris
Producer

Amanda Lipitz
Producer

Ruth Hendel
Producer

Chase Mishkin
Producer

Debra Black
Producer

Sharon Karmazin
Producer

Barbara Whitman
Producer

Jay Harris, Weissberger Theater Group (WTG)
Producer

Harvey Weinstein
Producer

Dirty Rotten Scoundrels

Andrew Asnes
Ensemble

Paula Leggett Chase
Ensemble

Sara Gettelfinger
Jolene Oakes

Nina Goldman
Swing

Grasan Kingsberry
Ensemble

Gina Lamparella
Swing

John Lithgow
Lawrence Jameson

Michael Paternostro
Ensemble

Sherie Rene Scott
Christine Colgate

Nick Wyman
*Standby for
Lawrence Jameson*

Lucie Arnaz
Muriel Eubanks

Jacqueline Bayne
*Understudy for
Christine Colgate*

Will Erat
Sailor #1; Ensemble

Nina Goldman
Swing

Timothy Edward Smith
Swing

(L-R): Mylinda Hull tries a cowboy hat on an unhappy Jonathan Pryce in the number "Oklahoma?."

Photo by Carol Rosegg

Dirty Rotten Scoundrels

Photo by Ben Strothmann

CAST AND CREW

Front Row (L-R):
Dina Steinberg (Assistant Company Manager), Bruce Kagel (Company Manager), Therese Costello (Assistant Stage Manager), Michael Brunner (Production Stage Manager), Dan Rosokoff (Assistant Stage Manager), Gregory Jbara (Cast), Greg Graham (Cast), Rhonda Barkow (Physical Therapist)

Second Row (L-R):
Tommy Thomson (Propman), Julie Connors (Cast), Jackie Bayne (Cast), Jenifer Foote (Cast), Norbert Leo Butz (Cast), Sally Mae Dunn (Cast), Jeremy Davis (Cast), Fred Lassen (Conductor)

Third Row (L-R):
Jack Scott (Dresser), Sonia Rivera (Hair Supervisor), Rachelle Rak (Cast), Laura Marie Duncan (Cast), Dennis Stowe (Cast), Timothy J. Alex (Cast), Rachel York (Cast), Roxane Barlow (Cast), Jan Rosenberg (Associate Conductor), Howard Joines (Percussionist), Kevin Kennedy (Doorman)

Fourth Row (L-R):
Kate McAleer (Dresser), Amber Isaac (Dresser), Enrique Vega (Hair), Jonathan Pryce (Cast), Rachel de Benedet (Cast), Jason Gillman (Cast), John Reid (Musician), Mark Thrasher (Musician)

Fifth Row (L-R):
Frank Scaccia (Dresser), Jessica Scoblick (Wardrobe Supervisor), Joe Whitmeyer (Hair), Chuck Saculla (Cast), Stephen Campanella (Cast), Will Erat (Cast)

Back Row (L-R):
John C. Cooper (Soundman), Pete Donovan (Electrician), Melanie Hansen (Dresser), Lonny McDougal (Electrician), Amy Heggins (Cast), Matt Wall (Cast), Dennis Parlato (Cast), Sara Gettelfinger (Cast), Tom Galantich (Cast)

Dirty Rotten Scoundrels

Dirty Rotten Scoundrels
SCRAPBOOK

Photos by Aubrey Reuben

Correspondent: Mylinda Hull, "Jolene Oakes"

Memorable Fan Letter: There is a young pair of fans, brother and sister, who live in Hilton Head, South Carolina. They're both great artists and have sent lovely letters with really great caricatures to me and many other Broadway folk.

Anniversary Party: On March 9, 2006 we had a "2nd Annual Opening Night" party, to celebrate the return of Jonathan Pryce to Broadway in the role of Lawrence Jameson, the addition of new cast members Rachel York and myself, and the overall excellent shape of the show thanks to the people who had already been there for the previous year. The party was at Madame Tussauds Wax Museum, and it was a little weird because those wax figures freak me out. There are so many people you don't know at an opening night party anyway, so to be polite many of us found ourselves starting a conversation with someone who turned out to be fake Shakira or fake Brad Pitt. After a couple of cocktails, things got a little rowdy in the "Heads of State" room. Fake Margaret Thatcher was put in a compromising position. I'll leave it at that.

Who Has Done the Most Shows: Production Stage Manager Mike Brunner and cast member Jason Gillman.

Easter Bonnet Skit: "A Change in My Life" by Chuck Saculla and Billy Strauss.

Backstage Ritual: Jonathan Pryce blasts music before every show. You never know what you'll hear coming out of his dressing room, Buddy Holly, Cat Powers, Miles Davis or some classical sh—.

Favorite Moment During Each Performance (Onstage or Off): Watching the crew do their work, setting and moving the show, over and over, eight times a week, with as much clarity and esprit as those of us onstage.

Favorite In-Theatre Gathering Place: The Imperial Theatre has limited backstage social space, so everyone crams into the stage managers' office, just off stage right.

Favorite Off-Site Hangout: McHale's (long may it live in our memories).

Mascot: A stuffed dog that plays "New York, New York."

Favorite Therapy: Ambien.

Memorable Ad-Libs: The audience was madly applauding Norbert and Jonathan for their big "Dirty Rotten Number" and an elderly couple, who must have thought the show was finished,

1. John Lithgow and Jonathan Pryce at the Theater Hall of Fame induction ceremony.
2. Cast applauds Lithgow (with rose) at his farewell performance.
3. Jenn Colella (L) and Jenifer Foote at an Absolut Vodka party for the show at the Paramount Hotel.
4: (L-R) Lithgow helps celebrate Butz' winning a TDF/Astaire Award.
5. Lithgow (2nd from L) and Butz (R) contemplate backstage visitors from the Moscow Cat Circus.

Dirty Rotten Scoundrels
SCRAPBOOK

1. The real David Yazbek (R) muses over the wax effigy of fellow composer Leonard Bernstein at the "2nd Annual Opening Night" party at Madame Tussauds.
2. (L-R): Lithgow, Butz, Yazbek and Greg Jbara at the cast album signing at Tower Records.
3. Cast clown Dennis Stowe boogies with the wax effigy of Beyoncé at Madame Tussauds.

started to make their way up the aisle. The whole audience could see them leaving and Norbert turned to Jonathan and loudly said "Well, they're not leaving because of me!" It brought the house down again. Also, the Sunday before Easter we had a rare technical malfunction with our turntable minutes after the show had started and had to pause briefly, so Jonathan and Joanna stayed onstage and danced for the audience while waiting to resume. When the turntable started up again and rotated into proper position, it was filled with nothing but palm trees and, as they all watched it come around, Jonathan said, "Look, Palm Sunday." Which of course it was.

Cell Phone Rings: One night there were three before we were even halfway through Act I.

Fastest Costume Change: The Jackal entrance. Not only is it fast, it's constantly in motion. Every night there's a backstage announcement: "Ladies and gentlemen, please clear the basement hallway for The Jackal."

Heaviest/Hottest Costume: Sally Mae Dunn as the Nun.

Who Wore the Least: Rachelle Rak and Amy Heggins, GORGEOUS in their bikinis.

Catchphrases Only the Company Would Recognize: "I know what to do."

Sweethearts Within the Company: Jonathan and Norbert during "Ruprecht."

Memorable Directorial Note: At one point, Norbert, Jonathan and myself were called for a rehearsal with Jack O'Brien. It lasted maybe three minutes. And it was truly very helpful. I loved it. That's Broadway, baby.

Understudy Anecdote: Joe Cassidy, who was on as Freddy, got hurt during "Great Big Stuff," so Jason Gillman got ready to take over mid-show. It was in between scenes so an announcement was made to the audience before the "Ruprecht" scene that the role of Freddy would now be played by Jason Gillman, but when it was time for Freddy's entrance, much to everyone's surprise, Joe marched back on. Jason wasn't quite dressed yet. Apparently it got quite a laugh.

Favorite Rehearsal Moment: I joined the company in January 2006 to replace Sara Gettelfinger. At my first rehearsal on the stage I finished singing through "Oklahoma?" and Fred Lassen, our wonderfully talented and incredibly sweet conductor, said in the most supportive manner, "That's just fantastic, Mylinda, really, really wonderful. Just one thing..." then he leaned down to Jan Rosenberg who was on the keyboard and said, "Hey Jan, can you play her the *melody*?" Picky, picky.

Embarrassing Moments: Jonathan Pryce says "Every night from 8 to 10:40."

Coolest Thing About Being in This Show: Being in a company of people who are experienced without being cynical. That's a great and rare combination.

Doubt

First Preview: March 9, 2005. Opened: March 31, 2005.
Still running as of May 31, 2006.

CAST

in order of appearance

Father Flynn .... RON ELDARD
Sister Aloysius .... EILEEN ATKINS
Sister James .... JENA MALONE
Mrs. Muller .... ADRIANE LENOX

Stage Manager: ELIZABETH MOLONEY

TIME:

Autumn, 1964

PLACE:

St. Nicholas Church School in the Bronx

STANDBYS

For Sister James:
NADIA BOWERS

For Mrs. Muller:
CAROLINE STEFANIE CLAY

For Father Flynn:
STEVIE RAY DALLIMORE

FROM THE PLAYWRIGHT

This play is dedicated to the many orders of Catholic nuns who devoted their lives to serving others in hospitals, schools and retirement homes. Though they have been much maligned and ridiculed, who among us has been so generous?

A JUJAMCYN THEATRE
ROCCO LANDESMAN
PRESIDENT

PAUL LIBIN   JACK VIERTEL
PRODUCING DIRECTOR   CREATIVE DIRECTOR

CAROLE SHORENSTEIN HAYS   MTC PRODUCTIONS, INC.
ARTISTIC DIRECTOR   EXECUTIVE PRODUCER
LYNNE MEADOW   BARRY GROVE

ROGER BERLIND   SCOTT RUDIN
PRESENT

EILEEN ATKINS   RON ELDARD

IN

DOUBT

BY

JOHN PATRICK SHANLEY

WITH

JENA MALONE   AND   ADRIANE LENOX

SCENIC DESIGN   COSTUME DESIGN   LIGHTING DESIGN   ORIGINAL MUSIC AND SOUND DESIGN
JOHN LEE BEATTY   CATHERINE ZUBER   PAT COLLINS   DAVID VAN TIEGHEM

PRODUCTION STAGE MANAGER   CASTING
CHARLES MEANS   NANCY PICCIONE/DAVID CAPARELLIOTIS

PRODUCTION MANAGEMENT   PRESS REPRESENTATIVE   MARKETING
AURORA PRODUCTIONS   BONEAU/BRYAN-BROWN   TMG – THE MARKETING GROUP

GENERAL MANAGEMENT   EXECUTIVE PRODUCER
STUART THOMPSON PRODUCTIONS/JAMES TRINER   GREG HOLLAND

DIRECTED BY

DOUG HUGHES

ORIGINALLY PRODUCED BY MANHATTAN THEATRE CLUB ON NOVEMBER 23, 2004.
THE PRODUCERS WISH TO EXPRESS THEIR APPRECIATION TO THEATRE DEVELOPMENT FUND FOR ITS SUPPORT OF THIS PRODUCTION.

LIVE BROADWAY

1/9/06

Jena Malone and Eileen Atkins as Sister James and Sister Aloysius.

Doubt

Eileen Atkins
Sister Aloysius

Ron Eldard
Father Flynn

Jena Malone
Sister James

Adriane Lenox
Mrs. Muller

Nadia Bowers
*Standby for
Sister James*

Caroline Stefanie Clay
*Standby for
Mrs. Muller*

Stevie Ray Dallimore
*Standby for
Father Flynn*

John Patrick Shanley
Playwright

Doug Hughes
Director

John Lee Beatty
Set Design

Catherine Zuber
Costume Design

Pat Collins
Lighting Design

Stuart Thompson,
Stuart Thompson
Productions
General Manager

Carole Shorenstein
Hays
Producer

Lynne Meadow
*Artistic Director,
Manhattan Theatre
Club*

Barry Grove
*Executive Producer,
Manhattan Theatre
Club*

Roger Berlind
Producer

Scott Rudin
Producer

Greg Holland
Executive Producer

Heather Goldenhersh
Sister James

Cherry Jones
Sister Aloysius

Chris McGarry
*Standby for
Father Flynn*

Brían F. O'Byrne
Father Flynn

Doubt

STAGE CREW and MEMBERS OF THE CAST
Front Row (L-R):
Jena Malone (Sister James),
Elizabeth Moloney (Stage Manager),
Eileen Atkins (Sister Aloysius),
Rebecca Heroff (Production Props) and
Sister Inflatus (Mascot).

Back Row (L-R):
Gina Gornik (Wardrobe),
James Gardner (Production Electrician),
Ron Eldard (Father Flynn),
Eileen Miller (Wardrobe Supervisor),
Stevie Ray Dallimore (Standby for Fr.
Flynn), George Fullum (House Carpenter),
Tim Bennet (House Props),
Charles Means (Production Stage
Manager), Caroline Anderson (Production
Assistant) and
Paul Delcioppo (Production Sound
Engineer).

2005-2006 Award

DRAMA LEAGUE AWARD
Honored Previous Recipient (Eileen Atkins)

BOX OFFICE
Stan Shaffer and Gail Yerkovich

FRONT OF HOUSE STAFF
Sitting (L-R):
Dayris Fana, Victoria Lauzun,
Elizabeth C. Taylor and Tatiana Gomberg.

Standing (L-R):
John Barker, Marjorie Glover, Aaron
Kendall, Laurie Garcia, Jennifer Artesi,
Kishan Redding, Brandon Houghton,
Virgilio Estrada, Ralph Santos and
Hector Rivera.

Doubt

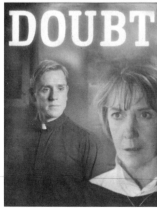
STAFF FOR *DOUBT*

GENERAL MANAGEMENT
STUART THOMPSON PRODUCTIONS
Stuart Thompson   Caroline Prugh   James Triner

COMPANY MANAGER
Bobby Driggers

GENERAL PRESS REPRESENTATIVE
BONEAU/BRYAN-BROWN
Chris Boneau Jim Byk Aaron Meier Heath Schwartz

PRODUCTION MANAGEMENT
AURORA PRODUCTIONS INC.
Gene O'Donovan
W. Benjamin Heller II   Elise Hanley
Bethany Weinstein

Production Stage Manager	**Charles Means**
Stage Manager	Elizabeth Moloney
Dialect Coach	Stephen Gabis
Associate Director	**Mark Schneider**
Associate Set Designer	Eric Renschler
Assistant Set Designer	Yoshinori Tanakura
Associate Lighting Designer	D.M. Wood
Assistant Costume Designers	T. Michael Hall, Michael Zecker
Assistant Sound Designer	Walter Trarbach
Production Electrician	James Gardner
Production Props	Rebecca Heroff
Production Sound	Paul Delcioppo
Wardrobe Supervisor	Eileen Miller
Dresser	Gina Gornik
Automation	Danny Braddish
Casting Assistant	Jennifer McCool
Production Assistants	Caroline Anderson, Anne Michelson
Assistant to Mrs. Hays	Kelly Hartgraves
Assistant to Mr. Berlind	Jeffrey Hillock
Assistant to Mr. Rudin	Michael Diliberti
General Management Assistant	Ryan Smith
Management Intern	Jeremy Blocker
Banking	Chase Manhattan Bank/ Richard L. Callian, Michele Gibbons
Payroll	Castellana Services, Inc./ Lance Castellana
Accountant	Robert Fried, CPA
Controller	Anne Stewart FitzRoy, CPA
Assistant Controller	Joseph S. Kubala
Insurance	DeWitt Stern Group, Inc./ Jolyon F. Stern, Peter Shoemaker, Anthony L. Pittari
Legal Counsel	Paul, Weiss, Rifkind, Wharton & Garrison/ John F. Breglio, Esq., Rachel Hoover, Esq.
Advertising	SpotCo/Drew Hodges, Jim Edwards, John Lanasa, Kim Smarsh
Marketing Consultants	The Marketing Group/ Tanya Grubich, Laura Matalon Trish Santini, Bob Bucci, Amber Glassberg, Liz Miller
Production Photographer	Joan Marcus
Cover Design by	SpotCo
Cover Photo Illustration by	Marc Yankus

CREDITS
Scenery and automation from Hudson Scenic Studio, Inc. Lighting equipment supplied by GSD Productions, Inc., West Hempstead, NY. Sound equipment by Masque Sound. *Doubt* rehearsed at Manhattan Theatre Club's Creative Center. Lozenges by Ricola.

STAFF FOR MANHATTAN THEATRE CLUB

Artistic Director	Lynne Meadow
Executive Producer	Barry Grove
General Manager	Florie Seery
Director of Artistic Production	Michael Bush
Director of Artistic Development	Paige Evans
Director of Artistic Operations	Mandy Greenfield
Artistic Associate/ Assistant to the Artistic Director	Amy Gilkes Loe
Director of Casting	Nancy Piccione
Casting Director	David Caparelliotis
Director of Development	Jill Turner Lloyd
Director of Marketing	Debra Waxman
Director of Finance	Jeffrey Bledsoe
Associate General Manager	Seth Shepsle
Company Manager/NY City Center	Lindsey T. Brooks
Assistant to the Executive Producer	Bonnie Pan
Director of Subscriber Services	Robert Allenberg
Director of Telesales and Telefunding	George Tetlow
Director of Education	David Shookhoff
Production Manager	Ryan McMahon

JUJAMCYN THEATERS

ROCCO LANDESMAN
President

PAUL LIBIN	**JACK VIERTEL**
Producing Director	Creative Director

JERRY ZAKS

DANIEL ADAMIAN	**JENNIFER HERSHEY**
General Manager	Director of Operations

MEREDITH VILLATORE
Chief Financial Officer

STAFF FOR THE WALTER KERR THEATRE

Manager	Susan Elrod
Treasurer	Stan Shaffer
Carpenter	George A. Fullum
Propertyman	Timothy Bennet
Electrician	Vincent Valvo, Jr.
Engineer	Ralph Santos

Doubt
SCRAPBOOK

Correspondents: Charles Means (Production Stage Manager) and Elizabeth Moloney (Stage Manager).

Memorable Note, Fax or Fan Letter: We receive random newspaper clippings about abuse in the Catholic Church, most often from people who have never seen the show.

Anniversary Parties and/or Gifts: A box of tea pots and cosies for the whole cast from the woman who made the original tea cosy used in the show.

Most Exciting Celebrity Visitor: A surprise Valentine's Day/Opening Night visit to Eileen Atkins from Colin Farrell.

"Gypsy of the Year": We didn't do a sketch for the 2005 "Gypsy of the Year" but we did raise the most money of any play on Broadway.

Actor Who Performed the Most Roles in This Show: Mark Schneider.

Who Has Done The Most Shows: Cherry Jones never missed a show, playing every performance both on and off Broadway (452).

Special Backstage Rituals: Saluting Cherry as she walked onstage during the curtain call. Eileen and Ron do a dance for each other in Eileen's dressing room between "Five" and "Places" every night.

Favorite Moment During Each Performance (Onstage or Off): Tea and gossip with Eileen Atkins every night at 6:45 in the stage management office.

Favorite In-Theatre Gathering Place: The stage management office.

Favorite Off-Site Hangouts: Vynl between shows and Joe Allen's after a Sunday matinee.

Favorite Snack Foods: Ron Eldard brings cookies from Levain Bakery every Saturday morning. Nadia's mom also sends excellent homemade cookies on every holiday or special occasion.

Mascot: Sister Inflatus.

Favorite Therapy: Hot water with lemon.

Memorable Ad-Lib: The night Adriane said "Not exactly no. I've seen him on the altar boys" instead of "Not exactly no. I've seen him on the altar."

Record Number of Cell Phone Rings During a Performance: Six rings on a single phone. The worst one was when a phone went off in the middle of the last line of the play: "I have doubts"—(ring ring)—"I have such doubts."

Busiest Week at the Box Office: We broke the house sales record for the sixth time on January 8, 2006.

Catchphrases Only the Company Would Recognize: "Manny, I love it already!"

Company Sweethearts: Beth got engaged to her girlfriend during the run.

Memorable Directorial Notes: "We want to stay on this side of the bizarre." "Easy breezy."

Company In-Jokes: The Atkins Diet, the Limerick, and the Dame Rap.

Company Legends: Both of our Sister Jameses (Heather Goldenhersh and Jena Malone) made their Broadway debuts with our show.

Tales from the Put-In: Our new cast got the flu and three of our four understudies went on for what was supposed to be the first performance of the new company.

Nicknames: Sister Delicious, Friar Five, Butch, Girlie, the Dame, the Singing Nun, and Fool.

Embarrassing Moments: When Eileen accidentally called Jena "Mister James" instead of "Sister James."

Superstitions That Turned Out To Be True: Someone made a joke the night before Eileen went on for the first time that "she'll never miss a show." She got the flu the very next day and was out for a week.

Coolest Thing About Being in This Show: Working on a long-running straight play and having the best crew on Broadway.

1. Ron Eldard and Eileen Atkins at a party for the replacement cast at Etcetera Etcetera restaurant.
2. Jena Malone and John Patrick Shanley at Etcetera Etcetera.
3. Moisés Kaufman with Cherry Jones.

Photos by Aubrey Reuben

The Drowsy Chaperone

First Preview: April 3, 2006. Opened: May 1, 2006.
Still running as of May 31, 2006.

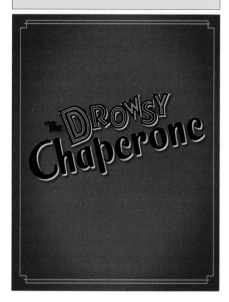

CAST
(in order of appearance)

Man in Chair	BOB MARTIN
Mrs. Tottendale	GEORGIA ENGEL
Underling	EDWARD HIBBERT
Robert Martin	TROY BRITTON JOHNSON
George	EDDIE KORBICH
Feldzieg	LENNY WOLPE
Kitty	JENNIFER SMITH
Gangster #1	JASON KRAVITS
Gangster #2	GARTH KRAVITS
Aldolpho	DANNY BURSTEIN
Janet Van De Graaff	SUTTON FOSTER
The Drowsy Chaperone	BETH LEAVEL
Trix	KECIA LEWIS-EVANS
Super	JOEY SORGE
Ensemble	LINDA GRIFFIN,
	ANGELA PUPELLO,
	JOEY SORGE,
	PATRICK WETZEL

SWINGS
ANDREA CHAMBERLAIN, JAY DOUGLAS,
STACIA FERNANDEZ, KILTY REIDY

Dance Captain:
ANGELA PUPELLO

Continued on next page

Continued on next page

⊰N⊱ MARQUIS THEATRE
UNDER THE DIRECTION OF JAMES M. NEDERLANDER AND JAMES L. NEDERLANDER

Kevin McCollum   Roy Miller   Boyett Ostar Productions
Stephanie McClelland   Barbara Freitag   Jill Furman
present

The DROWSY Chaperone

Music and Lyrics by   Book by
Lisa Lambert and Greg Morrison   Bob Martin and Don McKellar

by Special Arrangement with Paul Mack

Starring

Danny Burstein   Georgia Engel   Sutton Foster   Edward Hibbert   Troy Britton Johnson
Eddie Korbich   Garth Kravits   Jason Kravits   Beth Leavel
Kecia Lewis-Evans   Bob Martin   Jennifer Smith   Lenny Wolpe

and

Andrea Chamberlain   Jay Douglas   Stacia Fernandez   Linda Griffin
Angela Pupello   Kilty Reidy   Joey Sorge   Patrick Wetzel

Scenic Design	Costume Design	Lighting Design	Sound Design
David Gallo	Gregg Barnes	Ken Billington Brian Monahan	Acme Sound Partners

Casting	Hair Design	Makeup Design
Bernard Telsey Casting	Josh Marquette	Justen M. Brosnan

Orchestrations by	Dance and Incidental Music Arrangements by	Music Direction and Vocal Arrangements by
Larry Blank	Glen Kelly	Phil Reno

Music Coordinator	Production Supervisors	Production Stage Manager
John Miller	Brian Lynch Chris Kluth	Karen Moore

Associate Producers	Press Representative	Marketing	General Management
Sonny Everett Mariano Tolentino, Jr.	Boneau/Bryan-Brown	TMG - The Marketing Group	The Charlotte Wilcox Company

Directed and Choreographed by
Casey Nicholaw

American Premiere produced at the Ahmanson Theatre by Center Theatre Group, LA's Theatre Company
The producers wish to express their appreciation to Theatre Development Fund for its support of this production.

LIVE BROADWAY

5/1/06

The Company performs "Toledo Surprise."

The Drowsy Chaperone

MUSICAL NUMBERS

Overture .... Orchestra
"Fancy Dress" .... Company
"Cold Feets" .... Robert, George
"Show Off" .... Janet, Company
"As We Stumble Along" .... Drowsy Chaperone
"I Am Aldolpho" .... Aldolpho, Drowsy Chaperone
"Accident Waiting to Happen" .... Robert, Janet
"Toledo Surprise" .... Gangsters, Feldzieg, Kitty, Aldolpho,
George, Janet, Robert, Underling,
Mrs. Tottendale, Drowsy Chaperone and Company
"Message From a Nightingale" .... Kitty, Gangsters, Aldolpho, Drowsy Chaperone
"Bride's Lament" .... Janet, Company
"Love Is Always Lovely in the End" .... Mrs. Tottendale, Underling
"I Do, I Do in the Sky" .... Trix and Company
"As We Stumble Along" (Reprise) .... Company

(L-R): Linda Griffin, Angela Pupello, Sutton Foster, Patrick Wetzel, Jennifer Smith, Lenny Wolpe and Beth Leavel (seated).

Photo by Joan Marcus

Cast Continued

UNDERSTUDIES
For Man in Chair:
JAY DOUGLAS, PATRICK WETZEL
For Janet:
ANDREA CHAMBERLAIN, ANGELA PUPELLO
For Robert:
JAY DOUGLAS, JOEY SORGE
For The Drowsy Chaperone:
STACIA FERNANDEZ, LINDA GRIFFIN
For Mrs. Tottendale:
STACIA FERNANDEZ, LINDA GRIFFIN
For Aldolpho:
JAY DOUGLAS, JOEY SORGE
For Underling:
KILTY REIDY, PATRICK WETZEL
For Feldzieg:
JAY DOUGLAS, PATRICK WETZEL
For Kitty:
ANDREA CHAMBERLAIN, ANGELA PUPELLO
For George:
KILTY REIDY, PATRICK WETZEL
For Gangsters #1 and #2:
KILTY REIDY, JOEY SORGE
For Trix:
STACIA FERNANDEZ, LINDA GRIFFIN

ORCHESTRA
Conductor:
PHIL RENO
Associate Conductor:
LAWRENCE GOLDBERG

Reeds:
EDWARD JOFFE, TOM MURRAY,
TOM CHRISTENSEN, RON JANNELLI
Trumpets:
DAVE STAHL, GLENN DREWES,
JEREMY MILOSZEWICZ
Trombones:
STEVE ARMOUR, JEFF NELSON
Guitar:
ED HAMILTON
Bass:
MICHAEL KUENNEN
Drums:
PERRY CAVARI
Percussion:
BILL HAYES
Keyboards:
MATT PERRI, LAWRENCE GOLDBERG

Music Coordinator:
JOHN MILLER

The Drowsy Chaperone

Danny Burstein
Aldolpho

Georgia Engel
Mrs. Tottendale

Sutton Foster
Janet Van De Graaff

Edward Hibbert
Underling

Troy Britton Johnson
Robert Martin

Eddie Korbich
George

Garth Kravits
Gangster #2

Jason Kravits
Gangster #1

Beth Leavel
The Drowsy Chaperone

Kecia Lewis-Evans
Trix

Bob Martin
*Book,
Man in the Chair*

Jennifer Smith
Kitty

Lenny Wolpe
Feldzieg

Andrea Chamberlain
Swing

Jay Douglas
Swing

Stacia Fernandez
Swing

Linda Griffin
Ensemble

Angela Pupello
Ensemble

Kilty Reidy
Swing

Joey Sorge
Ensemble

Patrick Wetzel
Ensemble

Lisa Lambert
Music & Lyrics

Greg Morrison
Music & Lyrics

Don McKellar
Book

Casey Nicholaw
Director

David Gallo
Scenic Design

Gregg Barnes
Costume Design

Ken Billington
Co-Lighting Design

Brian Monahan
Co-Lighting Design

Tom Clark, Mark Menard and Nevin Steinberg,
Acme Sound Partners
Sound Design

Bernard Telsey
Casting
Casting

Justen M. Brosnan
Makeup Design

Larry Blank
Orchestrations

John Miller
Music Coordinator

The Drowsy Chaperone

Casey Hushion
Assistant Director

Charlotte Wilcox
General Manager

Kevin McCollum
Producer

Roy Miller
Producer

Bob Boyett
Producer

Bill Haber
OSTAR Enterprises
Producer

Stephanie McClelland
Producer

Jill Furman
Producer

Sonny Everett
Associate Producer

STAGE MANAGEMENT
(L-R): Joshua Halperin,
Karen Moore
and Rachel McCutchen.

Photos by Ben Strothmann

WARDROBE
(L-R):
Margiann Flanagan, David Ruble, Charlie Catanese,
Lyssa Everett, Joby Horrigan, Susan Checklick, Barry Hoff,
Pat Sullivan, Gregg Barnes, Julien Havard, Terri Purcell
and Phillip Rolfe.

STAGE CREW
Front Row (L-R):
Martin Van Beveren, Augie Mericola, Chris Weigel,
Timothy Shea, Tim Donovan.

Middle Row (L-R):
George Green, George Fullum, Ronnie Weigel, Jimmy Mayo,
Duke Wilson.

Back Row (L-R):
Mike "Jersey" Van Nest, Rick Poulin, Doug Purcell,
Keith Buchanan and Brady Jarvis.

The Drowsy Chaperone

HAIR DEPARTMENT
Front Row (L-R): Carla Muniz and
Nathaniel Hathaway
Back Row (L-R): Richard Orton and
Sandra Schlender.

2005-2006 AWARDS

TONY AWARDS
Best Book of a Musical (Bob Martin and
Don McKellar)
Best Music and Lyrics (Lisa Lambert and
Greg Morrison)
Best Performance by a Featured Actress in a
Musical (Beth Leavel)
Best Scenic Design of a Musical (David
Gallo)
Best Costume Design of a Musical (Gregg
Barnes)

NEW YORK DRAMA CRITICS' CIRCLE AWARD
Best Musical

OUTER CRITICS CIRCLE AWARDS
Outstanding New Score
Outstanding Featured Actress in a Musical
(Beth Leavel)
Outstanding Set Design (David Gallo)

Outstanding Costume Design (Gregg Barnes)

DRAMA DESK AWARDS
Outstanding Musical
Outstanding Featured Actress in a Musical
(Beth Leavel)
Outstanding Music (Lisa Lambert and Greg
Morrison)
Outstanding Lyrics (Lisa Lambert and Greg
Morrison)
Outstanding Book of a Musical (Bob Martin
and Don McKellar)
Outstanding Set Design of a Musical (David
Gallo)
Outstanding Costume Design (Gregg Barnes)

THEATRE WORLD AWARD
Outstanding Broadway Debut (Bob Martin)

FRONT OF HOUSE STAFF
Front Row (L-R):
David R. Calhoun (Manager), Lulu Caso
(Chief Usher), Carol Reilly, Barbara Corey,
Daisy Irizarry

Middle Row (L-R):
Charlie Spencer, Cecil Villar, Stanley Seidman,
Dixon Rosario, Jr., Frank Rosario

Back Row (L-R):
Phyllis Weinsaft, Matt Colton,
Orlando Concepcion and Odalis Concepcion.

ORCHESTRA
Front Row (L-R):
Don McGeen, Perry Cavari, Glenn Drewes,
Larry Goldberg

Back Row (L-R):
Phil Reno, Tom Christensen, Edward Joffe,
Jeff Nelson, Bill Hayes, Matt Perri, Tom Murray,
John Benthal, Dave Stahl, Steve Armour,
Jeremy Miloszewicz, and Michael Kuennen.

Photos by Ben Strothmann

The Drowsy Chaperone

STAFF FOR *THE DROWSY CHAPERONE*

GENERAL MANAGEMENT
THE CHARLOTTE WILCOX COMPANY
Charlotte W. Wilcox
Matthew W. Krawiec   Emily Lawson
Steve Supeck   Margaret Wilcox
Beth Cochran

GENERAL PRESS REPRESENTATION
BONEAU/BRYAN-BROWN
Chris Boneau   Joe Perrotta
Heath Schwartz

COMPANY MANAGER
Seth Marquette

ASSISTANT COMPANY MANAGER
Robert E. Jones

CASTING
BERNARD TELSEY CASTING, C.S.A.
Bernie Telsey, Will Cantler, David Vaccari,
Bethany Knox, Craig Burns,
Tiffany Little Canfield, Stephanie Yankwitt,
Betsy Sherwood, Carrie Rosson, Justin Huff

PRODUCTION
STAGE MANAGER ....KAREN MOORE
Stage Manager ....Joshua Halperin
Assistant Stage Manager ....Rachel S. McCutchen
Assistant Director ....Casey Hushion
Assistant Choreographer ....Josh Rhodes
Asst. to Mssrs. McCollum & Miller ...David Michael Roth
Assts. to Mr. Boyett ....Diane Murphy, Michael
Mandell
Assts. to Mr. Haber ....Theresa Pisanelli,
Andrew Cleghorn
Boyett-Ostar Development
and Strategic Planning ....Jan Gura
Associate Scenic Designer ....Charlie Smith
Assistant Scenic Designers ....Zhanna Gurvich,
Dustin O'Neill, Gaetane Bertol,
Bill Beilke, Mary Hamrick
Associate Costume Designer ....Sky Switser
Assistants to Costume Designers ....Cathy Parrot,
Sarah Sophia Turner
Costume Intern ....Katharine Sullivan
Associate Lighting Designer ....Stephen N. Boulmetis
Assistant Lighting Designer ....Anthony Pearson
Assistant Sound Designer ....Nick Borisjuk
Production Properties ....George Wagner
Moving Lights Programmer ....Hillary Knox
Head Carpenter ....Chris Kluth
Flyman ....Cheyenne Benson
Automation Carpenter ....Duke Wilson
Head Electrician ....Keith Buchanan
Assistant Electrician ....Brady Jarvis
Head Sound ....Daryl Kral
Head Properties ....Augie Mericola
Wardrobe Supervisor ....Terri Purcell
Assistant Wardrobe Supervisor ....Joby Horrigan
Dressers ....Charles Catanese, Susan Checklick,
Lyssa Everett, Margiann Flanagan,
Julien Havard, Barry Hoff,
Phillip R. Rolfe, David Ruble,
Pat Sullivan

Hair Supervisor ....Richard Orton
Hairdressers ....Nathaniel
Hathaway,
Carla Muniz, Sandy Schlender
Mr. Hibbert's Hair ......John Barrett, Bergdorf Goodman
Assistant to John Miller ....Kelly M. Rach
Synthesizer Programmer ....Jim Abbott
Music Preparation Service ....Hotstave, Ltd.
Music Copyists ....Anixter Rice Music Services
Rehearsal Pianists ....Lawrence Goldberg,
Glen Kelly, Matt Perri
Rehearsal Drummer ....Perry Cavari
Production Assistants ....Jeffrey Rodriguez,
Rachel Zack
Music Production Assistant ....Colleen Darnall
LA Casting ....Amy Lieberman, C.S.A.
NAMT Presentation Casting ....Cindi Rush Casting
Legal Counsel ....Levine, Plotkin & Menin LLP/
Loren Plotkin, Susan Mindell
Accountants ....Fried & Kowgios LLP/
Robert Fried
Advertising ....SpotCo/
Drew Hodges, Jim Edwards,
Pete Milano, Jim McNicholas
Marketing ....TMG – The Marketing Group/
Tanya Grubich, Laura Matalon,
Trish Santini, Ronni Seif,
Laura Laponte, Meghan Zaneski
Press Representative Staff ....Adrian Bryan-Brown,
Jim Byk, Brandi Cornwell,
Jackie Green, Juliana Hannett,
Hector Hernandez, Jessica Johnson,
Kevin Jones, Eric Louie,
Shanna Marcus, Aaron Meier,
Linnae Petruzzelli, Matt Polk,
Matt Ross, Susanne Tighe
Website Design ....Situation Marketing/
Damian Bazadona, Lisa Cecchini
Banking ..............................J.P. Morgan Chase/
Stephanie Dalton
Payroll ....Castellana Services Inc./
Lance Castellana, Norman Seawell,
James Castellana
Group Sales ....Group Sales Box Office
Merchandising ....Max Merchandising LLC
Travel Arrangements ....Tzell Travel
Insurance Broker ....................D.R. Reiff Associates/
Dennis R. Reiff, Sonny Everett
Computer Consultant ....Marion Taylor
Opening Night Coordinator ....Tobak Lawrence Co./
Joanna B. Koondel, Suzanne Tobak
Production Photographer ....Joan Marcus
Theatre Displays ....King Displays

CREDITS
Scenery by Hudson Scenic Studio, Inc. Automation by
Hudson Scenic Studio, Inc. Costume construction by Barbara
Matera Limited, Carelli Costumes and Rodney Gordon.
Custom made shoes built by Capri Shoes, J.C. Theatrical and
T.O. Dey. Special thanks to Bra*Tenders for hosiery and
undergarments. Chinese fan and feathers provided by
American Plum and Fancy Feathers, New York, NY. Lights by
Production Resource Group. Sound equipment by Sound
Associates. Wigs by Ray Marston Wig Studios and Anne
Devon Chambless. Natural herb cough drops courtesy of
Ricola USA, Inc. Crash cymbals courtesy of PAISTE America,
Brea, CA. Rehearsed at the New 42nd Street Studios.

SPECIAL THANKS
Best Man Productions
Matt Watts
Frederick P. Bimbler, Esq.
Mirvish Productions
Michael Jenkins

Makeup provided by
M•A•C Cosmetics

www.DrowsyChaperone.com

THE DROWSY CHAPERONE was presented

n|a|m|t   NATIONAL ALLIANCE
for MUSICAL THEATRE

at the 2004 Festival of New Musicals
Kathy Evans, Executive Director   www.namt.org

NEDERLANDER
Chairman ....James M. Nederlander
President ....James L. Nederlander

Executive Vice President
Nick Scandalios

Vice President   Senior Vice President
Corporate Development   Labor Relations
Charlene S. Nederlander   **Herschel Waxman**

Vice President   Chief Financial Officer
Jim Boese   **Freida Sawyer Belviso**

STAFF FOR THE MARQUIS THEATRE
Manager ....David Calhoun
Associate Manager ....Ava Probst
Treasurer ....Rick Waxman
Assistant Treasurer ....John Rooney
Carpenter ....Joseph P. Valentino
Electrician ....James Mayo
Property Man ....Roland Weigel

Bob Martin
as Man in
Chair.

Photo by Joan Marcus

The Drowsy Chaperone

Correspondent: Jennifer Smith, "Kitty."

Memorable Opening Night Note: Robert Jones, one of our company managers, took a picture of Bob Martin and photoshopped figures of the rest of us hopping up and down on him like Lilliputians.

Opening Night Gifts: On the theme that a good book, a blanket and a martini make for a perfect night, the producers gave us *Drowsy Chaperone* flasks, Tiffany champagne glasses, martini shakers, and lovely leather-bound journals with beautiful pens. The writers gave the entire company one turntable and we each got an album. Also, Casey Nicholaw and his assistants, Casey Hushion and Josh Rhodes, gave us each hilarious calendars documenting a year with *Drowsy*, featuring posed reproductions of the show's outtakes. I made a donation to Broadway Cares and made cards with a picture from the "Message From a Nightingale" scene at the top of Act II.

Most Exciting Celebrity Visitors: Liza Minnelli, Blythe Danner and Kellie Pickler (of "American Idol") were here on opening night.

Who Got the Gypsy Robe: Patrick Wetzel.

Actors Who Performed the Most Roles in This Show: The ensemble members all play maids and butlers and reporters and aviators and monkeys, and Joey Sorge also plays the Superintendent.

Who Has Done the Most Shows in Their Career: I've done the most Broadway shows (10) and Lenny Wolpe has done the most shows overall.

Special Backstage Rituals: We have a little group that gathers at five minutes to say a little prayer together. Also, at the very top of the show when Bob Martin starts talking in the dark, a group of us gather at an offstage video monitor to sort of feel out the temperature of the room. The monitor gives us a view of the house and we look for the sparkles that indicate bling. One of the offstage singers has an erasable marker and we circle the places where we see bling.

Favorite Moment During Each Performance: We have a special surprise at the top of Act II, and I love the reaction we get every night from the audience.

Favorite In-Theatre Gathering Place: We

1. (L-R): Christian Borle (of *Spamalot*) with Sutton Foster on opening night.
2. Troy Britton Johnson is hugged by guest Liza Minnelli at the cast party at Tavern on the Green.
3. (L-R): Producer Kevin McCollum with Lisa Lambert, Janet Van De Graaff, Greg Morrison, Don McKellar and Roy Miller at the opening night party.
4. Bob Martin and wife Janet Van De Graaff at the opening night party.
5. Jennifer Smith on opening night.

The Drowsy Chaperone

have a great greenroom in this theatre, which is very lucky. People warm up in there, eat in there, and use the vending machines in there. It's a great, great space.

Favorite Off-Site Hangout: We once went out to Luxia as a group, but so many in this cast have children, they tend to go home right after the show. It's not much of a party crowd.

Favorite Snack Food: Amy's Bakery Pink Cake.

Mascot: Our monkeys. One monkey in particular that showed up in L.A.—one of those windup monkeys that plays cymbals. It shows up periodically in different people's dressing rooms.

Favorite Therapy: We get physical therapy twice a week. Rollers and slant boards are our big PT toys.

Memorable Ad-Lib: Near the end of the tryout in L.A., Bob Martin was still trying out new lines. One night, in the dropped-walking-stick scene when the rest of us are supposed to be frozen on the stage, Bob was going through his rant and said, "And finally your relationship deteriorates into an animated annual email on your birthday. Last year it was a bunny… 'Hoppy Birthday'!" And we broke up. The entire stage was shaking with laughter.

Cell Phone Rings: Maybe because Bob makes so many references to it in the script, we haven't been so terrorized.

Memorable Stage Door Fan Encounters: When I walk out the door, people confuse me with Beth Leavel, who plays The Drowsy Chaperone. When they start gushing, "Oh, I love your number! You're fantastic! See you at the Tonys!," I have to tell them I actually play Kitty. It can be awkward. So now I tend to go out the secret door instead of the stage door.

Fastest Costume Change: Sutton Foster changes costume three or four times during her "Show Off" number.

Busiest Day at the Box Office: The day after opening.

Who Wore the Heaviest/Hottest Costume: Lenny Wolpe is layered pretty heavily.

Who Wore the Least: The gangsters, when they come out in their ridiculous swimsuits.

Catchphrases Only The Company Would Recognize: "Don't let it!"

Best In-House Parody Lyric: "I'm an asset that's made in Manhattan!"

Memorable Directorial Note: Casey Nicholaw told us, "In previews friends will come up to you with suggestions and ideas to improve the show. And to those people you say…'Shut up!'"

Nicknames: I call Beth Leavel "Betty" and she calls me "J-So."

Embarrassing Moments: An actor, not named, performed an entire scene with his zipper down.

Unwelcome Co-Stars: Our theatre is right under one of the ballrooms of the Marriott Marquis Hotel. One night there was a conven-

tion upstairs and they started playing dance music really loudly during our power blackout scene. Here it was, the quietest moment in our show, and from upstairs you can hear Gloria Estefan!

Coolest Thing About Being in This Show: To listen each night and hear that it's still a surprise to us and to the audience. Also, the fact that we get out before every other Broadway show. That's really cool!

1. Curtain call on opening night, with Bob Martin at center.
2. Beth Leavel on opening night.
3. Cast member Danny Burstein with guest Rebecca Luker.
4. Eddie Korbich at Tavern on the Green.

Edward Albee's Seascape

First Preview: October 28, 2005. Opened: November 21, 2005.
Closed January 8, 2006 after 27 Previews and 55 Performances.

PLAYBILL®

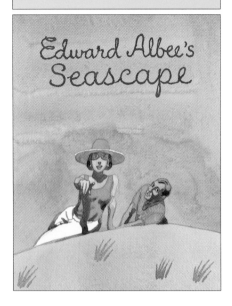

CAST

(in order of speaking)

Nancy .... FRANCES STERNHAGEN
Charlie .... GEORGE GRIZZARD
Leslie .... FREDERICK WELLER
Sarah .... ELIZABETH MARVEL

Assistant Stage Manager ...... ELIZABETH MILLER

UNDERSTUDIES

For Charlie – JACK DAVIDSON
For Nancy – JENNIFER HARMON
For Leslie – STEVE KAZEE
For Sarah – JENNIFER IKEDA

---

⑥ BOOTH THEATRE
222 West 45th Street
A Shubert Organization Theatre

Gerald Schoenfeld, *Chairman*   **Philip J. Smith,** *President*

Robert E. Wankel, *Executive Vice President*

LINCOLN CENTER THEATER
UNDER THE DIRECTION OF
André Bishop AND Bernard Gersten
PRESENTS

Edward Albee's Seascape

WITH (IN ALPHABETICAL ORDER)

George Grizzard   Elizabeth Marvel
Frances Sternhagen   Frederick Weller

SETS	COSTUMES	LIGHTING
Michael Yeargan	Catherine Zuber	Peter Kaczorowski

SOUND	MOVEMENT COORDINATOR
Aural Fixation	Rick Sordelet

STAGE MANAGER	CASTING	GENERAL PRESS AGENT
Michael McGoff	Daniel Swee	Philip Rinaldi

DIRECTOR OF DEVELOPMENT	DIRECTOR OF MARKETING
Hattie K. Jutagir	Linda Mason Ross

GENERAL MANAGER	PRODUCTION MANAGER
Adam Siegel	Jeff Hamlin

DIRECTED BY
Mark Lamos

LCT GRATEFULLY ACKNOWLEDGES AN EXTRAORDINARY GIFT FROM THE ESTATE OF EDITH K. EHRMAN.
AMERICAN AIRLINES IS THE OFFICIAL AIRLINE OF LINCOLN CENTER THEATER.
MERRILL LYNCH IS A 2005 LCT SEASON SPONSOR.

LCT WISHES TO EXPRESS ITS APPRECIATION TO THEATRE DEVELOPMENT FUND FOR ITS SUPPORT OF THIS PRODUCTION.

11/21/05

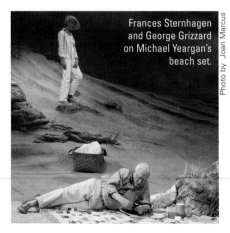

Frances Sternhagen and George Grizzard on Michael Yeargan's beach set.

Photo by Joan Marcus

George Grizzard
Charlie

Elizabeth Marvel
Sarah

Frances Sternhagen
Nancy

Frederick Weller
Leslie

Edward Albee's Seascape

Jack Davidson
Understudy for Charlie

Jennifer Harmon
Understudy for Nancy

Jennifer Ikeda
Understudy for Sarah

Steve Kazee
Understudy for Leslie

Edward Albee
Playwright

2005-2006 Award

DRAMA LEAGUE AWARD
Honored Previous Recipient
(Frances Sternhagen)

Mark Lamos
Director

Michael Yeargan
Sets

Catherine Zuber
Costumes

Peter Kaczorowski
Lighting

Guy Sherman
Aural Fixation
Sound

Rick Sordelet
Movement Coordinator

Baylen Thomas
Understudy for Leslie

BOX OFFICE
Rianna Bryceland

Photos by Ben Strothmann

STAGE CREW
(L-R): Brig Berney (Company Manager), Ronnie Burns Sr. (Head Electrician), Elizabeth Miller (Assistant Stage Manager), Rachel Zack (Production Assistant), Jimmy Keane (Prop Master), Brien Brannigan (Sound Operator), Nichole Amburg (Dresser), Kenny McDonough, Michael McGoff (Stage Manager) and Graeme McDonnell (Production Electrician).

Edward Albee's Seascape

FRONT OF HOUSE STAFF
(L-R): John Barbaretti, Bernadette Bokun, Frank Valdinoto, Nirmala Sharma, Teresa Aceves, Laurel Ann Wilson, Katherine Coscia, Jorge Velasquez and Chrissie Collins.

NOTE: The figure wearing a Santa Hat in the center is a bust of the theatre's namesake, Edwin Booth.

LINCOLN CENTER THEATER

ANDRÉ BISHOP	BERNARD GERSTEN
ARTISTIC DIRECTOR	EXECUTIVE PRODUCER

ADMINISTRATIVE STAFF

GENERAL MANAGER . . . . .ADAM SIEGEL
Associate General Manager . . . . .Melanie Weinraub
General Management Assistant . . . . .Beth Dembrow
Facilities Manager . . . . .Alex Mustelier
Assistant Facilities Manager . . . . .Michael Assalone
GENERAL PRESS AGENT . . . . .PHILIP RINALDI
Press Associate .Barbara Carroll
PRODUCTION MANAGER . . . . .JEFF HAMLIN
Associate Production Manager . . . . .Paul Smithyman
DIRECTOR OF
DEVELOPMENT . . . . .HATTIE K. JUTAGIR
Associate Director of Development . . . . . . .Rachel Norton
Manager of Special Events and
Young Patron Program . . . . .Karin Schall
Grants Writer . . . . .Neal Brilliant
Coordinator, Patron Program . . . . .Sheilaja Rao
Development Associate . . . . .Chris Chrzanowski
Assistant to the
Director of Development . . . . .Marsha Martinez
DIRECTOR OF FINANCE . . . . .DAVID S. BROWN
Controller . . . . .Susan Knox
Systems Manager .John N. Yen
Finance Assistant .Kellie Kroyer
DIRECTOR OF MARKETING . . . . . . .Linda Mason Ross
Marketing Associate . . . . .Denis Guerin
Marketing Assistant . . . . .Elizabeth Kandel
DIRECTOR OF EDUCATION . . . . . . .KATI KOERNER
Associate Director of Education . . . . .Dionne O'Dell
Assistant to the Executive Producer . . . . . .Barbara Hourigan
Office Assistant . . . . .Kenneth Collins
Messenger . . . . .Esau Burgess
Reception . . . . .Andrew Elsesser, Daryl
Watson

ARTISTIC STAFF

ASSOCIATE DIRECTORS . . . . . .GRACIELA DANIELE,
NICHOLAS HYTNER,
SUSAN STROMAN,
DANIEL SULLIVAN
DRAMATURG and DIRECTOR,
LCT DIRECTORS LAB . . . . .ANNE CATTANEO

CASTING DIRECTOR . . . . .DANIEL SWEE, CSA
MUSICAL THEATER
ASSOCIATE PRODUCER . . . . .IRA WEITZMAN
Artistic Administrator . . . . .Julia Judge
Casting Associate .Camille Hickman

In Loving Memory of
GERALD GUTIERREZ
Associate Director 1991-2003

SPECIAL SERVICES

Advertising . . . . .Serino-Coyne/
Jim Russek, Brad Lapin
Principal Poster Artist . . . . .James McMullan
Poster Art for *Edward Albee's Seascape* . . . . .James McMullan
Counsel . . . .Peter L. Felcher, Esq.; Charles H. Googe, Esq.;
and Rachel Hoover, Esq. of
Paul, Weiss, Rifkind, Wharton & Garrison
Immigration Counsel . . . . .Theodore Ruthizer,
Esq.;
Mark D. Koestler, Esq.
of Kramer, Levin, Naftalis & Frankel LLP
Auditor . . . . .Douglas Burack, C.P.A.
Lutz & Carr, L.L.P.
Insurance . . . . .Jennifer Brown of
DeWitt Stern Group
Photographer . . . . .Joan Marcus
Travel . . . . .Tygon Tours
Consulting Architect . . . . .Hugh
Hardy,
Hardy Holzman Pfeiffer Associates
Construction Manager . . . . .Yorke Construction
Payroll Service . . . . .Castellana Services, Inc.

STAFF FOR
EDWARD ALBEE'S SEASCAPE

COMPANY MANAGER . . . . .BRIG BERNEY
Assistant Director . . . . .Evan Cabnet
Fight Captain . . . . .Michael McGoff
Assistant to Mr. Albee . . . . .Jakob Holder
Assistant Set Designer . . . . .Mikiko Suzuki
Assistant Costume Designers . . . . .David Newell,
Michael Zecker
Assistant Lighting Designer . . . . .Hilary Manners
Associate Sound Designer . . . . .Tony Smolenski, IV
Assistant Sound Designer . . . . .Julie Pittman

---

Props . . . . .Faye Armon
Light Board Operator . . . . .Graeme McDonnell
Sound Operator . . . . .Brien Brannigan
Make-up Designer .Angelina Avallone
Wardrobe Supervisor . . . . .James Wilcox
Dresser . . . . .Nichole Amburg
Make-up and Hair . . . . .Susan Schectar
Assistant to the Director . . . . .Brendan Clifford
Production Assistant . . . . .Rachel Zack

Technical Supervision by
Walter Murphy and Patrick Merryman

CREDITS

Scenery constructed by Showman Fabricators, Inc., Long Island City, NY. Sound by Masque Sound. Costumes by Parsons-Meares. Lighting by PRG Lighting. Physical therapy provided by PhysioArts/Jennifer Green. Natural herb cough drops courtesy of Ricola USA, Inc.

 THE SHUBERT ORGANIZATION, INC.
Board of Directors

Gerald Schoenfeld	**Philip J. Smith**
Chairman	President
Wyche Fowler, Jr.	**John W. Kluge**
Lee J. Seidler	**Michael I. Sovern**

Stuart Subotnick

Robert E. Wankel
Executive Vice President

Peter Entin	**Elliot Greene**
Vice President -	Vice President -
Theatre Operations	Finance
David Andrews	**John Darby**
Vice President -	Vice President -
Shubert Ticketing Services	Facilities

House Manager . . . . .Laurel A. Wilson

Edward Albee's Seascape
SCRAPBOOK

Photos by Aubrey Reuben

Correspondent: Elizabeth Marvel, "Sarah."

Memorable Opening Night Gifts: Lizard-related paraphernalia in the form of mugs, plastic toys and shot glasses.

Most Exciting Celebrity Visitors: Paul Newman and Joanne Woodward.

Actor Who Has Done the Most Shows: Frannie Sternhagen.

Favorite Moment During Each Perfor-mance (Onstage or Off): Water break at intermission.

Mascot: Our hand puppet "Yips the Dog."

Favorite Therapy: Physical therapy two times a week.

Memorable Ad-Lib: George Grizzard's "Help me!"

Record Number of Cell Phone Rings During a Performance: Five.

Latest Audience Arrival: 8:35 p.m.

Who Wore the Heaviest/Hottest Costume: Elizabeth Marvel—pregnant in a lizard suit!

Who Wore the Least: George Grizzard.

Catchphrases Only the Company Would Recognize: "Sushi-cam."

Memorable Directorial Note: "When you quiver on top of her, you look like you're humping her tail."

Nicknames: Mark Lamos was "Butch." Edward Albee was "Eddie Scribblehands."

Ghostly Encounters Backstage: Strange female shrieking on two show days.

1. (L-R): Director Mark Lamos, playwright Edward Albee and leading man George Grizzard.
2. Frances Sternhagen arrives on opening night.
3. Frederick Weller and wife Ali at the opening night party at Tavern on the Green.
4. (L-R): Lincoln Center Theater alumni Alfred Uhry (*Parade*), Michael Berresse (*Light in the Piazza*) and Martha Clarke (*Belle Epoque*) are guests at the cast party.
5. Window card outside the Booth Theatre.

Photo by David Gewirtzman

Faith Healer

First Preview: April 18, 2006. Opened: May 4, 2006.
Still running as of May 31, 2006.

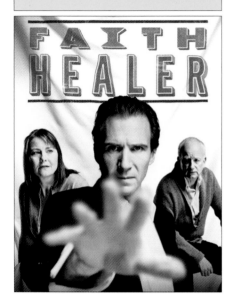

CAST
(in order of appearance)

Frank Hardy ....RALPH FIENNES
Grace Hardy ....CHERRY JONES
Teddy ....IAN McDIARMID

Part 1: Frank
Part 2: Grace
Part 3: Teddy
Part 4: Frank

STANDBYS

For Frank:
PATRICK BOLL

For Teddy:
JARLATH CONROY

For Grace:
ROBIN MOSELEY

*Ralph Fiennes and Ian McDiarmid are appearing with
the permission of Actors' Equity Association.*

2005-2006 Awards

Tony Award
Best Performance by a Featured Actor in a Play
(Ian McDiarmid)

Drama League Award
Honored Previous Recipient (Cherry Jones)

Theatre World Award
Outstanding Broadway Debut (Ian McDiarmid)

---

⑥ BOOTH THEATRE
222 West 45th Street
A Shubert Organization Theatre

Gerald Schoenfeld, *Chairman*   Philip J. Smith, *President*

Robert E. Wankel, *Executive Vice President*

Michael Colgan & Sonia Friedman Productions
The Shubert Organization   Robert Bartner   Roger Berlind
Scott Rudin   Spring Sirkin
present

Ralph Fiennes   Cherry Jones   Ian McDiarmid

in

the Gate Theatre Dublin production of

FAITH HEALER

by
Brian Friel

Set and Costume Design	Lighting Design	Sound Design
Jonathan Fensom	**Mark Henderson**	**Christopher Cronin**

Video Design	U.S. Casting	Production Stage Manager
Sven Ortel	**Jim Carnahan, C.S.A.**	**Jane Grey**

Production Management	Press Representative
Aurora Productions	**Barlow•Hartman**

General Management	Associate Producer
Stuart Thompson Productions/	**Lauren Doll**
James Triner	

Directed by
Jonathan Kent

LIVE BROADWAY

5/4/06

Ralph Fiennes
Photo by Anthony Woods

Cherry Jones
Photo by Joan Marcus

Ian McDiarmid
Photo by Joan Marcus

Faith Healer

Ralph Fiennes
Frank Hardy

Cherry Jones
Grace Hardy

Ian McDiarmid
Teddy

Patrick Boll
*Standby,
Frank Hardy*

Jarlath Conroy
Standby, Teddy

Robin Moseley
*Standby,
Grace Hardy*

Brian Friel
Playwright

Jonathan Kent
Director

Mark Henderson
Lighting Design

Christopher Cronin
Sound Design

Jim Carnahan
Casting

Stuart Thompson
Productions
General Manager

Michael Colgan
Artistic Director,
Dublin Gate
*Producer and
Original Presenter*

Sonia Friedman
Productions Ltd
Producer

Gerald Schoenfeld
Chairman,
The Shubert
Organization
Producer

Roger Berlind
Producer

Scott Rudin
Producer

Spring Sirkin
Producer

Lauren Doll
Producer

A photo of the Front of House staff for the Booth Theatre can be found in the chapter on Edward Albee's Seascape, *which played at the Booth just prior to* Faith Healer.

STAGE CREW
Kneeling (L-R):
Amanda Tramontazzi (Doorman), Jeffrey McGovney (Dresser), Sid King (Stage Manager), Mrs. James Kain (Wife of Production Propman).

Standing (L-R):
James Keane III (House Propman), Ronald Burns, Sr. (House Electrician), Brian McGarity (Production Electrician), Kenneth McDonough (House Carpenter), Jane Grey (Production Stage Manager), Sarah Kain (daughter of Production Propman), James Kain (Production Propman) and Kay Grunder (Wardrobe Mistress).

BOX OFFICE
Rianna Bryceland

Color photos by Ben Strothmann

Faith Healer

SCRAPBOOK

Correspondents: Jane Grey and Sid King, Stage Managers.

Memorable Opening Night Letter, Fax or Note: From the *History Boys* on opening night: "Ralph, Cherry and Ian—I think you will all go on and have careers after tonight."

Opening Night Gifts: Engraved *Faith Healer* bottle openers.

Which Actor Performed the Most Roles in This Show? Ralph Fiennes: 9 characters.

Special Backstage Rituals: Improvised song and dance numbers.

Favorite Snack Food: Jamesons!

Mascot: Buster, the Broadway Dog

Favorite Therapy: Jamesons, Ricola and Emer'gen-C.

Record Number of Cell Phone Rings During a Performance: 4!

Catchphrase Only the Company Would Recognize: "FANTASTIC!"

Photo by Ben Strothmann

(L-R): Director Jonathan Kent, Ian McDiarmid, Cherry Jones and Ralph Fiennes at the opening night party at the Bryant Park Grill.

STAFF CREDITS FOR *FAITH HEALER*

GENERAL MANAGEMENT
STUART THOMPSON PRODUCTIONS
Stuart Thompson Caroline Prugh James Triner

COMPANY MANAGER
Shawn M. Fertitta

GENERAL PRESS REPRESENTATIVE
BARLOW•HARTMAN
John Barlow   Michael Hartman
Dennis Crowley   Ryan Ratelle

PRODUCTION MANAGEMENT
AURORA PRODUCTIONS INC.
Gene O'Donovan W. Benjamin Heller II
Bethany Weinstein Hilary Austin Melissa Mazdra

Production Stage Manager	Jane Grey
Stage Manager	Sid King
Assistant to the Director	Will MacAdams
Associate Lighting Designer	Kristina Kloss
Production Electrician	Brian GF McGarity
Production Props	Jim Kane
Production Props Assistant	Donald "Buck" Roberts
Wardrobe Supervisor	Kay Grunder
Dresser	Jeff McGovney
Hair & Wig Supervisor	Cynthia Demand
Bob Bartner's Assistant	Mario Aiello
Assistant to Mr. Berlind	Jeffrey Hillock
Assistants to Mr. Rudin	Michael Diliberti, James P. Queen
Assistant to Ms. Sirkin	Annie Metheany-Pyle
General Management Assistant	Megan Curran
Management Intern	Jeremy Blocker

Press Associates	Leslie Baden, Jon Dimond, Carol Fineman, Bethany Larsen, Rick Miramontez, Gerilyn Shur, Andrew Snyder, Wayne Wolf
Banking	JP Morgan Chase/Michele Gibbons
Payroll	Castellana Services, Inc.
Accountant	Fried & Kowgios CPA's LLP/ Robert Fried, CPA
Controller	Joseph S. Kubala
Insurance	DeWitt Stern Group
Legal Counsel	Lazarus & Harris LLP/ Scott Lazarus, Esq., Robert C. Harris, Esq.
Opening Night Coordination	Tobak Lawrence Company/ Joanna B. Koondel, Suzanne Tobak
Advertising	SpotCo/Drew Hodges, Jim Edwards, Jim Aquino, Y. Darius Suyama
Production Photographer	Joan Marcus
Travel	Tzell Travel/Andi Henig
Immigration	Traffic Control Group, Inc.
Theatre Displays	King Displays, Inc.

Dialect Coach for Ms. Jones
Stephen Gabis

CREDITS
Scenery and scenic effects built and painted by Showmotion, Inc., Norwalk, CT. Scenic by Scenic Arts Studio, Inc. Fly automation, show control and finale effects by Showmotion, Inc., Norwalk, CT, using the AC2 computerized motion control system.

THE GATE THEATRE DUBLIN
Michael Colgan ....Director

Marie Rooney	Deputy Director
Teerth Chungh	Head of Production
Padraig Heneghan	Financial Controller

SONIA FRIEDMAN PRODUCTIONS
Sonia Friedman	Producer
Diane Benjamin	General Manager
Matthew Gordon	Associate Producer
Emily Merko	Production Assistant
Howard Panter, Rosemary Squire, Helen Enright	Board

 **THE SHUBERT ORGANIZATION, INC.**
Board of Directors

Gerald Schoenfeld	**Philip J. Smith**
Chairman	President
Wyche Fowler, Jr.	**John W. Kluge**
Lee J. Seidler	**Michael I. Sovern**

Stuart Subotnick
Robert E. Wankel
Executive Vice President

Peter Entin	**Elliot Greene**
Vice President - Theatre Operations	Vice President - Finance
David Andrews	**John Darby**
Vice President - Shubert Ticketing Services	Vice President - Facilities

House Manager ....Laurel A. Wilson

Festen

First Preview: March 23, 2006. Opened: April 9, 2006.
Closed May 20, 2006 after 20 Previews and 49 Performances.

PLAYBILL

FESTEN

CAST
(in order of appearance)

Christian	MICHAEL HAYDEN
Michael	JEREMY SISTO
Little Girl	MEREDITH LIPSON
	or RYAN SIMPKINS
Mette	CARRIE PRESTON
Lars	STEPHEN KUNKEN
Helene	JULIANNA MARGULIES
Else	ALI MacGRAW
Helge	LARRY BRYGGMAN
Pia	DIANE DAVIS
Helmut	CHRISTOPHER EVAN WELCH
Grandfather	JOHN CARTER
Poul	DAVID PATRICK KELLY
Kim	C.J. WILSON
Gbatokai	KEITH DAVIS

UNDERSTUDIES

For Christian, Michael, Helmut, Kim:
MICHAEL BAKKENSEN

For Helene, Else, Pia, Mette:
NATALIE GOLD

For Helge, Grandfather, Poul, Lars:
EDWARD JAMES HYLAND

For Gbatokai, Lars, Kim:
EZRA KNIGHT

THE MUSIC BOX
THE ESTATE OF IRVING BERLIN AND THE SHUBERT ORGANIZATION, OWNERS
239 W. 45th STREET

BILL KENWRIGHT and MARLA RUBIN
present
the ALMEIDA THEATRE PRODUCTION of

FESTEN

A dramatization by DAVID ELDRIDGE
Based on the DOGME film and play by
THOMAS VINTERBERG, MOGENS RUKOV and BO HR. HANSEN

LARRY MICHAEL ALI
BRYGGMAN HAYDEN MACGRAW

JULIANNA JEREMY
MARGULIES SISTO

DAVID PATRICK CARRIE CHRISTOPHER EVAN
KELLY PRESTON WELCH

JOHN DIANE KEITH STEPHEN MEREDITH RYAN C.J.
CARTER DAVIS DAVIS KUNKEN LIPSON SIMPKINS WILSON

Costumes by	Lighting by	Music by	Sound by
JOAN WADGE	JEAN KALMAN	ORLANDO GOUGH	PAUL ARDITTI

Casting by	Press Representatives	Fight Director
JIM CARNAHAN, CSA	THE PUBLICITY OFFICE	TERRY KING

Technical Supervisor	General Management	Production Stage Manager
LARRY MORLEY	ALAN WASSER ASSOCIATES	MICHAEL MCGOFF
	JIM BRANDEBERRY	

Directed by	Designed by
RUFUS NORRIS	IAN MACNEIL

The producers wish to express their appreciation to
Theatre Development Fund for its support of this production

LIVE BROADWAY

4/9/06

The company prepares for a birthday party none will ever forget.

Photo by Joan Marcus

Festen

Larry Bryggman
Helge

Michael Hayden
Christian

Ali MacGraw
Else

Julianna Margulies
Helene

Jeremy Sisto
Michael

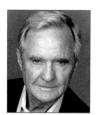

Michael Bakkensen
*Understudy for
Christian, Michael,
Helmut, Kim*

John Carter
Grandfather

Diane Davis
Pia

Keith Davis
Gbatokai

Natalie Gold
*Understudy for
Helene, Else, Pia,
Mette*

Edward James Hyland
*Understudy for
Helge, Grandfather,
Poul, Lars*

David Patrick Kelly
Poul

Ezra Knight
*Understudy for
Gbatokai, Lars, Kim*

Stephen Kunken
Lars

Meredith Lipson
Little Girl

Carrie Preston
Mette

Ryan Simpkins
Little Girl

Christopher Evan
Welch
Helmut

C. J. Wilson
Kim

David Eldridge
Playwright

Thomas Vinterberg
*Dogme Original Film/
Play*

Mogens Rukov
*Dogme Original Film/
Play*

Bo Hr. Hansen
*Dogme Original Film/
Play*

Rufus Norris
Director

Ian MacNeil
Set Design

Joan Wadge
Costume Design

Jean Kalman
Lighting Design

Jim Carnahan
Casting

Alan Wasser
Associates
General Manager

Bill Kenwright
Producer

BOX OFFICE
(L-R): Michael Taustine
(Treasurer) and
Robert Kelly (Head
Treasurer)

Photo by Ben Strothmann

Festen

STAGE CREW
Front Row (L-R):
Lee Iwanski (House Electrician),
Michael McGoff (Production Stage
Manager), Kristen Sauter (Wardrobe),
Richard C. Rauscher (Stage Manager),
Bill Lewis (Production Sound),
Brig Berney (Company Manager).

Back Row (L-R):
Candi Adams (Publicity),
Jerry Marshall (Production Props),
Michael Taylor (Electrics),
Dennis Maher (House Carpenter), and
Brian Maher (Fly Automation)

STAFF FOR *FESTEN*

GENERAL MANAGEMENT
ALAN WASSER ASSOCIATES
Alan Wasser   Allan Williams
Jim Brandeberry

GENERAL PRESS REPRESENTATION
THE PUBLICITY OFFICE
Bob Fennell   Marc Thibodeau
Candi Adams   Michael S. Borowski

COMPANY MANAGER
Brig Berney

TECHNICAL SUPERVISOR
Larry Morley

Associate Costume Designer	**Mitchell Bloom**
Associate Lighting Designer	**Fiona Simpson**
Associate Sound Designer	**Christopher Cronin**
Fight Coordinator	**Michael G. Chin**

Production Stage Manager	**Michael McGoff**
Stage Manager	**Richard C. Rauscher**

FOR BILL KENWRIGHT LTD.
Managing Director ....Bill Kenwright

NEW YORK
Associate Producer ....Dante Di Loreto
Assistant Marketing Manager ....Sarah Swanson

LONDON
Finance Director ....Guy Williams
Associate Producers ....Julius Green, Tom Siracusa
Marketing Manager ....Steve Potts
Production Manager ....David Stothard
Head of Touring ....Jamie Clark
Marketing Executives ....Rich Major, Julia Bailey
Graphic Designer ....Reg Schlieger
Production Executive ....David Bingham
Production Asst./Office Mgr. ....Geraldine Mackey
Production Assistant (Technical) ....Zoe Caldwell
Systems Co-ordinator (Marketing) ....John Collings
Systems Co-ordinator (Office) .....Patrick Crichton-Stuart
PA to the Marketing Manager ....Amy Taylor
Management Accountant ....Halyna Dyszkant
Senior Accountant ....Margaret Frame

Cost Accountant ....Kit Liu
Accounts Assistant ....Lesley-Anne Williams
PA to Bill Kenwright ....Emma Tyson
Theatre Consultant ....Rod H. Coton

Production Electrician ....Jeff Turner
Production Property ....Jerry Marshall
Production Sound ....Bill Lewis
Wardrobe Supervisor ....Rob Bevenger
Dressers ....Sandy Binion, Kristen Sauter
Wardrobe Day Work ....David Marquez
Vocal Coach ....Deborah Hecht
Fight Captain ....Michael McGoff
General Management Associates ....Thom Mitchell,
Aaron Lustbader
Press Intern ....Matt Fasano
Production Assistants ....Wesley Apfel, J.B McLendon,
Jamie Thoma
Immigration Lawyer ....Shannon K. Such
Insurance ....DeWitt Stern Group/
Peter Shoemaker
Banking ....JP Morgan Chase/
Richard Callian and Michele Gibbons
Accounting ......FK Partners/Fried & Kowglos CPAs, LLP
Robert Fried, Anne Stewart FitzRoy
Travel ....Road Rebel Entertainment
Payroll Service ....Castellana Services Inc.
Rehearsal Studio ....New 42nd Street Studios
Children's Chaperones ....Brooke Engen,
Tiffany Engen
Children's Tutor ....On Location Education/
Muriel Kester
Advertising..........................Eliran-Murphy Group/
Jon Bierman
Logo Art ....Dewynters & Fraver/EMG
Marketing ....Hugh Hysell Communications
Web Designer ....David Risley/Pygmalion Designs
Theatre Displays ....King Displays
Production Photographer ....Joan Marcus

CREDITS
Scenery constructed by Showman Fabricators, Inc., Long
Island City, NY. Computer motion control and automation
of scenery and rigging by Showman Fabricators, Inc.
Lighting equipment supplied by PRG Lighting. Sound
equipment supplied by PRG Audio. China provided by the
Homer Laughlin Co. Stemware provided by Cristal
D'Arques. Flatware provided by Oneida. Tabletop accessories provided by Michael C. Fina. Ricola natural herb
cough drops courtesy of Ricola USA, Inc. Coutts and Co.
were the original sponsor of *Festen* in London. *Festen* family
portrait taken at the New 42nd Street Studios.

SPECIAL THANKS
Maureen Sullivan,
Jen Green,
Physio Arts,
The Algonquin Hotel,
Dr. Judy Alpert,
Mud, Sweat & Tears

STAFF FOR THE MUSIC BOX THEATRE
HOUSE MANAGER ....Jonathan Shulman
Box Office Treasurer ....Robert D. Kelly
Assistant Treasurers ....Michael Taustine,
Brendan Berberich,
Victoria Radolinski
House Carpenter ....Dennis Maher
House Electrician ....F. Lee Iwanski
House Propertyman ....Kim Garnett
Chief of Staff ....Dennis Scanlon
Accountant ....William C. Grother

THE SHUBERT ORGANIZATION, INC.
Board of Directors

Gerald Schoenfeld   **Philip J. Smith**
Chairman   President

Wyche Fowler, Jr.   **John W. Kluge**

Lee J. Seidler   **Michael I. Sovern**

Stuart Subotnick

Robert E. Wankel
Executive Vice President

Peter Entin   **Elliot Greene**
Vice President -   Vice President -
Theatre Operations   Finance

David Andrews   **John Darby**
Vice President -   Vice President -
Shubert Ticketing Services   Facilities

Festen
SCRAPBOOK

1. Ali MacGraw arrives at the Music Box Theatre on opening night.
2. (L-R): Carrie Preston, Stephen Kunken, Diane Davis, Christopher Evan Welch at the opening night party at Tavern on the Green.
3. Lily Rabe (R) with mom, Jill Clayburgh, on opening night.
4. Meredith Lipson (L) and Ryan Simpkins at Tavern on the Green.

Correspondent: Stephen Kunken, "Lars"

Memorable Opening Night Letters, Faxes or Note: A photo of the entire British national tour company of *Festen* in costume on stage, toasting it's American counterparts. It was decided that upon our closing the American company would return a photo of our company flipping them the bird. (Strangely enough, it was our director's idea.)

Memorable Opening Night Gifts: Julianna's silver engraved necklaces for each company member. Jeremy Sisto's framed art panorama photo from rehearsal. Carrie Preston's DVD movie of behind the scenes footage. The entire movie was put to the hip-hop remaster of our director singing "The Big Old Teddy Bear." Bent fork sculptures from Rufus.

Gypsy of the Year Sketch: We felt that molestation dramas shouldn't field Gypsy sketches. Strangely the same policy did not hold true for softball.

Which Actor Performed the Most Roles in the Show: All actors were cast in only one role. The understudies each had to cover at least 2 and as many as 5. Way to go Natalie, Ezra, Michael, and Ed.

Who Has Done the Most Shows: Although all actors have done the same amount of shows, I'd give the edge to Michael Hayden who often performed the entire text in the shower.

Special Backstage Rituals: C.J. Wilson and Stephen Kunken's plate-smashing offstage silent theater sketch. David Patrick Kelley became a frequent guest artist in the show and Ali MacGraw, Larry Bryggman, and John Carter always the audience. Also, Larry Bryggman's famous and nightly intermission fishbowl full of Peanut M&M's giveaway.

Favorite Moment During Each Performance: Too many to choose. The Congas were up there, but Larry Bryggman's café speech (in all of its manifestations) was easily the most fun.

Favorite In-Theater Hangout: Warming up onstage before shows. The understudy/greenroom. Close second….around the cool and always stocked refrigerator in Stephen and Chris' room.

Favorite Off-Site Hangout: Bar Centrale. Angus McIndoe. West Side Sushi.

Mascot: Biscuit (terrier mix)—owner C.J. Wilson; Winston (King Charles Spaniel)—owner J. Sisto; Stella (black pug)—owner Stephen Kunken; Ty Simpkins (small child)—owner The Simpkins family.

Favorite Therapy: A filthy, dirty, tawdry Martini at Bar Centrale.

Snack Food: We all had to eat a full chicken dinner on stage in each performance. Snack Food?!?

Memorable Ad-Libs: Oh so many wonderous ones to choose from. Let's see...

AD LIB followed by *REAL LINE* in italics

"Michael you don't impress me as much of a large member"

"Michael you don't impress me as much of a lodge brother"

Perhaps tonight you can keep your fans to yourself.

Perhaps tonight you can keep your hands to yourself.

Are you CRAYNUTS? I'm not wearing these shoes to a dinner party.

Are you Nuts? I'm not wearing these shoes to a dinner party.

"We were all ready to fill these rooms with our music."

"We were all ready to fill these room with our laughter."

"To your brother…to MICHAEL"

"To your brother…to CHRISTIAN"

Michael and Linda were thrilled. And Christian…and Linda. Christian and Linda were also thrilled.

Christian and Linda were thrilled.

Record Number of Cell Phone Rings: Three.

Fastest Costume Change: Jeremy Sisto getting into his tuxedo. So fast it happened on stage during the singing of "It's Daddy's birthday."

Memorable Directorial Note: Director: "Okay, I know we all know that the press is all out there tonight so…."

Cast Member: "I didn't. Thanks for letting me know."

Fiddler on the Roof

First Preview: January 23, 2004. Opened: February 26, 2004.
Closed January 8, 2006 after 36 Previews and 781 Performances.

CAST

Tevye's Family:

Tevye	HARVEY FIERSTEIN
Golde	ROSIE O'DONNELL
Tzeitel	SALLY MURPHY
Hodel	LAURA SHOOP
Chava	TRICIA PAOLUCCIO
Shprintze	ALISON WALLA
Bielke	HANNAH DelMONTE

Yente, the Matchmaker .... NANCY OPEL

Papas

Lazar Wolf	DAVID WOHL
Rabbi	GEORGE BARTENIEFF
Mordcha	PHILIP HOFFMAN
Avram	NEAL BENARI
Jakov	MITCHELL JARVIS
Chaim	BRUCE WINANT

Mamas

Shandel	LORI WILNER
Mirala	ANN VAN CLEAVE
Fredel	DANA LYNN CARUSO
Rivka	JOY HERMALYN

Sons

Motel	MICHAEL THERRIAULT
Perchik	PAUL ANTHONY STEWART
Mendel	CHRIS GHELFI
Yussel	ENRIQUE BROWN
Yitzuk	RANDY BOBISH
Label	JEFF LEWIS
Shloime	FRANCIS TOUMBAKARIS

Daughters

Anya	JENNIFER BABIAK
Surcha	HAVILAND STILLWELL

Nachum, the Beggar .... JASON LACAYO

Fiddler ...... CHRISTOPHER PERRY CARDONA

Continued on next page

MINSKOFF THEATRE

UNDER THE DIRECTION OF
JAMES M. NEDERLANDER, JAMES L. NEDERLANDER,
SARA MINSKOFF ALLAN AND THE MINSKOFF FAMILY

JAMES L. NEDERLANDER
STEWART F. LANE/BONNIE COMLEY   HARBOR ENTERTAINMENT
TERRY ALLEN KRAMER   BOB BOYETT/LAWRENCE HOROWITZ   CLEAR CHANNEL ENTERTAINMENT

PRESENT

Harvey Fierstein

in

Also Starring

Rosie O'Donnell

Based on the Sholom Aleichem stories by special permission of Arnold Perl

Book by	Music by	Lyrics by
Joseph Stein	**Jerry Bock**	**Sheldon Harnick**

Choreography by and Original New York Stage Production Directed by

Jerome Robbins

Originally Produced on the New York Stage by Harold Prince

also starring

Christopher Perry Cardona   Patrick Heusinger   Philip Hoffman   Sally Murphy   Tricia Paoluccio
Richard Poe   Laura Shoop   Paul Anthony Stewart   Michael Therriault   David Wohl
George Bartenieff   Neal Benari   Hannah DelMonte   Chris Ghelfi   Jason Lacayo   Alison Walla
Jennifer Babiak   Randy Bobish   Shane Braddock   Enrique Brown   Kristin Carbone   Dana Lynn Caruso
Rachel Coloff   Craig D'Amico   Joy Hermalyn   Mitchell Jarvis   Jeff Lewis   Alphonse Paolillo
Roger Rosen   Daniel Rudin   Haviland Stillwell   Michael Tommer   Francis Toumbakaris
Ann Van Cleave   Robert Wersinger   Lori Wilner   Bruce Winant   Gustavo Wons   Adam Zotovich

and

Nancy Opel

Set Design	Costume Design	Lighting Design	Sound Design
Tom Pye	**Vicki Mortimer**	**Brian MacDevitt**	**Acme Sound Partners**

Hair & Wig Design	Casting by	Music Coordinator	Orchestrations	Additional Orchestrations
David Brian Brown	**Jim Carnahan**	**Michael Keller**	**Don Walker**	**Larry Hochman**

General Manager	Press Agent	Production Manager	Flying Sequences	Production Stage Manager
101 Productions, Ltd.	**Barlow•Hartman**	**Gene O'Donovan**	**ZFX, Inc.**	**Katherine Lee Boyer**

Music Director
Kevin Stites

Musical Staging by
Jonathan Butterell

Directed by

David Leveaux

9/26/05

Harvey Fierstein and
Rosie O'Donnell

Photo by Carol Rosegg

Fiddler on the Roof

MUSICAL NUMBERS

Cast Continued

ACT ONE

"Tradition" ....Full Company

"Matchmaker" ....Tzeitel, Hodel, Chava, Shprintze, Bielke

"If I Were a Rich Man" ....Tevye

"Sabbath Prayer" ....Family and Villagers

"To Life" ....Tevye, Lazar, Fyedka, Village Men

"Miracle of Miracles" ....Motel

"Tevye's Dream" ....Full Company

"Sunrise, Sunset" ....Family and Villagers

ACT TWO

"Now I Have Everything" ....Perchik, Hodel

"Do You Love Me?" ....Tevye, Golde

"Topsy-Turvy" ....Yente, Rivka and Mirala

"Far From the Home I Love" ....Hodel

"Chavaleh" ....Tevye

"Anatevka" ....Family and Villagers

Boy (Tues. – Sat. eves., Sat. mat.) ....
MICHAEL TOMMER
Boy (Wed. and Sun. mats.) ....
ALPHONSE PAOLILLO
Constable ....RICHARD POE
Russians
  Fyedka ....PATRICK HEUSINGER
  Sasha ....ADAM ZOTOVICH
  Vladek ....CRAIG D'AMICO
  Vladimir ....ROBERT WERSINGER
  Boris ....SHANE BRADDOCK
Grandma Tzeitel ....HAVILAND STILLWELL
Fruma Sarah ....JOY HERMALYN
Bottle Dancers ....RANDY BOBISH,
ENRIQUE BROWN,
CHRIS GHELFI, JEFF LEWIS,
FRANCIS TOUMBAKARIS

SWINGS
KRISTIN CARBONE, RACHEL COLOFF,
ROGER ROSEN, GUSTAVO WONS

UNDERSTUDIES
For Tevye:
NEAL BENARI, PHILIP HOFFMAN
For Golde:
ANN VAN CLEAVE, LORI WILNER
For Yente:
RACHEL COLOFF, LORI WILNER
For Tzeitel:
KRISTIN CARBONE, DANA LYNN CARUSO
For Hodel:
DANA LYNN CARUSO,
HAVILAND STILLWELL
For Chava:
JENNIFER BABIAK, ALISON WALLA
For Shprintze/Bielke:
JENNIFER BABIAK, HAVILAND STILLWELL
For Motel:
MITCHELL JARVIS, JEFF LEWIS
For Perchik:
RANDY BOBISH, MITCHELL JARVIS
For Fyedka:
SHANE BRADDOCK, ROBERT WERSINGER
For Lazar Wolf:
NEAL BENARI, PHILIP HOFFMAN
For Constable: NEAL BENARI, BRUCE WINANT
For Fiddler: GUSTAVO WONS
For Rabbi: BRUCE WINANT
For Mendel: RANDY BOBISH, ROGER ROSEN
For Mordcha: BRUCE WINANT
For Avram: RANDY BOBISH, ROGER ROSEN
For Boy:
ALPHONSE PAOLILLO, DANIEL RUDIN
For Nachum:
GUSTAVO WONS, ROGER ROSEN

Dance Captain ....ROGER ROSEN

ORCHESTRA

Conductor: KEVIN STITES
Associate Conductor: Charles duChateau

Music Coordinator: Michael Keller
Onstage Clarinet Solo: Jonathan Levine

Concertmaster: Martin Agee
Violins: Cenovia Cummins, Conrad Harris,
Heidi Stubner, Entcho Todorov
Violas: Debra Shufelt, Maxine Roach
Cellos: Peter Sachon, Charles duChateau
Lead Trumpet: Tim Schadt
Trumpets: Wayne duMaine, Joseph Reardon
Trombones/Euphonium: Ben Harrington
Flute: Brian Miller
Oboe: Matthew Dine
Clarinet/Flute: Jonathan Levine
Clarinet/Flute: Martha Hyde
Bassoon: Marc Goldberg
French Horns: Larry DiBello, Peter Schoettler
Drums/Percussion: Billy Miller
Bass: Peter Donovan
Accordion/Celeste: Elaine Lord
Guitar/Mandolin/Lute: Greg Utzig

Harvey Fierstein as Tevye
and Rosie O'Donnell
as Golde.

Photo by Carol Rosegg

SETTING
The Place:
Anatevka, a village in Russia

The Time:
1905, on the eve of the revolutionary period

Fiddler on the Roof

Harvey Fierstein
Tevye

Rosie O'Donnell
Golde

Nancy Opel
Yente

George Bartenieff
Rabbi

Neal Benari
Avram

Christopher Perry
Cardona
Fiddler

Hannah DelMonte
Bielke

Chris Ghelfi
Mendel

Patrick Heusinger
Fyedka

Philip Hoffman
Mordcha

Jason Lacayo
Nachum

Sally Murphy
Tzeitel

Tricia Paoluccio
Chava

Richard Poe
Constable

Laura Shoop
Hodel

Paul Anthony Stewart
Perchik

Michael Therriault
Motel

Alison Walla
Shprintze

David Wohl
Lazar Wolf

Jennifer Babiak
Anya

Randy Bobish
Yitzuk/Bottle Dancer

Shane Braddock
*Boris/Russian
Dancer*

Enrique Brown
Yussel/Bottle Dancer

Kristin Carbone
Swing

Dana Lynn Caruso
Fredel

Rachel Coloff
Swing

Craig D'Amico
*Vladek/
Russian Dancer*

Joy Hermalyn
Fruma Sarah/Rivka

Mitchell Jarvis
Jakov

Jeff Lewis
Label/Bottle Dancer

Alphonse Paolillo
Boy Understudy

Roger Rosen
Swing

Daniel Rudin
Boy Understudy

Haviland Stillwell
*Surcha/
Grandma Tzeitel*

Michael Tommer
Boy

Fiddler on the Roof

Francis Toumbakaris
Shloime/
Bottle Dancer

Ann Van Cleave
Mirala

Robert Wersinger
Vladimir/
Russian Dancer

Lori Wilner
Shandel

Bruce Winant
Chaim

Gustavo Wons
Swing

Adam Zotovich
Sasha/
Russian Dancer

David Leveaux
Director

Joseph Stein
Book

Jerry Bock
Music

Sheldon Harnick
Lyrics

Jerome Robbins
Choreographer/
Original Director

Tom Pye
Scenic Design

Brian MacDevitt
Lighting Design

Tom Clark, Mark Menard, and Nevin Steinberg/
Acme Sound Partners
Sound Design

David Brian Brown
Wig/Hair Design

Michael Keller
Music Coordinator

Paul Rubin
Flying Effects

Gustavo Zajac
Associate
Musical Staging

Jim Carnahan
Casting

James L. Nederlander
Producer

Stewart F. Lane/
Bonnie Comley
Producers

David Broser and Aaron Harnick,
Harbor Entertainment
Producers

Terry Allen Kramer
Producer

Bob Boyett
Producer

Fiddler on the Roof

Alumni 2005-2006

David Best
Boy
(Wednesday and
Sunday matinees)

Ward Billeisen
Vladek

Melissa Bohon
Anya/Bielke

Yusef Bulos
Rabbi

Molly Ephraim
Bielke

Betsy Hogg
Bielke

Leah Horowitz
Shandel/Swing

Anne Letscher
Anya

Mark Lotito
Avram

Andrea Martin
Golde

Janet Metz
Fruma Sarah/Rivka

Mark Moreau
Vladek/Swing

David Rossmer
Jakov

Elena Shaddow
Grandma
Tzeitel/Surcha

Tom Titone
Nachum/Swing

Entcho Todorov
Understudy Fiddler

Transfer Students 2005-2006

Stephen Lee Anderson
Constable

Melissa Bohon
Swing

Jacob Fischel
Motel

Rita Harvey
Hodel/Fredel

Gina Lamparella
Tzeitel

Fiddler on the Roof

WARDROBE AND HAIR DEPARTMENT
(L-R): "Suli"Hilda Garcia-Suli (Dresser), Tree Sarvay (Dresser), Theresa DiStasi, (Dresser), Joel Hawkins (Hair Supervisor), Wendall Goings (Assistant Wardrobe Supervisor), Maria Goya (Dresser), Jodi Jackson (Assistant Hair Supervisor), Timothy Greer (Wardrobe Supervisor) and Dawn E. Reynolds (Dresser).

COMPANY MANAGEMENT
(L-R): Gregg Arst (Company Manager) and Alex Gushin (Assistant Company Manager).

STAGE MANAGEMENT
(L-R): Jon Krause (Stage Manager), Jenny Dewar (Production Stage Manager) and Andrea Saraffian (Assistant Stage Manager).

STAGE CREW
(L-R): Erik Yans (Assistant Carpenter), Jeff Lunsford (Assistant Carpenter), Matt Lavaia (House Props), Jason Volpe (Automation), Kenny Brock, Tommy Richards, Frank Lavaia, Bob Adams (Production Props Supervisor), Steve Speer (Assistant House Electrician), Dave Lynch (Spot Operator), Mike Lynch (House Electrician), Rob Brenner (Assistant Props), Sean McMann, Don McKennan and Brad Gyorgak (Sound).

Photo by Ben Strothmann

Fiddler on the Roof

ORCHESTRA

Back Row (L-R): Maxine Roach (Viola), Martha Hyde (Clarinet/Flute), Billy Miller (Drums/ Percussion)
Middle Row (L-R): Adria Benjamin (Viola), Elaine Lord (Accordion/Celeste), Wayne duMaine (Trumpet), Heidi Stubner (Violin), Martin Agee (Concertmaster), Charles duChateau (Associate Conductor)
Front (L-R): Brian Miller (Flute) and Ben Harrington (Trombones/Euphonium).

Not Pictured: Kevin Stites (Conductor), Michael Keller (Music Coordinator), Jonathan Levine (Onstage Clarinet Solo/Clarinet/Flute), Cenovia Cummins (Violin), Conrad Harris (Violin), Entcho Todorov (Violin), Debra Shufelt (Viola), Peter Sachon (Cello), Tim Schadt (Lead Trumpet), Joseph Reardon (Trumpet), Matthew Dine (Oboe), Marc Goldberg (Bassoon), Larry DiBello (French Horn), Peter Schoettler (French Horn), Peter Donovan (Bass) and Greg Utzig (Guitar/Mandolin/Lute).

BOX OFFICE
(L-R): Tom Buda and Mike Kane.

Photos by Ben Strothmann

FRONT OF HOUSE STAFF
Standing (L-R): David Vaughn (House Manager), Christine Doyle, Judy Pirouz, Joanne Shannon, Elaine Healey, Joseph Melchiorre, Cheryl Budd, Chris Quartana (Assistant House Manager), Geraldine White, Marion Mooney, Alexis Garcia.

Sitting (L-R): Meryl Rosner, Martin Werner, Florence Coulter, Jason Burgos and Caryl Metneri.

Fiddler on the Roof

STAFF FOR *FIDDLER ON THE ROOF*

GENERAL MANAGEMENT
101 PRODUCTIONS, LTD.
Wendy Orshan   Jeffrey M. Wilson
David Auster

COMPANY MANAGER
Gregg Arst

GENERAL PRESS REPRESENTATIVE
BARLOW•HARTMAN
John Barlow   Michael Hartman
Wayne Wolfe   Andrew Snyder

PRODUCTION MANAGEMENT
Aurora Productions, Inc.
Gene O'Donovan
Melissa Mazdra   Tony Menditto
W. Benjamin Heller II

CASTING
Jim Carnahan, CSA
J.V. Mercanti, Associate

Production Stage Manager ....Katherine Lee Boyer
Stage Manager ....Jenny Dewar
Assistant Stage Manager ....Jon Krause
Assistant Company Manager ....Alex Gushin

ASSOCIATE MUSICAL STAGING ..GUSTAVO ZAJAC

Assistant Director ....Eli Gonda
Choreographic Consultant ....Newton Cole
Dance Captain ....Roger Rosen
Dialect Coach ....Kate Wilson
Associate Scenic Designer ....Larry Gruber
First Assistant Scenic Designer ....Dawn Robyn Petrilk
Assistant Scenic Designers ....John Deegan,
Todd Potter, Amy Smith
Assistants to Mr. Pye ....Alan Bain, Gaetane Bertol,
Daniela Galli, Joanie Schlafer
Associate Costume Designer ....Tracy L. Christensen
Assistant Costume Designers ....Lynette Mauro,
Brian J. Bustos, Amy Clark
Assistant to Ms. Mortimer ....Courtney Logan
Costume Intern ....Jennifer Fischer
Assistant Lighting Designers ....Charles Pennebaker,
Anne E. McMills
Moving Light Programmer ....David Arch
Assistant to Mr. MacDevitt ....Jennifer Schriever
Assistant Sound Designer ....Jeffrey Yoshi Lee

MAKEUP DESIGNER ..RANDY HOUSTON MERCER

Production Carpenter ....Hank Hale
Assistant Carpenters ....Donald "Buck" Roberts,
Jeff Lunsford
Automation ....Jason Volpe
Production Electrician ....Michael S. LoBue
Head Electrician ....Ron L. Martin
Assistant Electrician ....Brian Collins

Production Props Supervisor ....Robert G. Adams
Assistant Props ....Robert H. Brenner
Props Researcher/Purchaser ....Kathy Fabian
Assistant Props Researcher ....Eliza Brown
Production Sound Supervisor ....Scott Sanders
Sound ....Brad Gyorgak
Wardrobe Supervisor ....Timothy Greer
Assistant Wardrobe Supervisor ....Wendall Goings
Mr. Fierstein's Dresser ....Charlie Catanese
Ms. O'Donnell's Dresser ....Bobby Pearce
Dressers ....James Cavanaugh,
Jackie S. Freeman, Hilda Garcia-Suli,
Maria Goya, Victoria Grecki, William Jones,
Dawn Reynolds, Tree Sarvay, Kelly Smith
Hair Supervisor ....Richard Orton
Assistant Hair Supervisor ....Joel Hawkins
Additional
Music Copying ....Emily Grishman Music Preparation/
Katherine Edmonds, Emily Grishman
Incidental Music Arrangements ....Kevin Stites
Rehearsal Pianists ....Brad Garside, Paul Raiman,
Matthew Eisenstein
Production Assistants ....Jeff Cureton,
Karyn Meek, James Valletti
Assistants to Mr. Lane & Ms. Comley .....Jeanine Holiday,
Diane Prince
Assistant to Mr. Broser & Mr. Harnick ....Lisa Lapan
Harbor Entertainment thanks ....Josh Kagan,
Barry Funt, Robert Bertsch,
Jeff Ostrow of URL Productions,
Eric Brown, Rufus Collins, Steve Herz
Assistant to Ms. Kramer ....Sara Shannon
Assistant to Mr. Boyett ....Diane Murphy
Assistant to Dr. Horowitz ....Don Schnagl
Legal Counsel ....Levine, Plotkin & Menin LLP/
Loren Plotkin, Susan Mindell
Accountant ....Rosenberg, Neuwirth & Kuchner/
Chris Cacace, Pat Pedersen
Advertising ....Serino-Coyne/
Angelo Desimini, Jennifer Fleckner
101 Productions Ltd. ....Katharine Croke,
Clark Mims, Heidi Neven,
Mary Six Rupert, Aaron Slavik,
John Vennema
101 Intern ....Laura Dickinson
Press Associates ....Leslie Baden, Dennis
Crowley,
Jon Dimond, Carol Fineman,
Rick Miramontez, Ryan Ratelle
Press Office Manager ....Bethany Larsen
Production Photographer ....Carol Rosegg
Banking ....JP Morgan Chase/
Stephanie Dalton, Michele Gibbons
Insurance ....DeWitt Stern, Inc./
Peter Shoemaker, Jennifer Brown
Travel ....Altour International, Inc./
Melissa Casal
Housing ....Maison International/
Marie Claire Martineau
Children's Tutoring ....On Location Education/
Marsha Kobre Anderson, Ph.D.
Children's Guardians ....Martin
Tommer,

Maria Paolillo, Ellen Rudin
Theatre Displays ....King Displays, Inc.
Concessions ....SFX Theatrical Merchandising/
Larry Turk
Payroll Services ....Castellana Services, Inc.
Promotional Merchandising ....George Fenmore/
More Merchandising International

CREDITS

Scenery by Hudson Scenic Studio, Inc. Lighting equipment from Fourth Phase. Sound equipment from ProMix. Flying sequences provided by ZFX, Inc. Costume construction by Tricorne, Barbara Matera, Ltd., Carlos Campos and Grace Costume. Millinery by Lynne Mackey. Custom footwear by J.C. Theatrical and handmade shoes by Fred Longtin. Custom knitwear by Jeff Blumenkrantz and Vanessa Hopkins. Craftwork for the Dream by Marian J. Hose and Arnold Levine. Musician costumes constructed by Michael-Jon Costumes and Scafati. Percussion instruments by Kettles & Co. Emer'gen-C super energy booster provided by Alacer Corp. Ricola products used. Additional set and hand props courtesy of George Fenmore, Inc. In St. Petersburg, thanks to Alexey Korovin and the Pine Studio Vendors: Peter Molchanov, Peter Sirota and Igor Diakov. Costume designer's thanks to Tara L. Hawkes, Kaufman Army/Navy, Helen Uffner, Bec Chippendale, Stephen Merkel, Cosprop and Trouvaille Francaise. Havdala Candles provided by the Judaica House, Ltd., Teaneck, NJ. Light bulbs courtesy of Just Bulbs, the lightbulb store. Milk products generously donated by Parmalot.

Make-up provided by
M•A•C

Chairman ....**James M. Nederlander**	
President ....**James L. Nederlander**	

Executive Vice President
Nick Scandalios

Vice President	Senior Vice President
Corporate Development	Labor Relations
Charlene S. Nederlander	**Herschel Waxman**

Vice President	Chief Financial Officer
Jim Boese	**Freida Sawyer Belviso**

HOUSE STAFF FOR THE MINSKOFF THEATRE

House Manager ....David Vaughn
Treasurer ....Nicholas Loiacono
Assistant Treasurer ....Cheryl Loiacono
House Carpenter ....Gary Bender
House Electrician ....Michael Lynch
House Propertymaster ....Frank Lavaia

Fiddler on the Roof
SCRAPBOOK

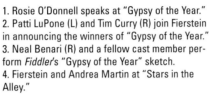

Photos by Aubrey Reuben

1. Rosie O'Donnell speaks at "Gypsy of the Year."
2. Patti LuPone (L) and Tim Curry (R) join Fierstein in announcing the winners of "Gypsy of the Year."
3. Neal Benari (R) and a fellow cast member perform *Fiddler*'s "Gypsy of the Year" sketch.
4. Fierstein and Andrea Martin at "Stars in the Alley."
5. Two cast members embody producers Fran and Barry Weissler in "Gypsy of the Year."

Correspondent: Jenny Dewar, Production Stage Manager.

Backstage Rituals: We have lots. Rosie O'Donnell has "Freebie Friday" every week. If you go to her dressing room, she has little gifts for everyone in the cast, everything from gumball machines to the DVD of Barbra Streisand's TV special. Streisand found out about that one and called her directly to thank her. She was thrilled. We also have "Dollar Friday": Everyone writes their name on a dollar and throws it in the pot. Then we pick out one of the dollars and that person gets to keep the pot.

"White Elephant Wednesday" began when Harvey Fierstein was moving and getting rid of a lot of stuff from his apartment. He would put together packages of stuff and raffle them off, with all the money going to Broadway Cares.

We have Shabbes every Friday evening in the Green Room, and every Saturday between shows there's a poker game in the upstairs lobby.

There's also "Saturday Night on Broadway." Harvey writes new verses to a little ditty about our show each week, and the boy who plays The Boy reads it over the PA system. Harvey always rhymes the last line, "It's Saturday night on Broadway, y'all."

Departing cast members always danced in the center of the circle dance at the bows, and Tevye (both Harvey and Fred) would give a speech to the audience mentioning something very special about that person.

"Carols for a Cure" Carol: "Light One Candle."

"Gypsy of the Year" Skit: No title. Created by Neal Benari.

Who Understudies the Most Roles: Roger Rosen, the four Russians.

Who Has Done the Most Shows: Philip Hoffman has never missed a performance in any show in his life, and he continued the tradition with *Fiddler*.

Favorite Moment: The circle dance at the bows is such a joyous way to end a show. That grew out of something we did in rehearsals: We'd start each day with traditional Jewish circle dances to set the mood and to teach movement. It was a way of establishing the community every day.

Favorite In-Theatre Gathering Place: The Green Room where we do all our rehearsals.

Favorite Off-Site Hangout: For a while the cast was going to Angus McIndoe's, but toward the end of the run Café Un Deux Trois became the place. Current stage management tends to steer toward Emmett's.

Favorite Snack Food: The challah bread. After each show, the girl playing Bielke would carry the challah up to Green Room where it would be scavenged. Everyone had an opinion on whether it was a good challah day or not.

Mascot: Michael Tommer.

Favorite Therapies: We get PT twice a week. Between the flying and the deck we need it! We've also gone through thousands of cans of Ricola.

Memorable Ad Libs: "It looks like a horse, It sounds like a horse, It WHINNIES!!!"

One night during "L'Chaim," Harvey yelled at someone to get their feet off the stage. I constantly had to go out front to ask people to take their coats and belongings off the edge of the stage. Once, somebody laid their lunch on the stage!

Memorable Fan Encounter: There was one uncomfortable one that had a nice ending. A girl in the second row started yelling stuff out and the house managers finally had to ask her to leave. But it turned out she had Tourette's Syndrome or

something. Rosie and Harvey felt so bad that they invited the family to come backstage and meet them at intermission, and they were thrilled.

Catchphrases Only the Company Would Recognize: "Woooooosh." "The rubber chicken."

Sweethearts: None started in the company, but we did have a young boyfriend and girlfriend who both got hired, Mitch Jarvis and Jen Babiak.

In-House Parody Lyrics: For the Spanish Company: "Es todo we loco, no, sí."

Company Legend: One night two of our actors fell through the trap.

Tales From the Put-In: Only thirteen original Equity members did the whole run, though seven people also returned. When we put in Harvey and Andrea Martin, the producers had a full dress rehearsal, which is unusual. We did it again when we put in Rosie. One thing I always found nice: any time an understudy or a new person had their first performance, the rest of the cast was in the wings, watching and supporting.

Nicknames: I'm called "Jenny Dew" or "Dew-dy Pie." Jonathan Butterell is Johnny B.

Best Flub: Unnamed cast member to Sheldon Harnick: "So you must be our new Rabbi."

Ghostly Encounters Backstage: One night I'm sure I saw a shadow behind me and there was definitely no one there. A member of the crew told me the Minskoff is too new to have a ghost, but I wonder. Jerome Robbins's sister passed away at the theatre just before the opening night performance. She was in her 90s, came in beautifully dressed, and then, poof, she was gone.

Coolest Thing About Being in This Show: It's being among those chosen by David Leveaux, Jonathan Butterell and Kevin Stites to be part of "our world."

The Glass Menagerie

First Preview: February 24, 2005. Opened: March 22, 2005.
Closed July 3, 2005 after 29 Previews and 120 Performances.

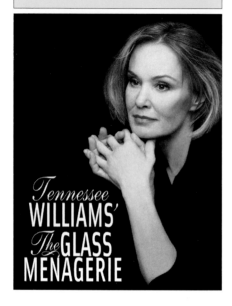

ⓈETHEL BARRYMORE THEATRE
243 West 47th Street
A Shubert Organization Theatre
Gerald Schoenfeld, *Chairman*   Philip J. Smith, *President*

Robert E. Wankel, *Executive Vice President*

BILL KENWRIGHT
presents

JESSICA LANGE

JOSH LUCAS   SARAH PAULSON
and
CHRISTIAN SLATER
in

Tennessee WILLIAMS'
The GLASS
MENAGERIE

| Scenic & Costume Design | Lighting Design |
| TOM PYE | NATASHA KATZ |

| Sound Design | Hair/Wig Design | Music Composed by |
| JON WESTON | DAVID BRIAN BROWN | DAN MOSES SCHREIER |

Technical Supervisor	Casting	Production Stage Manager
LARRY MORLEY	PAT McCORKLE, C.S.A./	BONNIE L. BECKER
	BONNIE GRISAN	

| Press | General Manager |
| PHILIP RINALDI PUBLICITY | RICHARDS/CLIMAN, INC. |

Directed by
DAVID LEVEAUX

The Glass Menagerie is presented by special arrangement with The University of the South, Sewanee, Tennessee.
The Producer wishes to express his appreciation to Theatre Development Fund for its support of this production.

6/1/05

CAST

Amanda Wingfield	JESSICA LANGE
Tom Wingfield	CHRISTIAN SLATER
Laura Wingfield	SARAH PAULSON
The Gentleman Caller	JOSH LUCAS

TIME
Now and the Past

UNDERSTUDIES

For Amanda Wingfield -
JENNIFER HARMON

for Tom Wingfield and The Gentleman Caller -
JOEY COLLINS

for Laura Wingfield -
CHEYENNE CASEBIER

Jessica Lange as Amanda Wingfield.

(L-R:) Sarah Paulson as Laura Wingfield and Josh Lucas as The Gentleman Caller.

Photos by Paul Kolnik

The Glass Menagerie

Jessica Lange
Amanda Wingfield

Christian Slater
Tom Wingfield

Sarah Paulson
Laura Wingfield

Josh Lucas
*The Gentleman
Caller*

Cheyenne Casebier
*Understudy for Laura
Wingfield*

Joey Collins
*Understudy for
Tom Wingfield and
The Gentleman
Caller*

Jennifer Harmon
*Understudy for
Amanda Wingfield*

David Leveaux
Director

Tom Pye
*Set & Costume
Design*

Natasha Katz
Lighting Design

David Brian Brown
Hair/Wig Design

Dan Moses Schreier
Original Music

Kate Maré
Dialect Coach

Bill Kenwright
Producer

Photo by Ben Strothmann

THE CREW
(L-R): Jim Bey (Sound Engineer), Manny Diaz (House Electrician), Catherine Osborne (Dresser), Victor Verdejo (House
Carpenter), Tree Sarvay (Dresser), Dan Landon (House Manager), Christel Murdock (Dresser), Diana Sikes (Hair Supervisor)
and Philip Feller (House Props).

The Glass Menagerie

Glengarry Glen Ross

First Preview: April 8, 2005. Opened: May 1, 2005.
Closed August 28, 2005 after 27 Previews and 137 Performances.

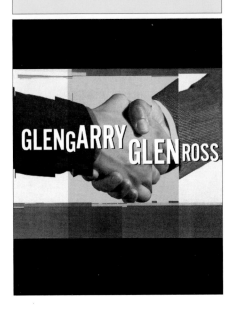

PLAYBILL

CAST
(in order of appearance)

Shelly Levene ....ALAN ALDA

John Williamson ....FREDERICK WELLER

Dave Moss ....GORDON CLAPP

George Aaronow.................JEFFREY TAMBOR

Richard Roma.....................LIEV SCHREIBER

James Lingk ....TOM WOPAT

Baylen ....JORDAN LAGE

STANDBYS

For Messrs. Schreiber and Weller:

JORDAN LAGE

For Messrs. Alda and Tambor:

JACK DAVIDSON

For Messrs. Wopat, Clapp and Lage:

JAY PATTERSON

⊛ **BERNARD B. JACOBS THEATRE**
242 West 45th Street
A Shubert Organization Theatre
Gerald Schoenfeld, *Chairman*   Philip J. Smith, *President*

Robert E. Wankel, *Executive Vice President*

JEFFREY RICHARDS   JERRY FRANKEL   JAM THEATRICALS
BOYETT OSTAR PRODUCTIONS   RONALD FRANKEL   PHILIP LACERTE
STEPHANIE P. MCCLELLAND/CJM PROD.   BARRY WEISBORD   ZENDOG PRODUCTIONS
in association with
HERBERT GOLDSMITH PRODUCTIONS
by special arrangement with THE ROUNDABOUT THEATRE COMPANY
Todd Haimes, Artistic Director
Ellen Richard, Managing Director
Julia C. Levy, Executive Director, External Affairs

present

ALAN ALDA   LIEV SCHREIBER
FREDERICK WELLER TOM WOPAT GORDON CLAPP
and **JEFFREY TAMBOR**

in

GLENGARRY GLENROSS

by **DAVID MAMET**

also with
JORDAN LAGE

Set By	Costumes By	Lighting By
SANTO LOQUASTO	**LAURA BAUER**	**KENNETH POSNER**

Casting by	Production Stage Manager	Company Manager
BERNARD TELSEY CASTING	**WILLIAM JOSEPH BARNES**	**BRUCE KLINGER**

Press Representative	General Management	Technical Supervision
IRENE GANDY	**ALBERT POLAND**	**NEIL A. MAZZELLA**

Directed by

JOE MANTELLO

6/1/05

Alan Alda (left)
and Liev Schreiber.

Photo by Scott Landis

Glengarry Glen Ross

Alan Alda
Shelly Levene

Liev Schreiber
Richard Roma

Jeffrey Tambor
George Aaronow

Frederick Weller
John Williamson

Tom Wopat
James Lingk

Gordon Clapp
Dave Moss

Jordan Lage
Baylen

Jack Davidson
*Standby for
Levene, Aaronow*

Jay Patterson
*Standby for
Moss, Lingk, Baylen*

David Mamet
Playwright

Joe Mantello
Director

Santo Loquasto
Set Design

Laura Bauer
Costume Design

Kenneth Posner
Lighting Design

Bernard Telsey
Casting, C.S.A
Casting

William Joseph
Barnes
*Production Stage
Manager*

Jill Cordle
Stage Manager

Neil A. Mazzella
*Technical
Supervision*

Albert Poland
General Manager

Jeffrey Richards
Producer

Jerry Frankel
Producer

Stephanie P.
McClelland
Producer

Jane Bergère
Producer

Morton Swinsky
Producer

Pun Bandhu,
ZenDog Productions
Producer

Marc Falato,
ZenDog Productions
Producer

Bill Haber
OSTAR Enterprises
Producer

Glengarry Glen Ross

Photos by Ben Strothmann

BACKSTAGE CREW
Front Row (L-R): Kimberly Baird (Dresser), Mike VanPraagh, Eddie Ruggiero,
William Joseph Barnes (Production Stage Manager).
Seated at Tables (L-R): Jim Fossi (Production Carpenter), Jessica Worsnop (Dresser), Danny Carpio,
Robert Guy (Wardrobe Supervisor), Herbert Messing, Brien Brannigan.
Standing (L-R): Jill Cordle (Stage Manager), Abe Morrison (Production Properties), Scott Shamenek (Dresser),
Jerry Klein, Kevin Keene and Brad Robertson (Head Electrician).

FRONT OF HOUSE STAFF
Sitting (L-R): William Mitchell (House Manager), Eva Laskow, Christian Borcan, Al Peay, Timothy Meyers
and John Minore.
Standing (L-R): Patanne McEvoy, Al Nazario, Sean Cutler and Monsoor Saidi.

Glengarry Glen Ross

Glengarry Glen Ross
SCRAPBOOK

1. (L-R): Jeffrey Tambor, Tom Wopat and Gordon Clapp at the opening of the 51st Season of the Broadway Softball League in Central Park.
2. Liev Schreiber on Tony night 2005 with his Tony Award as Best Featured Actor in a Play.
3. Jeffrey Tambor and friend at the "Broadway Barks 7!" event in Shubert Alley.
4. (L-R): Frederick Weller and Tom Wopat at the "Stars in the Alley" event.

Hairspray

First Preview: July 18, 2002. Opened: August 15, 2002.
Still running as of May 31, 2006.

PLAYBILL

hairspray

CAST
(in order of appearance)

Tracy Turnblad	SHANNON DURIG
Corny Collins	JONATHAN DOKUCHITZ
Amber Von Tussle	BECKY GULSVIG
Brad	MICHAEL CUNIO
Tammy	LINDSAY NICOLE CHAMBERS
Fender	ANDREW RANNELLS
Brenda	LESLIE GODDARD
Sketch	BRYAN WEST
Shelley	DONNA VIVINO
IQ	TODD MICHEL SMITH
Lou Ann	JACKIE SEIDEN
Link Larkin	RICHARD H. BLAKE
Prudy Pingleton	JULIE HALSTON
Edna Turnblad	JOHN PINETTE
Penny Pingleton	TRACY MILLER
Velma Von Tussle	BARBARA WALSH
Harriman F. Spritzer	KEVIN MEANEY
Wilbur Turnblad	STEPHEN DeROSA
Principal	KEVIN MEANEY
Seaweed J. Stubbs	CHESTER GREGORY II
Duane	TYRICK WILTEZ JONES
Gilbert	ARBENDER J. ROBINSON
Lorraine	TERITA R. REDD
Thad	TOMMAR WILSON
The Dynamites	CARLA J. HARGROVE, JUDINE SOMERVILLE, CANDICE MARIE WOODS
Mr. Pinky	KEVIN MEANEY
Gym Teacher	JULIE HALSTON
Little Inez	NIA IMANI SOYEMI
Motormouth Maybelle	DARLENE LOVE
Matron	JULIE HALSTON
Guard	KEVIN MEANEY

Continued on next page

Continued on next page

NEIL SIMON THEATRE
UNDER THE DIRECTION OF JAMES M. NEDERLANDER AND JAMES L. NEDERLANDER

Margo Lion   Adam Epstein   The Baruch · Viertel · Routh · Frankel Group
James D. Stern/Douglas L. Meyer   Rick Steiner/Frederic H. Mayerson
SEL & GFO   New Line Cinema
In Association With
Clear Channel Entertainment   A. Gordon/E. McAllister
D. Harris/M. Swinsky   J. & B. Osher
Present

HAIRSPRAY

Book By	Music By	Lyrics By
Mark O'Donnell	Marc Shaiman	Scott Wittman
Thomas Meehan		Marc Shaiman

Based upon the New Line Cinema film written and directed by John Waters

Starring
Shannon Durig   **John Pinette**

Also Starring
Richard H. Blake   Jonathan Dokuchitz
Chester Gregory II   Becky Gulsvig   Julie Halston   Blake Hammond   Kevin Meaney
Tracy Miller   Nia Imani Soyemi   Barbara Walsh

with Stephen DeRosa and Darlene Love

With
Joe Abraham   Joshua Bergasse   Gretchen Bieber   Lindsay Nicole Chambers   Michael Cunio
Michelle Dowdy   Leslie Goddard   Carla J. Hargrove   Tyrick Wiltez Jones   Abdul Latif
Rusty Mowery   Nicole Powell   Andrew Rannells   Terita R. Redd   Arbender J. Robinson   Jackie Seiden
Todd Michel Smith   Judine Somerville   Donna Vivino   Bryan West   Tommar Wilson   Candice Marie Woods

Scenery Designed by	Costumes Designed by	Lighting Designed by
David Rockwell	William Ivey Long	Kenneth Posner
Sound Designed by	Casting by	Wigs & Hair Designed by
Steve C. Kennedy	Bernard Telsey Casting	Paul Huntley
Production Stage Manager	Associate Director	Associate Choreographer
Frank Lombardi	Matt Lenz	Michele Lynch
Orchestrations by	Music Direction by	Arrangements by	Music Coordinator
Harold Wheeler	Lon Hoyt	Marc Shaiman	John Miller
General Management	Technical Supervisor	Press Representative	Associate Producers
Richard Frankel Productions	Tech Production	Richard Kornberg	Rhoda Mayerson
Laura Green	Services, Inc.	Don Summa	The Aspen Group, Daniel C. Staton

Choreography by
Jerry Mitchell

Direction by
Jack O'Brien

The world premiere of "HAIRSPRAY" was produced with the 5th Avenue Theatre in Seattle, Washington David Armstrong, Producing Artistic Director; Marilynn Sheldon, Managing Director

The producers wish to express their appreciation to Theatre Development Fund for its support of this production.

ORIGINAL BROADWAY CAST RECORDING ON SONY CLASSICAL

LIVE BROADWAY   10/1/05

John Pinette as Edna Turnblad.

Shannon Durig as Tracy Turnblad.

Photos by Paul Kolnik

Hairspray

SCENES & MUSICAL NUMBERS

Baltimore, 1962

ACT ONE

Prologue: "Good Morning Baltimore" ....Tracy & Company

Scene 1: TV Station WZZT & Turnblad Home
"The Nicest Kids in Town" ....Corny Collins & Council Members

Scene 2: At the Vanities
"Mama, I'm a Big Girl Now" ....Edna & Tracy, Velma & Amber, Penny & Prudy

Scene 3: TV Station WZZT
"I Can Hear the Bells" ....Tracy
"(The Legend of) Miss Baltimore Crabs" ....Velma & Council Members

Scene 4: Detention

Scene 5: Patterson Park High School Gymnasium
"The Madison" ....Corny & Company

Scene 6: WZZT & Turnblad Home
"The Nicest Kids in Town" (Reprise) ....Corny & Council Members
"It Takes Two" ....Link & Tracy

Scene 7: Turnblad Home and Streets of Baltimore
"Welcome to the '60s" ....Tracy, Edna, The Dynamites & Company

Scene 8: Patterson Park Playground
"Run and Tell That" ....Seaweed

Scene 9: Motormouth Maybelle's Record Shop
"Run and Tell That" ....Seaweed, Little Inez & Company
"Big, Blonde & Beautiful" ....Motormouth, Little Inez, Tracy, Edna, Wilbur

ACT TWO

Scene 1: Baltimore Women's House of Detention
"The Big Dollhouse" ....Women
"Good Morning Baltimore" (Reprise) ....Tracy

Scene 2: The Har-De-Har Hut
"Timeless to Me" ....Wilbur & Edna

Scene 3: Tracy's Jail Cell & Penny's Bedroom
"Without Love" ....Link, Tracy, Seaweed, Penny

Scene 4: Motormouth Maybelle's Record Shop
"I Know Where I've Been" ....Motormouth & Company

Scene 5: The Baltimore Eventorium
"Hairspray" ....Corny & Council Members
"Cooties" ....Amber & Council Members
"You Can't Stop the Beat" ....Tracy, Link, Penny, Seaweed,
Edna, Wilbur, Motormouth & Company

Hairspray

John Pinette
Edna Turnblad

Shannon Durig
Tracy Turnblad

Stephen DeRosa
Wilbur Turnblad

Darlene Love
Motormouth Maybelle

Richard H. Blake
Link Larkin

Jonathan Dokuchitz
Corny Collins

Chester Gregory II
Seaweed

Becky Gulsvig
Amber Von Tussle

Julie Halston
Prudy Pingleton/ Gym Teacher/Matron

Blake Hammond
Understudy Edna Turnblad, Wilbur Turnblad, Harriman F. Spritzer, Principal, Mr. Pinky, Guard

Kevin Meaney
Harriman F. Spritzer, Principal, Mr. Pinky, Guard

Tracy Miller
Penny Pingleton

Nia Imani Soyemi
Little Inez

Barbara Walsh
Velma Von Tussle

Joe Abraham
Swing

Joshua Bergasse
Swing

Gretchen Bieber
Swing

Lindsay Nicole Chambers
Tammy

Michael Cunio
Brad

Michelle Dowdy
Understudy Tracy Turnblad

Leslie Goddard
Brenda

Carla J. Hargrove
Dynamite

Tyrick Wiltez Jones
Duane

Abdul Latif
Swing

Rusty Mowery
Swing/ Production Dance Supervisor/ Dance Captain

Nicole Powell
Swing

Andrew Rannells
Fender

Terita R. Redd
Lorraine

Arbender J. Robinson
Gilbert

Jackie Seiden
Lou Ann

Todd Michel Smith
IQ

Judine Somerville
Dynamite

Donna Vivino
Shelley

Bryan West
Sketch

Tommar Wilson
Thad

Hairspray

Candice Marie Woods
Dynamite

Mark O'Donnell
Book

Thomas Meehan
Book

Marc Shaiman
*Music and Lyrics/
Arrangements*

Scott Wittman
Lyrics

Jack O'Brien
Director

Jerry Mitchell
Choreographer

David Rockwell
Scenic Designer

William Ivey Long
Costume Designer

Kenneth Posner
Lighting Designer

Steve Canyon Kennedy
Sound Designer

Paul Huntley
Wig and Hair Designer

John Waters
Consultant

Bernard Telsey,
Bernard Telsey
Casting, C.S.A
Casting

Richard Kornberg,
Richard Kornberg
and Associates
Press Representative

Harold Wheeler
Orchestrations

Lon Hoyt
Music Director

John Miller
Music Coordinator

Laura Green,
Richard Frankel
Productions
General Management

Michele Lynch
*Associate
Choreographer*

Margo Lion
Producer

Adam Epstein
Producer

Richard Frankel,
The Frankel Baruch
Viertel Routh Group
Producer

Steven Baruch,
The Frankel Baruch
Viertel Routh Group
Producer

Tom Viertel,
The Frankel Baruch
Viertel Routh Group
Producer

Marc Routh,
The Frankel Baruch
Viertel Routh Group
Producer

Douglas L. Meyer
Producer

Rick Steiner
Producer

Frederic H. Mayerson
Producer

Mark Kaufman,
New Line Cinema
Producer

Allan S. Gordon
Producer

Elan V. McAllister
Producer

Dede Harris
Producer

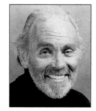
Morton Swinsky
Producer

John and Bonnie Osher
Producer

Hairspray

Daniel C. Staton
Associate Producer

Rhoda Mayerson
Associate Producer

alumni
2005-2006

Cameron Adams
*Brenda/Denizen of
Baltimore*

Jordan Ballard
Amber Von Tussle

Jim J. Bullock
*Principal/Guard/
Harriman F. Spritzer/
Mr. Pinky/Denizen of
Baltimore*

Eric L. Christian
*Gilbert/Denizen of
Baltimore*

Mary Bond Davis
Motormouth Maybelle

J.P. Dougherty
*Understudy
Edna Turnblad,
Wilbur Turnblad*

Carly Jibson
Tracy Turnblad

Leslie Kritzer
*Shelley/ Denizen of
Baltimore*

Liz Larsen
*Understudy Velma
Von Tussle, Prudy,
Gym Teacher,
Matron*

CJay Hardy Philip
*Dynamite/Denizen of
Baltimore*

Kathleen Shields
*Brenda/Denizen of
Baltimore*

Peter Matthew Smith
*Brad/Denizen of
Baltimore*

Todd Susman
Wilbur Turnblad

Bruce Vilanch
Edna Turnblad

Marissa Jaret Winokur
Tracy Turnblad

transfer
students
2005-2006

Cameron Adams
*Brenda/Tammy/
Denizen of
Baltimore/Swing*

Tevin Campbell
Seaweed J. Stubbs

Scott Davidson
*Understudy for
Edna Turnblad,
Wilbur Turnblad,
Spritzer, Principal,
Mr. Pinky, Guard*

Diana DeGarmo
Penny Pingleton

James Royce
Edwards
*Sketch/Denizen of
Baltimore*

Joanna Glushak
Velma Von Tussle

Tyler Hanes
*Fender/Denizen of
Baltimore*

Leah Hocking
Velma Von Tussle

Michelle Kittrell
*Dance Captain/
Swing*

Serge Kushnier
*Fender/Denizen of
Baltimore*

Liz Larsen
Velma Von Tussle

Caissie Levy
Penny Pingleton

Leslie McDonel
*Lou Ann/Denizen of
Baltimore*

Hairspray

Kenny Morris
Understudy for Edna Turnblad, Wilbur Turnblad, Spritzer, Principal, Mr. Pinky, Guard

Naturi Naughton
Inez

Rashad Naylor
Thad/Denizen of Baltimore

CJay Hardy Philip
Swing

Chloé Smith
Little Inez

Jason Snow
Dance Captain/Swing

Anne Warren
Lou Ann/Denizen of Baltimore

Willis White
Duane/Denizen of Baltimore

SCRAPBOOK

Correspondent: Judine Somerville, "Cindy Watkins"
Most Exciting Celebrity Visitor: Bruce Springsteen, came backstage with his wife and family and hung out for more than an hour. I introduced myself as one of the Dynamites and he said, "The whole show is dynamite!"
"Carols for a Cure" Carol: "All Alone on Christmas."
"Gypsy of the Year" Skit: "Love's In Need of Love Today" by The Company, music by Stevie Wonder.
"Easter Bonnet" Sketch: "Tracy's Nightmare" by Marc Shaiman and Donna Vivino. Directed by Abdul Latif.
Favorite Moment: When the Dyamites come to life.
Favorite Snack Food: Chips, chips and more chips.
Therapies: Water, tea, Emer'gen-C, Ricolas and honey.
Fastest Costume Change: In "Welcome to the '60s," John Pinette as Edna Turnblad goes from Plain-Jane mom to glam mom in seconds.
Coolest Things: Being part of such a wonderful group of people; having the opportunity to sing original, fun, fantastic music; looking fabulous; dancing fun numbers; and getting a great workout. I was a member of the original company and it was just a dream come true. I took a year off to have a baby. I'm back now and it's stronger than ever.

HAIR DEPARTMENT
Sitting (L-R): Isabelle Decauwert (Hair Assistant), Stephanie Barnes (Hair Assistant).
Standing (L-R): Mark Manalanasan (Hair Assistant), Jon Jordan (Hair and Make-up Supervisor), Adenike Wright (Assistant Hair Supervisor).

DANCE
(L-R): Michelle Kittrell (Dance Captain), Rusty Mowery (Production Dance Supervisor)

Photos by Ben Strothmann

STAGE CREW
Front Row (L-R):
Jason Brouillard (Assistant Stage Manager), Art Lutz (Deck Sound), Michael Pilipski (Head Property Master), Lorena Sullivan (Assistant Property Master), Scott Mecionis (House Propman), Jessica Morton (Assistant Electrician)

Second Row (L-R):
Marisha Ploski (Stage Manager), Lois L. Griffing (Production Stage Manager), John Kelly (Electrician)

Third Row (L-R):
Bryan Davis (Assistant Carpenter), Michael Boaden (Assistant Sound Engineer), Dawn Edmonds (Elevator Operator), Istvan Tamas (Carpenter), Mitch Cunistenson (Electrician), James Travers, Sr. (House Electrician), James Mosaphir (Doorman), Steve Vesa (Electrician)

Fourth Row (L-R):
Mike Bennet (Carpenter), Brian Monroe (Head Carpenter), Ron Culos (Propman), Richard Kirbey (Carpenter), Thomas Green (House Carpenter), Richard Aubrey (Treasurer)

Hairspray

ORCHESTRA
Front Row (L-R):
Sarah Hewitt-Roth (Cello), John Hines (Trumpet),
Carol Pool (Violin), Mike Davis (Trombone),
Francisco Centeno (Bass).

Middle Row (L-R):
Keith Cotton (Keyboard/Associate Conductor),
Belinda Whitney (Violin), John Tropea (Guitar),
Frank Pagano (Percussion), David Mann (Reeds).

Back Row (L-R):
Clint de Ganon (Drums), Jodie Moore
(Keyboard/Assistant Conductor), Lon Hoyt
(Keyboard/Music Director), David Riekenberg
(Reeds) and Al Orlo (Guitar).

Photos by Ben Strothmann

FRONT OF HOUSE STAFF
Front Row (L-R):
Evelyn Olivero (Usher), Jane Publik (Usher) and
Angel Diaz (Head Usher).

Second Row (L-R):
Deborah Peterson (Usher), Margie Montano
(Matron), Sharon Hauser (Usher),
Michelle Schechter (Usher),
Grace Darbasie (Usher).

Third Row (L-R):
Dolores Banyai (Usher), Adrienne Watson
(Usher), Maureen Santos (Ticket Taker),
Mary Ellen Palermo (Directress),
Dana Diaz (Usher).

Fourth Row (L-R):
Steven Ouellette (House Manager),
Sam Brookfield (Usher) and
Dylan Carusdna (Lines Co-Ordinator).

WARDROBE DEPARTMENT
Front Row (L-R):
Mindy Eng (Dresser) and Liz Goodrum (Dresser).

Middle Row (L-R):
Tanya Blue (Dresser), Sara Foster
(Day Worker/Swing), Del Miskie (Star Dresser).

Back Row (L-R):
Alex Bartlett (Dresser), Frankie Sancineto
(Day Worker/Swing) and Meghan Carsella
(Assistant Wardrobe Supervisor).

Todd Stern
Usher

Hairspray

STAFF FOR *HAIRSPRAY*

GENERAL MANAGEMENT
RICHARD FRANKEL PRODUCTIONS

Richard Frankel	Marc Routh	Laura Green
Rod Kaats	Jo Porter	Joe Watson

COMPANY MANAGER
Marc Borsak

Associate Company Manager .... Aliza Wassner

GENERAL PRESS REPRESENTATIVE
RICHARD KORNBERG & ASSOCIATES

Richard Kornberg	Don Summa
Tom D'Ambrosio	Carrie Friedman

CASTING
BERNARD TELSEY CASTING C.S.A.

Bernie Telsey   Will Cantler   David Vaccari

Bethany Berg   Craig Burns

Tiffany Little Canfield   Christine Dall

Stephanie Yankwitt

PRODUCTION STAGE MANAGER ..**Frank Lombardi**
Stage Manager .... Marisha Ploski
Assistant Stage Manager .... Jason Brouillard
Associate Director .... Matt Lenz
Associate Choreographer .... Michele Lynch
Production Dance Supervisor .... Rusty Mowery
Technical Supervision ......Tech Production Services, Inc./
Peter Fulbright, Elliot Bertoni,
Mary Duffe, Colleen Houlehen,
Jarid Sumner, Michael Altbaum
Associate Set Designer .... Richard Jaris
Assistant Set Designers .... Emily Beck,
Robert Bissinger, Ted LeFevre
Associate to David Rockwell .... Barry Richards
Assistants to David Rockwell .... Michael Dereskewicz,
Joanie Schlafer
Associate Costume Designer .... Martha Bromelmeier
Assistant Costume Designer .... Laura Oppenheimer
Assistants to William Ivey Long .....Melissa-Anne Blizzard,
Donald Sanders
Automated Light Programmer ....Paul J. Sonnleitner
Associate Lighting Designer .... Philip Rosenberg
Assistant Lighting Designer .... Paul Miller
Associate Sound Designer .... John Shivers
Associate Wig and Hair Designer .... Amy Solomon

Make-Up Design by .... Randy Houston Mercer

Supervising Production Carpenter .... Ken Fieldhouse
Head Carpenter .... Brian Monroe
Assistant Carpenters .... Bryan Davis, Ben Horrigan
Supervising Production Electrician .... Michael Lo Bue
Head Electrician .... Brent Oakley
Assistant Electrician .... Jessica Morton
Head Sound Engineer .... Andrew Keister
Assistant Sound Engineer .... Dave Dignazio
Deck Sound .... Art Lutz
Head Property Master .... Michael Pilipski
Assistant Property Master .... Lorena Sullivan
Wardrobe Supervisor .... Michael Sancineto

Assistant Wardrobe Supervisor .... Meghan Carsella
Star Dressers .... Kay Gowenlock,
Joseph Phillip Armon
Dressers .... Alex Bartlett, Mindy Eng, Larry Foster,
Laura Horner, Liz Goodrum, Tanya Guercio,
Kate McAleer, Vangel Kaseluris
Hair and Makeup Supervisor .... Jon Jordan
Assistant Hair Supervisor .... William Graham
Hair Assistants .... Stephanie Barnes, Lee Brock,
Isabelle Decauwert, Jodi Jackson,
Mark Manalanasan, John Roberson
Music Coordinator .... John Miller
Associate Conductor .... Keith Cotton
Drummer .... Clint DeGanon
Assistant Music Coordinator .... Matthew Ettinger,
Chuck Butler
Electronic Music System Design
and Programming .... Music Arts Technologies,
Jim Harp, Brett Sommer
Rehearsal Pianist .... Edward Rabin
Producing Assoc. to Ms. Lion .... Lily Hung
Assistant to Mr. Baruch .... Sonja Soper
Assistant to Mr. Viertel .... Tania Senewiratne
Associate Producer/
Adam Epstein Productions .... Lynn Shaw
Assistant to Mr. Steiner .... Kathy Wall
Assistant to Mr. Stern ....Leah Callaghan, Shira Sergant
Management Assistants ....Tracy Geltman, Eric Cornell
Juvenile Actors' Guardian .... Anna Rivera
Production Assistants .... Sharon DelPilar,
Daniel Kelly, Travis Milliken,
Adam M. Muller, Noah Pollock
Press Interns .... Samantha Borenstein,
Kathryn Calogero, Jennifer Pastrich
Advertising .... Serino Coyne, Inc./ Nancy Coyne,
Greg Coradetti, Joaquin Esteva,
Christina M. Prospero
Promotions/Marketing .....TMG - The Marketing Group/
Tanya Grubich, Laura Matalon
Photographer .... Paul Kolnik
Web Designer .... Simma Park
Theatre Displays .... King Displays
Insurance .... Marsh USA Inc., Margery Boyar
Legal Counsel ....Patricia Crown, Coblence & Warner
Banking .... Chase Manhattan Bank,
Richard Callian, Michael Friel
Payroll Service .... Castellana Services, Inc.
Accounting .... Fried and Kowgios Partners LLP
Travel Agency .... JMC Travel
Concessions .... Rick Steiner Productions
New York Rehearsals ....The New 42nd Street Studios
New York Opening Night Coordinator ....Tobak-Dantchik
Events and Promotions,
Suzanne Tobak, Jennifer Falik
New York Group Sales ....Show Tix (212) 302-7000

EXCLUSIVE TOUR DIRECTION:
On the Road

RICHARD FRANKEL PRODUCTIONS STAFF
Finance Director .... **Michael Naumann**
Assistant to Mr. Frankel .... Jeff Romley
Assistant to Mr. Routh .... Michael Sag

Assistant to Ms. Green .... Joshua A. Saletnik
Assistant Finance Director .... Liz Hines
Information Technology Manager .... Roddy Pimentel
Management Assistant .... Heidi Schading
Accounting Assistant .... Elsie Jamin-Maguire
National Sales and
Marketing Director .... **Ronni Mandell**
Director of Business Affairs ....**Carter Anne McGowan**
Marketing Coordinator .... Melissa Marano
Office Manager ....**Lori Steiger-Perry**
Office Assistant .... Stephanie Adamczyk
Receptionist .... Deniece Alvarado, Randy Rainbow
Interns .... Lauren Berger, Katie Berkshire,
Todd Blass, Eric Cornell,
Matthew Martin, Erin Porvaznik,
Kirsten Rega, Nathan Vernon,
Lucinda Walker

CREDITS AND ACKNOWLEDGEMENTS
Scenery and scenic effects built, painted, electrified and automated by Showmotion, Inc., Norwalk, Ct. Scenery automation by Showmotion, Inc., using the Autocue Computerized Motion Control System. Lighting equipment from Fourth Phase, New Jersey. Sound equipment by Sound Associates, Inc. Specialty props by Prism Production Services, Rahway, NJ. Costumes built by Euro Co Costumes Inc., Jennifer Love Costumes, Scafati Incorporated, Schneeman Studios, Tricorne New York City and Timberlake Studios, Inc. Custom shoes by LaDuca Shoes NYC. Champagne provided by Veuve Clicquot. Lite Brite Wall engineered, constructed and electrified by Showmotion, Inc. Soft goods by Rosebrand Textiles, Inc. Scenic painting by Scenic Art Studios. Hair Curtain Main Drape by I. Weiss and Sons, Inc.

NEDERLANDER

Chairman .... **James M. Nederlander**
President .... **James L. Nederlander**

Executive Vice President
Nick Scandalios

Vice President	Senior Vice President
Corporate Development	Labor Relations
Charlene S. Nederlander	**Herschel Waxman**

Vice President	Chief Financial Officer
Jim Boese	**Freida Sawyer Belviso**

STAFF FOR THE NEIL SIMON THEATRE
Theatre Manager .... Victor Irving
Treasurer .... Richard Aubrey
Associate Treasurer .... Eddie Waxman
House Carpenter .... Thomas Green
Flyman .... Douglas McNeill
House Electrician .... James Travers, Sr.
House Propman .... Scott Mecionis
House Engineer .... John Astras

The History Boys

First Preview: April 14, 2006. Opened: April 23, 2006.
Still running as of May 31, 2006.

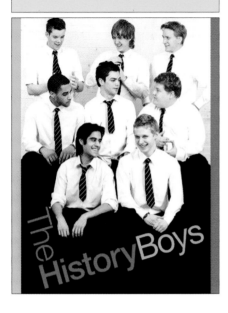

CAST

The Boys

Akthar	SACHA DHAWAN
Crowther	SAMUEL ANDERSON
Dakin	DOMINIC COOPER
Lockwood	ANDREW KNOTT
Posner	SAMUEL BARNETT
Rudge	RUSSELL TOVEY
Scripps	JAMIE PARKER
Timms	JAMES CORDEN

The Teachers

Headmaster	CLIVE MERRISON
Mrs. Lintott	FRANCES de la TOUR
Hector	RICHARD GRIFFITHS
Irwin	STEPHEN CAMPBELL MOORE
TV Director	COLIN HAIGH
Make-up Lady	PAMELA MERRICK
Other Boys	JOSEPH ATTENBOROUGH, TOM ATTWOOD, RUDI DHARMALINGAM

UNDERSTUDIES

For Lockwood, Timms, Rudge, TV Director:
JOSEPH ATTENBOROUGH
For Posner, Crowther, Scripps:
TOM ATTWOOD
For Akthar, Dakin:
RUDI DHARMALINGAM
For Hector, Headmaster:
COLIN HAIGH
For Mrs. Lintott:
PAMELA MERRICK

⑤ BROADHURST THEATRE

235 West 44th Street
A Shubert Organization Theatre

Gerald Schoenfeld, *Chairman*   **Philip J. Smith**, *President*

Robert E. Wankel, *Executive Vice President*

Boyett Ostar Productions
Roger Berlind   Debra Black   Eric Falkenstein   Roy Furman
Jam Theatricals   Stephanie P. McClelland   Judith Resnick
Scott Rudin   Jon Avnet/Ralph Guild   Dede Harris/Mort Swinsky

Present
NT The National Theatre of Great Britain's
production of

The HistoryBoys

A New Play By
Alan Bennett

with

Samuel Anderson   Joseph Attenborough   Tom Attwood
Samuel Barnett   Dominic Cooper   James Corden   Frances de la Tour
Rudi Dharmalingam   Sacha Dhawan   Richard Griffiths
Colin Haigh   Andrew Knott   Pamela Merrick   Clive Merrison
Stephen Campbell Moore   Jamie Parker   Russell Tovey

Designer	Lighting Designer
Bob Crowley	**Mark Henderson**

Music	Video Director	Sound Designer
Richard Sisson	**Ben Taylor**	**Colin Pink**

Press Representative	Marketing
Boneau/Bryan Brown	**HHC Marketing**

General Management	Production Stage Manager	Technical Supervisor
101 Productions, Ltd.	**Michael J. Passaro**	**David Benken**

Directed by
Nicholas Hytner

LIVE BROADWAY

4/23/06

(L-R): Jamie Parker, Andrew Knott, Dominic Cooper and James Corden

The History Boys

Samuel Anderson
Crowther

Joseph Attenborough
Company

Tom Attwood
Company/
Music Director

Samuel Barnett
Posner

Dominic Cooper
Dakin

James Corden
Timms

Frances de la Tour
Mrs. Lintott

Rudi Dharmalingam
Company

Sacha Dhawan
Akthar

Richard Griffiths
Hector

Colin Haigh
TV Director

Andrew Knott
Lockwood

Pamela Merrick
Make-up Lady

Clive Merrison
Headmaster

Stephen Campbell
Moore
Irwin

Jamie Parker
Scripps

Russell Tovey
Rudge

Alan Bennett
Playwright

Nicholas Hytner
Director

Bob Crowley
Scenic and Costume
Design

Mark Henderson
Lighting Design

Hugh Hysell,
HHC Marketing
Marketing

David Benken
Technical Supervisor

Bob Boyett
Producer

Bill Haber,
Ostar Enterprises
Producer

Roger Berlind
Producer

Debra Black
Producer

Eric Falkenstein
Producer

Roy Furman
Producer

Stephanie P.
McClelland
Producer

Scott Rudin
Producer

John Avnet
Producer

Dede Harris
Producer

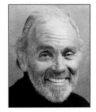
Mort Swinsky
Producer

The actors in The
History Boys *are*
appearing with
the permission of
Actors' Equity
Association.

The History Boys

Bill Buell
TV Director

LeRoy McClain
Company

Pippa Pearthree
Make-up Lady

Alex Tonetta
Company

Jeffrey Withers
Company

2005-2006 Awards

TONY AWARDS
Best Play
Best Performance by a Leading Actor in a Play (Richard Griffiths)
Best Performance by a Featured Actress in a Play (Frances de la Tour)
Best Direction of a Play (Nicholas Hytner)
Best Scenic Design of a Play (Bob Crowley)
Best Lighting Design of a Play (Mark Henderson)

NY DRAMA CRITICS' CIRCLE AWARD
Best Play

DRAMA DESK AWARDS
Outstanding Play
Outstanding Actor in a Play (Richard Griffiths)
Outstanding Featured Actor in a

Play (Samuel Barnett)
Outstanding Featured Actress in a Play (Frances de la Tour)
Outstanding Direction of a Play (Nicholas Hytner)

DRAMA LEAGUE AWARD
Distinguished Production of a Play

OUTER CRITICS CIRCLE AWARDS
Outstanding Broadway Play
Oustanding Featured Actor in a Play (Richard Griffiths)
Outstanding Featured Actress in a Play (Frances de la Tour)
Outstanding Direction of a Play (Nicholas Hytner)

THEATRE WORLD AWARD
Outstanding Broadway Debut (Richard Griffiths)

FRONT OF HOUSE STAFF
Front Row (L-R):
Karen Diaz (Usher), Henry Bethea (Ticket Taker), Hugh Barnett (Theatre Manager), Le'Shone Cleveland (Directress).

Middle Row (L-R): Jennifer Vega (Usher), Hugh Lynch (Usher), Juliette Cipriatti (Usher), Janet Kay (Usher).

Back Row (L-R): Juan "Tony" Lopez (Usher), Alfredo Rosario (Usher) and Matt Blank (Usher).

STAGE MANAGEMENT
(L-R):
Charlie Underhill (Stage Manager), Seth Sklar-Heyn (Production Assistant), and Michael Passaro (Production Stage Manager).

Photos by Ben Strothmann

STAGE CREW
Front Row (L-R):
Helen Toth (Wardrobe Supervisor), Maya Hardin (Dresser).

Back Row (L-R):
Geoffrey Polischuck (Dresser), Kevin Keene (Production Sound Supervisor), Ron Vitteli Jr. (House Properties) and Craig Laicata (Propman).

The History Boys

COMPANY MANAGER
Gregg Arst

BOX OFFICE
(L-R):
Michael Lynch and
Gerard O'Brien.

Photos by Ben Strothmann

STAFF FOR *THE HISTORY BOYS*

GENERAL MANAGEMENT
101 PRODUCTIONS, LTD.
Wendy Orshan   Jeffrey M. Wilson
David Auster

COMPANY MANAGER
Gregg Arst

GENERAL PRESS REPRESENTATIVE
BONEAU/BRYAN-BROWN
Adrian Bryan-Brown   Jim Byk
Juliana Hannett

CASTING
U.K. Casting .... Toby Whale
U.K. Casting Assistant .... Alastair Coomer
U.S. Casting .... Tara Rubin Casting/Laura Schutzel

Production Stage Manager .... Michael J. Passaro
Stage Manager .... Charlie Underhill
U.K. Musical Director .... Tom Attwood
Associate Lighting Designer .... Daniel Walker
U.K. Associate Production Manager .... Andy Ward
Assistant Technical Supervisor .... Rosemarie Palombo
Movement Director .... Jack Murphy

Production Carpenter .... Brian McGarty
Production Electrician .... Jon Lawson
Head Electrician .... Tom Lawrey
Production Props Supervisor .... Robert Adams
Production Sound Supervisor .... Kevin Keene
Moving Light Programmer .... Bobby Harrell
Wardrobe Supervisor .... Helen Toth
Dressers .... Geoffrey Polischuck, Maya Hardin
Production Assistant .... Seth Sklar-Heyn
Technical Production Assistant .... Will O'Hare

Boyett Ostar Senior Vice President,
Strategic Partnerships & Development .... Jan Gura

Assistants to Mr. Boyett .... Diane Murphy,
Ingrid Kloss, Michael Mandell
Assistants to Mr. Haber .... Theresa Pisanelli,
Andrew Cleghorn
Legal Counsel .... Lazarus & Harris, LLP/
Scott R. Lazarus, Esq.,
Robert C. Harris, Esq.
Accountant ...... Rosenberg, Neuwirth & Kushner, CPAs/
Chris Cacace
Comptroller .... Patricia Pedersen

Advertising .... SpotCo/
Drew Hodges, Jim Edwards,
Jim Aquino, Y. Darius Suyama
Marketing .... HHC Marketing/
Hugh Hysell, Michael Redman
Housing Coordinator .... Megan Trice
101 Productions, Ltd. Staff .... Katharine Croke,
Scott Falkowski, Heidi Neven,
Jason Paradine, David Renwanz,
Mary Six Rupert, John Vennema
101 Productions, Ltd. Intern .... Laura Dickinson
Press Assistant .... Matt Ross
Banking .... City National Bank/
Anne McSweeney
Insurance .... DeWitt Stern, Inc./
Jennifer Brown
Immigration .... Traffic Control Group, Inc./
David King
Theatre Displays .... King Displays, Inc.
Music Rights .... BZ Rights and Permissions, Inc./
Barbara Zimmerman
Merchandising .... Max Merchandising, LLC
Payroll Services .... Castellana Services, Inc.
Website Design .... Situation Marketing/
Damian Bazadona, Lisa Cecchini,
Tom Lorenzo
Opening Night
Coordinators .... Tobak Lawrence Company/
Suzanne Tobak,
Michael P. Lawrence

NATIONAL THEATRE, LONDON
Chairman of the Board .... Sir Hayden Phillips
Director .... Nicholas Hytner
Executive Director .... Nick Starr
Assistant Producer .... Tim Levy

SPONSOR
American Airlines is the associate sponsor of *The History Boys* on Broadway.

CREDITS
Lighting equipment from Hudson Sound and Light LLC. Sound equipment from Sound Associates. Video equipment from Scharff Weisberg, Inc. U.K. scenery properties and costumes constructed by the National Theatre of Great Britain. Additional scenery by Hudson Scenic Studio, Inc. Ricola natural herb cough drops courtesy of Ricola USA, Inc.

MUSIC CREDITS
"**Bewitched, Bothered and Bewildered,**" music by Richard

Rodgers, lyrics by Lorenz Hart. This selection is used by special arrangement with the Rodgers and Hammerstein Organization, 1065 Ave. of the Americas, Suite 2400, New York NY 10018. ©1941 (renewed), Chappell & Co. and Williamson Music Inc. All rights reserved. Used by permission. "**Now, Voyager,**" (Max Steiner). WB Music Corp. (ASCAP). All rights reserved. Used by permission. "**Sing As We Go,**" written by Harry Parr-Davies. Published by Colgems-EMI Music Inc. "**Wish Me Luck (As You Wave Me Goodbye),**" (Harry Parr-Davies, Phil Park). ©1939 Chappell Music Ltd., UK. All rights reserved. Used by permission. "**La Vie en Rose,**" (Louiguy, Edith Piaf, Mack Davis). ©1947 (renewed). Editions Paul Beuscher SA (SACEM) and WB Music Corp. (ASCAP). All rights admin. by WB Music Corp. All rights reserved. Used by permission.
Music Clearance: BZ/Rights & Permissions, Inc.

SPECIAL THANKS
The National Theatre wishes to thank Fiona Bardsley, Andrew Speed, Charles Evans, Bella Rodrigues, Mary Parker.

To learn more about upcoming National Theatre productions, please visit our website at
www.NTNY.org

 THE SHUBERT ORGANIZATION, INC.
Board of Directors

Gerald Schoenfeld	**Philip J. Smith**
Chairman	President
Wyche Fowler, Jr.	**John W. Kluge**
Lee J. Seidler	**Michael I. Sovern**

Stuart Subotnick

Robert E. Wankel
Executive Vice President

Peter Entin	**Elliot Greene**
Vice President -	Vice President -
Theatre Operations	Finance
David Andrews	**John Darby**
Vice President -	Vice President -
Shubert Ticketing Services	Facilities

House Manager .... Hugh Barnett

The History Boys
SCRAPBOOK

Correspondent: James Corden, "Timms"

Memorable Opening Night Letter, Fax or Note: We had done this play at the National Theatre in London and around the world, so the really amazing thing for us on opening night was being made to feel a part of this Broadway community we kept hearing about. We got faxes from all the other shows. It's really quite something to have people like Ralph Fiennes and Cherry Jones sending you good luck on your opening night. On a personal note, my parents sent me the biggest card in the world, which was really sweet.

Opening Night Gifts: Our producers gave us each a fantastic glass cube with the poster and the opening date in it. It's something we'll have forever and I was really blown away by it.

Celebrity Visitors: We've had the most extraordinary people in the audience—people like Steve Martin, Steven Spielberg and Dustin Hoffman. David Bowie was the first person to leap to his feet and applaud the night he came. But none of them have come backstage to meet us! Maybe we're giving off the wrong vibrations?

Who Has Done the Most Shows in Their Career: Frances de la Tour, and then probably Richard Griffiths and Clive. They're way ahead of the rest of us.

Special Backstage Rituals: At the start of the show, four boys are standing in one wing and four boys in the other. The four on our side, we always have a huddle. The rule is you must say the first thing that comes into your head. Sometimes it's quite silly. Generally we start with the words, "Is it wrong if…?"

Favorite Moment During Each Performance: Me and my friend Andrew get to do a scene where we replicate a scene from *Now, Voyager*. I

1. Richard Griffiths toasts opening night at the cast party at Tavern on the Green.
2. (L-R): Russell Tovey and Dominic Cooper on opening night.
3. (L-R): Director Nicholas Hytner and playwright Alan Bennett at Tavern on the Green.
4. (L-R): Sacha Dhawan and James Corden.
5. Curtain call on opening night at the Broadhurst Theatre.

always quite enjoy that.

Favorite In-Theatre Gathering Place: There's a little alley where people go to have a smoke. And we sometimes gather in Richard's dressing room.

Favorite Off-Site Hangout: If anyone wants to find The History Boys after the show, we're always in Angus McIndoe, where they always look after us. There's one waitress in particular, Stephanie, who's very popular amongst all the boys.

Favorite Snack Food: We all revert to being school boys and eat all the candy we can. The crew will always be eating the biggest bag of pretzels you ever saw in your life. We're like vultures around any food.

Favorite Therapy: We don't have anything like that. We're probably the most unprofessional cast on Broadway. We don't even warm up before the show. Most of us start to get dressed at "five minutes." Sam Anderson is known not even to be dressed at "places." There he is in the wings, yeah, putting on his pants in a leisurely way.

Memorable Ad-Lib: You can't ad-lib on Alan's words. It sticks out like a sore thumb.

Memorable Press Encounter: When we did the shoot for Vanity Fair in Hong Kong, the photographer wanted us all to kneel on the floor and pile onto each other like cheerleaders. The answer to that was a resounding "no."

Memorable Stage Door Fan Encounters: Everyone asks how old we are. Some are known to ask, "Are you actors? Is this your job?" To which we go, "Uh, *yeah*." They think they picked us up on a street. That never goes down well with the boys, I can tell you.

Nicknames: I'll tell you the nicknames, but you'll have to guess who is who: "Zammo," "Moon," "Levine," "Scripps," "Rusty," "Cheesebox," "Dirtbox" and "Sashkins." We call Sam just "Sam"—he never developed a nickname. Frances is J-Lo, Rizzo or Rizzler. We all call each other "Babe."

Memorable Directorial Note: Nick's notes are always great, always fantastic. Mostly he tells us to "Keep the pace." It's quite easy for this play to get quite slow.

Ghostly Encounter Backstage: We thought we saw a ghost, and it caused a huge amount of ruckus. There was a man standing in a corner, and after we came offstage he was gone! Then, when we turned around, he was there again! Richard said we should throw a pen at the ghost. That's when we found it was the fire inspector. He wasn't very happy.

Superstitions: We don't go in for all that. We're as untheatrical as we can be. We're all too arrogant.

Coolest Thing About Being in This Show: I get to travel around the world with a group of my best friends, experiencing all these cities and cultures and getting paid to do it. Then we go to work for three and a half hours in this great and original play, and then 1000 people tell us we're brilliant. It's just the best job in the world and we're having the greatest time in the world.

Photos by Aubrey Reuben

Hot Feet

First Preview: April 20, 2006. Opened: April 30, 2006.
Still running as of May 31, 2006.

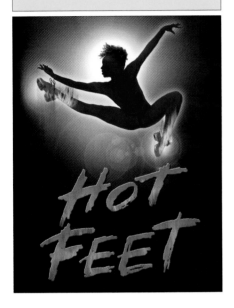

PLAYBILL

CAST

(in order of appearance)

Louie	ALLEN HIDALGO
Emma	SAMANTHA POLLINO
Kalimba	VIVIAN NIXON
Mom	ANN DUQUESNAY
Anthony	MICHAEL BALDERRAMA
Victor	KEITH DAVID
Naomi	WYNONNA SMITH
Ensemble	KEVIN AUBIN,

GERRARD CARTER,
DIONNE FIGGINS,
RAMÓN FLOWERS,
KARLA PUNO GARCIA,
NAKIA HENRY,
DUANE LEE HOLLAND,
IQUAIL S. JOHNSON,
DOMINIQUE KELLEY,
STEVE KONOPELSKI,
SUMIE MAEDA,
JON-PAUL MATEO,
VASTHY MOMPOINT,
TERA-LEE POLLIN,
MONIQUE SMITH,
DARYL SPIERS,
FELICITY STIVERSON,
HOLLIE E. WRIGHT

PLACE: New York City
TIME: Present

Continued on next page

HILTON THEATRE
A LIVE NATION VENUE

TRANSAMERICA
PRESENTS
A NEW DANCE MUSICAL PRODUCED BY
RUDY DURAND
IN ASSOCIATION WITH
KALIMBA ENTERTAINMENT, INC.
Meir A & Eli C, LLC   Polymer Global Holdings   Godley Morris Group, LLC

CONCEIVED BY
MAURICE HINES

BOOK BY
HERU PTAH

MUSIC & LYRICS BY*
MAURICE WHITE

NEW SONGS ADDITIONAL MUSIC & LYRICS BY
CAT GRAY, BRETT LAURENCE, BILL MEYERS, HERU PTAH, and ALLEE WILLIS

starring

KEITH DAVID
ALLEN HIDALGO
MICHAEL BALDERRAMA

ANN DUQUESNAY
WYNONNA SMITH
SAMANTHA POLLINO

and
VIVIAN NIXON

with

KEVIN AUBIN   BRENT CARTER   GERRARD CARTER   DIONNE FIGGINS   RAMON FLOWERS
KEITH ANTHONY FLUITT   KARLA PUNO GARCIA   NAKIA HENRY   DUANE LEE HOLLAND
IQUAIL S. JOHNSON   DOMINIQUE KELLEY   STEVE KONOPELSKI   SARAH LIVINGSTON
SUMIE MAEDA   JON-PAUL MATEO   VASTHY MOMPOINT   TERA-LEE POLLIN   MONIQUE SMITH
DARYL SPIERS   FELICITY STIVERSON   THERESA THOMASON   HOLLIE E. WRIGHT

SET DESIGN	COSTUME DESIGN	LIGHTING DESIGN	SOUND DESIGN
JAMES NOONE	**PAUL TAZEWELL**	**CLIFTON TAYLOR**	**ACME SOUND PARTNERS**

HAIR DESIGN	MUSIC DIRECTOR & CONDUCTOR	ARRANGEMENTS & ORCHESTRATIONS	MUSIC COORDINATOR
QODI ARMSTRONG	**JEFFREY KLITZ**	**BILL MEYERS**	**JOHN MILLER**

PRODUCTION MANAGER	CASTING	ASSISTANT DIRECTOR	PRODUCTION STAGE MANAGER
ARTHUR SICCARDI	**STUART HOWARD, AMY SCHECTER & PAUL HARDT**	**RICARDO KHAN**	**MICHAEL E. HARROD**

MARKETING	PRESS REPRESENTATIVE	GENERAL MANAGEMENT
HHC MARKETING	**SPRINGER ASSOCIATES PR JOE TRENTACOSTA**	**LEONARD SOLOWAY STEVEN M. LEVY**

DIRECTED & CHOREOGRAPHED BY
MAURICE HINES

*ADDITIONAL MUSIC & LYRICS : Philip Bailey, Reginald Burke, Valerie Carter, William B. Champlin, Peter Cor, Eddie Del Barrio, Larry Dunn, David Foster, Garry Glenn, Jay Graydon, James N. Howard, Jonathan G. Lind, Al McKay, Skip Scarbrough, Skylark, Charles Stepney, Beloyd Taylor, Wayne Vaughn, Wanda Vaughn, Verdine White, Allee Willis

LIVE BROADWAY

4/30/06

Vivian Nixon (center) and the Ensemble perform "Africano."

Photo by Paul Kolnik

Hot Feet

MUSICAL NUMBERS

ACT I

Overture	The Band
"Hot Feet (Latin)"	Louie
"In the Stone"	The Band
"Rock That/Boogie Wonderland"	The Band
"When I Dance"	The Band
"Dearest Heart"	Mom, Kalimba
"September"	The Band
"Turn It Into Something Good"	The Band
"Ponta de Areia"	The Band
"Thinking of You"	The Band
"Mighty Mighty"	The Band
"Serpentine Fire"	The Band
"Fantasy"	The Band

ACT II

"Louie's Welcome"	Louie
"Getaway"	The Band
"Dirty"	The Band
"After the Love Has Gone"	The Band
"Can't Hide Love"	Victor
"You Don't Know"	Mom, Victor
"Kali"	Mom

Hot Feet Ballet

Ballet Intro	The Band
"Hot Feet (Funky)"	Louie
"Let Your Feelings Show"	The Band
"System of Survival"	The Band
"Saturday Night"	The Band
"Africano"	The Band
"Star"	The Band
"Faces"	The Band
"Kali Reprise"	Mom
"Mega Mix"	The Band
"September/Gratitude"	The Band

All background vocals are sung by live band vocalists.

Allen Hidalgo with the magical shoes of the title.

Photo by Paul Kolnik

SWINGS

JESSICA HOPE COHEN, DANA MARIE INGRAHAM, TERACE JONES, MATTHEW WARNER KIERNAN, DANITA SALAMIDA

BAND VOCALISTS

BRENT CARTER, KEITH ANTHONY FLUITT, THERESA THOMASON

BAND VOCALIST SWINGS

MARVEL J. ALLEN, JOHN A. JAMES

UNDERSTUDIES/STANDBYS/ALTERNATES

Standby for Victor:
ADRIAN BAILEY
for Mom:
SANDRA REAVES-PHILLIPS
Alternate/Standby for Emma:
SARAH LIVINGSTON
Understudy for Kalimba:
DIONNE FIGGINS
For Louie:
CAESAR SAMAYOA
For Anthony:
DARYL SPIERS
For Naomi:
NAKIA HENRY

THE ORCHESTRA

Conductor: JEFFREY KLITZ
Associate Conductor: ANDY EZRIN

Guitar:
KEITH ROBINSON, BERND SCHOENHART
Electric Bass/Bass Synthesizer:
ARTIE C. REYNOLDS, III
Drums:
BRIAN DUNNE
Percussion:
ERROL CRUSHER BENNETT
Synthesizer:
JEFFREY KLITZ, ANDY EZRIN, DAVE KEYES
Saxophones:
SCOTT KREITZER
Trumpets:
DON DOWNS, DAVID TRIGG
Trombone:
KEITH O'QUINN

Music Coordinator:
JOHN MILLER

Hot Feet

Vivian Nixon
Kalimba

Keith David
Victor

Ann Duquesnay
Mom

Allen Hidalgo
Louie

Wynonna Smith
Naomi

Michael Balderrama
Anthony

Samantha Pollino
Emma

Marvel J. Allen
Band Vocalist

Kevin Aubin
Ensemble

Adrian Bailey
Standby Victor

Brent Carter
Band Vocalist

Gerrard Carter
Ensemble

Jessica Hope Cohen
Swing

Dionne Figgins
Ensemble

Ramón Flowers
Ensemble

Keith Anthony Fluitt
Band Vocalist

Karla Puno Garcia
Ensemble

Nakia Henry
Ensemble

Duane Lee Holland
Ensemble, Assistant Dance Captain, Assistant Choreographer

Dana Marie Ingraham
Swing

John A. James
Band Vocalist Swing

Iquail S. Johnson
Ensemble

Terace Jones
Swing

Dominique Kelley
Ensemble

Matthew Warner Kiernan
Swing

Steve Konopelski
Ensemble

Sarah Livingston
Alternate/ Standby Emma

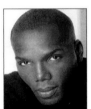
Sumie Maeda
Ensemble

Jon-Paul Mateo
Ensemble

Vasthy Mompoint
Ensemble

Tera-Lee Pollin
Ensemble

Sandra Reaves-Phillips
Standby Mom

Danita Salamida
Swing, Dance Captain, Assistant Choreographer

Caesar Samayoa
Standby Louie

Monique Smith
Ensemble

Hot Feet

Daryl Spiers
Ensemble

Felicity Stiverson
Ensemble

Theresa Thomason
Band Vocalist

Hollie E. Wright
Ensemble

Maurice Hines
Creator, Director and Choreographer

Maurice White
Music and Lyrics/ Associate Producer

Heru Ptah
Book

James Noone
Scenic Design

Paul Tazewell
Costume Design

Clifton Taylor
Lighting Design

Tom Clark, Mark Menard and Nevin Steinberg, Acme Sound Partners
Sound Design

Arthur Siccardi
Production Manager

Michael E. Harrod
Production Stage Manager

John Miller
Music Coordinator

Jeffrey Klitz
Musical Director and Conductor

Bill Meyers
Arrangements and Orchestrations

Leonard Soloway
General Manager

Steven M. Levy
General Manager

Ricardo Khan
Assistant Director

Alexandra Gushin
Company Manager

Rudy Durand
Producer

Art Macnow, Kalimba Entertainment
Associate Producer

Lon Olejniczak, Transamerica
Producer

Gary Springer and Joe Trentacosta, Springer Associates
Publicity

Bill Blackstock
Doorman

Gabriel Maysonette
Doorman

Photo by Ben Strothmann

HAIR DEPARTMENT
(L-R):
Laverne Long (Assistant to Hair Designer), Leslie (Goddess) Zeigler (Hair Assistant), Qodi Armstrong (Hair Designer), and Caroline (C.C.) Campbell (Hair Stylist).

Hot Feet

WARDROBE DEPARTMENT
Front Row (L-R):
Jocelyn Wilkosz (Dresser), Andrea Gonzalez
(Dresser), Christina Foster (Dresser),
Ginene Licata (Dresser), Gerbie Connolly
(Wardrobe Supervisor)

Middle Row (L-R):
Marc Borders (Stitcher), Teri Pruitt (Dresser),
Mary Miles (Master Stitcher), Bob Kwiatkowski
(Dresser), Donna Hulland (Dresser),
Marisa Tchornobai (Dresser), Timothy Hanlon
(Dresser) and Michael P. Murphy
(Assistant Wardrobe Supervisor).

Back Row:
Paul Riner (Dresser).

STAGE CREW
Front Row (L-R):
Mike Kondrat (Laser Tech), Sean Jones
(Carpenter), Joe Goldman (Carpenter),
John Warburton (Props).

Second Row (L-R):
John Santagata (Carpenter), Richard Fedeli
(Carpenter).

Back Row (L-R):
Jim Harris (Head Carpenter), Bill Garvey
(Road Carpenter), Rob Presley (Road Props),
Art Friedlander (House Electrician), Jeff Wever
(Frontlight) and Jim Stapleton (Carpenter).

ORCHESTRA
Front Row (L-R):
Artie C. Reynolds (Bass/Bass Synth),
Theresa Thomason (Singer), Marvel Allen
(Singer), Donald Downs (Trumpet).

Middle Row (L-R):
John Miller (Music Coordinator),
Errol "C" Bennett (Congas & Miscellaneous
Percussion), Andy Ezrin (Synthesizer),
Keith O'Quinn (Trombone),
Keith Robinson (Guitar #1).

Back Row (L-R):
Jeffrey Klitz (Conductor/Synthesizer),
Bernd Schoenhart (Guitar), Brian Dunne (Drums),
Dave Keyes (Synthesizer), Scott Kreitzer
(Saxophone/Flute), Brent Carter (Singer),
Keith Fluitt (Singer), John James (Singer),
and Dave Trigg (Trumpet).

Hot Feet

BOX OFFICE
(L-R): Michelle Smith (Treasurer) and Spencer Taustine (Treasurer)

Photos by Ben Strothmann

STAGE MANAGEMENT
(L-R): Dan Shaheen (Stage Manager), Michael E. Harrod (Production Stage Manager), Frances W. Falcone (Assistant Stage Manager), and Michael Krug (Production Assistant)

FRONT OF HOUSE STAFF
Front Row (L-R):
Jeffrey Dobbins (House Manager), Delilah Lloyd (Assistant House Manager), Edward Griggs (Usher), Alysha Wright (Usher), Charles Catt (Usher), Jason McKelvy (Usher), Nicole March (Usher), Ryan Tschetter (Usher).

Second Row (L-R):
John Wescott (Assistant House Manager), Deborah Langenfeld (Usher), Juana Rivas (Usher), Lisa Lopez (Usher), Cristin Whitley (Usher), Anna Robillard (Usher).

Third Row (L-R):
Billy Pena (Usher), Robert Phelps (Usher), Lydia Soto (Usher), Mike Chavez (Usher), Vicki Herschman (Usher), Tommie Williams (Usher), Danielle Fazio (Usher).

Back Row (L-R):
Kirssy Toribio (Usher), Erroll Worthington (Usher), Alan Toribio (Usher), Shoanna Charles (Usher), Sharon Hawkins (Usher), Ken Fuller (Usher), Dario Puccini (Usher) and Christina Gutierrez (Usher).

PRODUCTION STAFF FOR *HOT FEET*

GENERAL MANAGEMENT
Leonard Soloway   Steven M. Levy

COMPANY MANAGER
Alexandra Gushin

PRESS REPRESENTATION
SPRINGER ASSOCIATES PR
Gary Springer/Joe Trentacosta
Michelle Moretta   D'Arcy Drollinger

CASTING
Stuart Howard   Amy Schecter   Paul Hardt

Production Stage Manager .... Michael E. Harrod

Stage Manager .... Dan Shaheen
Assistant Stage Manager .... Frances W. Falcone
Assistant Director .... Ricardo Khan
Assistant Choreographer .... Danita Salamida
Assistant Choreographer .... Duane Lee Holland
Production Manager .... Arthur Siccardi
Assistant Set Designer .... Jon Savage
Assistants to James Noone .... Kenichi Takahashi,
                                                        Eric Allgeier
Associate Costume Designer .... Dennis Ballard
Assistant Costume Designers .... Stacey Galloway,
                                                        Michael McAleer
Costume Assistant .... Caitlin Kanapka Hunt
Associate Lighting Designer .... Ed McCarthy
Assistant Lighting Designer .... Greg Guarnaccia
Automated Lighting Programmer .... Paul J. Sonnleitner
Assistant Sound Designer .... Michael A. Creason

Production Carpenter .... Bill Van DeBogart
Deck Automation .... Stephen Burns
Automation Flyman .... Gabe Harris
Production Electrician .... Drayton L. Allison
Head Electrician .... Joe "Fish" Cangelosi
Deck Electrician .... Craig Aves
Follow Spot Operator .... Jennifer Lerner
Production Sound Engineer .... Scott Sanders
Advance Production Sound .... John Dory
Monitor Mixer .... Dan Robillard
Synthesizer Programmer .... Kenny Seymour
Production Property Master .... Mike Pilipski
Wardrobe Supervisor .... Gerbie Connoly
Wardrobe Assistant .... Michael Murphy
Wynonna Smith Hair Design .... Lillie Frierson King
Hair Supervisor .... Qodi Armstrong
Hairstylist .... Caroline (C.C.) Campbell

Hot Feet

Assistant to Hair Designer ....Laverne Long
New Vocal Arrangements ....Cat Gray, Brett Laurence, Bill Meyers, Maurice White
Additional Orchestrations ....Ray Brown, Michael Rubino
Associate Conductor ....Andy Ezrin
Assistant to John Miller ....Kelly M. Rach
Digital Music Editor ....Jimi Randolph
Music Copyist ....Robert Nowak and Associates, Inc.
Production Assistant ....Michael Krug
Advertising...................Eliran Murphy Group LTD/ Barbara Eliran, Ann Murphy, Steve Knight, Betsy Gershaw
Artwork ....Frank Fraver Verlizzo
Artwork Concept ....Rudy Durand
Artwork Photography ....Lois Greenfield
Marketing ....HHC Marketing/ Hugh Hysell, Amanda Pekoe, Jennifer Scherer, Jessica Hinds, Mandi Messina, Matt Sicoli, Caitlin Strype, Michael Redman, Keita Williams
Marketing ....Marketing On Demand/Davett Singletary
Multicultural Marketing ....Gwendolyn Quinn, Sandie M. Smith
Viral Marketing ....TheatreMAMA/Michelin Hall, Timothy Wooster
Merchandising ....LTS Enterprises, LLC/ Larry Turk, Randi Grossman
Production Photographer.......................Paul Kolnik
Rehearsal Photographer ....Alexandra Seegers
General Management Staff ....Errolyn Rosa
Kalimba Entertainment Staff ....Robert Weissman
Theatre Displays ....King Displays
Opening Night Coordination ....Tobak Lawrence
Insurance Services ....Tanenbaum Harber Insurance Group Carol A. Bressi-Cilona
Legal Counsel ....Cowan, DeBaets, Abrahams & Sheppard LLP/ Frederick Bimbler
Payroll ....Castellana Services, Inc.
Production Accountant ....Annemarie Aguanno, CPA
Accounting ....Rosenberg, Neuwirth & Kuchner CPAs/ Chris Cacace, CPA
Travel Agent ....Express Travel/Michael Dietz
Hotel Booking ....Road Rebel
Massage Therapist ....Ryan Blanchard
Web Design ....Carrie Schoenfeld
Child Wrangler ....Vanessa Brown
Tutoring....................On Location Education

EXCLUSIVE BOOKING DIRECTION
WILLIAM MORRIS AGENCY, INC.
Susan Weaving
1325 Avenue of the Americas
New York, NY 10019
Phone: (212) 903-1170
Fax: (212) 903-1446

CREDITS AND ACKNOWLEDGEMENTS
Scenery constructed by Hudson Scenic Studios. Costumes executed by John Kristiansen New York Inc.; Parsons-Meares, Ltd.; Eric Winterling, Inc., New York, New York; Donna Langman; Barbara Matera Ltd; C.C. Wei. Electronic costumes by Janet Hansen. Hosiery and undergarments provided by Bra*Tenders. Shoes by Capezio; T.O. Dey. Hats by Arnold Levine. Lighting equipment from PRG Lighting. Laser equipment provided by Nth Degree Creative. Soft goods, digitally printed drops and fiberoptics hangers by I. Weiss. Sound equipment by Sound Associates, Inc. Production properties by Spoon Group.

SPECIAL THANKS
Ricola natural herb cough drops courtesy of Ricola USA. Thanks to Stanley Kaye, Sherrie Maricle. Special thanks to Beverley Randolph.

MUSIC & PUBLISHER CREDITS
"**Africano**," music by Lorenzo Dunn and Maurice White. Published by EMI. "**After the Love Is Gone,**" music by William B. Champlin, David Foster, and Jay Graydon. Published by EMI Blackwood Music, Inc., Foster Frees Music, Garden Rake Music, Inc., Music Sales Corp. and Noted for the Record. "**Boogie Wonderland**," music by Jonathan G. Lind and Allee Willis. Published by Big Mystique Music and EMI Blackwood Music, Inc. "**Can't Hide Love**," music by Skip Scarborough. Published by Alexscarmusic and UniChappell Music. "**Dearest Heart**," music by William Keith Meyers, Maurice White and Allee Willis. Published by Electric Bill Music, Maurice White Music and Tonepet Music. "**Dirty**," music by Maurice White. Published by Maurice White Music and Sony/ATV Tunes LLC. "**Faces**," music by Philip Bailey, Lorenzo Dunn, Maurice White and Verdine White. Published by Cherubim Music, EMI April Music, Inc., Sir & Trini Music and Verdine White Songs. "**Fantasy**," music by Eduardo Del Barrio, Maurice White and Verdine White. Published by Criga Music and EMI April Music, Inc. "**Getaway**," music by Peter Cor and Bernard Taylor. Published by EMI April Music, Inc. "**Gratitude**," music by Lorenzo Dunn, Maurice White and Verdine White. Published by EMI April Music. "**Hot Feet**," music by Brett Laurence, William Keith Meyers and Maurice White. Published by Digable Tunes, Electric Bill Music and Maurice White Music. "**In the Stone**," music by David Foster, Maurice White, Allee Willis. Published by EMI April Music, EMI Blackwood Music, Foster Frees Music, Irving Music. "**Kali**," music by Brett Laurence, William Keith Meyers and Maurice White. Published by Digable Tunes, Electric Bill Music and Maurice White Music. "**Let Your Feelings Show**," music by David Foster, Maurice White and Allee Willis. Published by EMI April Music, Inc.; EMI Blackwood Music, Inc.; Foster Frees Music; and Irving Music, Inc. "**Let's Groove**," music by Wayne Vaughn and Maurice White. Published by EMI April Music Inc. and Music Sales Corp. "**Louie's Welcome**," music by Cat Gray and Heru Ptah. Published by Heru Ptah Music and Pretty Little Kitty Music. "**Mighty Mighty**," music by Maurice White and Verdine White. Published by EMI April Music, Inc. "**Ponta De Areia**," music by Fernando Brant and Milton Nascimento. Published by EMI April Music and BMG Songs. "**Reasons**," music by Philip James Bailey, Charles Stepney and Maurice White. Published by EMI April Music, Inc.; Eibur Music; Embassy Music; and Music Sales Corporation. "**Rock That**," music by David Foster and Maurice White. Published by EMI April Music, Foster Frees Music and Irving Music, Inc. "**Saturday Night**," music by Philip J. Bailey, Albert Phillip McKay and Maurice White. Published by EMI April Music, Inc. "**September**," music by Albert Phillip McKay, Maurice White and Allee Willis. Published by EMI April Music, Inc., EMI Blackwood Music, Inc., Irving Music, Inc. and Steel Chest Music. "**Serpentine Fire**," music by Reginald Burke, Maurice White and Verdine White. Published by EMI April Music, Inc. "**Star**," music by Eduardo Del Barrio, Maurice White and Allee Willis. Published by Criga Music, EMI April Music, EMI Blackwood Music and Irving Music. "**System of Survival**," music by Skylark. Published by EMI April Music, Inc. and Sputnik Adventure Music. "**That's the Way of the World**," music by Charles Stepney, Maurice White and Verdine White. Published by Eibur Music, EMI April Music, Inc. and Embassy Music Corp. "**Thinking of You**," music by Wanda Vaughn, Wayne Vaughn and Maurice White. Published by EMI April Music and Music Sales Corp. "**Turn It Into Something Good**," music by Valerie Carter, James Howard and Maurice White. Published by Careers BMG Music Publishing, EMI April Music, Inc., Newton House Music and River Honey Music. "**When I Dance**," music by William Keith Meyers, Maurice White and Allee Willis. Published by Electric Bill Music, Maurice White Music and Tonepet Music. "**You Don't Know**," music by William Keith Meyers, Maurice White and Heru Ptah. Published by Electric Bill Music, Heru Ptah Music and Maurice White Music.

HILTON THEATRE STAFF
General Manager ....Micah Hollingworth
Assistant General Manager ....Jorelle Aronovitch
House Manager ....Jeffrey Dobbins
Facility Manager ....Jeff Nuzzo
Box Office Treasurer ....Peter Attanasio Jr.
Head Carpenter ....James C. Harris
Head Electrician ....Art J. Friedlander
Head of Properties ....Joseph P. Harris Jr.
Head of Sound ....John R. Gibson
Asst. Box Office Treasurer ....Spencer Taustine
Regional Accounting
Manager ....Patricia Busby O'Shaughnessy
Payroll Administrator ....Carmen Martinez
Shipping/Receiving ....Dinara Ferreira
Administrative Assistant ....Jenny Kirlin

LIVE NATION
President and Chief Executive Officer ......Michael Rapino

LIVE NATION – VENUES
President....................................Bruce Eskowitz
CFO ....Alan Ridgeway
Vice President, Finance ....Kathy Porter
Executive Vice President ....Ned Collette
Senior Vice President NY and CT Venues ....John Huff
Director of Labor Relations...............Chris Brockmeyer

LIVE NATION – THEATRICAL
Chairman, Global Theatre ....David Ian
CEO Theatrical, North America ....Steve Winton
President and COO, North America...David M. Anderson
CFO, North America ....Paul Dietz
Senior Vice President, Producing ....Jennifer Costello
Executive Vice President/CMO ....Susie Krajsa
Senior Vice President, Operations ....Dan Swartz
Senior Vice President, Business Affairs ....David Lazar
Senior Vice President, Sales & Ticketing ...Courtney Pierce
Vice President, Marketing ....Jennifer DeLange
Vice President, Finance ....Chante Moore
Vice President, Programming ....Alison Spiriti

Hot Feet

Scrapbook

Correspondent: Michael E. Harrod, Production Stage Manager.

Memorable Opening Night Letter, Fax or Note: A personal note and flowers from Judith Jamison.

Opening Night Gifts : *The Color Purple* sent us two very generous gift baskets filled with goodies that would delight any Broadway company (Emer'gen-C, Throat Coat, and other treats).

Most Exciting Celebrity Visitor and What They Did/Said: Chita Rivera, who took pictures with the company after the show. Afterward, she sent a thank-you gift basket.

Who Got the Gypsy Robe: Ramón Flowers.

Most Roles: Each person in the ensemble is extremely talented. They dance their feet off 8 times a week.

Most Shows: Adrian Bailey (Victor standby).

Special Backstage Rituals: During the overture, most of the cast continues warming up in the wings, choreographed to the music.

Cell Phone Incident: At an early preview I witnessed an audience member take out her cell phone, call a friend, shout into the phone, "You gotta hear this!" She then held the phone high up in the air to share the music. Our sensational usher team quickly swooped down to confiscate the offending device.

Memorable Press Encounter: We were recently featured, live, on a Japanese morning show. Of course this was at 6 P.M. Eastern time. I guess we have a large demographic in central Tokyo.

Latest Audience Arrival: Twenty minutes before the end of the performance.

Heaviest/Hottest Costume: Allen Hidalgo's "Bag Man" costume consists of numerous heavy layers, including just over a dozen shoes tied to the inside of the coat. He also wears a cape covered with neon footprints powered by 8 batteries.

Honorable mention: Vivian Nixon. She dances the strenuous "Hot Feet Ballet" in a pair of light-up shoes. Each shoe contains 50 light bulbs wired in 5 separate circuits, powered by 2 batteries.

Who Wore the Least: Most of the ensemble costumes leave nothing to the imagination. Including women in black lace lingerie, and men in exaggerated codpieces.

Catchphrase Only the Company Would Recognize: "Baseball, Baseball, Baseball."

Orchestra Member Who Played the Most Performances Without a Sub : Our Maestro, Jeff Klitz, has never missed a performance

Memorable Directorial Note: "FULL OUT NO MARKING!!!"

Company In-Jokes: We have a sheet going around that lists potential titles for the sequel.

Nickname: I'm "Peanut."

Embarrassing Moments: A certain actress playing the role of Naomi made her entrance for a scene too early and had to be told by the actor playing Anthony to come back later.

Also: During the curtain call, our extraordinary pit singers consistently get the largest round of applause, and numerous cheers. Most of the audience members think that they are Earth, Wind & Fire.

1. Vivian Nixon and Michael Balderrama at the opening night party at the Hilton New York Hotel.
2. Wynonna Smith on opening night.
3. Nixon (R) with mom, Debbie Allen.
4. Curtain call on opening night (L-R): Keith David, composer Maurice White, director Maurice Hines, Vivian Nixon and Ann Duquesnay.
5. Samantha Pollino at the opening night party.

In My Life

First Preview: September 30, 2005. Opened: October 20, 2005.
Closed December 11, 2005 after 23 Previews and 61 Performances.

CAST
(in order of appearance)

Vera ....CHIARA NAVARRA
J.T. ....CHRISTOPHER J. HANKE
Jenny ....JESSICA BOEVERS
Winston ....DAVID TURNER
Al ....MICHAEL J. FARINA
Samantha ....LAURA JORDAN
Liz ....ROBERTA GUMBEL
Nick ....MICHAEL HALLING
Ensemble ....COURTNEY BALAN,
CARMEN KEELS,
KILTY REIDY, BRYNN WILLIAMS

UNDERSTUDIES

For Vera: BRYNN WILLIAMS

For J.T.: MICHAEL HALLING,
JONATHAN GROFF

For Jenny: LAURA JORDAN,
COURTNEY BALAN

For Winston: KILTY REIDY

For Liz: CARMEN KEELS

For Al: KILTY REIDY

For Nick: JONATHAN GROFF, KILTY REIDY

For Samantha: COURTNEY BALAN,
CARMEN KEELS

Swing/Dance Captain:
JONATHAN GROFF

THE MUSIC BOX
THE ESTATE OF IRVING BERLIN AND THE SHUBERT ORGANIZATION, OWNERS
239 W. 45th STREET

_____

WATCH HILL PRODUCTIONS AND TBF MUSIC CORP.
present

IN MY LIFE

Music, Lyrics and Book by
Joseph Brooks

Starring

Jessica Boevers   Christopher J. Hanke

David Turner   Michael J. Farina
Roberta Gumbel   Michael Halling   Laura Jordan
Courtney Balan   Jonathan Groff   Carmen Keels   Kilty Reidy   Brynn Williams
and introducing
Chiara Navarra

Scenic Design	Costume Design	Lighting Design
Allen Moyer	**Catherine Zuber**	**Christopher Akerlind**
Sound Design	Projection Design	Hair and Wig Design
John H. Shivers	**Wendall K. Harrington**	**Tom Watson**

Casting	Associate Director	Production Manager	Production Stage Manager
Dave Clemmons Casting	**Dan Fields**	**Arthur Siccardi**	**Jane Grey**
Press Agent	Marketing	General Management	
Richard Kornberg Associates	**HHC Marketing**	**NLA/Devin Keudell**	
Music Director	Orchestrations	Music Coordinator	
Henry Aronson	**Kinny Landrum**	**Michael Keller**	

Musical Staging by
Richard Stafford

Directed by
Joseph Brooks

10/20/05

Chiara Navarra and
Michael J. Farina

Photo by Joan Marcus

In My Life

MUSICAL NUMBERS

"Life Turns on a Dime" .... Vera, J.T., Jenny
"It Almost Feels Like Love" .... J.T., Jenny
"Perfect for an Opera" .... Winston
"What a Strange Life We Live" .... Jenny
"Doomed" .... Winston, Nick and Ensemble
"What a Strange Life We Live" .... Vera
"Sempre Mio Rimani" .... Liz
"I Am My Mother's Son" .... J.T.
"Life Turns on a Dime" (Reprise) .... Jenny
"Volkswagen" .... Al
"What a Strange Life We Live" .... Nick
"Headaches" .... Winston, Nick, Liz, Vera and Ensemble
"When I Sing" .... J.T.
"Secrets" .... Winston and Ensemble
"In My Life" .... Jenny, J.T.
"A Ride on the Wheel" .... Nick, Samantha, J.T., Ensemble
"Perfect for an Opera" (Reprise) .... Winston, Liz, Nick, Vera
"Didn't Have to Love You" .... Jenny, J.T.
"Listen to Your Mouth" .... Winston, Al
"When She Danced" .... Liz, Vera
"Volkswagen" (Reprise) .... Al
"Not This Day" .... Al
"Floating on Air" .... J.T.
"Not This Day" .... J.T., Jenny, Liz, Nick, Vera, Al and Ensemble
"Life Turns on a Dime" (Reprise) .... Vera and Full Company

Jessica Boevers
Jenny

Christopher J. Hanke
J.T.

David Turner
Winston

Michael J. Farina
Al

Roberta Gumbel
Elizabeth

Michael Halling
Nick

Laura Jordan
Samantha, Doctor

Chiara Navarra
Vera

Courtney Balan
Ensemble

Jonathan Groff
Swing

David Turner (above) and (L-R:) Kilty Reidy and Christopher J. Hanke.

Photo by Joan Marcus

BAND

Conductor: HENRY ARONSON
Associate Conductor/Keyboard: GREG DLUGOS

Keyboards:
TED KOOSHIAN,
MAGGIE TORRES,
FRAN MINARIK

Guitars:
BRUCE UCHITEL, J.J. MCGEEHAN

Bass:
RANDY LANDAU

Drums:
BRIAN BRAKE

Music Coordinator: Michael Keller

In My Life

Carmen Keels
Ensemble

Kilty Reidy
Ensemble

Brynn Williams
Ensemble

Joseph Brooks
*Director, Composer,
Author, Producer*

Dan Fields
Associate Director

Richard Stafford
Musical Staging

Allen Moyer
Set Design

Catherine Zuber
Costume Designer

Christopher Akerlind
Lighting Designer

John H. Shivers
Sound Design

Wendall K. Harrington
Projection Designer

Tom Watson
Hair Designer

Henry Aronson
Music Director

Kinny Landrum
Orchestrations

Michael Keller
Music Coordinator

Jane Grey
*Production
Stage Manager*

Dave Clemmons
Casting

Arthur Siccardi
Production Manager

Richard Kornberg
Public Relations

Christopher J. Hanke
and Jessica Boevers (C)
sing "Not This Day."

Photo by Joan Marcus

In My Life

In My Life
SCRAPBOOK

Photos by Aubrey Reuben

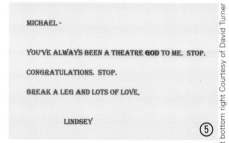

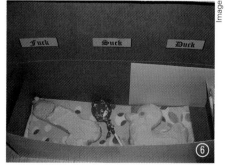

Images at bottom right Courtesy of David Turner

Correspondent: David Turner, "Winston."

Opening Night Gifts: Everyone got 30G iPods from Joe Brooks. One of us received a Cuisinart juicer. (For making lemonade. Lots of lemonade.)

Celebrity Visitor: Dame Edna: "Winston, possum, this is my stage." Honestly, no celebrities have come. Or if they have, they've come in disguise.

Who Got the Gypsy Robe: Twelve-year-old Brynn Williams, the youngest Gypsy ever. She attached trinkets to her section of the Gypsy Robe: pirates, lemons, skeletons and a mock-up of our Playbill.

"Gypsy of the Year" Sketch: "Broadway Baby." Courtney Balan, Kilty Reidy, and Laura Jordan wrote it. Most of the cast participated in the presentation. In it, our adorable Gypsy, young Brynn, belted the hell out of "I'm Still Here." Because, improbably, after almost 75 performances, um...we're still here.

Actor Who Performed the Most Roles an This Show: Kilty Riedy: Heaven Worker, Sal the diner man, Good Samaritan with backpack, Doctor's Aide.

Who Has Done the Most Shows: Probably Michael J. Farina.

Backstage Rituals: Sneaking candy from stage management. Calling each other "Boo." Singing the "Dance Belts on Broadway" song.

Favorite Moment During Each Performance: Listening to Jess give the Broadway Cares speech.

Favorite In-Theatre Gathering Place: The quick-change booth when Michael Halling is changing.

Favorite Off-Site Hangout: David Turner's Apartment

Favorite Snack Food: Emer'gen-C, lemon wedges.

Mascot: Jane (PSM) and Sandy's dog, "Buster." Followed by the irrepressible and uncooperative Mr. Bones.

Favorite Therapy: Paychecks.

1. Arriving at the cast party at the Millennium Broadway Hotel (L-R): Michael Halling, Michael J. Farina, David Turner, Joe Brooks, Chiara Navarra, Jessica Boevers, Christopher J. Hanke and Roberta Gumbel.
2. Cast members Carmen Keels, Kilty Reidy and Courtney Balan at the cast party.
3. Taking bows on opening night.
4. Hanke and Boevers at the "Broadway on Broadway" event.
5. An opening-night telegram to Michael J. Farina.
6. Laura Jordan's opening-night gift diorama of one of the show's memorable lines.

In My Life
SCRAPBOOK

Most Memorable Ad-Lib: "Do You Believe in Fairies?"

Record Number of Cell Phone Rings During a Performance: Many. Many rings on many separate occasions. And, in rehearsals, they were all Joe Brooks's.

Memorable Press Encounter: Performing "Doomed" at press day 48 hours after it was added to the show in rehearsal.

Fastest Costume Change: Kilty Reidy: from Good Samaritan with Backpack into Doctor's Aide. A lascivious Jessica Boevers would hang around stage left to ogle Kilty's dance belt.

Busiest Day at the Box Office: The day we were on Oprah.

Who Wore the Heaviest/Hottest Costume: David Turner: full-length, blue-haired fur coat (a.k.a. "Cookie Monster.")

Who Wore The Least: Jessica Boevers's tank/mini-skirt

Catchphrases Only the Company Would Recognize: "He's talented, you're having fun—and this is gonna work." "We'd have literally dozens of dollars."

Best In-House Parody Lyrics: "What a strange show this is . . .."

Embarrassing Moment: Christopher J. Hanke, instead of singing, "She touched my soul, she moved my heart," accidentally came out with "She touched my hole, she moved my heart."

Nicknames: C.J. Hanks, Cotes Totes, Mr. Bones, DT, Slim, Berta, Jonath-Ann.

Sweethearts Within the Company: Kilty and Rubberband Ball. David and Mr. Bones. Carmen and I.A.T.S.E.

Coolest Thing About Being in This Show: Seven Broadway debuts; the twelve-year-old received the Gypsy Robe.

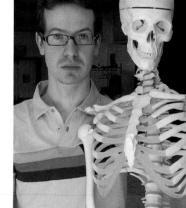

1. Chiara Navarra ad-libs with a headless Mr. Bones.
2. David Turner getting into makeup as Winston.
3. Michael Halling, Courtney Balan, Jonathan Groff and Michael J. Farina.
4. David Turner confers with "Mr. Bones."
5. Brynn Williams sings "I'm Still Here" while wearing the Gypsy Robe at "Gypsy of the Year."

Jackie Mason: Freshly Squeezed

First Preview: March 8, 2005. Opened: March 23, 2005.
Closed September 4, 2005 after 14 Previews and 172 Performances.

THE HELEN HAYES THEATRE

MARTIN MARKINSON   DONALD TICK

Jyll Rosenfeld, Jon Stoll and James Scibelli
present

JACKIE MASON
freshly squeezed

Lighting Design by   *Sound Design by*
Paul Miller   **Peter Hylenski**

General Press Representative   *Marketing*   *Advertising*
Larry Weinberg   **Keith Hurd**   **Echo Advertising**

General Management   *Production Stage Manager*   *Company Manager*
Theatre Production Group   **Don Myers**   **G. Eric Muratalla**

Written and Directed by
Jackie Mason

6/1/05

Jackie Mason
Himself, Writer and Director

Peter Hylenski
Sound Design

Keith Hurd
Marketing

Raoul Lionel Felder
Legal Counsel

Larry Weinberg
*General Press
Representative*

Alan Markinson
House Manager

Jackie Mason: Freshly Squeezed

THE CREW
Back Row (L-R): Roger Keller, Jessica Bailey, Olivia Goode, John Biancamano, Don Myers, Joe Beck, Michael Lynch, Bobby Seymour.
Middle Row (L-R): Gary Stocker, David Heveran, Eric Muratalla, Shannon Taylor, Berdine Vaval, Hirendra Joshi.
Front Row (L-R): Ron Mooney, Jyll Rosenfeld, Jackie Mason and Linda Maley-Biancamano.

STAFF FOR
JACKIE MASON: FRESHLY SQUEEZED;
JUST ONE JEW TALKING

GENERAL MANAGEMENT
THEATRE PRODUCTION GROUP LLC
Frank P. Scardino
in association with
Joseph P. Harris

COMPANY MANAGER
G. ERIC MURATALLA

GENERAL PRESS REPRESENTATIVE
LARRY WEINBERG

PRODUCTION STAGE MANAGER ....**Don Myers**
Production Carpenter ....Ron Mooney
Production Electrician ....Joe Beck
Production Prop ....Roger Keller
Sound Engineer ....Bob Etter
Front Light Operator ....Thomas Galinski
Assistant to General Manager ....Tegan Meyer
Assistant to Jyll Rosenfeld ....Melissa Flores
Assistant to Jon Stoll ....Susan Christopher
Advertising ....Echo Advertising/Barry Avrich, Tracy
Chang
Marketing ....Keith Hurd
Insurance ....C&S Int'l Insurance Brokers, Inc./Debra Kozee

Legal Counsel ....Raoul Lionel Felder
Accounting ....Rosenberg, Neuwirth & Kuchner/Michele Gugliero
Payroll Services ....Castellana Services, Inc.
Banking ....Commerce Bank/Barbara von Borstel, Ashley Elezi
Web-Site Design ....Sarah DiSanti

CREDITS
Lighting equipment provided by PRG Lighting. Sound equipment provided by PRG Audio. Soft goods provided by Rosebrand, Inc. Company boards and sliders by King Displays.

THE HELEN HAYES THEATRE
owned and operated by
MARTIN MARKINSON and DONALD TICK
General Manager ....Susan S. Myerberg
Associate General Manager ....Jeffrey T. Hughes

STAFF FOR THE HELEN HAYES THEATRE
HOUSE MANAGER ....ALAN R. MARKINSON
Treasurer ....David Heveran
Assistant Treasurers ....Michael A. Lynch,
Manuel Rivera
Head Carpenter ....Ron Mooney
Head Electrician ....Joseph Beck
Head Propertyman ....Roger Keller
Engineer/Maintenance ....Hector Angulo
Head Usher ....John Biancamano
Stage Door ....Vincent Kwasnicki, Robert Seymour
Accountant ....Chen-Win Hsu, CPA., P.C.

Jersey Boys

First Preview: October 4, 2005. Opened: November 6, 2005.
Still running as of May 31, 2006.

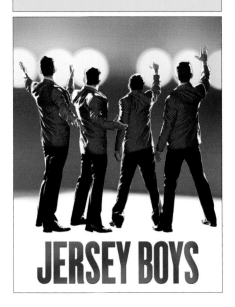

CAST
(in alphabetical order)

Hal Miller (and others) ....TITUSS BURGESS
Hank Majewski (and others) .....STEVE GOUVEIA
Bob Crewe (and others) ....PETER GREGUS
Tommy DeVito ....CHRISTIAN HOFF
Norm Waxman (and others) ....DONNIE KEHR
Joey (and others) ....MICHAEL LONGORIA
Gyp DeCarlo (and others) ....MARK LOTITO
Mary Delgado (and others) .....JENNIFER NAIMO
Lorraine (and others) ....ERICA PICCININNI
Bob Gaudio ....DANIEL REICHARD
Francine (and others) ....SARA SCHMIDT
Nick Massi ....J. ROBERT SPENCER
Frankie Valli ....JOHN LLOYD YOUNG

UNDERSTUDIES

For Frankie Valli:
MICHAEL LONGORIA, DOMINIC NOLFI

For Tommy DeVito:
DONNIE KEHR, JOHN LEONE

For Bob Gaudio:
STEVE GOUVEIA, DOMINIC NOLFI

For Nick Massi:
STEVE GOUVEIA, JOHN LEONE

For Gyp DeCarlo:
DONNIE KEHR, JOHN LEONE

SWINGS

HEATHER FERGUSON, JOHN LEONE,
DOMINIC NOLFI

Dance Captain: PETER GREGUS

♩ AUGUST WILSON THEATRE
A JUJAMCYN THEATRE
ROCCO LANDESMAN
PRESIDENT

PAUL LIBIN   JACK VIERTEL
PRODUCING DIRECTOR   CREATIVE DIRECTOR

Dodger Theatricals Joseph J. Grano Pelican Group Tamara and Kevin Kinsella
in association with Latitude Link Rick Steiner/Osher/Staton/Bell/Mayerson Group

present

JERSEY BOYS

The Story of Frankie Valli & The Four Seasons

Book by   Music by   Lyrics by
Marshall Brickman & Rick Elice   **Bob Gaudio**   **Bob Crewe**

with

Christian Hoff Daniel Reichard J. Robert Spencer and John Lloyd Young

Tituss Burgess Heather Ferguson Steve Gouveia Donnie Kehr
John Leone Michael Longoria Jennifer Naimo Dominic Nolfi
Erica Piccininni Sara Schmidt with Peter Gregus and Mark Lotito

Scenic Design	Costume Design	Lighting Design	Sound Design
Klara Zieglerova	Jess Goldstein	Howell Binkley	Steve Canyon Kennedy

Projection Design	Wig and Hair Design	Fight Director	Production Stage Manager
Michael Clark	Charles LaPointe	Steve Rankin	Richard Hester

Orchestrations	Music Coordinator
Steve Orich	John Miller

Technical Supervisor	East Coast Casting	West Coast Casting	Company Manager
Peter Fulbright	Tara Rubin Casting	Sharon Bialy C.S.A. Sherry Thomas C.S.A.	Sandra Carlson

Associate Producers	Executive Producer	Promotions	Press Representative
Lauren Mitchell Rhoda Mayerson Stage Entertainment	Sally Campbell Morse	HHC Marketing	Boneau/Bryan-Brown

Music Direction, Vocal Arrangements & Incidental Music
Ron Melrose

Choreography
Sergio Trujillo

Directed by
Des McAnuff

World Premiere Produced by La Jolla Playhouse, La Jolla, CA
Des McAnuff, Artistic Director & Steven B. Libman, Managing Director

The producers wish to thank Theatre Development Fund for it's support of this production.

11/6/05

Photo by Joan Marcus

(L-R): J. Robert Spencer, John Lloyd Young, Daniel Reichard and Christian Hoff

Jersey Boys

MUSICAL NUMBERS

ACT ONE

"Ces Soirées-La (Oh What a Night)" – Paris, 2000 ....French Rap Star, Backup Group
"Silhouettes" ....Tommy DeVito, Nick Massi, Nick DeVito, Frankie Castelluccio
"You're the Apple of My Eye" ....Tommy DeVito, Nick Massi, Nick DeVito
"I Can't Give You Anything But Love" ....Frankie Castelluccio
"Earth Angel" ....Tommy DeVito, Full Company
"Sunday Kind of Love" ....Frankie Valli, Tommy DeVito, Nick Massi, Nick's Date
"My Mother's Eyes" ....Frankie Valli
"I Go Ape" ....The Four Lovers
"(Who Wears) Short Shorts" ....The Royal Teens
"I'm in the Mood for Love/Moody's Mood for Love" ....Frankie Valli
"Cry for Me" ....Bob Gaudio, Frankie Valli, Tommy DeVito, Nick Massi
"An Angel Cried" ....Hal Miller and The Rays
"I Still Care" ....Miss Frankie Nolan and The Romans
"Trance" ....Billy Dixon and The Topix
"Sherry" ....The Four Seasons
"Big Girls Don't Cry" ....The Four Seasons
"Walk Like a Man" ....The Four Seasons
"December, 1963 (Oh What a Night)" ....Bob Gaudio, Full Company
"My Boyfriend's Back" ....The Angels
"My Eyes Adored You" ....Frankie Valli, Mary Delgado, The Four Seasons
"Dawn (Go Away)" ....The Four Seasons
"Walk Like a Man" (reprise) ....Full Company

ACT TWO

"Big Man in Town" ....The Four Seasons
"Beggin'" ....The Four Seasons
"Stay" ....Bob Gaudio, Frankie Valli, Nick Massi
"Let's Hang On (To What We've Got)" ....Bob Gaudio, Frankie Valli
"Opus 17 (Don't You Worry 'Bout Me)" ....Bob Gaudio, Frankie Valli and The New Seasons
"Bye Bye Baby" ....Frankie Valli and The Four Seasons
"C'mon Marianne" ....Frankie Valli and The Four Seasons
"Can't Take My Eyes Off of You" ....Frankie Valli
"Working My Way Back to You" ....Frankie Valli and The Four Seasons
"Fallen Angel" ....Frankie Valli
"Rag Doll" ....The Four Seasons
"Who Loves You" ....The Four Seasons, Full Company

ORCHESTRA
Conductor: Ron Melrose

Associate Conductor: Deborah N. Hurwitz
Keyboards: Deborah N. Hurwitz, Ron Melrose,
Stephen "Hoops" Snyder
Guitars: Joe Payne
Bass: Ken Dow
Drums: Kevin Dow
Reeds: Matt Hong, Ben Kono
Trumpet: David Spier
Music Coordinator: John Miller

2005-2006 AWARDS
TONY AWARDS
Best Musical
Best Performance by a Lead Actor in a Musical
(John Lloyd Young)
Best Performance by a Featured Actor in a
Musical (Christian Hoff)
Best Lighting Design of a Musical
(Howell Binkley)

DRAMA LEAGUE AWARD
Distinguished Production of a Musical

OUTER CRITICS CIRCLE AWARDS
Outstanding Broadway Musical
Outstanding Actor in a Musical
(John Lloyd Young)
Outstanding Lighting Design (Howell Binkley)

DRAMA DESK AWARDS
Outstanding Actor in a Musical
(John Lloyd Young)
Outstanding Sound Design
(Steve Canyon Kennedy)

(L-R): J. Robert Spencer, John Lloyd Young, Daniel Reichard, Christian Hoff.

Photo by Joan Marcus

Jersey Boys

Christian Hoff
Tommy DeVito

Daniel Reichard
Bob Gaudio

J. Robert Spencer
Nick Massi

John Lloyd Young
Frankie Valli

Peter Gregus
Bob Crewe and others

Mark Lotito
Gyp DeCarlo and others

Tituss Burgess
Hal Miller and others

Heather Ferguson
Swing

Steve Gouveia
Hank Majewski and others

Donnie Kehr
Norm Waxman and others

John Leone
Swing

Michael Longoria
Joey and others

Jennifer Naimo
Mary Delgado and others

Dominic Nolfi
Swing

Erica Piccininni
Lorraine and others

Sara Schmidt
Francine and others

Marshall Brickman
Book

Rick Elice
Book

Bob Gaudio
Composer

Bob Crewe
Lyricist

Des McAnuff
Director

Sergio Trujillo
Choreographer

Klara Zieglerova
Set Design

Jess Goldstein
Costume Design

Howell Binkley
Lighting Design

Steve Canyon Kennedy
Sound Design

Steve Rankin
Fight Director

Steve Orich
Orchestrations

John Miller
Music Coordinator

Tara Rubin,
Tara Rubin Casting
East Coast Casting

Stephen Gabis
Dialect Coach

Rick Steiner
Producer

John and
Bonnie Osher
Producers

Dan Staton
Producer

Joop van den Ende,
Stage Entertainment
Producer

Jersey Boys

Frederic H. Mayerson
Producer

Rhoda Mayerson
Associate Producer

TRANSFER STUDENTS
2005-2006

Ken Dow
Thug

Joe Payne
Thug

Matthew Scott
Swing

Photos by Ben Strothmann

BAND
(L-R): Matt Hong (Baritone Sax), Kevin Dow (Drums), Joe Payne (Guitar), David Spier (Trumpet), Deborah Hurwitz (Keyboard), Steve Gibb (Guitar and Drums) and Stephen "Hoops" Snyder (Keyboard).

Gustavo Catuy (Doorman)

Ron Melrose
(Music Direction, Vocal Arrangements & Incidental Music)

Julie M. Randolph (Head Sound Engineer)

Jersey Boys

WARDROBE DEPARTMENT
Front Row (L-R):
Nancy Ronan (Assistant Wardrobe Supervisor),
Kelly Kinsella (Dresser), Lee Austin
(Wardrobe Supervisor).

Second Row (L-R):
Wendy Lorenz (Dresser), Nick Staub (Dresser).

Third Row (L-R):
Sandy Binion (Dresser), Hazel Higgins (Dresser),
Jessica Worsnop (Dresser).

Back Row (L-R):
Ricky Yates (Dresser) and Davis Duffield
(Dresser).

STAGE MANAGEMENT
(L-R): Michael T. Clarkston, Richard
Hester and Michelle Bosch.

BOX OFFICE
(L-R): Kevin Dublynn (Assistant Treasurer),
Jeanne Halal (Assistant Treasurer)
and Nick Russo (Head Treasurer).

Jersey Boys

FRONT OF HOUSE STAFF
Front Row (L-R):
Judy Jones (Bartender), David McKoy (Security), Antoin Ramirez (Bartender).

Middle Row (L-R):
Arthur Van Salisbury (Engineer), Maria Theresa Farenbach (Usher), Rose Balsamo (Head Usher), Anne Cavanaugh (Ticket Taker), Sally Lettieri (Usher), Gail Worthman (Usher) and Paula Gallo-Kcira (Usher).

STAGE CREW
Front Row (L-R): Michael Lyons (Electrics), Sean Fedigan (Electrician), Dave Shepherd (Sound), Brian Aman (Electrician).

Back Row (L-R):
Robert Fehribach (House Electrician), Steve Pugilese (Electrician), and Mike Terestra (Sound).

STAGE CREW
Front Row (L-R):
Emiliano Pares (Props), Ron Fucarino (Automation), Ken Harris (Props).

Back Row (L-R):
Dan Dour (House Carpenter), Scott Mulrain (House Props), Mike Kelly (Carpenter), Peter Wright (Carpenter), John Thomson (Props) and Greg Burton (Automation).

Jersey Boys

STAFF FOR *JERSEY BOYS*

GENERAL PRESS REPRESENTATION
BONEAU/BRYAN-BROWN
Adrian Bryan-Brown Susanne Tighe
Heath Schwartz

COMPANY MANAGER
Sandra Carlson

PRODUCTION STAGE MANAGER .... RICHARD HESTER
Stage Manager .... Michelle Bosch
Assistant Stage Manager .... Michael T. Clarkston
Assistant Stage Manager .... Michelle Reupert
Associate General Manager .... Jennifer F. Vaughan
Technical Supervision .... Tech Production Services/ Peter Fulbright, Mary Duffe, Colleen Houlehen, Lauren A. Duffy
Music Technical Design .... Deborah N. Hurwitz
Assistant Director .... Holly-Anne Ruggiero
Second Assistant Director .... Alex Timbers
Assistant Choreographer .... Kelly Devine
Dialect Coach .... Stephen Gabis
Assistant Company Manager .... Tim Sulka
Fight Captain .... Peter Gregus
Associate Scenic Designers .... Nancy Thun, Todd Ivins
Assistant Scenic Designers .... Sonoka Gozelski, Matthew Myhrum
Associate Costume Designer .... Alejo Vietti
Assistant Costume Designers .... China Lee, Elizabeth Flauto
Associate Lighting Designer .... Patricia Nichols
Assistant Lighting Designer .... Sarah E. C. Maines
Associate Sound Designer .... Andrew Keister
Assistant Projection Designers .... Jason Thompson, Chris Kateff
Story Board Artist .... Don Hudson
Casting Associates .... Dunja Vitolic, Eric Woodall, Laura Schutzel
Casting Assistants ...... Mona Slomsky, Rebecca Carfagna
Automated Lighting Programmer .... Hillary Knox
Projection Programming .... Paul Vershbow
Set Model Builder .... Anne Goelz
Costume Intern .... Jessica Reed
Production Carpenter .... Michael W. Kelly
Deck Automation .... Greg Burton
Fly Automation .... Ron Fucarino
Flyman .... Peter Wright
Production Electrician .... James Fedigan
Head Electrician .... Jon Mark Davidson
Assistant Electrician .... Brian Aman
Follow Spot Operator .... Sean Fedigan
Production Sound Engineer .... Andrew Keister
Head Sound Engineer .... Julie M. Randolph
Production Props .... Emiliano Pares
Assistant Props .... Kenneth Harris Jr.
Wardrobe Supervisor .... Lee J. Austin
Assistant Wardrobe Supervisor .... Nancy Ronan
Wardrobe Department ...... Davis Duffield, Kelly Kinsella, Shaun Ozminski, Nicholas Staub, Jessica Worsnop, Ricky Yates
Hair Supervisor .... Amy Neswald
Hair Assistant .... Craig Kilander
Hair Department .... Frederick G. Waggoner
Assistant to John Miller .... Charles Butler
Synthesizer Programming .... Deborah N. Hurwitz, Steve Orich
Guitar Technician .... Gin Beck
Music Copying .... Anixter Rice Music Service
Music Production Assistant .... Alexandra Carlson
Production Assistants .... Kerry McGrath, Michelle Reupert, Bryan Rountree, Deborah Wolfson
Dramaturg .... Allison Horsley
Associates to Messrs. Michael David and Ed Strong .... Pamela Lloyd, James Love
Advertising .... Serino Coyne, Inc./ Scott Johnson, Sandy Block, Ben Downing
Marketing .... Dodger Marketing/ Gordon Kelly, Jessica Ludwig
Promotions .... HHC Marketing/ Hugh Hysell, Michael Redman, Jim Glaub, Jay Johnson, Amanda Pekoe, Matt Sicoli, Caitlin Strype
Press Representative Staff .... Chris Boneau, Jim Byk, Brandi Cornwell, Jackie Green, Juliana Hannett, Hector Hernandez, Jessica Johnson, Kevin Jones, Eric Louie, Aaron Meier, Joe Perrotta, Linnae Petruzzelli, Matt Polk, Matt Ross
Sponsorship/ Partnership Marketing .... Kobin Enterprises. Ltd.
Banking .... Commerce Bank/Barbara von Borstel
Payroll .... Castellana Services Inc./ Lance Castellana, Norman Seawell, James Castellana
Accountants .... Schall and Ashenfarb, C.P.A.
Finance Director .... Paula Maldonado
Insurance .... AON/ Albert G. Rubin Insurance Services, Inc./ George Walden, Claudia Kaufman
Counsel .... Nan Bases, Esq.
Special Events .... John L. Haber
Travel Arrangements .... The "A" Team at Tzell Travel/ Andi Henig
MIS Services .... Rivera Technics: Sam Rivera
Web Design/Maintenance ...... Curious Minds Media, Inc. www.curiousm.com
Production Photographer .... Joan Marcus
Theatre Displays .... King Displays

DODGERS
Dodger Theatricals
Sandra Carlson, Michael David, John L. Haber, Gordon Kelly, Pamela Lloyd, James Elliot Love, Jessica Ludwig, Paula Maldonado, Lauren Mitchell, Sally Campbell Morse, Samuel Rivera, Maureen Rooney, Bill Schaeffer, Edward Strong, Tim Sulka, Jennifer F. Vaughan.

LA JOLLA PLAYHOUSE
Artistic Director .... Des McAnuff
Managing Director .... Steven B. Libman
Associate Artistic Director .... Shirley Fishman
Literary Manager .... Allison Horsley
General Manager .... Debby Buchholz
Director of Communications .... Lendre Kearns
Marketing Manager .... Gigi Cantin
Public Relations Manager .... Jill McIntyre
Director of Finance .... Elizabeth Doran
Director of Operations .... Ellery Brown
Director of Institutional Advancement .... James Forbes
Individual Gifts Officer .... Jill Smayo
Manager, Special Events .... Mary Reitz
Production Manager .... Peter J. Davis
Company Manager .... Jenny Case
Technical Director .... Chad Woerner
Corporate/Legal Counsel .... Robert C. Wright, Wright & L'Estrange
Theatre/Legal Counsel .... F. Richard Pappas, Esq.

CREDITS
Scenery, show control and automation by ShowMotion, Inc., Norwalk, CT. Lighting equipment from PRG Lighting. Sound equipment by Masque Sound. Projection equipment by Sound Associates. Selected men's clothing custom made by Saint Laurie Merchant Tailors, New York City. Costumes executed by Carelli Costumes, Studio Rouge, Carmen Gee, John Kristiansen New York, Inc. Selected menswear by Carlos Campos. Props provided by The Spoon Group, Downtime Productions, Tessa Dunning. Laundry services provided by Ernest Winzer Theatrical Cleaners. Additional set and hand props courtesy of George Fenmore, Inc. Rosebud matches by Diamond Brands, Inc., Zippo lighters used. Rehearsed at the New 42nd Street Studios. Natural herb cough drops courtesy of Ricola USA, Inc. Emer'gen-C by Alacer Corporation. PLAYBILL® cover photo by Chris Callis.

Scenic drops adapted from *George Tice: Urban Landscapes*/W.W. Norton. Other photographs featured are from *George Tice: Selected Photographs 1953–1999*/David R. Godine. (Photographs courtesy of the Peter Fetterman Gallery/Santa Monica.)

SONG CREDITS
"Ces Soirees-La ("Oh What a Night")" (Bob Gaudio, Judy Parker, Yannick Zolo, Edmond David Bacri). Jobete Music Company Inc., Seasons Music Company (ASCAP). **"Silhouettes"** (Bob Crewe, Frank Slay, Jr.), Regent Music Corporation (BMI). **"You're the Apple of My Eye"** (Otis Blackwell), EMI Unart Catalog Inc. (BMI). **"I Can't Give You Anything But Love"** (Dorothy Fields, Jimmy McHugh), EMI April Music Inc., Aldi Music Company, Cotton Club Publishing (ASCAP). **"Earth Angel"** (Jesse Belvin, Curtis Williams, Gaynel Hodge), Embassy Music Corporation (BMI). **"A Sunday Kind of Love"** (Barbara Belle, Anita Leanord Nye, Stan Rhodes, Louis Prima), LGL Music Inc, Universal MCA Music Publishing (ASCAP). **"My Mother's Eyes"** (Abel Baer, L. Wolfe Gilbert), Abel Baer Music Company, EMI Feist Catalog Inc. (ASCAP). **"I Go Ape"** (Bob Crewe, Frank Slay, Jr.), MPL Music Publishing Inc. (ASCAP). **"(Who Wears) Short Shorts"** (Bill Crandall, Tom Austin, Bob Gaudio, Bill Dalton), EMI Longitude Music, Admiration Music Inc., Third Story Music Inc., and New Seasons Music (BMI). **"I'm in the Mood for Love"** (Dorothy Fields, Jimmy McHugh), Famous Music Corporation (ASCAP). **"Moody's Mood for Love"** (James Moody, Dorothy Fields, Jimmy McHugh), Famous Music Corporation (ASCAP). **"Cry for Me"** (Bob Gaudio), EMI Longitude Music, Seasons Four Music (BMI). **"An Angel Cried"** (Bob Gaudio), EMI Longitude Music (BMI). **"I Still Care"** (Bob Gaudio), Hearts Delight Music, Seasons Four Music (BMI). **"Trance"** (Bob Gaudio), Hearts Delight Music, Seasons Four Music (BMI). **"Sherry"** (Bob Gaudio), MPL Music Publishing Inc. (ASCAP). **"Big Girls Don't Cry"** (Bob Crewe, Bob Gaudio), MPL Music Publishing Inc. (ASCAP). **"Walk Like a Man"** (Bob Crewe, Bob Gaudio), Gavadima Music, MPL Communications Inc. (ASCAP). **"December, 1963 (Oh What a Night)"** (Bob Gaudio, Judy Parker), Jobete Music Company Inc, Seasons Music Company (ASCAP). **"My Boyfriend's Back"** (Robert Feldman, Gerald Goldstein, Richard Gottehrer), EMI Blackwood Music Inc. (BMI). **"My Eyes Adored You"** (Bob Crewe, Kenny Nolan), Jobete Music Company Inc, Kenny Nolan Publishing (ASCAP), Stone Diamond Music Corporation, Tannyboy Music (BMI). **"Dawn, Go Away"** (Bob Gaudio, Sandy Linzer), EMI Full Keel Music, Gavadima Music, Stebojen Music Company (ASCAP). **"Big Man in Town"** (Bob Gaudio), EMI Longitude Music (BMI), Gavadima Music (ASCAP). **"Beggin'"** (Bob Gaudio, Peggy Farina), EMI Longitude Music, Seasons Four Music (BMI). **"Stay"** (Maurice Williams), Cherio Corporation (BMI). **"Let's Hang On (To What We've Got)"** (Denny Randell, Bob Crewe, Sandy Linzer), EMI Longitude Music, Screen Gems-EMI Music Inc., Seasons Four Music (BMI). **"Opus 17 (Don't You Worry 'Bout Me)"** (Denny Randell, Sandy Linzer) Screen Gems-EMI Music Inc, Seasons Four Music (BMI). **"Everybody Knows My Name"** (Bob Crewe, Bob Gaudio), EMI Longitude Music, Seasons Four Music (BMI). **"Bye Bye Baby"** (Bob Crewe, Bob Gaudio), EMI Longitude Music, Seasons Four Music (BMI). **"C'mon Marianne"** (L. Russell Brown, Ray Bloodworth), EMI Longitude Music and Seasons Four Music (BMI). **"Can't Take My Eyes Off of You"** (Bob Crewe, Bob Gaudio), EMI Longitude Music, Seasons Four Music (BMI). **"Working My Way Back to You"** (Denny Randell, Sandy Linzer), Screen Gems–EMI Music Inc, Seasons Four Music (BMI). **"Fallen Angel"** (Guy Fletcher, Doug Flett), Chrysalis Music (ASCAP). **"Rag Doll"** (Bob Crewe, Bob Gaudio), EMI Longitude Music (BMI), Gavadima Music (ASCAP). **"Who Loves You?"** (Bob Gaudio, Judy Parker), Jobete Music Company Inc, Seasons Music Company (ASCAP).

SPECIAL THANKS
Peter Bennett, Elliot Groffman, Karen Pals, Janine Smalls, Chad Woerner of La Jolla Playhouse, Alma Malabanan-McGrath and Edward Stallsworth of the New 42nd Street Studios, David Solomon of the Roundabout Theatre Company, Dan Whitten. The authors, director, cast and company of *Jersey Boys* would like to express their love and thanks to Jordan Ressler.

Original cast album coming soon from Rhino Records.

JUJAMCYN THEATERS

ROCCO LANDESMAN
President

PAUL LIBIN
Producing Director

JACK VIERTEL
Creative Director

JERRY ZAKS

DANIEL ADAMIAN
General Manager

JENNIFER HERSHEY
Director of Operations

MEREDITH VILLATORE
Chief Financial Officer

STAFF FOR THE AUGUST WILSON THEATRE
Manager .... Matt Fox
Treasurer .... Nick Russo
Assistant Manager .... Albert T. Kim
Carpenter .... Dan Dour
Propertyman .... Scott Mulrain
Electrician .... Robert Fehribach
Engineer .... Arthur VanSalisbury

The Playbill Broadway Yearbook 2005-2006

183

Jersey Boys
SCRAPBOOK

Photos by Aubrey Reuben

1. (L-R): J. Robert Spencer, Daniel Reichard, John Lloyd Young, Christian Hoff recording the cast album at Right Track Studios.
2. (L-R): Sara Schmidt, Erica Piccininni and Jennifer Naimo arrive at the Marriott Marquis Hotel for the opening night party.
3. Curtain call on opening night. The cast welcomes special guests Joe Pesci (3rd from L) and (L-R) original Four Seasons Tommy DeVito, Bob Gaudio and Frankie Valli.

Correspondent: Michael Clarkston, Stage Manager.

Opening Night Gifts: 1) Sterling silver key chain from Frankie Valli, Bob Gaudio, Rick Elice, Marshall Brickman.
2) Luggage from the producers.
3) Thermos mugs from stage management.
4) Backstage water bottles.

Most Exciting Visitors: Frankie Valli, Bob Gaudio, Bob Crewe, Tommy DeVito and the cast of "The Sopranos."

Who Got the Gypsy Robe: Sara Schmidt.

"Carols for a Cure" Carol: "Merry Christmas and Happy New Year."

"Easter Bonnet" Skit: "Broadway—Jersey Style" by Rick Elice, Marshall Brickman and Richard Hester, making fun of the whole jukebox musical genre.

Actor Who Has Done the Most Shows: Mark Lotito.

Special Backstage Rituals: 1) On Saturday Night, we serenade the cast of *Hairspray* across the street with "Hello Broadway" and a kick line to "New York, New York."
2) Saturday night X-rated shot provided by stage management.

In-Theatre Gathering Place: Ongoing competition between the female dressing room and the male swings.

Off-Site Hangout: Thursday night bowling.

Favorite Snacks: York Peppermint Patties and Starburst in the stage management office.

Mascot: No, but we have a Matt Scott.

Favorite Therapies: 1) Self-flagellating massage mallet.
2) Tongue-pulling exercises from Katie Agresta, the vocal coach to all our Frankies.
3) Nasal spray.

Memorable Ad-Libs: 1) "You gotta do what you gotta do." –Christian Hoff as Tommy DeVito.
2) "Get that" –Bob Spencer (Nick Massi) referring to a cell phone ring in the audience during a performance.

Latest Audience Arrival: Last 20 minutes of the show.

Fastest Costume Change: Nine seconds: Jen Naimo.

Busiest Day at Box Office: The day after a color full-page ad appeared in *The New York Times*.

Who Wears the Least: Sara Schmidt—bra and panties.

Catchphrases Only the Company Would Recognize: 1) "Unclear."
2) "Phone's ringing."
3) "It's hard to say."
4) "Why you so mad?"
5) "Keep on Rockin'—Don't Stop the Rock"

Orchestra Member Who Played the Most Instruments: Ben Kono, alto sax, clarinet, flute, oboe.

Orchestra Member Who Played the Most Performances Without A Sub: Kevin Dow.

Memorable Directorial Note: "Studio glass coming in was ALMOST LATE."

Jersey Boys
SCRAPBOOK

Photos 1, 2, 3, 4 by Aubrey Reuben

Best In-House Parody Lyrics: "I'll be a big manatee," from "I'll Be A Big Man in Town."
"This key's too high," from "Big Girls Don't Cry."
Company In-Joke: "As cast."
Nicknames: "Mary Thomas" is Michael Clarkston. "Chihuahua" is Jen Naimo.
Company Sweethearts: Michael Clark and Michelle Bosch.
Embarrassing Moment: Sara Schmidt relieved by the end of "My Boyfriend's Back."
Ghostly Encounters: Props missing during tech.
Coolest Thing About Being in This Show: Playing to audiences who love the show and Frankie Valli and come back again and again and again.

1. John Lloyd Young (L) and Frankie Valli at the opening night party.
2. The creative team and cast at the recording session.
3. (L-R): Rick Elice (book), Bob Gaudio (music), Marshall Brickman (book), Des McAnuff (director) at the recording session.
4. Erica Piccininni and Sara Schmidt in rehearsal.
5. The Thursday night bowling team.
On floor: Deborah N. Hurwitz.
Kneeling: (L-R) Donnie Kehr, Shaun Ozminski, Richard Hester, Steve Gouveia.
Third Row (L-R): Michael T. Clarkston, Michael Clark, Angelique Orsini, Jennifer Alam, Preston Mock.
Back Row (L-R): Kevin Dow, Jessica Worsnop, Joe Leone, Paul Vershbow, Michelle Bosch, Matthew Scott, Lee Austin and Heather Ferguson.

Photo by Michael Clarkston

Julius Caesar

First Preview: March 8, 2005. Opened: April 3, 2005.
Closed June 12, 2005 after 31 Previews and 81 Performances.

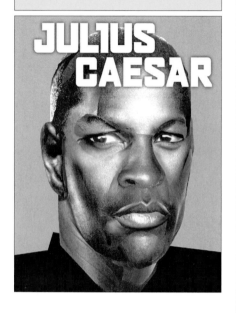

CAST
(in order of appearance)

Soothsayer	STEPHEN LEE ANDERSON
Marcus Brutus	DENZEL WASHINGTON
Portia	JESSICA HECHT
Artemidora	JACQUELINE ANTARAMIAN
Flavius	JOHN DOUGLAS THOMPSON
Marullus	HENRY WORONICZ
Carpenter	HOWARD W. OVERSHOWN
Cobbler	KEITH DAVIS
Guards to Caesar	MARK MINEART, DAN MORAN
Mark Antony	EAMONN WALKER
Julius Caesar	WILLIAM SADLER
Calpurnia	TAMARA TUNIE
Casca	JACK WILLIS
Decius Brutus	PATRICK PAGE
Cassius	COLM FEORE
Cicero	DAVID CROMWELL
Cinna	RICHARD TOPOL
Metellus Cimber	PETER JAY FERNANDEZ
Trebonius	HENRY WORONICZ
Lucius	MAURICE JONES
Servant to Caesar	SETH FISHER
Popilius Lena	JASON MANUEL OLAZÁBAL
Servant to Mark Antony	ED ONIPEDE BLUNT
Servant to Octavius Caesar	QUENTIN MARÉ
Cinna the Poet	DAVID CROMWELL
Octavius Caesar	KELLY AuCOIN
Lepidus	RICHARD TOPOL
Lucilius	PETER JAY FERNANDEZ
Pindarus	KEITH DAVIS
Messala	PATRICK PAGE
Titinius	STEPHEN LEE ANDERSON
Messenger	QUENTIN MARÉ
Cato	ED ONIPEDE BLUNT
First Soldier	SETH FISHER

Continued on next page

Continued on next page

Carole Shorenstein Hays   Freddy DeMann

present

Denzel Washington

in

JULIUS CAESAR

by

William Shakespeare

with

Colm Feore   Jessica Hecht   William Sadler   Tamara Tunie   Eamonn Walker   Jack Willis

Stephen Lee Anderson   Jacqueline Antaramian   Kelly AuCoin   Ed Onipede Blunt   David Cromwell   Keith Davis
Peter Jay Fernandez   Seth Fisher   Effie Johnson   Maurice Jones   Ty Jones   Aaron Krohn   Quentin Maré
Christopher McHale   Mark Mineart   Dan Moran   Jason Manuel Olazábal   Howard W. Overshown   Patrick Page
Kurt Rhoads   John Douglas Thompson   Richard Topol   Henry Woronicz

Set Design Ralph Funicello	*Costume Design* Jess Goldstein	*Lighting Design* Mimi Jordan Sherin	*Original Music and Sound Design* Dan Moses Schreier
Fight Director Robin H. McFarquhar	*Special Effects Design* Gregory Meeh	*Wig and Hair Design* Charles Lapointe	*Make-up Design* Angelina Avallone
Dramaturge Dakin Matthews	*Vocal Consultant* Elizabeth Smith	*Production Management* Aurora Productions	*Production Stage Manager* Lisa Dawn Cave
Casting Daniel Swee C.S.A.	*Marketing* Eric Schnall	*Press Representative* Boneau/Bryan-Brown	*Company Manager* Edward Nelson	*General Management* Stuart Thompson Productions/ James Triner

Executive Producers
Pilar DeMann   Greg Holland

Directed by
Daniel Sullivan

LIVE BROADWAY

6/1/05

(L-R) Denzel Washington, Patrick Page and William Sadler.

Photo by Joan Marcus

Julius Caesar

UNDERSTUDIES

For Marcus Brutus:
PETER JAY FERNANDEZ

For Mark Antony:
TY JONES

For Julius Caesar:
HENRY WORONICZ

For Cassius:
PATRICK PAGE

For Calpurnia/Portia:
JACQUELINE ANTARAMIAN

For Casca:
RICHARD TOPOL

For Soothsayer/Titinius/Octavius/Volumnius:
TY JONES

For Marullus/Trebonius:
QUENTIN MARÉ

For Cato/Lucius/Messenger/Clitus/
Servant to Octavius:
AARON KROHN

For Metellus Cimber/Lucilius/
Decius Brutus/Messala/Cinna/Lepidus:
CHRISTOPHER McHALE

For Artemidora:
EFFIE JOHNSON

For Carpenter/Volumnius/Popilius/
Dardanius/Flavius:
MARK MINEART

For Cobbler/Pindarus:
DAN MORAN

For Cicero/Cinna the Poet/
Metellus Cimber/Lucilius/Cinna/Lepidus/
Decius Brutus/Messala/Marullus/Trebonius:
KURT RHOADS

Denzel Washington
Marcus Brutus

Colm Feore
Cassius

Jessica Hecht
Portia

William Sadler
Julius Caesar

Tamara Tunie
Calpurnia

Eamonn Walker
Mark Antony

Jack Willis
Casca

Stephen Lee
Anderson
*Soothsayer, Titinius,
Ensemble*

Jacqueline
Antaramian
*Artemidora,
Ensemble*

Kelly AuCoin
*Octavius Caesar,
Ensemble*

Ed Onipede Blunt
*Servant to Mark
Antony, Cato,
Ensemble*

David Cromwell
*Cicero, Cinna the
Poet, Ensemble*

Keith Davis
*Cobbler, Pindarus,
Ensemble*

Peter Jay Fernandez
*Metellus Cimber,
Lucilius, Ensemble*

Seth Fisher
*Servant to Caesar,
First Soldier,
Ensemble*

Effie Johnson
Ensemble

Maurice Jones
Lucius, Ensemble

Ty Jones
Ensemble

Aaron Krohn
Ensemble

Quentin Maré
*Servant to Octavius,
Messenger, Clitus,
Ensemble*

Julius Caesar

Christopher McHale
Second Soldier,
Ensemble

Mark Mineart
Ensemble, Fight
Captain

Dan Moran
Guard to Caesar,
Volumnius, Ensemble

Jason Manuel
Olazábal
Popilius Lena,
Ensemble

Howard W.
Overshown
Carpenter,
Dardanius, Ensemble

Patrick Page
Decius Brutus,
Messala, Ensemble

Kurt Rhoads
Ensemble

John Douglas
Thompson
Flavius, Ensemble

Richard Topol
Cinna, Lepidus,
Ensemble

Henry Woronicz
Marullus, Trebonius,
Ensemble

Daniel Sullivan
Director

Ralph Funicello
Set Design

Jess Goldstein
Costume Design

Mimi Jordan Sherin
Lighting Design

Angelina Avallone
Make-Up and
Special Effects
Design

Dan Moses Schreier
Original Music and
Sound Design

Robin H. McFarquhar
Fight Direction

Dakin Matthews
Dramaturge

Elizabeth Smith
Vocal Consultant

Stuart Thompson,
Stuart Thompson
Productions
General Manager

Greg Holland
Executive Producer

Carole Shorenstein
Hays
Producer

Julius Caesar

Photo by Ben Strothmann

**THE CREW AND
FRONT OF HOUSE STAFF**

Front Row (kneeling, L-R):
Kathleen Dunn,
Selena Nelson, Daniel Rosario, Tasha Allen,
Tadese Bartholomew, Gwendolyn Coley,
Mindy Lutz, Meaghan McElroy.

Second Row (L-R):
Devlani James, Eugenia Raines, Derek Moreno,
Nancy Ronan, Sakie Onazawa, Jen Kievit,
Kathleen Powell, Susan Goulet.

Third Row (L-R):
Eric "Speed" Smith,
Lisa Dawn Cave, Brian Meister,
Jenny Montgomery, Rick Dal Curtivo, Mia Neal,
Jared Beasley, Scott McLelland.

Back Row (L-R):
Davis Duffield, Charles Loesche, Curtis Croome,
Kevin Bertolacci, Lee J. Austin, Amanda Ezell,
Mike LoBue, George Dummitt,
Joe Moritz, Dexter L. Luke.

STAFF FOR *JULIUS CAESAR*

GENERAL MANAGEMENT

STUART THOMPSON PRODUCTIONS

Stuart Thompson   James Triner

COMPANY MANAGER

Edward Nelson

GENERAL PRESS REPRESENTATIVE

BONEAU/BRYAN-BROWN

Chris Boneau   Adriana Douzos   Erika Creagh

PRODUCTION MANAGEMENT

AURORA PRODUCTIONS INC.

Gene O'Donovan   W. Benjamin Heller II
Elise Hanley   Bethany Weinstein

PRODUCTION STAGE MANAGER ....
.... LISA DAWN CAVE
Stage Manager ....Brian Meister
Assistant Stage Manager ....Kevin Bertolacci
Assistant Company Manager ....Laura Penney
Assistant to the Director ....Tre Garrett
Fight Captain ....Mark Mineart
Assistant Set Designer ....Randall Richards
Associate Costume Designer ....Alejo Vietti
Assistant Costume Designers ....Elizabeth Flauto,
China Lee
Associate Lighting Designer ...................D.M. Wood
Assistant Lighting Designer ....Ruth Pitzer
Assistant Sound Designer ....Fitz Patton, Phillip Peglow
Production Electrician ....Michael LoBue
Production Props ....Vera Pizzarelli
Production Sound ....Jenny Scheer Montgomery
Production Carpenter.........................James Kane
Production Flyman ....Eric Smith
Automated Lighting Programmer ....Steve Garner
Wardrobe Supervisor ....Lee J. Austin
Dressers ....Anita-Ali Davis, Davis Duffield,
Delvan C. James, Derek Moreno,
Nancy Ronan
Hair Supervisor ....Mia Neal

Hair Assistant ....Sakie Onozawa
Casting Associate ....Kristin McTigue
Production Assistants ....Alyssa Gardner,
Paige van den Burg
Assistant to Mrs. Hays ....Kelly Hartgraves
Assistant to Mr. DeMann ....Renee Sandmann
Assistant to Mr. Thompson ....Caroline Prugh
General Management Assistants ....Ryan Smith,
John Vennema
Management Intern ....Barry Branford, Joel Solari
Banking ....Chase Manhattan Bank/
Richard L. Callian, Michele Gibbons
Payroll ....Castellana Services, Inc./
Lance Castellana
Controller ....Sarah Galbraith
Accountant ....Fried & Kowgios CPA's LLP/
Robert Fried, CPA
Insurance ....DeWitt Stern Group, Inc./
Jolyon F. Stern, Peter Shoemaker,
Anthony L. Pittari
Legal Counsel ....Paul, Weiss, Rifkind,
Wharton & Garrison/
John F. Breglio, Esq.,
Rachel Hoover, Esq.
Advertising...SpotCo/
Drew Hodges, Jim Edwards,
Ilene Rosen, Jim McNicholas
Production Photographer ....Joan Marcus
Website Design/
Online Marketing...............Situation Marketing LLC/
Damian Bazadona, Ian Bennett
Travel ....Tzell Travel Group/
Andi Henig
Opening Night Coordination ....Tobak-Dantchik
Events & Promotions, Inc./
Suzanne Tobak, Michael P. Lawrence
Merchandising ....George Fenmore/
More Merchandising International

CREDITS

Scenery and automation from Hudson Scenic Studio, Inc.
Lighting equipment supplied by GSD Productions, Inc.,
West Hempstead, NY. Sound equipment provided by
Masque Sound and Recording Corporation. Special effects
equipment by Jauchem & Meeh Inc. Denzel Washington's

suits courtesy of Valentino. Costumes by Carmen Gee
Design New York and Carelli Costumes. Zippo lighters
used. Additional set and hand props courtesy of George
Fenmore, Inc. Special thanks to June Haynes. Cough drops
provided by Ricola.

Rehearsed at the New 42nd Street Studios.

JULIUS CAESAR online
www.caesaronbroadway.com

An earlier production of *Julius Caesar* was directed by
Daniel Sullivan at THE OLD GLOBE, SAN DIEGO, CA.

Jack O'Brien   Louis G. Spisto
Artistic Director   Executive Director

 THE SHUBERT ORGANIZATION, INC.
Board of Directors

Gerald Schoenfeld   **Philip J. Smith**
Chairman   President

John W. Kluge   **Michael I. Sovern**

Lee J. Seidler   **Stuart Subotnick**

Stuart Subotnick

Robert E. Wankel
Executive Vice President

Peter Entin   **Elliot Greene**
Vice President -   Vice President -
Theatre Operations   Finance

David Andrews   **John Darby**
Vice President -   Vice President -
Shubert Ticketing Services   Facilities

House Manager ....Carol Flemming

La Cage aux Folles

First Preview: November 11, 2004. Opened: December 9, 2004.
Closed June 26, 2005 after 31 previews and 229 performances.

CAST
(in order of appearance)

Georges	ROBERT GOULET
"Les Cagelles"	
Chantal	T. OLIVER REID
Monique	CHRISTOPHER FREEMAN
Dermah/Slaveboy	ERIC OTTE
Nicole	NATHAN PECK
Hanna	BRAD MUSGROVE
Mercedes	JOSH WALDEN
Bitelle	JOEY DUDDING
Lo Singh	JERMAINE R. REMBERT
Odette	CHARLIE SUTTON
Angelique/White Bird	ANDY PELLICK
Phaedra	WILL TAYLOR
Clo-Clo	PAUL CANAAN
Francis	JOHN SHUMAN
Jacob	MICHAEL BENJAMIN WASHINGTON
Albin	GARY BEACH
Jean-Michel	GAVIN CREEL
Anne	ANGELA GAYLOR
Jacqueline	RUTH WILLIAMSON
St. Tropez Townspeople	
M. Renaud	MERWIN FOARD
Mme. Renaud	DOROTHY STANLEY
Paulette	EMMA ZAKS
Hercule	JOEY DUDDING
Etienne	JOHN HILLNER
Fisherman	DALE HENSLEY
Colette	PATTY GOBLE
Fisherman	ADRIAN BAILEY
Edouard Dindon	MICHAEL MULHEREN
Mme. Dindon	LINDA BALGORD

TIME:
Summer

PLACE:
St. Tropez, France

Continued on next page

Continued on next page

Gary Beach (left) with Robert Goulet.

Photo by Carol Rosegg

La Cage aux Folles

MUSICAL NUMBERS

ACT I

Overture

"We Are What We Are" .... Les Cagelles

"A Little More Mascara" .... Albin and Friends

"With Anne on My Arm" .... Jean-Michel and Georges

"With You on My Arm" (Reprise) .... Georges and Albin

"The Promenade" .... Townspeople

"Song on the Sand" .... Georges

"La Cage aux Folles" .... Albin and Les Cagelles

"I Am What I Am" .... Albin

ACT II

Entr'acte

"Song on the Sand" (Reprise) .... Georges and Albin

"Masculinity" .... Georges, Albin and Townspeople

"Look Over There" .... Georges

"Cocktail Counterpoint" .... Georges, Dindon,

Mme. Dindon, Jacob, Jean-Michel and Anne

"The Best of Times" .... Albin, Jacqueline and Patrons

"Look Over There" (Reprise) .... Jean-Michel

Grand Finale .... Full Company

Cast Continued

SWINGS
CLARK JOHNSEN, PAUL MCGILL,
ERIC STRETCH, LEAH HOROWITZ

STANDBY
BRYAN BATT

DANCE CAPTAIN: Nathan Peck
ASSISTANT DANCE CAPTAIN: Charlie Sutton

UNDERSTUDIES
Understudies for Albin: Bryan Batt, Dale Hensley; for Georges: Dale Hensley, John Hillner; for Jean-Michel: Joey Dudding, Will Taylor; for Anne: Leah Horowitz, Emma Zaks; for Jacqueline: Patty Goble, Dorothy Stanley; for Edouard Dindon: Merwin Foard, John Hillner; for Mme. Dindon: Patty Goble, Dorothy Stanley; for Francis: Adrian Bailey, John Hillner; for Jacob: Adrian Bailey, T. Oliver Reid.

ORCHESTRA
Conductor:
Patrick Vaccariello

Associate Conductor:
Jim Laev

Concertmaster:
Paul Woodiel

Violins:
Mary Whitaker, Victor Heifets, Dana Ianculovici

Cellos:
Peter Prosser, Vivian Israel

Lead Trumpet:
Jeff Kievit

Trumpets:
Trevor Neumann, Earl Gardner

Trombones:
Michael Seltzer, Randy Andos

French Horn:
Roger Wendt

Reeds:
Ted Nash, Ben Kono, David Young, Ron Jannelli

Drums:
Ron Tierno

Percussion:
Dan McMillan

Bass:
Bill Sloat

Keyboard 1:
Jim Laev

Keyboard 2:
Maggie Torre

Guitar/Banjo:
JJ McGeehan

Music Coordinator:
Michael Keller

Music Copying:
Kaye-Houston Music/Annie Kaye
and Doug Houston

Photo by Carol Rosegg

Robert Goulet (center left) and Gary Beach (center right) with Les Cagelles.

La Cage aux Folles

Robert Goulet
Georges

Gary Beach
Albin

Gavin Creel
Jean-Michel

Angela Gaylor
Anne

Ruth Williamson
Jacqueline

Michael Mulheren
Edouard Dindon

Linda Balgord
Mme. Dindon

John Shuman
Francis

Michael Benjamin Washington
Jacob

Adrian Bailey
Fisherman

Bryan Batt
Standby Albin

Paul Canaan
Clo-Clo

Joey Dudding
Bitelle, Hercule

Merwin Foard
M. Renaud

Christopher Freeman
Monique

Patty Goble
Colette

Dale Hensley
Fisherman

John Hillner
Etienne

Leah Horowitz
Swing

Clark Johnsen
Swing

Paul McGill
Swing

Brad Musgrove
Hanna

Eric Otte
Dermah/Slaveboy

Nathan Peck
Nicole

Andy Pellick
Angelique

T. Oliver Reid
Chantal

Jermaine R. Rembert
Lo Singh

Dorothy Stanley
Mme. Renaud

Eric Stretch
Swing

Charlie Sutton
Odette

Will Taylor
Phaedra

Josh Walden
Mercedes

Emma Zaks
Paulette

Jerry Herman
Composer/Lyricist

Harvey Fierstein
Book

La Cage aux Folles

 Jerry Zaks
Director

 Jerry Mitchell
Choreographer

 Scott Pask
Set Design

 William Ivey Long
Costume Design

 Donald Holder
Lighting Design

 Paul Huntley
Hair & Wig Design

 Patrick Vaccariello
Music Director

 Larry Blank
Additional Orchestrations

 Michael Keller
Music Coordinator

 Arthur P. Siccardi
Technical Supervisor

 Chic Silber
Special Effects

 Jim Carnahan
Casting

 Steven Beckler
Production Supervisor

 Marc Bruni
Associate Director

 Robert Tatad
Assistant Choreographer

 James L. Nederlander
Producer

 Kenneth D. Greenblatt
Producer

 Terry Allen Kramer
Producer

SCRAPBOOK

1. Michael Mulheren at "Broadway Barks."
2. Choreographer Jerry Mitchell flashes his newly-won 2005 Tony Award for Best Choreography, accompanied by Angie Schworer of *The Producers* at Bryant Park Grill.
3. Gary Beach at "Stars in the Alley."

La Cage aux Folles

Latinologues

First Preview: September 13, 2005. Opened: October 13, 2005.
Closed December 31, 2005 after 34 Previews and 93 Performances.

CAST

EUGENIO DERBEZ

RICK NAJERA

RENE LAVAN

SHIRLEY A. RUMIERK

UNDERSTUDIES

CARLO D'AMORE

IVETTE SOSA

THE HELEN HAYES THEATRE

MARTIN MARKINSON   DONALD TICK

TATE ENTERTAINMENT GROUP
PROUDLY PRESENTS
IN ASSOCIATION WITH
JUAN CARLOS ZAPATA
RICK NAJERA, AEG LIVE, RENE LAVAN
ICON ENTERTAINMENT, TATI INCORPORATED
RICHARD MARTINI ENTERTAINMENT & ALAN SPIVAK

LATINOLOGUES

A Comedy About Life in America

CREATED AND WRITTEN BY
RICK NAJERA

STARRING

EUGENIO DERBEZ
RICK NAJERA
RENE LAVAN
SHIRLEY A. RUMIERK

LIGHTING DESIGN	SOUND DESIGN	VIDEO DESIGN	COSTUME DESIGN
KEVIN ADAMS	T. RICHARD FITZGERALD	DENNIS DIAMOND	SANTIAGO

PRODUCTION STAGE MANAGER	CASTING	ASSOCIATE PRODUCER
ARABELLA POWELL	ELSIE STARK/STARK NAKED PRODUCTIONS	KEVIN BENSON

PRESS REPRESENTATIVES
JIM RANDOLPH/BILL EVANS & ASSOCIATES
SUSIE ALBIN/TRINA BARDUSCO

ADVERTISING/MARKETING	GENERAL MANAGEMENT
JIM WEINER/WEINER ASSOCIATES	MORER/BOWMAN PRODUCTIONS
DANIEL HASTINGS	

DIRECTED BY
CHEECH MARIN

10/13/05

An alternate cover used later in the run.

Photo by Joan Marcus

(L-R): Rick Najera, Eugenio Derbez, Rene Lavan and Shirley A. Rumierk in character.

Latinologues

Rick Najera
Writer and Creator

Eugenio Derbez
Performer

Rene Lavan
Performer

Shirley A. Rumierk
Performer

Carlo D'Amore
Understudy

Ivette Sosa
Understudy

Cheech Marin
Director

Santiago
Costume Design

Jonathan Solari
Costume Design Assistant

Eugenio Derbez as Erasmo.

Author and co-star Rick Najera as Buford Gomez.

Photos by Joan Marcus

STAFF FOR *LATINOLOGUES*

GENERAL MANAGEMENT
Morer/Bowman Productions
Paul Morer, Jill Bowman
Management Assistant: Wilmary Alindato

GENERAL PRESS REPRESENTATIVE
Jim Randolph
Bill Evans & Associates

Company Manager ....Jill Bowman
Production Stage Manager ....Arabella Powell
Stage Manager ....Pat Sosnow
Assistant Lighting Designer ....Aaron Sporer
Associate Video Designers ....Kevin Frech,
Marc Gamboa
Production Electrician..........................Joseph Beck
Production Carpenter ....Ron Mooney
Production Propertyman ....Roger Keller
Wardrobe Supervisor ....Kara Volkmann
Production Sound................................Bob Etter
Wardrobe Assistant ....Wilmary Alindato
Advertising/Marketing ....Jim Weiner/
Weiner Associates

Hispanic Press ....Susie Albin
Additional Marketing ....Latino Media Works/
Trina Bardusco
Audience Development and Promotions .....MATCH-TIX
Jeff Duchin, Joe Aiello
Legal ....Kaufmann, Feiner, Yamin, Gildin & Robbins/
Ronald E Feiner/ Pamela Golinski
Accounting ....Rosenberg, Neuwirth & Kuchner/
Michele Gugliaro
Payroll ....Castellana Services, Inc.
Banking ....JPMorgan Chase/
Richard Callian
Additional Promotions ....Daniel Hastings
Graphic Design ....Very Memorable Design/
Weiner Associates/
Claudia Hernandez

CREDITS
Sound equipment provided by Sound Associates.
Video equipment provided by Video D Studios, Inc.
Still photographs by Thea Bellos.

SPECIAL THANKS
Special thanks to Tere Miranda, Dalilah Polanco, Gus

Rodriguez, Jose Sierra, Eduardo Cisneros, Elias Solorio, Mauricio Martinez, Lydia Hidalgo, Carolina Calderon, Susie Najera, Jacob Vargas, Carlos Gomez, Elaina Sotomayor, Chi-Town crew por ever, Fernando Carrillo, Sam Woodhouse, Art Rutter, Mary Najera, Mr. Mo Casanova, Luis Marin, Bahiye Fashions, Karoline Hood, Samantha Levitt, Birkenstock USA, Kevin Benson, Robin Tate

THE HELEN HAYES THEATRE
owned and operated by
MARTIN MARKINSON and DONALD TICK
GENERAL MANAGER ....SUSAN S. MYERBERG
Associate General Manager ....Jeffrey T. Hughes

STAFF FOR THE HELEN HAYES THEATRE
HOUSE MANAGER ....Alan R. Markinson
Treasurer ....David Heveran
Assistant Treasurers ....Michael A. Lynch,
Manuel Rivera
Engineer/Maintenance ....Hector Angulo
Head Usher ....John Biancamano
Stage Door ....Vincent Kwasnicki, Robert Seymour
Accountant ....Chen-Win Hsu, CPA., P.C.

Latinologues

STAGE CREW
Front Row (L-R): Kara Volkmann (Wardrobe), Wilmary Alindato (Wardrobe Assistant), Jill Bowman (Company Manager), Ron Mooney (Production Carpenter), Arabella Powell (Production Stage Manager).
Back Row (L-R): Robert Etter (Production Sound), Roger Keller (Production Propertyman) and Victor Seastone (Substitute Production Electrician).

Not Pictured: Joseph Beck (Production Electrician).

FRONT OF HOUSE STAFF:
Front Row (L-R): Berdine Vaval (Ticket Taker), C. J. Gelfand (Usher), Linda Maley (Usher), Frank Biancamano (Usher).
Back Row (L-R): Harry Joshi (Usher), Robert Seymour (Stage Doorman), Yuri Ivanov (Usher) and Alan Markinson (House Manager).

Latinologues
SCRAPBOOK

①

②

③

Correspondents: Rick Najera, playwright, "Elian Gonzalez," "Buford Gomez," "The Manic Hispanic," "Metrosexual Latino," "The Drug Lord."
Eugenio Derbez, "Erasmo," "Mexican Moses," "Vampire's Mama" "Drug Lord's Bodyguard."
Memorable Celebrity Visitors/Opening Night Note: (Najera:) Geraldo Rivera attended the opening, and I told him I'd love to get him to review the show. Later, he handed me a napkin and said, "Here's my review." It was a beautiful statement of how much the play meant to him. Rosie Perez was also there and said how much she loved the show.
Opening Night Gifts: (Najera:) Producer Robin Tate gave me a beautiful live orchid and told me that the show would run until that flower died. I bought my wife Susie a Tiffany diamond pendant, but on my way back I couldn't get a cab, so I had to walk from Tiffany's, which almost made me late for my opening night!
Superstitions That Turned Out To Be True: (Najera:) Robin Tate was right: When my orchid died, the show closed.
Which Actor Performed the Most Roles in This Show: (Najera:) I'd have to say it was me.
Special Backstage Rituals: (Najera:) Every night we did a circle and a prayer. We'd put our hands together in the middle and we'd say, "One, two three—*Latinologues!*" Also, every night I always prayed for ticket sales. Sometimes I'd also bring my son to the theatre and put him on the stage. He'd run around and use his hands to make shadows in the lights, and I loved watching how much fun he was having.
Favorite Moment: (Najera:) Before the show

1. (L-R): Shirley A. Rumierk, Eugenio Derbez, Cheech Marin, Lauren Velez and Rosie Perez at the opening night party at Havana Central.
2. Susie and Rick Najera on opening night.
3. Producer Juan Carlos Zapata with actress Rosina Grosso at Havana Central.

started we had a pre-show, a series of slides we'd project on the stage, kind of spoofing Broadway. We'd show logos for things like *Madre Mia!, Mariachi on the Roof* and *Cholo Cholo Bang Bang: The Drive-By Musical.* The audience would start noticing this, and would start to laugh more and more. I'd hear them over the sound system and I'd think, "I've already made people laugh even before I hit the stage!" No matter how bad the day had been, once the audience started laughing I'd feel great.
(Derbez:) I loved all my characters, but my personal favorite was Mama. For the entire cast, the favorite moment was when we'd get a standing ovation. After the show we'd all go outside and hold hands and look up at the marquee and say, "Oh my God, we're on Broadway!"
Favorite In-Theatre Gathering Place: (Derbez:) The greenroom couch. Everybody fought for a place there. The girls did their knitting there. It was the hottest place in the theatre. (Najera:) It's such a beautiful old theatre that a lot of times, before half-hour, everyone would gather in the first two rows of the house and just look around, watch the crew prepare, and relax. It was a moment of calm before the storm. Once we all went downstairs and they locked the door, it was like we were entombed. But sitting there in the house, we'd get a feeling for the show from the audience's perspective. It was just a beautiful little moment.
Favorite Off-Site Hangout: (Najera:) Two places: Angus McIndoe and Sardi's, both right on our block. We gave the employees free tickets to our show. Whenever we'd go to Sardi's, the busboys, the dishwashers and the waiters would treat us like family. When they put my picture up at Sardi's one of the busboys came up to me and said, "I love your show because it gives people like me a voice." At Angus, all the waiters and waitresses are struggling actors. I'd tell them, "Listen guys, this is one of the truly best times in your life. I never realized that when I was starting out, but I hope you guys do." One of the waiters was cast in *The Wedding Singer* while I was there. I said, "That's the beauty of Broadway. You can start as a waiter and wind up on Broadway. Next year, I'll come to see you in your show!" It's a dream I share with them.
(Derbez:) Sardi's. We all wanted our portraits there, but just two of us got it, Rick Najera and me. All the waiters knew me, and a lot of the clients who were Spanish people. A lot of us also went to Ollie's later in the run.
Mascot: (Najera:) I found a mouse backstage just about the time there was an article in the paper about some mice with anthrax who escaped from a laboratory. I used to say, "I swear that's the anthrax mouse!" But really, I wouldn't let anyone hurt that mouse. It became our mascot.
Favorite Therapies: (Derbez:) Number one was Throat Coat Tea, then Emer'gen-C. And earplugs—for Rick's jokes. He was always making bad jokes backstage.

Latinologues
SCRAPBOOK

Favorite Snack Foods: (Derbez:) The coffee from Starbucks. And Jolly Rancher candies.

Memorable Ad-Libs: (Najera:) Once in a while, Eugenio Derbez's English would fail him. If he couldn't say the word in English, he's switch to Spanish and it would make the house roar. He had trouble one night saying, "Miraculous," so, after a few tries, he just went to "Milagrosamente," and it brought the house down.

(Derbez:) One day, during the Vampire's Mama scene, a girl in the audience distracted me and I completely forgot my lines. English is not my first language. I can't improvise as well as I can in Spanish. So I began crying. And I kept crying and crying and crying, hoping I'd remember something. Finally I found one of my lines and grabbed it and went ahead. The audience thought it was part of the show, but I sweated like never before in my life.

Cell Phone Rings: (Najera:) Never. But we got people taking photographs and even videos all the time. They thought they had the right. The stage manager would go out and stop them. One woman who had pretty much videotaped the whole show was asked to surrender the tape. She begged me to let her keep it, but I told her it was a rule from Equity.

Memorable Press Encounter: (Najera:) One Spanish magazine didn't get an interview they wanted and threatened to create a scandal about our show. I told them, "Please! I'd love the publicity! Say that a famous actress is in love with me! Any publicity is good publicity!" I gave them a few more ideas, too, but they finally backed off.

(Derbez:) We had a guy from Univision who did a very tough interview with us. He was trying to get us to fight with him and said what we were doing wasn't all that hard. So I challenged him to step onto that stage and see how hard it is to be an actor. He took us up on it and did a monologue one night. He was terrible. Awful. But it was funny because we made fun of him all night.

Memorable Stage Door Fan Encounters: (Derbez:) On the day before the end of the run a Brazilian woman showed up with a bag of DVDs of all my television shows—there must have been fifty or more—and asked me to autograph them all. It took me a half hour! She said she wanted to give copies to all her friends, but I suspect she was planning to sell them.

(Najera:) We had a joke in our show about how Guatemalans are short, the leprechauns of Central America. One day, waiting for me at the stage door was a seven-foot Guatemalan! A lot of people told us it was their first Broadway show. One woman wanted me to sign a program for *Phantom of the Opera* across the street. She said she'd had such a good time at our show that she came back the next night and bought tickets for *Phantom*! She just loved the theatre experience. Not that *Phantom* needed my help….

Catchphrases Only the Company Would Recognize: (Najera:) "I'll sue 'em!"

(Derbez:) Whenever the audience failed to laugh at a joke, we'd say, "I see dead people."

Latest Audience Arrival: (Derbez:) Latinos are always late, but the latest was twenty minutes before the end of the show. That's more than an hour after the show began.

Fastest Costume Change: (Derbez:) Shirley had 90 seconds to go from the blonde in a negligee to the pregnant teenager

Memorable Directorial Notes: (Najera:) Cheech Marin was a very precise director. He said to me, "Rick, they usually bring a white guy in to run our shows. I guess on this production, *I'm* the white guy!" He's the godfather of Latino comedy, and he was very encouraging. When things got tough, he'd say to me, "Believe in your show, because I do." He'd seen it all and was able to get us through rough spots. One time he turned to our production stage manager, Arabella Powell, and said, "Relax. You're like the cowboy in the whorehouse!"

(Derbez:) On the very last day before the opening, Cheech Marin told us, "I think you guys need a director."

Coolest Thing About Being in This Show:

(Derbez:) Being on Broadway itself was the coolest thing that happened in our careers. And maybe when I met Matthew Broderick at Angus McIndoe. We were colleagues!

(Najera:) The cops out in front of the theatre. I'd walk down 44th Street to work and they'd recognize me and say, "Hey Rick, howya doin'?" I was just a guy in the neighborhood. It's just a neighborhood that happened to be Broadway. There's was a great friendliness to it. It was like falling in love with New York itself.

Also: (Najera:) We were all very excited about being *on Broadway*. There was a moment when we'd come onstage and they would name what number performance it was that we were *on Broadway*. Every Saturday night there would be a special excitement because it was Saturday night *on Broadway*. We felt like we were part of history. Someone once told me that the real beauty of Broadway is the way it reflects all of America. The great thing about *Latinologues* is that it made Broadway truly more reflective of America, and brought in an audience that Broadway didn't get to see too often. That was my proudest achievement.

1. Shirley A. Rumierk (bottom) gets into her pregnant costume, while the men of the cast pretend to argue about who's the father.
2. At the final performance: Front Row: Rumierk, Derbez. 2nd Row: Carlo D'Amore (understudy), Arabella Powell (Production Stage Manager), Jill Bowman (General Management). 3rd Row: Kara Volkmann (Wardrobe), Shirley A. Rumierk, Wilmary Alindato (Wardrobe). 4th Row: Najera, Robin Tate (Producer), Juan Carlos Zapata (Producer), Rene Lavan.
3. Derbez holds a plaque celebrating that *Latinologues* had become the first play written, directed and performed by Latinos to reach 100 performances on Broadway.

Lennon

First Preview: July 7, 2005. Opened: August 14, 2005.
Closed September 24, 2005 after 42 previews and and 49 performances.

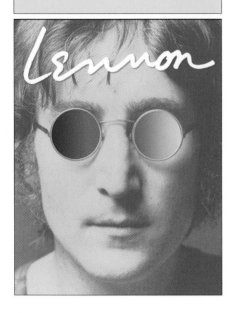

PLAYBILL

CAST
(in alphabetical order)

WILL CHASE
CHUCK COOPER
JULIE DANAO-SALKIN
MANDY GONZALEZ
MARCY HARRIELL
CHAD KIMBALL
TERRENCE MANN
JULIA MURNEY
MICHAEL POTTS

STANDBYS

For Julie and Mandy:
RONA FIGUEROA

For Chuck, Terrence and Michael:
MARK RICHARD FORD

For Marcy and Julia:
NICOLE LEWIS

For Will, Chad and Terrence:
DARIN MURPHY

Continued on next page

---

⑥ BROADHURST THEATRE
235 West 44th Street
A Shubert Organization Theatre

Gerald Schoenfeld, *Chairman*   **Philip J. Smith,** *President*

Robert E. Wankel, *Executive Vice President*

| ALLAN McKEOWN | EDGAR LANSBURY | CLEAR CHANNEL ENTERTAINMENT | JEFFREY A. SINE |

present

Lennon

Music & Lyrics by
JOHN LENNON

Book by
DON SCARDINO

with

Special Thanks to **YOKO ONO LENNON**

starring

WILL CHASE   CHUCK COOPER   JULIE DANAO-SALKIN

MANDY GONZALEZ   MARCY HARRIELL   CHAD KIMBALL

TERRENCE MANN   JULIA MURNEY   MICHAEL POTTS

RONA FIGUEROA   MARK RICHARD FORD   NICOLE LEWIS   DARIN MURPHY

| Scenic/Projection Design **JOHN ARNONE** | Costume Design **JANE GREENWOOD** | Lighting Design **NATASHA KATZ** | Sound Design **BOBBY AITKEN** |

| Music Coordinator **JOHN MILLER** | Music Director **JEFFREY KLITZ** | Creative Consultants **BOB EATON** **BRIAN HENDEL** | Casting **JANET FOSTER, CSA** |

| Press Representative **BONEAU/BRYAN-BROWN** | Marketing **TMG — THE MARKETING GROUP** | General Management **NLA/MAGGIE EDELMAN** |

| Production Manager **ARTHUR SICCARDI** | Production Stage Manager **ARTHUR GAFFIN** | Executive Producer **NINA LANNAN** | Associate Producer **LOUISE FORLENZA** |

| Orchestrator **HAROLD WHEELER** | Music Supervisor/Arranger **LON HOYT** |

Choreographed by
JOSEPH MALONE

Directed/Conceived by
DON SCARDINO

LIVE BROADWAY

8/14/05

The cast gives peace a chance.

Photo by Joan Marcus

Lennon

MUSICAL NUMBERS

ACT I

"New York City" ....Will with All
"Mother" ....Chad, Will, Julie with All
"Look At Me" ....All
"Money" ....Mandy, Marcy, Julia, Julie
"Twist and Shout" ....Mandy, Marcy, Julia, Julie
"Instant Karma" ....Chuck with All
"India, India" ....Julia, Mandy, Will with All
"Real Love (Boys and Girls)" ....Chuck, Will
"Mind Games" ....Chad, Julie with All
"The Ballad of John and Yoko" ....All
"How Do You Sleep?" ....Mandy
"God" ....Michael with All
"Give Peace a Chance" ....Terrence with All

ACT II

"Power to the People" ....All
"Woman Is the Nigger of the World" ....Marcy with Women
"Attica State" ....Michael, Julie
"Gimme Some Truth" ....Will with All
"I'm Losing You/I'm Moving On" ....Chad, Julie
"I'm Stepping Out" ....Will, Chuck with All
"I Don't Want to Lose You" ....Terrence, Julie, Chad
"Whatever Gets You Through the Night" ....Marcy, Will
"Woman" ....Will with All
"Beautiful Boy" ....Julia with All
"Watching the Wheels" ....Will, Chad, Michael, Terrence
"(Just Like) Starting Over" ....Chuck with All
"Grow Old With Me" ....Julie
"Imagine" ....John with All

ORCHESTRA

Music Director, Keyboards
Jeffrey Klitz
Associate Music Director, Keyboards
Dave Keyes

Guitars – John Benthal, Jack Cavari
Bass – David Anderson
Drums – Warren Odze
Percussion – Dave Yee
Reeds – Tom Murray
Trumpet – Tony Kadleck
Trombone – Larry Dean Farrell

Music Coordinator – John Miller

Music Copying: Emily Grishman Music
Preparation
Emily Grishman/Katharine Edmonds

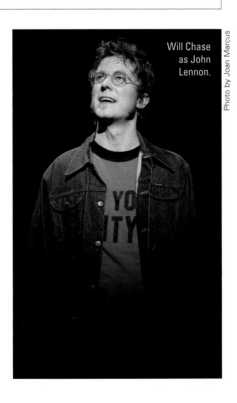

Will Chase
as John
Lennon.

Photo by Joan Marcus

Will Chase
Performer

Chuck Cooper
Performer

Julie Danao-Salkin
Performer

Mandy Gonzalez
Performer

Marcy Harriell
Performer

Chad Kimball
Performer

Terrence Mann
Performer

Julia Murney
Performer

Michael Potts
Performer

Rona Figueroa
*Standby for Julie
Danao-Salkin and
Mandy Gonzalez*

Lennon

Mark Richard Ford
Standby for Chuck Cooper, Terrence Mann and Michael Potts

Nicole Lewis
Standby for Marcy Harriell and Julia Murney

Darin Murphy
Standby for Will Chase, Chad Kimball and Terrence Mann

Don Scardino
Conceiver, Director and Book Writer

John Lennon
Music and Lyrics

Yoko Ono
Producer

Jane Greenwood
Costume Design

Natasha Katz
Lighting Design

Bobby Aitken
Sound Design

Joseph Malone
Choreographer

Lon Hoyt
Music Supervisor

Harold Wheeler
Orchestrations

John Miller
Music Contractor

Janet Foster
Casting

John Arnone
Scenic/Projection Design

Jeffrey Klitz
Music Director

Chic Silber
Special Effects

Arthur Siccardi
Production Manager

Christopher Morey (Company Manager)

BOX OFFICE
(L-R): Debbie Giarratano (Assistant Treasurer) and Noreen Morgan (Assistant Treasurer)

Shaun W. Moorman
(Associate Company Manager)

Photos by Melissa Merlo

Lennon

STAGE MANAGEMENT
(L-R): Arthur Gaffin (Production Stage Manager), Justin Scribner (Assistant Stage Manager) and Laurie Goldfeder (Stage Manager).

(L-R): Christopher C. Sloan (Sound Engineer) and Drayton Allison (Head Electrician/Board Operator).

Charles J. DeVerna (House Electrician).

(L-R): Jonathan Cohen (Electrician) and Andrew Funk (Sound Technician).

Seated on Floor: Stephen Abbott II (Follow Spot Operator)
Second Row (L-R): Craig Licata (Props), Robert Presley (Head Props), Ron Vitelli (House Props), Timothy Welch (Assistant Carpenter/Flyman) and Michael Cornell (Follow Spot Operator).

Lennon

WARDROBE DEPARTMENT
(L-R):
Kathryn Guida (Wardrobe Supervisor),
Rodd Sovar (Dresser),
Kristin Gardner (Dresser),
Susan Gomez (Dresser)
and Franklin Hollenbeck (Dresser).

FRONT OF HOUSE STAFF
Front Row (L-R):
Lisa Houghton (Usher),
Jennifer Vega (Usher),
Linda Ruik (Usher),
Rose Ann Cipriano (Head Usher)
and Janet Kay (Usher).

Back Row (L-R):
Joe Pittman (Usher),
Karen Diaz (Usher)
and Hugh Lynch (Usher).

Not Pictured:
Hugh Barnett (House Manager).

BAND
(L-R):
David Anderson (Bass),
John Benthal (Guitar),
Dave Keyes
(Associate Conductor/Keyboards),
Jeffrey Klitz (Conductor/Keyboards),
Warren Odze (Drums)
and Larry Dean Farrell (Trombone).

Not Pictured:
Jack Cavari (Guitar),
David Yee (Percussion),
Tom Murray (Reeds)
and Tony Kadleck (Trumpet).

Photos by Melissa Merlo

Lennon

STAFF FOR *LENNON*

Company Manager ....CHRIS MOREY
Associate Company Manager ....Shaun W. Moorman

GENERAL PRESS REPRESENTATIVE

BONEAU/BRYAN-BROWN

Chris Boneau, Susanne Tighe, Juliana Hannett

Associate Director ....Dianne Trulock
Assistant to the Director ....Ellie Dvorkin
Assistant Choreographer ....Allison Leo

Production Stage Manager ....ARTHUR GAFFIN
Stage Manager ....Laurie Goldfeder
Assistant Stage Manager ....Justin Scribner
Dance Captain ....Marcy Harriell

Consultant Assistant ....Bea Soong

Associate Scenic Designer ....Brian Webb
Associate Projection Designer ....Michael Clark
Assistant Projection Designers ....Jennifer Kievit,
Jason Thompson
Projection Programmer ....Paul Vershbow
Associate Costume Designers ....Wade Laboissonniere,
MaryAnn D. Smith
Assistant Costume Designer ....Jessica Ford
Associate Lighting Designer ....Yael Lubetzky
Assistant Lighting Designer ....Daniel Walker
Automated Lighting Programmer ....David Arch
Associate Sound Designer ....Tony Smolenski
Special Effects ....Chic Silber
Special Effects Associate ....Aaron Waitz
Makeup Consultant ....Angelina Avallone

Production Carpenter ....Curtis Cowley
Assistant Carpenter/Flyman ....Timothy Welch
Production Electrician ....James J. Fedigan
Head Electrician/Board Operator ....Drayton Allison
Moving Lights ....Gary Marlin
Follow Spot Operator ....Michael Cornell
Sound Engineer ....Christopher C. Sloan
Assistant Sound Engineer.......................Marcus Ross
Production Properties ....Abraham Morrison
Head Properties ....Robert Presley
Wardrobe Supervisor ....Kathryn Guida
Dressers ....Kristin Gardner, Susan Gomez,
Franklin Hollenbeck, Rodd Sovar
Synthesizer Programmer ....Justin Malakhow
Dialect Coach ....Stephen Gabis
Signing Coach ....Candace Broecker-Penn
Production Assistants...........Lauren Jones, Ryan J. Bell,
Roseanna M. Sharrow, Melissa Jernigan
Music Copyist ....Emily Grishman Music Preparation
Audition Pianist ....Keith Cotton

Assistant to John Miller ....Charles Butler
Press Intern ....T. Rick Hayashi

Advertising ....SpotCo/Drew Hodges, Jim Edwards,
Tom McCann, Kim Smarsh, Aaliytha Davis
Marketing ....TMG-The Marketing Group/
Tanya Grubich, Laura Matalon,
Trish Santini, Steve Tate
Web Design and
Online Marketing Strategy ......Situation Marketing LLC/
Damian Bazadona, Ian Bennett,
Sara Fitzpatrick
Legal Counsel ....M. Graham Coleman and
Robert J. Driscoll/
Davis Wright Tremaine LLP
Accounting ....Rosenberg, Neuwirth and Kuchner/
In Woo
Production Photographer ....Joan Marcus
General Management Associates ....Jon Ferrari,
Amy Jacobs, Katherine McNamee
Creative Videography and Film ....Jojo Pennebaker
Study Guide ....Peter Royston
Illustrator ....Jesse Poleshuck
Archivist ....Karla Merrifield
Insurance ....DeWitt Stern Group Inc./Yasmine Ramos
Banking ....Commerce Bank/Barbara Von Borstel
Payroll ....Castellana Services, Inc.
Merchandising ....Max Merchandising/Randi Grossman
Travel Agent ....Tzell Travel/The "A" Team
Immigration Counsel ....Kramer Levin Haftalis &
Frankel, LLP

Assistant to Mr. McKeown ....Jennifer Hart

www.LennonTheMusical.com

MUSIC CREDITS

"Give Peace a Chance," John Lennon, Sony/ATV Tunes LLC (ASCAP) 100%; "The Ballad of John and Yoko," John Lennon, Paul McCartney, Sony/ATV Tunes LLC (ASCAP) 100%; "Twist and Shout," Bert Russell (BMI), Phil Medley (BMI), Sony/ATV Songs LLC (BMI) 66.67% USA, Sloopy II Music (BMI). "Money (That's What I Want)" by Berry Gordy and Janie Bradford; ©1959, renewed 1987 Jobete Music Co., Inc. All rights controlled and administered by EMI April Music Inc. (ASCAP) and EMI Blackwood Music Inc. (BMI) on behalf of Jobete Music Co., Inc. and Stone Agate Music (a division of Jobete Music Co., Inc.) All rights reserved. International copyright secured. Used by permission. "Nixon's the One" by Vic Caesar. ©Babaji Music. All rights reserved. Used by permission. "Blue Suede Shoes" by Carl Lee Perkins. Used by permission of Carl Perkins Music, Inc., administered by Wren Music Co., a division of MPL Music Publishing, Inc. (BMI). "I'm Moving On" by Yoko Ono. "Luck of the Irish" by John Lennon.

CREDITS AND ACKNOWLEDGEMENTS

Scenery constructed by F&D Scene Changes LTD. Costumes executed by Eric Winterling, Parsons-Meares, Mark Astbury for Beatwear.co.uk. Beatle boots by Beatwear. Hosiery and undergarments by Bra*Tenders, Inc. Audio props provided by Omnitech. Other props built by Spoon Group and Cigar Box Studios. Lighting equipment by PRG Lighting. Projection equipment by Scharff-Weisberg. Sound equipment supplied by Masque Sound. Automation equipment provided by Hyde Power Systems. Effects equipment by Sunshine Scenic Studios. Photo images provided by Starfile Photo Agency Ltd.; Corbis/Bettman Archives; Getty/Hulton Archives; Magnum Photos; Alamy Photos Ltd; AP/World Wide Photos; Astrid Kirchherr; Bob Gruen. Video images provided by Historic Films; BBC. Gretsch Country Classic guitar courtesy of Fender Musical Instruments Corp. Cymbals provided by Zildjian. Epiphone guitars and Slingerland drums provided courtesy of Gibson Family of Brands. Rehearsed at the New 42nd Street Studios, Hilton Theatre Studios and Roundabout Theatre Company Studios. Natural herb cough drops supplied by Ricola USA Inc. Throat Coat provided by Traditional Medicinals. Special Thanks: Peter S. Shukat, Jonas E. Herbsman, Amanda Keeley, Helen Barden, Robert Young and Tom Watson. The director would like to acknowledge the contributions of those who participated in the developmental readings: Joe McGinty, Matthew Bennett, Samrat Chakrabarti, Luther Creek, Daniel Jenkins, Dee Dee Magno, Aasif Mandvi, Euan Morton, Aiko Nakasone, Sara Ramirez, Sharon Scruggs, Ivette Sosa, Wayne Wilcox.

SHUBERT ORGANIZATION, INC.

Board of Directors

Gerald Schoenfeld	Philip J. Smith
Chairman	President
John W. Kluge	Michael I. Sovern
Lee J. Seidler	Stuart Subotnick

Irving M. Wall

Robert E. Wankel

Executive Vice President

Peter Entin	Elliot Greene
Vice President - Theatre Operations	Vice President - Finance
David Andrews	John Darby
Vice President - Shubert Ticketing Services	Vice President - Facilities

House Manager ....Hugh Barnett

Lennon
SCRAPBOOK

1. Charlotte D'Amboise and Terrence Mann at the opening night party at Sardi's.
2. Director Don Scardino at Sardi's.
3. Yoko Ono and Sean Lennon arrive at the Broadhurst Theatre on opening night.
4. Marcy Harriell and Julia Murney at Sardi's.
5. Ono with Chad Kimball.

Photos by Aubrey Reuben

Correspondent: Chad Kimball, "John"

Memorable Opening Night Telegram: We had a great one from the cast of *Mamma Mia!* They took our poster and Photoshopped it to say Lenin instead of Lennon, and the rest of the lettering was in Russian.

Opening Night Gifts: Yoko Ono gave the entire company iPods. Each cast member also got an Epiphone acoustic guitar from director Don Scardino.

Celebrity Visitors: Yoko and Sean Lennon came on opening night. We've also had Lindsay Lohan, Geraldo Rivera, Paul Shaffer, Roberta Flack, Al Sharpton and Ralph Nader. Quite a selection!

Who Plays the Most Roles: Terrence Mann, eight.

Who Has Done the Most Shows: Terrence Mann or Chuck Cooper.

Ritual: We form a circle on the stage before curtain time and do a concentration exercise.

Favorite Moment During Each Performance: When we sing "Imagine." The audience has completely let down their guard and accepted us as one of them.

Favorite In-Theatre Gathering Place: The basement under the Broadhurst.

Favorite Off-Site Hangout: The cast doesn't really hang out. The crew goes to John's Pizzeria down the block.

Cast's Favorite Snack Foods: Pringles and Ho-Ho's.

Mascot: We have a Jerry Rubin puppet that was axed the first day we used it, and now lives in Marcy Harriell's dressing room.

Favorite Therapies: We have different cliques. Some use Dr. Kessler's Vapors. Some do licorice and pineapple. I guess just about everyone uses Throat-Coat Tea.

Memorable Ad-Lib: I had a line, "Cynthia was away. My childhood chum Pete was there," and then another actor had a line. But the night his line was cut, I didn't realize until the middle of the show that he wasn't going to be there to say the next line. So I ad-libbed, "Cynthia was away. My childhood chum Pete was there…but he left."

"Carols for a Cure" Carol: "Christmas and Beyond."

Record Number of Cell Phone Rings: Around four. It hasn't been that bad.

Memorable Stage Door Fan Encounter: We have what we call the "Lennonites," who see the show over and over. One man asked me to sign his poster. After I did, he said, "Could you please sign it better?" I said, "But that's my signature!" He said, "But I can't read it." So I signed it better.

Fastest Costume Change: Julia Murney: 21 seconds from jeans into a sari as an Indian dancer.

Best In-House Parody Lyric: "Cold Turkey was banned" in the number "Cold Turkey."

Memorable Directorial Note: "Change the anecdote in 'Beautiful Boy'." The director wanted to change the lines, and gave that note about five times, but every time the company convinced him not to.

Company In-Joke: "Green Larry. First in Amsterdam and then in Montreal."

Nicknames: Mandy Gonzales is "Mandrew." Terrence Mann is "Jingles." Will Chase is "Willerton Chasmarian." Michael Potts is "Michael Props." Mine is "Ball Chimwick."

Coolest Thing About Being In This Show: Becoming one with the company, and with John.

Lestat

First Preview: March 25, 2006. Opened: April 25, 2006.
Closed May 28, 2006 after 33 Previews and 39 Performances.

PLAYBILL

CAST

Lestat	HUGH PANARO
Gabrielle	CAROLEE CARMELLO
Armand	DREW SARICH
Louis	JIM STANEK
Nicolas	RODERICK HILL
Marius	MICHAEL GENET
Claudia	ALLISON FISCHER
Magnus	JOSEPH DELLGER
Marquis	WILL SWENSON
Laurent	WILL SWENSON
Beautiful Woman	MEGAN REINKING

ENSEMBLE

RACHEL COLOFF,
NIKKI RENÉE DANIELS,
JOSEPH DELLGER,
COLLEEN FITZPATRICK,
PATRICK MELLEN,
CHRIS PELUSO,
DOMINIQUE PLAISANT,
MEGAN REINKING, WILL SWENSON,
TOMMAR WILSON

SWINGS

SEAN MACLAUGHLIN,
SARAH SOLIE,
STEVE WILSON

Dance Captain: SARAH SOLIE

Continued on next page

⇒N⇐ PALACE THEATRE
UNDER THE DIRECTION OF
STEWART F. LANE, JAMES M. NEDERLANDER AND JAMES L. NEDERLANDER

WARNER BROS. THEATRE VENTURES

presents

LESTAT

Based on "The Vampire Chronicles" by ANNE RICE

Music by	Lyrics by	Book by
ELTON JOHN	BERNIE TAUPIN	LINDA WOOLVERTON

Starring
HUGH PANARO
CAROLEE CARMELLO   DREW SARICH
JIM STANEK   RODERICK HILL   MICHAEL GENET   ALLISON FISCHER

Featuring
RACHEL COLOFF   NIKKI RENEE DANIELS   JOSEPH DELLGER   COLLEEN FITZPATRICK   SEAN MACLAUGHLIN   PATRICK MELLEN   CHRIS PELUSO
DOMINIQUE PLAISANT   MEGAN REINKING   SARAH SOLIE   AMY SPARROW   WILL SWENSON   STEVE WILSON   TOMMAR WILSON

Set Design	Costume Design	Lighting Design	Sound Design
DEREK MCLANE	SUSAN HILFERTY	KENNETH POSNER	JONATHAN DEANS

Visual Concept Design	Wig & Hair Design	Make-Up Design	Fight Director	Projections Coordinator
DAVE MCKEAN	TOM WATSON	ANGELINA AVALLONE	RICK SORDELET	HOWARD WERNER

Musical Supervisor	Orchestrations	Additional Orchestrations	Music Direction, Incidental Music & Additional Vocal Arrangements	Vocal Arrangements
GUY BABYLON	STEVE MARGOSHES & GUY BABYLON	BRUCE COUGHLIN	BRAD HAAK	TODD ELLISON

Casting	Production Stage Manager	Music Coordinator	Associate Director	Associate Scenic Design
JAY BINDER, C.S.A./ MARK BRANDON	BONNIE L. BECKER	JOHN MILLER	SAM SCALAMONI	BRYAN JOHNSON

General Management	Technical Supervision	Press Representative	Marketing
ALAN WASSER ASSOCIATES ALLAN WILLIAMS	JUNIPER STREET PRODUCTIONS	BARLOW•HARTMAN	TMG – THE MARKETING GROUP

Musical Staging by
MATT WEST

Directed by
ROBERT JESS ROTH

4/25/06

Hugh Panaro (center) and the company perform "Welcome To the New World."

Photo by Paul Kolnik

Lestat

MUSICAL NUMBERS

ACT I

From the Dead
Beautiful Boy
In Paris
The Thirst
Right Before My Eyes
Make Me As You Are
To Live Like This
Morality Play
The Crimson Kiss

ACT II

Welcome to the New World
Embrace It
I Want More
I'll Never Have That Chance
Sail Me Away
To Kill Your Kind
Embrace It (Reprise)
After All This Time
Finale

Carolee Carmello performs "Make Me As You Are."

Photos by Paul Kolnik

Hugh Panaro performs "Sail Away."

Cast Continued

Standby for Claudia: AMY SPARROW

UNDERSTUDIES

For Lestat:
DREW SARICH, WILL SWENSON
For Gabrielle:
RACHEL COLOFF, COLLEEN FITZPATRICK
For Armand:
SEAN MACLAUGHLIN, WILL SWENSON
For Nicolas:
CHRIS PELUSO, TOMMAR WILSON
For Louis:
CHRIS PELUSO, TOMMAR WILSON
For Marius:
JOE DELLGER, STEVE WILSON

ORCHESTRA

Conductor:
BRAD HAAK
Associate Conductor/Keyboard II:
ANDY GROBENGIESER

Concertmaster:
MARTIN AGEE
Violins:
NATALIE CENOVIA CUMMINS,
CECELIA HOBBS GARDNER
Viola:
MAXINE L. ROACH
Celli:
STEPHANIE L. CUMMINS, CHUNGSUN KIM
Flute/Clarinet:
CHUCK WILSON
Oboe/English Horn:
LYNNE A. COHEN
French Horns:
CHRIS KOMER,
BRADLEY C. GEMEINHARDT
Trombone/Euphonium:
MATT INGMAN
Keyboard I:
JASON DeBORD
Keyboard III:
JOSE SIMBULAN
Guitars:
BRUCE UCHITEL
Bass:
BRIAN HAMM
Drums/Percussion:
DAVE RATAJCZAK
Percussion/Assistant Conductor:
THAD WHEELER

Music Coordinator: JOHN MILLER

Lestat

Hugh Panaro
Lestat

Carolee Carmello
Gabrielle

Drew Sarich
Armand

Jim Stanek
Louis

Roderick Hill
Nicolas

Michael Genet
Marius

Allison Fischer
Claudia

Rachel Coloff
Ensemble

Nikki Renée Daniels
Eleni/Ensemble

Joseph Dellger
Magnus/Ensemble

Colleen Fitzpatrick
Ensemble

Sean MacLaughlin
Swing

Patrick Mellen
Ensemble

Chris Peluso
Ensemble

Dominique Plaisant
Ensemble

Megan Reinking
*Beautful Woman/
Ensemble*

Sarah Solie
*Swing/
Dance Captain*

Amy Sparrow
Standby Claudia

Will Swenson
*Marquis/Laurent/
Ensemble*

Steve Wilson
Swing

Tommar Wilson
Ensemble

Anne Rice
Source Material

Elton John
Music

Bernie Taupin
Lyrics

Linda Woolverton
Book

Robert Jess Roth
Director

Matt West
Musical Staging

Derek McLane
Set Design

Susan Hilferty
Costume Design

Kenneth Posner
Lighting Design

Tom Watson
Hair Design

Angelina Avallone
Make-up Design

Rick Sordelet
Fight Director

Guy Babylon
*Musical Supervisor/
Orchestrations*

Bruce Coughlin
*Additional
Orchestrations*

Lestat

John Miller
Music Coordinator

Todd Ellison
Vocal Arrangements

Jay Binder, C.S.A.
Casting

Mark Brandon
Casting

Bonnie L. Becker
*Production
Stage Manager*

J. Philip Bassett
Stage Manager

Alan Wasser
Associates
General Manager

Guy Kwan, John Paull III, Hillary Blanken,
Kevin Broomell, Ana Rose Greene,
Juniper Street Productions
Technical Supervisor

Allison Fischer and Hugh Panaro perform
"I Want More."

Photo by Paul Kolnik

Lestat

STAFF FOR *LESTAT*

WARNER BROS. THEATRE VENTURES

Raymond Wu ....Vice Pres., Business and Legal Affairs
Laura Valan ....Chief Financial Officer
Mark Coker ....Vice Pres., Finance
Maria Gonzalez ....Director, Finance
Carol Wood ....Executive Assistant
Jennifer Kim ....Executive Assistant

GENERAL MANAGEMENT
ALAN WASSER ASSOCIATES
Alan Wasser   Allan Williams
Aaron Lustbader

GENERAL PRESS REPRESENTATION
BARLOW•HARTMAN
John Barlow   Michael Hartman
Wayne Wolfe   Andrew Snyder

CASTING
JAY BINDER CASTING
Jay Binder CSA
Jack Bowdan CSA, Mark Brandon, Megan Larche
Assistants: Rachel Shapiro-Cooper, Nikole Vallins

COMPANY MANAGER
MARK SHACKET

ASSOCIATE COMPANY MANAGER
MARIA MAZZA

TECHNICAL SUPERVISION
JUNIPER STREET PRODUCTIONS
Kevin Broomell   Hillary Blanken
John Paul III   Guy Kwan   Ana Rose Greene

PRODUCTION STAGE MANAGER
BONNIE L. BECKER

Stage Manager ....J. Philip Bassett
Assistant Stage Manager ....Kimberly Russell
Associate General Manager ....Aaron Lustbader
Asst. Projections Coordinator ....Andrew Bauer
Dance Captain ....Sarah Solie
Fight Captain ....Steve Wilson
Assistant Scenic Designers ....Shoko Kambara, Michael Auszura, Raul Abrego, Court Watson
Associate Lighting Designer ....Philip Rosenberg
Assistant Lighting Designer ....Patricia Nichols
Assistant Sound Designer ....Brian Hsieh
Associate Costume Designers ....Maiko Matsushima, Nancy Palmatier
Assistant Costume Designer ....Amy Clark
Production Carpenter ....Rick Howard
Production Electrician ....James Maloney
Production Properties ....Heidi L. Brown
Head Carpenter ....Jack Anderson
Assistant Carpenters ....Robert Hentze, Robert Kelly, Matt Lynch, Geoffrey Vaughn
Head Electrician ....Carlos Martinez
Assistant Electricians ....Andy Catron, Brad Robertson

Automated Lights Programmer ....David Arch
Lighting Intern ....Joel Shier
Video Projections Electrician ....Justin Freeman
Video Projections Programmer ....Drew Findley
Video Projectionist ....Bob Loney
Head Sound Engineer ....Simon Matthews
Assistant Sound Engineer ....Dan Hochstine
Head Properties Supervisor ....Eric Castaldo
Assistant Properties Supervisor ....David Cohen
Production Wardrobe Supervisor ....Rory Powers
Assistant Wardrobe Supervisor ....Shana Dunbar
Hair Supervisor ....Craig Kilander
Assistant Hair Supervisor ....Chris Calabrese
Assistant Hair Dressers ....Mary Mulligan, Daryl J. Terry
Music Preparation ....Paul Holderbaum/ Chelsea Music
Synthesizer Programmer ....Guy Babylon
Assistant to John Miller ....Charles Butler
Press Office Manager ....Bethany Larsen
Press Associates ....Leslie Baden, Dennis Crowley, Jon Dimond, Carol Fineman, Rick Miramontez, Ryan Ratelle, Gerilyn Shur
Production Assistants ....Toni Ostini, Scott Rowen, Jessica Schiavoni, Elena Soderblom, Rachel Sterner, Chris Zaccardi
Legal Counsel ....Paul Weiss, Rifkind, Wharton & Garrison L.L.P./ John F. Breglio
Insurance ....AON Insurance
Banking ....JP Morgan Chase & Co./ Richard Callian, Michele Gibbons
Accounting ....Rosenberg Neuwirth & Kuchner/ Chris Cacace, In Woo
Travel ....Road Rebel Entertainment Touring
Payroll Service ....Castellana Services Inc./ Lance Castellana
Advertising ....SpotCo/Drew Hodges, Jim Edwards, Tom Greenwald, Pete Milano, Jim McNicholas
Marketing ....The Marketing Group/ Laura Matalon, Tanya Grubich, Trish Santini, Bob Bucci, Amber Glassberg, Liz Miller
General Management Associates ....Jim Brandeberry, Jake Hirzel, Lane Marsh, Thom Mitchell, Robert Nolan, Connie Yung
General Management Office ....Chris Betz, Chris D'Angelo, Jason Hewitt, Jennifer Mudge, Kimberly Jade Tompkins
Merchandising ....Max Merchandising, LLC/ Randi Grossman
Website Design/Online Marketing ....Situation Marketing/ Damian Bazadona, Ian Bennett, Sara Fitzpatrick
Study Guide ....Peter Royston/GUIDEWRITE
New York Rehearsal Space ....New 42nd Street Studios
Theatre Displays ....King Displays, Inc.
Production Photographer ....Paul Kolnik
Orthopedic Consultant ....Phillip Bauman, M.D.
Physical Therapy ....Performing Arts Physical Therapy

CREDITS AND ACKNOWLEDGMENTS

Scenery and scenic effects built and electrified by PRG Scenic Technologies, New Windsor, NY; Hudson Scenic Studio, Inc., Yonkers, NY; and Beyond Imagination, Newburgh, NY. Scenery painted by Scenic Art Studios, Cornwall, NY. Show control and scenic motion control featuring Stage Command Systems® by PRG Scenic Technologies, New Windsor, NY. Softgoods built by I. Weiss and Sons, Inc., Long Island City, NY. Video projection equipment provided by PRG Video, Mt. Vernon, NY. Lighting equipment provided by PRG Lighting, North Bergen, NJ. Sound equipment provided by PRG Audio, Mt. Vernon, NY. Furniture and props executed by The Spoon Group, Rahway, NJ; John Creech Design and Production, Brooklyn, NY; and Jerard Studio, Brooklyn, NY. Additional set and hand props courtesy of George Fenmore, Inc. Special effects equipment by Jauchem & Meeh Inc. Costumes by Eric Winterling Costumes; TRICORNE, Inc.; Euro Co.; Schneeman Studio Limited; Marc Happel; Seamless Costume; and Martin Izquierdo Studio. Millinery by Rodney Gordon Studio and Lynne Mackey Studio. Shoes by La Duca and Fred Longtin. Fur by Fur and Furgery. Digital printing of fabrics by Olympus and Supersample. Custom wigs executed by Watson Associates. Interstate hauling by Clark Transfer, Inc. Rehearsed at New 42nd Street Studios.

No animals were harmed
in the making of this production.

Cover illustration by Dave McKean © Warner Bros.

Makeup provided by M•A•C Cosmetics.

SPECIAL THANKS
Yamaha Corporate Artists Affairs, John Conway, Tracey Dobkowski, Derrick Kardos.

GROUP SALES
TDI/Broadway.com: 1-800-Broadway

⟫N⟪

NEDERLANDER

Lestat
SCRAPBOOK

Correspondent: Allison Fischer, "Claudia"

Opening Night Gifts: Personally-engraved Tiffany picture frame from Elton John, a toy Smurf set from Jim Stanek (ha ha!), a jewelry box from Linda Woolverton, cards, flowers, fruit baskets, a leather bag from Warner Bros., et cetera.

Most Exciting Celebrity Visitor: Either Alice Cooper or Jon Bon Jovi. I was able to talk to both and received compliments without fainting!

Who Got the Gypsy Robe: Sarah Solie. We took some fabric that represented the show and we all signed it.

Who Has Done the Most Shows in Their Career: Sarah has done the most Broadway productions.

Special Backstage Ritual: Jim Stanek and I usually talk each other's ears off. Then I will do some voice warm-ups, drink my calm tea from Starbucks, suck on a million cough drops, say a quick prayer, and I'm set!

Favorite Moment During Each Performance: The second I step on the stage, all my troubles and worries in life disappear and I'm taken to a whole new world with wonderful people.

Amazing Fan Letter: I got a fan letter from a young girl telling me how much she admired and respected what I did. She told me I inspired her to not only pursue what she loves, but to be a better person as well. That was the most amazing fan letter I have ever gotten.

Favorite In-Theatre Gathering Places: Jim's and Drew's dressing rooms. In Jim's dressing room I usually talk with him about life and the show. In Drew's dressing room we sing and play guitar.

Favorite Snack Food: Goldfish, Verona cookies, Milano cookies, and potato chips and onion dip.

Mascot: Hmm… A vampire? He he!

Favorite Therapy: Cherry Hall's, Ricolas, lemon, honey, calm tea, and snickerdoodle cookies!

Memorable Ad-Lib: Probably when Jim called Lestat "Claudia"! Ha ha!

Most Cell Phone Rings During a Performance: Two? Maybe?

Memorable Press Encounter: Opening night for *Lestat*! There is nothing like walking down the red carpet, getting your pictures taken, and being interviewed!

Memorable Stage Door Fan Encounter: I had two people act out one of the scenes in the show for me and then give me two porcelain dolls! That would have to be the coolest!

Latest Audience Arrival: I have heard people came in at intermission!

Heaviest/Hottest Costume: Drew (Armand). The only skin you saw on him was his face!

Who Wore the Least?: Chris Peluso in "The Morality Play." He was shirtless.

Catchphrases Only the Company Would Recognize: "Wooooosh"

Memorable Directorial Note: "Just have fun with it!"

Company In-Jokes: "Quote on Quotes."

Nicknames: Al, Kiddo, Lady Bug, Allison Fishcakes, Hughy (Hugh), Drewy (Drew) and Jimples (Jim). We all gave each other poker

names as well. We played it a lot on our own time.

Embarrassing Moments: I won't mention any names (he he), but one cast member just simply forgot to sing a solo line. Another cast member tripped down the staircase in the old finale, back in San Francisco, and I fell flat on my face during "I Want More" once.

Ghostly Encounters Backstage: None. But I played a trick on some of the cast members, telling them I heard Judy Garland's voice singing "Over the Rainbow."

Coolest Thing About Being in This Show: Working and becoming friends with the most amazing people I have ever met.

Photos by Aubrey Reuben

1. Anne Rice (R) shares a curtain call with Elton John on opening night.
2. Hugh Panaro and Carolee Carmello at the opening night party at the Time Warner Center.
3. David Furnish (L) and Elton John arrive at the Palace Theatre for opening night.
4. Anne Rice and son Chris at the opening night party.
5. (L-R): Roderick Hill, Hugh Panaro, Jim Stanek at the party.
6. Librettist Linda Woolverton arrives at the Time Warner Center.

The Lieutenant of Inishmore

First Preview: April 18, 2006. Opened: May 3, 2006.
Still running as of May 31, 2006.

CAST
(in order of speaking)

Davey .... DOMHNALL GLEESON
Donny .... PETER GERETY
Padraic .... DAVID WILMOT
James .... JEFF BINDER
Mairead .... ALISON PILL
Christy .... ANDREW CONNOLLY
Joey .... DASHIELL EAVES
Brendan .... BRIAN D'ARCY JAMES

TIME/PLACE
The play is set in 1993
on the island of Inishmore, County Galway.

UNDERSTUDIES
For Donny & Christy:
JOHN AHLIN

For Padraic, Joey, Davey, James & Christy:
BRIAN AVERS

For Mairead:
CRISTIN MILIOTI

*Domhnall Gleeson and David Wilmot are appearing
with the permission of Actors' Equity Association
pursuant to an exchange program between
American Equity and U.K. Equity.*

2005-2006 AWARD

THEATRE WORLD AWARD
Outstanding Broadway Debut (David Wilmot)

☺ LYCEUM THEATRE
149 West 45th Street
A Shubert Organization Theatre

Gerald Schoenfeld, *Chairman*   Philip J. Smith, *President*

Robert E. Wankel, *Executive Vice President*

RANDALL L. WREGHITT   DEDE HARRIS   ATLANTIC THEATER COMPANY
DAVID LEHRER   HARRIET NEWMAN LEVE & RON NICYNSKI
ZAVELSON MEYRELLES GREINER GROUP
MORT SWINSKY & REDFERN GOLDMAN PRODUCTIONS
and   RUTH HENDEL
present

THE LIEUTENANT OF INISHMORE

by
MARTIN McDONAGH

with
JEFF BINDER   ANDREW CONNOLLY   DASHIELL EAVES
PETER GERETY   DOMHNALL GLEESON
BRIAN D'ARCY JAMES   ALISON PILL   DAVID WILMOT

set design SCOTT PASK	costume design THERESA SQUIRE	lighting design MICHAEL CHYBOWSKI
sound design OBADIAH EAVES	music MATT McKENZIE	arrangements ANDREW RANKEN
casting PAT McCORKLE, CSA	fight director J. DAVID BRIMMER	dialect coach STEPHEN GABIS
production stage manager JAMES HARKER	production management AURORA PRODUCTIONS	general management RICHARDS/CLIMAN, INC.
associate producer BRAUN-McFARLANE PRODUCTIONS	marketing HHC MARKETING	press representative BONEAU/BRYAN-BROWN

directed by
WILSON MILAM

Originally produced by Atlantic Theater Company on February 27th, 2006
by special arrangement with Randall L. Wreghitt & Dede Harris.

The producers wish to express their appreciation to the
Theatre Development Fund for its support of this production.

LIVE BROADWAY

5/3/06

David Wilmot
and Alison Pill.

Photo by Monique Carboni

The Lieutenant of Inishmore

Jeff Binder
James

Andrew Connolly
Christy

Dashiell Eaves
Joey

Peter Gerety
Donny

Domhnall Gleeson
Davey

Brian d'Arcy James
Brendan

Alison Pill
Mairead

David Wilmot
Padraic

John Ahlin
*Understudy for
Donny & Christy*

Brian Avers
*Understudy for
Padraic, Joey, Davey,
James & Christy*

Cristin Milioti
*Understudy for
Mairead*

Martin McDonagh
Playwright

Wilson Milam
Director

Scott Pask
Set Designer

Theresa Squire
Costume Designer

Michael Chybowski
Lighting Designer

Obadiah Eaves
Sound Designer

J. David Brimmer
Fight Director

Stephen Gabis
Dialect Coach

James Harker
*Production
Stage Manager*

Randall L. Wreghitt
Producer

Dede Harris
Producer

David Lehrer
Producer

Harriet Newman Leve
Producer

Mort Swinsky
Producer

Katrin Redfern,
Redfern Goldman
Productions
Producer

Eric Warren Goldman,
Redfern Goldman
Productions
Producer

Ruth Hendel
Producer

Thom Clay
Company Manager

FRONT OF HOUSE STAFF
Front Row (L-R): Joann Swanson
(House Manager), Merida Cohen
(Chief Usher), Elsie Grosvenor (Directress),
Lorraine Bellaflores (Usherette)

Middle Row (L-R): Susan Houghton
(Ticket Taker), Rosie Rodriguez
(Head Porter), Gerry Belitsis (Usher),
Tim Moran (Assistant Treasurer),
Sonia Moreno (Usherette)

Back Row (L-R): Judy Pinouz (Usher),
Ramona (Usherette), Jack Kearns
(Security), John Donovan
(Night Doorman), Robert Dejesus (Usher)

Photo by Ben Strothmann

The Lieutenant of Inishmore

Photos by Ben Strothmann

BOX OFFICE
(L-R):
Sidney J. Burgoyne (Assistant Treasurer)
and Tim Moran (Assistant Treasurer)

STAGE CREW
(L-R): Jim Harker (Production Stage Manager), Leah Nelson (House Props), Jenny Montgomery (Production Sound), Anmaree Rodibaugh (Production Props), Adam Braunstein (House Carpenter), Heather Richmond Wright (Hair & Makeup), Freda Farrell (Stage Manager), Laura Koch (House Props), Cathy Prager (House Props), Bill Rowland (House Electrician). The sign refers to the play's cat.

STAFF FOR *THE LIEUTENANT OF INISHMORE*

GENERAL MANAGEMENT
RICHARDS/CLIMAN, INC.
David R. Richards   Tamar Haimes
Laura Janik Cronin

COMPANY MANAGER
Thom Clay

GENERAL PRESS REPRESENTATIVE
BONEAU/BRYAN-BROWN
Chris Boneau   Susanne Tighe
Heath Schwartz

PRODUCTION
STAGE MANAGER ....JAMES HARKER
Stage Manager ....Freda Farrell
Assistant to the Director ....Nick Leavens
Assistant Set Designer ....Nancy Thun, Lauren Alvarez
Assistant Costume Designer   ....Renee Mariotti
Assistant Lighting Designer ....Dale Knoth
Assistant Sound Designer ....Ryan Powers
Production Management ....Aurora Productions/
Gene O'Donovan,
W. Benjamin Heller II,
Bethany Weinstein, Hillary Austin,
Melissa Mazdra
Head Carpenter...........................Adam Braunstein
Advance Carpenter ....Paul Wimmer
Head Electrician ....William Rowland
Production Electrician ....James Gardner
Production Sound ....Jenny Montgomery
Production Properties Supervisor .....Anmaree Rodibaugh
Head Props ....Leah Nelson
Wardrobe Supervisor ....Nancy Schaefer
Hair Supervisor ....Heather Richmond Wright
Fight Captain ....Jeff Binder
Dresser ....Edmund Harrison
Prop Shopper ....Peter Sarafin
Casting Associate ....Kelly Gillespie
Casting Assistant ....Joe Lopick
Production Assistant ....Kirsten Lake
Press Associates ....Adrian Bryan-Brown,
Jim Byk, Brandi Cornwell,
Jackie Green, Juliana Hannett,
Hector Hernandez, Jessica Johnson,

Kevin Jones, Eric Louie,
Shanna Marcus, Aaron Meier,
Joe Perrotta, Linnae Petruzzelli,
Matt Polk, Matt Ross
Banking ....Commerce Bank/
Ashley Elezi, Barbara Von Borstel
Payroll ....Castellana Services, Inc./Lance Castellana
Accountant ....FK Partners/
Robert Fried, Elliott Aronstam
Insurance ....DeWitt Stern Group, Inc./
Anthony Pittari
Legal ....Cowan DeBaets Abrahams & Sheppard LLP
Frederick P. Bimbler
Advertising....................................SpotCo/
Drew Hodges, Jim Edwards,
Amelia Heape, Jen McClelland
Marketing ....HHC Marketing/
Hugh Hysell, Amanda Pekoe,
Jennifer Scherer
Group Sales.............................Shubert Group Sales
Merchandising ....Matt Murphy
Website ....Late August Design
Production Photographer ....Monique Carboni

ATLANTIC THEATER COMPANY STAFF
Artistic Director ....Neil Pepe
Managing Director ....Andrew D. Hamingson
School Executive Director ....Mary McCann
General Manager ....Melinda Berk
Associate Artistic Director ....Christian Parker
Development Director ....Erika Mallin
Development Associate ....Rose Yndigoyen
Production Manager ....Lester Grant
Marketing Director ....Jodi Sheeler
Membership Coordinator ....Sara Montgomery
Operations Manager ....Brian Isaacs
Company Manager ....Nick Leavens
Assistant to the Artistic and
Managing Directors ....Laura Savia
School Associate Director ....Kate Blumberg
School Associate Director ....Steven Hawley
Business Manager ....Diana Ascher
Education Director ....Frances Tarr
School Production Director ....Geoff Berman
School Production Manager ....Eric Southern
School Admissions ....Brandon Thompson
Resident Director ....William H. Macy

Resident Lighting Designer ....Howard Werner
Resident Fight Director ....Rick Sordelet
Box Office Treasurer ....Frances Tarr
House Managers ....   Josh Cole, Sarah Heartley, Nick
Leavens, David Toomey

CREDITS
Scenery constructed and painted by Showmotion, Inc.
Original scenery constructed by Tom Carroll Scenery.
Lighting and sound equipment by GSD Productions.
Costumes constructed by Lee Purdy, Kyra Svetlovsky, Piort
Candelario. Aerographic services by Flying by Foy. Special
effects by Waldo Warshaw. Mannequins by Peter Sarafin,
Craig Grigg. Firearms provided by IAR, Inc.

SPECIAL THANKS
Bill Berloni and Mr. Ed, Lester Grant, Camryn Duff, Erin
Lorek, Griffith Maloney, Anton Nadler, Stephanie Parsons,
Austin Tidwell, Barbara Milam, Mary McDonagh and the
use of her music library

www.InishmoreOnBroadway.com

 THE SHUBERT ORGANIZATION, INC.
Board of Directors

Gerald Schoenfeld	**Philip J. Smith**
Chairman	President
Wyche Fowler, Jr.	**John W. Kluge**
Lee J. Seidler	**Michael I. Sovern**

Stuart Subotnick
Robert E. Wankel
Executive Vice President

Peter Entin	**Elliot Greene**
Vice President -	Vice President -
Theatre Operations	Finance
David Andrews	**John Darby**
Vice President -	Vice President -
Shubert Ticketing Services	Facilities

House Manager ....Joann Swanson

The Lieutenant of Inishmore
SCRAPBOOK

Photos by Aubrey Reuben

①

②

③

④

⑤

⑥

Photo by David Gewirtzman

Correspondent: James Harker, Production Stage Manager
Memorable Opening Night Note: Kerry Condon's Happy Opening "order" to "Knock 'em dead from 60 yards."
Most Exciting Celebrity Visitors: Robert De Niro and Liam Neeson.
Most Shows in Their Career: Peter Gerety with 13,000-plus performances.
Favorite Moment in the Show: Post-show showers.
Favorite Gathering Place: David Wilmot's dressing room.
Favorite Off-Site Hangout: O'Lunney's.
Favorite Snack Food: Honey
Favorite Therapy: Throat Coat Tea, Ricolas and darts in Dashiell's dressing room.
Company Catchphrase: "Lob it up me boss."
Memorable Directorial Notes: "There's no art in this blood." "One of these days just shoot him—see what happens."
Theatrical Superstitions That Turned Out To Be True: Black cats are nasty bad luck.

1. (L-R): Alison Pill, Peter Gerety, director Wilson Milam, Domhnall Gleeson, Dashiell Eaves, playwright Martin McDonagh, David Wilmot and Andrew Connolly at the opening night party at B.B. King's Blues Club.
2. (L-R) Domhnall Gleeson, Amy Ryan and Brian d'Arcy James at the opening night party.
3. Rebecca Luker and Dashiell Eaves at B.B. King's.
4. Monique Carboni and Martin McDonagh at the Lyceum Theatre on opening night.
5. (L-R): David Wilmot and Alison Pill at the opening night party.
6. The window card outside the Lyceum Theatre.

The Light in the Piazza

First Preview: March 17, 2005. Opened: April 18, 2005.
Still running as of May 31, 2006.

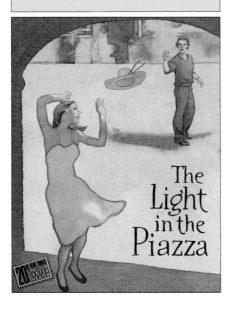

PLAYBILL

The Light in the Piazza

CAST

(in order of appearance)

Margaret Johnson ....VICTORIA CLARK

Clara Johnson, her daughter ....KELLI O'HARA

Fabrizio Naccarelli ....AARON LAZAR

Signor Naccarelli,
    Fabrizio's father ....CHRIS SARANDON

Giuseppe Naccarelli,
    Fabrizio's brother ....MICHAEL BERRESSE

Franca Naccarelli,
    Giuseppe's wife.........SARAH URIARTE BERRY

Signora Naccarelli,
    Fabrizio's mother ....PATTI COHENOUR

Roy Johnson,
    Margaret's husband ....BEAU GRAVITTE

Tour Guide ....FELICITY LaFORTUNE

Priest ....JOSEPH SIRAVO

Ensemble ....DAVID BONANNO,
                        DAVID BURNHAM,
                        LAURA GRIFFITH,
            PRUDENCE WRIGHT HOLMES,
                        JENNIFER HUGHES,
                    FELICITY LaFORTUNE,
                        MICHEL MOINOT,
                        JOSEPH SIRAVO

Continued on next page

LINCOLN CENTER THEATER AT THE VIVIAN BEAUMONT

under the direction of
André Bishop and Bernard Gersten
presents

The Light in the Piazza

book
Craig Lucas

music and lyrics
Adam Guettel

based on the novel by Elizabeth Spencer

with (in alphabetical order)

Glenn Seven Allen   Michael Berresse   Sarah Uriarte Berry   David Bonanno
David Burnham   Victoria Clark   Patti Cohenour   Beau Gravitte
Laura Griffith   Prudence Wright Holmes   Jennifer Hughes
Felicity LaFortune   Catherine LaValle   Aaron Lazar   Michel Moinot
Kelli O'Hara   Peter Samuel   Chris Sarandon   Joseph Siravo   Diane Sutherland

sets
Michael Yeargan

costumes
Catherine Zuber

lighting
Christopher Akerlind

sound
ACME Sound Partners

orchestrations
Ted Sperling and Adam Guettel

additional orchestrations
Bruce Coughlin

conductor
Kimberly Grigsby

casting
Janet Foster, C.S.A.

production stage manager
Peter Wolf

general press agent
Philip Rinaldi

musical theater
associate producer
Ira Weitzman

general
manager
Adam Siegel

production
manager
Jeff Hamlin

director of
development
Hattie K. Jutagir

director of
marketing
Linda Mason Ross

music direction
Ted Sperling

musical staging
Jonathan Butterell

direction
Bartlett Sher

This production of "The Light in the Piazza" is dedicated to the memory of Andrew Heiskell,
who, during his lifetime, gave off a lovely light of his own.

LCT thanks the Blanchette Hooker Rockefeller Fund for its outstanding support.
Major support is provided by The Shen Family Foundation.
LCT gratefully acknowledges an extraordinary gift from the Estate of Edith K. Ehrman.
Special thanks to The Harold and Mimi Steinberg Charitable Trust for supporting new American plays at LCT.

American Airlines is the official airline of Lincoln Center Theater.
Merrill Lynch is a 2005 LCT Season Sponsor.

LCT wishes to express its appreciation to Theatre Development Fund for its support of this production.

The World Premiere of THE LIGHT IN THE PIAZZA was produced by the Intiman Theatre, Seattle, Washington; Bartlett Sher, Artistic Director,
Laura Penn, Managing Director; and the Goodman Theatre, Chicago, Illinois; Robert Falls, Artistic Director, Roche Schulfer, Executive Director.
Developed with the Assistance of the Sundance Institute Theatre Laboratory.
Produced by arrangement with Turner Entertainment Co, Owner of the original motion picture "Light in the Piazza."

9/26/05

(L-R): Aaron Lazar and Katie Clarke
as Fabrizio and Clara.

Photo by Joan Marcus

The Light in the Piazza

MUSICAL NUMBERS

ACT ONE

Overture
Statues and Stories .... Margaret and Clara
The Beauty Is .... Clara
Il Mondo Era Vuoto .... Fabrizio
Passeggiata .... Fabrizio and Clara
The Joy You Feel .... Franca
Dividing Day .... Margaret
Hysteria .... Clara and Margaret
Say It Somehow .... Clara and Fabrizio

ACT TWO

Aiutami .... The Naccarelli Family
The Light in the Piazza .... Clara
Octet .... Company
Tirade .... Clara
Octet (Reprise) .... Company
The Beauty Is (Reprise) .... Margaret
Let's Walk .... Signor Naccarelli and Margaret
Love to Me .... Fabrizio
Fable .... Margaret

ORCHESTRA

Conductor:
KIMBERLY GRIGSBY

Associate Conductor, Piano, Celesta:
MARK MITCHELL

Violins:
SYLVIA D'AVANZO (Concertmaster),
MATTHEW LEHMANN, JAMES TSAO,
LISA MATRICARDI, KARL KAWAHARA
KATHERINE LIVOLSI-STERN,
Cello:
ARIANE LALLEMAND, ROBERT BURKHART
Harp:
VICTORIA DRAKE
Bass:
BRIAN CASSIER
Clarinet/English Horn/Oboe:
DENNIS ANDERSON
Bassoon/Contrabassoon:
GILI SHARETT
Percussion:
MATTHEW GOLD
Guitar/Mandolin:
ANDREW SCHWARTZ

Music Coordinator: SEYMOUR RED PRESS

(L-R): Victoria Clark and Katie Clarke.

Photo by Joan Marcus

Cast Continued

TIME AND PLACE

The Light in the Piazza takes place in
Florence and Rome in the summer of 1953,
with occasional side trips to America.

Assistant Stage Managers .... CLAUDIA LYNCH,
MATTHEW MELCHIORRE

Swings .... GLENN SEVEN ALLEN,
CATHERINE LaVALLE,
PETER SAMUEL

UNDERSTUDIES

For Margaret:
PATTI COHENOUR, DIANE SUTHERLAND

For Clara:
LAURA GRIFFITH, JENNIFER HUGHES

For Fabrizio:
GLENN SEVEN ALLEN, DAVID BURNHAM

For Signor Naccarelli and Roy Johnson:
PETER SAMUEL, JOSEPH SIRAVO

For Signora Naccarelli:
FELICITY LaFORTUNE,
DIANE SUTHERLAND

For Giuseppe:
GLENN SEVEN ALLEN, DAVID BONANNO

For Franca:
LAURA GRIFFITH, CATHERINE LaVALLE

For Tour Guide:
CATHERINE LaVALLE, DIANE SUTHERLAND

For Priest:
GLENN SEVEN ALLEN, PETER SAMUEL

The Light in the Piazza

Glenn Seven Allen
Swing

Michael Berresse
Giuseppe Naccarelli

Sarah Uriarte Berry
Franca Naccarelli

David Bonanno
Ensemble

David Burnham
Ensemble

Victoria Clark
Margaret Johnson

Patti Cohenour
Signora Naccarelli

Beau Gravitte
Roy Johnson

Laura Griffith
Ensemble

Prudence Wright
Holmes
Ensemble

Jennifer Hughes
Ensemble

Felicity LaFortune
*Tour Guide,
Ensemble*

Catherine LaValle
Swing

Aaron Lazar
Fabrizio Naccarelli

Michel Moinot
Ensemble

Kelli O'Hara
Clara Johnson

Peter Samuel
Swing

Chris Sarandon
Signor Naccarelli

Joseph Siravo
Priest, Ensemble

Craig Lucas
Book

Adam Guettel
*Music and Lyrics,
Orchestrations*

Bartlett Sher
Director

Ted Sperling
*Orchestrations,
Musical Direction*

Michael Yeargan
Sets

Catherine Zuber
Costumes

Christopher Akerlind
Lighting

Tom Clark, Mark Menard and Nevin Steinberg/
Acme Sound Partners
Sound

Bruce Coughlin
*Additional
Orchestrations*

Kimberly Grigsby
Conductor

Janet Foster, C.S.A.
Casting

André Bishop and Bernard Gersten,
Lincoln Center Theatre
Producers

The Light in the Piazza

Mark Harelik
Signor Naccarelli

Matthew Morrison
Fabrizio Naccarelli

Katie Clarke
Clara Johnson

Adam Overett
Swing

HAIR DEPARTMENT
(L-R): Alice Ramos (Hair Assistant), Mary Micari (Hair Assistant) and Lazaro Arencibia (Hair Supervisor).

STAGE MANAGEMENT
Front Row (L-R):
Jen Nelson (Production Assistant) and Claudia Lynch (Assistant Stage Manager).

Back Row (L-R):
Matthew Melchiorre (Assistant Stage Manager) and Peter Wolf (Production Stage Manager).

Photos by Ben Strothmann

ORCHESTRA
Front Row (L-R):
Kimberly Grigsby (Music Director).

Second Row (L-R):
Katherine Livolsi-Stern (Violin).

Third Row (L-R):
Andrew Schwartz (Guitar) and Victoria Drake (Harp).

Fourth Row (L-R):
Sylvia D'Avanzo (Concertmaster), Dennis Anderson (Reeds), Karl Kawahara (Violin), James Tsao (Violin).

Fifth Row (L-R):
Matthew Gold (Percussion), Mark Mitchell (Piano/Associate Conductor), Gili Sharett (Bassoon/Contra-Bassoon), Matthew Lehmann (Violin), David Calhoun (Cello, sub).

Back Row (L-R):
Lisa Matricardi (Violin), Robert Burkhart (Cello), David Phillips (Bass, sub).

Not Pictured:
Brian Cassier (Bass) and Ariane Lallemand (Cello).

The Light in the Piazza

STAGE CREW

Front Row (L-R):
Nick Irons (Electrician/Follow Spot Operator), Walter Murphy (Production Carpenter), John Ross (Props), Karl Rausenberger (Production Props), Rudy Wood (Props), Will Coholan (Props), Ray Skillin (Carpenter).

Back Row (L-R):
Frank Linn (Electrician/Automated Tech), Bruce Rubin (Electrician/Board Operator), Marc Salzberg (Production Soundman), Gary Simon (Deck Sound), Juan Bustamante (Automation Carpenter), Pat Merryman (Production Electrician), Linda Heard (Electrician), Jeff Ward (Electrician/Follow Spot Operator), Kristina Clark (Electrician), John Howie (Carpenter), Matt Altman (Electrician/Follow Spot Operator), Scott Jackson (Props), Kevin McNeill (Automation Carpenter) and Andrew Belits (Carpenter).

Not Pictured:
Mark Dignam (Props),
Bill Nagle (Production Flyman),
Joe Pizzuto (Electrician/Follow Spot).

BOX OFFICE
(L-R): Bob Belkin, Marc Friedenreich and Fred Bonis.

WARDROBE DEPARTMENT
(L-R): Sarah Rochford (Dresser), Jerome Parker (Dresser), Cathy Cline (Dresser), Lynn Bowling (Wardrobe Supervisor), Liam O'Brien (Dresser), Tony Hoffman (Dresser) and Amanda Scott (Dresser).

FRONT OF HOUSE STAFF
Front Row (L-R):
Miriam Miller, Jodi Gigliobianco, Susan Lehman, Barbara Hart.

Middle Row (L-R):
Larry Hincher, Alexandra Zavilowicz, Justin McCulla.

Back Row (L-R):
Nick Andors, Manny Billingslea, Mim Pollock, Margareta Shakridge-Cottington, Judith Fanelli and Steve Spear.

Not Pictured:
Rheba Flegelman (House Manager)

The Light in the Piazza

LINCOLN CENTER THEATER

ANDRÉ BISHOP   **BERNARD GERSTEN**
ARTISTIC DIRECTOR   **EXECUTIVE PRODUCER**

ADMINISTRATIVE STAFF

GENERAL MANAGER ....ADAM SIEGEL
Associate General Manager ....Melanie Weinraub
General Management Assistant ....Beth Dembrow
Facilities Manager ....Alex Mustelier
Assistant Facilities Manager ....Michael Assalone
GENERAL PRESS AGENT ....PHILIP RINALDI
Press Associate ....Barbara Carroll
PRODUCTION MANAGER ....JEFF HAMLIN
Associate Production Manager ....Chris Akins
DIRECTOR OF
DEVELOPMENT ....HATTIE K. JUTAGIR
Associate Director of Development ....Rachel Norton
Manager of Special Events and
Young Patron Program ....Karin Schall
Grants Writer ....Neal Brilliant
Coordinator, Patron Program ....Sheilaja Rao
Development Associate...............Chris Chrzanowski
Assistant to the
Director of Development ....Marsha Martinez
DIRECTOR OF FINANCE..........DAVID S. BROWN
Controller ....Susan Knox
Systems Manager ....John N. Yen
Finance Assistant ....Kellie Kroyer
DIRECTOR OF MARKETING ..LINDA MASON ROSS
Marketing Associate ....Denis Guerin
Marketing Assistant ....Elizabeth Kandel
DIRECTOR OF EDUCATION ....KATI KOERNER
Associate Director of Education ....Dionne O'Dell
Assistant to the
Executive Producer ....Barbara Hourigan
Office Assistant ....Kenneth Collins
Messenger ....Esau Burgess
Reception ....Andrew Elsesser, Daryl Watson

ARTISTIC STAFF

ASSOCIATE DIRECTORS ......GRACIELA DANIELE,
NICHOLAS HYTNER,
SUSAN STROMAN,
DANIEL SULLIVAN
DRAMATURG and DIRECTOR,
LCT DIRECTORS LAB ....ANNE CATTANEO
CASTING DIRECTOR ....DANIEL SWEE, CSA
MUSICAL THEATER
ASSOCIATE PRODUCER ....IRA WEITZMAN
Artistic Administrator ....Julia Judge
Casting Associate ....Camille Hickman

HOUSE STAFF

HOUSE MANAGER ....RHEBA FLEGELMAN
Production Carpenter ....Walter Murphy
Production Electrician ....Patrick Merryman
Production Propertyman ....Karl Rausenberger
Production Flyman ....William Nagle
House Technician ....Bill Burke
Chief Usher ...................................M.L. Pollock
Box Office Treasurer ....Fred Bonis
Assistant Treasurer ....Robert A. Belkin

SPECIAL SERVICES

Advertising ....Serino-Coyne/
Jim Russek, Brad Lapin, Jennifer Gelhar
Principal Poster Artist ....James McMullan
Poster Art for
The Light in the Piazza ....James McMullan
Counsel ....Peter L. Felcher, Esq.;
Charles H. Googe, Esq.;
and Rachel Hoover, Esq. of
Paul, Weiss, Rifkind, Wharton & Garrison
Immigration Counsel ....Theodore Ruthizer, Esq.;
Mark D. Koestler, Esq.
of Kramer, Levin, Naftalis & Frankel LLP
Auditor ....Douglas Burack, C.P.A.
Lutz & Carr, L.L.P.
Insurance ....Jennifer Brown of
DeWitt Stern Group
Photographer ....Joan Marcus
Travel ....Tygon Tours
Web Design and
Development ....Four Eyes Productions
Consulting Architect ....Hugh
Hardy,
Hardy Holzman Pfeiffer Associates
Construction Manager ....Yorke Construction
Payroll Service ....Castellana Services, Inc.

STAFF FOR *THE LIGHT IN THE PIAZZA*

COMPANY MANAGER ....Matthew Markoff
Assistant Company Manager ... Jessica Perlmeter Cochrane
Assistant Director ....Sarna Lapine
Assistant to Mr. Lucas ....Troy Miller
Dance Captain ....Laura Griffith
Assistant Set Designer ....Mikiko Suzuki
Assistant Costume Designers ....David Newell,
Michael Zecker
Assistant Lighting Designer ....Michael J. Spadaro
Assistant Sound Designer ....Jeffrey Yoshi Lee
Associate Orchestrator ....Bruce Coughlin
Rehearsal Pianist ....Adam Ben-David

Music Copyist ....Emily Grishman Music Preparation/
Emily Grishman, Katharine Edmonds
Dialect Coach ....Ralph Zito
Props ....Christopher Schneider
Production Soundman ....Marc Salzberg
Light Board Operator ....Bruce Rubin
Moving Light Programmer ....Victor Seastone
Wardrobe Supervisor ....Lynn Bowling
Dressers.............Cathy Cline, Kimberly Mark-Sirota,
Virginia Neininger, Liam O'Brien,
Pat Sullivan, James Wilcox
Hair and Wig Designer ....Jerry Altenburg
Make-up Designer ....Angelina Avallone
Hair Supervisor ....Lazaro Arencibia
Hair Assistants ....Jun Kim, Alice Ramos
Production Assistants ....Andrew Einhorn,
Melanie T. Morgan, Jen Nelson

Italian translation for "Il Mondo Era Vuoto"
by Judith Blazer.

L.A. Casting Consultant ....Julia Flores

CREDITS

Show control and scenic motion control featuring stage command systems by Scenic Technologies, a division of Production Resource Group, LLC, New Windsor, NY. Scenery fabrication by PRG Scenic Technologies, a division of Production Resource Group, LLC, New Windsor, NY. Men's costumes executed by Tim McKelvey, Angels the Costumier and Vos Savant, Inc. Women's costumes by Parson-Meares, Ltd. and Euro Co. Costumes. Millinery by Hugh Hanson for Carelli Costumes Inc. Shoes by LaDuca Shoes NYC. Lighting equipment from PRG Lighting. Sound equipment by Sound Associates. Piano by Steinway & Sons. Natural herb cough drops courtesy of Ricola USA, Inc.

Stock and amateur performance rights to *The Light in the Piazza* are licensed by R&H Theatricals: rnhtheatricals.com

Mr. Guettel would like to thank the following people:
Loy Arcenas, Judith Blazer, Ted Chapin, Mary Cleere Haran, Alison Cochrill, Stephanie Coen, Eric Ebbenga, Michael Feinstein, Peter Franklin, Father John Fraser, Pat Graney, Michael Greif, John Guare, Robert Hurwitz, Celia Keenan-Bolger, Tina Landau, Arthur Laurents, Marcella Lorca, John McDermott, Steven Pasquale, Stephen Sondheim, Alfred Uhry, and Wayne Wilcox.

Lobby refreshments by Sweet Concessions

 Developed with the assistance of the Sundance Institute Theatre Laboratory.

The Light in the Piazza
SCRAPBOOK

Correspondent: David Bonanno, Ensemble

Cast Parties: In late August, Lincoln Center took the entire company and everyone working at Lincoln Center Theater on a Harbor Dinner Cruise. We spent the evening cruising around the harbor and had a wonderful party, the highlight of which was when we pulled along side The Statue of Liberty and watched a spectacular fireworks display.

On New Year's Day, our producer, Bernie Gersten threw a huge bash at his place, stipulating that the dress be "All White." I don't own any white clothes except underwear, so that's what I wore: my white boxers and T-shirt. There I was, with Cherry Jones and Terrence McNally, in nothing but my underwear. Bernie loved it and everyone else was horrified. André Bishop completely ignored me.

Backstate Rituals: About every six weeks, Chris Sarandon and I put on a huge Sunday brunch before our final show of the week. We set up tables in the endlessly long hallways of the Vivian Beaumont and Chris mans the bacon and sausage griddles while I make the pancakes. Our Easter Sunday brunch was our biggest with the entire crew and orchestra joining us. It was a HUGE spread. On our brunch days, the audience walks in to the smell of bacon.

For Christmas, Chris Sarandon and Aaron Lazar had show hats made for everyone in the company. On the back of the hat is a hoof print where Clara was kicked in the head by the pony.

When we get bored backstage, David Burnham and I, along with our dresser Liam O'Brien, pick a character in the show and deliver all their lines like Cartman from "South Park."

We all look forward to our weekly visits from our producer Bernie Gersten. He hangs out in our dressing rooms during half hour and regales us with tales of Broadway's yesteryear. Bernie has an endless supply of very colorful mismatched socks!

"Carols for a Cure" Carol: "Show Song (It's Coming Down)."

In-Jokes: Our crew had T-shirts made that say "I don't want to do what you want me to do!" the dramatic line that Clara says to Margaret right before she sings the title song.

Memorable Ad-Lib: David Burnham makes his first entrance in the show on a bicycle as "Nino the bike boy." He delivers a bundle of newspapers to me and the mail to Signore Naccarelli. One night his bike was experiencing technical difficulties and he rode on stage without any of his props. He rode up and delivered his line "*Journale!*" (newspapers), but not the *Journales* themselves, as they were still sitting on the prop table. I cursed at him in Italian and he shrugged and rode away.

Mascot: Our company mascot is named Edwina. She's been around since Halloween when Vickie Clark brought in a mask to

1. Victoria Clark (orange dress) unveils her caricature at Sardi's with the help of friends and fellow cast members.
2. Kelli O'Hara at the annual "Broadway Flea Market" event.
3. Clark with show mascot, "Edwina."

"BOO" Beau Gravitte. The mask made its way through all the dressing rooms and ended up on a dress dummy in the hallway. She is always dressed in the season's finest and for Easter was given a beautiful handmade dress by one of our dressers, Jerome Parker. The dress is made out of one of David Bonanno's old T-shirts.

Nickname: When Patti Cohenour performs the role of Margaret twice a week, we call her "Mini Margaret," as she is six inches shorter than Vickie.

Favorite After Show Hangout: O'Neal's.

Least Favorite Snack Food: One night, Michael Berresse came out of his dressing room with a bad stomachache. He had gone to Whole Foods for dinner and said "There are two types of food you should NEVER mix in the same meal: sushi and Indian!"

Audience Encounters: During Chris Sarandon's first week in the show, two audience members got sick. One passed out and Aaron Lazar stopped the show and called out, "Is there a doctor in the house?" Another night a man wandered onto the stage, into the wings, and threw up outside of Kelli O'Hara's dressing room door. Chris tried not to take either incident personally!

Also: During the course of our run, our wardrobe supervisor, Lynn Bowling had both hips replaced: one on Labor Day and the other on New Year's Eve. He was back on the job within two weeks with each!

The Lion King

First Preview: October 15, 1997. Opened: November 13, 1997.
Still running as of May 31, 2006.

CAST
(in order of appearance)

RAFIKI .... Tshidi Manye
MUFASA .... Alton Fitzgerald White
SARABI .... Jean Michelle Grier
ZAZU .... Jeff Binder
SCAR .... Derek Smith
YOUNG SIMBA .... Jarrell J. Singleton
(Wed. Mat., Thurs., Sat. Mat., Sun. Mat.)
YOUNG SIMBA .... Aaron D. Conley
(Wed. Eve., Fri., Sat. Eve., Sun. Eve.)
YOUNG NALA .... Alex de Castro
(Wed. Mat., Thurs., Sat. Eve., Sun. Eve.)
YOUNG NALA .... Natalie Guerrero
(Wed. Eve., Fri., Sat. Mat., Sun. Mat.)
SHENZI .... Jacquelyn Renae Hodges
BANZAI .... Benjamin Sterling Cannon
ED .... Enrique Segura
TIMON .... Danny Rutigliano
PUMBAA .... Tom Alan Robbins
SIMBA .... Josh Tower
NALA .... Kissy Simmons
ENSEMBLE SINGERS .... Lindiwe Dlamini,
Michelle Dorant, Bongi Duma,
Jean Michelle Grier, Michael Alexander Henry,
Keswa, Ron Kunene, Brian M. Love,
Sheryl McCallum, S'bu Ngema, Mpume Sikakane,
L. Steven Taylor, Rema Webb,
Kenny Redell Williams
ENSEMBLE DANCERS .... Kristina Michelle
Bethel, Kylin Brady, Camille M. Brown,
Michelle Aguilar Camaya, Gabriel A. Croom,

Continued on next page

Continued on next page

THE PROGRAM

Disney
PRESENTS

THE LION KING

Music & Lyrics by
ELTON JOHN & TIM RICE
Additional Music & Lyrics by
LEBO M, MARK MANCINA, JAY RIFKIN, JULIE TAYMOR, HANS ZIMMER
Book by
ROGER ALLERS & IRENE MECCHI

Starring
DEREK SMITH   ALTON FITZGERALD WHITE   TSHIDI MANYE
JEFF BINDER   TOM ALAN ROBBINS   DANNY RUTIGLIANO
JOSH TOWER   KISSY SIMMONS
BENJAMIN STERLING CANNON   JACQUELYN RENAE HODGES   ENRIQUE SEGURA
AARON D. CONLEY   ALEX de CASTRO   NATALIE GUERRERO   JARRELL J. SINGLETON

KRISTINA MICHELLE BETHEL   JOHN E. BRADY   KYLIN BRADY   CAMILLE M. BROWN
MICHELLE AGUILAR CAMAYA   GABRIEL A. CROOM   GARLAND DAYS   LINDIWE DLAMINI   MICHELLE DORANT
BONGI DUMA   IAN YURI GARDNER   JEAN MICHELLE GRIER   MICHAEL ALEXANDER HENRY
TONY JAMES   DENNIS JOHNSTON   CORNELIUS JONES, JR.   KESWA   GREGORY A. KING   JACK KOENIG
RON KUNENE   LISA LEWIS   NIKKI LONG   BRIAN M. LOVE   SHERYL McCALLUM   IAN VINCENT McGINNIS
RAY MERCER   JENNIFER HARRISON NEWMAN   S'BU NGEMA   ANGELICA EDWARDS PATTERSON
MPUME SIKAKANE   SOPHIA N. STEPHENS   L. STEVEN TAYLOR   RYAN BROOKE TAYLOR   TORYA
STEVEN EVAN WASHINGTON   REMA WEBB   KENNY REDELL WILLIAMS

Adapted from the screenplay by
IRENE MECCHI & JONATHAN ROBERTS & LINDA WOOLVERTON

Produced by
PETER SCHNEIDER & THOMAS SCHUMACHER

Scenic Design	*Costume Design*	*Lighting Design*	*Mask & Puppet Design*
RICHARD HUDSON	JULIE TAYMOR	DONALD HOLDER	JULIE TAYMOR & MICHAEL CURRY
Hair & Makeup Design	*Casting*	*Associate Director*	*Production Dance Supervisor*
MICHAEL WARD	BINDER CASTING/ MARK BRANDON	ANTHONY LYN	MAREY GRIFFITH
Associate Producers	*Technical Director*	*Production Stage Manager*	*Production Supervisor*
TODD LACY AUBREY LYNCH II	DAVID BENKEN	JIMMIE LEE SMITH	DOC ZORTHIAN
Music Director	*Associate Music Producer*	*Music Coordinator*	*Press Representative*
KARL JURMAN	ROBERT ELHAI	MICHAEL KELLER	BONEAU/ BRYAN-BROWN

Music Produced for the Stage & Additional Score by	*Additional Vocal Score, Vocal Arrangements & Choral Director*	*Orchestrators*
MARK MANCINA	LEBO M	ROBERT ELHAI DAVID METZGER BRUCE FOWLER

Choreography by
GARTH FAGAN

Directed by
JULIE TAYMOR

Disney ON BROADWAY

10/3/05

The opening number, "The Circle of Life."

Photo by Joan Marcus

The Lion King

SCENES AND MUSICAL NUMBERS

ACT ONE

Scene 1 Pride Rock
"Circle of Life" with "Nants' Ingonyama" ....Rafiki, Ensemble

Scene 2 Scar's Cave

Scene 3 Rafiki's Tree

Scene 4 The Pridelands
"The Morning Report" ....Zazu, Young Simba, Mufasa

Scene 5 Scar's Cave

Scene 6 The Pridelands
"I Just Can't Wait to Be King" ....Young Simba, Young Nala, Zazu, Ensemble

Scene 7 Elephant Graveyard
"Chow Down".......................................Shenzi, Banzai, Ed

Scene 8 Under the Stars
"They Live in You"......................................Mufasa, Ensemble

Scene 9 Elephant Graveyard
"Be Prepared" ....Scar, Shenzi, Banzai, Ed, Ensemble

Scene 10 The Gorge

Scene 11 Pride Rock
"Be Prepared" (Reprise) ....Scar, Ensemble

Scene 12 Rafiki's Tree

Scene 13 The Desert/The Jungle
"Hakuna Matata" ....Timon, Pumbaa, Young Simba, Simba, Ensemble

ACT TWO

Entr'acte "One by One" ....Ensemble

Scene 1 Scar's Cave
"The Madness of King Scar" ....Scar, Zazu, Banzai, Shenzi, Ed, Nala

Scene 2 The Pridelands
"Shadowland" ....Nala, Rafiki, Ensemble

Scene 3 The Jungle

Scene 4 Under the Stars
"Endless Night" ....Simba, Ensemble

Scene 5 Rafiki's Tree

Scene 6 The Jungle
"Can You Feel the Love Tonight" ....Timon, Pumbaa, Simba, Nala, Ensemble
"He Lives in You" (Reprise) ....Rafiki, Simba, Ensemble

Scene 7 Pride Rock
"King of Pride Rock"/"Circle of Life" (Reprise) ....Ensemble

SONG CREDITS

All songs by Elton John (music) and Tim Rice (lyrics) except as follows:

"Circle of Life" by Elton John (music) and Tim Rice (lyrics)
with "Nants' Ingonyama" by Hans Zimmer and Lebo M
"He Lives in You" ("They Live in You"): Music and lyrics by Mark Mancina, Jay Rifkin, and Lebo M
"One by One": Music and lyrics by Lebo M
"Shadowland": Music by Lebo M and Hans Zimmer, lyrics by Mark Mancina and Lebo M
"Endless Night": Music by Lebo M, Hans Zimmer, and Jay Rifkin, lyrics by Julie Taymor
"King of Pride Rock": Music by Hans Zimmer, lyrics by Lebo M

ADDITIONAL SCORE

Grasslands chant and Lioness chant by Lebo M; Rafiki's chants by Tsidii Le Loka.

Cast Continued

Michelle Dorant, Gregory A. King, Lisa Lewis, Nikki Long, Ian Vincent McGinnis, Ray Mercer, Ryan Brooke Taylor, Steven Evan Washington

UNDERSTUDIES

RAFIKI: Sheryl McCallum, Mpume Sikakane, Rema Webb; MUFASA: Michael Alexander Henry, L. Steven Taylor; SARABI: Camille M. Brown, Sheryl McCallum; ZAZU: John E. Brady, Enrique Segura; SCAR: Jeff Binder, Jack Koenig; SHENZI: Angelica Edwards Patterson, Sophia N. Stephens, Rema Webb; BANZAI: Garland Days, Cornelius Jones, Jr.; Kenny Redell Williams; ED: Ian Yuri Gardner, Dennis Johnston, Cornelius Jones Jr.; TIMON: John E. Brady, Enrique Segura; PUMBAA: John E. Brady, Jack Koenig; SIMBA: Dennis Johnston; Cornelius Jones, Jr.; Brian M. Love; NALA: Kylin Brady, Sophia N. Stephens, Rema Webb

SWINGS

Garland Days, Ian Yuri Gardner; Tony James, Dennis Johnston, Cornelius Jones, Jr., Jennifer Harrison Newman, Angelica Edwards Patterson, Sophia N. Stephens, Torya

DANCE CAPTAINS

Garland Days, Torya

SPECIALTIES

CIRCLE OF LIFE VOCALS: Bongi Duma, S'bu Ngema
MOUSE SHADOW PUPPET: Brian M. Love ANT HILL LADY: Kristina Michelle Bethel
GUINEA FOWL: Ryan Brooke Taylor
BUZZARD POLE: Gregory A. King
GAZELLE WHEEL: Michelle Aguilar Camaya
BUTTERFLIES: Michelle Aguilar Camaya
GAZELLE: Steven Evan Washington
LIONESS CHANT VOCAL: S'bu Ngema
ACROBATIC TRICKSTER: Ray Mercer
STILT GIRAFFE CROSS: Gabriel A. Croom
GIRAFFE SHADOW PUPPETS: Steven Evan Washington, Kenny Redell Williams
CHEETAH: Lisa Lewis
SCAR SHADOW PUPPETS: Ryan Brooke Taylor, Steven Evan Washington, Kenny Redell Williams
SIMBA SHADOW PUPPETS: Gregory A. King, Ian Vincent McGinnis, Ray Mercer
ONE BY ONE VOCAL: Bongi Duma, Keswa
ONE BY ONE DANCE: Bongi Duma, Ron Kunene, S'bu Ngema
FIREFLIES: Camille M. Brown

Continued on next page

The Lion King

Cast Continued

PUMBAA POLE PUPPET: Kenny Redell Williams
NALA POLE PUPPET: Lisa Lewis
FLOOR DANCERS: Kristina Michelle Bethel,
Ryan Brooke Taylor
FLYING DANCERS: Michelle Aguilar Camaya,
Gabriel A. Croom,
Lisa Lewis, Keena Smith, Steven Evan Washington
LIONESS/HYENA SHADOW PUPPETS:
Lindiwe Dlamini, Keswa, Ron Kunene,
Sheryl McCallum, Mpume Sikakane, Rema Webb

*Keswa and Mpume Sikakane are appearing with the
permission of Actors' Equity Association.*

ORCHESTRA
CONDUCTOR–KARL JURMAN

KEYBOARD SYNTHESIZER/
ASSOCIATE CONDUCTOR:
Cherie Rosen
SYNTHESIZERS:
Ted Baker, Paul Ascenzo
WOOD FLUTE SOLOIST/FLUTE/PICCOLO:
David Weiss
CONCERTMASTER:
Francisca Mendoza
VIOLINS:
Krystof Witek, Avril Brown
VIOLIN/VIOLA:
Ralph Farris
CELLOS:
Eliana Mendoza, Bruce Wang
FLUTE/CLARINET/BASS CLARINET:
Bob Keller
FRENCH HORNS:
Alexandra Cook, Katie Dennis, Greg Smith
TROMBONE:
Rock Ciccarone
BASS TROMBONE/TUBA:
George Flynn
UPRIGHT AND ELECTRIC BASSES:
Tom Barney
DRUMS/ASSISTANT CONDUCTOR:
Tommy Igoe
GUITAR:
Kevin Kuhn
PERCUSSION/ASSISTANT CONDUCTOR:
Rolando Morales-Matos
MALLETS/PERCUSSION:
Valerie Dee Naranjo, Tom Brett
PERCUSSION:
Junior "Gabu" Wedderburn

Music Coordinator–Michael Keller

Derek Smith
Scar

Alton Fitzgerald White
Mufasa

Tshidi Manye
Rafiki

Jeff Binder
Zazu

Tom Alan Robbins
Pumbaa

Danny Rutigliano
Timon

Josh Tower
Simba

Kissy Simmons
Nala

Benjamin Sterling
Cannon
Banzai

Jacquelyn Renae
Hodges
Shenzi

Enrique Segura
Ed

Aaron D. Conley
Young Simba

Alex de Castro
Young Nala

Natalie Guerrero
Young Nala

Jarrell J. Singleton
Young Simba

Kristina Michelle
Bethel
Ensemble

John E. Brady
*Standby Timon,
Pubaa, Zazu*

Kylin Brady
Ensemble

Camille M. Brown
Ensemble

Michelle Aguilar
Camaya
Ensemble

The Lion King

Gabriel A. Croom
Ensemble

Garland Days
*Swing,
Dance Captain*

Lindiwe Dlamini
Ensemble

Michelle Dorant
Ensemble

Bongi Duma
Ensemble

Ian Yuri Gardner
Ensemble

Jean Michelle Grier
Ensemble, Sarabi

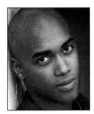
Michael Alexander
Henry
Ensemble

Tony James
Swing

Dennis Johnston
Swing

Cornelius Jones, Jr.
Swing

Keswa
Ensemble

Gregory A. King
Ensemble

Jack Koenig
*Standby for
Scar and Pumbaa*

Ron Kunene
Ensemble

Lisa Lewis
Ensemble

Brian M. Love
Ensemble

Sheryl McCallum
Ensemble

Ian Vincent McGinnis
Ensemble

Ray Mercer
Ensemble

Jennifer Harrison
Newman
Swing

S'bu Ngema
Ensemble

Angelica Edwards
Patterson
Swing

Mpume Sikakane
Ensemble

Sophia N. Stephens
Swing

L. Steven Taylor
Ensemble

Ryan Brooke Taylor
*Ensemble,
Fight Captain*

Torya
*Swing,
Dance Captain*

Steven Evan
Washington
Ensemble

Rema Webb
Ensemble

Kenny Redell Williams
Ensemble

Sir Elton John
Music

Tim Rice
Lyrics

Julie Taymor
*Director,
Costume Design,
Mask/Puppet
Co-Design,
Additional Lyrics*

Garth Fagan
Choreographer

The Lion King

Lebo M
Additional Music & Lyrics, Additional Vocal Score, Vocal Arrangements, Choral Director

Donald Holder
Lighting Design

Mark Brandon/ Binder Casting
Casting

David Benken
Technical Director

Anthony Lyn
Associate Director

Karl Jurman
Music Director/ Conductor

Brian Hill
Resident Director

Robert Elhai
Associate Music Producer, Orchestrator

Michael Keller
Music Coordinator

Thomas Schumacher/ Disney Theatrical Productions
Producer

Kyle R. Banks
Ensemble Singer

Kailani M. Coba
Young Nala

LaTrisa A. Coleman
Ant Hill Lady, Cheetah, Ensemble Dancer, Floor Dancer

Bobby Daye
Ensemble Singer, Mouse Shadow Puppet

Zipporah G. Gatling
Young Nala

Bonita J. Hamilton
Shenzi

Marva Hicks
Understudy Rafiki

Dennis Lue
Swing

Kyle Wrentz
Circle of Life Vocals, Ensemble Dancer, Lioness Chant Vocal, One by One Dance

Frank Wright II
Swing

Kyle R. Banks
Swing

Alvin Crawford
Ensemble Singer

Alicia Fisher
Ensemble Dancer

Christopher Freeman
Gazelle, Ensemble Singer and Dancer, Flying Dancer, Mouse, Giraffe and Scar Shadow

Tony Freeman
Zazu

Bonita Hamilton
Shenzi

The Lion King

Rod Harrelson
*Swing, Buzzard Pole,
Simba Shadow
Puppet*

Ashley Renee Jordan
*Young Nala
(at certain
performances)*

Joel Karie
*Ensemble Singer,
Pumbaa Pole
Puppet, Giraffe, Scar
and Mouse Shadow
Puppets*

Justin Martin
*Young Simba
(at certain
performances)*

Brandon Louis
Matthieus
Ensemble Singer

Sinclair Mitchell
*Ensemble Singer,
One by One Dance,
Swing*

Brandon O'Neal
*Gazelle,
Ensemble Dancer,
Flying Dancer,
Giraffe and Scar
Shadow Puppets*

Patrick Page
Scar

Dawn Noel Pignuola
*Cheetah,
Ensemble Dancer,
Flying Dancer,
Nala Pole Puppet*

Jacqueline Rene
*Ensemble Singer,
Lioness/Hyena
Shadow Puppet*

Thom Christopher
Warren
*Understudy for
Timun and Zazu*

Kyle Wrentz
Ensemble Singer

SCRAPBOOK

Correspondents: Stage Managers Jimmie Lee Smith, Victoria Epstein, Antonia Gianino, Kristin Newhouse and Ron Vodicka.

Memorable Note, Fax or Fan Letter: We once received an audition CD with a performer singing "Be Prepared" with his own accordion accompaniment. It sounded like "Pirates of the Caribbean."

"Gypsy of the Year" Skit: "I Remember He Said" created by Ray Mercer, music by Moby. Winner: Best Sketch Presentation.

"Carols for a Cure: Carol: "Chant" and "What Child Is This?"

Easter Bonnet Sketch: "Movin' On Up" (about our upcoming moved to the Minskoff Theatre) by Enrique Segura, Ray Mercer, Rod Harrelson, Tony Freeman and Josh Tower.

Actors Who Performed the Most Roles: Frank Wright II and Angelica Edwards.

Who Has Done the Most Shows: Camille M. Brown, Lindiwe Dlamini, Tom Robbins and Ron Kunene.

Favorite Moment During Each Performance: "Circle of Life."

Favorite In-Theatre Gathering Place: Physical Therapy.

Favorite Off-Site Hangout: The Above Bar, The Hilton.

Favorite Snack Food: Baked goods from Adrian Bailey.

Mascot: Jillian, the Lawn Flamingo

Favorite Therapy: Ricola; Dropping out of the "He Lives in You" reprise.

Memorable Ad-Lib: The correct line: "Give me one good reason why I shouldn't rip you apart." What was said: "Give me one good reason why I shouldn't rip your clothes off."

Fastest Costume Change: The entire cast as they change into street clothes to catch the early bus after the Finale.

Busiest Day at the Box Office: Every day. It's *The Lion King.*

Who Wore the Heaviest/Hottest Costume: Pumbaa or Principal Hyena; it's a tossup.

Who Wore the Least: Young Simba.

Catchphrases Only the Company Would Recognize: "This is your seventh and final places call."

Sweethearts Within the Company: Sweethearts? We've got offspring!

Orchestra Member Who Played the Most Instruments: Rolando Morales-Matos House Right Percussion.

Most Exciting Celebrity Visitor: Dakota Fanning. (Not yet but we've got our fingers crossed.)

The Lion King

CAST AND CREW

Front Row (Kneeling and Seated L-R):
Guy Bentley, Lindiwe Dlamini, Ron Kunene, Angelica Edwards, Bill Romanello, Bonita J. Hamilton, Antonia Gianino, Victoria Epstein, Joel Karie, Ashley Renee Jordan, Niki White, Kissy Simmons, Kristina Bethel, Justin Martin, Jennifer Harrison Newman, Jacqueline Rene, Michelle Camaya, Michelle Dorant, Tshidi Manye, Rod Harrelson, Tony James, Lisa Lewis, Donna Doiron, Alicia Fisher, Jimmie Lee Smith

Second Row (L-R):
Andrew Grennan, Sheryl McCallum, Dawn Bentley, Jonathan Hanson, Rema Webb, Scott Stauffer, Suyin Chan, Cynthia Boardman, BJ Cannon, Sheila Little Terrell, Cornelius Jones, Jr., Tony Freeman, Danny Rutigliano, Ted Baker, Jean Michelle Grier, Alton F. White, Kylin Brady, Alexis Vazquez-Riggs, Walter Weiner, Steve Stackle, April Taylor-Stackle, Dennis Johnston, Douglas Hamilton, Meredith Chase-Boyd, Ray Mercer, Gabriel Croom, Aubrey Lynch

Third Row (L-R):
Brian T. Hill, Laura Eichholz, Sara Stith, David Weiss, Garland Days, Karl Jurman, Kjeld Andersen, Tom Robbins, Jack Koenig, Thomas Schlenk, Paul Ascenzo, Ian Yuri Gardner, Alex de Jesus, S'bu Ngema, Tania Velez, Karla Fromm, Angela Skinner, Bongi Duma, Sylvia Brown

Fourth Row (L-R):
Al "Skip" Manganaro, Drew Siccardi, James Maloney, Tara Engler, Elizabeth Cohen, Milagros Medina-Cerdeira, Dylan Trotto, Chris Passalacqua, Jimmy Maher, Pamela Pierzina, Sara Jablon, Mariah Torres, Tom Daniels, Dave Tisue, Mark Houston, Peter Candela, John Loiacono, Keith Guarlchuk, James McKenna

Back Row (L-R):
David Helk, Mike Trotto, Doug Graf, Mike Corbett, Richie Maloney, John Saye, Tommy Igoe, Ryan Brooke Taylor, Kyle Wrentz, L. Steven Taylor, Michael Henry, Joe Garvey, Aldo "Butch" Servilio, Tom Barney, Dave Ehle and Cherie Rosen.

(L-R):
Kathy Kong (Ticket Taker)
and Michele Adornato
(Usher).

The Lion King

Staff for *THE LION KING* Worldwide

Associate Producer ....Todd Lacy
Associate Producer ....Aubrey Lynch II
Associate Director ....Anthony Lyn
Production Dance Supervisor ....Marey Griffith
Production Manager ....Anne Quart
Production Supervisor ....,.....Doc Zorthian
Supervising Resident Director ....John Stefaniuk
Dance Supervisor ....Celise Hicks
Associate Scenic Designer ....Peter Eastman
Associate Costume Designer ....Mary Nemecek Peterson
Associate Mask & Puppet Designer ....Louis Troisi
Associate Sound Designer ....John Shivers
Associate Hair & Makeup Designer ....Carole Hancock
Associate Lighting Designer ....Jeanne Koenig
Assistant Lighting Designer ....Marty Vreeland
Automated Lighting Programmer ....Aland Henderson
Production Coordinator ....Jane Abramson
Management Assistants ....Suyin Chan, Tara Engler

GENERAL PRESS REPRESENTATIVES
BONEAU/BRYAN-BROWN

Chris Boneau   Jackie Green   Matt Polk   Aaron Meier

Staff for *THE LION KING* New York

Company Manager ....DAVE EHLE
Production Stage Manager ....Jimmie Lee Smith
Resident Director ....Brian Hill
Resident Dance Supervisor ....Leonora Stapleton
Musical Director/Conductor ....Karl Jurman

Stage Managers ....Victoria Epstein, Antonia Gianino,
Kristin Newhouse, Ron Vodicka
Assistant Company Manager ....Laura Eichholz
Fight Captain ....Ryan Brooke Taylor
Assistant Choreographers ....Norwood J. Pennewell,
Natalie Rogers
Fight Consultant ....Rick Sordelet
South African Dialect Coach ....Ron Kunene
Casting Associates ....Jack Bowdan, C.S.A.,
Megan Larche, Leah Alter, Sarah Prosser
Show Accountant ....Alma LaMarr
Corporate Counsel ....Michael Rosenfeld
Physical Therapy ....Neuro Tour Physical Therapy,
Emelie Vulcain
Consulting Orthopedist ....Philip A. Bauman, M.D.
Child Guardian ....Niki White
Executive Travel ....Robert Arnao, Patt McRory
Production Travel ....Jill Citron
Advertising ....Serino Coyne Inc.

Production Carpenter ....Drew Siccardi
Assistant Carpenters ....Michael P. Corbett,
Mike Phillips, Michael Trotto
Automation Carpenters ....Steve Stackle,
George Zegarsky
Carpenters ....Kirk Bender, Fudie Carriocia,
Ray King, Jimmy Maher,
Mike Rahilly, Aldo "Butch" Servilio,
Dylan Trotto
Production Flyman ....Brad Ingram
Production Electrician ....James Maloney

Key Spot Operator ....Joseph P. Garvey
Board Operator ....Edward M. Greenberg
Automated Lighting Technician ....Sean Strohmeyer
Production Electricians ....Gregory Dunkin,
Douglas Graf, Joe Lynch,
Al Manganaro, Kevin Strohmeyer
Production Propman ....Victor Amerling
Assistant Propman ....Tim Abel
Props ....Joe Bivone, Bo Metzler
Production Sound Engineer ....Scott Stauffer
Assistant Sound Engineer ....Marie Renee Foucher
Sound Assistant ....Bill Romanello
Production Wardrobe Supervisor ....Kjeld Andersen
Assistant Wardrobe Supervisor ....Cynthia Boardman
Puppet Supervisor ....Pamela Pierzina
Puppet Dayworkers...................Islah Abdul-Rahiim,
Ilya Vett
Mask/Puppet Studio ....Jeff Curry
Dressers ....Meredith Chase-Boyd, Elizabeth Cline,
Andy Cook, Donna Doiron, Joelyn Draut,
April Fernandez-Taylor, Michelle Gore,
Kimberly Greenberg, Douglas Hamilton,
Mark Houston, Sara Jablon,
Mark Lauer, Michelle Palladino,
Sheila Little Terrell, Dave Tisue,
Gregory Young, Walter Weiner
Stitcher ....Janeth Iverson
Production Hair Supervisor ....Monica Costea
Assistant Hair Supervisor ....Alison Wadsworth
Production Makeup Supervisor ....Elizabeth Cohen
Assistant Makeup Supervisor ....Angela Johnson
Makeup Artist ....Milagros Medina-Cerdeira

Music Development ....Nick Glennie-Smith
Music Preparation ....Donald Oliver and Evan Morris/
Chelsea Music Service, Inc.
Synthesizer Programmer ....Ted Baker
Orchestral Synthesizer Programmer ......Christopher Ward
Electronic Drum Programmer ....Tommy Igoe
Addt'l Percussion Arrangements ....Valerie Dee Naranjo
Music Assistant ....Elizabeth J. Falcone
Personal Assistant to Elton John ....Bob Halley
Assistant to Tim Rice ....Eileen Heinink
Assistants to Mark Mancina ....Chuck Choi,
Kevin Mayfield

Associate Scenic Designer ....Jonathan Fensom
Assistant Scenic Designer ....Michael Fagin
Lighting Design Assistant ....Karen Spahn
Automated Lighting Tracker ....Lara Bohon
Projection Designer ....Geoff Puckett
Projection Art ....Caterina Bertolotto
Assistant Sound Designer ....Kai Harada
Assistant Costume Designer ....Tracy Dorman
Stunt Consultant ....Peter Moore
Children's Tutoring ....On Location Education
Production Photography ....Joan Marcus,
Marc Bryan-Brown
Associate Producer 1996–1998 ....Donald Frantz
Project Manager 1996–1998 ....Nina Essman
Associate Producer 1998–2002 ....Ken Denison
Associate Producer 2000-2003 ....Pam Young
Original Music Director ....Joseph Church

Disney's *The Lion King* is a registered trademark owned by The Walt Disney Company and used under special license by Disney Theatrical Productions, Ltd.

Cover Art Design © Disney.

CREDITS

Scenery built and mechanized by Hudson Scenic Studio, Inc. Additional scenery by Chicago Scenic Studios, Inc.; Edge & Co., Inc.; Michael Hagen, Inc.; Piper Productions, Inc.; Scenic Technologies, Inc.; I. Weiss & Sons, Inc. Lighting by Westsun, vari*lite® automated lighting provided by Vari-Lite, Inc. Props by John Creech Design & Production. Sound equipment by Pro-Mix, Inc. Additional sound equipment by Walt Disney Imagineering. Rehearsal Scenery by Brooklyn Scenic & Theatrical. Costumes executed by Barbara Matera Ltd., Parsons-Meares Ltd., Donna Langman, Eric Winterling, Danielle Gisiger, Suzie Elder. Millinery by Rodney Gordon, Janet Linville, Arnold Levine. Emer'gen-C, the Super Energy Booster, provided by Alacer Corp. Ricola provided by Ricola, Inc. Shibori dyeing by Joan Morris. Custom dyeing and painting by Joni Johns, Mary Macy, Parsons-Meares Ltd., Gene Mignola. Additional Painting by J. Michelle Hill. Knitwear by Maria Ficalora. Footwear by Sharlot Battin, Robert W. Jones, Capezio, Vasilli Shoes. Costume Development by Constance Hoffman. Special Projects by Angela M. Kahler. Custom fabrics developed by Gary Graham and Helen Quinn. Puppet Construction by Michael Curry Design, Inc. and Vee Corporation. Shadow puppetry by Steven Kaplan. Pumbaa Puppet Construction by Andrew Benepe and Flying by Foy. Trucking by Clark Transfer. Wigs created by Wig Workshop of London. Marimbas by De Morrow Instruments, Ltd. Latin Percussion by LP Music Group. Drumset by DrumWorkshop. Cymbals by Zildjian. Bass equipment by Eden Electronics. House Video monitors provided by Mitsubishi Electronics.

SONG EXCERPTS (used by permission): "It's a Small World" written by Richard M. Sherman and Robert B. Sherman; "Five Foot Two, Eyes of Blue" written by Sam Lewis, Joe Young, and Ray Henderson; "The Lion Sleeps Tonight" written by Hugo Peretti, George David Weiss, and Luigi Creatore.

Staff for the New Amsterdam Theatre

Theatre Manager ....John Loiacono
Guest Services Manager ....Keith Guralchuk
Box Office Treasurer ....Helen Cullen
Assistant Treasurer ....Harry Jaffie
Coordinator, Special Events ....Amy Andrews
Chief Engineer ....Frank Gibbons
Engineers ....John Burke, Dan Milan
Security Supervisor ....Richard Gonzalez
Head Usher ....Susan Linder
Lobby Refreshments ....Sweet Concessions
Special Thanks ....Lynn Beckemeyer, Amy Bawden, Nancy Holland

The Lion King

DISNEY THEATRICAL PRODUCTIONS

President ....Thomas Schumacher
Senior Vice President & General Manager ....Alan Levey
Senior Vice President, Managing Director & CFO ....David Schrader

General Management

Vice President, International ....Ron Kollen
Vice President, Operations ....Dana Amendola
Vice President, Labor Relations ....Allan Frost
Director, Human Resources ....June Heindel
Director, Domestic Touring ....Michele Gold
Manager, Labor Relations ....Stephanie Cheek
Manager, Human Resources ....Cynthia Young
Manager, Information Systems ....Scott Benedict
Senior Computer Support Analyst ....Kevin McGuire

Production

Executive Music Producer ....Chris Montan
Senior Vice President, Creative Affairs.......................Michele Steckler
Vice President, Creative Affairs ....Greg Gunter
Vice President, Physical Production ....John Tiggeloven
Purchasing Manager ....Joseph Doughney
Staff Associate Director ....Jeff Lee
Staff Associate Designer ....Dennis W. Moyes
Staff Associate Dramaturg ....Ken Cerniglia

Marketing

Vice President, Domestic Touring ....Jack Eldon
Director, New York ....Andrew Flatt
Manager, New York ....Michele Holland
Manager, New York ....Leslie Barrett
Manager ....Joel Hile

Sales

Vice President, Ticketing ....Jerome Kane
Manager, Group Sales ....Jacob Lloyd Kimbro
Assistant Manager, Group Sales ....Juil Kim
Group Sales Representative ....Jarrid Crespo

Business and Legal Affairs

Vice President ....Jonathan Olson
Vice President ....Robbin Kelley
Director ....Harry S. Gold
Attorney ....Seth Stuhl
Paralegal/Contract Administration ....Colleen Lober

Finance

Director ....Joe McClafferty
Manager, Finance ....Justin Gee
Manager, Production Accounting ....Bill Hussey
Senior Business Planner ....Jason Fletcher
Production Accountants ....Wilson Liu, Barbara Toben
Analyst ....Ronnie Cooper

Controllership

Director, Accounting ....Leena Mathew
Manager, Accounting ....Erica McShane
Senior Analysts ....Stephanie Badie, Mila Danilevich, Adrineh Ghoukassian
Analyst ....Ken Herrell

Administrative Staff

Elliot Altman, Amy Andrews, Alice Baeza, Gregory Bonsignore, Craig Buckley, Karl Chmielewski, Dayna Clark, Matthew Cronin, Cristi Finn, Cristina Fornaris, Dayle Gruet, Gregory Hanoian, Jonathan Hanson, Jay Hollenback, Connie Jasper, Kristine Lee, Janine McGuire, Jeff Parvin, Ryan Pears, Giovanna Primak, Roberta Risafi, Susan Rubio, Kisha Santiago, Lynne Scheurer

Disney Theatrical Productions • 1450 Broadway • New York, NY 10018
mail@disneytheatrical.com

BUENA VISTA THEATRICAL MERCHANDISE, L.L.C.

Vice President ....Steven Downing
Manager ....John F. Agati
Operations Manager ....Shawn Baker
Assistant Manager, Inventory ....Suzanne Jakel
Buyer ....Suzanne Araneo
Retail Supervisor ....Mark Nathman
Merchandising Assistant ....Ed Pisapia
On-site Retail Manager ....Jackie Velazquez
On-Site Assistant Retail Manager ....Anjie Maraj

Tshidi Manye (C) and the chorus perform "Shadowland."

Photo by Joan Marcus

Mamma Mia!

First Preview: October 5, 2001. Opened: October 18, 2001.
Still running as of May 31, 2006.

PLAYBILL

A NEW MUSICAL BASED ON THE SONGS OF ABBA

MAMMA MIA!

CAST
(in order of speaking)

Sophie Sheridan	CAREY ANDERSON
Ali	OLIVIA OGUMA
Lisa	SAMANTHA EGGERS
Tanya	JUDY McLANE
Rosie	OLGA MEREDIZ
Donna Sheridan	MICHELE PAWK
Sky	ANDY KELSO
Pepper	BEN GETTINGER
Eddie	ALBERT GUERZON
Harry Bright	DAVID BEACH
Bill Austin	MARK L. MONTGOMERY
Sam Carmichael	JOHN DOSSETT
Father Alexandrios	BRYAN SCOTT JOHNSON

THE ENSEMBLE

MEREDITH AKINS, BRENT BLACK,
JEN BURLEIGH-BENTZ,
ANGELA ARA BROWN,
ISAAC CALPITO,
CHRISTOPHER CARL,
SHAKIEM EVANS,
BRYAN SCOTT JOHNSON,
CAROL LINNEA JOHNSON,
MEGAN OSTERHAUS,
SANDY ROSENBERG,
PATRICK SARB,
RYAN-MICHAEL SHAW,
BRITT SHUBOW,
MACKENZIE THOMAS, LEAH ZEPEL

Continued on next page

CADILLAC WINTER GARDEN THEATRE

1634 Broadway
A Shubert Organization Theatre

Gerald Schoenfeld, *Chairman*　　　Philip J. Smith, *President*

Robert E. Wankel, *Executive Vice President*

JUDY CRAYMER, RICHARD EAST AND BJÖRN ULVAEUS
FOR LITTLESTAR IN ASSOCIATION WITH UNIVERSAL

PRESENT

MAMMA MIA!

MUSIC AND LYRICS BY
BENNY ANDERSSON
BJÖRN ULVAEUS

AND SOME SONGS WITH STIG ANDERSON

BOOK BY CATHERINE JOHNSON

PRODUCTION DESIGNED BY
MARK THOMPSON

LIGHTING DESIGNED BY
HOWARD HARRISON

SOUND DESIGNED BY
**ANDREW BRUCE &
BOBBY AITKEN**

MUSICAL SUPERVISOR, ADDITIONAL MATERIAL
& ARRANGEMENTS
MARTIN KOCH

CHOREOGRAPHY
ANTHONY VAN LAAST

DIRECTED BY
PHYLLIDA LLOYD

LIVE BROADWAY

10/17/05

Andy Kelso as Sky and Carey Anderson as Sophie.

Photo by Joan Marcus

Mamma Mia!

MUSICAL NUMBERS

(in alphabetical order)

CHIQUITITA
DANCING QUEEN
DOES YOUR MOTHER KNOW
GIMME! GIMME! GIMME!
HONEY, HONEY
I DO, I DO, I DO, I DO, I DO
I HAVE A DREAM
KNOWING ME, KNOWING YOU
LAY ALL YOUR LOVE ON ME
MAMMA MIA
MONEY, MONEY, MONEY
ONE OF US
OUR LAST SUMMER
SLIPPING THROUGH MY FINGERS
S.O.S.
SUPER TROUPER
TAKE A CHANCE ON ME
THANK YOU FOR THE MUSIC
THE NAME OF THE GAME
THE WINNER TAKES IT ALL
UNDER ATTACK
VOULEZ-VOUS

On a Greek Island, a wedding is about to take place...

PROLOGUE
Three months before the wedding
ACT ONE
The day before the wedding
ACT TWO
The day of the wedding

(L-R): Olivia Oguma, Carey Anderson and Samantha Eggers perform "Honey, Honey."

Photo by Joan Marcus

Cast Continued

UNDERSTUDIES

For Sophie Sheridan: SAMANTHA EGGERS, MEGAN OSTERHAUS, BRITT SHUBOW

For Ali: ANGELA ARA BROWN, LEAH ZEPEL

For Lisa: MEREDITH AKINS, BRITT SHUBOW

For Tanya: JEN BURLEIGH-BENTZ, CAROL LINNEA JOHNSON

For Rosie: JEN BURLEIGH-BENTZ, SANDY ROSENBERG

For Donna Sheridan: JEN BURLEIGH-BENTZ, CAROL LINNEA JOHNSON

For Sky: RYAN SANDER, PATRICK SARB

For Pepper: ISAAC CALPITO, RYAN-MICHAEL SHAW

For Eddie: SHAKIEM EVANS, RYAN SANDER

For Harry Bright: CHRISTOPHER CARL, BRYAN SCOTT JOHNSON

For Bill Austin: BRENT BLACK, CHRISTOPHER CARL, BRYAN SCOTT JOHNSON

For Sam Carmichael: BRENT BLACK, CHRISTOPHER CARL

For Father Alexandrios: BRENT BLACK, CHRISTOPHER CARL

SWINGS
LANENE CHARTERS, JON-ERIK GOLDBERG, RYAN SANDER, COLLETTE SIMMONS

DANCE CAPTAIN
JANET ROTHERMEL

THE BAND
Music Director/Conductor/Keyboard 1: DAVID HOLCENBERG

Associate Music Director/Keyboard 3: ROB PREUSS

Keyboard 2: STEVE MARZULLO
Keyboard 4: MYLES CHASE
Guitar 1: DOUG QUINN
Guitar 2: JEFF CAMPBELL
Bass: PAUL ADAMY
Drums: RAY MARCHICA
Percussion: DAVID NYBERG
Music Coordinator: MICHAEL KELLER
Synthesizer Programmer: NICHOLAS GILPIN

Mamma Mia!

Michele Pawk
Donna Sheridan

Carey Anderson
Sophie Sheridan

Judy McLane
Tanya

Olga Merediz
Rosie

John Dossett
Sam Carmichael

David Beach
Harry Bright

Mark L. Montgomery
Bill Austin

Andy Kelso
Sky

Samantha Eggers
Lisa

Olivia Oguma
Ali

Ben Gettinger
Pepper

Albert Guerzon
Eddie

Meredith Akins
Ensemble

Angela Ara Brown
Ensemble

Brent Black
Ensemble

Jen Burleigh-Bentz
Ensemble

Isaac Calpito
Ensemble

Christopher Carl
Ensemble

Lanene Charters
Swing

Shakiem Evans
Ensemble

Jon-Erik Goldberg
Swing

Bryan Scott Johnson
Father Alexandrios,
Ensemble

Carol Linnea Johnson
Ensemble

Megan Osterhaus
Ensemble

Sandy Rosenberg
Ensemble

Janet Rothermel
Dance Captain

Patrick Sarb
Ensemble

Ryan Sander
Swing

Ryan-Michael Shaw
Ensemble

Britt Shubow
Ensemble

Collette Simmons
Swing

Mackenzie Thomas
Ensemble

Leah Zepel
Ensemble

Tom Capps
Production
Supervisor

Catherine Johnson
Book

Mamma Mia!

Björn Ulvaeus
Music & Lyrics

Benny Anderson
Music & Lyrics

Phyllida Lloyd
Director

Anthony van Laast
Choreographer

Mark Thompson
Production Designer

Howard Harrison
Lighting Designer

Andrew Bruce
Sound Designer

Bobby Aitken
Sound Designer

Martin Koch
Musical Supervisor

Nichola Treherne
*Associate
Choreographer*

Martha Banta
Resident Director

Tara Rubin,
Tara Rubin Casting
Casting

David Grindrod
Casting Consultant

Arthur Siccardi,
Arthur Siccardi
Theatrical Services,
Inc.
Production Manager

Michael Keller,
Music Coordinator

Judy Craymer
Producer

Richard East
Producer

ALUMNI
2005-2006

Robin Baxter
Rosie

Carolee Carmello
Donna Sheridan

Joanna Chozen
Swing

Meghann Dreyfuss
Ensemble

Matthew Farver
Swing

Keisha T. Fraser
Lisa

Peter Kelly Gaudreault
Sam Carmichael

Kurt Andrew Hansen
Ensemble

Rebecca Kasper
Ali

Sara Kramer
Sophie Sheridan

Amber Kryzs
Ensemble

Liz McCartney
Rosie

Daniel McDonald
Sam Carmichael

Mamma Mia!

Corinne Melançon
Ensemble

Whitney Osentoski
Ensemble

Joi Danielle Price
Ali, Ensemble

Aaron Staton
Sky

Joanna Chozen
Swing

Meghann Dreyfuss
Ensemble

Matthew Farver
Swing

Lori Haley Fox
Ensemble

Veronica J. Kuehn
Ali

Erica Mansfield
Ensemble

Corinne Melançon
*Donna Sheridan,
Ensemble*

Steve Morgan
Ensemble

Lauren Mufson
Donna Sheridan

Gerard Salvador
Ensemble

Michael James Scott
Eddie

Which one is Sophie's Dad? (L-R): John Dossett, David Beach and Mark L. Montgomery.

Photo by Joan Marcus

Mamma Mia!

COMPANY
Front Row (L-R): Ray Marchica (Band), Paul Adamy (Band), Jeff Campbell (Band), Carey Anderson (Cast), Olga Merediz (Cast), Michael James Scott (Cast), Meredith Akins (Cast), Andy Fenton (Stage Manager), Leah Zepel (Cast), Britt Shubow (Cast), Judy McLane (Cast).

Middle Row (L-R): Malcolm Perry (FOH), Michael Bosch (Doorman), Officer Steven Fabb (Theatre Cop), David Holcenberg (Musical Director), Doug Quinn (Band), David Nyberg (Band), Janet Rothermel (Dance Supervisor), Tom Capps (Production Supervisor), Charlene Speyerer (SM Sub), Ben Gettinger (Cast), Laurie Dank (FOH), Christopher Carl (Cast), Ryan-Michael Shaw (Cast), Matthew Farver (Cast), Jen Burleigh-Bentz (Cast), Collette Simmons (Cast), Andy Kelso (Cast), Shakiem Evans (Cast), Mark Montgomery (Cast).

Back Row (L-R): Rina Saltzman (Company Manager), Liza Garcia (Asst. Company Manager), Sherry Cohen (Stage Manager), Lori Haley Fox (Cast), Sandy Rosenberg (Cast), Angela Ara Brown (Cast), Olivia Oguma (Cast), Isaac Calpito (Cast), Bryan Scott Johnson (Cast), Megan Osterhaus (Cast), Ryan Sander (Cast), Corinne Melancon (Cast), Lee Cobb (Box Office) and Dean R. Greer (Stage Manager).

STAGE CREW and FRONT OF HOUSE STAFF
Seated (L-R): Jessica Boyd (Wardrobe), Elvia Pineda (Wardrobe), I Wang (Wardrobe), Dennis Marion (FOH), Vinnie Macaluso (FOH), Sabiel Almonte (FOH).

Front Row (L-R): Lolly Totero (Wardrobe), Josh Marquette (Hair), Vickey Walker (Hair), Craig Cassidy (Sound), Irene Bunis (Wardrobe), Celeste Belhoucine (Operations), Lauren Kievet (Wardrobe), Sherry McIntyre (FOH), Richie McQuail (Crew), Frank Lofgren (Crew).

Back Row (L-R): Aarne Lofgren (Crew), John Mitchell (FOH), Art Soyk (Crew), Reggie Carter (Crew), Butch Oeser (Crew), Eric Anthony Pregent (Wardrobe), Carey Bertini (Wardrobe), Mendy Levine (House Manager), John Maloney (Crew), Andy Sather (Crew), Don Lawrence (Crew), Will Martin (Crew), Ken Costigan (FOH), Meredith Kievit (Crew), Mai-Linh DeVirgilio (Crew), Patricia Zwicker (FOH) and Dottie Arney (FOH).

Mamma Mia!

LITTLESTAR SERVICES LIMITED

Directors ....Judy Craymer,
Richard East,
Benny Andersson,
Björn Ulvaeus
International Executive Producer ....Andrew Treagus
Business & Finance Director ....Ashley Grisdale
Administrator.....................................Peter Austin
PA to Judy Craymer ....Mel Bartram
Communications Co-ordinator ....Claire Teare
Communications Assistant ....Liz McGinity
Head of Accounts ....Jo Reedman
Accountant ....Sheila Egbujie
Accountant ....Kerri Jordan
Administrative Assistant ....Matthew Willis
Receptionist ....Bryony Fraser
Legal Services...................................Barry Shaw
Howard Jones at Sheridans
Production Insurance Services ....Walton & Parkinson Ltd.
Business Manager for
Benny Andersson and
Björn Ulvaeus &
Scandinavian Press ....Görel Hanser

NINA LANNAN ASSOCIATES

GENERAL MANAGERS ....AMY JACOBS,
DEVIN M. KEUDELL
COMPANY MANAGER ....RINA L. SALTZMAN
Assistant Company Manager ....Liza Garcia
Management Associates ....Jon Ferrari,
Katherine McNamee

ANDREW TREAGUS ASSOCIATES LIMITED

GENERAL MANAGER ....JULIAN STONEMAN
Production Coordinator ....Daniel Sparrow
PA to Andrew Treagus ....Jacki Harding
PA to Julian Stoneman ....Stella Warshaw
Production Assistant ....Maria Persson

PRODUCTION TEAM

ASSOCIATE
CHOREOGRAPHER ....NICHOLA TREHERNE
DANCE SUPERVISOR ....JANET ROTHERMEL
PRODUCTION SUPERVISOR ....TOM CAPPS
RESIDENT DIRECTOR ....MARTHA BANTA
ASSOCIATE
MUSIC SUPERVISOR ....DAVID HOLCENBERG
ASSOCIATE
SCENIC DESIGNER (US) ....NANCY THUN
ASSOCIATE
SCENIC DESIGNER (UK) ....JONATHAN ALLEN
ASSOCIATE
COSTUME DESIGNERS ....LUCY GAIGER
SCOTT TRAUGOTT
ASSOCIATE HAIR DESIGNER ..JOSH MARQUETTE
ASSOCIATE
LIGHTING DESIGNERS ....DAVID HOLMES,
ED MCCARTHY,
ANDREW VOLLER
ASSOCIATE SOUND DESIGNERS ....BRIAN
BEASLEY,
DAVID PATRIDGE
MUSICAL TRANSCRIPTION ......ANDERS NEGLIN
CASTING CONSULTANT ....DAVID GRINDROD

CASTING
TARA RUBIN CASTING (U.S.)

PRESS REPRESENTATIVE
BONEAU/BRYAN-BROWN
Adrian Bryan-Brown   Joe Perrotta

MARKETING U.S.
TMG – THE MARKETING GROUP
TANYA GRUBICH   LAURA MATALON
Trish Santini   Ronni Seif
Gregory Ramos

MUSIC PUBLISHED BY EMI GROVE PARK MUSIC, INC. AND EMI WATERFORD MUSIC, INC.

STAFF FOR MAMMA MIA!
PRODUCTION
STAGE MANAGER................ANDREW FENTON
Stage Managers ....Sherry Cohen, Dean R. Greer
Assistant Dance Captain ....Meredith Akins

PRODUCTION MANAGER.....ARTHUR SICCARDI

HEAD CARPENTER....................PAT SULLIVAN
Assistant Carpenters ....Richie McQuail, Chris Nass
Production Electrician ....Rick Baxter
Head Electrician ....Don Lawrence
Assistant Electrician ....Andy Sather
Vari*Lite Programmer ....Andrew Voller
Production Sound ....David Patridge
Head Sound ....Craig Cassidy
Assistant Sound ....George Huckins
Production Properties ....Simon E.R. Evans
Head Properties ....Gregory Martin
Wardrobe Supervisor ....Irene L. Bunis
Assistant Wardrobe ....Ron Glow
Dressers ....Carey Bertini, Jessica Boyd,
Jim Collum, Lauren Kievit,
Elvia Pineda, Eric Pregent,
Christine Richmond, I Wang
Hair Supervisor ....Josh Marquette
Assistant Hair Supervisor ....Vickey Walker
Assistant Lighting Designer ....Jeffrey Lowney
Assistant Costume Designers ....Angela Kahler,
Brian Russman
Assistant to the Costume Designer ....Meghan Healey
House Crew   Richard Carney, Reginald Carter,
Gregory Chabay, Rick Dalcortivo,
Gary DeVirgilio, Meredith Kievit,
Aarne Lofgren, Francis Lofgren,
John Maloney, Glenn Russo,
Tanya Smith, Dennis Wiener
Box Office   Mary Cleary, Lee Cobb,
Lenny Cobb, Steve Cobb, Sue Giebler,
Bob McCaffrey, Ron Schroeder
Casting Directors ....Tara Rubin CSA, Eric Woodall
Casting Associates ....Dunja Vitolic, Laura Schutzel
Casting Assistants ....Mona
Slomsky,
Rebecca Carfagna
Canadian Casting ....Stephanie Gorin Casting, C.D.C.
Associate to Casting Consultant ....Stephen Crockett
London Casting Assistant ....James Orange
Legal Counsel (U.S.) ....Lazarus & Harris LLP/
Scott Lazarus, Esq. Robert Harris, Esq.
Immigration
Counsel ....Kramer, Levin, Naftalis & Frankel LLP
Accounting ....Rosenberg, Neuwirth and Kuchner/
Chris Cacace, In Woo
Advertising ....Serino Coyne, Inc./
Nancy Coyne, Greg Corradetti,
Ryan Greer, Ruth Rosenberg
Press Office Staff...................Chris Boneau, Jim Byk,
Brandi Cornwell, Jackie Green,
Juliana Hannett, Hector Hernandez,
Jessica Johnson, Kevin Jones,
Eric Louie, Aaron Meier, Linnae Petruzzelli,
Matthew Polk, Heath Schwartz, Susanne Tighe
Production Photographer ....Joan Marcus

Merchandising ....Max Merchandise, LLC/
Randi Grossman, Todd Coolidge
Theater Displays ....King Display
Insurance ....Marsh Inc.,
Walton & Parkinson Ltd.
Banking ...................................J.P. Morgan Trust
Travel Agent ....Tzell Travel
Tour Direction ....The Booking Group/Meredith Blair
(212) 869-9280
Original Logo Design ....© Littlestar Services Limited

CREDITS AND ACKNOWLEDGMENTS
Scenery constructed and painted by Hudson Scenic Studio, Inc. and Hamilton Scenic Specialty. Computer motion control and automation by Feller Precision, Inc. SHOWTRAK computer motion control for scenery and rigging. Sound equipment supplied by Masque Sound. Lighting equipment supplied by Fourth Phase and Vari*Lite, Inc. Soft goods by I. Weiss and Sons. Costumes by Barbara Matera, Ltd., Tricorne New York City and Carelli Costumes, Inc. Additional costume work by Allan Alberts Productions. Millinery by Lynne Mackey. Wet suits by Aquatic Fabricators of South Florida. Custom men's shirts by Cego. Custom knitting by C.C. Wei. Custom fabric printing and dyeing by Dye-namix and Gene Mignola. Shoes by Native Leather, Rilleau Leather and T. O. Dey. Gloves by Cornelia James - London. Hair color by Redken. Properties by Paragon Theme and Prop Fabrication. Cough drops provided by Ricola U.S.A. Physical therapy provided by Sean Gallagher.

Mamma Mia! was originally produced in London by LITTLESTAR SERVICES LIMITED on April 6, 1999.

Experience *Mamma Mia!* in these cities:
London Las Vegas
Hamburg Utrecht Stuttgart
Madrid Osaka Stockholm
U.S. National Tour
International Tour

Coming soon: Seoul

For more information and tour schedules visit:
www.mamma-mia.com

 ### THE SHUBERT ORGANIZATION, INC.
Board of Directors

Gerald Schoenfeld   **Philip J. Smith**
Chairman   President

Wyche Fowler, Jr.   **John W. Kluge**

Lee J. Seidler   **Michael I. Sovern**

Stuart Subotnick

Robert E. Wankel
Executive Vice President

Peter Entin   **Elliot Greene**
Vice President -   Vice President -
Theatre Operations   Finance

David Andrews   **John Darby**
Vice President -   Vice President -
Shubert Ticketing Services   Facilities

House Manager ....Manuel Levine

Mamma Mia!
SCRAPBOOK

Photos by Aubrey Reuben

Correspondent: Judy McLane, "Tanya"

Fourth Anniversary Party: We had a great party at a bar on Tenth Avenue. There was a Champagne toast and they got a cake from The Cupcake Café. It was my second of these anniversary parties, and I like them because you get to see who's been around the whole five years. The resident director came and the choreographer came. It was good fun.

Anniversary Gifts: They give us so many cool gifts at *Mamma Mia!* One of the coolest was a coffee press with a beautiful silver cup that says *Mamma Mia!* Judy Craymer, the producer, sent us all beautiful bouquets. It's like every anniversary is an opening night.

Most Exciting Celebrity Visitors: Andy Fenton, our PSM, is always up to something to build spirit. This year he had a Christmas Tree door competition, which was judged by Huey Lewis and Debra Monk. You had to deck out the door of your dressing room. We had everything from these elaborate scenes to just one little Post-it. Andy Kelso had a door with a whole "Charlie Brown Christmas" theme, and somebody else did a Kwanzaa door. It was great fun—so festive. I think the Post-it won! Huey couldn't believe what we'd done. He said, "Wow, the energy over here is so great!" It's really like one great big family.

"Gypsy of the Year" Sketch: "A Minute of Your Time" by David Beach, who plays Harry.

"Carols for a Cure" Carol: "Silent Night."

"Easter Bonnet" Sketch: "Money Mia!" by Bryan Scott Johnson, Ryan Sander and David Beach.

Actor Who Performs the Most Roles in This Show: Matt Farver and Ryan Sander.

Special Backstage Rituals: At "five minutes" I do this thing called Angel Cards. It's my way of saying hello to people. I have a little bag filled with slips of paper. Each slip has a word

1. (L-R): Judy McLane, Michele Pawk, Olga Merediz take curtain call on the show's anniversary at the Cadillac Winter Garden.
2. (L-R): McLane, Pawk and Merediz at the party to celebrate the anniversary at 44 1/2.
3. L-R) Carol Linnea Johnson, Resident Director Martha Banta and Janet Rothermel at 44 1/2.
4. Cast and crew members at the summer 2005 "Broadway on Broadway" event.

Mamma Mia!
SCRAPBOOK

on it. Each person digs into the bag and the word they pick is their word of the show. Say you pick "understanding." It's your word to think about that day. You can sing it to yourself, say it to others, figure out how it applies to your part in the show.

Also whenever anyone is leaving, we do a Top Ten list, like a David Letterman Top Ten. David Beach is usually the writer and they're always brilliant. They basically roast the person. Then you sign your name on a huge map of Greece we have in the greenroom, and we take your picture, which goes up on the wall. All the people who have done the show are on the wall in the green room.

For birthdays around here you get a cake from the person who had the last birthday, and then it's your job to buy the cake for the next person's birthday.

Favorite Moment During Each Performance (Onstage or Off): After I come off from the Arrival scene, Olga Meredi z and I come around to Isaac Calpito, Michael and Christopher Carl in the backstage booth where they sing. Christopher brings *The New York Post* and Isaac reads our horoscopes in this bizarre accent. It's silly but we look forward to it.

Favorite In-Theatre Gathering Place: Mark Montgomery and David Beach's dressing room. After the show we sometimes gather there for a drink. It's not the biggest room but we all squeeze in there.

Favorite Off-Site Hangout: There's a new place we go called Harmony View. It's a big open place right on 50th Street kitty-corner to our theatre. We've been going there to celebrate birthdays and stuff.

Favorite Snack Food: Dunkin' Donuts is pretty much the popular thing. You find them on the table as you come up the stairs from the stage door.

Mascots: We have a plastic Charlie Brown in the window of Andy Fenton's room, and we have a fish tank in the stage manager's office. We also had an ant farm this year.

Favorite Therapy: Ice! Knees are a big problem on this show because of the raked stage. A physical therapy person comes in regularly. But everybody also has these foam rollers to help stretch their leg muscles. I also get acupuncture for my knees.

Memorable Ad-Lib: One night there was a loud noise on the stage, something with the lights, I think. We were practically screaming the lines at each other. But when Carolee Carmello made her entrance the noise suddenly stopped. And she said, "Oh, the power I have!"

Record Number of Cell Phone Rings During a Performance: Cell phones are becoming less of a problem, but cell phone

photographs are even worse! Sometimes a dozen people at a time will take pictures, especially during the Megamix at the end of the show. Sometimes they even use video cameras!

Memorable Press Encounter: We did a publicity shoot at the Stage Door Deli when they named a sandwich after us. The three Dynamos had to take pictures with these giant sandwiches in our mouths.

Memorable Fan Encounters: We have a couple of girls who have come a hundred or something times. They make us chocolate and other goodies. One time a woman invited Corinne to her house in the Hamptons.

Latest Audience Arrival: On Sundays we have a two o'clock show that everybody thinks is a three o'clock show. At about forty minutes into the show, here they come. I call them "comedy-killers."

Fastest Costume Change: When Sophie comes out of "Voulez-Vous," she actually has to jump out of her pants and change her costume on stage while the set is turning.

Orchestra Member Who Plays the Most Instruments: David Nyberg.

Orchestra Member Who Has Played the Most Performances Without a Sub: Doug Quinn.

Who Wore the Heaviest/Hottest Costume: The Dynamos. Spandex is hotter than you think!

Who Wore the Least: Andy Kelso (as Sky) and the ensemble men in their bathing suits and flippers.

Best In-House Parody Lyrics: For "Chiquitita": "Take your teeth out/Tell me what's wrong."
For "Slipping Through My Fingers": "Slipping in two fingers." (Wrong, I know.)

Nicknames: Tranny and Tina.

Company In-Jokes: PSM Andy Fenton puts out the monthly "Taverna Gazette" filled with fun surprises. No comment on its validity.

Catchphrases Only People in the Company Would Recognize: "You always have a home here at the *Mia!*"
Also: "Beatrice and the late Colonel William Hastings."

Tales From the Put-In: Everyone who joins the cast gets the warning: If you're too far downstage at the end of "Voulez-Vous" you will get knocked down when the curtain comes down. Move upstage!

Coolest Thing About Being in This Show: The audience at the end of the show dancing in the aisles and going crazy. On my first night I was coming on in Spandex at the end of the show and I heard this *roar*, and I wondered, what the heck was that? And then I realized: it's the audience! I thought, oh my God, I'm in a rock concert! It's a fun show and a fun backstage.

1. (L-R): Olivia Oguma and Samantha Eggers at the party to celebrate the fourth anniversary at 44 1/2.
2. Carolee Carmello at the "Stars in the Alley" event.

Photos by Aubrey Reuben

Mark Twain Tonight!

First Preview June 6, 2005. Opened June 9, 2005.
Closed June 26, 2005 after 3 Previews and 15 Performances.

Hal Holbrook
Mark Twain

Scott Rudin
Producer

Ben Sprecher
Producer

Emanuel Azenberg
Producer

SCRAPBOOK

Correspondent: Richard Costabile, Production Supervisor

Memorable Opening Night Note: The one that *Spamalot* sent us was hilarious. It was a big piece of oaktag with a picture of Mark Twain in the middle and many Spam-related Mark Twain items, like a copy of "Spam and Old Times on the Mississippi." It was addressed, "To Hal and Company…OK, just Hal. Have a magnificent opening."

Opening Night Gifts: His wife, Dixie Carter, sent him a whole raft of peonies.

Exciting Celebrity Visitors: On opening night we had Glenn Close, Cherry Jones and, of course, Dixie. The conversation was wonderful and just went on and on.

Backstage Ritual: He takes two and a half hours to get into makeup. He does it all himself and always has.

Favorite Moments During Each Performance: I'd say the Huck Finn "number." He has five excerpts he chooses from. My other favorite moment is when he first walks out. He gets a thunderous ovation every single performance. It does wonderful things for my heart when I hear it for him. It's such a privilege to do this show.

Favorite Snack Food: About an hour before he goes on, he eats a can of Progresso chicken and barley or chicken and wild rice soup with Saltines and cottage cheese.

Favorite Therapy: At 80, he just takes really good care of himself.

Record Number of Cell Phone Rings During a Performance: Only one. I do a really good announcement before the show begins. I say that it's set in the era before cell phones, so to preserve the illusion, everyone should shut them off. It works.

Memorable Stage Door Fan Encounter: A young man with from Santa Barbara, California told us he was thrilled to be here. When Mr. Holbrook told him we'll be appearing in Santa Barbara at the end of the year, he almost cried, he was so happy to be able to see him again.

Latest Arrival: We don't let late arrivals in—we shoot them.

Ghostly Encounters: We had forty members of the National Corporate Theatre Fund one night. At the Q&A afterward we mentioned that the only light cues were lights up at the beginning and lights down at the end, and that we had no sound effects. But one man was convinced that he heard water flowing during the Huck Finn number and another one was convinced that he heard birds chirping during the Blue Jay number. We said, "It must be the ghosts."

Nickname: He calls me "Dad." But then, he calls a lot of people "Dad." It's his all-purpose honorific.

Sweethearts: Hal and Dixie.

Catchphrase: Every night when I do my checklist before he goes on, I say, "And how's your hearing aid, sir?" And he says, "What?"

Mark Twain Tonight!

Selections

NOTE: While Mr. Twain's selections will come from the complete list below, we have been unable to pin him down as to which of them he will do. He claims it would cripple his inspiration. However, he has generously conceded to a printed program for the benefit of those who are in distress and wish to fan themselves.

SELECTION	SOURCE
Compliments Collection	Miscellaneous
Chaucer, Sailor, Tennessee Girl	Miscellaneous
Slow Train, Long Dog	Following the Equator
Charity, Reform, Cats	Miscellaneous
My Cigar Habit?	Miscellaneous
The Marienbad Cure	Essays
A Cyclopedia of Sin	Miscellaneous
Smoke Rings	Miscellaneous
A Moral Pauper	Following the Equator
Hunting the Water Closet	Mark Twain's Notebook
Virginia City	Roughing It
Shoveling Sand	Roughing It
The Ant	A Tramp Abroad
The Great Landslide Case	Roughing It
The Lord Will Provide	Autobiography
The German Opera	A Tramp Abroad
A Genuine Mexican Plug	Roughing It
San Francisco	Miscellaneous
Crippling the Accordion	Sketches
The Anarchist Story	Speeches
Baker's Bluejay	A Tramp Abroad
The Sweet Bye and Bye	Essays: The Invalid Story
His Grandfather's Old Ram	Mark Twain's Notebook
Congress: The Grand Old Asylum	Miscellaneous
The Press	Speeches
Down There in Washington	Miscellaneous
Running for President	Miscellaneous
The Sandwich Islands	Roughing It
The Italian Guide	Innocents Abroad
My Encounter With an Interviewer	Sketches
Accident Insurance	Speeches
The Supreme Art	Letters From the Earth
White Suit	Speeches
Requesting a Hymn Book	Mark Twain in Eruption
Money Is God	Notebooks
Decay in the Art of Lying	Essays and Miscellaneous
Advice to Youth	Speeches
Taming the Bicycle	Essays
The Evolution of Man	Biography
Insanity: Elections, War and Petrified Opinions	Miscellaneous
Huck and Jim	Huckleberry Finn
Shooting of Boggs	Huckleberry Finn
Huck, Jim and 'Lizbeth	Huckleberry Finn
Huck's Conscience	Huckleberry Finn
Lost in the Fog	Huckleberry Finn
Lynching and China	Essays
A Helluva Heaven	Letters From the Earth
Slavery: A Holy Thing	Autobiography
Man, That Poor Thing	Biography
Noah's Ark	Letters From the Earth
Chief Love	Mark Twain in Eruption
The Creator's Pet	Letters From the Earth
The War Prayer	Europe and Elsewhere
The Christian Bible	Miscellaneous
Circumstances	Mark Twain in Eruption
Our Civilization	Autobiography
A Ghost Story	Short Stories
Sunrise on the River	Life on the Mississippi
The Get Rich Quick Disease	Miscellaneous
The Thin Skin	Mark Twain's Notebook
The Virgin Mary	Ladies Home Journal
Praying for Gingerbread	Autobiography
Boyhood on the Farm	Autobiography
Taking Along the Window Sash	Innocents Abroad
My Trained Presbyterian Conscience	Autobiography
How I Stole My Name	Life on the Mississippi
Livy	Autobiography
How to Be Seventy	Speeches
My Ancestor Satan	Short Stories
The Hartford Home	Letters
Susy's Prayer	Autobiography
Halley's Comet	Biography
Mary Ann	Speeches

STAFF FOR *MARK TWAIN TONIGHT!*

GENERAL MANAGER
ABBIE M. STRASSLER

PRESS REPRESENTATIVE
BILL EVANS & ASSOCIATES
JIM RANDOLPH

PRODUCTION SUPERVISOR .... **RICHARD COSTABILE**

Company Manager	Sean Free
Technical Supervisor	Theatretech, Inc./Brian Lynch
Prop Shopper	Christine M. Barnes
Sound Engineer	Wally Flores
Light Board Operator	Manuel Becker
Wardrobe Supervisor	Kelly Saxon
Assistant to Mr. Holbrook	Joyce Cohen
General Management Staff	Eduardo Castro, Shelley Ott, Michael Salonia
Production Carpenter	Thomas A. Lavaia
Production Properties	Joseph P. DePaulo
Production Assistant	Betty Tung
Car Service	Elegant Limousine
Banking	JPMorgan Chase/Richard Callian
Accountants	Fried and Kowgios CPAs LLP/ Robert Fried, CPA Sarah Galbraith
Insurance	Tanenbaum Harber of Florida/ Carol Bressi-Cilona
Legal Counsel	Brooks & Distler/ Marsha S. Brooks Tom R. Distler
Advertising	Serino Coyne Inc./ Angelo Desimini
Theatre Displays	King Displays, Inc.
Exclusive Tour Direction	Klaus W. Kolmar/ The Booking Group, Inc.
Opening Night Coordination	Tobak-Dantchik Events & Promotions/ Suzanne Tobak, Michael Lawrence

---

CREDITS

Soft goods and lighting equipment by Hudson Scenic Studio. Sound equipment by Sound Associates. Props by Christine M. Barnes.

The television special of HAL HOLBROOK in

MARK TWAIN TONIGHT!

is now available on video and DVD.

www.kultur.com

STAFF FOR THE BROOKS ATKINSON THEATRE

House Manager	Barbara Carrellas
Treasurer	Keshave Sattaur
Assistant Treasurers	William Dorso, William O'Brien, Mohammed Sattaur
House Carpenter	Thomas A. Lavaia
House Flyman	Joseph J. Maher
House Properties	Joseph P. DePaulo

Chairman	**James M. Nederlander**
President	**James L. Nederlander**

Executive Vice President
Nick Scandalios

Vice President • Corporate Development **Charlene S. Nederlander**	Senior Vice President • Labor Relations **Herschel Waxman**
Vice President **Jim Boese**	Chief Financial Officer **Freida Sawyer Belviso**

www.nederlander.org

Monty Python's Spamalot

First Preview: February 14, 2005. Opened: March 17, 2005.
Still running as of May 31, 2006.

PLAYBILL

CAST

(in order of appearance)

Historian, Not Dead Fred, French Guard, Minstrel, Prince Herbert	CHRISTIAN BORLE
Mayor, Patsy, Guard 2	MICHAEL McGRATH
King Arthur	SIMON RUSSELL BEALE
Sir Robin, Guard 1, Brother Maynard	DAVID HYDE PIERCE
Sir Lancelot, The French Taunter, Knight of Ni, Tim the Enchanter	HANK AZARIA
Sir Dennis Galahad, The Black Knight, Prince Herbert's Father	CHRISTOPHER SIEBER
Dennis's Mother, Sir Bedevere, Concorde	STEVE ROSEN
The Lady of the Lake	LAUREN KENNEDY
Sir Not Appearing	KEVIN COVERT
Monk	KEVIN COVERT
Nun	BRIAN SHEPARD
God	JOHN CLEESE
French Guards	THOMAS CANNIZZARO, GREG REUTER
Minstrels	BRAD BRADLEY, EMILY HSU, GREG REUTER
Sir Bors	BRAD BRADLEY

Continued on next page

SAM S. SHUBERT THEATRE
225 West 44th Street
A Shubert Organization Theatre

Gerald Schoenfeld, *Chairman*   **Philip J. Smith,** *President*

Robert E. Wankel, *Executive Vice President*

Boyett Ostar Productions   The Shubert Organization
Arielle Tepper   Stephanie McClelland/Lawrence Horowitz   Elan V. McAllister/Allan S. Gordon
Independent Presenters Network   Roy Furman   GRS Associates
Jam Theatricals   TGA Entertainment   Clear Channel Entertainment

present

Monty Python's
SPAMALOT

Book & Lyrics by   Music by
Eric Idle   **John Du Prez & Eric Idle**

A new musical lovingly *ripped off from the motion picture*
"Monty Python and the Holy Grail"
from the original screenplay by
Graham Chapman, John Cleese, Terry Gilliam, Eric Idle, Terry Jones, Michael Palin

starring

David Hyde Pierce   Simon Russell Beale   Hank Azaria

also starring

Christopher Sieber

Michael McGrath   Steve Rosen   Christian Borle

with

Brad Bradley   Thomas Cannizzaro   Kevin Covert   Jennifer Frankel
Lisa Gajda   Rosena M. Hill   Emily Hsu   Beth Johnson   Lorin Latarro   James Ludwig
Drew McVety   Abbey O'Brien   Ariel Reid   Pamela Remler   Greg Reuter
Brian Shepard   Rick Spaans   Scott Taylor   Lee A. Wilkins

and

Lauren Kennedy

Set & Costume Design by **Tim Hatley**		Lighting Design by **Hugh Vanstone**	
Sound Design by **Acme Sound Partners**	Hair & Wig Design by **David Brian Brown**	Special Effects Design by **Gregory Meeh**	Projection Design by **Elaine J. McCarthy**
Music Director/Vocal Arrangements **Todd Ellison**	Orchestrations by **Larry Hochman**	Music Arrangements by **Glen Kelly**	Music Coordinator **Michael Keller**
Casting by **Tara Rubin Casting**	Associate Director **Peter Lawrence**	Associate Choreographer **Darlene Wilson**	Production Management **Gene O'Donovan**
General Management **101 Productions, Ltd.**	Press Representative **Boneau/Bryan-Brown**	Marketing **HHC Marketing**	Associate Producers **Randi Grossman Tisch/Avnet Financial**

Choreography by
Casey Nicholaw

ORIGINAL CAST ALBUM
AVAILABLE ON DECCA BROADWAY

Directed by
Mike Nichols

LIVE BROADWAY

12/26/05

A Chorus Line? (L-R): Martin Moran, Steve Kazee, Christopher Sieber, Steve Rosen, Harry Groener and Michael McGrath sing "All for One."

Photo by Joan Marcus

Monty Python's Spamalot

SCENES & MUSICAL NUMBERS

ACT I

Overture
Scene 1: The Mighty Portcullis
Scene 2: Moose Village
      "Fisch Schlapping Song" ....Historian, Mayor, Villagers
Scene 3: Mud Castle
      "King Arthur's Song" ....King Arthur, Patsy
Scene 4: Plague Village
      "I Am Not Dead Yet" ....Not Dead Fred, Lance, Robin and Bodies
Scene 5: Mud Village
Scene 6: The Lady of the Lake and The Laker Girls
      "Come With Me"..........................King Arthur, Lady of the Lake and Laker Girls
      "The Song That Goes Like This" ....Sir Galahad and Lady of the Lake
Scene 7: The Knights
      "All for One" ....King Arthur, Patsy, Sir Robin, Sir Lancelot,
                                                                      Sir Galahad and Sir Bedevere
Scene 8: Camelot
      "Knights of the Round Table" ....Lady of the Lake, King Arthur, Patsy,
                                                                      Sir Robin, Sir Lancelot, Sir Galahad,
                                                                      Sir Bedevere and The Camelot Dancers
      "The Song That Goes Like This (Reprise)" ....Lady of the Lake
Scene 9: The Feet of God
Scene 10: Find Your Grail
      "Find Your Grail" ....Lady of the Lake, King Arthur, Patsy, Sir Robin,
                                                      Sir Lancelot, Sir Galahad, Sir Bedevere, Knights and Grail Girls
Scene 11: The French Castle
      "Run Away"................................French Taunters, King Arthur, Patsy, Sir Robin,
                                                                      Sir Lancelot, Sir Galahad, Sir Bedevere,
                                                                      French Guards and French Citizens

ACT II

Scene 1: The Mighty Portcullis
Scene 2: A Very Expensive Forest
      "Always Look on the Bright Side of Life" ....Patsy, King Arthur, Knights and
                                                                      The Knights of Ni
Scene 3: Sir Robin and His Minstrels
      "Brave Sir Robin" ....Sir Robin and Minstrels
Scene 4: The Black Knight
Scene 5: Another Part of the Very Expensive Forest
      "You Won't Succeed on Broadway" ....Sir Robin and Ensemble
Scene 6: A Hole in the Universe
      "The Diva's Lament" ....Lady of the Lake
Scene 7: Prince Herbert's Chamber
      "Where Are You?" ....Prince Herbert
      "Here Are You" ....Prince Herbert
      "His Name Is Lancelot" ....Sir Lancelot, Prince Herbert and Ensemble
Scene 8: Yet Another Part of the Very Expensive Forest
      "I'm All Alone" ....King Arthur, Patsy and Knights
      "The Song That Goes Like This (Reprise)" ....Lady of the Lake and
                                                                      King Arthur
Scene 9: The Killer Rabbit
      "The Holy Grail" ....King Arthur, Patsy, Sir Robin, Sir Lancelot,
                                                                      Sir Galahad, Sir Bedevere and Knights
      Finale
      "Find Your Grail Finale - Medley" ....The Company

Monty Python's Spamalot

David Hyde Pierce
Sir Robin, Guard 1, Brother Maynard

Simon Russell Beale
King Arthur

Hank Azaria
Lancelot, The French Taunter, Knight of Ni, Tim the Enchanter

Christopher Sieber
Sir Dennis Galahad, The Black Knight, Prince Herbert's Father

Michael McGrath
Mayor, Patsy, Guard 2

Steve Rosen
Dennis's Mother, Sir Bedevere, Concorde

Christian Borle
Historian, Not Dead Fred, French Guard, Minstrel, Prince Herbert

Lauren Kennedy
The Lady of the Lake

Brad Bradley
Minstrel, Sir Bors, Ensemble

Thomas Cannizzaro
French Guard, Ensemble

John Cleese
God

Kevin Covert
Sir Not Appearing, Monk, Ensemble

Jennifer Frankel
Ensemble

Lisa Gajda
Ensemble

Rosena M. Hill
Standby for Lady of the Lake

Emily Hsu
Minstrel, Ensemble

Beth Johnson
Swing

James Ludwig
Standby for Robin, Bedevere, Patsy, Historian, Not Dead Fred, Prince Herbert, Lancelot

Drew McVety
Standby for Arthur, Lancelot, Galahad, Robin, Bedevere

Abbey O'Brien
Ensemble

Ariel Reid
Ensemble

Pamela Remler
Swing, Dance Captain

Greg Reuter
French Guard, Minstrel, Ensemble, Fight Captain

Brian Shepard
Nun, Ensemble

Rick Spaans
Swing

Scott Taylor
Ensemble, Dance Captain

Lee A. Wilkins
Swing

Mahlon Kruse
Production Stage Manager

Jim Woolley
Stage Manager

Rachel A. Wolff
Stage Manager

Eric Idle and John Du Prez
Book, Lyrics and Music; Composer

Mike Nichols
Director

Casey Nicholaw
Choreography

Tim Hatley
Set and Costume Design

Monty Python's Spamalot

Hugh Vanstone
Lighting Design

Tom Clark, Mark Menard and Nevin Steinberg,
Acme Sound Partners
Sound Design

David Brian Brown
Wig and Hair Design

Todd Ellison
*Musical Director/
Vocal Arranger*

Larry Hochman
Orchestrations

Michael Keller
Music Coordinator

Peter Lawrence
Associate Director

Tara Rubin,
Tara Rubin Casting
Casting

Bill Haber,
Ostar Enterprises
Producer

Bob Boyett
Producer

Gerald Schoenfeld,
The Shubert
Organization
Producer

Arielle Tepper
Producer

Stephanie P.
McClelland
Producer

Lawrence Horowitz,
M.D.
Producer

Elan V. McAllister
Producer

Allan S. Gordon
Producer

Roy Furman
Producer

Elie Landau
Ergo Entertainment
*Company Manager
and Producer*

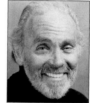

Morton Swinsky
GRS Associates,
Producer

Steve Tisch,
Tisch-Avnet Financial
Associate Producer

Jon Avnet,
Tisch-Avnet Financial
Associate Producer

Harry Groener (left, as King
Arthur) finds his grail
with the help of
Lauren Kennedy as The
Lady of the Lake.

Photo by Joan Marcus

Monty Python's Spamalot

John Bolton
Standby

Tim Curry
King Arthur

Jenny Hill
Ensemble

Sara Ramirez
The Lady of the Lake

Alan Tudyk
*Sir Lancelot,
The French Taunter,
Knight of Ni,
Tim the Enchanter*

Darlene Wilson
Standby

Asmeret
Ghebremichael
Minstrel, Ensemble

Harry Groener
King Arthur

Steve Kazee
*Sir Lancelot, The
French Taunter,
Knight of Ni, Tim the
Enchanter*

Kristie Kerwin
Ensemble

Joanne Manning
Ensemble

Martin Moran
*Sir Robin, Guard 1,
Brother Maynard*

Billy Sprague, Jr.
Ensemble

Simon Russell Beale (R, as
King Arthur) wields
Excalibur, to the delight of
Michael McGrath (as Patsy).

Monty Python's Spamalot

Photos by Ben Strothmann

BOX OFFICE STAFF
Names withheld at request of theatre.

FRONT OF HOUSE STAFF
Front Row (L-R): Eva Torres (Bartender), Maura Gaynor (Directress), Joanne Blessington (Usher), Delia Pozo (Usher), Aspacia Savas (Directress), Luis Maldonado (Usher), Chris Caoili (Usher)
Back Row (L-R): Sean Becktel (Bartender), Susan Snow (Usher), Stephen Ivelja (Ticket Taker), Luis Rodriguez (Bartender), Brian Gaynair (Theatre Manager), Paul Rodriguez (Usher), Richard Guzman (Usher), Elvis Caban (Usher), Susan Maxwell (Head Usher), Tomas Ortiz (Usher), Joe Lupo (Bar Manager) and Doreen Barnard (Bartender).

CREW
Front Row (L-R): Mike Hyman (Production Electrician), Karen Zitnick (Assistant Electrician), Mahlon Kruse (Production Stage Manager), Sheri K. Turner (Assistant Stage Manager), Chad Lewis (Assistant Stage Manager), Meredith Benson (Wardrobe Dresser), Jennie Naughton (Wardrobe Dresser).
Second Row (L-R): James Spadling (Head House Electrician), Ray Wright, Jr. (House Props), Kelly Saxon (Assistant to Simon Russell Beale), Jim Woolley (Stage Manager), Gus Poitras (Production Flyman), Elie Landau (Company Manager), Jackie Green (Press Agent).
Third Row (L-R): Charles Peak (House Electrician), Timothy Altman (Follow Spot Operator), Lair Paulsen (Hairdresser), Larry Boyette (Hair Supervisor), Adam Biscow (Assistant Electrician-Pyro), Randy Morrison (House Sound), Thomas Manoy (House Head Carpenter), R. J. Styles (House Electrician), Carl Keator (House Carpenter), Bill Partello (Production Automation), Amelia Haywood (Dresser), Jennifer Kievit (Props Department), Linda Lee (Wardrobe Supervisor), Sonya Wysocki (Assistant Wardrobe Supervisor), Mike Wojchik (Assistant Sound), Rose Alaio (Stage Doorperson).
Back Row (L-R): Greg Gould (House Carpenter), Joe Luongo (House Carpenter), John Kenny (House Carpenter), Mike Martinez (Production Carpenter), Andrea Roberts (Dresser), Brian Gaynair (House Manager) and Keith Shaw (Dresser).

Monty Python's Spamalot

Monty Python's Spamalot

Correspondent: Christopher Sieber, "Sir Dennis Galahad, The Black Knight, Prince Herbert's Father."

Memorable Quote From Director Mike Nichols: "Have fun, for God's sake. When it comes down to it, we're all going to die!"

Memorable Press Event: The day we set the "Guinness Book of World Records" record for Largest Coconut Orchestra. The official count was something like 1700, but I say there had to be more than 2000 people, all playing coconuts over their heads. It was INSANE.

Fastest Costume Change: Mike McGrath has to go from Mayor of Finland to Patsy in 20 seconds or less.

Fastest Dismemberment: We were sued by a model whose image appeared on the side of the theatre, looking out a window. One day she was there and the next, there were just hands. I don't think those were even her hands anymore. I think they might even be Mike Nichols' hands.

Favorite Snack Food: Saturday morning doughnuts.

Another Memorable Mike Nichols Quote: "You can't make lemonade without killing a few patrons."

"Carols for a Cure" Carol: "I'm Dreaming of Christmas and You."

Busiest Day at the Box Office: The day after we won the Tony Awards we did two million dollars in one day.

Easily Misunderstood Michael McGrath Quote: At one vocal rehearsal he said, "You want me to join on top? Because we've got a lot of bottom."

Heaviest and Hottest Costumes: Steve plays the Knight of Ni and his costume has got to weigh sixty pounds. My costume as the Father in the "Where Are You?" scene is the second heaviest but it's got to be the hottest. It's like a big stuffed animal you might wear.

Who Wore the Least: Abbey O'Brien plays the naughty girl in nasty tights.

A Not Quite As Memorable and Yet *Rather* Memorable Mike Nichols Quote: "I think we've just learned something: No acting!"

Near-Dismemberment: Myself, Christopher Sieber, being stabbed by a sword during the Black Knight scene. I'm supposed to be impaled on a wall, but one night King Arthur actually drew blood and left a major bruise. So that was uncomfortable.

Latest Audience Arrival: Literally as we were doing the final verse of "Run Away" and exiting for the end of Act I, a couple came in and were seated down front.

In-House Parody Lyric: Mike McGrath, in "The Song That Ends Like This," sang, "This is the show that ends my career."

Catchphrase Only the Company Would Recognize: "DOOOON'T!"

Special Moment: At the final performance for David Hyde Pierce and Hank Azaria, the guys were standing there at curtain call with flowers

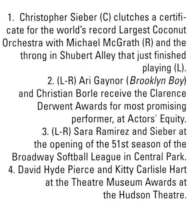

1. Christopher Sieber (C) clutches a certificate for the world's record Largest Coconut Orchestra with Michael McGrath (R) and the throng in Shubert Alley that just finished playing (L).
2. (L-R) Ari Gaynor (*Brooklyn Boy*) and Christian Borle receive the Clarence Derwent Awards for most promising performer, at Actors' Equity.
3. (L-R) Sara Ramirez and Sieber at the opening of the 51st season of the Broadway Softball League in Central Park.
4. David Hyde Pierce and Kitty Carlisle Hart at the Theatre Museum Awards at the Hudson Theatre.

and the audience was screaming. Everyone in the cast was in tears because we love these guys so much. Then Mike Nichols came out with a microphone and said, "Ladies and gentlemen, what you saw here today was open heart surgery because right here, these two guys are the heart of this show." He got so choked up, he couldn't speak. And that's a strange and wonderful thing because Mike is one guy who always knows exactly what to say. We all just lost it.

Final Memorable Series of Quotes from Mike Nichols and Librettist Eric Idle: Mike (talking to the actors who will play monks who smack their heads with giant Bibles): "Don't hurt yourselves." Eric: "It's comedy, Mike." Mike: "Oh. Right. Hurt yourselves."

Movin' Out

First Preview: September 30, 2002. Opened: October 24, 2002.
Closed December 11, 2005 after 28 Previews and 1,303 Performances.

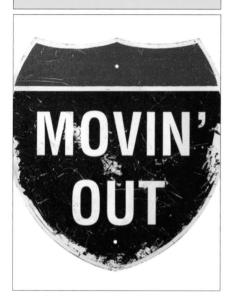

CAST

Eddie ....JOHN SELYA

Brenda ....ELIZABETH PARKINSON

Tony ....KEITH ROBERTS

Judy ....ASHLEY TUTTLE

James ....BENJAMIN G. BOWMAN

Sergeant O'Leary/Drill Sergeant ....SCOTT WISE

Piano/Lead Vocals ....MICHAEL CAVANAUGH

THE ENSEMBLE

MICHAEL BALDERRAMA, ALEXANDER BRADY,
RON DeJESUS, MELISSA DOWNEY, PASCALE FAYE,
TIGER MARTINA, JILL NICKLAUS,
RIKA OKAMOTO,
JUSTIN PECK, KARINE PLANTADIT

SWINGS

IAN CARNEY, CAROLYN DOHERTY, TREY GILLEN,
CODY GREEN, CHARLIE HODGES,
TRAVIS KELLEY, MARTY LAWSON,
BRIAN LETENDRE, LORIN LATARRO,
MABEL MODRONO, ERIC OTTO,
MEG PAUL, LAWRENCE RABSON,
JESSICA WALKER, RYAN WATKINSON

Dance Supervisor – STACY CADDELL

Dance Captains – IAN CARNEY and MEG PAUL

Continued on next page

Continued on next page

RICHARD RODGERS THEATRE
UNDER THE DIRECTION OF JAMES M. NEDERLANDER AND JAMES L. NEDERLANDER

James L. Nederlander
Hal Luftig   Scott E. Nederlander   Terry Allen Kramer
Clear Channel Entertainment   Emanuel Azenberg
present

Conceived by
Twyla Tharp

Music and Lyrics by
Billy Joel

starring

John Selya   Elizabeth Parkinson   Keith Roberts
Ashley Tuttle
Scott Wise   Benjamin G. Bowman
and
Michael Cavanaugh

with

Michael Balderrama   Alexander Brady   Ian Carney   Ron DeJesus
Carolyn Doherty   Melissa Downey   Pascale Faye   Trey Gillen
Cody Green   Henry Haid   Charlie Hodges   Travis Kelley   Lorin Latarro
Marty Lawson   Brian Letendre   Tiger Martina   Mabel Modrono   Jill Nicklaus
Rika Okamoto   Eric Otto   Meg Paul   Justin Peck   Karine Plantadit
Wade Preston   Lawrence Rabson   Jessica Walker   Ryan Watkinson

Scenic Design	Costume Design	Lighting Design
Santo Loquasto	**Suzy Benzinger**	**Donald Holder**

Sound Design	Additional Musical Arrangements and Orchestrations
Brian Ruggles **Peter J. Fitzgerald**	**Stuart Malina**

Hair Design	Synthesizer Programmer	Music Coordinator	Musical Consultant
Paul Huntley	**David Rosenthal**	**John Miller**	**Tommy Byrnes**

Assistant Choreographer/ Assistant Director	Production Associate	Technical Supervision	Casting
Scott Wise	**Jesse Huot**	**Brian Lynch**	**Jay Binder Casting** **Sarah Prosser**

Press Representative	Marketing	Production Stage Manager	General Manager
Barlow • Hartman	**TMG** **The Marketing Group**	**Kim Vernace**	**Abbie M. Strassler**

Musical Continuity and Supervision
Stuart Malina

Directed and Choreographed by
Twyla Tharp

LIVE BROADWAY

9/26/05

Elizabeth Parkinson (front) and members of the cast of *Movin' Out.*

Photo by Joan Marcus

Movin' Out

MUSICAL NUMBERS

ACT I

Overture: "It's Still Rock and Roll to Me" ....The Company

Scene 1: Brenda and Eddie Split
"Scenes from an Italian Restaurant" ....Brenda, Eddie, Tony, James,
Judy, Sergeant O'Leary and Ensemble

Scene 2: Tony Moves Out
"Movin' Out (Anthony's Song)" ....Tony, Eddie, James and Sergeant O'Leary

Scene 3: James and Judy Are Forever
"Reverie (Villa D'Este)/Just the Way You Are" ....James, Judy and Ensemble

Scene 4: Brenda Is Back
"For the Longest Time/Uptown Girl" ....Brenda, Eddie, Tony and Ensemble

Scene 5: Tony and Brenda Get Together
"This Night" ....Tony, Brenda and Ensemble

Scene 6: Eddie Knows
"Summer, Highland Falls" ....Eddie, Brenda, Tony and Ensemble

Scene 7: Off to War
"Waltz #1 (Nunley's Carousel)" ....Tony, Eddie, James, Drill Sergeant and Ensemble

Scene 8: The Sky Falls
"We Didn't Start the Fire" ....Judy, Brenda, James, Tony, Eddie and Ensemble

Scene 9: Two Bars: Hicksville/Saigon
"She's Got a Way" ....Tony, Brenda and Ensemble

Scene 10: Coming Home
"The Stranger" ....Judy and Ensemble
"Elegy (The Great Peconic)" ....Judy, Brenda, Tony, Eddie, Drill Sergeant and Ensemble

ACT II

Scene 1: Vets Cast Out
"Invention in C Minor" ....Eddie and Ensemble

Scene 2: Eddie Rages
"Angry Young Man" ....Eddie and Ensemble

Scene 3: Tony Disconnects
"Big Shot" ....Tony, Brenda and Ensemble

Scene 4: A Contest of Pain
"Big Man on Mulberry Street" ....Tony, Brenda and Ensemble

Scene 5: Eddie Gets High
"Captain Jack" ....Eddie and Ensemble

Scene 6: Eddie Reaches Out
"Innocent Man" ....Eddie and Ensemble

Scene 7: Eddie's Nightmares
"Pressure" ....Judy, Eddie and Ensemble

Scene 8: Eddie's Journey Back
"Goodnight Saigon" ....Eddie, Judy, James, Tony and Ensemble

Scene 9: Brenda's Lost Dreams
"Air (Dublinesque)" ....Brenda

Scene 10: Tony and Brenda Reconcile
"Shameless" ....Brenda and Tony

Scene 11: Judy Releases Eddie
"James" ....Judy and Eddie

Scene 12: Eddie Attains Grace
"River of Dreams/Keeping the Faith/Only the Good Die Young" ....Eddie and Ensemble

Scene 13: The Reunion Begins
"I've Loved These Days" ....Tony, Brenda, Eddie and Ensemble

Scene 14: Reunion/Finale
"Scenes From an Italian Restaurant (Reprise)" ....The Company

---

WEDNESDAY MATINEE & SATURDAY MATINEE

Eddie ....CHARLIE HODGES

Brenda ....KARINE PLANTADIT

Tony ....CODY GREEN

Judy ....MABEL MODRONO

James ....ERIC OTTO

Sergeant O'Leary/Drill Sergeant ....SCOTT WISE

Piano/Lead Vocals ....WADE PRESTON

UNDERSTUDIES

For Eddie –
CODY GREEN, CHARLIE HODGES,
MARTY LAWSON, LAWRENCE RABSON

For Brenda –
CAROLYN DOHERTY, LORIN LATARRO,
MEG PAUL, KARINE PLANTADIT

For Tony –
MICHAEL BALDERRAMA, IAN CARNEY,
CODY GREEN, LAWRENCE RABSON

For Judy –
MELISSA DOWNEY, MEG PAUL,
MABEL MODRONO

For James –
ALEX BRADY, CODY GREEN, CHARLIE HODGES,
BRIAN LETENDRE, ERIC OTTO

For Sergeant O'Leary/Drill Sergeant –
MICHAEL BALDERRAMA, IAN CARNEY,
TIGER MARTINA

For Piano/Lead Vocals –
WADE PRESTON, HENRY HAID

THE MOVIN' OUT BAND

Piano/Lead Vocals – MICHAEL CAVANAUGH

Leader/Guitar – TOMMY BYRNES

Keyboard – WADE PRESTON

Lead Guitar – DENNIS DELGAUDIO

Bass – GREG SMITH

Drums – CHUCK BÜRGI

Lead Sax/Percussion – JOHN SCARPULLA

Sax – SCOTT KREITZER

Trumpet – CARL FISCHER

Trombone/Whistler/Vocals – KEVIN OSBORNE

Music Coordinator – John Miller

Movin' Out

John Selya
Eddie

Elizabeth Parkinson
Brenda

Keith Roberts
Tony

Ashley Tuttle
Judy

Scott Wise
*Sgt. O'Leary/
Drill Sgt./
Assistant Director &
Choreographer*

Benjamin G. Bowman
James

Michael Cavanaugh
Piano/Lead Vocals

Michael Balderrama
Ensemble

Alexander Brady
Ensemble

Ian Carney
*Swing/Dance
Captain*

Ron DeJesus
Ensemble

Carolyn Doherty
Swing

Melissa Downey
Ensemble

Pascale Faye
Ensemble

Trey Gillen
Swing

Cody Green
Swing/matinee Tony

Henry Haid
*Understudy
Piano/Lead Vocal*

Charlie Hodges
*Swing/matinee
Eddie*

Travis Kelley
Swing

Lorin Latarro
Swing

Marty Lawson
Swing

Brian Letendre
Swing

Tiger Martina
Ensemble

Mabel Modrono
*Swing/ matinee
Judy*

Jill Nicklaus
Ensemble

Rika Okamoto
Ensemble

Eric Otto
*Swing/matinee
James*

Meg Paul
*Swing/
Dance Captain*

Karine Plantadit
*Ensemble/
matinee Brenda*

Justin Peck
Ensemble

Wade Preston
*Synthesizer/
matinee Piano/Lead
Vocals*

Lawrence Rabson
*Swing/
matinee Eddie*

Greg Smith
Bass

Jessica Walker
Swing

Ryan Watkinson
Swing

Movin' Out

Twyla Tharp
Conception, Choreography, Direction

Billy Joel
Music & Lyrics

Santo Loquasto
Scenic Design

Suzy Benzinger
Costume Design

Donald Holder
Lighting Design

Paul Huntley
Hair Designer

John Miller
Music Coordinator

Kim Vernace
Production Stage Manager

Terry Allen Kramer
Producer

James M. Nederlander
Producer

James L. Nederlander
Producer

Hal Luftig
Producer

Emanuel Azenberg
Executive Producer

ALUMNI 2005-2006

Kristine Bendul
Ensemble

Timothy W. Bish
Swing

Christopher Body
Swing/ Understudy Eddie, James, Tony

Stuart Capps
Swing/ Understudy James, Tony, Sergeant O'Leary, Drill Sergeant

Kurt Froman
Swing/ Understudy James

Philip Gardner
Ensemble, Understudy Sergeant O'Leary, Drill Sergeant

Darren Holden
Piano/Lead Vocals

Marc Mann
Swing

Lynda Sing
Ensemble/Swing

Michael Snipe, Jr.
Ensemble/Swing

Ron Todorowski
Swing/ Understudy Eddie

TRANSFER STUDENTS 2005-2006

Stuart Capps
Swing/ Understudy James, Tony, Sergeant O'Leary, Drill Sergeant

Mary Nesvaba
Swing

Movin' Out

Photos by Ben Strothmann

CREW
Front Row (L-R): Angie Simpson Phillips (Wardrobe Supervisor), Alicia Aballi (Stitcher), Shannon Koger (Dresser), Robin Baxter (Hair Dresser), Andrea Gonzalez (Dresser), Cheree Collucelli, Laisi Rogovin (Dresser), Russell Easley (Dresser), Caroline Ranald Curvan (Asst. Stage Manager), Stacy Caddell (Dance Supervisor).
Second Row (L-R): Duke Wilson (Automation), Linda Lee (Production Wardrobe Supervisor), Fred Mecionis, Jack Curtain, Lara Greene (Dresser), Brian Frankel, Sean Quinn (House Engineer), Dan Tramon (Synthesizer Programmer), Betty Gillispie (Dresser), Kim Vernace (PSM).
Third Row (L-R): Stuart Capps (Swing), Angelo Grasso (Flyman), Charles Dague (Head Props), Sean Hughes (Automation), John Senter (Production Monitor Engineer), Jack Culver (Production Electrician).
Back Row (L-R): Tommy Maher, Kevin Camus (House Carpenter), Mike "Jesey" Van Nest (Front Light Operator), Joe Ippolito (Head Carpenter), Janet Netzke (Dresser) and Gregory Victor (Stage Manager).

THE BAND
Back Row (L-R): Dave Richards (Bass), Michael Cavanaugh (Piano/Lead Vocal), Dennis DelGaudio (Lead Guitar), Scott Burrows, Doug Kistner, Unidentified and Tobias Ralph (Drums).
Front Row (L-R): Carl Fischer (Trumpet) and Scott Kreitzer (Saxophone).

Not Pictured: Tommy Byrnes (Leader/Guitar), Wade Preston (Keyboard), Greg Smith (Bass), Chuck Bürgi (Drums), John Scarpulla (Lead Sax/Percussion), Kevin Osborne (Trombone/Vocals/Whistler).

FRONT OF HOUSE STAFF
Front Row (L to R): Maureen Dabreo (Usherette), Dianne Hosang (Usherette), Frances Eppy (Usherette), Carmen Frank (Usherette), Beverly Thornton (Usherette), Eileen Roig (Usherette), Barbara Rodell (Usherette), Rosanne Kelly (Usherette), and Dorothy Darby (Usherette).
Middle Row (L-R): Darnell Smith (Usher), Nadiah Earle (Usherette), Robyn Corrigan (Usherette), Joseph Melchiorre (Usher) and Vinceta Gishard (Usherette).
Back Row (L-R): Jacqueline Corrigan (Usherette), Kevin Corrigan (Usher), Giovanny Lopez (Usherette), Richard Dahlia (Usher), Robert Rea (Usher) and Timothy Pettolina (House Manager).

Movin' Out

STAFF FOR *MOVIN' OUT*

GENERAL MANAGER
ABBIE M. STRASSLER

COMPANY MANAGER
SHELLEY OTT

PRODUCTION ASSOCIATE
GINGER MONTEL

PRESS REPRESENTATIVE
BARLOW•HARTMAN

Michael Hartman	John Barlow
Carol R. Fineman	Leslie Baden

CASTING
JAY BINDER CASTING
Jay Binder CSA, Jack Bowdan CSA,
Mark Brandon, Laura Stanczyk,
Sarah Prosser

DANCE SUPERVISOR
Stacy Caddell

Production Stage Manager ....Kim Vernace
Stage Manager ....Gregory Victor
Assistant Stage Manager ....Caroline Ranald Curvan
Associate Company Manager ....Eduardo Castro
Assistant Director/Choreographer ....Scott Wise
Dance Captains ....Ian Carney, Meg Paul

Associate Set Designer ....David Swayze
Associate Costume Designer ....Rory Powers
Associate Lighting Designers ....Jeanne Koenig,
Karen Spahn
First Assistant Lighting Designer ....Michelle Habeck
Assistant Lighting Designers ....Hilary Manners,
Traci Klainer, Thomas Hague
Associate Lighting Design/
Automated Lighting ....Aland Henderson
Associate Hair Designer ....Amy Solomon

Assistant Set Designer ....Emily Beck
Assistant Costume Designer ....Mitchell Bloom
Assistant Sound Designer ....Janet Smith
Assistant Musical Supervisor ....David Rosenthal
Sound Effects ....Randy Hansen
Technical Supervision ....Theatretech, Inc./Brian Lynch
Production Carpenter ....Michael Connors
Head Carpenter ....Joe Ippolito
Flyman ....Angelo Grasso
Automation ....Duke Wilson, Sean Hughes
Production Electrician ....Jack Culver
Front Light Operator ....Mike Van Nest
Moving Light Operator ....Bruce Liebenow
Production Properties ....George Wagner
Head Props ....Augie Mericola
Production Sound Engineer ....Dan Tramontozzi
Production Monitor Engineer ....Craig Van Tassel
Production Wardrobe Supervisor ....Linda Lee
Wardrobe Supervisor ....Angie Simpson Phillips
Asst. Wardrobe Supervisor ....Jennifer Griggs
Dressers ....Betty Gillispie, Janet Netzke,
Timothy Hanlon, Nicholas Staub,

Russell Easley, Laisi Rogovin,
Lara Greene, Shannon Koger,
Tracey Boone
Stitcher ....Alicia Aballi
Laundry ....Ruth Goya
Production Hair Supervisor ....Natasha Steinhagen
Hair Dresser ....Marion Geist
Music Copying ....John Leonard
Assistant to Mr. Miller ....Matthew P. Ettinger
Assistant to Mr. Joel ....Stepanie Rosenzweig
Production Assistants ....Megan Durden, Victor Lukas,
Tessa Peterson
Research/Historian ....Gregory Victor
Drill Instruction ....Stephan Wolfert
Company Orthopedist ....Dr. Philip Bauman
Company Physical Therapists ....Physio Arts, PLLC
Company Massage Therapist ....Russ Beasley
Makeup Design ....M•A•C Cosmetics/
Patrick Eichler
Banking ....JPMorgan Chase/Richard Callian
Payroll ....Castellana Services, Inc./Lance Castellana
Assistant to Mr. Luftig ....Shannon R. Morrison
Accountants ....Fried and Kowgios CPAs LLP
Robert Fried, CPA
Sarah Galbraith
Insurance ....Tanenbaum Harber of FL, LLC
Carol A. Bressi-Cilona
Legal Counsel ....Lazarus & Harris LLP/
Scott R. Lazarus, Esq.,
Robert C. Harris, Esq.,
David H. Friedlander, Esq.
Immigration Counsel ....Shannon K. Such,
Attorney At Law
Press Office Manager ....Bethany Larsen
Advertising ....Serino Coyne, Inc./Angelo Desimini,
Diane Niedzialek
Marketing ....TMG The Marketing Group/
Tanya Grubich, Laura Matalon, Trish Santini,
Bob Bucci, Erica Lynn Schwartz
Education Program ....StudentsLive/Amy Weinstein,
Laura Sullivan, Marcie Sturiale
Production Photographer ....Joan Marcus
Onstage Merchandising ....George Fenmore/
More Merchandising International
Souvenir Merchandising ....Clear Channel Entertainment/
Larry Turk
Theater Displays ....King Displays, Inc.
Group Sales ....Nederlander Group Sales
Travel Agency ....Tzell Travel/The "A" Team
Opening Night
Coordination ......Tobak-Dantchik Events & Promotions/
Suzanne Tobak, Jeffry Gray

Classical pieces performed by Stuart Malina. Classical pieces
recorded and produced by David Rosenthal.

CREDITS
Scenery and Automation by Hudson Scenic Studio, Inc.
Lighting equipment by GSD. Sound equipment by Sound
Associates, Inc. Costumes executed by D. Barak Stribling,
Carelli Costumes, Euroco Costumes, Schneeman Studios,
Seamless Costumes, Donna Langman Studio, Barbara
Matera Ltd. and Tricorne New York City. Fabric painting
and aging by Jeffrey Fender and Dean Batten. Custom
footware by La Duca, JC Theatrical and T.O. Dey. Wigs by

Paul Huntley. Makeup provided by M•A•C. Rehearsed at
the New 42nd Street Studios. Clearances provided by
Wendy Cohen. Military surplus items provided by S-4
Military Surplus Hackensack, NJ. Military uniforms by Jim
Korn/Kaufman's Army Navy Surplus. Natural herb cough
drops courtesy of Ricola USA, Inc.

SPECIAL THANKS
Elizabeth Nehls, Terence Dale, Matt Stern, Jim Corona, Jesse
Huot, Sony Music Studios (Mike Negri & Daphne Walter),
Prism Production Services, David O'Brien, Erica Schwartz,
Kurzweil/Jeff Allen, American Ballet Theatre, City Center,
Dana Calanan, Cameron Roberts, Larry Moss, Claire
Mercuri, Teddy Krause, Lee Eastman and Ed London.

BAND CREDITS
Mr. Bürgi uses Tama drums, Paiste cymbals, Pro-Mark
drumsticks. Mr. Smith uses Hartke amplification, GMP 5-
string basses and Fender basses, Mr. DelGaudio uses pedal
boards from Pedalboards.com. Mr. Scarpulla uses Vandoren
reeds distributed by J. D'addario & Co., SKB cases and Kiwi
wind products. Mr. Byrnes uses Gibson guitars, Marshall
amplifiers and B'Aquisto strings. Mr. Danielian uses
Calicchio trumpets, custom mouthpieces by GR
Technologies. Support provided by Yamaha Artist Services.
Piano custom built by Young Chang America.

Yamaha is the official piano of the
Nederlander Organization.

Drumheads courtesy of Evans Drumheads.

MUSIC CREDITS
All compositions written by Billy Joel
and published by Impulsive Music (ASCAP)
and Joelsongs (BMI).

Original cast recording available on SONY CLASSICAL

NEDERLANDER

Chairman	**James M. Nederlander**
President	**James L. Nederlander**

Executive Vice President
Nick Scandalios

Vice President•	Senior Vice President•
Corporate Development	Labor Relations
Charlene S. Nederlander	**Herschel Waxman**

Vice President	Chief Financial Officer
Jim Boese	**Freida Sawyer Belviso**

HOUSE STAFF FOR
THE RICHARD RODGERS THEATRE
House Manager ....Timothy Pettolina
Box Office Treasurer ....Fred Santore Jr.
Assistant Treasurer ....Daniel Nitopi
Electrician...................................Steve Carver
Carpenter ....Kevin Camus
Propertymaster ....Steve DeVerna
Engineer ....Sean Quinn

Movin' Out
SCRAPBOOK

1. Elizabeth Parkinson and John Selya take part in the "Stars in the Alley" event in Shubert Alley.
2. Parkinson and Scott Wise at the opening night for *The Odd Couple* at the Brooks Atkinson Theatre.

Correspondent 1: Greg Smith, musician.

Anniversary Party: For our first Christmas party Billy Joel rented out a nice Italian restaurant and played Christmas carols for us all night.

Celebrity Visitors: There have been many. Ex Israeli prime minister Ariel Sharon, Dick Gephardt, Hillary Clinton, Jack Nicholson, Nicole Kidman, Jason Alexander, Henry Winkler and Christopher Reeve.

Which Actor Performed the Most Roles: Probably Lawrence Rabson who has done the roles of Eddie, Tony, and various ensemble roles.

Most Shows: In the band that would probably be Wade Preston who not only is the Matinee Piano man, but when Michael Cavanaugh is Piano man, Wade plays synth.

"Carols for a Cure" Carol: "Jingle Bells."

"Gypsy of the Year" Sketch: "One Perfect Sunrise" by Ron DeJesus, music by Orbital.

Special Backstage Rituals: For the band, Patron Tequila.

Favorite Moment During Each Performance: Probably off stage just laughing with the guys in the band and ranking on subs. Onstage would probably be the "Keeping the Faith" / "River of Dreams" / "Only the Good Die Young" medley.

In-Theatre Gathering Place: Band dressing room

Favorite Off-Site Hangout: Definitely McHale's and we're all sorry to see it closing.

Favorite Snack Food: Popcorn

Memorable Ad Lib: When Michael Cavanaugh left out part of "Goodnight Saigon." Watching the dancers "wing it" was amazing. Nobody knew what a big screw-up it was!

Stage Door Fan Encounter: Stage door encounters always surprise me. Sometimes there are a ton of people, other times nobody. They always make you feel appreciated.

Fastest Costume Change: During "We Didn't Start the Fire" when the male principals change almost instantly from street clothes to army fatigues including flak jacket.

Busiest Day at the Box Office: The busiest week was Christmas 2004, so probably sometime that week.

Heaviest/Hottest Costume: Probably Eddie with a leather biker jacket and blue jeans.

Who Wore the Least: The female ensemble during "Captain Jack." One of my favorite moments!

Sweethearts Within the Company: Quite a few that didn't last.

Orchestra Member Who Played the Most Consecutive Performances Without a Sub: Wade Preston or Dennis DelGaudio.

Who Played the Most Instruments: Probably John Scarpulla. Tenor sax, baritone sax, alto sax, tambourine, triangle and the in-house contractor.

Embarassing Moment: Probably when one of the ensemble girls fell off the stage into the audience.

Company Legends: The two incredibly talented dancers that are no longer with us: William Marrie and Mark Arvin.

Coolest Thing About Being in This Show: The camaraderie between dancers and musicians and the brotherhood that was formed within the band members. I'm told it isn't always like that on Broadway. I've met some of the most amazing people working on this show and would consider it an honor to work with any of them again. It was the most memorable three years of my life.

Correspondent 2: Travis Kelley, Swing.

Most Roles: Ian Carney

Most Shows: Ashley Tuttle

Backstage Rituals: When Jill Nicklaus gives me her special massage in the Michael Balderrama track after "Italian Restaurant."

Favorite Moment: Getting pumped up in the wings before "Angry Young Man."

In-Theatre Gathering Place: Male Swing dressing room.

Mascot: "Charlie the bad dancer."

Favorite Therapy: Cheap beer.

Memorable Ad-Lib: Watching Keith, Marty, and Scott dance "Movin' Out" without a car.

Fastest Costume Change: Justin track— "Captain Jack" into "Innocent Man"—33 seconds to completely undress halter top, glasses, head wrap, heels, and scarf, and put on shirt, pants, belt, SOCKS, and shoes, and get to the other side of the stage.

Most Minimal Costume: Rika Okamoto by design, Karine Plantadit by personal choice.

Sweethearts Within the Company: Alex Brady and Rika Okamoto.

Best In-House Parody Lyric: Jill Nicklaus: Instead of ". . . I'm Shameless" says, "I Shave This"!

Memorable Directorial Note: On different occasions: "That choice you made during _____? Don't."

Nickname: Baby Giraffe.

Embarrassing Moments: 1. Farting really loudly at my first rehearsal. 2. Joking around during the bows (curtain still up) and turning to exit, only to smack my face on the boom.

Coolest Thing About Being in This Show: Awesome dancing, great people, and bellbottoms!

A Naked Girl on the Appian Way

First Preview: September 13, 2005. Opened: October 6, 2005.
Closed December 4, 2005 after 27 Previews and 69 Performances.

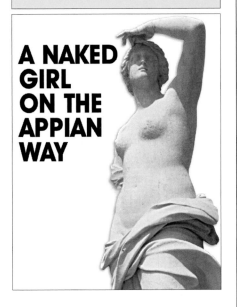

PLAYBILL®

A NAKED GIRL ON THE APPIAN WAY

CAST
(in order of appearance)

Bess Lapin	JILL CLAYBURGH
Jeffrey Lapin	RICHARD THOMAS
Sadie	ANN GUILBERT
Elaine	LESLIE AYVAZIAN
Juliet Lapin	SUSAN KELECHI WATSON
Thad Lapin	MATTHEW MORRISON
Bill Lapin	JAMES YAEGASHI

TIME AND PLACE

Present day. A beautiful house in some Hampton.
Early June.

UNDERSTUDIES/STANDBYS

For Bess Lapin:
CHARLOTTE MAIER

For Jeffrey Lapin:
RAY VIRTA

For Juliet Lapin:
PHYLLIS JOHNSON

For Thad Lapin:
TERRENCE RIORDAN

For Bill Lapin:
JAMES SEOL

For Sadie:
NANCY FRANKLIN

For Elaine:
CHARLOTTE MAIER

Production Stage Manager: LESLIE C. LYTER
Stage Manager: AMY PATRICIA STERN

Special thanks to Marc Felix, culinary consultant.

AMERICAN AIRLINES THEATRE

ROUNDABOUT THEATRE COMPANY
TODD HAIMES, Artistic Director
HAROLD WOLPERT, Managing Director
JULIA C. LEVY, Executive Director

Presents

Jill Clayburgh   Richard Thomas
in

A NAKED GIRL ON THE APPIAN WAY

by
Richard Greenberg

with

Matthew Morrison   Susan Kelechi Watson   James Yaegashi
Leslie Ayvazian   Ann Guilbert

Set Design John Lee Beatty	*Costume Design* Catherine Zuber	*Lighting Design* Peter Kaczorowski	*Original Music and Sound Design* David Van Tieghem
Production Stage Manager Leslie C. Lyter	*Casting by* Jim Carnahan, C.S.A. Mele Nagler, C.S.A. Joanne DeNaut	*Technical Supervisor* Steve Beers	*General Managers* Sydney Beers Nichole Larson
Founding Director Gene Feist	*Associate Artistic Director* Scott Ellis	*Press Representative* Boneau/Bryan-Brown	*Director of Marketing* David B. Steffen

Directed by
Doug Hughes

Commissioned and first produced by South Coast Repertory.
Roundabout Theatre Company is a member of the League of Resident Theatres.
www.roundabouttheatre.org

10/6/05

(L-R): Jill Clayburgh, Susan Kelechi Watson, Richard Thomas and Matthew Morrison.

Photo by Joan Marcus

A Naked Girl on the Appian Way

Jill Clayburgh
Bess Lapin

Richard Thomas
Jeffrey Lapin

Matthew Morrison
Thad Lapin

Susan Kelechi Watson
Juliet Lapin

James Yaegashi
Bill Lapin

Leslie Ayvazian
Elaine

Ann Guilbert
Sadie

Nancy Franklin
Understudy Sadie

Phyllis Johnson
*Understudy
Juliet Lapin*

Charlotte Maier
*Understudy
Bess Lapin, Elaine*

Terrence Riordan
*Understudy
Thad Lapin*

James Seol
*Understudy
Bill Lapin*

Ray Virta
*Understudy
Jeffrey Lapin*

Richard Greenberg
Playwright

Doug Hughes
Director

John Lee Beatty
Set Design

Catherine Zuber
Costume Design

Peter Kaczorowski
Lighting Design

Jim Carnahan
Casting

Todd Haimes
*Artistic Director,
Roundabout Theatre
Company*

Gene Feist
*Founding Director
Roundabout Theatre
Company*

James Yaegashi and
Jill Clayburgh.

Matthew Morrison
and
Susan Kelechi
Watson.

Photos by Joan Marcus

A Naked Girl on the Appian Way

ROUNDABOUT THEATRE COMPANY STAFF
ARTISTIC DIRECTOR ....TODD HAIMES
MANAGING DIRECTOR .... HAROLD WOLPERT
EXECUTIVE DIRECTOR ....JULIA C. LEVY
ASSOCIATE ARTISTIC DIRECTOR ..SCOTT ELLIS

ARTISTIC STAFF
DIRECTOR OF ARTISTIC DEVELOPMENT/
DIRECTOR OF CASTING ....Jim Carnahan
Artistic Consultant ....Robyn Goodman
Resident Director ....Michael Mayer
Associate Artists ....Scott Elliott, Doug Hughes,
Bill Irwin, Joe Mantello
Consulting Dramaturg ....Jerry Patch
Artistic Assistant ....Jill Rafson
Casting Director ....Mele Nagler
Casting Associate ....Carrie Gardner
Casting Associate .............................J.V. Mercanti
Casting Assistant ....Kate Schwabe
Casting Assistant ....Stephen Kopel
Artistic Intern ....Deborah Friedman

EDUCATION STAFF
EDUCATION DIRECTOR ....Megan Kirkpatrick
Director of Instruction and
Curriculum Development ....Renee Flemings
Education Program Associate ....Lindsay Erb
Education Program Associate ....Stacey L. Morris
Education Assistant ....Cassidy Jones
Education Intern ....Amelia Stanley
Education Dramaturg ....Ted Sod
Teaching Artists ....Zakiyyah Alexander,
Phil Alexander, Cynthia Babak,
Victor Barbella, Brigitte Barnett-Loftis,
Caitlin Barton, Joe Basile, LaTonya Borsay,
Bonnie Brady, Mike Carnahan, Joe Clancy,
Melissa Denton, Stephen DiMenna,
Joe Doran, Tony Freeman,
Sheri Graubert, Susan Hamburger,
Karla Hendrick, Jim Jack, Alvin Keith,
Rebecca Lord, Erin McCready,
Andrew Ondrejcak, Laura Poe,
Nicole Press, Chris Rummel,
Drew Sachs, Anna Saggese, David Sinkus,
Vickie Tanner, Olivia Tsang,
Jennifer Varbalow, Leese Walker,
Eric Wallach, Diana Whitten,
Gail Winar, Kirche Zeile

ADMINISTRATIVE STAFF
GENERAL MANAGER ....Sydney Beers
Associate Managing Director ....Greg Backstrom
General Manager of the
Steinberg Center.........................Don-Scott Cooper
General Counsel ....Nancy Hirschmann
Office Manager ....Scott Kelly
Human Resources Manager ....Stephen Deutsch
Network Systems Manager ....Jeff Goodman
Manager of Corporate and Party Rentals ....Jetaun Dobbs
Facilities Manager ....Keith A. Smalls
Assistant to the General Manager ....Maggie Cantrick
Management Assistant ....Nicholas Caccavo
MIS Associate ....Lloyd Alvarez
MIS Associate ....Anthony Foti
Receptionists..............Candice Alustiza, Andre Fortson,
Elisa Papa, Monica Sidorchuk,
Nina Wheeler
Messenger ....Robert Weisser
Management Intern ....Tania Camargo

FINANCE STAFF
CONTROLLER ....Susan Neiman
Assistant Controller..........................John LaBarbera
Accounts Payable Administrator ....Frank Surdi
Customer Service Coordinator ....Trina Cox
Business Office Associate ....David Solomon
Financial Associate ....Yonit Kafka
Business Intern ....Myra Wong

DEVELOPMENT STAFF
DIRECTOR OF DEVELOPMENT ....Jeffory Lawson
Director, Institutional Giving ....Julie K. D'Andrea
Director, Individual Giving ....Julia Lazarus
Director, Special Events ....Steve Schaeffer
Manager, Donor Information Systems ....Tina Mae Bishko
Capital Campaign Manager ....Mark Truscinski
Manager, Friends of RTC ....Jeff Collins
Institutional Giving Associate ....Kristen Bolibruch
Development Assistant ....Stephenie L. Overton
Assistant to the Executive Director ....Robert Weinstein
Patrons Services Assistant ....Dawn Kusinski
Development Assistant ....Chelsea Glickfield
Individual Giving Assistant ....Dominic Yacobozzi
Special Events Assistant ....Ginger Vallen
Individual Giving Intern ....Alicia Hogan
Special Event Intern ....Katie Cush

MARKETING STAFF
DIRECTOR OF MARKETING ....David B. Steffen
Marketing/Publications Manager ....Tim McCanna
Marketing Associate ....Sunil Ayyagari
Marketing Associate ....Rebecca Ballon
Website Consultant ....Keith Powell Beyland
Marketing Intern ....Ruth Fink
DIRECTOR OF TELESALES
SPECIAL PROMOTIONS ....Tony Baksa
Telesales Manager ....Anton Borissov
Telesales Office Coordinator ....................J.W. Griffin

TICKET SERVICES STAFF
DIRECTOR OF SALES OPERATIONS ..Jim Seggelink
Ticket Services Manager ....Ellen Holt
Subscription Manager ....Charlie Garbowski
Box Office Managers ....Edward P. Osborne,
Jaime Perlman, Jessica Bowser
Group Sales Manager ....Jeff Monteith
Assistant Box Office Managers ..Paul Caspary, Steve Howe,
Robert Morgan
Assistant Ticket Services Managers ....Robert Kane,
David Meglino, Ethan Ubell
Ticket Services ....Solangel Bido,
Daniel Carlisle, Andrew Clements,
Nisha Dhruna, Adam Elsberry,
Lindsay Ericson, Scott Falkowski,
Catherine Fitzpatrick, Amanda Genovese,
Tova Heller, Dottie Kenul,
Bill Klemm, Alexander LaFrance,
Krystin MacRitchie, Mead Margulies,
Chuck Migliaccio, Carlos Morris,
Nicole Nicholson, Jillian Owdier,
Adam Owens, Shannon Paige,
Thomas Protulipac, Amy Robinson,
Jacki Rocha, Heather Siebert,
Monté Smock, Lillian Soto,
Greg Thorson, Ryan Weible
Ticket Services Intern ....Lauren Cartelli

SERVICES
Counsel ....Jeremy Nussbaum,
Cowan, Liebowitz & Latman, P.C.
Counsel ....Rosenberg & Estis
Counsel ....Rubin and Feldman, P.C.
Counsel ....Andrew Lance,
Gibson, Dunn, & Crutcher, LLP
Counsel ....Harry H. Weintraub,
Glick and Weintraub, P.C.
Immigration Counsel ....Mark D. Koestler and
Theodore Ruthizer
House Physicians ....Dr. Theodore Tyberg,
Dr. Lawrence Katz
House Dentist ....Neil Kanner, D.M.D.
Insurance ....Marsh USA Inc.
Accountant ....Brody, Weiss, Zucarelli &
Urbanek CPAs, P.C.
Advertising ....Eliran Murphy Group/Denise Ganjou
Events Photography ....Anita and Steve Shevett
Production Photographer ....Joan Marcus

Theatre Displays..............King Displays, Wayne Sapper

MANAGING DIRECTOR EMERITUS ....Ellen Richard

Roundabout Theatre Company
231 West 39th Street, New York, NY 10018
(212) 719-9393.

GENERAL PRESS REPRESENTATIVES
BONEAU / BRYAN-BROWN

Adrian Bryan-Brown   Matt Polk
Jessica Johnson   Joe Perrotta

CREDITS FOR
A NAKED GIRL ON THE APPIAN WAY

GENERAL MANAGERS ....Sydney Beers and
Nichole Larson
Company Manager ....Denys Baker
Production Stage Manager ....Leslie C. Lyter
Stage Manager ....Amy Patricia Stern
Assistant Director ....Mark Schneider
Assistant Set Designers ....Eric Renschler,
Yoshi Tanokura
Assistant Costume Designer ....David Newell
Assistant Lighting Designer ....Aaron Spivey
Associate Sound Designer ....Jill BC DuBoff
Dialect Consultant ....Kate Mare
Assistant Technical Supervisor ....Elisa Kuhar
Production Carpenter ....Glenn Merwede
Production Electrician ....Brian Maiuri
House Properties ....Andrew Forste
Wardrobe Supervisor ....Susan J. Fallon
Sound Engineer ....Dann Wojnar
Dressers ....Melissa Crawford
Properties Supervisor ....Denise Grillo
Properties Assistant ....Kevin Crawford
Production Assistant ....Lauren B. Conlon
IATSE Apprentice ....Jill Anania
Scenery constructed by ....Great Lakes Scenic Studios
Scenic drop provided by ....Paper Mill Playhouse
Sound equipment provided by ....Sound Associates
Lighting equipment provided by ....PRG Lighting
Plumbing products by ....Kohler Co.
Special thanks to ....Lincoln Center Theater

Roundabout Theatre Company would like to thank
Goldman Associates of New York for their generous donation of the Sub Zero refrigerator and Wolf oven range.

MUSIC CREDIT
"Heart" by Richard Adler and Jerry Ross, ©1955, renewed
Lakshmi Puja Music and J&J Ross Music. Permission
secured. All rights reserved.

AMERICAN AIRLINES THEATRE STAFF
General Manager ....Sydney Beers
House Carpenter ....Glenn Merwede
House Electrician ....Brian Maiuri
Wardrobe Supervisor ....Susan J. Fallon
Box Office Manager ....Edward P. Osborne
House Manager ....Stephen Ryan
Associate House Managers ....Zipporah Aguasvivas,
Jack Watanachaiyot
Head Usher ....Edwin Camacho
House Staff ....Peter Breaden, Oscar Castillo,
Ruth Conley, Ilia Diaz, Anne Ezell,
Sherra Johnston, Jacklyn Rivera
Security ....Julious Russell
Additional Security Provided by ....Gotham Security
Maintenance ......Chucky Fernandez, RonHenry, Kenrick
Johnson, Maggie Western
Lobby Refreshments ....Sweet Concessions

A Naked Girl on the Appian Way
SCRAPBOOK

Photos by Aubrey Reuben

①

②

1. The cast takes curtain calls on opening night.
2. James Yaegashi, Susan Kelechi Watson and Matthew Morrison at rehearsals at the Roundabout Studios.
3. Richard Thomas, Jill Clayburgh, playwright Richard Greenberg and Roundabout Artistic Director Todd Haimes at the opening night party at The Hard Rock Cafe.

③

Correspondent: James Yaegashi, "Bill Lapin."

Celebrity Visitors: We've had lots: Dana Ivey, Patricia Clarkson, Blair Brown, Tony Roberts. Meryl Streep is very good friends with Jill Clayburgh, and she seemed to really enjoy the show. I bumped into her in the hallway, and she said, "Very nice work." Meryl came during previews, at which point we still had an intermission. She said she liked the show, but thought it could do without an intermission. The next day, we came to rehearsal and our director, Doug Hughes, cut the intermission.

Backstage Rituals: There is a brunch for the entire company every Sunday that's a lot of fun. My roommate Matt Morrison does his vocal warmups before each show. He just can't shake the habit from his musical theatre days. Matt and I take out our computers and surf the web whenever we get a chance.

Favorite Moment During Each Performance: There is one joke that comes almost at the end of the play, and it refers to the fact that there is a baby named Pearl mentioned several pages back. My line is, "As in Harbor," and it takes the audience a couple of beats to catch on. It's fun to see the audience slowly catch on to it.

Favorite Snack Food: Anything made by Susan Fallon, our wardrobe person. She used to be a pastry chef and she's an amazing cook. Any time there is an announcement that "There's food downstairs," everybody runs.

Favorite Therapy: We have Ricola candies on every level. Fallon makes this killer ginger and lemon tea. It's intense but really great.

Memorable Ad-Lib: Matt Morrison and Richard Thomas have a moment in the show that's been dangerous ever since rehearsals because it's so funny they almost crack each other up. One night they just broke. The audience saw that, and they were on the floor for a good few minutes.

Memorable Press Encounter: Our shoot for *The New Yorker* was kind of strange. The photographer was very intense and "artsy." We were, like, "Just take our picture already!" He put us in all these strange poses, and we kept going along with it with pasted smiles on our faces. At one point he gave me a toy gun with flag that says "Bang" and put dog ears on Matt. And we were going "Okaaay."

Memorable Stage Door Fan Encounter: Old ladies are always fun because they're never shy. One lady said, "You were so good, but there was one moment where you're sitting there on the couch with a cushion and the cushion kept getting in the way." And, actually, that was very helpful. Now I use my arm to push it down.

Nicknames: We call Richard and Jill "Dad" and "Mom." Before the show opened, *The Times* ran an article on Doug Hughes that spelled his name "Hayes." So now we call him "Hayes."

Coolest Thing About Being in This Show: Sharing a dressing room with Matt Morrison. Personally being in a Rich Greenberg play that's so different from anything else he's written.

The Odd Couple

First Preview: October 4, 2005. Opened: October 27, 2005.
Still running as of May 31, 2006.

CAST
(in order of appearance)

Speed .... ROB BARTLETT
Murray .... BRAD GARRETT
Roy .... PETER FRECHETTE
Vinnie .... LEE WILKOF
Oscar Madison .... NATHAN LANE
Felix Ungar .... MATTHEW BRODERICK
Gwendolyn Pigeon .... OLIVIA d'ABO
Cecily Pigeon .... JESSICA STONE

TIME:
1965

PLACE:
Oscar Madison's Riverside Drive apartment

ACT I
Scene 1: A hot summer night
Scene 2: Two weeks later, about 11 PM

ACT II
Scene 1: A few days later, about 8 PM
Scene 2: The next evening, about 7:30 PM

UNDERSTUDIES

For Felix Ungar:
PETER FRECHETTE

For Oscar Madison, Murray, Speed, Roy, Vinnie:
GENE GABRIEL

For Felix Ungar, Murray, Speed, Roy, Vinnie:
MARC GRAPEY

For Gwendolyn Pigeon, Cecily Pigeon:
CHRISTY PUSZ

BROOKS ATKINSON THEATRE
UNDER THE DIRECTION OF JAMES M. NEDERLANDER AND JAMES L. NEDERLANDER

Ira Pittelman   Jeffrey Sine   Ben Sprecher   Max Cooper   Scott E. Nederlander   and   Emanuel Azenberg
Present

NATHAN LANE   MATTHEW BRODERICK
IN
NEIL SIMON'S

THE ODD COUPLE

With
Rob Bartlett   Olivia d'Abo   Peter Frechette
Jessica Stone   Lee Wilkof
And
BRAD GARRETT

Scenic Design	Costume Design	Lighting Design
John Lee Beatty	Ann Roth	Kenneth Posner

Sound Design	Original Music	Casting
Peter Fitzgerald	Marc Shaiman	Bernard Telsey Casting

Hair Design	Production Stage Manager	Technical Supervision
David Brian Brown	William Joseph Barnes	Brian Lynch

Associate Producers	Press Representative	General Manager
Roy Furman & Jay Binder	Bill Evans & Associates	Abbie M. Strassler

Directed by
JOE MANTELLO

10/27/05

(L-R):
Matthew Broderick
and Nathan Lane

Photo by Chris Callas

The Odd Couple

Nathan Lane
Oscar Madison

Matthew Broderick
Felix Ungar

Brad Garrett
Murray

Rob Bartlett
Speed

Olivia d'Abo
Gwendolyn Pigeon

Peter Frechette
Roy

Jessica Stone
Cecily Pigeon

Lee Wilkof
Vinnie

Gene Gabriel
*Understudy for
Oscar Madison,
Murray, Speed, Roy,
Vinnie*

Marc Grapey
*Understudy for
Felix Ungar, Murray,
Speed, Roy, Vinnie*

Christy Pusz
*Understudy for
Gwendolyn Pigeon,
Cecily Pigeon*

Neil Simon
Playwright

Joe Mantello
Director

John Lee Beatty
Scenic Design

Ann Roth
Costume Design

Kenneth Posner
Lighting Design

Marc Shaiman
Original Music

Bernard Telsey,
Bernard Telsey
Casting, C.S.A
Casting

David Brian Brown
Hair Design

Roy Furman
Associate Producer

Jay Binder
Associate Producer

Ben Sprecher
Producer

Emanuel Azenberg
Producer

Kate Blumberg
*Understudy for
Gwendolyn*

Mike Starr
Murray

The Odd Couple

STAGE CREW
Front Row (L-R): Augie Mericola (Head Props), William (Billy) Joseph Barnes (Production Supervisor), Jill Cordle (Stage Manager), Michael Attianese, Joseph DePaulo (House Properties).
Second Row (L-R): Manuel Becker (Production Electrician), Carmel Vargyas, Richard Costabile (Stage Manager), Ken Brown (Star Dresser), Wallace Flores (Production Sound Engineer), Douglas Petitjean (Wardrobe Supervisor), Kelly Smith (Dresser), Mark Trezza (Star Dresser), Maura Clifford (Dresser), Danny Paulos (Props), Thomas A. Lavaia (House Carpenter).

FRONT OF HOUSE STAFF
Front Row (L-R): Kimberlee Imperato, Brenda Brauer (Head Usher), Barbara Carrellas (Theatre Manager), Khadija Dib.
Middle Row (L-R): Marie Gonzalez, Judith Pirouz, Michele Gonzalez, Stephen Flaherty.
Back Row (L-R): James Holley, Timothy Newsome, Arlene Reilly, Robert Prensa.

The Odd Couple

STAFF FOR *THE ODD COUPLE*

GENERAL MANAGEMENT
ABBIE M. STRASSLER

COMPANY MANAGER
JOHN E. GENDRON

GENERAL PRESS REPRESENTATIVE
BILL EVANS & ASSOCIATES
JIM RANDOLPH

CASTING
BERNARD TELSEY CASTING, C.S.A.:
Bernie Telsey, Will Cantler, David Vaccari,
Bethany Knox, Craig Burns, Tiffany Little Canfield,
Stephanie Yankwitt, Betsy Sherwood

ASSISTANT DIRECTOR
Lisa Leguillou

Production Supervisor ....William Joseph Barnes
Stage Manager ....Jill Cordle
Associate Scenic Designer ....Eric Renschler
Assistant Scenic Designer ....Yoshi Tanokura
Assistant Costume Designer ....John Glaser
Associate Lighting Designer ....Philip Rosenberg
Associate Sound Designer ....Jill B.C. DuBoff
Technical Supervision ....Brian Lynch,
                                                                                 Neil A. Mazzella
Production Electrician ....Manuel Becker
Production Sound Engineer ....Wallace Flores
Production Properties ....George Wagner
Head Props ....Augie Mericola
Wardrobe Supervisor ....Douglas C. Petitjean
Star Dressers ....Ken Brown, Mark Trezza
Dressers ....Maura Clifford, Kelly Smith
Hair Supervisor ....Carole Morales
Makeup Design ....Angelina Avallone
Production Assistants..Annette Verga-Lagier,
                                                                                      Maura Farver
Management Assistant ....Michael Salonia
Assistant to Ms. Roth ....Melissa Haley
Asst. to Mr. Lane ....Andrea Wolfson
Asst. to Mr. Broderick ....Melanie Hansen
Accountants ....Fried & Kowgios CPAs LLP/
                                                              Robert Fried, CPA, Elliott Aronstam
Advertising...Serino Coyne Inc./Angelo Desimini
Insurance ....Tanenbaum Harber of Florida/
                                                                                      Carol Bressi-Cilona
Legal Counsel ....Brooks & Distler/
                                                               Marsha S. Brooks, Thomas R. Distler
Merchandising ....Max Merchandising
Production Photographer ....Carol Rosegg
Banking ....JPMorgan Chase/Richard Callian
Payroll Service ....Castellana Services Inc./
                                                                                      Lance Castellana
Rehearsals ....The New 42nd Street Studios
Displays...King Displays
Opening Night Coordination ....Tobak Lawrence Company/
                                                               Suzanne Tobak, Michael P. Lawrence

CREDITS AND ACKNOWLEDGEMENTS
Scenery by Hudson Scenic Studio, Inc. Lighting equipment from Hudson Sound and Light LLC. Sound equipment by Sound Associates, Inc. Costumes constructed by Werner Russold. Additional costume construction by Studio Rouge, Inc. Custom upholstery and draperies provided by Martin-Albert Interiors, Manhattan, NY. Graphic props provided by Proper Decorum, Inc., Kinnelon, NJ. Playing cards courtesy of US Playing cards, Cincinnati, OH. Utz potato chip bags provided by Utz Quality Foods, Inc., Hanover, PA. Period furniture provided by Chatsworth Auction Rooms, Mamaroneck, NY.

STAFF FOR THE BROOKS ATKINSON THEATRE
House Manager ....Barbara Carrellas
Treasurer ....Keshave Sattaur
Assistant Treasurers ....William Dorso,
                                                                                 William O'Brien,
                                                                              Mohammed Sattaur
House Carpenter ....Thomas A. Lavaia
House Flyman..Joseph J. Maher
House Properties ....Joseph P. DePaulo
House Electrician ....Manuel Becker
Engineer ....Kevin Mac

NEDERLANDER
Chairman ....**James M. Nederlander**
President ....**James L. Nederlander**

Executive Vice President
Nick Scandalios

Vice President
Corporate Development
Charlene S. Nederlander

Senior Vice President
Labor Relations
Herschel Waxman

Vice President
Jim Boese

Chief Financial Officer
Freida Sawyer Belviso

The Odd Couple
SCRAPBOOK

Photos by Aubrey Reuben

Correspondent: William Joseph Barnes, Production Stage Manager

Opening Night Gifts: The producers had ladles made for everyone with the show logo on them. Rob Bartlett had playing cards made using pictures of the cast for the face cards. We got our stage managers goldfish—they died. really fast.

Most Exciting Celebrity Visitor And What They Did/Said: Rip Taylor came a lot. A lot.

"Gypsy of the Year": Brad Garrett and Lee Wilkof were the hosts of "Gypsy of the Year."

Who Has Done the Most Shows: We're gonna say Nathan. He's pretty famous.

Special Backstage Rituals: The understudies host a talk show "Live From the Greenroom" and interview members of the cast and crew with a panel of celebrity guests.

Also, we inherited a Xerox machine from *Movin' Out* and have used it to photocopy the faces of the entire cast and crew. We have created a huge art installation in the basement with them.

Favorite Moment During Each Performance (On Stage or Off): A pickle in the audience gets them every time.

Favorite In-Theatre Gathering Place: The greenroom, it's like hanging out on the surface of the sun.

Favorite Off-Site Hangout: Joe Allen, Bar Centrale, Angus McIndoe.

Favorite Snack Food: Fruits and vegetables...preferably deep fried and dipped in chocolate.

Mascot: Suzanne Somers. Her one-woman show played in our theater immediately prior to us, and we have old programs, copies of her autobiography and cases of her bottled water hanging around.

Favorite Therapy: Emer'gen-C.

Most Memorable Ad-Libs: Felix usually tells

1. Nathan Lane and Matthew Broderick on opening night.
2. Broderick and wife Sarah Jessica Parker arrive at the theatre on opening night.
3. Cast member Olivia d'Abo (R) and son Oliver, 9, arrive at the opening night party at the Marriott Marquis Hotel.
4. Comedian Jerry Seinfeld and wife Jessica walk the red carpet into the Brooks Atkinson Theatre on opening night.

The Odd Couple
SCRAPBOOK

Oscar to "blow on" his burnt London broil. One night Matthew told Nathan to "blow it," and they both lost it.

Also Speed (Rob Bartlett) has the line "I'm three blocks away. I could be here in five minutes," but one night he said, "I live three minutes away. I can be here in five minutes." One of the legs on the couch broke and what followed was an amazing ad-lib between Matthew and Nathan about losing weight that brought the audience to tears with laughter.

Nickname: Lee Wilkof is lovingly referred to as "Pumpkin Pants."

Record Number of Cell Phone Rings During a Performance: None, but we once had a seeing-eye monkey in the audience. Seriously.

Catchphrase Only the Company Would Recognize: "Don't eat the ravioli."

Photos by Aubrey Reuben

1. Playwright Neil Simon (C) accepts applause from the cast and audience on stage opening night.
2. Guest Martin Short arrives at the Biltmore.
3. Director Joe Mantello arrives at the cast party.
4. Cast member Rob Bartlett.
5. Cast member Lee "Pumpkin Pants" Wilkof conducts an interview.
6. Guests Tom Kirdahy and playwright Terrence McNally arrive at the theatre.

On Golden Pond

First Preview: March 22, 2005. Opened: April 7, 2005.
Closed June 26, 2005 after 19 Previews and 93 Performances.

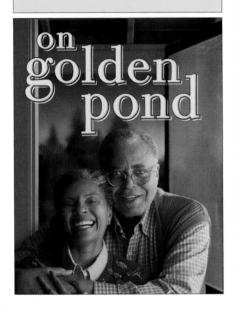

PLAYBILL

CAST
(in order of appearance)

Norman Thayer, Jr. ....JAMES EARL JONES
Ethel Thayer ....LESLIE UGGAMS
Charlie Martin ....CRAIG BOCKHORN
Chelsea Thayer Wayne ....LINDA POWELL
Billy Ray..................ALEXANDER MITCHELL
Bill Ray.....................PETER FRANCIS JAMES

TIME
The Present

PLACE
The Thayers' summer home
on Golden Pond in Maine

STANDBYS
For Norman –
CHARLES TURNER

For Ethel –
PETRONIA PALEY

For Chelsea –
OPAL ALLADIN

For Bill and Charlie –
CORNELL WOMACK

For Billy –
RYDELL ROLLINS

☒ CORT THEATRE
138 West 48th Street
A Shubert Organization Theatre

Gerald Schoenfeld, *Chairman*   Philip J. Smith, *President*

Robert E. Wankel, *Executive Vice President*

Jeffrey Finn
Arlene Scanlan
Stuart Thompson

present

JAMES EARL JONES   LESLIE UGGAMS

in

on golden pond

by

Ernest Thompson

with

Linda Powell   Peter Francis James
Craig Bockhorn   Alexander Mitchell

| Scenic Design | Costume Design | Lighting Design | Original Music and Sound Design |
| Ray Klausen | Jane Greenwood | Brian Nason | Dan Moses Schreier |

| Technical Supervisor | Production Stage Manager |
| Christopher C. Smith/Smitty | Kelley Kirkpatrick |

| Press Representative | Marketing | Casting |
| The Publicity Office | TMG The Marketing Group | Stuart Howard/Amy Schecter/ Paul Hardt |

| General Management | Associate Producers |
| Stuart Thompson Productions/ James Triner | Magnesium.com, Inc./ Neal Edelson/Andy Sawyer |

Directed by

Leonard Foglia

The Producers wish to express their appreciation to Theatre Development Fund for its support of this production.

6/1/05

Photo by Scott Suchman

(L-R): James Earl Jones, Leslie Uggams, Alexander Mitchell (lying down), Peter Francis James and Linda Powell work out family issues in *On Golden Pond*.

On Golden Pond

James Earl Jones
Norman Thayer, Jr

Leslie Uggams
Ethel Thayer

Linda Powell
Chelsea Thayer Wayne

Peter Francis James
Bill Ray

Craig Bockhorn
Charlie Martin

Alexander Mitchell
Billy Ray

Charles Turner
Standby for Norman

Petronia Paley
Standby for Ethel

Opal Alladin
Standby for Chelsea

Cornell Womack
Standby for Bill And Charlie

Rydell Rollins
Standby for Billy Ray

Ernest Thompson
Playwright

Leonard Foglia
Director

Ray Klausen
Scenic Designer

Jane Greenwood
Costume Designer

Brian Nason
Lighting Designer

Dan Moses Schreier
Original Music and Sound Designer

Christopher C. Smith,
Theatersmith, Inc.
Technical Supervisor

Stuart Thompson
Producer

Arlene Scanlan
Producer

Jeffrey Finn
Producer

STANDBYS
(L-R):
Cornell Womack,
Rydell Rollins,
Petronia Paley
and Charles Turner.

Not Pictured: Opal Alladin

Photo by Ben Strothmann

On Golden Pond

BACKSTAGE CREW
(L-R):
Grantley A. McIntyre (Hair & Makeup Supervisor), Michael S. Borowski (Press Agent), Thomas B. Grasso (Production Sound Man), James Fedigan (Production Electrician), Emiliano Pares (Original Production Prop Supervisor), Marti Mcintosh (Stage Manager), Valerie Gladstone (Dresser To Ms. Uggams), Christopher "Smitty" C. Smith (Technical Supervisor), Dylan Foley (Current Production Prop Supervisor), Kathryn B. Guida (Original Wardrobe Supervisor) and Kelley Kirkpatrick (Production Stage Manager).

Not pictured: Lee J. Austin (Replacement Wardrobe Supervisor).

STAFF FOR
ON GOLDEN POND

GENERAL MANAGEMENT
STUART THOMPSON PRODUCTIONS
Stuart Thompson   James Triner

COMPANY MANAGER
Julie Crosby, Ph.D.

GENERAL PRESS REPRESENTATIVE
THE PUBLICITY OFFICE
Marc Thibodeau   Bob Fennell   Michael S. Borowski

TECHNICAL SUPERVISOR
Christopher C. Smith/Smitty

Production Stage Manager	**Kelley Kirkpatrick**
Stage Manager	Marti McIntosh
Assistant to the Director	Tyler Marchant
Assistant Scenic Designer	Randall Parsons
Assistant Costume Designer	MaryAnn D. Smith
Assistant Lighting Designer	John Burkland
Assistant Sound Designers	Jeremy J. Lee, Phillip Peglow
Dialect Coach	Kate Maré
Production Electrician	James Fedigan
Production Prop Supervisor	Dylan Foley
Production Sound	Thomas B. Grasso
Wardrobe Supervisor	Kathryn B. Guida
Dressers	Valerie Gladstone, Christine Kuhn
Hair Supervisor	Grantley A. McIntyre
Children's Supervisor	Sharon Mitchell
Children's Tutoring	On Location Education
Transportation	Earnest McRae; Danny Ibanez/IBA Limousine
Production Assistant	Emily Roberts
Assistant to the Lighting Designer	Rachel Gilmore
Assistants to Jeffrey Finn	Richard Rainville, Anne Tanaka
Assistant to Stuart Thompson	Caroline Prugh
General Management Assistants	Ryan Smith,

	John Vennema
Management Interns	Barry Branford, Joel Solari
Press Associate	Candi Adams
Press Interns	Jaclyn DeGiorgio, Michelle Greene
Banking	Chase Manhattan Bank/ Richard L. Callian, Michele Gibbons
Payroll	Castellana Services, Inc./ Lance Castellana
Accountant	Fried & Kowgios CPAs LLP/ Robert Fried, CPA
Controller	Anne Stewart Fitzroy, CPA
Assistant Controller	Joseph S. Kubala
Insurance	DeWitt Stern Group, Inc./ Jolyon F. Stern, Peter Shoemaker, Anthony L. Pittari
Legal Counsel	Jason Baruch/ Franklin, Weinrib, Rudell & Vassallo
Advertising	SpotCo/ Drew Hodges, Jim Edwards, Tom McCann, Kim Smarsh
Marketing Consultants	The Marketing Group/ Tanya Grubich, Laura Matalon Trish Santini, Lesley Alpert, Laura LaPonte
Website Design	Damian Bazadona, Situation Marketing
Production Photographers	Joan Marcus, Scott Suchman
Key Art Photography	Gregory Heisler
Displays	King Displays/Wayne Sapper
Opening Night Coordinator	Tobak-Dantchik Events & Promotions Cathy Dantchik, Joanna B. Koondel

Visit the Official
ON GOLDEN POND website at:
www.goldenpondonbroadway.com

Jeffrey Finn would like to acknowledge the support of Michael Kaiser, Max Woodward and The Kennedy Center in the initial presentation of this new production of *On Golden Pond*.

CREDITS
Scenery supplied by Atlas Scenic Studios, Ltd. Lighting equipment supplied by GSD Productions Inc, West Hempstead, NY. Sound equipment supplied by Masque Sound. Wig fabricated by Tom Watson. Ricola natural herb cough drops courtesy of Ricola USA, Inc. Rehearsed at The New 42nd Street Studios.

Special thanks to Rick Sordelet.

SPECIAL THANKS
Thomas A. Katzenmeyer and L. Glenn Poppleton

On Golden Pond is presented by arrangement with Graham Agency, New York.

THE SHUBERT ORGANIZATION, INC.
Board of Directors

Gerald Schoenfeld Chairman	**Philip J. Smith** President
Wyche Fowler, Jr.	**John W. Kluge**
Lee J. Seidler	**Michael I. Sovern**

Stuart Subotnick

Robert E. Wankel
Executive Vice President

Peter Entin Vice President - Theatre Operations	**Elliot Greene** Vice President - Finance
David Andrews Vice President - Shubert Ticketing Services	**John Darby** Vice President - Facilities

CORT THEATRE
House Manager .... Joseph Traina

The Pajama Game

First Preview: January 19, 2006. Opened: February 23, 2006.
Still running as of May 31, 2006.

PLAYBILL

CAST
(in order of appearance)

Factory Workers:

Prez	PETER BENSON
Mae	JOYCE CHITTICK
Virginia	BRIDGET BERGER
Charlie	STEPHEN BERGER
Martha	KATE CHAPMAN
Brenda	PAULA LEGGETT CHASE
Poopsie	JENNIFER CODY
Lewie	DAVID EGGERS
Cyrus	MICHAEL HALLING
Carmen	BIANCA MARROQUIN
Jake	VINCE PESCE
Joe	DEVIN RICHARDS
Ralph	JEFFREY SCHECTER
Shirley	DEBRA WALTON
Hines	MICHAEL McKEAN
Mr. Hasler	RICHARD POE
Gladys	MEGAN LAWRENCE
Mabel	ROZ RYAN
Ganzenlicker/Pop	MICHAEL McCORMICK
Sid Sorokin	HARRY CONNICK, JR.
Babe Williams	KELLI O'HARA

TIME: 1954
PLACE: Cedar Rapids, Iowa

40TH ANNIVERSARY SEASON

ROUNDABOUT THEATRE COMPANY

TODD HAIMES, Artistic Director
HAROLD WOLPERT, Managing Director
JULIA C. LEVY, Executive Director

By Special Arrangement with Jeffrey Richards, James Fuld, Jr., and Scott Landis

Present

Harry Connick, Jr.

Kelli O'Hara   Michael McKean

in

THE PAJAMA GAME

Book by George Abbott *and* Richard Bissell
Music & Lyrics by Richard Adler *and* Jerry Ross
Based on the Novel *"7 ½ Cents"* by Richard Bissell
Book Revisions for this Production by Peter Ackerman

Peter Benson   Joyce Chittick   Megan Lawrence
Michael McCormick   Richard Poe   Roz Ryan

Bridget Berger   Stephen Berger   Kate Chapman   Paula Leggett Chase   Jennifer Cody
David Eggers   Michael Halling   Bianca Marroquin   Michael O'Donnell   Vince Pesce
Devin Richards   Jeffrey Schecter   Amber Stone   Debra Walton

Set Design Derek McLane	*Costume Design* Martin Pakledinaz	*Lighting Design* Peter Kaczorowski	*Sound Design* Brian Ronan
Production Stage Manager David O'Brien	*Hair & Wig Design* Paul Huntley	*Music Coordinator* Seymour Red Press	*Casting* Jim Carnahan, C.S.A.
Associate Director Marc Bruni	*Associate Choreographer* Vince Pesce	*Musical Director* Rob Berman	*Technical Supervisor* Steve Beers	*General Manager* Sydney Beers
Press Representative Boneau/Bryan-Brown	*Director of Marketing* David B. Steffen	*Founding Director* Gene Feist	*Associate Artistic Director* Scott Ellis

Orchestrations
Dick Lieb and Danny Troob

Musical Supervisor/Vocal and Dance Arranger
David Chase

Directed and Choreographed by
Kathleen Marshall

Major support for this production provided by The Kaplen Foundation and JPMorgan Chase

Roundabout Theatre Company is a member of the League of Resident Theatres. www.roundabouttheatre.org

2/23/06

Kelli O'Hara, Harry Connick, Jr. (C) and the chorus perform "Once-a-Year Day."

The Pajama Game

MUSICAL NUMBERS

ACT ONE

Overture	The Orchestra
"Racing with the Clock"	Factory Workers
"A New Town Is a Blue Town"	Sid
"I'm Not at All in Love"	Babe, Factory Girls
"I'll Never Be Jealous Again"	Hines, Mabel
"Hey There"	Sid
"Racing with the Clock" (Reprise)	Factory Workers
"Sleep Tite"	Joe, Brenda, Martha, Cyrus
"Her Is"	Prez, Gladys
"Once-a-Year-Day"	Sid, Babe, Company
"Her Is" (Reprise)	Prez, Mae
"Small Talk"	Sid, Babe
"There Once Was a Man"	Sid, Babe
"Hey There" (Reprise)	Sid

ACT TWO

"Steam Heat"	Mae, Lewie, Jake
"The World Around Us"	Sid
"Hey There" (Reprise) / "If You Win, You Lose" *	Babe, Sid
"Think of the Time I Save"	Hines, Factory Girls
"Hernando's Hideaway"	Gladys, Sid, Company
"The Three of Us" *	Hines, Gladys
"Seven and a Half Cents"	Prez, Babe, Factory Workers
"There Once Was a Man" (Reprise)	Babe, Sid
"The Pajama Game"	Full Company

* "If You Win, You Lose" and "The Three of Us" – music and lyrics by Richard Adler

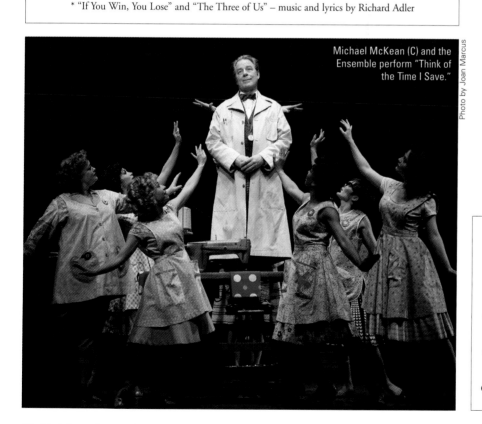

Michael McKean (C) and the Ensemble perform "Think of the Time I Save."

Photo by Joan Marcus

The Pajama Game

Harry Connick, Jr.
Sid Sorokin

Kelli O'Hara
Babe Williams

Michael McKean
Hines

Peter Benson
Prez

Joyce Chittick
Mae

Megan Lawrence
Gladys

Michael McCormick
Ganzenlicker/Pop

Richard Poe
Mr. Hasler

Roz Ryan
Mabel

Bridget Berger
Virginia

Stephen Berger
Charlie

Kate Chapman
Martha

Paula Leggett Chase
Brenda

Jennifer Cody
Poopsie

David Eggers
Lewie,
Dance Captain

Michael Halling
Cyrus

Bianca Marroquin
Carmen

Michael O'Donnell
Swing

Vince Pesce
Associate
Choreographer,
Jake

Devin Richards
Joe

Jeffrey Schecter
Ralph

Amber Stone
Swing

Debra Walton
Shirley

George Abbott
Book

Kathleen Marshall
Director &
Choreographer

Dick Lieb
Orchestrator

Danny Troob
Orchestrator

Derek McLane
Set Design

Martin Pakledinaz
Costume Design

Peter Kaczorowski
Lighting Design

Brian Ronan
Sound Design

Rob Berman
Music Director/
Conductor

Paul Huntley
Wig Design

Marc Bruni
Associate Director

Jim Carnahan
Casting

The Pajama Game

Jeffrey Richards
Associate Producer

Gene Feist
*Founding Director
Roundabout Theatre
Company*

Todd Haimes
*Artistic Director
Roundabout Theatre
Company*

BOX OFFICE
(L-R):
Robert Morgan and
Mead Margulies

Color photos by Ben Strothmann

STAGE CREW
Front Row (L-R):
Leslie C. Lyter, David O'Brien,
Stephen Gruse.

Second Row (L-R):
Patty McKeever, Tammy Kopko,
Susan Fallon, Jackie Freeman,
Julie Hilimire, Victoria Grecki.

Third Row (L-R):
Eddie Camacho, Bruce Harrow,
Melissa Crawford, Thom Carlson,
Brandon Claflin, Nellie LaPorte,
Anne Ezell.

Fourth Row (L-R):
Nelson Vaughn, Glenn Merwede,
Chris Mattingly, Jeremy Lewit,
Andrew Forste, Jill Anania.

Back Row (L-R):
Mike Faralla, Benjamin Barnes,
Jefferson Rowland, Barb Bartel,
Sean Haines, Dann Wojnar and Brian Maiuri.

ROUNDABOUT THEATRE COMPANY STAFF
ARTISTIC DIRECTOR .... **TODD HAIMES**
MANAGING DIRECTOR .... **HAROLD WOLPERT**
EXECUTIVE DIRECTOR .... **JULIA C. LEVY**
ASSOCIATE ARTISTIC DIRECTOR ...**SCOTT ELLIS**

ARTISTIC STAFF
DIRECTOR OF ARTISTIC DEVELOPMENT/
DIRECTOR OF CASTING .... **Jim Carnahan**
Artistic Consultant ....Robyn Goodman
Resident Director ....Michael Mayer
Associate Artists ....Scott Elliott, Doug Hughes,
Bill Irwin, Joe Mantello
Consulting Dramaturg ....Jerry Patch
Artistic Assistant ....Jill Rafson
Casting Director ....Mele Nagler
Casting Associate...........................Carrie Gardner
Casting Associate ..........................J.V. Mercanti
Casting Assistant ....Kate Schwabe
Casting Assistant ....Stephen Kopel
Artistic Intern ....Rachel Balik

---

EDUCATION STAFF
EDUCATION DIRECTOR ...**Margie Salvante-McCann**
Director of Instruction and
Curriculum Development ....Renee Flemings

Education Program Associate ....Stacey L. Morris
Education Program Associate ....Carrie Soloman
Education Coordinator ....Jennifer DeBruin
Education Interns ....Allison Barcom, Molly Glenn
Education Dramaturg ....Ted Sod
Teaching Artists ....Phil Alexander, Tony Angelini,
Cynthia Babak, Victor Barbella,
Brigitte Barnett-Loftis, Caitlin Barton,
Joe Basile, LaTonya Borsay, Bonnie Brady,
Lori Brown-Niang, Michael Carnahan,
Stella Cartaino, Joe Clancy, Melissa Denton,
Joe Doran, Katie Down, Tony Freeman,
Aaron Gass, Katie Gorum, Sheri Graubert,
Adam Gwon, Susan Hamburger, Karla Hendrick,
Lisa Renee Jordan, Alvin Keith, Rebecca Lord,
Robin Mates, Erin McCready, Jordana Oberman,
Andrew Ondrejcak, Laura Poe, Nicole Press,
Jennifer Rathbone, Chris Rummel, Drew Sachs,
Anna Saggese, Robert Signom, David Sinkus,
Derek Straat, Vickie Tanner, Olivia Tsang,
Jennifer Varbalow, Leese Walker, Eric Wallach,
Diana Whitten, Gail Winar

ADMINISTRATIVE STAFF
GENERAL MANAGER ....**Sydney Beers**
Associate Managing Director ....Greg Backstrom

General Manager, Steinberg Center ....Rebecca Habel
General Counsel ....Nancy Hirschmann
Human Resources Manager ....Stephen Deutsch
MIS Director ....Jeff Goodman
Manager of Corporate and Party Rentals ....Jetaun Dobbs
Office Manager ....Scott Kelly
Assistant to the General Manager ....Maggie Cantrick
Management Assistant ....Nicholas Caccavo
Management Assistant ....Tania Camargo
MIS Assistant ....Micah Kraybill
Receptionists ....Candice Alustiza, John Haynes,
Elisa Papa, Monica Sidorchuk
Messenger ....Robert Weisser
Management Intern ....Michelle Bergmann

FINANCE STAFF
CONTROLLER ....**Susan Neiman**
Assistant Controller ....John LaBarbera
Accounts Payable Administrator ....Frank Surdi
Customer Service Coordinator ....Trina Cox
Business Office Associate ....David Solomon
Financial Associate ....Yonit Kafka
Business Intern ....Virginia Graham

DEVELOPMENT STAFF
DIRECTOR OF DEVELOPMENT .....**Jeffory Lawson**

The Pajama Game

Director, Institutional Giving ....Julie K. D'Andrea
Director, Individual Giving ....Julia Lazarus
Director, Special Events ....Steve Schaeffer
Manager, Donor Information Systems ....Tina Mae Bishko
Capital Campaign Manager ....Mark Truscinski
Manager, Friends of Roundabout ....Jeff Collins
Institutional Giving Associate ....Kristen Bolibruch
Assistant to the Executive Director ....Robert Weinstein
Patrons Services Liaison ....Dawn Kusinski
Development Assistant ....Chelsea Glickfield
Individual Giving Assistant ....Dominic Yacobozzi
Special Events Assistant ....Ginger Vallen
Development Assistant ....Elissa Sussman
Special Events Intern ....Casey Cipriani
Development Intern ....Trey Gilpin

MARKETING STAFF
DIRECTOR OF MARKETING ....**David B. Steffen**
Marketing/Publications Manager .....Margaret Casagrande
Assistant Marketing Director ....Sunil Ayyagari
Marketing Associate ....Rebecca Ballon
Website Consultant ....Keith Powell Beyland
DIRECTOR OF TELESALES
SPECIAL PROMOTIONS ....**Tony Baksa**
Telesales Manager ....Anton Borissov
Telesales Office Coordinator ..................J.W. Griffin
Marketing Intern ....Carla Borras

TICKET SERVICES STAFF
DIRECTOR OF SALES OPERATIONS ..**Jim Seggelink**
Ticket Services Manager ....Ellen Holt
Subscription Manager ....Charlie Garbowski, Jr.
Box Office Managers ....Edward P. Osborne,
Jaime Perlman, Jessica Bowser
Group Sales Manager ....Jeff Monteith
Assistant Box Office Managers..............Paul Caspary,
Steve Howe, Robert Morgan
Assistant Ticket Services Managers ....Robert Kane,
David Meglino, Ethan Ubell
Assistant Director of Sales Operations ......Nancy Mulliner
Ticket Services ....Solangel Bido, Jacob Burstein-Stern,
William Campbell, David Carson,
Andrew Clements, Johanna Comanzo,
Nisha Dhruna, Adam Elsberry,
Lindsay Ericson, Scott Falkowski, John Finning,
Catherine Fitzpatrick, Amanda Genovese,
Tova Heller, Dottie Kenul, Alexander LaFrance,
Krystin MacRitchie, Mead Margulies,
Chuck Migliaccio, Carlos Morris,
Nicole Nicholson, Adam Owens,
Shannon Paige, Thomas Protulipac,
Jacki Rocha, Heather Siebert, Monté Smock,
Lillian Soto, Greg Thorson,
Pam Unger, Tiffany Wakely, Ryan Weible
Ticket Services Interns ....Rachel Bauder, Elisa Mala

SERVICES
Counsel ....Jeremy Nussbaum,
Cowan, Liebowitz & Latman, P.C.
Counsel ....Rosenberg & Estis
Counsel ....Rubin and Feldman, P.C.
Counsel ....Andrew Lance,
Gibson, Dunn, & Crutcher, LLP
Counsel ....Harry H. Weintraub,
Glick and Weintraub, P.C.
Immigration Counsel ....Mark D. Koestler and
Theodore Ruthizer

House Physicians ....Dr. Theodore Tyberg,
Dr. Lawrence Katz
House Dentist ....Neil Kanner, D.M.D.
Insurance ....DeWitt Stern Group, Inc.
Accountant ....Brody, Weiss, Zucarelli &
Urbanek CPAs, P.C.
Advertising.........................Eliran Murphy Group/
Denise Ganjou, Katie Koch
Events Photography ....Anita and Steve Shevett
Production Photographer ....Joan Marcus
Theatre Displays..............King Displays, Wayne Sapper

MANAGING DIRECTOR
EMERITUS ....ELLEN RICHARD

Roundabout Theatre Company
231 West 39th Street, New York, NY 10018
(212) 719-9393.

GENERAL PRESS REPRESENTATIVES
BONEAU / BRYAN-BROWN
Adrian Bryan-Brown   Matt Polk
Jessica Johnson   Shanna Marcus

CREDITS FOR *THE PAJAMA GAME*
GENERAL MANAGER ....Sydney Beers
Company Manager ....Denys Baker
Production Stage Manager ....David John O'Brien
Assistant Stage Managers ....Stephen R. Gruse,
Leslie C. Lyter
Assistant to the Director ....Jenny Hogan
Dance Captain ....David Eggers
Assistant Technical Supervisor ....Elisa Kuhar
Associate Set Designer ....Shoko Kambara
Assistant Costume Designer ....Martin Lopez
Associate Lighting Designer ....Karen Spahn
Assistant Lighting Designer ....Jen Schriever
Assistant Sound Designer ....Mike Creason
Make-up Design ....Angelina Avallone
Production Carpenter ....Glenn Merwede
Production Electrician ....Brian Maiuri
House Properties ....Andrew Forste
Wardrobe Supervisor ....Susan J. Fallon
House Sound Engineer ....Dann Wojnar
Hair and Wig Supervisor ....Manuela LaPorte
Production Properties ....Al Steiner
Production Sound Engineer ....Mike Farfalla
Deck Electrician ....Barb Bartel
Moving Light Programmer ....Josh Weitzman
Follow Spot Operators ....Benjamin Barnes,
David Sean Haines, Jeff Rowland
Automation Operator ....Paul Ashton
Flyman..Jeremy Lewit
Deck Stagehand ....Chris Mattingly
Properties ....Nelson Vaughn
Local One IATSE Apprentice ....Jill Anania
Dressers ....Jackie Freeman, Vicki Grecki,
Bruce Harrow, Julie Hilimire,
Tammy Kopko, Patty McKeever,
Gosia Slota
Day Workers ....Elizabeth Barton, Melissa Crawford
Hair and Wig Assistant ....Jodi Jackson
Assistant to Mr. Connick, Jr. ....Stephanie Conway
Hairstylist for Mr. Connick, Jr. ....Martial Corneville
Company Management Intern ....Sherra Johnston
Costume Assistant to Mr. Pakledinaz ...Courtney McClain

Costume Intern ....Jessica Lustig
Assistant to Martin Pakledinaz ....Wendy Hill
Copyist ....Anixter Rice Music Service
Production Assistant ....Gregory T. Livoti
SDCF Observer ....Wendy Seyb
Company Orthopedist ....Dr. Phillip Bauman
Company Physical Therapist ....Physio Arts
Scenery Automation by ....Hudson Scenic Studio
Properties Fabricated by ....Birch Street Design,
Cigar Box Studios, Factory at 54
Lighting Equipment by .PRG, Production Resource Group
Sound Equipment Provided by ....Sound Associates
Mr. Connick Jr.'s Costumes
Executed by ....Barbara Matera Ltd.
Costumes Executed by ....Carelli Costumes Inc.;
Eric Winterling, Inc.; Marc Happel;
Paul Chang Custom Tailors; Studio Rouge;
Timberlake Studios, Inc.
Screen Printing & Fabric Dyeing by ...Gene Mignola, Inc.
Shoes by ....Celebrity Ballroom Dance Shoes,
J.C. Theatrical & Custom Footwear Inc.,
LaDuca Shoes, T.O. Dey Shoes, WorldTone
Embroidery by ....Vogue Too
Custom Knitwear by ...........................C.C. Wei
Assorted Millinery by ....Arnold Levine
and Arnold Hatters, Inc.
Vintage Eyewear by ....Fabulous Fanny's
Transportation Provided by ....John Walker
Onstage Merchandising ....George Fenmore/
More Merchandising International
Merchandising ....Max Merchandising, LLC/
Randi Grossman

SPECIAL THANKS
Special thanks to Altenburg Piano House, Anheuser-Busch
Companies, Bra*Tenders, Channel Manufacturing Inc.,
Diamond Brands Inc., Nestle Confections and Snacks,
Emeco: The Aluminum Chair Co., Lakeside Manufacturing
Inc., N.G. Slater Corp., The Homer Laughlin China Co.,
Spalding Division, Russell Corp., United Thread Mills
Corp., Westbridge PET Containers and Zippo
Manufacturing Co., Keen Gat

Stock and amateur rights for *The Pajama Game* are available through Music Theatre International, New York, NY.
www.mtishows.com

AMERICAN AIRLINES THEATRE STAFF
General Manager ....Sydney Beers
House Carpenter ....Glenn Merwede
House Electrician ....Brian Maiuri
Wardrobe Supervisor ....Susan J. Fallon
Box Office Manager ....Edward P. Osborne
House Manager ....Stephen Ryan
Associate House Manager ....Zipporah Aguasvivas
Head Usher ....Edwin Camacho
House Staff ....Peter Breaden, Oscar Castillo,
Ilia Diaz, Anne Ezell,
Vince Allen Rawles,
Jacklyn Rivera, Tiesha Rivers
Security ....Julious Russell
Additional Security Provided by ....Gotham Security
Maintenance ....Chucke Fernandez, Ron Henry,
Kenrick Johnson, Maggie Western
Lobby Refreshments ....Sweet Concessions

The Pajama Game
SCRAPBOOK

Photos by Aubrey Reuben

Correspondent: Jennifer Cody, "Poopsie."

Opening Night Gifts: Harry gave us all Tiffany keychains. It's always nice to see that Tiffany bag! Kathleen Marshall gave us great *Pajama Game* robes. The producers gave us a framed photo of the entire company. We had started rehearsals right before Christmas and didn't know each other that well yet. So, for opening night, we did a Secret Santa, and gave each other pajamas.

Most Exciting Celebrity Visitor and What They Did/Said: My favorite was Tracey Ullman who had just done the movie of *Once Upon a Mattress* with Kathleen. But we have such great celebrities right in our own cast. Just sitting with Michael McKean and hearing him tell us stories is much more of a highlight to me than any celebrity visitor.

Who Got the Gypsy Robe: Vince Pesce. This is first time I've done a show where there were five or six of us who had already gotten it. It's a cast of old gypsies. It's so great to work on a show where people come in and they know exactly what to do.

"Easter Bonnet" Sketch: "Full View" by Chris Fenwick, Jeffrey Schacter, Peter Benson and Paula Leggett Chase.

Who Has Done the Most Shows: Vince Pesce has done eleven, but most of us in the ensemble have done nine to eleven shows.

Backstage Ritual: A bunch of us stand behind the curtain and dance and sing to the overture.

Favorite Moments: I love the end of "Hernando's Hideaway." The audience is always so ecstatic. There are so few numbers on Broadway where the audience is completely caught off-guard. It's also nice, sitting offstage right, when Harry sings for the first time. I remember the first time I heard him, losing my breath. Oh my God! It's nice to hear the audience have the same reaction.

Favorite Off-Site Hangout: We go right across the street to the bar at the Hilton. It's always half price to the actors in our show. It's a nice place and there's plenty of room.

Favorite Snack Food: Kelli O'Hara has a box in her dressing room full of Starbursts and Reisen chocolate caramels. We always dip into that box before we go on stage. Sometimes that candy makes it with us onto the stage, too! "Hernando" is all about eating our candy.

Mascot: Harry's kind of our mascot.

Favorite Therapy: Feet are a problem on this show because we all have to run up and down five flights of cement stairs. They've said they're going to put down carpet, but in the meantime

1. The cast takes curtain calls on opening night, wearing pajamas.
2. Roz Ryan arrives at the theatre.
3. Joyce Chittick in the lobby of the American Airlines Theatre on opening night.
4. Harry Connick, Jr. on opening night with (L) wife Jill Goodacre and (C) daughter Georgia.
5. (L-R): Former *Urinetown* castmates Hunter Foster and Jennifer Cody.

The Pajama Game
SCRAPBOOK

we have these great vibrating foot rollers that we pass around.

Memorable Ad-Libs: Every night Kelli and Harry try to crack each other up during "There Once Was a Man." We call it "The Ad-Lib Song." We all sit in the wings and listen to what they do. Harry tries to improvise dance steps during it, but he's not really a dancer. Kathleen tells him "OK, you can do the Russian [steps] but no jetés, no passés—nothing French!" Sometimes he does some *Chorus Line*.

Memorable Stage Door Fan Encounters: A lot of women come just to see Harry, and many of them have never seen a musical before. A lot of people at the stage door have been in productions of the show at one time or another, and all of them want to tell us about their *Pajama Game*. One guy said his whole production was played on a giant sewing machine. And everyone's been Poopsie, let me tell ya.

Fastest Costume Change: At the end of the show six dancers who go into what we call the "'Jama Jive," which we do in pajamas. We have about 30 seconds to change costumes.

Orchestra Member Who Plays the Most Instruments: That's probably our percussionist, Paul Pizzuti. We have a lot of Harry's own band in our pit and, in the scene where he ad-libs on the piano, some of his guys in the pit ad-lib right along with him. That's cool.

Best In-House Parody Lyrics: In "I'm Not at All in Love," a group of us are supposed to be talking in the background while Kelli is singing. We started saying limericks to each other, usually written by Paula Leggett Chase. The limerick has to be about a character or a person in the show. They're hysterical, and sometimes R-rated. We're saving them in a book.

Memorable Directorial Note: None of us know how to sew. In the opening scene where we're all supposed to be working on the sewing machines we couldn't make the song cues. The first time we went through it, it was such a train wreck! Everyone crashed and burned. Kathleen Marshall just quietly said, "OK, how can we make this work?" Everybody cracked up. We got it now, but we never thought we would.

Embarrassing Moments: A couple of pants rips. A lot of hat drama in "Steam Heat."

Catchphrase That Only People in the Company Will Understand: "Uh appow?"

Nicknames: Harry Connick, Jr. is "Swamp Dog."

Coolest Things About Being in This Show: That it's a hit. I've done some bad shows and let me tell you, it's really cool to be in a hit. Also, we get to bow in pajamas.

1. Michael McKean salutes the troops as he arrives for opening night.
2. Kelli O'Hara arrives at the Marriott Marquis Hotel for the opening night party.
3. The entire company poses for a class photo on the first day of rehearsal at 42nd Street Studios.
4. (L-R): Richard Poe, Roz Ryan and Michael McCormick at the first day of rehearsal.

Photos by Aubrey Reuben

The Phantom of the Opera

First Preview: January 9, 1988. Opened: January 26, 1988.
Still running as of May 31, 2006.

PLAYBILL

7486
The Record-Breaking Performance
January 9, 2006

CAST

The Phantom of the Opera .HOWARD McGILLIN
Christine Daaé ....SANDRA JOSEPH
Christine Daaé (at certain
performances) ....REBECCA PITCHER
Raoul,
Vicomte de Chagny .....TIM MARTIN GLEASON
Carlotta Giudicelli ....ANNE RUNOLFSSON
Monsieur André ....GEORGE LEE ANDREWS
Monsieur Firmin ....TIM JEROME
Madame Giry ....MARILYN CASKEY
Ubaldo Piangi ....LARRY WAYNE MORBITT
Meg Giry ....HEATHER McFADDEN
Monsieur Reyer/
Hairdresser (in *Il Muto*) ....RICHARD POOLE
Auctioneer ....CARRINGTON VILMONT
Jeweler (in *Il Muto*) ....DAVID GASCHEN
Monsieur Lefèvre/Firechief ....JOHN JELLISON
Joseph Buquet ....RICHARD WARREN PUGH
Don Attilio
(in *Il Muto*) ...GREGORY EMANUEL RAHMING
Passarino (in *Don Juan*
Triumphant) ....CARRINGTON VILMONT
Slave Master (in *Hannibal*)/
Solo Dancer (in *Il Muto*) ....DANIEL RYCHLEC
Flunky/Stage Hand......................JACK HAYES
Page (in *Don Juan Triumphant*) ....KRIS KOOP
Porter/Fireman ....JOHN WASINIAK
Spanish Lady
(in *Don Juan Triumphant*) ....SALLY WILLIAMS
Wardrobe Mistress/
Confidante (in *Il Muto*) ......MARY LEIGH STAHL

Continued on next page

☺ MAJESTIC THEATRE
247 West 44th Street
A Shubert Organization Theatre
Gerald Schoenfeld, *Chairman*   **Philip J. Smith**, *President*

Robert E. Wankel, *Executive Vice President*

CAMERON MACKINTOSH and
THE REALLY USEFUL THEATRE COMPANY, INC.
present

The
PHANTOM
of the
OPERA.

starring

HOWARD McGILLIN
SANDRA JOSEPH
TIM MARTIN GLEASON

GEORGE LEE ANDREWS   TIM JEROME   ANNE RUNOLFSSON
MARILYN CASKEY   LARRY WAYNE MORBITT   HEATHER McFADDEN

At certain performances
REBECCA PITCHER
plays the role of 'Christine'

Music by
ANDREW LLOYD WEBBER
Lyrics by **CHARLES HART**
Additional lyrics by **RICHARD STILGOE**
Book by **RICHARD STILGOE & ANDREW LLOYD WEBBER**
Based on the novel 'Le Fantôme de L'Opéra' by **GASTON LEROUX**
Production Design by **MARIA BJÖRNSON**   *Lighting by* **ANDREW BRIDGE**
Sound by **MARTIN LEVAN**   *Musical Supervision & Direction* **DAVID CADDICK**
Musical Director **DAVID LAI**   *Production Supervisor* **PETER von MAYRHAUSER**
Orchestrations by **DAVID CULLEN & ANDREW LLOYD WEBBER**
Casting by **TARA RUBIN CASTING**   *Original Casting by* **JOHNSON-LIFF ASSOCIATES**
General Management **ALAN WASSER**

Musical Staging & Choreography by **GILLIAN LYNNE**

Directed by **HAROLD PRINCE**

LIVE
BROADWAY

1/9/06

Sandra Joseph and Howard McGillin as Christine and The Phantom.

The Phantom of the Opera

MUSICAL NUMBERS

PROLOGUE
The stage of the Paris Opéra House, 1911

OVERTURE

ACT ONE—PARIS 1881

Scene 1—The dress rehearsal of *Hannibal*
"Think of Me" .... Carlotta, Christine, Raoul
Scene 2—After the Gala
"Angel of Music" .... Christine and Meg
Scene 3—Christine's dressing room
"Little Lotte/The Mirror" (Angel of Music) .... Raoul, Christine, Phantom
Scene 4—The Labyrinth underground
"The Phantom of the Opera" .... Phantom and Christine
Scene 5—Beyond the lake
"The Music of the Night" .... Phantom
Scene 6—Beyond the lake, the next morning
"I Remember/Stranger Than You Dreamt It" .... Christine and Phantom
Scene 7—Backstage
"Magical Lasso" .... Buquet, Meg, Madame Giry and Ballet Girls
Scene 8—The Managers' office
"Notes/Prima Donna" .... Firmin, André, Raoul, Carlotta, Giry, Meg, Piangi and Phantom
Scene 9—A performance of *Il Muto*
"Poor Fool, He Makes Me Laugh" .... Carlotta and Company
Scene 10—The roof of the Opéra House
"Why Have You Brought Me Here/Raoul, I've Been There" .... Raoul and Christine
"All I Ask of You" .... Raoul and Christine
"All I Ask of You" (Reprise) .... Phantom

ENTR'ACTE

ACT TWO—SIX MONTHS LATER

Scene 1—The staircase of the Opéra House, New Year's Eve
"Masquerade/Why So Silent" .... Full Company
Scene 2—Backstage
Scene 3—The Managers' office
"Notes/Twisted Every Way" ... André, Firmin, Carlotta, Piangi, Raoul, Christine, Giry and Phantom
Scene 4—A rehearsal for *Don Juan Triumphant*
Scene 5—A graveyard in Peros
"Wishing You Were Somehow Here Again" .... Christine
"Wandering Child/Bravo, Bravo" .... Phantom, Christine and Raoul
Scene 6—The Opéra House stage before the Premiere
Scene 7—*Don Juan Triumphant*
"The Point of No Return" .... Phantom and Christine
Scene 8—The Labyrinth underground
"Down Once More/Track Down This Murderer" .... Full Company
Scene 9—Beyond the lake

Cast Continued

Princess (in *Hannibal*) .... SUSAN OWEN
Madame Firmin .... MELODY RUBIE
Innkeeper's Wife (in *Don Juan Triumphant*) .... WREN MARIE HARRINGTON
Marksman .... STEPHEN R. BUNTROCK
The Ballet Chorus of the Opéra Populaire .... POLLY BAIRD, KARA KLEIN, GIANNA LOUNGWAY, JESSICA RADETSKY, CARLY BLAKE SEBOUHIAN, DIANNA WARREN
Ballet Swing .... HARRIET CLARK
Swings .... SCOTT MIKITA, JAMES ROMICK, JANET SAIA

UNDERSTUDIES

For the Phantom—STEPHEN R. BUNTROCK, DAVID GASCHEN, TIM MARTIN GLEASON, JAMES ROMICK; for Christine—KRIS KOOP, SUSAN OWEN; for Raoul—STEPHEN R. BUNTROCK, JAMES ROMICK, CARRINGTON VILMONT; for Monsieur Firmin—JOHN JELLISON, RICHARD WARREN PUGH, GREGORY EMANUEL RAHMING, JAMES ROMICK; for Monsieur André—SCOTT MIKITA, RICHARD POOLE, JAMES ROMICK; for Carlotta—WREN MARIE HARRINGTON, KRIS KOOP, MELODY RUBIE, JANET SAIA; for Mme. Giry—KRIS KOOP, JANET SAIA, SALLY WILLIAMS; for Piangi—DAVID GASCHEN, RICHARD WARREN PUGH, JOHN WASINIAK; for Meg Giry—POLLY BAIRD, KARA KLEIN, CARLY BLAKE SEBOUHIAN; for Slave Master and for Solo Dancer (*Il Muto*)—JACK HAYES

Dance Captain—Harriet Clark
Assistant Dance Captain—Heather McFadden

ORCHESTRA

CONDUCTORS:
David Caddick, Kristen Blodgette, David Lai, Tim Stella, Norman Weiss

Violins—Joyce Hammann (Concert Master), Jan Mullen, Alvin E. Rogers, Gayle Dixon, Kurt Coble, Karen Milne; Violas—Stephanie Fricker, Veronica Salas; Cellos—Jeanne LeBlanc, Ted Ackerman; Bass—Melissa Slocum; Harp—Henry Fanelli; Flute—Sheryl Henze; Flute/Clarinet—Ed Matthew; Oboe—Melanie Feld; Clarinet—Matthew Goodman; Bassoon—Atsuko Sato; Trumpets---Lowell Hershey, Francis Bonny; Bass Trombone—William Whitaker; French Horns—Daniel Culpepper, David Smith, Peter Reit; Percussion—Eric Cohen, Jan Hagiwara; Keyboards—Tim Stella, Norman Weiss.

The Phantom of the Opera

Howard McGillin
The Phantom of the Opera

Sandra Joseph
Christine Daaé

Tim Martin Gleason
Raoul, Vicomte de Chagny

George Lee Andrews
Monsieur André

Tim Jerome
Monsieur Firmin

Anne Runolfsson
Carlotta Giudicelli

Marilyn Caskey
Madame Giry

Larry Wayne Morbitt
Ubaldo Piangi

Heather McFadden
Meg Giry

Rebecca Pitcher
Christine Daaé at certain performances

Polly Baird
Ballet Chorus

Stephen R. Buntrock
Marksman

Harriet Clark
Dance Captain/ Swing

David Gaschen
Jeweler

Wren Marie Harrington
Innkeeper's Wife

Jack Hayes
Flunky/Stagehand

John Jellison
Monsieur Lefèvre/ Firechief

Kara Klein
Ballet Chorus

Kris Koop
Page

Gianna Loungway
Ballet Chorus

Scott Mikita
Swing

Susan Owen
Princess

Richard Poole
Monsieur Reyer/ Hairdresser

Richard Warren Pugh
(1951-2006)
Joseph Buquet

Jessica Radetsky
Ballet Chorus

Gregory Emanuel Rahming
Don Attilio

James Romick
Swing

Melody Rubie
Madame Firmin

Daniel Rychlec
Slave Master/ Solo Dancer

Janet Saia
Swing

Carly Blake Sebouhian
Ballet Chorus

Mary Leigh Stahl
Wardrobe Mistress/ Confidante

Carrington Vilmont
Auctioneer/ Passarino

Dianna Warren
Ballet Chorus

John Wasiniak
Porter/Fireman

The Phantom of the Opera

Sally Williams
Spanish Lady

Andrew Lloyd Webber
*Composer/Book/
Co-Orchestrator*

Harold Prince
Director

Charles Hart
Lyrics

Richard Stilgoe
*Book and
Additional Lyrics*

Gillian Lynne
*Musical Staging and
Choreographer*

Maria Björnson
(1949-2002)
Production Design

Andrew Bridge
Lighting Designer

Martin Levan
Sound Designer

David Caddick
*Musical Supervision
and Direction*

Kristen Blodgette
*Associate Musical
Supervisor*

David Cullen
Co-Orchestrator

Ruth Mitchell
(1919-2000)
*Assistant to
Mr. Prince*

Denny Berry
*Production
Dance Supervisor*

Craig Jacobs
*Production
Stage Manager*

Bethe Ward
*Stage Manager from
the beginning*

David Lai
Musical Director

Johnson-Liff Associates/
Vincent Liff and Geoffrey Johnson
Original Casting

Tara Rubin,
Tara Rubin Casting
Casting

Alan Wasser,
Alan Wasser
Associates
General Management

Cameron Mackintosh
Producer

*Alumni
2005-2006*

Dara Adler
*The Ballet Chorus of
the Opéra Populaire*

Emily Adonna
*The Ballet Chorus of
the Opéra Populaire*

Harlan Bengel
*Slave Master
("Hannibal")/
Solo Dancer
("Il Muto")*

Marie Danvers
*Princess
("Hannibal")*

Julie Hanson
*Christine Daaé
at certain
performances*

Jeff Keller
Monsieur Firmin

Michael Shawn Lewis
Marksman

Sabra Lewis
*The Ballet Chorus of
the Opéra Populaire*

Peter Lockyer
*Porter/Fireman/
Jeweler ("Il Muto")*

Hugh Panaro
*The Phantom
of the Opera*

Fred Rose
*Marksman/Auctioneer
/ Passarino ("Don
Juan Triumphant")/
Monsieur Reyer/
Hairdresser ("Il Muto")*

Julie Schmidt
*Carlotta Giudicelli/
Page/Inkeeper's
Wife ("Don Juan
Triumphant")*

The Phantom of the Opera

Jim Weitzer
Swing/ u/s Raoul

Dara Adler
Ballet Chorus

Emily Adonna
Ballet Chorus

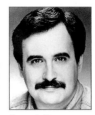

David Cryer
Monsieur Firmin

Kenneth Kantor
Don Attilio ("Il Muto")

Michael Shawn Lewis
Raoul

Peter Lockyer
Marksman

Justin Peck
Flunky/Stage Hand

Patricia Phillips
Carlotta

Roland Rusinek
Ubaldo Piangi

Julie Schmidt
Spanish Lady

Stephen Tewksbury
Joseph Buquet

Jennifer Hope Wills
Christine Daaé at certain performances

7,486

*"What a night! What a crowd!
Makes you glad! Makes you proud!"*

January 9, 2006

Welcome to a very special evening.

With performance #7,486, **THE PHANTOM OF THE OPERA** shatters the ultimate Broadway record to become the longest-running show in Broadway history.

For this phenomenal achievement, Cameron Mackintosh, The Really Useful Theatre Company, Inc., Andrew Lloyd Webber and Harold Prince thank all the wonderful actors, musicians, staff and crew that have worked under the guidance of our inspired production team.

We also thank our amazing creators Gillian Lynne, Charles Hart and Richard Stilgoe, as well as designers Andrew Bridge and Martin Levan, and pay special tribute to our dearly missed designer, the brilliant Maria Björnson, who was such an integral part of this show's success.

We acknowledge the thousands of people that worked on the three national tours in every capacity, all of whom are represented here tonight by the current cast of The Music Box Company, joining us direct from the road.

We also thank the millions of fans across America and around the world that have embraced this extraordinary musical with such unbridled and unparalleled enthusiasm.

Amazingly, the best years are nowhere near behind us. **PHANTOM** continues to play to packed Broadway houses; ends 2005 as the highest-grossing year in its history; gets ready to celebrate an unprecedented 18 years (which it will on January 26); and is about to open in a spectacular new reincarnation in Las Vegas. Additionally, every performance from here on out sets a new record, and all with absolutely no end in sight.

We're all thrilled that "The Music of the Night" has struck such a powerful chord in so many people. May it play forever!

Thank you, and enjoy tonight.

THE CITY OF NEW YORK
OFFICE OF THE MAYOR
NEW YORK, N.Y. 10007

January 9, 2006

Dear Friends:

It is a great pleasure to welcome everyone to the 7,486[th] performance of *The Phantom of the Opera*. Tonight's show is a tremendous milestone for the musical as it becomes the longest-running show in Broadway history.

Since its opening night in New York eighteen years ago, *Phantom* has established itself as one of Broadway's most memorable productions, making its mark on the Great White Way with inspired music and amazing theatrics. Andrew Lloyd Webber, Harold Prince and Cameron Mackintosh have dazzled audiences with a true classic which I hope will be enjoyed for many more years to come.

On behalf of over eight million New Yorkers, I congratulate all those who have contributed to this incredible run of *Phantom* over the years bringing the joy and humanity of theater to audiences night after night. A special congratulations to everyone performing both onstage and behind the scenes in this evening's show. You have made an indelible contribution to Broadway, and I thank you for your support of our City's rich cultural community.

Please accept my best wishes for an enjoyable performance and many more to come.

Sincerely,

Michael R. Bloomberg
Mayor

The Phantom of the Opera

The Phantom of the Opera

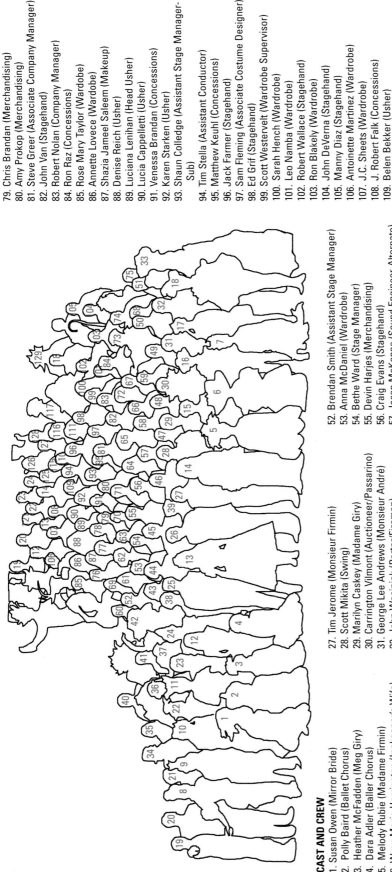

CAST AND CREW

1. Susan Owen (Mirror Bride)
2. Polly Baird (Ballet Chorus)
3. Heather McFadden (Meg Giry)
4. Dara Adler (Ballet Chorus)
5. Melody Rubie (Madame Firmin)
6. Wren Marie Harrington (Innkeeper's Wife)
7. Gianna Loungway (Ballet Chorus)
8. Kris Koop (Ensemble)
9. Dianna Warren (Ballet Chorus)
10. Larry Wayne Morbitt (Piangi)
11. Anne Runolfsson (Carlotta)
12. Kara Klein (Ballet Chorus)
13. Sandra Joseph (Christine Daaé)
14. Rebecca Pitcher (Christine Daaé-Alternate)
15. Carly Blake Sebouhian (Ballet Chorus)
16. Jessica Radetsky (Ballet Chorus)
17. Harriet Clark (Dance Captain/Swing)
18. Janet Saia (Swing)
19. Michael Borowski (Press Agent)
20. Peter von Mayrhauser (Production Supervisor)
21. Craig Jacobs (Production Stage Manager)
22. Gregory Emanuel Rahming (Don Attilio)
23. Sally Williams (Spanish Lady)
24. John Jellison (Monsieur Lefèvre/Firechief)
25. Howard McGillin (The Phantom of the Opera)
26. Tim Martin Gleason (Raoul)
27. Tim Jerome (Monsieur Firmin)
28. Scott Mikita (Swing)
29. Marilyn Caskey (Madame Giry)
30. Carrington Vilmont (Auctioneer/Passarino)
31. George Lee Andrews (Monsieur André)
32. John Wasiniak (Porter/Fireman)
33. Mary Leigh Stahl (Wardrobe Mistress/Confidante)
34. Daniel Rychlec (Slave Master)
35. Thelma Pollard (Makeup Supervisor)
36. George Dumit (Stagehand)
37. Richard Poole (Monsieur Reyer/Hairdresser)
38. Jack Hayes (Flunky/Stagehand/Ensemble)
39. John Galdieri (Stagehand)
40. Alan Lampel (Head Electrician)
41. Robert Strong Miller (Assistant Wardrobe Supervisor)
42. James Romick (Swing)
43. Sylvia Bailey (Usher)
44. Georgia Bibeau (Merchandising)
45. Stephen R. Buntrock (Marksman)
46. Richard Warren Pugh (Buquet)
47. Charlie Grieco (Sound Engineer-Alternate)
48. Fred Smith (Stagehand)
49. John Alban (Stagehand)
50. Randy Brown (Stagehand)
51. Michael Girman (Automation)
52. Brendan Smith (Assistant Stage Manager)
53. Anna McDaniel (Wardrobe)
54. Bethe Ward (Stage Manager)
55. Devin Harjes (Merchandising)
56. Craig Evans (Stagehand)
57. Jason McKenna (Sound Engineer-Alternate)
58. Frank Billings (Stagehand)
59. Joe Grillman (Stagehand)
60. Barbara Roman (Hairdresser)
61. Charise Champion (Hairdresser)
62. Jennifer Arnold (Wardrobe)
63. Peter McIver (Wardrobe)
64. Tanesha Warren (Merchandising)
65. Jake Hirzel (Assistant Company Manager)
66. Zack Arkin (Stagehand)
67. Dan Dashman (Stagehand)
68. Russell Tiberio III (Head Carpenter)
69. Angie Finn (Wardrobe)
70. Giavani Laduke (Usher)
71. Julia McDarris (Merchandising)
72. Erna Diaz (Wardrobe)
73. Mannequin
74. Tim Higgins (Stagehand)
75. Dick Miller (Stagehand)
76. Linda Schultz (Wardrobe)
77. Pearleta N. Price (Makeup Assistant)
78. Santos Sanchez (Automation)
79. Chris Brandan (Merchandising)
80. Amy Prokop (Merchandising)
81. Steve Greer (Associate Company Manager)
82. John Van (Stagehand)
83. Robert Nolan (Company Manager)
84. Ron Raz (Concessions)
85. Rose Mary Taylor (Wardrobe)
86. Annette Lovece (Wardrobe)
87. Shazia Jameel Saleem (Makeup)
88. Denise Reich (Usher)
89. Luciana Lenihan (Head Usher)
90. Lucia Cappelletti (Usher)
91. Venessa Brandan (Concessions)
92. Karen Starken (Usher)
93. Shaun Colledge (Assistant Stage Manager-Sub)
94. Tim Stella (Assistant Conductor)
95. Matthew Keuhl (Concessions)
96. Jack Farmer (Stagehand)
97. Sam Fleming (Associate Costume Designer)
98. Ed Grif (Stagehand)
99. Scott Westervelt (Wardrobe Supervisor)
100. Sarah Hench (Wardrobe)
101. Leo Namba (Wardrobe)
102. Robert Wallace (Stagehand)
103. Ron Blakely (Wardrobe)
104. John DeVerna (Stagehand)
105. Manny Diaz (Stagehand)
106. Antoinette Martinez (Wardrobe)
107. J.C. Sheets (Wardrobe)
108. J. Robert Falk (Concessions)
109. Belen Bekker (Usher)
110. Terence Doherty (Wardrobe)
111. Lisa Brownstein (Wardrobe)
112. Matt Mezick (Head Properties)
113. Russell Easley (Wardrobe)
114. Michael Jacobs (Wardrobe)
115. Giancarlo Cottignoli (Assistant Carpenter)
116. Lisa Herrell (Hairdresser)
117. Kelly Reed (Hairdresser)
118. Brian Colona (Stagehand)
119. Alex DaPonte (Apprentice)
120. Spencer Bell (Assistant Properties)
121. Margie Marchionnie (Wardrobe)
122. Matt Goodman (Orchestra)
123. Karen Parlato (Assistant Stage Manager-Sub)
124. Hector Lugo (Wardrobe)
125. Jan Hagiwara (Orchestra)
126. Mary Lou Rios (Wardrobe)
127. Ed Matthew (Orchestra)
128. Eileen Casey (Wardrobe)
129. Jonathan Tessero (Devil)

The Phantom of the Opera

The Phantom of the Opera
SCRAPBOOK

Correspondent: Kris Koop Ouellette, Ensemble and Understudy for "Christine," "Carlotta" and "Madame Giry"

In the months leading up to January 9, 2006, every person involved with every aspect of the production put in many extra hours in preparation to celebrate *Phantom* becoming the longest running show in Broadway history.

This event demanded that we deliver an even higher standard of excellence. Every important person in the industry would be in attendance, from the spouses and partners of the cast, crew and orchestra, show alumni, to distinguished members of the press, supporters of our favorite charities, all of our union leaders, big directors, producers, casting agents, stars of stage and screen…not to mention the incredible production team who put this show together in the first place.

So here was the original creative team, the current cast and crews, a liaison from the tour…all gathered at the Majestic to stage a special version of "Masquerade" and a top-secret addition we started referring to as "Act III."

Laurie Volney, the Dance Captain from the Music Box Company, served as liaison between *Phantom* on Broadway and *Phantom* on tour. She commuted between NYC and Pittsburgh to translate what she, Harriet Clark (Dance Captain, Broadway), and Denny Berry (Production Dance Supervisor) gleaned from Gillian Lynne: little changes, enhancements, and subtleties.

The ballerinas, rehearsing in studios around the city, described "Gillie" as "amazing" and "inspirational." The rest of us were quite curious about "Act III," but we had to wait to find out what this top-secret project was all about.

The entire cast then received lyric sheets, with a new verse to "Masquerade," written especially for this big celebration by Charles Hart. On Friday, January 6, 2006, we met quickly in the lower lobby of the theatre to sing through the new words, and begin the memorization process. Up on our feet, on stage, Gillie started to choreograph the big finale, introducing to the entire company a lovely young dancer named Abby Simon, who would perform in "Act III" as "Victoria," the White Cat from *Cats*. She would symbolically pass the torch to Howard McGillin, our Phantom.

We rehearsed all day, and though we were happy about the upcoming events, the tone felt pretty serious. Not tense, per se, but serious. We

1. Curtain calls on the night the show became the longest-running in Broadway history.
2. Andrew Lloyd Webber (C) addresses the audience while producer Cameron Mackintosh (L), director Harold Prince (R) and the cast look on.
3. Eighteen years worth of Phantoms reunite for a group curtain call.

The Phantom of the Opera
SCRAPBOOK

worked hard to learn new lyrics and new choreography simultaneously. Gillie had her hands full with so many people to place onstage, yet she remained in good humor, often gathering the entire group of us into a tight circle so that she could speak to us in private, and then whispering into her hand-held microphone so that the entire theatre could hear. Lovely, lovely lady.

David Caddick, conducting from the pit, created a kind of dance of his own, to serve as a reminder of which lyric was to come. His charm and impeccable musicality kept us all engaged as the hours wore longer and longer. We reminded ourselves that this celebration was because of David's and Gillie's incredible gifts. What an honor to work with them in this way!

We tied *Cats*' record before a sold-out crowd on Saturday night, January 7, 2006. We quietly acknowledged it during the curtain call, there were Champagne toasts and backstage pizza, and then we all raced home to rest. The holidays had been especially tough, with a grueling schedule, the transit strike and two kinds of flu working their way through the company.

Before we knew it, we were back at the Majestic on Monday morning.

The Big Day

The air inside the theatre absolutely hummed with energy.

The call-boards backstage at the Majestic Theatre were crowded with dozens and dozens of faxes, telegrams, cards and letters from every show on Broadway, most of the tours, and all *Phantom* companies, worldwide, congratulating us on becoming the longest running Broadway show. Our favorite card was from Broadway's *Mamma Mia!* company, incorporating the slogan from Lord Lloyd Webber's *former* record-holder, a.k.a. "The Kitty Play": "*The Phantom of the Opera*—Now And Forever."

Very loved, very welcomed faces of the touring company started to cross the threshold, exhausted from their bus-trip in from Pittsburgh that left at some ungodly hour in the morning. Audible in every corner of the theatre was some group reviewing the new "Masquerade" lyrics.

The normally tight spaces backstage were crowded now with some of the most famous and important people in theatre history…everyone a little giddy, everyone a little nervous, all of us openly in awe of what was taking place. We had under our roof 17 Phantoms (including the first, Michael Crawford), 14 Christines, other original cast members, and many, many more!

1. Choreographer Gillian Lynne (L) with *Woman in White* star Maria Friedman at the record-breaking celebration.
2. Andrew Lloyd Webber jokes with original Phantom, Michael Crawford, at the celebration.
3. Lloyd Webber (R) and family at the Majestic Theatre.

We started to feel like hosts of this amazing party, and we began to act the part. Sweet Abby, our "White Cat" was adopted by the crew first, then by the entire cast and management…we kept her well fed, encouraged, even stroked her ego a bit. What a tremendously pressured Broadway debut she would be making in a few hours!

Howard McGillin was now being asked to perform a role that challenged his confidence. He was to "dance" with Abby, as she, in all of her ballet-trained elegance, symbolically passed the *Cats* torch to *Phantom*. Howard was dubious about his being featured in a dance piece, but he trusted Gillie and gave it his all. Those of us who had performed in *Cats* stole moments with Howard and with each other to translate the poignancy of Gillie's choreography…the parallel between The Phantom, disfigured, abandoned, alone…and Grizabella, a similarly lonely character who received redemption at the hands of Victoria, the White Cat. We knew what Gillie knew, what David knew, what Hal Prince, Lord Lloyd Webber and Sir Cameron Mackintosh saw when they quietly entered the theatre to watch…When The Phantom and Victoria embraced each other, it was magical. This moment was going to bring the audience and all of us onstage to laughter and tears. The energy, the importance, the sense of occasion of every little thing carried the feeling of an opening night. Just a few more hours to go….

We had successfully added all the extras for "Act III," and we were about to be released for dinner. We had heard from Cameron Mackintosh, Andrew Lloyd Webber and everyone who made this incredible piece of theatre possible—the people who created a show that generated thousands of jobs for people in every aspect of the industry. They laughed with us, they thanked us—imagine that!—and they shared old stories about a time before they knew that this was possible. Unforgettable.

We were ordered to leave the theatre and move to the lower lobby. The press had moved into the theatre, and we were being kicked out. As we exited, we saw that each and every seat now held a souvenir program, specially re-shot with this cast in all of the scenes, and a black or white or multi-colored feathered mask was affixed to the right corner of the back of the chair. A huge section of the orchestra, house left, was labeled as reserved for specific alumni. Breathtaking.

We all met in the lower lobby for one last moment before we went to dinner. Clad in our rehearsal-wear, looking both tired and exhilarated, we sat on the stairs and on the couches and on the floor. David Caddick thanked us all for our hard work, for our talent, and then offered something like this: "You've all been working so hard for so long, and when it's over, you may wonder what all of the fuss was about. This celebration is for you. For what you do every show

The Phantom of the Opera
Scrapbook

of the week. Try to enjoy this."

My paraphrasing cannot capture his eloquence, his sincerity, nor the power of that moment. He brought us all together and made us all feel ready, without making a big deal out of it at all. Quite wonderful.

The Performance

We went up at 6:30 p.m. One of the stomach-flu sufferers was feeling "a little bit better" and the other had turned simply green, upchucking in the WC six times throughout the performance. Stage makeup barely concealed her discomfort, yet she'd even make it through "Act III"! The Music Box Company has made themselves at home at the Jacobs Theatre, opened to us for this event. Abby has a home there, as well.

At the Majestic, the excitement and nervousness of the afternoon had blended in with the usual show vibe, and I felt proud that everyone here would be delivering their same performance tonight as ever. "Invited crowd of important guests…you're getting our show, the way we do it eight times a week!" Nice!

The audience, however, felt too excited to contain themselves. They erupted into applause at the announcement to turn off cell phones. This was going to be a good night!

The show vibe backstage remained the same as always…lots of laughs, general silliness, some of us worried to death over the "sickie." The Auction Scene went well, and the audience cheered for the Chandelier as it rose from the stage to its place under the domed roof of the theatre. We began the Hannibal Scene, and the audience was eating it up! Every laugh line was received with uproarious laughter, and it began to settle in the company at once, like honey sifting through the comb: we were in the midst of something truly incredible.

George Lee Andrews (original cast, plays M. André) entered the scene quietly, from a concealed upstage-right corner. The audience greeted George with performance-stopping applause, befitting his contribution to this record-breaking show. It brought tears to the eyes, but we were doing a play here, so we continued the scene, and the show began to overpower this powerful audience. Though they were always generous in their laughter, shock and applause, we gave them the show they came to see. The focus of the evening truly became about the story being told on stage and not just the celebration at hand. Even this crowd, so determined to contribute to this extraordinary event, settled back and became mesmerized by the show. That's theatre magic!

Behind The Scenes at the Jacobs

Just a snapshot from behind the scenes: The touring company had made their temporary quarters at the Jacobs, just two steps away from our stage door. Without a video feed to watch,

A symbolic passing of the torch on the night *Phantom* surpassed *Cats* to become the longest running show in Broadway history.

Photos by Aubrey Reuben

they clustered around an audio monitor to listen to the show as it was happening, some dressed for their appearance in Act II's "Masquerade," some dressed in street clothes, some dressed in equal parts street-wear and costume. With plastic-sheeted chairs in a dimly lit auditorium as the background, the scene resembled a 1940's Radio Hour broadcast, with good friends huddled by the monitor, breaking out in laughter, turning to question each other. "What do you think that audience reaction was about?" A couple of revelers sipped Dixie cups of Champagne in the back of the theatre. A few people were heard chanting the new lyrics to "Masquerade" and marking through the movement.

Several Tour members were making their Broadway debut singing "Masquerade" on the stairs, and we, as happy hosts, took a moment to congratulate them and make sure everyone felt welcome. The show was going beautifully, and though Intermission ran long (we heard that Champagne was being served in the lobby, and we all pretended that we're pissed that we weren't invited), we're back in action. Our thoughts turn to the subtle changes we've rehearsed. Diamonds. Diamonds. Diamonds. The electricity in the air was palpable.

The audience was ready. We were ready. Act II began. Here were go!

"Act III"

The show ended, the audience forgot that they were watching their friends and family, and they were weeping for these ill-fated lovers. The performance was a success. The standing-ovation couldn't happen fast enough, and our swings—the hardest working people in this building— joined us, in costume, for the curtain call. We rushed downstage in our final bow with Gillie's other great invention—"WHOOSH!"—and the audience went simply wild! We went back into our places, as though the curtain would fall and the evening was ending, but then this slow, throbbing "shark music" (a lot like the theme from *Jaws*) began to sound from the orchestra. The room went mostly silent, but now the reactions from the audience resembled those at a rock concert or comedy show. We exited the stage in very dramatic fashion, and revealed all of the ballerinas (Broadway and tour) dressed in their white costumes, and the audience hushed.

The girls parted slowly to reveal Abby costumed as Victoria, the white Jellicle Cat. The

The Phantom of the Opera
SCRAPBOOK

audience shrieked with recognition, some laughing, some ooh-ing and aww-ing, but everyone touched and impressed. Abby performed a segment of the *Cats* choreography most closely associated with her character, then departed the corps and moved towards The Phantom, Howard McGillin, isolated in the downstage-left corner.

Quietly, softly, powerfully, the stage behind these two began to fill with the principal actors of the show, and us chorus-folk. It was all so subtle, it happened without the audience noticing. "Victoria" nudged the "Phantom" to let her in. He relented, finally, and suddenly, the audience realized that everyone in the company was on stage behind them. The Phantom and Victoria reveled in their newfound friendship for just a moment, and then she started to exit, stage right.

The entire company, sensing her importance and the significance of her visit…and her departure…gathered together and followed her for a few steps. She then stopped to bow to us, her back to the audience, saying: 'This honor belongs to you, now.' The entire group bowed to her, and she continued her proud exit. We continued to shadow her exit for three more steps, leaning forward, one arm outstretched to wish her well. She never turned back to see it (a suggestion by Cameron, actually!) And then, the *Phantom* Company, members of the longest-running-show in Broadway history began to celebrate, and in doing so, prepared to receive the rest of our special guests onstage.

There were dance segments with all of the Raouls and Christines, the Carlottas and Piangis, the original cast, The Phantoms, all masked, the production team, and then Michael

Crawford charged to center stage and proclaimed this a celebration worth happening. The air was filled with balloons, streamers, confetti and smoke. The spotlights scoped the room, and from my vantage point way the hell upstage-left, I couldn't stop the tears that streamed down my face. WE DID IT! And we did it with the sense of occasion that Hal Prince had once mentioned. It was important, it was poetic, it was powerful.

Most Exciting Celebrity Visitors: The Warren Beatty family made quite an impression on all of us…and we have to include all of the stars of stage and screen that attended our record-breaking performance and party thereafter.

Actors Who Performed the Most Roles: Peter Lockyer, Jim Romick, and Kris Koop all cover the most principal contracts in the show.

"Carols for a Cure" Carol: "Help Is on the Way."

"Gypsy of the Year" Skit: No title. Crafted by Jim Weitzer, Harriet Clark, Polly Baird, Shaun Colledge and John Wasiniak.

"Easter Bonnet" Skit: "Help Is on the Way" performed by members of the entire cast, crew and orchestra.

Fave Offsite Hangouts: Angus McIndoe and McHale's (RIP).

Mascot: Teddy: Howard McGillin's sweetest, cuddliest, never-howls-when-Daddy's-singing, most-loveable, adorable backstage puppy dog that we all love. Too much? You haven't met Teddy.

Backstage Rituals: George Lee Andrews has created and maintained a stunningly accurate, up-to-date Wall of Fame (now, adorning most of the walls in the basement of the theatre), with a

photograph of every individual who has performed under contract on our stage, either in a chorus or principal role, EVER…but the trick is, you have to have left the show to have the honor. George even lovingly labeled the original cast members' photos with "OC" before the gala. An amazing and inspiring tribute from an amazing and inspiring man!

George Lee also maintains a different Wall of Fame, this one dedicated to the children, both two and four-legged, that belong to the Phantom Family. Some are newborns, some ready to graduate from college, and some have had children of their own! WOW. That puts the length of this run into perspective for you!

Each year, at the Holidays, George Dummitt draws a Christmas Tree and a Menorah in colored chalk on the back of the SR2 hard masking, and the Menorah is "lit" each night of Chanukah. All drawings remain, though some are covered by a bolster that was installed a few years into the run.

The Hair Room putting out mouse traps on every Saturday night. Unloading them on Monday night is not a favorite, but it is a backstage ritual. RIP.

Ken Kantor screams—no, shrieks like a woman with her ass on fire—while the Phantom descends the stairs at the end of the Masquerade Scene. Every show, always funny!

Lottery picks and discussions about the numbers, a la Erna and Leon. Luck—or science? The debate rages on!

Ballerinas hitting the "barre" under the stage, warming up their footwear—toe spacers, bunheads, pointe-shoes themselves—by holding the pieces right up to their mouths and blowing. Then, back onto their feet they go! Mind-boggling, the dedication to their craft! I don't even want to smell my own breath when I sing, let alone my footwear!

Catchphrases: 1.) "Restore" (said with a distinctly Southern accent, often).
2.) "Diamonds" (Gillie's new word for what used to be "Twitches." It makes sense to us!)
3.) "Welcome back, BITCH" (an acronym for Back In The Chorus, Honey): a congratulatory understudy welcome to other understudies, after they've had a run in the spotlight.

Memorable Ad-Libs: "I'm sorry sir! There weren't any bullets!" (Shouted in defense when a gun didn't fire on cue.)

"Firmin, DEAD…I mean Piangi…" (Tim Jerome, as M. Firmin, accidentally pronouncing himself dead.)

"Please Monsieur, there's no one there…there's no one there, there's no one there, there's no one there…there's no one there, there's no one there…." (Buquet)

Favorite Moment During the Performance: I think we have a hands-down winner…our new final bow, with the WOOOOOSH, newly added by Gillie for the record-breaker. It's a keeper, and most of us still say WOOOOOSH every time.

Cast members John Jellison and Daniel Rychlec at the "Gypsy of the Year" Competition.

Photo by Aubrey Reuben

The Pillowman

First Preview: March 21, 2005. Opened: April 10, 2005.
Closed September 18, 2005 after 23 Previews and 188 Performances.

PLAYBILL

CAST
(in order of appearance)

Tupolski . . . . .JEFF GOLDBLUM
Katurian . . . . .BILLY CRUDUP
Ariel . . . . .ŽELJKO IVANEK
Michal . . . . .MICHAEL STUHLBARG
Father .TED KŌCH
                    VIRGINIA LOUISE SMITH
Boy . . . . .JESSE SHANE BRONSTEIN
Girl . . . . .MADELEINE MARTIN
Man . . . . .RICK HOLMES

UNDERSTUDIES

For Tupolski and Ariel: TED KŌCH
For Katurian, Michal and Father: RICK
HOLMES
For Mother: KATE GLEASON
For Boy and Girl: COLBY MINIFIE

---

⑤ BOOTH THEATRE
222 West 45th Street
A Shubert Organization Theatre

Gerald Schoenfeld, *Chairman*   Philip J. Smith, *President*

Robert E. Wankel, *Executive Vice President*

Boyett Ostar Productions   Robert Fox
Arielle Tepper   Stephanie P. McClelland   Debra Black   Dede Harris/Morton Swinsky
Roy Furman/Jon Avnet in association with Joyce Schweickert

present

BILLY CRUDUP   JEFF GOLDBLUM
ŽELJKO IVANEK   MICHAEL STUHLBARG

in

NT The National Theatre of Great Britain's
production of

THE PILLOWMAN

by MARTIN McDONAGH

with

JESSE SHANE BRONSTEIN   KATE GLEASON   RICK HOLMES
TED KŌCH   MADELEINE MARTIN   COLBY MINIFIE   VIRGINIA LOUISE SMITH

Scenic/Costume Designer
SCOTT PASK

Lighting Design
BRIAN MacDEVITT

Sound Design   Music by
PAUL ARDITTI   PADDY CUNNEEN

Casting   Press Representative   Marketing   Production Manager
JIM CARNAHAN   BARLOW•HARTMAN   HHC MARKETING   ARTHUR SICCARDI

General Management   Fight Director   Production Stage Manager
NINA LANNAN ASSOCIATES   J. STEVEN WHITE   JAMES HARKER

Directed by
JOHN CROWLEY

Special thanks to British Airways for their generous support of the National Theatre on Broadway.

6/1/05

Madeleine Martin

Billy Crudup, Željko Ivanek and Jeff Goldblum.

The Pillowman

Billy Crudup
Katurian

Jeff Goldblum
Tupolski

Željko Ivanek
Ariel

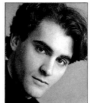
Michael Stuhlbarg
Michal

Ted Koch
Father

Virginia Louise Smith
Mother

Jesse Shane Bronstein
Boy

Madeleine Martin
Girl

Rick Holmes
Blind Man

Kate Gleason
Standby for Mother

Colby Minifie
*Standby for
Boy and Girl*

Martin McDonagh
Playwright

John Crowley
Director

Scott Pask
*Scenic &
Costume Designer*

Brian MacDevitt
Lighting Designer

Jim Carnahan
Casting

J. Steven White
Fight Director

James Harker
*Production
Stage Manager*

Thea Bradshaw Gillies
Stage Manager

Arielle Tepper
Producer

Stephanie P.
McClelland
Producer

Morton Swinsky
Producer

Jon Avnet
Producer

Debra Black
Associate Producer

Bob Boyett
Producer

Roy Furman
Producer

Dede Harris
Producer

Bill Haber,
Ostar Enterprises
Producer

Arthur P. Siccardi
Technical Supervisor

The Pillowman

Stage Management
Thea Gillies and Jim Harker.

Hair
Leone Gagliardi and Tom Denier Jr.

Box Office
(L-R): Vincent Whittaker and Edward Whittaker.

*Not Pictured: Marshall Colbrunner, Rianna Bryceland,
Head Usher Katherine Coscia and Nirmala Sharma.*

Stage Crew
Front Row (L-R): Chris Cronin (Associate Sound Designer),
Amanda Tramontozzi (Children's Guardian), Kelly Kinsella (Dresser).
Second Row (L-R): Jimmy Keane (House Props), Denise Grillo (Props Sub),
Kathleen Gallagher (Production Wardrobe Supervisor), Jessica Chaney (Dresser).
Third Row (L-R): Brian GF McGarity (Head Electrician), Ronnie Burns (House Electrician),
Thea Bradshaw Gillies (1st Asst. Stage Manager), Patrick Shea (Production Carpenter),
Leone Gaglardi (Hair Supervisor) and James Harker (Production Stage Manager).

Front of House
Front (L-R): Ralph Jett, Chrissie Collins, Theresa Aceves, Laurel Ann Wilson (House Manager)
and Bernadette Bokun.
Back: Jorge Colon, Vincent Whittaker, Jaime Wilhelm, Marjorie Glover, Dara Cohen and Tim Wilhelm.

Wardrobe
Kelly Kinsella, Jessica Chaney
and Kathleen Gallagher.

The Pillowman

The Pillowman Playbill: March 2005

The Pillowman Playbill: April 2005

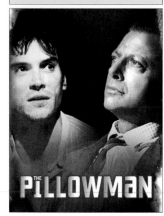

The Pillowman Playbill: July 2005

PRODUCTION STAFF FOR
THE PILLOWMAN

GENERAL MANAGER
NINA LANNAN ASSOCIATES

Associate General Manager ....MAGGIE EDELMAN
Company Manager ....LESLIE A. GLASSBURN

GENERAL PRESS REPRESENTATIVE
BARLOW•HARTMAN PUBLIC RELATIONS

John Barlow	Michael Hartman
Dennis Crowley	Ryan Ratelle

CASTING
Jim Carnahan Casting
Carrie Gardner, Mele Nagler, CSA
JV Mercanti, Kate Schwabe,
Stephen Kopel

Production Stage Manager ....**James Harker**	
Stage Manager ....**Thea Bradshaw Gillies**	

Assistant Director ....Todd Lundquist
Associate Scenic Designers ....Orit Jacoby Carroll,
Nancy Thun
Scenic Design Assistant ....Tobin Ost
Associate Costume Designer (US) ....Brian Russman
Associate Costume Designer (UK) ....Irene Bohan
Associate Lighting Designer ....Jason Lyons
Assistant Lighting Designer ....Rachel Eichorn
Associate Sound Designer ....Christopher Cronin

Makeup Design ....Angelina Avallone
Hair Supervisor ....Leone Gagliardi

Production Carpenter ....Patrick Shea
Production Electrician ....Michael Pitzer
Head Electrician ....Brian GF McGarity
Production Sound ....Christopher Cronin
Production Properties ....Joe Redmond
Fight Captain ....Rick Holmes
Production Wardrobe Supervisor ....Kathleen Gallagher
Dressers ....Jessica Chaney, Kelly
Kinsella
Makeup Supervisor ....Tom Denier,
Jr.
Production Assistant ....Bethany Russell
Lighting Intern ....Ali Cruso
Assistants to Mr. Boyett   Diane Murphy, Tom Alberg
Assistant to Mr. Haber ....Theresa Pisanelli
Advertising ....SpotCo/Drew Hodges, Jim Edwards,
Jim Aquino, Lauren Hunter
Marketing ......HCC Marketing/Hugh Hysell, Adam Jay,
Michael Redman, Jillian Boeni, Matt Sicoli,
Amanada Marcus, Caitlin Strype, Jason Zammit
Production Photographer ....Joan Marcus
Production Web Design ....Situation Marketing/
Damian Bazadona
NTNY Web Design ....Dotmeta
Accounting ....Fried & Kowgios CPA's LLP,
Robert Fried, CPA
Controller ....Anne Stewart FitzRoy, CPA
Legal Counsel ....Lazarus & Harris, LLP/
Scott Lazarus, Esq., Robert Harris, Esq.,
David Friedlander, Esq.
Immigration Counsel ....Kramer Levin Naftalis &
Frankel LLP,

Mark D. Koestler
Company Management Associate ....Jon Ferrari
General Management Associates   Kristy Bronder,
Ethan Brown, Katherine McNamee
Press Office Manager ....Bethany Larsen
Press Associates ....Leslie Baden, Jon Dimond,
Carol Fineman, Rick Miramontez,
Mark Pino, Miguel Raya,
Gerilyn Shur, Andy Snyder,
Wayne Wolf
Insurance ....Yasmine Ramos, MARSH USA, Inc.
Banking ....JP Morgan Chase
Payroll ....Castellana Services, Inc.
Merchandising ....Max Merchandising
Travel Agent ....Andi Henig, Tzell Travel
Children's Tutoring ....On-Location Education
Children's Wrangler ....Bridget Walders
Sign Language Consultant ....Jackie Roth

NATIONAL THEATRE, LONDON
Chairman of the NT Board ....Sir Hayden Phillips
Director ....Nicholas Hytner
Executive Director ....Nick Starr
Assistant Producer ....Tim Levy

CREDITS
Scenery constructed and painted by Hudson Scenic Studio, Inc. Lighting and sound equipment from PRG. UK properties constructed by the National Theatre of Great Britain. Costumes by Barbara Matera Ltd., Tricorne Inc., Arel Studio. Costume painting by Hochi Asiatico. Custom shirts by Allmeier. Wigs by The Wig Party. Smoking accessories by Nat Sherman. Rehearsed at Roundabout Rehearsal Studio.

SPECIAL THANKS
National Theatre: Katrina Gilroy, James Manley, Jason Barnes, Alison Rankin, David Milling, Nic Haffenden; Jo Nield, Suzie Fairchild and the American Associates of the Royal National Theatre.

 THE SHUBERT ORGANIZATION, INC.
Board of Directors

Gerald Schoenfeld	**Philip J. Smith**
Chairman	President
John W. Kluge	**Lee J. Seidler**
Michael I. Sovern	**Stuart Subotnick**

Irving M. Wall

Robert E. Wankel
Executive Vice President

Peter Entin	**Elliot Greene**
Vice President -	Vice President -
Theatre Operations	Finance
David Andrews	**John Darby**
Vice President -	Vice President -
Shubert Ticketing Services	Facilities

House Manager ....Laurel A. Wilson

The Pillowman
SCRAPBOOK

Photos by Aubrey Reuben

1. Billy Crudup at "Broadway Barks 7!"
2. Jeff Goldblum (R) with members of the cast at the unveiling of his portrait for the Broadway Wall of Fame at Tony's Di Napoli restaurant.
3. Goldblum and Madeleine Martin at "Broadway Barks 7!"
4. Michael Stuhlbarg (L) and Željko Ivanek at Tony's Di Napoli.
5. Goldblum at the unveiling.

Primo

First Preview: July 8, 2005. Opened: July 11, 2005.
Closed August 14, 2005 after 4 previews and 35 performances.

Antony Sher
as Primo Levi

Photo by Ivan Kyncl

Cast

Primo Levi .... ANTONY SHER

Antony Sher's adaptation is from Stuart Woolf's
English translation of
Primo Levi's *Se questo e un uomo*.

THE MUSIC BOX

THE ESTATE OF IRVING BERLIN AND THE SHUBERT ORGANIZATION, OWNERS
239 W. 45th STREET

BILL KENWRIGHT and THELMA HOLT
present
THE NATIONAL THEATRE OF GREAT BRITAIN PRODUCTION

ANTONY SHER
in
primo

Based on "If This Is A Man" by
PRIMO LEVI

Adapted by
ANTONY SHER

Scenic & Costume Design	Original Lighting Design	Lighting Recreated by
HILDEGARD BECHTLER	**PAUL PYANT**	**DAVID HOWE**

Sound Design	Music Composed by
RICH WALSH	**JONATHAN GOLDSTEIN**

Technical Supervisor	Production Supervisor
LARRY MORLEY	**ERNEST HALL**

Press	General Management
PHILIP RINALDI PUBLICITY	**RICHARDS/CLIMAN, INC.**

PROGRAM NOTE

Directed by
RICHARD WILSON

The Producers wish to express their appreciation to Theatre Development Fund for its support of this production.

NT   **LIVE BROADWAY**

7/11/05

Antony Sher
Primo Levi

Richard Wilson
Director

Jonathan Goldstein
Music

Paul Pyant
*Original Lighting
Design*

Primo

Hildegard Bechtler
Scenic and Costume Design

David Howe
Lighting Re-creation

Thelma Holt
Producer

Bill Kenwright
Producer

CREW

Front Row (L-R): Jim Bay (Sub-Sound Engineer), Thomas Vowles (Stage Manager), Kim Garnett (House Propertyman), Jonathan Schulman (House Manager).
Back Row (L-R): F. Lee Iwanski (House Electrician), Brig Berney (Company Manager), Antony Sher (Performer/Star), David Hyslop (Stage Manager), Rob Bevenger (Wardrobe Supervisor) and Dennis Maher (House Carpenter).

Not pictured: Jared Sayeg (Assistant Lighting Designer), Christopher Cronin (Assistant Sound Designer), Bill Lewis (Assistant Sound Designer), Tony Polemeni (Sound Engineer), Robin Thompson-Clarke (Cello), Paul Beniston (Trumpet), Andy Findon (Piccolo), Tristan Fry (Percussion), Oren Marshall (Tuba) and Ian Watson (Accordion).

Photo by Ben Strothmann

Primo
Scrapbook

Photos by Aubrey Reuben

1. Antony Sher at the opening night party at Sardi's restaurant.
2. Sher is joined by Nobel laureate and Holocaust survivor Elie Wiesel.
3. Producer Bill Kenwright on opening night.
4. Director Richard Wilson (L) and Antony Sher celebrate at Sardi's
5. Guests model/actress Silviya Peneva (L) and Lynn Redgrave.

2005-2006 Awards

DRAMA DESK AWARD
Outstanding Solo Performance
(Sir Antony Sher)

OUTER CRITICS CIRCLE AWARD
Outstanding Solo Performance
(Sir Antony Sher)

The Producers

First Preview: March 21, 2001. Opened: April 19, 2001.
Still running as of May 31, 2006.

PLAYBILL

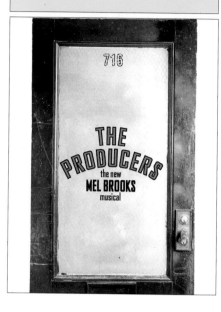

CAST
(in order of appearance)

The Usherettes	MELISSA RAE MAHON, JENNIFER SMITH
Max Bialystock	BRAD OSCAR
Leo Bloom	HUNTER FOSTER
Hold-me Touch-me	MADELEINE DOHERTY
Mr. Marks	KEVIN LIGON
Franz Liebkind	JOHN TREACY EGAN
Carmen Ghia	BRAD MUSGROVE
Roger DeBris	GARY BEACH
Bryan	PETER MARINOS
Kevin	KEVIN LIGON
Scott	JIM BORSTELMANN
Shirley	KATHY FITZGERALD
Ulla	ANGIE SCHWORER
Lick-me Bite-me	JENNIFER SMITH
Kiss-me Feel-me	KATHY FITZGERALD
Jack Lepidus	PETER MARINOS
Donald Dinsmore	JIM BORSTELMANN
Jason Green	KEVIN LIGON
Lead Tenor	ERIC GUNHUS
Sergeant	KEVIN LIGON
O'Rourke	WILL TAYLOR
O'Riley	CHRIS KLINK
O'Houllihan	ROBERT H. FOWLER
Guard	JIM BORSTELMANN
Bailiff	WILL TAYLOR
Judge	PETER MARINOS
Foreman of Jury	KATHY FITZGERALD

Continued on next page

ST. JAMES THEATRE
A JUJAMCYN THEATRE
ROCCO LANDESMAN
PRESIDENT

PAUL LIBIN
PRODUCING DIRECTOR

JACK VIERTEL
CREATIVE DIRECTOR

Rocco Landesman   Clear Channel Entertainment   The Frankel • Baruch • Viertel • Routh Group
Bob and Harvey Weinstein   Rick Steiner   Robert F.X. Sillerman   Mel Brooks
In Association with James D. Stern/Douglas Meyer

present

Brad Oscar   Hunter Foster

in

THE PRODUCERS

the new
Mel Brooks
musical

Book by **Mel Brooks and Thomas Meehan**   Music and Lyrics by **Mel Brooks**
and by Special Arrangement with StudioCanal

also starring

Gary Beach   John Treacy Egan   Brad Musgrove   Angie Schworer

With

Madeleine Doherty   Kathy Fitzgerald   Eric Gunhus
Kevin Ligon   Peter Marinos   Jennifer Smith

Jim Borstelmann   Angie C. Creighton   Robert H. Fowler   Justin Greer   Kimberly Hester   Stacey Todd Holt
Shauna Hoskin   Kimberly Catherine Jones   Renée Klapmeyer   Chris Klink   Melissa Rae Mahon
Liz McKendry   Jessica Perrizo   Jason Patrick Sands   Will Taylor   Courtney Young

Scenery Designed by	Costumes Designed by	Lighting Designed by
Robin Wagner	William Ivey Long	Peter Kaczorowski
Sound Designed by	Casting by	Original Casting by
Steve C. Kennedy	Tara Rubin Casting	Johnson-Liff Associates
Associate Director	Associate Choreographer	Wigs & Hair Designed by
Steven Zweigbaum	Warren Carlyle	Paul Huntley
Music Direction and Vocal Arrangements by	Orchestrations by	Music Coordinator
Patrick S. Brady	Doug Besterman	John Miller

General Management	Technical Supervisor	Press Representative	Associate Producers
Richard Frankel Productions Laura Green	Juniper Street Productions	Barlow • Hartman	Frederic H. and Rhoda Mayerson Jennifer Costello

Musical Arrangements and Supervision by
Glen Kelly

Direction and Choreography by
Susan Stroman

10/1/05

(L-R) Gary Beach, Hunter Foster, Brad Oscar and Brad Musgrove.

Photo by Paul Kolnik

The Producers

SCENES and MUSICAL NUMBERS

ACT ONE
New York, 1959

Scene 1: Shubert Alley
"Opening Night" ....The Ensemble
"The King of Broadway" ....Max & Ensemble
Scene 2: Max's Office, June 16, 1959
"We Can Do It" ....Max & Leo
Scene 3: The Chambers Street Offices of Whitehall and Marks
"I Wanna Be A Producer" ....Leo & The Accountants
Scene 4: Max's Office
"We Can Do It" (Reprise) ....Max & Leo
Scene 5: Max's Office Early the Following Morning
Scene 6: The Rooftop of a Greenwich Village Apartment Building
"In Old Bavaria" ....Franz
"Der Guten Tag Hop Clop" ....Franz, Max, Leo
Scene 7: The Living Room of Renowned Theatrical Director Roger DeBris' Elegant Upper
East Side Townhouse on a Sunny Tuesday Afternoon in June
"Keep It Gay" ....Roger, Carmen, Bryan, Kevin, Scott, Shirley, Max, Leo
Scene 8: Max's Office
"When You Got It, Flaunt It" ....Ulla
Scene 9: Little Old Lady Land
"Along Came Bialy" ....Max, Little Old Ladies
"Act One Finale" ......Max, Leo, Franz, Ulla, Roger, Carmen, Bryan, Kevin, Scott, Shirley, Ensemble

ACT TWO

Scene 1: Max's Office, late morning, a few weeks later
"That Face" ....Leo, Ulla, Max
Scene 2: The Bare Stage of a Broadway Theatre
"Haben Sie Gehoert Das Deutsche Band?" ....Jason, Franz
Scene 3: Shubert Alley
"Opening Night" (Reprise) ....The Usherettes
"You Never Say 'Good Luck' On Opening Night" ....Roger, Max, Carmen, Franz, Leo
Scene 4: The Stage of The Shubert Theatre
"Springtime For Hitler" ....Lead Tenor, Roger, Ulla, Ensemble
Scene 5: Max's Office, later that night
"Where Did We Go Right?" ....Max, Leo
Scene 6: The Holding Cell of a New York Courthouse, ten days later.
"Betrayed" ....Max
Scene 7: A New York Courtroom
" 'Til Him" ....Leo, Max
Scene 8: Sing Sing
"Prisoners Of Love" ....The Convicts
Scene 9: The Stage of The Shubert Theatre
"Prisoners Of Love" (continued) ....Roger, Ulla, The Ensemble
Scene 10: Shubert Alley
"Prisoners of Love (Reprise): Leo and Max" ....Leo, Max
Curtain Call
"Goodbye!" ....The Company

ORCHESTRA
Conductor: PATRICK S. BRADY
Associate Conductor: PHIL RENO

Woodwinds: Vincent Della Rocca, Steven J.
Greenfield, Jay Hassler, Alva F. Hunt, Frank
Santagata
Trumpets: David Rogers, Nick Marchione,
Frank Greene
Tenor Trombones: Dan Levine, Tim Sessions
Bass Trombone: Chris Olness
French Horn: Nancy Billman

Concert Master: Rick Dolan
Violins: Ashley D. Horne, Louise Owen,
Karen M. Karlsrud, Helen Kim
Cello: Laura Bontrager
Harp: Anna Reinersman
String Bass: Robert Renino
Drums: Larry Lelli
Percussion: Benjamin Herman
Keyboard: Phil Reno

Music Coordinator: JOHN MILLER
Additional Orchestrations: LARRY BLANK

Angie Schworer and Hunter Foster.

The Producers

Brad Oscar
Max Bialystock

Hunter Foster
Leo Bloom

Gary Beach
Roger DeBris

John Treacy Egan
Franz Liebkind

Brad Musgrove
Carmen Ghia

Angie Schworer
Ulla

Madeleine Doherty
Hold-me Touch-me

Kathy Fitzgerald
Shirley,
Kiss-me Feel-me,
Foreman of Jury

Eric Gunhus
Lead Tenor

Kevin Ligon
Mr. Marks, Kevin,
Jason Green,
Sergeant, Trustee

Peter Marinos
Bryan, Jack Lepidus,
Judge

Jennifer Smith
Usherette,
Lick-me Bite-me

Jim Borstelmann
Blind Violinist, Scott,
Donald Dinsmore,
Guard

Angie C. Creighton
Swing

Robert H. Fowler
O'Houllihan

Justin Greer
Swing

Kimberly Hester
Ensemble

Stacey Todd Holt
Swing

Shauna Hoskin
Ensemble

Kimberly Catherine
Jones
Ensemble

Renée Klapmeyer
Ensemble

Chris Klink
O'Riley

Melissa Rae Mahon
Usherette

Liz McKendry
Swing

Jessica Perrizo
Dance Captain,
Ensemble

Jason Patrick Sands
Swing

Will Taylor
O'Rourke, Bailiff

Courtney Young
Resident
Choreographer,
Swing

Mel Brooks
Book, Composer and
Lyricist

Thomas Meehan
Book

Susan Stroman
Director/
Choreographer

Robin Wagner
Set Design

William Ivey Long
Costume Designer

Peter Kaczorowksi
Lighting Designer

Steve Canyon Kennedy
Sound Designer

The Producers

Tara Rubin,
Tara Rubin Casting
Casting

Vincent Liff and Geoffrey Johnson,
Johnson-Liff Associates
Original Casting

Lisa Shriver
*Assistant
Choreographer*

Paul Huntley
Wig and Hair Design

Doug Besterman
Orchestrations

John Miller
Music Coordinator

Laura Green,
Richard Frankel
Productions
*General
Management*

Guy Kwan, John Paull, Hillary Blanken,
Kevin Broomell, Ana-Rose Greene,
Juniper Street Productions
Technical Supervisor

Rocco Landesman
Producer

Steven Baruch,
The Frankel•Baruch•
Viertel•Routh Group
Producer

Tom Viertel
The Frankel•Baruch•
Viertel•Routh Group
Producer

Marc Routh
The Frankel•Baruch•
Viertel•Routh Group
Producer

Richard Frankel,
The Frankel•Baruch•
Viertel•Routh Group
Producer

Harvey Weinstein
Producer

Bob Weinstein
Producer

Rick Steiner
Producer

Robert F.X. Sillerman
Producer

Douglas L. Meyer
Producer

Frederic H. Mayerson
Associate Producer

Rhoda Mayerson
Associate Producer

Brooks Ashmanskas
Carmen Ghia

Roger Bart
Leo Bloom

Jonathan Freeman
Roger DeBris

Chris Holly
O'Riley, Ensemble

Richard Kind
Max Bialystock

Mike McGowan
*Bailiff, O'Rourke,
Ensemble*

Patrick Wetzel
Swing

The Producers

Roger Bart
Leo Bloom

DJ Gray
*Usherette,
Lick-me Bite-me,
Ensemble, Swing*

Chris Holly
O'Riley, Ensemble

**Christina Marie
Norrup**
*Lick-me Bite-me,
Usherette, Ensemble*

Bill Nolte
Franz Liebkind

Jai Rodriguez
Carmen Ghia

André Ward
*O'Houlihan,
Ensemble*

Wendy Waring
Ensemble

Ashley Yeater
Usherette, Ensemble

STAGE MANAGEMENT
(L-R): Ira Mont (Stage Manager),
Alexis Shorter (Assistant Stage
Manager), Casey Aileen Rafter
(Assistant Stage Manager) and
Steven Zweigbaum (Associate
Director).

Color photos by Ben Strothmann

BOX OFFICE
(L-R): Vinny Sclafani (Head Treasurer),
Carmine Loiacono (Treasurer) and
Michael Milione (Treasurer).

The Producers

CREW

Kneeling (L-R): Joe Pearson (Head Electrician), David Gotwald (Head Sound Engineer), Joe Caputo (Props), Bob Miller (Follow Spot Operator).
Standing (L-R): Jim Devins (Carpenter), Timothy McDonough (House Carpenter), Scott Silvian (Assistant Sound Engineer), Timothy McDonough, Jr. (Flyman), Tom Galinski (Electrician), Tom Ferguson (Assistant Electrician), Albert Sayers (House Electrician), Ryan McDonough (Carpenter), Julia Rubin (Follow Spot Operator), Tom Maloney (Electrician) and Joe Lenihan (Sound Engineer).

FRONT OF HOUSE STAFF

Kneeling (L-R): Cynthia Lopiano (Head Usher) and Ashley Devlin (Usher).
Standing (L-R): Lenny Baron (Ticket Taker), Scott Rippe (Usher), Catherine Junior (Usher), Donna Van Der Linden (Ticket Taker), Murray Bradley (Usher), Heather Jewels (Usher) and Lauren Vadino (House Manager).

WARDROBE AND HAIR DEPARTMENT

Kneeling (L-R): Roy Seiler (Dresser), Dennis Birchall (Dresser), Douglas C. Petitjean (Production Wardobe Supevisor).
Standing (L-R): Adam Girardet (Dresser), Laura Beattie (Dresser), Misty Fernandez (Dresser), Scotty Cain (Dresser), Ron Fleming (Dresser), Jessica Minczeski (Assistant Wardrobe Supervisor), Jessica Dermody (Dresser), Judith Farley Haugh (Wig Stylist), Michele Rutter (Wig Supervisor), Constance Holperin (Dresser), Shanah-Ann Kendall (Wig Stylist), Mary Kay Yezerski (Wig Stylist), Ron Mack (Assistant Wig Supervisor), and Susie Ghebresillassie (Dresser).

The Producers

GENERAL MANAGEMENT
RICHARD FRANKEL PRODUCTIONS

Richard Frankel   Marc Routh   Laura Green
Rod Kaats   Jo Porter   Joe Watson

COMPANY MANAGER
Kathy Lowe
Associate Company Manager .... Jackie Newman

GENERAL PRESS REPRESENTATIVE
BARLOW • HARTMAN

John Barlow   Michael Hartman
Rick Miramontez   Jon Dimond

CASTING
TARA RUBIN CASTING
Tara Rubin, CSA
Dunja Vitolic, Eric Woodall, Laura Schutzel,
Mona Slomsky, Rebecca Carfagna

Production Stage Manager	**Steven Zweigbaum**
Stage Manager	**Ira Mont**
Assistant Stage Managers	Casey Aileen Rafter, Alexis Shorter
Associate Choreographer	Warren Carlyle
Assistant Director	Scott Bishop
Assistant Choreographer	Lisa Shriver
Resident Choreographer	Courtney Young
Dance Captain	Jessica Perrizo
Technical Supervisor	Juniper Street Productions, Hillary Blanken, John H. Paul III
Technical Associates	Kevin Broomell, Lonnie Goertz, Guy Kwan
Associate Set Designer	David Peterson
Assistant Set Designers	Atkin Pace, Thomas Peter Sarr
Associate Costume Designer	Martha Bromelmeier
Assistant Costume Designer	Tom Beall
Assistants to William Ivey Long	Laura Oppenheimer, Heather Bair
Automated Light Programmer	Josh Weitzman
First Assistant Lighting Designer	Paul Miller
Assistant Lighting Designers	Mick Addison Smith, Philip S. Rosenberg
Associate Sound Designer	John Shivers
Supervising Production Carpenter	Joe Patria
Head Carpenter	Jack Cennamo
Assistant Carpenters	Michael Cennamo, Christopher Morcone, Guy Patria, Richard Patria
Supervising Production Electrician	Rick Baxter
Head Electrician	Joe Pearson
Assistant Electrician	Tom Ferguson
Head Sound Engineer	David Gotwald
Assistant Sound Engineer	Scott Silvian
Supervising Property Master	Laura Koch
Production Wardrobe Supervisor	Douglas C. Petitjean
Wardrobe Supervisor	Dede LaBarre
Assistant Wardrobe Supervisor	Jessica Minczeski
Mr. Oscar's Dresser	Terry LaVada
Mr. Foster's Dresser	Scotty Cain
Dressers	Laura Beattie, Dennis Birchall, Jessica Dermody, Ron Fleming, Susie Ghebresillassie, Constance Halperin, Shannon Munn, John Rinaldi, Roy Seiler
Wig Supervisor	Michele Rutter
Assistant Wig Supervisor	Ron Mack
Wig Stylists	Judith Farley Haugh, Shanah-Ann Kendall, Mary Kay Yezerski
Makeup Design	Randy Houston Mercer
Music Coordinator	John Miller

Assistant Music Coordinator	Todd Cutrona
Assistant to Mr. Miller	Matthew P. Ettinger
Associate Conductor	Philip Reno
Synthesizer Programming	Music Arts Technologies, Brett Sommer
Rehearsal Drummer	Cubby O'Brien
Music Preparation	Miller Music Services
Additional Orchestrations	Larry Blank
Make-up Consultant	Melissa Silver
Physical Therapy Services	PhysioArts
Associate to Mr. Brooks	Leah Zappy
Assistant to Mr. Brooks	Jennifer Yale
Assistant to Mr. Landesman	Nicole Kastrinos
Asstistants to Mr. Sillerman	Gini Smythe, Matthew Morse, Manuela Perea
Assistant to Mr. Steiner	Kathy Wall
Assistants to Mr. Stern	Debbie Bisno, Leah Callaghan
Assistant to Mr. Baruch	Sonja Soper
Assistant to Mr. Viertel	Tania Senewiratne
Management Assistants	Tracy Geltman, Eric Cornell
Production Assistants	Kate Sullivan, Donald Fried, Adam M. Muller, Erin J. Riggs, Leah Richardson, Sharon Del Pilar
Advertising	Serino Coyne, Inc., Nancy Coyne, Sandy Block, Thomas Mygatt, Brad Lapin, Jennifer Richman
Promotions/Marketing	The Marketing Group
Photographers	Paul Kolnik, Norman Jean Roy
Theatre Displays	King Displays
Insurance	Marsh USA Inc., Anthony Catanzaro
Legal Counsel	Elliot Brown, Jason Baruch; Franklin Weinrib, Rudell & Vassallo, P.C.; Alan U. Schwartz; Greenberg Traurig, LLP
Banking	Chase Manhattan Bank, Stephanie Dalton, Michelle Gibbons
Payroll Service	Castellana Service, Inc.
Accounting	Fried and Kowgios Partners, LLP
Travel Agencies	JMC Travel, Navigant International
Exclusive Tour Direction	On The Road, The Booking Group
On-Stage Merchandising	George Fenmore/ More Merchandising International
Concessions	Clear Channel Entertainment, Theatrical Merchandising
New York Rehearsals	The New 42nd Street Studios
Opening Night Coordinator	Tobak-Dantchik Events and Promotions, Suzanne Tobak, Jennifer Falik, Rebakah Sale
Group Sales	Show Tix (212) 302-7000

RICHARD FRANKEL PRODUCTIONS STAFF

Finance Director	**Michael Naumann**
Assistant to Mr. Frankel	Jeff Romley
Assistant to Mr. Routh	Michael Sag
Assistant to Ms. Green	Joshua A. Saletnik
Assistant Finance Director	Liz Hines
Information Technology Manager	Roddy Pimentel
Management Assistant	Heidi Schading
Accounting Assistant	Elsie Jamin-Maguire
National Sales and	
Marketing Director	**Ronni Mandell**
Director of Business Affairs	**Carter Anne McGowan**
Marketing Coordinator	Melissa Marano
Office Manager	Lori Steiger-Perry
Office Assistant	Stephanie Adamczyk
Receptionist	Deniece Alvarado, Randy Rainbow
Interns	Lauren Berger, Katie Berkshire, Todd Blass, Eric Cornell, Matthew Martin, Erin Porvaznik, Kirsten Rega, Nathan Vernon, Lucinda Walker

CLEAR CHANNEL ENTERTAINMENT — THEATRICAL

Miles C. Wilkin, Scott Zeiger, David Ian,
Steve Winton, David Anderson, Lauren Reid,
Lynn Blandford, Bradley Broecker, Philip Brohn,
Jennifer Costello, Jennifer DeLange, Joanna Hagan,
Eric Joseph, Susan Krajsa, David Lazar,
Hailey Lustig, Carl Pasbjerg, Debra Peltz,
Denise Perry, Courtney Pierce, Dominic Roncace,
Alison Spiriti, Dan Swartz

Make-up courtesy of M.A.C Cosmetics

CREDITS AND ACKNOWLEDGEMENTS
Scenery and scenic effects built, painted, electrified and automated by Showmotion, Inc., Norwalk, CT; Scenery fabrication by Entolo/Scenic Technologies, a division of Production Resource Group, L.L.C., New Windsor, NY; Additional scenery built by Hudson Scenic Studios; Scenery automation by Showmotion, Inc., using the Autocue Computerized Motion Control System; Show control and scenic motion control featuring Stage Command Systems by Entolo, a division of Production Resource Group, L.L.C., New Windsor, NY; Soft goods by I. Weiss, New York; Water fountain effect by Waltzing Waters; Stormtrooper puppets designed and fabricated by Eoin Sprott; Tanks and pigeon puppets designed and fabricated by Jerard Studio; Lighting equipment from Fourth Phase New Jersey; Sound equipment from ProMix.; Costumes by Euro Co., Timberlake Studios, Inc., Tricorne New York City, Jennifer Love Costumes; Tailoring by Scafatti Custom Tailors; Shoes by LaDuca Shoes NYC, T.O. Dey; Hosiery provided by Hue; Specialty props fabricated by Prism Production Services, Rahway, N.J.; Max's office furniture, the script stacks and Roger's furniture by the Rabbit's Choice; Assorted hand props by Jennie Marino, Moon Boot Prod.; Vintage lighting fixture courtesy of Four Star Lighting; MP40 Schmeissers machine guns by Costume Armour; Walkers through J & J Medical Supplies, Teaneck, NJ; Champagne by Mumm's; Krylon spray paint by Siperstein's Paints; Custom shirts by Cego; Millinery by Rodney Gordon and Henry Ewoskio; Showgirl specialty costumes by Martin Adams; Set poster art by Jim Miller; Lozenges provided by Ricola, Inc.; Parker jotter pens courtesy of the Parker Corporation. The use of Village People characters and costumes is by kind courtesy and permission of Can't Stop Productions Inc. and Scorpio Music S.A. The name Village People and the trade-dress of the Village People are registered trademarks.

MUSIC CREDITS
Words and Music by Mel Brooks. Songs published by Mel Brooks Music, except for "Have You Ever Heard the German Band," "Springtime for Hitler" and "Prisoners of Love," published by Legation Music Corp.

⊞ JUJAMCYN THEATERS

ROCCO LANDESMAN
President

PAUL LIBIN   **JACK VIERTEL**
Producing Director   Creative Director

JERRY ZAKS

DANIEL ADAMIAN   **JENNIFER HERSHEY**
General Manager   Director of Operations

MEREDITH VILLATORE
Chief Financial Officer

STAFF FOR THE ST. JAMES THEATRE

Manager	Daniel Adamian
Treasurer	Vincent Sclafani
Carpenter	Timothy McDonough
Propertyman	Barnett Epstein
Electrician	Albert Sayers
Engineer	James Higgins

The Producers
SCRAPBOOK

Photos by Aubrey Reuben

1. Brad Oscar and Hunter Foster (4th and 5th from L) take curtain call after the performance that welcomed them back to the leading roles at the St. James Theatre.
2. Star struck? Just back from the International Space Station, astronaut Charles Camarda (L) and Shuttle Commander Eileen Collins (C) visit backstage with Hunter Foster, Brad Oscar and Angie Schworer.
3. Brad Oscar takes part in the annual "Broadway Barks" event.

Correspondents: Angie Schworer ("Ulla") and Stage Manager Ira Mont.

Most Exciting Celebrity Visitors: Shuttle astronauts Eileen Collins and Charles Camarda, who were in town doing press and decided to come see our show. They couldn't have been nicer.

Actors Who Perform the Most Roles in This Show: Kevin Ligon does 14 enemble roles and 16 costumes changes, plus he understudies three principals. Kathy Fitzgerald is the woman who plays the most parts: 10 ensemble roles with 12 costume changes.

Who Has Done the Most Shows: Robert Fowler, the man who sings, "I debits all the morning…." He's been in the show since the beginning, as have Kathy and myself [Schworer].

Special Backstage Rituals: During "Springtime for Hitler," I high-five the whole crew as I do my fast cross behind. Also, the crew and cast members do a little jig just offstage left during "Haben Sie Gehoert."

"Carols for a Cure" Carol: "In the Bleak Midwinter."

Favorite In-Theatre Gathering Place: The dressing room of the actor playing Leo Bloom (now Hunter Foster). We have all our little parties there. Also, people like to congregate in my dressing room.

Favorite Off-Site Hangout: Angus McIndoe, of course, which is right next door. And now also Bar Centrale, the new upstairs place at Joe Allen's.

Favorite Snack Foods: Anything that the wardrobe department puts out on their table: chocolate, pretzels, Cheez-its, that kind of thing.

Mascot: Shirley Markowitz, the lesbian lighting designer, currently played by Kathy Fitzgerald.

Favorite Therapy: Ricolas are a big hit. Ira Mont also puts out Advil and Aleve, which I guess we use the most.

Memorable Ad-Lib: Jimmy Borstelmann, who understudies Roger DeBris, is supposed to say the line, "This crazy kraut is crackers. He crashed in here and crassly tried to kill us." Carmen Ghia is supposed to reply, "Roger, what alliteration!" One night, Jimmy said, "He's a terrible man and he must be expelled." I have no idea why.

Busiest Day at the Box Office: The day the tickets went on sale for Nathan Lane's and Matthew Broderick's return.

Memorable Fan Encounter: One night we all became aware of a woman sitting in the audience with a tissue up her nose. We thought it was so funny. At the end of the show, when we were collecting for Broadway Cares, we handed her a tissue box signed by the cast. She topped us by sending back a letter saying something to the effect, "It was the first time this Jewish-American Princess accepted something from a Nazi."

The Producers
SCRAPBOOK

Memorable Press Encounter: The Gold Girls [who appear in "I Wanna Be a Producer"] were asked to take part in a Times Square event to form the world's largest kick line. It was fun but they froze their butts off.

Fastest Costume Change: In "Springtime for Hitler," one of the showgirls has 13 seconds to come out of her puppet costume, rip off her pants, change her hat and leap out to center stage to do the button on the number.

Who Wore the Least: Chris Klink as Sabu.

Sweethearts Within the Company: Carpenter Eddie Ackerman and Madeleine Doherty, who plays Hold-me Touch-me. They met while working on the show.

Coolest Thing About Being in This Show: Two words: Mel Brooks.

1. Angie Schworer at "Broadway on Broadway."
2. (L-R) Carson Kressley joins fellow "Queer Eye for the Straight Guy" cast member Jai Rodriguez, along with Gary Beach and John Treacy Egan, at a party to welcome Egan and Rodriguez to the cast.
3. Schworer (C) presents Hunter Foster (L) and Brad Oscar (R) with champagne upon their return to the cast.
4. Brad Musgrove (L) and Schworer (C) welcome Gary Beach back to the cast.
5. Director Susan Stroman (C) is honored by her fellow choreographers at the Elan Awards.

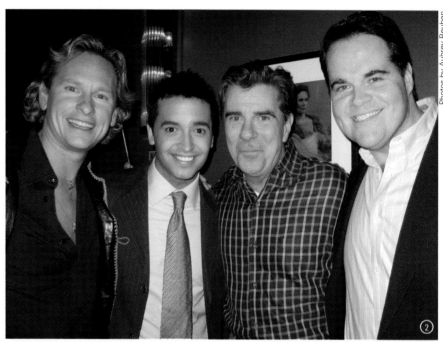

Rabbit Hole

First Preview: January 12, 2006. Opened: February 2, 2006.
Closed April 9, 2006 after 23 Previews and 77 Performances.

PLAYBILL

RABBIT HOLE

CAST
(in order of appearance)

Izzy .... MARY CATHERINE GARRISON
Becca .... CYNTHIA NIXON
Howie .... JOHN SLATTERY
Nat .... TYNE DALY
Jason .... JOHN GALLAGHER JR.

Stage Manager: Bruce A. Hoover

UNDERSTUDIES
For Nat:
CYNTHIA DARLOW

For Jason:
TROY DEUTSCH

For Becca and Izzy:
ERIKA ROLFSRUD

2005-2006 Award

TONY AWARD
Best Performance by a Leading Actress in a
Play (Cynthia Nixon)

BILTMORE THEATRE

MANHATTAN THEATRE CLUB
BILTMORE THEATRE

Artistic Director
LYNNE MEADOW

Executive Producer
BARRY GROVE

Presents

RABBIT HOLE

by
DAVID LINDSAY-ABAIRE

with
TYNE DALY   JOHN GALLAGHER JR.

MARY CATHERINE GARRISON

CYNTHIA NIXON   JOHN SLATTERY

Scenic Design
JOHN LEE BEATTY

Costume Design
JENNIFER VON MAYRHAUSER

Lighting Design
CHRISTOPHER AKERLIND

Original Music and Sound Design
JOHN GROMADA

Production Stage Manager
ROY HARRIS

Directed by
DANIEL SULLIVAN

Casting
**NANCY PICCIONE/
DAVID CAPARELLIOTIS**

*Director of
Artistic Operations*
MANDY GREENFIELD

*Production
Manager*
RYAN McMAHON

*Director of
Development*
JILL TURNER LLOYD

*Director of
Marketing*
DEBRA A. WAXMAN

*Press
Representative*
**BONEAU/
BRYAN-BROWN**

General Manager
FLORIE SEERY

*Director of
Artistic Development*
PAIGE EVANS

*Director of
Artistic Production*
MICHAEL BUSH

Special funding for new American works is provided by the Harold and Mimi Steinberg Charitable Trust.
Manhattan Theatre Club wishes to express its appreciation to Theatre Development Fund for its support of this production.
Rabbit Hole was originally commissioned by South Coast Repertory.

2/2/06

(L-R): John Slattery, Cynthia Nixon, Tyne Daly and
Mary Catherine Garrison.

Photo by Joan Marcus

Rabbit Hole

Tyne Daly
Nat

John Gallagher Jr.
Jason

Mary Catherine
Garrison
Izzy

Cynthia Nixon
Becca

John Slattery
Howie

Cynthia Darlow
Understudy for Nat

Troy Deutsch
*Understudy for
Jason*

Erika Rolfsrud
*Understudy for
Becca and Izzy*

David Lindsay-Abaire
Playwright

Daniel Sullivan
Director

John Lee Beatty
Scenic Design

Jennifer Von
Mayrhauser
Costume Design

Christopher Akerlind
Lighting Design

John Gromada
*Original Music and
Sound Design*

Lynne Meadow
*Artistic Director,
Manhattan Theatre
Club, Inc.*

Barry Grove
*Executive Producer,
Manhattan Theatre
Club, Inc.*

BOX OFFICE
(L-R): David Dillon (Box Office Treasurer)
and Tevy Bradley
(Assistant Box Office Treasurer).

Photo by Ben Strothmann

Rabbit Hole

Photos by Ben Strothmann

STAGE CREW
Seated (L-R): Rosie Goldman (Production Assistant), Daniel Kerrigan (Apprentice) and Denise Cooper (Company Manager).

Standing (L-R): Tracey Boone (Dresser), Chris Wiggins (Head Carpenter), Louis Shapiro (Sound Engineer), Timothy Walters (Head Propertyman), Patrick Murray (Automation), Sue Poulin (Apprentice) and Jeff Dodson (Master Electrician).

FRONT OF HOUSE STAFF
Front Row (L-R): Miranda Scopel (Biltmore Intern), Patricia Polhill (Usher), Purple Bear (Substitute for Valerie Simmons, Theatre Manager), Rebecca Rozin (Patron Lounge Attendant), Kenneth Harlin (Assistant House Manager/Sub).

Middle Row (L-R): Danita Johnson (Usher), Catherine Burke (Usher), Wendy Wright (Chief Usher), Johannah-Joy Magyawe (Assistant House Manager).

Back Row (L-R): Meghann Early (Usher), Beren Willwerth (Sweet Concessions Bar Manager), Jackson Ero (Usher) and Edward Brashear (Ticket Taker).

Rabbit Hole

Tyne Daly and
Cynthia Nixon

Photo by Joan Marcus

Rabbit Hole
SCRAPBOOK

Correspondent: Roy Harris, Production Stage Manager

Most Exciting Celebrity Visitor: All of our celebrity visitors have loved the show. The ones we value the most are other playwrights, like Jon Robin Baitz, who was incredibly moved by the play, calling it "one of the most transparently perfect plays I've ever seen."

Who Has Done the Most Shows: We're very lucky with this show. All five actors have done all 23 previews and 77 regular performances, though we have a very gifted cast of understudies, who were always ready to go on.

Special Backstage Rituals: Cynthia kept hand and nail cream at the stage manager's calling desk. Just before her entrance into the second act she would use both on her hands and cuticles.

Favorite Therapy: Ricola was without question the therapy of choice.

Record Number of Cell Phone Rings During a Performance: Six, all during the second act. Once we had a ring on the final two lines of the first act. Company was so incensed at first that they asked stage management to make a special "live" announcement.

Latest Audience Arrival: At an early preview, an agent of one of our cast members arrived at 8:25, flounced down the aisle so she could see the client's only scene in the first act.

Fastest Costume Change: John Slattery putting on a different shirt and shoes, then running up the off-stage stairs as the turntable was moving into place. He always made it.

1. (L-R) Peter Solomon, playwright David Lindsay-Abaire, wife Chris, Barry Grove and Lynne Meadow of Manhattan Theatre Club in front of the Biltmore Theatre on opening night.
2. Director Daniel Sullivan arrives on opening night.
3. Leading lady Cynthia Nixon at the opening night party at The China Club.
4. Curtain call on opening night. (L-R:) John Gallagher, Tyne Daly, Cynthia Nixon, John Slattery and Mary Catherine Garrison.

Rent

First Preview: April 16, 1996. Opened: April 29, 1996.
Still running as of May 31, 2006.

CAST
(in order of appearance)

Roger Davis .... CARY SHIELDS
Mark Cohen .... MATT CAPLAN
Tom Collins .... DESTAN OWENS
Benjamin Coffin III .... D'MONROE
Joanne Jefferson .... MERLE DANDRIDGE
Angel Schunard .... JUSTIN JOHNSTON
Mimi Marquez .... KARMINE ALERS
Maureen Johnson .... AVA GAUDET
Mark's mom and others .... NICOLETTE HART
Christmas caroler, Mr. Jefferson,
a pastor, and others .... MARCUS PAUL JAMES
Mrs. Jefferson, woman with bags,
and others .... FRENCHIE DAVIS
Gordon, the man,
Mr. Grey, and others .... COLIN HANLON
Steve, man with squeegee,
a waiter, and others .... ENRICO RODRIGUEZ
Paul, a cop, and others .... SHAUN EARL
Alexi Darling, Roger's mom,
and others .... MAYUMI ANDO

UNDERSTUDIES
For Roger:
COLIN HANLON, OWEN JOHNSTON II,
JAY WILKISON

For Mark:
COLIN HANLON, JAY WILKISON

Continued on next page

NEDERLANDER THEATRE
UNDER THE DIRECTION OF
JAMES M. NEDERLANDER AND JAMES L. NEDERLANDER

Jeffrey Seller   Kevin McCollum   Allan S. Gordon
and New York Theatre Workshop

present

Book, Music and Lyrics by
Jonathan Larson

Karmine Alers   Mayumi Ando   Matt Caplan   Merle Dandridge
Frenchie Davis   D'Monroe   Shaun Earl   Ava Gaudet   Colin Hanlon
Nicolette Hart   Marcus Paul James   Justin Johnston
Destan Owens   Enrico Rodriguez   Cary Shields
Crystal Monée Hall   Owen Johnston II   Diana Kaarina
Philip Dorian McAdoo   Dominique Roy   Jay Wilkison

| Set Design | Costume Design | Lighting Design | Sound Design |
| Paul Clay | Angela Wendt | Blake Burba | Kurt Fischer |

| Original Concept/Additional Lyrics | Musical Arrangements | Dramaturg |
| Billy Aronson | Steve Skinner | Lynn M. Thomson |

| Casting | Publicity |
| Bernard Telsey Casting | Richard Kornberg/Don Summa |

| Music Director | Production Stage Manager |
| Boko Suzuki | John Vivian |

| General Manager | Technical Supervision |
| John Corker | Unitech Productions, Inc. |

| Music Supervision and Additional Arrangements | Choreography |
| Tim Weil | Marlies Yearby |

Director
Michael Greif

Original cast recording available on DreamWorks Records' CD's and cassettes

LIVE BROADWAY

9/26/05

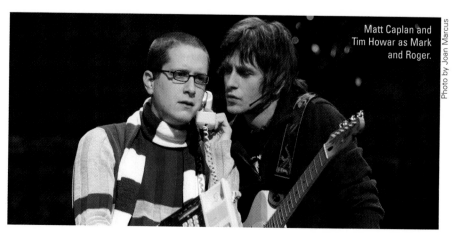

Matt Caplan and
Tim Howar as Mark
and Roger.

Photo by Joan Marcus

313

Rent

MUSICAL NUMBERS

ACT ONE

Tune Up/Voice Mail #1 ....Mark, Roger, Mrs. Cohen, Collins, Benny
Rent ....The Company
You Okay Honey?… ....Angel, Collins
One Song Glory ....Roger
Light My Candle ....Roger, Mimi
Voice Mail #2 ....Mr. & Mrs. Jefferson
Today 4 U ....Angel
You'll See ....Benny, Mark, Collins, Roger, Angel
Tango: Maureen ....Mark, Joanne
Life Support ....Paul, Gordon, The Company
Out Tonight ....Mimi
Another Day ....Roger, Mimi, The Company
Will I? ....Steve, The Company
On the Street ....The Company
Santa Fe ....Collins and The Company
I'll Cover You ....Angel, Collins
We're Okay ....Joanne
Christmas Bells ....The Company
Over the Moon ....Maureen
La Vie Boheme/I Should Tell You ....The Company

ACT TWO

Seasons of Love ....The Company
Happy New Year/Voice Mail #3 ....Mimi, Roger, Mark, Maureen, Joanne,
Collins, Angel, Mrs. Cohen, Alexi Darling, Benny, The man
Take Me or Leave Me ....Maureen, Joanne
Without You ....Roger, Mimi
Voice Mail #4 ....Alexi Darling
Contact ....The Company
I'll Cover You: Reprise ....Collins, The Company
Halloween ....Mark
Goodbye, Love ....Mark, Mimi, Roger,
Maureen, Joanne, Collins, Benny
What You Own ....Pastor, Mark, Collins, Benny, Roger
Voice Mail #5 ....Roger's Mom, Mimi's Mom, Mr. Jefferson, Mrs. Cohen
Your Eyes/Finale ....Roger, The Company

Cast Continued

For Tom Collins:
MARCUS PAUL JAMES,
PHILIP DORIAN MCADOO

For Benjamin:
MARCUS PAUL JAMES,
PHILIP DORIAN MCADOO

For Joanne:
FRENCHIE DAVIS, CRYSTAL MONÉE HALL

For Angel:
SHAUN EARL, OWEN JOHNSTON II,
ENRICO RODRIGUEZ

For Mimi:
AVA GAUDET, DIANA KAARINA,
DOMINIQUE ROY

For Maureen:
NICOLETTE HART, DIANA KAARINA

SWINGS

CRYSTAL MONÉE HALL, OWEN JOHNSTON
II, DIANA KAARINA, PHILIP DORIAN
MCADOO, DOMINIQUE ROY, JAY
WILKISON

DANCE CAPTAIN

Owen Johnston II

THE BAND

Conductor, Keyboards–Boko Suzuki
Bass–Steve Mack
Guitar–Bobby Baxmeyer
Drums–Jeff Potter
Keyboards, Guitar–John Korba

FILM BY

Tony Gerber

The cast sings "La Vie Boheme."

Photo by Joan Marcus

Rent

Karmine Alers
Mimi

Mayumi Ando
Ensemble

Matt Caplan
Mark

Merle Dandridge
Joanne

Frenchie Davis
Ensemble

D'Monroe
Benny

Shaun Earl
Ensemble

Ava Gaudet
Maureen

Colin Hanlon
Ensemble

Nicolette Hart
Ensemble

Marcus Paul James
Ensemble

Justin Johnston
Angel

Destan Owens
Collins

Enrico Rodriguez
Ensemble

Cary Shields
Roger

Crystal Monée Hall
Understudy

Owen Johnston II
Understudy

Diana Kaarina
Understudy

Philip Dorian McAdoo
Understudy

Dominique Roy
Understudy

Jonathan Larson
Book, Music, Lyrics

Michael Greif
Director

Marlies Yearby
Choreography

David Santana
*Wig, Hair and
Makeup Design*

Bernard Telsey,
Bernard Telsey
Casting, C.S.A.
Casting

Richard Kornberg,
Richard Kornberg
and Associates
Publicity

Jeffrey Seller
Producer

Kevin McCollum
Producer

Allan S. Gordon
Producer

James C. Nicola,
Artistic Director
New York Theatre
Workshop
Producer

Rent

Danielle Lee Greaves
*Joanne Jefferson,
Swing*

Sala Iwamatsu
*Alexi Darling,
Roger's mom,
and others*

Stu James
Benjamin Coffin III

Catrice Joseph
Swing

Kelly Karbacz
Maureen Johnson

Joshua Kobak
*Gordon, the man,
Mr. Grey, and others/
Swing*

Caren Lyn Manuel
*Mark's mom
and others*

Nick Sanchez
*Paul, a cop,
and others*

Robin De Jesús
*Steve, the man with
squeegee, a waiter,
and others*

Joshua Kobak
*Roger Davis/
Steve, the man with
squeegee, a waiter,
and others*

Moesha McGill
*Understudy Joanne,
Mimi*

Kenna J. Ramsey
Joanne Jefferson

Antonique Smith
Mimi Marquez

Justin Brill
Swing

Haven Burton
Mark's Mom

Will Chase
Roger Davis

Luther Creek
*Gordon, Mr. Grey
and others*

Mark Richard Ford
Tom Collins

Tim Howar
Roger Davis

Caren Lyn Manuel
Maureen Johnson

Peter Matthew Smith
*Gordon, Mr. Grey,
and others*

Rent

BOX OFFICE
(L-R): Peggy Loiacono, Michael Loiacono and Scott Kenny.

STAGE DOOR
(L-R): Antonio Ferrao (Engineer) and Joe Santiago (Doorman).

MANAGEMENT
(L-R): Nick Kaledin (Company Manager) and John Vivian (Production Stage Manager).

Rent

BAND
(L-R): Boko Suzuki, John Korba, Bobby Baxmeyer and Jeff Potter.

Not Pictured: Steve Mack

HAIR & MAKEUP
(L-R): Antonique Smith (Mimi) and David Santana (Hair & Makeup Designer)

STAGE CREW
Seated (L-R):
Susan Ash (Sound), Cleo Matheos (Wardrobe),
Paula Inocent (Wardrobe),
Karen Lloyd (Wardrobe),
Crystal Huntington (Stage Manager),
Ken McGee (Assistant Stage Manager).

Standing (L-R):
Brian Ronan (Sound), Steve Clem (Electrician),
Jan Marasek (Props), Richie Beck (Electrician),
William T. Wright (Props), Billy Wright (Props),
Eric Carney (Sound), Joe Ferreri, Jr. (Carpenter)
and Joe Ferreri (Carpenter)

Rent

FRONT OF HOUSE STAFF
(L-R): Terrence Cummiskey, Lee Bonacci, Joaquin Quintana, Willie Figueroa, Shep Pamplin (Special Infared Service), Iris Cortes, Derek King, Junesse Cartagena, Marion Pichardo and Michael Angelino.

Not Pictured: Samuel A. Morris (Education).

STAFF FOR RENT

GENERAL MANAGER
JOHN CORKER

GENERAL PRESS REPRESENTATIVE
RICHARD KORNBERG & ASSOCIATES
RICHARD KORNBERG, CARRIE FRIEDMAN

BERNARD TELSEY CASTING, C.S.A.:
Bernie Telsey, Will Cantler, David Vaccari,
Bethany Berg, Craig Burns,
Tiffany Little Canfield, Christine Dall,
Stephanie Yankwitt

COMPANY MANAGER ....NICK KALEDIN

PRODUCTION STAGE MANAGER ....JOHN VIVIAN
Stage Manager..........................Crystal Huntington
Assistant Stage Manager ....Kenneth J. McGee
Technical Supervision ....Unitech Productions, Inc.
Brian Lynch, Ken Keneally,
Manuel Becker & Jack Culver
Assistant Director.............................Martha Banta
Resident Assistant Director ....Evan Ensign
Associate Conductor ....John Korba
Company Manager Associates ......Dawn Marie Bernhard,
Ginger Montel
Wig, Hair and Makeup Designer ....David Santana
Assistant Costume Designer ....Lisa Zinni
Wardrobe Supervisor ....Karen Lloyd
Hair and Makeup Supervisor ....David Santana
House Manager ....Louise Angelino
Treasurer ....Gary Kenny
House Electrician ....Richard J. Beck
Console Operator ....Stephen Clem
Follow Spot Operators ....Tom O'Neill,
Holli Shevett
Sound Board Operators ....Greg Freedman,
Brian Ronan
Deck Electrician ....Emile LaFargue
House Carpenter ....Joe Ferreri
Assistant House Carpenter ....Joe Ferreri, Jr.
House Prop Master ....Billy Wright
Prop Master ....Jan Marasek
Assistant House Prop Master............William T. Wright
Dressers......................Paula Inocent, Cleo Matheos

Wardrobe Daywork ....Lynne Wilson
Assistant to Messrs. Seller & McCollum ....Ryan Hill
Assistant to John Corker ....Kim Vasquez
Receptionist ....Dan Weisberg
Dramaturg ....Lynn M. Thomson
Merchandise Manager ....Toni Ostini
Special Garment Construction ....Colleen Morris
Front of House/Lobby Creative Assistant ....Jamie Leo
Lobby Ceiling Murals ....Billy Miller
Music Preparation ....Eva Gianono
Marketing ....TMG-The Marketing Group/
Laura Matalon, Tanya Grubich,
Trish Santini, Jenny Richardson, Steve Tate
Advertising ....SpotCo
Ilene Rosen, Jim McNicholas
Rent Education Program ....Students Live!/
Amy Weinstein, President
Allyson Morgan, Petol Weekes, Directors
Merchandising ....Max Merchandising, LLC
Title Treatment Design ....Spot Design
Poster Artwork ....Amy Guip
Legal Counsel ....Levine Plotkin & Menin, LLP/
Loren H. Plotkin
Accounting ....Lutz & Carr
Insurance ....DeWitt Stern Group
Banking ....JP Morgan
Payroll Service ....ADP
Production Photographers ....Joan Marcus/
Carol Rosegg
Theatre Displays ....King Display
Product Placement ....George Fenmore/
More Merchandising International
Press Interns ....Jennifer Pastrich, Kathryn Calogero,
Samantha Borenstein

New York Theatre Workshop

Artistic Director   Managing Director
James C. Nicola   Lynn Moffat

The Producing Office

Kevin McCollum   Jeffrey Seller
John Corker

Allan S. Gordon Productions
Allan S. Gordon
Elan Vital McAllister
Anne Caruso   David R. Gerson

Credits

Scenery by Hudson Scenic Inc. Lighting equipment by Four Star, Inc., Vari*Lite Inc. Costumes by Euro Co. Sound equipment by ProMix, Inc. Angel and Maureen's costumes by Izquierdo Studio. Drums by Pearl Drums. Bed linens by Martex. Additional musical instruments courtesy of Sam Ash Music Stores. Motorcycle helmets courtesy of Bell Helmets. 16 mm Projectors by Elmo Mfg. Corp. Acrylic drinkware by US Acrylic, Inc. Candles courtesy of Will & Baumer, Inc. Diamond Brand matches used. Some skin care and hair products provided by Kiehl's. Guitar strings supplied by D'Addario & Co. Some denim wear by Lee Apparel and Rider. Make-up provided by Francois Nars. Tattoos by Temptu Marketing. Throat lozenges provided by Ricola, Inc. Plastic cups by Polar Plastic, Inc. Emer'gen-C Super Energy Booster provided by Alacer Corp.

Special Thanks to:

Allan and Nanette Larson; Julie Larson; Victoria Leacock.

"White Christmas" used by arrangement with the Irving Berlin Music Company. "Do You Know the Way to San Jose," written by Burt Bacharach and Hal David, used by permission of Casa David and New Hidden Valley Music. "The Christmas Song (Chestnuts Roasting on an Open Fire)" by Mel Torme and Robert Wells, used by permission of Edwin H. Morris & Company, a division of MPL Communications, Inc. "Rudolph the Red-Nosed Reindeer" written by Johnny Marks used by permission of St. Nicholas Music, Inc.

NEDERLANDER

Chairman ....James M. Nederlander
President ....James L. Nederlander

Executive Vice President
Nick Scandalios

Vice President   Senior Vice President
Corporate Development   Labor Relations
Charlene S. Nederlander **Herschel Waxman**

Vice President   Chief Financial Officer
Jim Boese   **Freida Sawyer Belviso**

Rent
SCRAPBOOK

Photos by Aubrey Reuben

1. Cast members warm up for the "Broadway on Broadway" event in Times Square.
2. Frenchie Davis gets set to perform at Broadway's "Stars in the Alley" event in Shubert Alley.

Correspondent: Marcus Paul James, "Christmas caroler, Mr. Jefferson, a pastor, and others."

Anniversary Parties and or Gifts: We're celebrating our 10th anniversary this year so the partying is unbelievable. The concert performed by the original cast was unbelievable. As a gift the producers made a video that showed everyone who has ever been in Rent 1996-2006. It was such good memento.

"Carols for a Cure" Carol: "This Is Christmas."

Special Backstage Ritual: Right outside the stage manager's office above our sign-in board is a wooden plaque that says "Thank You Jonathan" crafted by one of Jonathan's family members. This plaque is mentioned at almost every commemorative event as the perfect thing to be said. A new plaque is crafted for every new company of the show so that we don't forget the real lives behind the show. It has become a ritual for some of us, as we do our last bits of warming up on the way to places, to just touch or rub the plaque for luck and remembrance. It just feels good.

Favorite Moment During Each Performance: I guess I will have to take the cheesy road and say that "Seasons of Love" is my favorite moment in the show. We get to sing one of the most truth-telling songs ever written and we get to share it and really share with the audience. I figure it's really hard to sit in the first 15 rows and not smile and clap while the cast are singing their hearts out and grooving in the love of the message. Some still don't participate,

but the ones that do make us feel we are all taking another step forward.

Favorite In-Theatre Gathering Place: The greenroom is our watering hole. It is directly under the stage and is passed by anyone who has to cross to stage left—which is everyone at some point. And seeing that most of our dressing rooms are upstairs, it's easier for the few minutes some of us have between scenes to hang in the green room. And some characters, like me, have a 20 minute break in which we like to play games mostly, talk, eat that dinner we missed, crochet, anything to fill the time. And we mostly end up running to our next entrance cause we know exactly how much time we have or don't.

Favorite Off-Site Hangout: Next door to our theatre is a bar called Bar 41, we call it our second greenroom. Some of the time it serves as a shelter from the mob of people taking pictures and waving Playbills outside the theatre. But most of the time it is our rally place where we figure out what to do next, see old friends and, if we are lucky, get some food. But we also get a discount there so that helps as well.

Favorite Snack Food: It is very safe to say the Rent favorite snack food is "everything." During a show at any time anyone can be eating what ever can be delivered or brought to the theatre. From sushi, to Indian, to deli, we eat it all at all times.

Favorite Therapy: I believe anything that has to do with quiet, relaxing, or resetting is very much frequented by Rent cast members. We have chiropractors and a massage therapist on

call at all times. Aside from that professional help, I think most of us like to keep it pretty natural when it comes to upkeep. I don't know how many cans of Ricolas and boxes of Emer'gen-C we go through, but stage management keeps us pretty stocked up on them. And when one person gets sick, out comes the Airborne and the Wellness Formula.

Memorable Stage Door Encounter: There are no other people in the world like our "Rent-Heads." They are always there and always want you to know that they're there. And it's hard to forget coming out of the theatre and seeing someone dressed up like the character you have been playing for the past two hours. There are wanna-be Marks, Angels, Rogers, and Maureens. No one ever comes as the Christmas caroler and other. What about him??

Fastest Costume Change: I believe this award has to go to anyone who plays Alexi Darling in the show, played now by our lovely Mayumi Ando. In Act II Alexi does a voicemail that is followed immediately by "Contact." In the dark on the first downbeat of the music, she has to run to the stage left corner of the stage, slightly past the proscenium, and change out of a track suit, wig, headband, and glasses and join in the dance in less than three counts of eight. And there are some nights she just doesn't make it till later on in the dance.

Busiest Day at the Box Office: Our Friday and Saturday nights end up being packed regularly. Though with all the press around since November 2005 the words "sold out" have been heard all the time. We have been breaking

Rent
SCRAPBOOK

attendance records by leaps and bounds. Let's just say that I am sure the producers are happy.

Catchphrases Only the Company Would Recognize: Anyone who has been in the show can agree that "Christmas Bells" or "Big Bells" is just a headache between all the crossing vocal parts and the fast intricate singing that everyone has to do. So in rehearsals we spend a huge chunk of our time on big "Christmas Bells" and when we have to run it, yet again, from the top, the phrase "All right, hats bats everyone" is yelled and we giggle and wearily head to our beginning positions.

Which Orchestra Member Played the Most Instruments: I was told by our music conductor Boko Suzuki that the infamous Robert Baxmeyer plays everything. But not only does he play them, he is great at them all too.

Memorable Directorial Note: I think every one in the history of *Rent* who has worked with Michael Greif, at some point got the note starting with "This is three years late but could you …?" This usually leaves every one going "well it was fine for three years." But it always serves a good chuckle when heard.

Nicknames: Mayumi Ando—"Mayuumsdog, Moonbeam"
Frenchie Davis—"Frenchell"
Peter Matthew Smith—"PMS"
Karmine Alers—"Carmina"
Justin Brill—"Brillo"
Matt Caplan—"Capitan"
Merle Dandridge—"Squirrel"

Superstition That Turned Out To Be True: It's always said that it feels like Jonathan Larson is with us every show. On the anniversary of Jonathan's passing Victoria Leacock, one his best friends, said that he was cremated and some of his ashes were spread across the Nederlander stage. And that at the rate our theatre gets cleaned, she was sure that a part of Jonathan is indeed with us…literally.

Coolest Thing About Being in This Show: I think the coolest thing about being in the cast of *Rent* is being a part of an endless family. Being at the tenth anniversary celebration was like being in a glamorous heavenly event. Seeing new and old faces from previous casts was just enough to bring me and a few others to tears, and the show hadn't even started yet. The original cast members met us with open arms; welcoming arms. And then realizing that I, in one view, am seeing a group of people that has affected, infected, and changed musical theatre, individual lives, and the world. I think every actor dreams of achieving greatness and in turn doing good and meaningful work. And I think trading a starring name on a marquee for being in the rank of *Rent* is choosing the dream. Best thing I have ever done in my career was sign my first *Rent* contract. Also it was the coolest. Thank you, Jonathan.

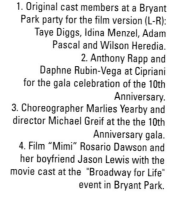

1. Original cast members at a Bryant Park party for the film version (L-R): Taye Diggs, Idina Menzel, Adam Pascal and Wilson Heredia.
2. Anthony Rapp and Daphne Rubin-Vega at Cipriani for the gala celebration of the 10th Anniversary.
3. Choreographer Marlies Yearby and director Michael Greif at the the 10th Anniversary gala.
4. Film "Mimi" Rosario Dawson and her boyfriend Jason Lewis with the movie cast at the "Broadway for Life" event in Bryant Park.

Ring of Fire

First Preview: February 8, 2006. Opened: March 12, 2006.
Closed April 30, 2006 after 38 Previews and 57 Performances.

PLAYBILL

CAST

JEB BROWN
JASON EDWARDS
JARROD EMICK
BETH MALONE
CASS MORGAN
LARI WHITE

DAVID M. LUTKEN ......Banjo, Dobro, Evoharp,
Guitar, Harmonica, Mandolin
RANDY REDD ....Keyboards, Mandolin
JEFF LISENBY ...Conductor, Accordion, Keyboards
ERIC ANTHONY ....Electric Guitar, Mandolin
LAURIE CANAAN ....Fiddle, Mandolin
DAN IMMEL ....Bass
RON KRASINSKI............................Drums
BRENT MOYER ....Guitar, Cornet

UNDERSTUDIES

For Jeb:
ROD WEBER, JIM PRICE
For Jason:
SCOTT WAKEFIELD, JIM PRICE
For Jarrod:
MARK LUNA, ROD WEBER
For Beth:
SHERRIÉ AUSTIN
For Cass:
MELANIE VAUGHAN, GAIL BLISS
For Lari:
GAIL BLISS, SHERRIÉ AUSTIN

Continued on next page

⑤ ETHEL BARRYMORE THEATRE

243 West 47th Street
A Shubert Organization Theatre
Gerald Schoenfeld, *Chairman*   Philip J. Smith, *President*

Robert E. Wankel, *Executive Vice President*

WILLIAM MEADE   CTM PRODUCTIONS   BOB CUILLO   GFOUR PRODUCTIONS

and

JAMES B. FREYDBERG

present

★ RING of FIRE ★
THE JOHNNY CASH MUSICAL SHOW

Created by

RICHARD MALTBY, JR.

Conceived by

WILLIAM MEADE

Starring

**JEB BROWN   JASON EDWARDS   JARROD EMICK
BETH MALONE   CASS MORGAN   LARI WHITE**

with

DAVID M. LUTKEN   RANDY REDD

and

**ERIC ANTHONY   LAURIE CANAAN   DAN IMMEL
RON KRASINSKI   JEFF LISENBY   BRENT MOYER**

Scenic Production Design **NEIL PATEL**	Costume Design **DAVID C. WOOLARD**	Lighting Design **KEN BILLINGTON**	Sound Design **PETER FITZGERALD & CARL CASELLA**
Projection Design **MICHAEL CLARK**	Musical Director **JEFF LISENBY**	Technical Supervisor **BRIAN LYNCH**	Associate Technical Supervisor **MATT MARAFFI**
Press Representative **BONEAU/BRYAN-BROWN**	Marketing **HHC MARKETING**	Producing Associate **DOUG MACARTHUR**	Production Stage Manager **MARK DOBROW**
Additional Arrangements & Music Continuity by **JEFF LISENBY & DALE M. HERR**	Casting **DAVE CLEMMONS CASTING**	Associate Producer **IDT ENTERTAINMENT**	Associate Producers **TAMLYN FREUND YERKES DAVID MALTBY**
Company Manager **SUSAN BELL**	General Management **SNUG HARBOR PRODUCTIONS STEVEN CHAIKELSON & BRANNON WILES**		Executive Producer **JAMES B. FREYDBERG**

Choreographed by

LISA SHRIVER

Directed by

RICHARD MALTBY, JR.

This production done in cooperation with the John R. Cash Revocable Trust.
Ring of Fire was first presented at Studio Arena Theatre in Buffalo, New York.
The Producers would like to express their appreciation to Theatre Development Fund for its support of this production.

3/12/06

(L-R): Jason Edwards, Cass Morgan, Beth Malone, Jarrod Emick, Jeb Brown and Lari White sing "Country Boy."

Photo by Joan Marcus

Ring of Fire

MUSICAL NUMBERS

ACT ONE

All music and lyrics by John R. Cash except where otherwise indicated.
Dates indicate year of Johnny Cash recording or release.

"Hurt" (2002) ....Jason & Company
By Michael Trent Reznor
"Country Boy" (1957) ....Company
"Thing Called Love" (1972) ....Jarrod, Beth & Company
By Jerry Hubbard
"There You Go" (1956) ....Beth & Company
"While I've Got It on My Mind" (1974) ....Jeb & Lari
"My Old Faded Rose" (1964) ....Jason, Cass & Ron, David, Randy, Dan
By John R. Cash & June Carter Cash
"Daddy Sang Bass" (1969) ....Company
By John R. Cash & Carl L. Perkins
"Straight A's in Love" (1959) ....Jarrod
"Big River" (1957) ....Jason, Jarrod, Jeb & Dan
"I Still Miss Someone" (1959) ....Beth
By John R. Cash & Roy Cash, Jr.
"Five Feet High and Rising" (1959) ....Jason, Jarrod, Lari, Beth, Jeb, Cass
"Flesh and Blood" (1970) ....Lari & Jeb, Cass & Jason
"Look at Them Beans" (1975) ....Jarrod & Beth, Cass, Lari
By Joseph Arrington, Jr.
"Get Rhythm" (1956) ....Company
"Flushed…" (1968) ....Cass
By Jack H. Clement
"Dirty Old…Dog" (1966) ....Randy, Brent, David
By Jack H. Clement
"Angel Band" (1979) ....Company
"If I Were a Carpenter" (1970) ....Jarrod & Beth
By James Timothy Hardin
"Ring of Fire" (1963) ....Jarrod & Beth
By June Carter & Merle Kilgore
"Jackson" (1967) ....Jarrod & Beth, Jeb & Lari, Jason & Cass
By Jerry Leiber & Billy Edd Wheeler

ACT TWO

Prologue: "Big River" reprise ....Company
"I've Been Everywhere" (1996) ....Company
By Geoff Mack
"Sunday Mornin' Comin' Down" (1970) ....Jeb
By Kris Kristofferson
"Temptation" (2003) ....Lari & Jeb
By Arthur Freed & Nacio Herb Brown
"I Feel Better All Over" (1960) ....Jeb & Lari
By Ken Rogers & Ferlin Husky
"A Boy Named Sue" (1969) ....Jeb, Jarrod, Jason
By Shel Silverstein
"Going to Memphis" (1960) ....Men
"Delia's Gone" (1962) ....David
By John R. Cash, Karl M. Silbersdorf & Richard Toops
"Austin Prison" (1966) ....Randy & Company
"Orleans Parish Prison" (1974) ....Cass, Lari, Beth & Company
By Dick Feller
"Folsom Prison Blues" (1955) ....Jarrod
"Man in Black" (1971) ....Jeb
"All Over Again" (1958) ....Lari
"I Walk the Line" (1956) ....Jeb & Lari, Jason & Cass, Jarrod & Beth
"The Man Comes Around" (2002) ....Jason & Beth, Cass, Jarrod, Jeb, Lari
"Waiting on the Far Side Banks of Jordan" (1976) ....Cass & Jason
By Terry Smith
"Why Me" (1994) ....Jason & Company
By Kris Kristofferson
"Hey Porter" (1955) ....Company

For David:
SCOTT WAKEFIELD, JIM PRICE
For Jeff:
AUGUST ERIKSMOEN
For Randy:
ERIC ANTHONY, MILES AUBREY,
AUGUST ERIKSMOEN
For Eric and Brent:
MILES AUBREY
For Laurie:
DeANN WHALEN
For Dan:
ERIC ANTHONY, SCOTT WAKEFIELD
For Ron:
STEVE BARTOSIK

Resident Choreographer:
MICHELLE WEBER
Associate Musical Director:
AUGUST ERIKSMOEN

Production Stage Manager:
MARK DOBROW
Assistant Stage Managers:
BEVERLY JENKINS,
NANCY ELIZABETH VEST

Jason Edwards in the "The Man Comes Around" scene.

Photo by Joan Marcus

Ring of Fire

John R. Cash
Composer/Lyricist

Jeb Brown
Performer

Jason Edwards
Performer

Jarrod Emick
Performer

Beth Malone
Performer

Cass Morgan
Performer

Lari White
Performer

David M. Lutken
Performer

Randy Redd
Performer

Eric Anthony
Performer

Laurie Canaan
Performer

Dan Immel
Performer

Ron Krasinski
Performer

Jeff Lisenby
Performer

Brent Moyer
Performer

Miles Aubrey
Understudy
Eric, Brent, Randy

Sherrié Austin
Understudy
Beth, Lari

Steve Bartosik
Understudy Ron

Gail Bliss
Understudy
Lari, Cass

August Eriksmoen
Understudy
Jeff, Randy

Mark Luna
Understudy Jarrod

Jim Price
Understudy
Jeb, Jason, David

Melanie Vaughan
Understudy Cass

Scott Wakefield
Understudy
Jason, Dan, David

Rod Weber
Understudy
Jeb, Jarrod

DeAnn Whalen
Understudy Laurie

Richard Maltby, Jr.
Creator/Director

Lisa Shriver
Choreographer

Neil Patel
Scenic Production
Designer

David C. Woolard
Costume Designer

Ken Billington
Lighting Designer

Carl Casella
Sound Designer

Dave Clemmons
Casting
Casting

Kenneth Greenblatt,
GFour Productions
Producer

Ring of Fire

Photos by Ben Strothmann

STAGE CREW
Front Row (L-R): Bruce Liebenow, James Crayton, Steve Abbott, Beverly Jenkins, Philip Feller, Valarie LaMour, Joseph Ippolito, Kathleen Gallagher, Adam Miller, Matt Maraffi, Josh Marks.

Back Row: Dan Landon, Jim Bay, Matthew Lackey, Clark Middleton, Peter Condos, Laura Ellington, Ray Panelli, Kathryn Guida and Bruce Thiel.

BOX OFFICE
Kikki Lenoue and Bill Friendly.

Ring of Fire

FRONT OF HOUSE STAFF
(L-R): Dan Landon, John Barbetti and Sandy Califano.

STAGE MANAGEMENT
Beverly Jenkins (Stage Manager).

In the photograph (L-R): Beverly Jenkins (Stage Manager), Mark Dobrow (Production Stage Manager) and Nancy Elizabeth Vest (Assistant Stage Manager).

STAFF FOR *RING OF FIRE*

GENERAL MANAGEMENT
SNUG HARBOR PRODUCTIONS
Steven Chaikelson   Brannon Wiles

COMPANY MANAGER
Susan Bell

PRESS REPRESENTATIVE
BONEAU/BRYAN-BROWN
Chris Boneau   Matt Polk
Jessica Johnson   Shanna Marcus

ASSOCIATE COMPANY MANAGER
Adam J. Miller

CASTING
DAVE CLEMMONS CASTING
Dave Clemmons C.S.A.
Rachel Hoffman   Sara Schatz
Geoff Josselson   Nikole Vallins

Production Stage Manager ....Mark Dobrow
Stage Manager ....Beverly Jenkins
Assistant Stage Manager ....Nancy Elizabeth Vest
Associate General Manager ....Jamie Tyrol
Associate Choreographer ....Michelle Weber

Associate Casting Director ....Sara Schatz
Associate Scenic Designer ....Tim Mackabee
Assistant Scenic Designer ....Arnulfo Maldonado
Associate Costume Designer .... Kevin Brainerd
Assistants to the Costume Designer ...Matthew Pachtman,
                                          Angela Harner
Associate Lighting Designer ....John Demous
Assistant Lighting Designer .... Stephen Boulmetis
Moving Light Programmer ....David Arch
Associate Sound Designer ....Dominic Sack
Assistant Sound Designer ....Janet Smith
Assistant Projection Designer ....Jennifer Kievit
Assistant to the Projection Designer ....Chris Kateff

Ring of Fire

Projection Programmer ....Paul Vershbow
Production Carpenter ....Matt Maraffi
Production Automation ....McBrien Dunbar
Production Electrician ....Bruce Liebenow
Moving Lights ....James Crayton
Production Properties Supervisor ....George Wagner
Prop Master ....Joseph Ippolito
Production Sound ....Matthew Lackey
Monitor Operator ....Josh Marks
Wardrobe Supervisor ....Kathleen Gallagher
Assistant Wardrobe Supervisor ....Kathryn Guida
Dressers ....Laura Ellington, Kristin Gardner,
Ray Panelli
Guitar Techs ....Miles Aubrey, Jim
Price

Assistant to Mr. Maltby ....Ben Stein
Advertising..SpotCo/
Drew Hodges, Jim Edwards,
Tom McCann, Aaliytha Davis
Marketing ....HHC Marketing/
Hugh Hysell, Amanda Pekoe,
Jennifer Scherer, Katharine Boies,
Jessica Hinds, Michael Redman,
Matt Sicoli, Caitlin Strype,
Keita H. Williams
Web Design and
Online Marketing Strategy ....Situation Marketing/
Damian Bazadona, Sara Fitzpatrick
Souvenir Merchandise Design
and Creation ....Araca Merch, LLC
Theatre Displays ....King Displays
Assistants to the General Manager .... Kendra Bator,
Jacquelyn Green, Stacey McMath
Press Office ....Adrian Bryan-Brown, Jim Byk,
Brandi Cornwell, Juliana Hannett,
Jackie Green, Kevin Jones, Eric Louie,
Aaron Meier, Joe Perrotta, Linnae Petruzzelli,
Matt Ross, Heath Schwartz, Susanne Tighe
Production Assistants .... Mary Kathryn Flynt,
Michael Krug
Legal Counsel .... Kaufman, Feiner, Yamin,
Gildin & Robbins LLP/
Ronald Feiner, Pamela Golinski
Accountant .... Fried & Kowgios CPAs LLP/
Robert Fried, CPA
Comptroller ....Elliott Aronstam
Banking ....Commerce Bank/
Barbara von Borstel, Ashley Elezi
Insurance .... Dewitt Stern Group/Anthony Pittari
Payroll Service ....Castellana Services, Inc.
Production Photographer ....Joan Marcus
Rehearsal Pianist ....JoLynn Burks
Rehearsal Studio ... Roundabout Theatre Rehearsal Studios
Travel Agent ....Road Rebel Entertainment Touring
Ground Transportation ....IBA Transportation/
Danny Ibanez
Opening Night Coordination ....Carrie Mahoney

CREDITS

Scenery constructed by Atlas Scenic Studios. Computer motion control and automation of scenery and rigging by Hyde Power Systems. Computer motion control for scenery and rigging by SHOWTRAK®. Lighting equipment by PRG Lighting. Costumes built by Tricorne, Inc., Studio Rouge Inc., Studio Arena Theatre, Paul Chang Custom Tailor. Millinery by Arnold S. Levine, Inc.; Gary White/The Custom Hatter. Dyeing/painting by Gene Mignola, Inc.; DYE-NAMIX. Sound and video equipment by Sound Associates, Inc. L.E.D. equipment by Daktronics. Props by John Creech Design & Productions. Trucking by Clark Transfer.

INSTRUMENT CREDITS

Acoustic guitars courtesy of CF Martin & Company. Drums courtesy of Pearl Drums. Cymbals courtesy of Bosphorous Cymbals. Fiddle strings courtesy of Super Sensitive Strings. Electric guitar strings courtesy of Black Diamond Strings. Keyboards courtesy of Yamaha Corporation of America. Acoustic guitar strings courtesy of D'Addario Strings. Amplifiers and electric guitars courtesy of Fender Musical Instruments Corporation. Mandolins, banjos and dobro courtesy of Gibson Guitars. Accordion courtesy of Titano Accordion Company. Drum sticks and brushes courtesy of Regal Tip. Guitar tuners courtesy of Peterson Tuners. Evoharp courtesy of The Dulcimer Shop. Double bass stand courtesy of Kolstein Music. Violins courtesy of Gregory Singer Fine Violins.

MUSIC CREDITS

"**Hurt**" (Michael Trent Reznor) © Leaving Hope Music. "**Country Boy**" (John R. Cash) © House of Cash, Inc. "**In the Highways**" (Maybelle Carter) © Peermusic Inc. "**Thing Called Love**" (Jerry Hubbard) © Sixteen Stars Music/Vector Music. "**There You Go**" (John R. Cash) © House of Cash, Inc. "**Orange Blossom Special**" (Ervin T. Rouse) © Universal MCA Publishing. "**While I've Got It on My Mind**" (John R. Cash) © Song of Cash Music. "**My Old Faded Rose**" (John R. Cash, June Carter) © 1964 (renewed), Unichappell Music Inc. (BMI). All rights reserved. Used by permission. "**Daddy Sang Bass**" (John R. Cash and Carl L. Perkins) © Universal Cedarwood Publishing. "**Straight A's in Love**" (John R. Cash) © 1958 (renewed), Chappell & Co. (ASCAP). All rights reserved. Used by permission. "**Big River**" (John R. Cash) © House of Cash, Inc. "**I Still Miss Someone**" (John R. Cash, Roy Cash Jr.) © 1958 (renewed), Unichappell Music Inc. (BMI). All rights reserved. Used by permission. "**Five Feet High and Rising**" (John R. Cash) © 1959 (renewed), Chappell & Co., Inc. (ASCAP). All rights reserved. Used by permission. "**Flesh and Blood**" © Song of Cash Music/House of Cash, Inc. "**Look at Them Beans**" (Joseph Arrington, Jr.) © Sony/ATV Tree Publishing, Trio/Windwept Pacific & Fort Knox Music. "**Get Rhythm**" (John R. Cash) © House of Cash, Inc. "**Flushed From the Bathroom of Your Heart**" (Jack H. Clement) © Universal Songs of Polygram, Inc. "**Dirty Old Egg Sucking Dog**" (Jack H. Clement) © Universal Songs of Polygram, Inc. "**Angel Band**" (John R. Cash) © Song of Cash Music. "**If I Were a Carpenter**" (James Timothy Hardin) © Allen Stanton Productions. "**Ring of Fire**" (Written by June Carter and Merle Kilgore). Used by permission of Painted Desert Music Corp. All rights reserved. International copyright secured. "**Jackson**" (Jerry Leiber & Billy Edd Wheeler) © Bexhill Music Corp., Jerry Leiber Music (ASCAP) & Mike Stoller Music (ASCAP). "**I've Been Everywhere**" (Geoff Mack) © 1962 (renewed), Belinda Music (Australia) Pty. Ltd. (APRA). All rights administered by Unichappell Music Inc. All rights reserved. Used by permission. "**Sunday Mornin' Comin' Down**" (written by Kris Kristofferson), published by Combine Music Corp. "**Temptation**" (written by Arthur Freed and Nacio Herb Brown), published by EMI Robbins Catalog Inc. "**I Feel Better All Over**" (written by Ken Rogers and Ferlin Husky), published by Beechwood Music Corporation. "**A Boy Named Sue**" (words & music by Shel Silverstein) TRO – Evil Eye Music, Inc. – ASCAP. "**Going to Memphis**" (John R. Cash) © 1960 (renewed), Unichappell Music Inc. (BMI). All rights reserved. Used by permission. "**Delia's Gone**" (John R. Cash, Karl M. Silberdorf & Richard Toops) © Song of Cash Music. "**Austin Prison**" (John R. Cash) © 1966 Chappell & Co., Inc. (ASCAP). All rights Reserved. Used by permission. "**Orleans Parish Prison**" (Dick Feller) © Cyberphonic Publishing. "**Folsom Prison Blues**" (John R. Cash) © House of Cash, Inc. "**Man in Black**" (John R. Cash) © Song of Cash Music. "**All Over Again**" (John R. Cash) © 1958 (renewed), Chappell & Co., Inc. (ASCAP). All rights administered by Chappell & Co., Inc. All rights reserved. Used by permission. "**I Walk the Line**" (John R. Cash) © House of Cash, Inc. "**The Man Comes Around**" (John R. Cash) © Song of Cash Music/House of Cash, Inc. "**Waiting on the Far-Side Banks of Jordan**" (Terry Smith) © 1975 (renewed), Warner-Tamerlane Publishing Corp. (BMI). All rights reserved. Used by permission. "**Why Me**" (written by Kris Kristofferson), published by Resaca Music Publishing Co. "**Hey Porter**" (John R. Cash) © House of Cash, Inc.

SPECIAL THANKS

John Carter Cash, Rosanne Cash, Lou Robin and Karen Wilder Robin (Artist Consultants Productions, Inc.), Robert Sullivan, Katherine Sullivan, Denise Stevens, Gerald Schoenfeld, Ken Neufeld and all the staff and crew at Studio Arena Theatre, John Miller, Gail Anderson, Jenn Colella, Kayce Glasse, Dale M. Herr, Dave Martin, Pat McRoberts, Dave Roe Rorick, David Shire, Collette Simmons, Ken Triwush, Mark Winchester, Kevin Lind, Fred Hemminger, Sharon Rosen. Also thanks to Guitar Center, Boulet Boots, Engelhardt-Link Basses, Justin Boots, Beaver Brand Hats and Frontier Outfitter. Pickup for the upright bass provided by K & K Sound.

THE SHUBERT ORGANIZATION, INC.
Board of Directors

Gerald Schoenfeld	**Philip J. Smith**
Chairman	President
Wyche Fowler, Jr.	**John W. Kluge**
Lee J. Seidler	**Michael I. Sovern**

Stuart Subotnick

Robert E. Wankel
Executive Vice President

Peter Entin	**Elliot Greene**
Vice President -	Vice President -
Theatre Operations	Finance
David Andrews	**John Darby**
Vice President -	Vice President -
Shubert Ticketing Services	Facilities

Staff for The Ethel Barrymore

House Manager ....Dan Landon

Ring of Fire
SCRAPBOOK

Photos by Aubrey Reuben

Correspondent: Cass Morgan, Performer

Memorable Opening Night Visitors: Johnny Cash's children John Carter Cash, Rosanne Cash and Carlene Carter. Also, Larry Gatlin and Cowboy Jack Clements. They all loved the show and said that it meant a great deal to them, and that Johnny and June would have loved it. The cast has become such a family under Richard Maltby's guidance, and Johnny's family was the most important thing to him.

Opening Night Gifts: We all got special opening night posters of the show made by Hatch Show Prints (those old-fashioned block letter show posters made in Nashville). It's a Country Music thing. They're wonderful and very different from the beautiful glossy Broadway posters you see everywhere. Everyone had a personal favorite gift. Jeb Brown was given a suit by Manuel (a designer who outfitted Johnny and Elvis), but the shoulders were too big, so he passed it on to Jason Edwards. But Jason's favorite gift was having his parents in the audience. The most meaningful gift was the one given to Richard Maltby. Our producers got him a gorgeous black Epiphone guitar, like the one Johnny played, and we all signed it and presented it to him the first day back after opening.

Who Has Done the Most Broadway Shows: Melanie Vaughan, my understudy, leads the pack with 10. Among the six principals, I've done six and Jarrod Emick has done five. But more importantly most of our 14-member ensemble has never even done a show in New York before, let alone a Broadway show. Over half of us relocated for this. That's eight of the 14-member ensemble, plus five of our 11 understudies. That's over half of the total performing company. Some left behind their homes and spouses, others packed up and moved their entire families, putting other careers on hold.

Special Backstage Ritual: There are two times when several of us are in the wings singing backup. We're changing costumes and we're individually miked so we don't need to stand together, but we stop mid-change and come stand next to each other and sing. Then we go back to our costume changes.

Most Fun Ritual: Once a week we get together at a bar after the show and have a hootenanny. David Lutken started it when we were out of

1. (L-R): Assistant choreographer Michelle Weber, cast members Beth Malone and Jason Edwards, understudy Gail Bliss (in front) and musician Laurie Canaan at a cast party at Tony's Di Napoli restaurant.
2. Lari White, Eric Anthony and David M. Lutken have a musical battle at a preview for reporters.
3. Director Richard Maltby Jr. arrives at the Ethel Barrymore Theatre.
4. Rosanne Cash at the Barrymore Theatre on opening night.
5. Country singer Larry Gatlin arrives at the Barrymore.

Ring of Fire
SCRAPBOOK

(L-R) Lari White, Jarrod Emick, Jason Edwards, Beth Malone, Jeb Brown and Cass Morgan at the opening night party at the Marriott Marquis Hotel.

town with the show at Buffalo Studio Arena. It's for anybody and everybody who wants to play: stagehands, understudies, band and actors. When people in the cast have friends in to see the show, we invite them too. One night I was playing the spoons, and I played them so hard and so long I got a spoon wound! I had to wear Band-Aids on my fingers for a week. It's a lot of fun, but it's also a way of honing our listening skills. You have to really listen to play together as closely as we do, and our hootenannies are one way to stay connected.

Favorite Moment During Each Performance: There's a moment right near the end, as Jason and I are singing "The Far Side Banks of Jordan," when I can feel something different happening in the audience, in the way they react. They've gotten to know all of us so well during the show that they really identify with us. The show takes a really personal turn at this point, as we deal with the death of a spouse. Then two songs later the whole company is onstage singing and dancing so powerfully and joyfully with "Hey Porter." We take them low, but we leave them on a high. Ending the show with those three songs is magical.

Favorite In-Theatre Gathering Place: Stage manager's office.

Favorite Off-Site Hangout: The place where we have our hootenanny. It's a bar on Eighth Avenue, in the Theatre District, but I'm going to keep the name our secret.

Favorite Therapy: Once again, our weekly hootenanny.

Favorite Snack Food: We have a cross-under beneath the stage and there's always cake, doughnuts and cookies. The cast bought an espresso machine so there'd be coffee to go along with the treats. But then again, since we tried out the show in Buffalo last fall, we all ate A LOT of Buffalo chicken wings. Possibly enough for a lifetime.

Mascot: The black guitar. It's very specifically passed from one player to another throughout the show.

Funniest Costumes: The silly apron I wear in the Opry sequence.

Inadvertently Funny Costume: Lari White's yellow rain slicker and hat she wears in "Five Feet High and Risin'. " It's very Paddington Bear.

Memorable Press Event: It was very moving to sing the national anthem at the opening day of the Mets season. Right before we sang, as they finished introducing the players, the powerful roar from the record-breaking crowd was thrilling!

Memorable Stage Door Fan Encounters: There are always people waiting to talk to us. Many of them are older people, and are thrilled by what they saw and heard. I feel that this show touches something in an age group that a lot of shows ignore. But ours is a show at which young and old both have a great time.

Catchphrase Only the Company Would Recognize: "I'd like to wear a rainbow every day, please."

Memorable Directorial Note: During "A Boy Named Sue" we women are behind bar, watching while the men are fighting. Richard Maltby Jr. told us, "You're way too interesting. You need be actively boring."

"Easter Bonnet" Sketch: "The Ballad of Johnny Cash," written by Jeb Brown and Randy Redd and performed by them, plus Eric Anthony, Miles Aubrey, Gail Bliss, Laura Ellington, Jeff Lisenby, Beth Malone, DeAnn Whalen, Jarrod Emick, Dan Immel, and me. The bonnet was built, designed and worn by Ray Panelli.

Fastest Costume Change: Laurie Canaan exits stage right, drops off her violin, slips her arms into a jacket that's held out for her and is back onstage in just a couple of seconds. That's fast. But I have the fastest top-to-bottom change,

going from "Flushed From the Bathroom of Your Heart" into my glittering blue suede "Angel Band" outfit. It's so fast that Beth Malone is creating a drink in its honor called "The Blue Tornado."

Nicknames: Laurie Canaan, in her other life, is also a professional clown, whose name is "Buttons."

Embarrassing Moment: We all turned to Eric at the top of Act II, for "Pasadena, Catalina" in "I've Been Everywhere," and he wasn't there. Missed his entrance.

Company In-Jokes: This is somewhere between ritual and inside joke: Jim Price and Miles Aubrey have invented their own union. It's called GUI-ATSE (GUI for guitar and IATSE for...well, IATSE). They keep the instruments tuned, replace broken strings, picks, etc. They've claimed a corner of stage left for themselves, which they call "GUIATSE International Headquarters." They mark the fire door with chalk to keep track of who has broken the most strings or guitar picks or drumsticks. Jeb Brown seems to break a string almost every show.

Understudy Anecdote: First of all, they prefer to call themselves "Principals in Waiting." In their down time, they are writing a novel, as a group. The second chapter is well under way. The manuscript is done in longhand, and makes its rounds, a page per person. The main character in the book is a quadruple amputee, Susie Mendlebaum, who dreams of being a Broadway star. It's guaranteed to offend everyone.

Orchestra Member Who Played the Most Instruments: Everyone in the cast and band plays at least two, but David Lutken is the winner with six: guitar, mandolin, banjo, dobro, harmonica and Evoharp.

Coolest Thing About Being in This Show : That we get to celebrate a man like Johnny Cash on Broadway.

700 Sundays

First Preview: November 12, 2004. Opened: December 5, 2004.
Closed June 12, 2005 after 21 Previews and 163 Performances.

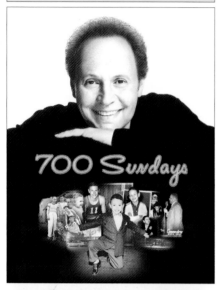

Billy Crystal.

Photo by Carol Rosegg

⑤ BROADHURST THEATRE

235 West 44th Street
A Shubert Organization Theatre

Gerald Schoenfeld, *Chairman*   Philip J. Smith, *President*

Robert E. Wankel, *Executive Vice President*

Janice Crystal, Larry Magid
and Face Productions

Present

BILLY CRYSTAL

In

700 Sundays

Written by

Billy Crystal

Additional material by	Scenic Design	Lighting Design	Production Design
Alan Zweibel	**David F. Weiner**	**David Lee Cuthbert**	**Michael Clark**

Sound Design	Clothing Stylist	Technical Supervisor	Production Stage Manager
Steve Canyon Kennedy John Shivers	**David C. Woolard**	**Don Gilmore-DSG Entertainment**	**Lurie Horns Pfeffer**

General Manager	Company Manager	Press Representative
Niko Companies, Ltd	**Brig Berney**	**Barlow • Hartman**

Directed By

Des McAnuff

700 SUNDAYS was originally produced by the La Jolla Playhouse
Des McAnuff, Artistic Director & Terrence Dwyer, Managing Director

Presented in association with Clear Channel Entertainment

LIVE BROADWAY

6/1/05

Billy Crystal
Playwright/Performer

Des McAnuff
Director

Alan Zweibel
Additional Material

John Shivers
Sound Design

700 Sundays

Steve Canyon
Kennedy
Sound Design

Manny Kladitis,
Niko Companies
General Manager

Brig Berney
Company Manager

Lurie Horns Pfeffer
*Production
Stage Manager*

Janice Crystal
Producer

SCRAPBOOK
Billy Crystal (L) grins as his
caricature is added to the wall at
Sardi's restaurant by managing
partner Max Klimavicius.

FRONT OF HOUSE
Front Row (L-R): Sabiel Almonte,
Marie Gonzalez, Rose Ann Cipriano,
Marie Mangelli
Standing (L-R): Henry Bathea,
Carmen Rodriguez, Lashone
Cleveland, Latoya Sewell, Hugh
Lynch, Karen Diaz and Hugh Barnett
(House Manager).

700 Sundays

700 SUNDAYS CREDITS

MUSIC CREDITS

"The Alley Cat" written by Frank Bjorn. Used by permission of Music Sales Group. All rights reserved. Used by permission.

"American Collection Theme" (John Williams). © Marjer Publishing (BMI). All rights on behalf of Marjer Publishing (BMI). Administered by Warner-Tamerlane Publishing Corp. (BMI). All rights reserved. Used by permission.

"Baby Won't You Please Come Home" written by Charles Warfield and Clarence Williams. All rights owned or administered by Universal-MCA Music Publishing, a division of Universal Studios, Inc. and Great Standard's Music c/o The Songwriters Guild. Used by permission.

"Butterfly's Day Out" by Mark O'Connor. © Mark O'Connor Musik International (administered by MCS Music America, Inc.). All rights reserved. Used by permission,

"Candy" by Alex Kramer, Joan Whitney and Mack David. © 1944 by Bourne Co. and PolyGram International Pub. Copyright renewed. All rights reserved. International copyright secured, ASCAP.

"Cute" instrumental (Neal Hefti). © 1958 (renewed) WB Music Corp. All rights reserved. Used by permission.

"It's a Lovely Day," "My Walking Stick," "Steppin' Out With My Baby" and "They Say It's Wonderful": music and lyrics by Irving Berlin. These selections are used by special arrangement with The Rodgers and Hammerstein Organization, on behalf of the Estate of Irving Berlin, 1065 Avenue of the Americas, Suite 2400, New York, New York 10018. All rights reserved.

"Love Is Just Around the Corner" written by Leo Robin/Louis Gensler. Published by Famous Music Corporation (ASCAP). Used by permission. All rights reserved.

"Memories of You" written by Eubie Blake and Andy Razaf. Used by permission of Shapiro, Bernstein & Co., Inc. and Razaf Music, c/o The Songwriters Guild. All rights reserved. International copyright secured.

"Muskrat Ramble" written by Edward Ory. Used by permission of Slick Tongue Ory Music care of Bughouse, a division of Bug Music, Inc. All rights reserved. Used by permission.

"On the Sunny Side of the Street" written by Dorothy Fields and Jimmy McHugh. Used by permission of Shapiro, Bernstein & Co., Inc. and Cotton Club Publishing c/o EMI Music Publishing. All rights reserved. International copyright secured.

"One B" written by Edgar A. Meyer. Used by permission of Hendon Music, Inc. All rights reserved. Used by permission.

"Someone to Watch Over Me" (George Gershwin, Ira Gershwin). © 1926 (renewed), WB MUSIC CORP. (ASCAP). All rights reserved. Used by permission.

"Sunrise, Sunset" music by Jerry Bock, lyrics by Sheldon Harnick. This selection is used by special arrangement with Jerry Bock Enterprises and with R&H Music, on behalf of Mayerling Productions Ltd.

"Vocalise" written by Sergei Rachmaninoff. Used by permission of Boosey and Hawkes, Inc. All rights reserved. Used by permission.

"Wrap Your Troubles in Dreams (And Dream Your Troubles Away)" written by Harry Barris, Ted Kochler, and Billy Moll. Used by permission of Shapiro, Bernstein & Co., Inc. and the Fred Ahlert Music Corporation. All rights reserved. International copyright secured.

"You Always Hurt the One You Love" written by Doris Fisher and Allan Roberts. All rights owned or administered by Universal-MCA Music Publishing, a division of Universal Studios, Inc. and Doris Fisher Music Corporation. Used by permission.

Incidental music performed by Stephen "Hoops" Snyder (piano), Ken Dow (bass), and Kevin Dow (drums).

VIDEO CREDITS

Shane courtesy of Paramount Pictures. Jazz dance film provided by Mark Cantor/Celluloid Improvisations Film Archive.

Photo by Ben Strothmann

Backstage Crew and Cast
Front Row (L-R): Ron Vitelli (House Properties), Lurie Horns Pfeffer (Production Stage Manager, Robert Thurber (Stage Manager), Steve Abbott (Follow Spot Operator), Billy Crystal (Star), Janice Crystal (Producer), Hugh Barnett (House Manager), Phil Lojo (Production Sound Engineer) and Charlie DeVerna (House Electrician).

Back Row (L-R): Brig Berney (Company Manager), Bill Staples (Spot Operator), Dan Novi (Follow Spot Operator), Brian McGarty (House Carpenter), Jonathan Cohen (Deck Sound), Brian Bullard (House Flyman) and Marcie Olivi (Wardrobe Supervisor).

700 Sundays

STAFF FOR *700 SUNDAYS*

GENERAL MANAGEMENT

NIKO COMPANIES, LTD.

Manny Kladitis

David Cole   James Lawson

Maia Sutton   Walter Shepherd

COMPANY MANAGER

Brig Berney

GENERAL PRESS REPRESENTATIVE

BARLOW•HARTMAN

Michael Hartman	John Barlow
Carol Fineman	Leslie Baden

Production Stage Manager	Lurie Horns Pfeffer
Stage Manager	Donald Fried
Production Assistant	Sarah Kirby
Assistant to the Director	Holly-Anne Ruggiero
Associate Scenic Designer	Christopher T. Borreson
Associate Lighting Designer	Patricia Nichols
Associate Sound Designers	Chris Luessman, Walter Trarbach
House Carpenter	Brian McGarty
House Properties	Ron Vitelli
House Electrician	Charlie DeVerna
House Flyman	Brian Bullard
Production Electrician	John Michael Pitzer, Jr.
Assistant Production Electrician	Shannon January
Follow Spot Operators	Steve Abbott, Jr.; Dan Novi
Production Sound Engineer	Phillip Lojo
Deck Sound	Jonathan Cohen
Wardrobe Supervisor	Marcie Olivi
Video Coordinator	Chris Luessman
Projection Programmer	Paul Vershbow
Properties Supervisor	Emiliano Pares
Assistant to Mr. Crystal	Carol Sidlow
Assistant to Mr. Magid	Carrie Cunningham
Assistant to Mr. McAnuff	Jim Roderick
Legal Counsel	Franklin, Weinrib, Rudell & Vasallo Elliot Brown, Daniel Wasser
Accountant	Rosenberg, Neuwirth, & Kuchner CPAs Mark A. D'Ambrosi, Sandra Lattanzio, Jana Jevnikar
Advertising	Serino Coyne Inc. Nancy Coyne, Angelo Desimini, Sandy Block, Ben Downing
Marketing	Clear Channel Marketing Jennifer DeLange, Carolyn Christensen
Production Photographer	Carol Rosegg
Groups Sales	Clear Channel Group Sales Nicholas Falzon

Souvenir Merchandise	Clear Channel Theatrical/ Larry Turk
Opening Night Coordinators	Tobak-Dantchik Suzanne Tobak, Joanna Koondel
Banking	JP Morgan Chase Mary Ann Viafore
Insurance	Tanenbaum Harber of FL, LLC Carol Bressi-Cilona
Theatre Displays	King Displays, Inc.
Payroll Services	Castellana Services, Inc.

CREDITS

Scenery by PRG Scenic Technologies. Lighting equipment from Fourth Phase. Sound equipment by Masque Sound. Projection equipment from Scharff Weisberg. Mr. Crystal's gym equipment provided by Gym Source. Security provided by RL Security, Inc. Fiber Optics by TPR Enterprises.

SPECIAL THANKS

American Express, The New York Yankees, The New York Times, UPS, Carl Pasbjerg, Eric Joseph, David Steinberg, Steve Tennenbaum, Bob Sheppard.

The photo of Billy Crystal on the cover

of the PLAYBILL® is by Nigel Parry/CPi.

CLEAR CHANNEL ENTERTAINMENT - Theatrical

Brian Becker, Miles C. Wilkin, Scott Zeiger, Steve Winton, David Anderson, Lauren Reid, Lynn Blandford, Bradley Broecker, Jennifer Costello, Jennifer DeLange, Joanna Hagan, Eric Joseph, Susan Krajsa, David Lazar, Hailey Lustig, Drew Murphy, Carl Pasbjerg, Debra Peltz, Denise Perry, Courtney Pierce, Alison Spiriti, Dan Swartz.

THE SHUBERT ORGANIZATION, INC.

Board of Directors

Gerald Schoenfeld Chairman	**Philip J. Smith** President
Wyche Fowler, Jr.	**John W. Kluge**
Lee J. Seidler	**Michael I. Sovern**

Stuart Subotnick

Robert E. Wankel

Executive Vice President

Peter Entin Vice President - Theatre Operations	**Elliot Greene** Vice President - Finance
David Andrews Vice President - Shubert Ticketing Services	**John Darby** Vice President - Facilities

House Manager	Hugh Barnett

Shining City

First Preview: April 20, 2006. Opened: May 9, 2006.
Still running as of May 31, 2006.

PLAYBILL®

CAST
(in order of appearance)

Ian	BRÍAN F. O'BYRNE
John	OLIVER PLATT
Neasa	MARTHA PLIMPTON
Laurence	PETER SCANAVINO

PLACE
An office in Dublin.

TIME
Present. Roughly two months separate each scene.

Stage Manager: Francesca Russell

UNDERSTUDIES
For Ian/Laurence:
CHRIS GENEBACH

For Neasa:
FIANA TOIBIN

BILTMORE THEATRE

MANHATTAN THEATRE CLUB
Artistic Director
LYNNE MEADOW

Executive Producer
BARRY GROVE

By Special Arrangement with
SCOTT RUDIN   ROGER BERLIND   DEBRA BLACK

Presents

Shining City

by
CONOR McPHERSON

with

BRÍAN F. O'BYRNE   OLIVER PLATT
MARTHA PLIMPTON   PETER SCANAVINO

Scenic Design
SANTO LOQUASTO

Costume Design
KAYE VOYCE

Lighting Design
CHRISTOPHER AKERLIND

Sound Design
OBADIAH EAVES

Dialect Coach
DEBORAH HECHT

Production Stage Manager
BARCLAY STIFF

Directed by
ROBERT FALLS

Casting
**NANCY PICCIONE/
DAVID CAPARELLIOTIS**

Director of Artistic Operations
MANDY GREENFIELD

Production Manager
RYAN McMAHON

Director of Development
JILL TURNER LLOYD

Director of Marketing
DEBRA A. WAXMAN

Press Representative
**BONEAU/
BRYAN-BROWN**

General Manager
FLORIE SEERY

Director of Artistic Development
PAIGE EVANS

Director of Artistic Production
MICHAEL BUSH

SHINING CITY was first presented by The Royal Court Theatre, London and The Gate Theatre, Dublin on June 4, 2004. Manhattan Theatre Club wishes to express its appreciation to Theatre Development Fund for is support of this production.

5/9/06

Widower Oliver Platt (L) tells therapist Brían F. O'Byrne (R) about the ghost of his late wife.

Photo by Joan Marcus

Shining City

Brían F. O'Byrne
Ian

Oliver Platt
John

Martha Plimpton
Neasa

Peter Scanavino
Laurence

Chris Genebach
*Understudy for
Ian, Laurence*

Fiana Toibin
*Understudy for
Neasa*

Robert Falls
Director

Conor McPherson
Playwright

Santo Loquasto
Scenic Design

Kaye Voyce
Costume Design

Christopher Akerlind
Lighting Design

Obadiah Eaves
Sound Design

Lynne Meadow
*Artistic Director,
Manhattan Theatre
Club, Inc.*

Barry Grove
*Executive Producer,
Manhattan Theatre
Club, Inc.*

Photo by Ben Strothmann

FRONT OF HOUSE STAFF AND CREW
Front Row (L-R):
Tevy Bradley (Assistant Box Office Treasurer), Valerie D. Simmons (Theatre Manager), Johannah-Joy Magyawe (Assistant Theatre Manager), Francesca Russell (Stage Manager) and David Dillon (Box Office Treasurer).

Second Row (L-R):
Ingrid Pohle, Sue Poulin (Apprentice), Miranda Scopel, Tim Walters (Head Propertyman), Tracey Boone (Dresser), Angela Simpson (Wardrobe Supervisor), Walter Cordero, Catherine Burke and Wendy Wright.

Back Row (L-R):
Barclay Stiff (Production Stage Manager), Louis Shapiro (Sound Engineer), Jeff Dodson (Master Electrician), Taurance Williams, Daniel Kerrigan (Apprentice), Jackson Ero, Edward Brashear, Bruce Dye, Patricia Polhill and Beren Willwerth.

Shining City

MANHATTAN THEATRE CLUB STAFF

Artistic Director	**Lynne Meadow**
Executive Producer	**Barry Grove**
General Manager	**Florie Seery**
Director of Artistic Production	**Michael Bush**
Director of Artistic Development	**Paige Evans**
Director of Artistic Operations	**Mandy Greenfield**
Artistic Associate/ Assistant to the Artistic Director	Amy Gilkes Loe
Artistic Assistant	Kacy O'Brien
Director of Casting	**Nancy Piccione**
Casting Director	**David Caparelliotis**
Casting Assistant	Kristin Svenningsen
Literary Manager	**Emily Shooltz**
Play Development Associate/ Sloan Project Manager	Aaron Leichter
Play Development Assistant	Annie MacRae
Director of Musical Theatre	**Clifford Lee Johnson III**
Artistic Consultant	Ethan Youngerman
Director of Development	**Jill Turner Lloyd**
Director, Corporate Relations	Karen Zornow Leiding
Director, Individual Giving	Casey Reitz
Director, Special Events	Allison Gutstein
Director, Foundation and Government Relations	Josh Jacobson
Senior Development Associate, Individual Giving	Antonello Di Benedetto
Development Associate/ Foundation & Gov't Relations	Andrea Gorzell
Development Associate/ Planning & Projects	Liz Halakan
Development Associate/ Corporate Relations	Jessica Sadowski
Development Database Coordinator	Rey Pamatmat
Patrons' Liaison	Sage Young
Director of Marketing	**Debra A. Waxman**
Marketing Manager	Dale Edwards
Marketing Associate/Website Manager	Ryan M. Klink
Director of Finance	**Jeffrey Bledsoe**
Business Manager	Holly Kinney
HR/Payroll Manager	Darren Robertson
Senior Business Associate & HR Coordinator	Denise L. Thomas
Business Assistant	Thomas Casazzone
Manager of Systems Operations	Avishai Cohen
Systems Analyst	Andrew Dumawal
Associate General Manager	**Lindsey T. Brooks**
Company Manager/New York City Center	Erin Moeller
Assistant to the Executive Producer	Bonnie Pan
Director of Subscriber Services	**Robert Allenberg**
Associate Subscriber Services Manager	Andrew Taylor
Subscriber Services Representatives	Mark Bowers, Alva Chinn, Rebekah Dewald, Matthew Praet, Rosanna Consalvo Sarto
Director of Telesales and Telefunding	**George Tetlow**
Assistant Manager	Terrence Burnett
Director of Education	David Shookhoff
Asst. Director of Education/Coordinator, Paul A. Kaplan Theatre Management Program	Amy Harris
Education Assistants	Kayla Cagan, Sarah McLellan

MTC Teaching Artists ...Stephanie Alston, David Auburn, Michael A. Bernard, Carl Capotorto, Chris Ceraso, Charlotte Colavin, Gilbert Girion, Andy Goldberg, Elise Hernandez, Jeffrey Joseph, Kate Long, Samantha Mascali, Lou Moreno, Michaela Murphy, Melissa Murray, Angela Pietropinto, Alfonzo Ramirez, Carmen Rivera, Judy Tate, Candido Tirado, Joe White

Theatre Management Interns ...Jill Amato, Maureen Cavanaugh, Kari Foster, Kristin Miller, Bonnie Pipkin, Emily Plumb, Alexa Polmer, Rebecca Rozin, Sarah Ryndak, Sarah Schacter, Miranda Scopel, Caitlin Smith, Christopher Taggart, Angela Taylor, Shayla Titley, Christina Trivigno, Romana Zajac

---

The Paul A. Kaplan Theatre Management Program, MTC's internship program, is designed to train the next generation of theatre leaders.

Randy Carrig Casting Intern	Drew Ross
Reception/Studio Manager	Lauren Snyder
Production Manager	**Ryan McMahon**
Associate Production Manager	Bridget Markov
Assistant Production Manager	Ian McNaugher
Technical Director	William Mohney
Assistant Technical Director	Peter Gilchrist
Shop Foreman	Shayne Izatt
Assistant Shop Foreman	Nicholas Morales
Carpenter	Brian Corr
Scenic Painting Supervisor	**Jenny Stanjeski**
Lights and Sound Supervisor	**Matthew T. Gross**
Properties Supervisor	**Scott Laule**
Assistant Properties Supervisor	Dana Lewman
Props Carpenter	Peter Grimes
Costume Supervisor	**Erin Hennessy Dean**
Assistant Costume Supervisor	Michelle Sesco

GENERAL PRESS REPRESENTATIVES
BONEAU/BRYAN-BROWN
Chris Boneau   Jim Byk
Aaron Meier   Heath Schwartz

Script Readers	Sadie Foster, Liz Jones, Lara Mottolo, Mark von Sternberg, Michelle Tattenbaum, Kathryn Walat, Ethan Youngerman
Musical Theatre Reader	Emily King

SERVICES

Accountants	ERE, LLP
Advertising	SpotCo/ Drew Hodges, Jim Edwards, Tom McCann, Aaliytha Davis
Marketing Consultants	The Marketing Group/ Tanya Grubich, Laura Matalon, Trish Santini, Bob Bucci, Amber Glassberg, Liz Miller
Web Design	Pilla Marketing Communications
Legal Counsel	John Breglio, Deborah Hartnett/ Paul, Weiss, Rifkind, Wharton and Garrison LLP
Real Estate Counsel	Marcus Attorneys
Labor Counsel	Harry H. Weintraub/ Glick and Weintraub, P.C.
Immigration Counsel	Theodore Ruthizer/ Kramer, Levin, Naftalis & Frankel, LLP
Special Projects	Elaine H. Hirsch
Insurance	DeWitt Stern Group Inc/ Anthony Pittari

Opening Night Coordination	Joanna B. Koondel, Suzanne Tobak/ Tobak Lawrence Company
Maintenance	Reliable Cleaning
Production Photographer	Joan Marcus
Cover Photo	Frank Ockenfels 3
Cover Design	SpotCo
Theatre Displays	King Display

For more information visit
www.ManhattanTheatreClub.com

PRODUCTION STAFF FOR *SHINING CITY*

Company Manager	**Denise Cooper**
Production Stage Manager	**Barclay Stiff**
Stage Manager	Francesca Russell
Assistant Director	Henry Wishcamper
Associate Scenic Designer	Jenny B. Sawyers
Assistant Scenic Designer	Wilson Chin
Assistant Costume Designer	Sarah Laux
Assistant Lighting Designer	Michael Spadaro
Assistant Sound Designer	Mark Huang
Wigs	Tom Watson
Hair & Makeup Supervisor	Marion M. Geist
Dresser	Tracey Boone
Production Assistant	Kyle Gates

CREDITS

Scenic elements by Showman Fabricators, Inc. Backdrop by USA Image Technologies, Inc. Lighting equipment provided by PRG Lighting. Sound equipment provided by Masque Sound. Natural herbal cough drops courtesy of Ricola USA.

MUSIC CREDITS

"**Polly Come Home**," written by Gene Clark. All rights owned or administered by ©Irving Music, Inc./BMI. Used by permission. "**Through the Morning, Through the Night**," written by Gene Clark. All rights owned or administered by ©Irving Music, Inc./BMI. Used by permission. "**Fair and Tender Ladies**," written by Gene Clark. All rights owned or administered by ©Bug Music, Inc./BMI. Used by permission. "**Razor Love**," written by Neil Young. All rights owned or administered by ©Silver Fiddle Music/ASCAP. Used by permission.

SPECIAL THANKS

Hudson Photographic, Downtime Productions

MANHATTAN THEATRE CLUB/ BILTMORE THEATRE STAFF

Theatre Manager	**Valerie D. Simmons**
Assistant House Manager	Johannah-Joy Magyawe
Box Office Treasurer	**David Dillon**
Assistant Box Office Treasurers	Tevy Bradley, Stephanie Valcarcel
Head Carpenter	Chris Wiggins
Head Propertyman	Timothy Walters
Sound Engineer	Louis Shapiro
Master Electrician	Jeff Dodson
Wardrobe Supervisor	Angela Simpson
Apprentices	Daniel Kerrigan, Sue Poulin
Engineers	Deosarran, Richardo Deosarran, Byron Johnson
Security	OCS/Initial Security
Lobby Refreshments	Sweet Concessions

Shining City

1. Oliver Platt on opening night.
2. (L-R): Brían F. O'Byrne, Oliver Platt, Martha Plimpton and Peter Scanavino at the opening night party at the Bryant Park Grill.
3. Playwright Conor McPherson and wife Fionnuala Ni Chiosain arrive at Bryant Park Grill.
4. Director Robert Falls (L) and Barry Grove at the opening night party.
5. (L-R): Fionnuala Ni Chiosain, McPherson and the cast react to news of the rave review in *The New York Times*.
6. (L-R): Scanavino and O'Byrne at one of the many *Shining-City*-goes-to-the-Mets-game events.

Souvenir

First Preview: October 28, 2005. Opened: November 10, 2005.
Closed January 8, 2006 after 14 Previews and 68 Performances.

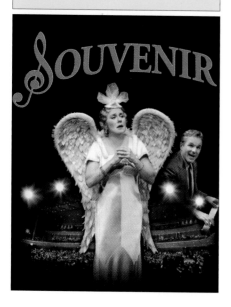

CAST

Florence Foster Jenkins ....JUDY KAYE
Cosme McMoon ....DONALD CORREN

The Time:

1964

The Place:

A supper club with resident pianist somewhere in
Greenwich Village, New York City

STANDBYS

For Florence Foster Jenkins: MEG BUSSERT
For Cosme McMoon: BOB STILLMAN

⊛LYCEUM THEATRE
149 West 45th Street
A Shubert Organization Theatre
Gerald Schoenfeld, *Chairman*   Philip J. Smith, *President*

Robert E. Wankel, *Executive Vice President*

TED SNOWDON
in association with JANICE MONTANA
by arrangement with
THE YORK THEATRE COMPANY
presents

JUDY KAYE
in
SOUVENIR
A FANTASIA ON THE LIFE OF FLORENCE FOSTER JENKINS

also starring
DONALD CORREN

A New Play with Music by
STEPHEN TEMPERLEY

Scenic Designer	Costume Designer	Lighting Designer
R. MICHAEL MILLER	TRACY CHRISTENSEN	ANN G. WRIGHTSON

Sound Designer	Musical Supervision	Casting	Production Stage Manager
DAVID BUDRIES	TOM HELM	BARRY MOSS, C.S.A./ BOB KALE	JACK GIANINO

Production Manager	Press Representative	Marketing	General Manager
SHOWMAN FABRICATORS	RICHARD KORNBERG & ASSOCIATES	HHC MARKETING	ROY GABAY

Directed by
VIVIAN MATALON

Original New York Production by The York Theatre Company,
James Morgan, *Artistic Director*   W. David McCoy, *Chairman*

Subsequently presented by the Berkshire Theatre Festival, Kate Maguire, *Executive Director*
The producers wish to express their appreciation to Theatre Development Fund for its support of this production.

11/10/05

Judy Kaye

Donald Corren and
Judy Kaye

Photos by Carol Rosegg

Souvenir

Judy Kaye
Florence Foster Jenkins

Donald Corren
Cosme McMoon

Meg Bussert
Standby, Florence Foster Jenkins

Bob Stillman
Standby, Cosme McMoon

Stephen Temperley
Author

Vivian Matalon
Director

R. Michael Miller
Scenic Designer

Tracy Christensen
Costume Designer

Roy Gabay
General Manager

Ann. G. Wrightson
Lighting Designer

Richard Kornberg,
Richard Kornberg & Associates
Press Representative

Bob Kale
Casting

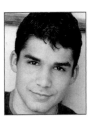
Jonathan Solari
Costume Design Assistant

SCRAPBOOK

①

②

③

④

Photos by Aubrey Reuben

Correspondent: Jack Gianino, Production Stage Manager

Actors Who Performed the Most Roles in This Show: Judy Kaye and Donald Corren.

Who Has Done the Most Shows: Judy Kaye or our PSM Jack Gianino.

Favorite Moment During Each Performance (On Stage Or Off): The first bad notes Ms. Kaye sings as Florence Foster Jenkins.

Favorite In-Theatre Gathering Place: At the back edge of the deck where our Christmas tree lived.

Favorite Off-Site Hangout: Joe Allen.

Favorite Snack Food: Sugar-free Ricola.

Mascot: If there had to be one I would say it should be Ms. Kaye in her angel wings.

Record Number of Cell Phone Rings During a Performance: A lot!

Fastest Costume Change: Five seconds

Who Wore the Heaviest/Hottest Costume: Judy Kaye's Carnegie Hall costumes.

Who Wore the Least: Donald Corren's suit; no changes.

Catchphrase Only the Company Would Recognize: "Not quite secure. Secure. Not quite."

Company In-Joke: "Fantastic."

Sweethearts Within the Company: Everyone.

Coolest Thing About Being in This Show: The Lyceum—both the theatre and the crew.

1. Judy Kaye on opening night.
2. Donald Corren and Kaye take bows on opening night.
3. Kaye and Corren arrive at the cast party.
4. (L-R): York Theatre Company artistic director James Morgan with arts patron Anita Jaffe and York's board chairman David McCoy.

Souvenir

Steel Magnolias

First Preview: March 15, 2005. Opened: April 4, 2005.
Closed July 31, 2005 after 23 Previews and 136 Performances.

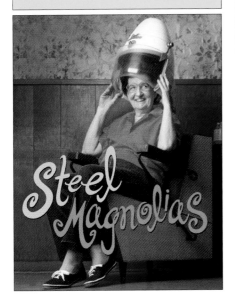

PLAYBILL

CAST
(in order of appearance)

Truvy . . . . .DELTA BURKE
Annelle . . . . .LILY RABE
Clairee . . . . .FRANCES STERNHAGEN
Shelby . . . . .REBECCA GAYHEART
M'Lynn . . . . .CHRISTINE EBERSOLE
Ouiser . . . . .MARSHA MASON

STANDBYS
PATRICIA KILGARRIFF,
GINIFER KING,
SALLY MAYES

TIME:
1987

PLACE:
Chinquapin, Louisiana

ACT ONE
Scene 1: April
Scene 2: December

ACT TWO
Scene 1: June, 18 months later
Scene 2: November

⑤LYCEUM THEATRE
220 West 48th Street
A Shubert Organization Theatre
Gerald Schoenfeld, *Chairman*   **Philip J. Smith,** *President*

Robert E. Wankel, *Executive Vice President*

Roy Gabay   Robyn Goodman

Danzansky Partners Ergo Entertainment Ruth Hendel Sharon Karmazin

Susan Dietz/Ina Meibach Michael Galvis/Billy Huddleston Elsa Daspin Suisman/Martha R. Gasparian

present

Delta   Christine   Rebecca   Marsha   Lily   Frances
Burke   Ebersole   Gayheart   Mason   Rabe   Sternhagen

in

Steel Magnolias

By Robert Harling

Set Design by	Costume Design by	Lighting Design by
Anna Louizos	David Murin	Howell Binkley

Sound Design by	Hair Design & Supervision by	Production Stage Manager
Ken Travis	Bobby H. Grayson	James FitzSimmons

Press Representative	Casting by	Dialect Coach
Boneau/Bryan-Brown	Bernard Telsey Casting	Stephen Gabis

Props Coordinator	Production Manager	General Manager	Associate Producers
Kathy Fabian	Showman Fabricators, Inc.	Roy Gabay	Stephen Kocis Bill Goodman

Directed by
Jason Moore

Originally produced by the WPA Theatre, New York City, 1987
(Kyle Renick, Artistic Director)

The producers wish to thank Theatre Development Fund for their support of this production.

LIVE BROADWAY

6/1/05

(L-R): Rebecca Gayheart as Shelby, Delta Burke as Truvy, Lily Rabe as Annelle and Christine Ebersole as M'Lynn in *Steel Magnolias*.

Photo by Joan Marcus

Steel Magnolias

Delta Burke
Truvy

Christine Ebersole
M'Lynn

Rebecca Gayheart
Shelby

Marsha Mason
Ouiser

Lily Rabe
Annelle

Frances Sternhagen
Clairee

Patricia Kilgarriff
Standby

Ginifer King
Standby

Sally Mayes
Standby

Robert Harling
Playwright

Jason Moore
Director

Anna Louizos
Set Design

David Murin
Costume Design

Howell Binkley
Lighting Design

Bernard Telsey
Casting, C.S.A.
Casting

Jen Bender
Assistant Director

Roy Gabay
Producer/General Manager

Robyn Goodman
Producer

Ruth Hendel
Producer

Sharon Karmazin
Producer

Transfer Students 2005-2006

Kathleen Early
Standby

Darrie Lawrence
Standby

Steel Magnolias

FRONT OF HOUSE
Front Row (L-R): Lorraine Bellaflores, Merida Colon (Chief Usher), Chip Jorgensen (Head Treasurer) and Joann Swanson (House Manager).
Middle Row (L-R): Kevin Pinzon, Susan Houghton, Elsie Grosvenor, Sonia Moreno.
Back Row (L-R): Saviel Almonte, Robert De Jesus and Nicole McIntyre.

BACKSTAGE CREW
(L-R): Leah Nelson, William Rowland, Gerry Stein, Steve Loehle, Neil Krasnow, Adam Braunstein, Kim Prentice, James FitzSimmons (Production Stage Manager), Kay Grunder and Nancy Lawson.

Steel Magnolias

Photo by Ben Strothmann

HAIR DEPARTMENT
Susan Corrado (Assistant Hair Supervisor)
and Bobby H. Grayson
(Hair Designer/Supervisor).

STAFF FOR *STEEL MAGNOLIAS*

GENERAL MANAGEMENT

ROY GABAY THEATRICAL
PRODUCTION & MANAGEMENT

Cheryl Dennis, Daniel Kuney,
Shawn Murphy, Cori Silberman

GENERAL PRESS REPRESENTATION
BONEAU/BRYAN-BROWN
Chris Boneau   Susanne Tighe
Heath Schwartz

COMPANY MANAGER
CHERYL DENNIS

CASTING

BERNARD TELSEY CASTING, C.S.A.
Bernie Telsey, Will Cantler, David Vaccari,
Bethany Knox, Craig Burns,
Tiffany Little Canfield, Christine Dall,
Stephanie Yankwitt

PRODUCTION SUPERVISION

SHOWMAN FABRICATORS, INC.

Production Strategies
Kai Brothers, Jason Block

PRODUCTION STAGE MANAGER

James FitzSimmons

Stage Manager . . . . .Neil Krasnow
Assistant Director . . . . .Jen Bender
Associate Set Designer . . . . .Donyale Werle
Set Design Assistants . . . . .Michael Carnahan,
Heather Dunbar
Assistant Costume Designer . . . . .Leslie Fuhs Allen
Associate Lighting Designer . . . . .Aaron Copp
Assistant Sound Designer . . . . .Shannon Slaton
Production Sound Operator . . . . .Gerry Stein
On Stage Styling Instruction . . . . .Bobby H. Grayson
Assistant Wig Design . . . . .Inga Thrasher
Assistant Hair Supervisor . . . . .Susan Corrado
Production Carpenter . . . . .Chris Wiggins
Production Electrician . . . . .Graeme McDonnell
Production Props . . . . .Steven Loehle

Props Assistants . . . . . . .Carrie S. Hash, Carrie Mossman
Wardrobe Supervisor . . . . .Kay Grunder
Dressers . . . . Nancy Lawson, Kim Prentice
Production Assistants . . . . .Amy Birnbaum,
Cyrille Blackburn
Assistant to Aged in Wood . . . . .Josh Fiedler
Press Representative Staff . . . . .Adrian Bryan-Brown,
Jim Byk, Brandi Cornwell,
Erika Creagh, Adriana Douzos,
Jackie Green, Juliana Hannett,
Hector Hernandez, Jessica Johnson,
Kevin Jones, Eric Louie,
Aaron Meier, Joe Perrotta,
Linnae Petruzzelli, Matt Polk
Accountant . . . . .Fried & Kowgios CPAs LLP/
Robert Fried, CPA
Controller . . . . .Elliott Aronstam
Banking . . . . .JPMorgan Chase
Insurance . . . . .DeWitt Stern Group Inc
Legal . . . . .John Silberman & Associates,
Karen Levinson
Advertising .Serino Coyne, Inc./
Greg Corradetti, Joaquin Esteva
Ruth Rosenberg, Sue Wozny
Production Photographer . . . . .Joan Marcus
Theatre Displays . . . . .King Displays
Car Service . . . . .I.B.A. Luxury Sedan Service,
Danny Ibanez
Rehearsal Studios . . . . .Playwrights Horizons
Payroll Services . . . . .Castellana Services, Inc.
On Stage Merchandising . . . . .George Fenmore, Inc.
Opening Night Coordination . . . . .Toback-Dantchik
Events & Promotion

CREDITS

Scenery supplied by SMI Showmotion. Lighting equipment
supplied by PRG Lighting. Sound equipment supplied by
Masque Sound. Costume construction by The Costume
Lab. Wig construction by Ray's Marston and Victoria
Wood. Beauty parlor equipment by Veeco Manufacturing,
Inc., David S.S. Davis. Additional period props courtesy of
George Fenmore, Inc. Hair care products and styling tools
provided by ConairPro and Rusk. Makeup provided By
M·A·C. Manicure products provided by OPI Products, Inc.
Ms. Gayheart's jeans provided by Joe's Jeans. Some of Ms.
Ebersole's wardrobe provided by Talbots. Salon decor and

hair accessories by Ray's Beauty Supply. Skincare products
used in the show are provided by Murad. Children's bath
and body products provided by Circle of Friends. Natural
herb cough drops courtesy of Ricola USA, Inc. Playbill cover
photo by Lee Crum.

www.steelmagnoliasbroadway.com

SPECIAL THANKS

Midge Lucas (Painter), Elizabeth Payne (Crafts and
Painting), Kevin Mark Harris (Tailor), Virginia Johnson
(Draper), Ray Beauty Supply, Catherine Small, Anne Guay,
Erin Eagleton, John Kilgore, Michael Pilipski, Robin
Santos, Trattoria Dopo Teatro, Playwrights Horizons
Costume Shop

THE SHUBERT ORGANIZATION, INC.
Board of Directors

Gerald Schoenfeld
Chairman

Philip J. Smith
President

Wyche Fowler, Jr.

John W. Kluge

Lee J. Seidler

Michael I. Sovern

Stuart Subotnick

Robert E. Wankel
Executive Vice President

Peter Entin
Vice President -
Theatre Operations

Elliot Greene
Vice President -
Finance

David Andrews
Vice President -
Shubert Ticketing Services

John Darby
Vice President -
Facilities

House Manager .Joann Swanson

Steel Magnolias
SCRAPBOOK

Photos by Aubrey Reuben

1. (Standing L-R): Rebecca Gayheart, Robert Harling, Lily Rabe, Christine Ebersole; (sitting L-R): Frances Sternhagen, Delta Burke, visiting film star Shirley MacLaine with Burke's long-haired chihuahua Lola, and Marsha Mason with Rebecca Gayheart's maltese Jackie backstage at the Lyceum Theatre.
2. Ebersole at "Broadway Barks 7!" in Shubert Alley.
3. Gayheart with Jackie backstage.
4. Burke (L) and her Aunt Ruth from Mississippi backstage at the Lyceum.
5. Burke delights in a gift of chicken spaghetti from her Aunt Ruth.
6. Playwright Robert Harling with MacLaine (who played Ouiser on film) and Mason (who plays Ouiser in Broadway) backstage.

A Streetcar Named Desire

First Preview: March 26, 2005. Opened: April 26, 2005.
Closed July 3, 2005 after 33 Previews and 73 Performances.

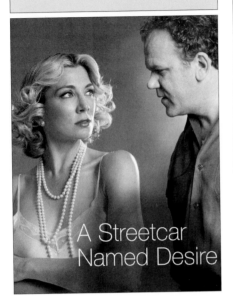

PLAYBILL®

CAST

A Negro Woman	WANDA L. HOUSTON
Eunice Hubbell	KRISTINE NIELSEN
Stanley Kowalski	JOHN C. REILLY
Harold Mitchell (Mitch)	CHRIS BAUER
Stella Kowalski	AMY RYAN
Blanche DuBois	NATASHA RICHARDSON
Steve Hubbell	SCOTT SOWERS
Pablo Gonzales	FRANK PANDO
A Young Collector	WILL TOALE
A Mexican Woman	TERESA YENQUE
A Doctor	JOHN CARTER
A Nurse	KATE BUDDEKE
Street People	JOHN CARTER, WILL TOALE, TERESA YENQUE, ALFREDO NARCISO, STARLA BENFORD, FRANK PANDO

SETTING: New Orleans, 1947

UNDERSTUDIES/STANDBYS

For Blanche and Stella: ANGELA PIERCE

For Stanley and Mitch: CHARLES BORLAND

For Eunice, Negro Woman, Mexican Woman and Nurse: STARLA BENFORD

For Steve and Doctor: ROBERT EMMET LUNNEY

For Pablo and Collector: ALFREDO NARCISO

Production Stage Manager: JANE GREY
Stage Manager: PHILIP CUSACK

STUDIO 54

ROUNDABOUT THEATRE COMPANY

TODD HAIMES, Artistic Director
ELLEN RICHARD, Managing Director
JULIA C. LEVY, Executive Director, External Affairs

Presents

Natasha Richardson   John C. Reilly

in

Tennessee Williams'

A Streetcar Named Desire

with

Amy Ryan   Chris Bauer

Starla Benford   Kate Buddeke   John Carter   Wanda L. Houston
Alfredo Narciso   Kristine Nielsen   Frank Pando
Scott Sowers   Will Toale   Teresa Yenque

Set Design by Robert Brill	*Costume Design by* William Ivey Long	*Lighting Design by* Donald Holder	*Original Music and Sound Design by* John Gromada
Hair and Wig Design by Paul Huntley	*Production Stage Manager* Jane Grey	*Dialect Coach* Deborah Hecht	*Fight Direction by* Rick Sordelet
Casting by Jim Carnahan, C.S.A.	*Associate Director* Barbara Rubin	*Technical Supervisor* Steve Beers	*General Manager* Sydney Beers
Founding Director Gene Feist	*Associate Artistic Director* Scott Ellis	*Press Representative* Boneau/Bryan-Brown	*Director of Marketing* David B. Steffen

Directed by

Edward Hall

Major support for this production provided by JPMorgan Chase.
Additional support provided by the Eleanor Naylor Dana Charitable Trust and
the National Endowment for the Arts.

Presented by arrangement with The University of the South, Sewanee, Tennessee
Roundabout Theatre Company is a member of the League of Resident Theatres. www.roundabouttheatre.org

6/1/05

(L-R) Natasha Richardson and Amy Ryan.

Photo by Joan Marcus

A Streetcar Named Desire

Natasha Richardson
Blanche DuBois

John C. Reilly
Stanley Kowalski

Amy Ryan
Stella Kowalski

Chris Bauer
Harold Mitchell

Starla Benford
Street Person

Kate Buddeke
Nurse

John Carter
Doctor, Street Person

Wanda L. Houston
Negro Woman

Alfredo Narciso
Street Person

Kristine Nielsen
Eunice Hubbell

Frank Pando
Pablo, Street Person

Scott Sowers
Steve Hubble

Will Toale
Young Collector, Street Person

Teresa Yenque
Mexican Woman, Street Person

Charles Borland
Standby Stanley, Mitch

Robert Emmet Lunney
Standby Steve, Doctor

Angela Pierce
Standby Blanche, Stella

Tennessee Williams (1911-1983)
Playwright

Edward Hall
Director

Robert Brill
Set Design

William Ivey Long
Costume Design

Donald Holder
Lighting Design

John Gromada
Original Music and Sound Design

Paul Huntley
Hair and Wig Design

Rick Sordelet
Fight Direction

Jane Grey
Production Stage Manager

Philip Cusack
Stage Manager

Barbara Rubin
Associate Director

Jim Carnahan
Casting Director

Julia C. Levy
Roundabout Theatre Company
Producer

Gene Feist
Founding Director, Roundabout Theatre
Producer

Todd Haimes
Artistic Director Roundabout Theatre Company
Producer

A Streetcar Named Desire

WARDROBE
(L-R): Sandy Binion, Nadine Hettel, Kevin Mark Harris, Gerald Crawford and Jay Woods.

COMPANY MANAGEMENT
(L-R): Nancy Mulliner and Lauren Parker.

CREW
(L-R): Dan Hoffman, John Wooding, Josh Weitzman, Erin Delaney, Greg Peeler and Lawrence Jenino.

STAGE MANAGEMENT
(L-R): Philip Cusack and Jane Grey.

FRONT OF HOUSE
Front Row (L-R): Mary Ann Ehlshlager, Laconya Robinson, Jack Watanachaiyot.
Middle Row (L-R): Jonathan Martinez, Anthony Roman, Kate Longosky, Latiffa Marcus, Jay Watanachaiyot.
Back Row (L-R): Maman Garba, Ralph Mohan, Nick Wheatly and Jason Fernandez.

BOX OFFICE
(L-R): Krystin MacRitchie, Steve Howe and Scott Falkowski.

A Streetcar Named Desire

ROUNDABOUT THEATRE COMPANY STAFF

ARTISTIC DIRECTOR ....TODD HAIMES
MANAGING DIRECTOR...........ELLEN RICHARD
EXECUTIVE DIRECTOR,
EXTERNAL AFFAIRS.................JULIA C. LEVY
ASSOCIATE ARTISTIC DIRECTOR ...SCOTT ELLIS

ARTISTIC STAFF

**DIRECTOR OF ARTISTIC DEVELOPMENT/
DIRECTOR OF CASTING** .... **Jim Carnahan**
Artistic Consultant ....Robyn Goodman
Resident Director ....Michael Mayer
Associate Artists....................Scott Elliott, Bill Irwin,
Joe Mantello, Mark Brokaw
Consulting Dramaturg ....Jerry Patch
Artistic Associate............................Samantha Barrie
Casting Director ....Mele Nagler
Casting Associate ....Carrie Gardner
Casting Associate............................J.V. Mercanti
Casting Assistant ....Kate Schwabe
Casting Assistant ....Stephen Kopel
Artistic Intern ....Corinne Hayoun

EDUCATION STAFF

EDUCATION DIRECTOR .... **Megan Kirkpatrick**
Director of Instruction and
Curriculum Development ....Renee Flemings
Education Program Associate ....Lindsay Erb
Education Program Associate...............Stacey L. Morris
Education Assistant ....Cassidy Jones
Education Interns ...Fumiko Eda, Tommy Marr, Catherine
Taylor
Education Dramaturg ....Ted Sod
Teaching Artists ....Zakiyyah Alexander,
Phil Alexander, Cynthia Babak,
Victor Barbella, Brigitte Barnett-Loftis,
Caitlin Barton, Joe Basile, LaTonya Borsay,
Bonnie Brady, Mike Carnahan, Joe Clancy,
Melissa Denton, Stephen DiMenna, Joe Doran,
Tony Freeman, Shana Gold, Sheri Graubert,
Dennis Green, Susan Hamburger,
Karla Hendrick, Jim Jack, Alvin Keith,
Rebecca Lord, Erin McCready,
Andrew Ondrejcak, Laura Poe,
Nicole Press, Chris Rummel,
Drew Sachs, Anna Saggese, David Sinkus,
Vickie Tanner, Olivia Tsang,
Jennifer Varbalow, Leese Walker,
Eric Wallach, Diana Whitten,
Gail Winar, Kirche Zeile

ADMINISTRATIVE STAFF

GENERAL MANAGER .... **Sydney Beers**
General Counsel ....Laura O'Neill
Associate Managing Director ....Greg Backstrom
General Manager of the
Steinberg Center.........................Don-Scott Cooper
Assistant to the General Manager ....Maggie Cantrick
Management Assistant ....Nicholas Caccavo
Office Operations Manager ....Bonnie Berens
Human Resources Manager ....Stephen Deutsch
Network Systems Manager ....Jeff Goodman
Manager of Corporate and Party Rentals ....Jetaun Dobbs
MIS Associate ....Lloyd Alvarez
MIS Assistant ....Anthony Foti
Receptionists ....Jennifer Decoteau,
Andre Fortson, Carolyn Miller,
Elisa Papa
Messenger ....Robert Weisser
Management Intern ....Chris Aniello

FINANCE STAFF

CONTROLLER .... **Susan Neiman**
Assistant Controller........................John LaBarbera
Accounts Payable Administrator ....Frank Surdi
Customer Service Coordinator ....Trina Cox
Business Office Associate ....David Solomon
Business Assistant ....Yonit Kafka
Business Intern ....Chelsea Glickfield

DEVELOPMENT STAFF

DIRECTOR OF DEVELOPMENT ......**Jeffory Lawson**
Director, Institutional Giving ....Julie K. D'Andrea
Director, Individual Giving ....Julia Lazarus
Director, Special Events ....Steve Schaeffer
Manager, Donor Information Systems ....Tina Mae Bishko
Special Events Associate ....Elaina Grillo
Institutional Giving Associate ....Kristen Bolibruch
Annual Giving Associate ....Justin D. Steensma
Development Associate ....Adam Gwon
Development Assistant ....Stephenie L. Overton
Assistant, External Affairs ....Robert Weinstein
Patrons Services Assistant ....Dawn Kusinski
Development Intern ....Lauren Hoshibata

MARKETING STAFF

DIRECTOR OF MARKETING ....**David B. Steffen**
Marketing/Publications Manager ....Tim McCanna
Marketing Associate ....Sunil Ayyagari
Marketing Assistant ....Rebecca Ballon
Marketing Intern ....Alejandro Lojo
Website Consultant ....Keith Powell Beyland
Director of Telesales Special Promotions ....Tony Baksa
Telesales Manager ....Anton Borissov
Telesales Office Coordinator ...................J.W. Griffin

TICKET SERVICES STAFF

DIRECTOR OF SALES OPERATIONS . **Jim Seggelink**
Ticket Services Manager ....Ellen Holt
Subscription Manager ....Charlie Garbowski
Box Office Managers ....Edward P. Osborne,
Jaime Perlman, Jessica Bowser
Group Sales Manager ....Jeff Monteith
Assistant Box Office Managers ....Paul
Caspary,
Steve Howe, Megan Young
Assistant Ticket Services Managers ....Robert Kane,
David Meglino, Robert Morgan
Ticket Services ....Solangel Bido,
Andrew Clements, Johanna Comanzo,
Sean Crews, Thomas Dahl, Nisha Dhruna,
Adam Elsberry, Lindsay Ericson,
Scott Falkowski, Catherine Fitzpatrick,
Erin Frederick, Steven Gottlieb, Julie Hilimire,
Bill Klemm, Talia Krispel, Alexander LaFrance,
Krystin MacRitchie, Mead Margulies,
Chris Migliaccio, Carlos Morris, Nicole Nicholson,
Shannon Paige, Hillary Parker,
Thomas Protulipac, Amy Robinson,
Heather Siebert, Monté Smock,
Melissa Snyder, Lillian Soto, Justin Sweeney,
Greg Thorson, Pamela Unger
Ticket Services Intern ....Jesse Blum

SERVICES

Counsel ....Jeremy Nussbaum,
Cowan, Liebowitz & Latman, P.C.
Counsel ....Rosenberg & Estis
Counsel ....Rubin and Feldman, P.C.
Counsel ....Cleary, Gottlieb, Steen & Hamilton
Counsel ....Harry H. Weintraub,
Glick and Weintraub, P.C.
Immigration Counsel ....Mark D. Koestler and
Theodore Ruthizer
House Physicians ....Dr. Theodore Tyberg,
Dr. Lawrence Katz
House Dentist ....Neil Kanner, D.M.D.
Insurance ....Marsh USA Inc.
Accountant ....Brody, Weiss, Zucarelli &
Urbanek CPAs, P.C.
Advertising ....Eliran Murphy Group/Denise Ganjou
Events Photography ....Anita and Steve Shevett
Production Photographer ....Joan Marcus
Theatre Displays............King Displays, Wayne Sapper

GENERAL PRESS REPRESENTATIVES
BONEAU / BRYAN-BROWN

Adrian Bryan-Brown   Matt Polk

Jessica Johnson   Joe Perrotta

Roundabout Theatre Company
231 West 39th Street, New York, NY 10018
(212) 719-9393.

CREDITS FOR
A STREETCAR NAMED DESIRE

GENERAL MANAGER .... Sydney Beers
Associate General Manager/
Company Manager .... Nichole Larson
Associate Company Manager ....Nancy Mulliner
Production Stage Manager .... Jane Grey
Stage Manager .... Philip Cusack
Assistant to the Technical Supervisor ....Elisa R. Kuhar
Assistant Set Designers .... Dustin O'Neill,
Jenny Sawyers
Set Design Assistants .... Michael Byrnes,
Erica Hemminger
Associate Costume Designer .... Rachel Attridge
Costume Shopper ....Matthew Pachtman
Associate Lighting Designer .... Hilary Manners
Assistant Sound Designer .... Christopher Cronin
Assistant Sound Designer .... Ryan Rumery
Additional Music Research ....Rian Murphy
Production Electrician ....Josh Weitzman
Assistant Production Electrician ....John Wooding
House Head Electrician ....Josh Weitzman
Deck Electrician ....John Wooding
Sound Engineer ....Greg Peeler
Wardrobe Supervisor .... Nadine Hettel
Dresser to Ms. Richardson ....Kevin Mark Harris
Dresser to Mr. Reilly ....Gerald Crawford
Dresser ....Jay Woods
Hair Supervisor ....Cynthia Demand
Makeup Artist ....Melissa Silver
Production Carpenter ....Dan Hoffman
House Head Carpenter .... Dan Hoffman
Production Properties .... Denise J. Grillo
Assistant Production Properties ....Keen Gat
House Head Properties...................Lawrence Jennino
Properties ....Erin Delaney
Assistant to the Stage Managers .... Ry Pepper
Production Assistant ....Sara Sahin
Intern to the Company Manager ....Lauren Parker
Ms. Richardson's Hair
for Production Designed by ....J. Roy Helland
Scenery Provided by..................Showman Fabricators
Additional Scenery Provided by ....Atlas Scenic Studios
Lighting Equipment Provided by ....PRG,
Production Resource Group
Sound Equipment Provided by ....Sound Associates
Natasha Richardson's Clothes by ....Euroco Costumes
Costumes and Alterations by ....Jennifer Love Costumes
Army Clothing by ....Kaufman's Army & Navy
Zippo Lighters Used
Rosebud matches by ....Diamond Brands, Inc.
Additional set and
hand props courtesy of ....George Fenmore, Inc.
Merchandising ....George Fenmore/
More Merchandising International

MUSIC CREDITS

"Doctor Jazz" (Walter Melorse, Joseph Oliver). Administered
by Edwin H. Morris & Co. Inc., Universal Music Publishing
Group. All rights reserved. Used by permission.

STUDIO 54 THEATRE STAFF

Theatre Manager ....Mary Ann Ehlshlager
House Manager .... LaConya Robinson
Assistant House Managers ....Jack Watanachaiyot,
Jay Watanachaiyot
House Staff ..Onercida Concepcion, Elicia Edwards, Linda
Edwards, Jason Fernandez,
Jen Kneeland, Kate Longosky,
Latiffa Marcus, Nicole Marino,
Jonathan Martinez, Dana McCaw,
Kevin Owens, Nicole Ramirez,
Anthony Roman, Stella Varriale,
Nick Wheatley
Security ....Gotham Security
Maintenance .... Ralph Mohan, Maman Garba
Refreshments and Merchandising ... Studio 54 Promotions

Sweeney Todd

First Preview: October 3, 2005. Opened: November 3, 2005.
Still running as of May 31, 2006.

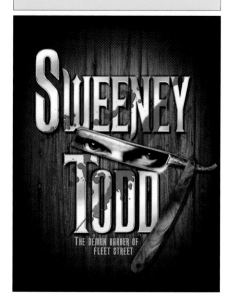

PLAYBILL®

CAST

Mrs. Lovett .... PATTI LuPONE
Tuba, Orchestra Bells, Percussion

Sweeney Todd .... MICHAEL CERVERIS
Guitar, Orchestra Bells, Percussion

Judge Turpin .... MARK JACOBY
Trumpet, Orchestra Bells, Percussion

Pirelli .... DONNA LYNNE CHAMPLIN
Accordion, Keyboard, Flute

Tobias .... MANOEL FELCIANO
Violin, Clarinet, Keyboard

The Beadle .... ALEXANDER GEMIGNANI
Keyboard, Trumpet

Jonas Fogg .... JOHN ARBO
Bass

Beggar Woman .... DIANA DIMARZIO
Clarinet

Anthony .... BENJAMIN MAGNUSON
Cello, Keyboard

Johanna .... LAUREN MOLINA
Cello

STANDBYS

For Sweeney Todd, Judge Turpin:
MERWIN FOARD, *Orchestra Bells, Percussion*

For Mrs. Lovett, Pirelli:
DOROTHY STANLEY, *Violin, Keyboard, Orchestra Bells, Percussion*

For Anthony, Tobias, The Beadle:
BENJAMIN EAKELEY, *Keyboard, Clarinet*

For Johanna, Beggar Woman:
ELISA WINTER, *Cello, Accordion, Keyboard, Guitar*

EUGENE O'NEILL THEATRE
A JUJAMCYN THEATRE
ROCCO LANDESMAN
PRESIDENT

PAUL LIBIN — JACK VIERTEL
PRODUCING DIRECTOR — CREATIVE DIRECTOR

TOM VIERTEL   STEVEN BARUCH   MARC ROUTH   RICHARD FRANKEL
AMBASSADOR THEATRE GROUP   ADAM KENWRIGHT   TULCHIN/BARTNER/BAGERT

present

PATTI LuPONE   MICHAEL CERVERIS

in

SWEENEY TODD
THE DEMON BARBER OF FLEET STREET

Music and Lyrics by — Book by
STEPHEN SONDHEIM — HUGH WHEELER

From an Adaptation by CHRISTOPHER BOND

Originally Directed on Broadway by HAROLD PRINCE

with

DONNA LYNNE CHAMPLIN   MANOEL FELCIANO   ALEXANDER GEMIGNANI
JOHN ARBO   DIANA DIMARZIO   BENJAMIN MAGNUSON   LAUREN MOLINA
MERWIN FOARD   DOROTHY STANLEY   BENJAMIN EAKELEY   ELISA WINTER

and

MARK JACOBY

Lighting Design	Sound Design	Wig & Hair Design
RICHARD G. JONES	DAN MOSES SCHREIER	PAUL HUNTLEY
Resident Music Supervisor	Casting	Music Coordinator
DAVID LOUD	BERNARD TELSEY CASTING	JOHN MILLER

General Management — Production Stage Manager — Press Representative — Production Management
RICHARD FRANKEL PRODUCTIONS, INC.   ADAM JOHN HUNTER   BARLOW•HARTMAN   SHOWMAN FABRICATORS, INC.
JO PORTER

Musical Supervision and Orchestrations by
SARAH TRAVIS

Directed and Designed by
JOHN DOYLE

Originally produced on Broadway by Richard Barr, Charles Woodward, Robert Fryer, Mary Lea Johnson, Martin Richards
in association with Dean and Judy Manos.

Proudly sponsored by Fidelity Investments

The Producers wish to express their appreciation to the Theatre Development Fund for its support of this production.

LIVE BROADWAY

11/3/05

Patti LuPone and
Michael Cerveris.

Photo by Paul Kolnik

Sweeney Todd

MUSICAL NUMBERS

Act I

The Ballad of Sweeney Todd .... Company
No Place Like London .... Anthony, Sweeney Todd, Beggar Woman
The Barber and His Wife .... Sweeney Todd
The Worst Pies in London .... Mrs. Lovett
Poor Thing .... Mrs. Lovett
My Friends .... Sweeney Todd, Mrs. Lovett
Green Finch and Linnet Bird .... Johanna
Ah, Miss .... Anthony, Beggar Woman
Johanna .... Anthony
Pirelli's Miracle Elixir .... Tobias, Sweeney Todd, Mrs. Lovett, Company
The Contest .... Pirelli
Johanna .... Judge Turpin
Wait .... Mrs. Lovett
Kiss Me .... Johanna, Anthony
Ladies in Their Sensitivities .... The Beadle
Quartet .... Johanna, Anthony, The Beadle, Judge Turpin
Pretty Women .... Sweeney Todd, Judge Turpin
Epiphany .... Sweeney Todd
A Little Priest .... Sweeney Todd, Mrs. Lovett

Act II

God, That's Good! .... Tobias, Mrs. Lovett, Sweeney Todd, Company
Johanna .... Anthony, Sweeney Todd, Johanna, Beggar Woman
By the Sea .... Mrs. Lovett
Not While I'm Around .... Tobias, Mrs. Lovett
Parlor Songs .... The Beadle, Mrs. Lovett
City on Fire! .... Tobias, Johanna, Anthony, Company
Final Sequence .... Anthony, Beggar Woman, Sweeney Todd,
Judge Turpin, Mrs. Lovett, Johanna, Tobias
The Ballad of Sweeney Todd .... Company

(Clockwise, starting at top):
Patti LuPone,
Donna Lynne Champlin,
Manoel Felciano and
Michael Cerveris.

Photo by Paul Kolnik

Patti LuPone
Mrs. Lovett

Michael Cerveris
Sweeney Todd

Mark Jacoby
Judge Turpin

Donna Lynn Champlin
Pirelli

Manoel Felciano
Tobias

Alexander Gemignani
The Beadle

John Arbo
Jonas Fogg

Diana DiMarzio
Beggar Woman

Benjamin Magnuson
Anthony

Lauren Molina
Johanna

Sweeney Todd

Merwin Foard
*Standby for
Sweeney Todd,
Judge Turpin*

Dorothy Stanley
*Standby Mrs. Lovett,
Pirelli*

Benjamin Eakeley
*Standby Tobias,
Anthony, The Beadle*

Elisa Winter
*Standby Johanna,
Beggar Woman*

Stephen Sondheim
Music & Lyrics

John Doyle
*Director and
Designer*

Richard G. Jones
Lighting Designer

Dan Moses Schreier
Sound Designer

Paul Huntley
Wig & Hair Designer

Angelina Avallone
Make-up Designer

John Miller
Music Coordinator

Bernard Telsey
Casting, C.S.A.
Casting

Darren Bagert
Producer

Richard Frankel,
The Frankel•Baruch•
Viertel•Routh Group
Producer

Steven Baruch,
The Frankel•Baruch•
Viertel•Routh Group
Producer

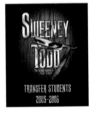

Tom Viertel
The Frankel•Baruch•
Viertel•Routh Group
Producer

Marc Routh
The Frankel•Baruch•
Viertel•Routh Group
Producer

David Hess
*Standby for
Sweeney Todd,
Judge Turpin, The
Beadle, Fogg*

Stephen McIntyre
Standby for Fogg

Jessica Wright
*Standby for Beggar
Woman, Pirelli*

2005-2006 Awards

DRAMA DESK AWARDS
Outstanding Revival of a Musical
Outstanding Director of a Musical
(John Doyle)
Outstanding Orchestrations
(Sarah Travis)
Outstanding Lighting Design
(Richard G. Jones)

TONY AWARDS
Best Direction of a Musical
(John Doyle)
Best Orchestrations (Sarah Travis)

OUTER CRITICS CIRCLE AWARDS
Outstanding Revival of a Musical
Outstanding Direction of a Musical
(John Doyle)

DRAMA LEAGUE AWARD
Distinguished Revival of a Musical

NY DRAMA CRITICS CIRCLE AWARD
Special Citation (John Doyle,
Sarah Travis and Company)

Sweeney Todd

Photos by Ben Strothmann

FRONT OF HOUSE STAFF
Sitting (L-R):
Charlotte Brauer (Usher), Sarah Jane Runser (Merchandise Manager).
Second Row (L-R):
Bryon Vargas (Porter), Carmella Galante (Usher), Verna Hobson (Usher).
Back Row (L-R):
Dorothy Lennon (Usher), John Dapolito (Usher), Jim Higgins (Engineer), Adrian Atkinson-Bleakley (Usher),
Christine Ehren (Stage Door), Lauren Vadino (House Manager) and Irene Vincent (Usher).

STAGE CREW
Front Row (L-R):
Penny Davis (Wardrobe Supervisor), Adam John Hunter (Production Stage Manager),
Vanessa Anderson (Hair and Wig Supervisor).
Back Row (L-R):
Todd D'Aiuto (Production Electrician), Christopher Cronin (Production Sound Engineer),
Christopher Beck (Production Property Master), Patricia White (Ms. LuPone's Dresser),
Donny Beck (Stagehand Emeritus), Kevin O'Brien (Dresser), Karen Zabinski (Deck Sound),
Mary McGregor (Deck Electrician), Newton Cole (Stage Manager), Michelle Gutierrez (Board Operator)
and Aja Kane (Assistant Stage Manager).

Sweeney Todd

GENERAL MANAGEMENT

RICHARD FRANKEL PRODUCTIONS

Richard Frankel   Marc Routh   Jo Porter

Laura Green   Rod Kaats   Joe Watson

COMPANY MANAGER

Sammy Ledbetter

Associate Company Manager .... Jason Pelusio

GENERAL PRESS REPRESENTATIVE

BARLOW•HARTMAN

John Barlow   Michael Hartman

Rick Miramontez   Leslie Baden

CASTING

BERNARD TELSEY CASTING, C.S.A.

Bernie Telsey   Will Cantler   David Vaccari

Bethany Knox   Craig Burns

Tiffany Little Canfield   Stephanie Yankwitt

Betsy Sherwood

Production Stage Manager	Adam John Hunter
Stage Manager	Julia P. Jones
Assistant Stage Manager	Newton Cole
Production Management	Showman Fabricators, Inc., Kai Brothers, Annie Jacobs
Associate Set Designer, Broadway Production	Ted LeFevre
Associate Costume Designer, Broadway Production	Patrick Chevillot
Make-Up Designer	Angelina Avallone
Assistant Costume Designer	Rosemary Lepre
Associate Lighting Designer, Broadway Production	Paul Miller
Associate Sound Designer, Broadway Production	David Bullard
Production Carpenter	Donald Robinson
Production Electrician	Todd D'Aiuto
Production Property Master	Christopher Beck
Board Operator	Michelle Gutierrez
Production Sound Engineer	Christopher Cronin
Flyman	Kevin Maher
Wardrobe Supervisor	Penny Davis
Miss LuPone's Dresser	Patricia White
Dresser	Kevin O'Brien
Hair Design Assistant	Giovanna Calabretta
Hair & Wig Supervisor	Vanessa Anderson
Assistant to Mr. Sondheim	Steven Clar

Assistant to John Miller	Tom Dannenbaum
Assistant to Mr. Baruch	Sonja Soper
Assistant to Mr. Viertel	Tania Senewiratne
Creative Director for Mr. Bagert	Russell Owen
Management Assistant	Katie Berkshire
Production Assistants	Ryan Bell, David Redman Scott
Advertising	Serino Coyne, Inc./ Sandy Block, Greg Corradetti, Brad Lapin, Natalie Serota
Press Associates	Dennis Crowley, Jon Dimond, Carol Fineman, Gerilyn Shur, Andrew Shamer, Stephen Sosnowski, Wayne Wolfe
Press Office Manager	Bethany Larsen
Photography	Paul Kolnik, Nigel Perry
Web Designer	Simma Park
Theatre Displays	King Displays
Music Copying	Kaye-Houston Music/ Anne Kaye, Doug Houston
Insurance	Acordia Northeast
Legal Counsel	Patricia Crown, Esq., Coblence & Associates
Banking	Chase Manhattan Bank/Michele Gibbons
Payroll Service	Castellana Services, Inc.
Accounting	Fried & Kowgios Partners, CPAs, LLP
Travel Agency	JMC Travel, Judith Marinoff
Exclusive Tour Direction	On the Road
New York Rehearsals	Ripley-Grier Studios
Opening Night Coordinator	Tobak-Lawrence Company/ Suzanne Tobak, Michael Lawrence

RICHARD FRANKEL PRODUCTIONS STAFF

Finance Director	**Michael Naumann**
Assistant to Mr. Frankel	Jeff Romley
Assistant to Mr. Routh	Michael Sag
Assistant to Ms. Porter	Myriah Perkins
Assistant Finance Director	Liz Hines
Information Technology Manager	Roddy Pimentel
Management Assistant	Heidi Schading
Accounting Assistant	Elsie Jamin-Maguire
National Sales and Marketing Director	**Ronni Mandell**
Director of Business Affairs	**Carter Anne McGowan**
Marketing Coordinator	Melissa Marano
Office Manager	**Lori Steiger-Perry**
Office Assistant	Stephanie Adamczyk
Receptionists	Deniece Alvarado, Randy Rainbow

Interns	Lauren Berger, Todd Blass, Casey Cipriani, Eric Cornell, Matt Martin, Nicole Monente, Erin Porvaznik, Kirsten Rega, Nathan Vernon, Lucinda Walker

AMBASSADOR THEATRE GROUP LTD.

Chairman	Sir Eddie Kulukundis, OBE
Deputy Chairman	Peter Beckwith
Managing Director	Howard Panter
Executive Director	Rosemary Squire

For *Sweeney Todd* New York:

Associate Producer	Angela Edwards
Business Affairs Manager	Diane Benjamin

CREDITS AND ACKNOWLEDGEMENTS

Scenery built and painted by Showmotion, Inc. Lighting equipment from PRG Lighting. Sound equipment from PRG Audio. Miss LuPone's costume built by Barbara Matera, Ltd. Special thanks to Novelet Knight, Steven Clar, Matthew Goldenberg, Grant A. Rice, Walter W. Kuehr, Charles Butler, Stas Iavorski, Daedalus Productions, The Spoon Group, Heidi Ettinger and Ian Goldrich.

---

www.SweeneyToddonBroadway.com

STAFF FOR EUGENE O'NEILL THEATRE

Manager	Hal Goldberg
Treasurer	Dean Gardner
Carpenter	Donald Robinson
Propertyman	Christopher Beck
Electrician	Todd D'Aiuto
Engineer	Padraig Mullen

JUJAMCYN THEATERS

ROCCO LANDESMAN

PRESIDENT

PAUL LIBIN
Producing Director

JACK VIERTEL
Creative Director

JERRY ZAKS

DANIEL ADAMIAN
General Manager

JENNIFER HERSHEY
Director of Operations

MEREDITH VILLATORE
Chief Financial Officer

Sweeney Todd
SCRAPBOOK

(L-R): Patti LuPone, Stephen Sondheim, Michael Cerveris and Mark Jacoby autograph CDs at the O'Neill Theatre.

Correspondent: Donna Lynne Champlin, "Pirelli"

Memorable Opening Night Telegram or Note: Manoel Felciano wrote the whole company a great sonnet, as follows:

"Sweeney Sonnet 11/03/05"
At first, my friends, it did seem rather tough,
No music stands, a coffin, ladder, chairs:
Director Doyle assuring 'twas enough,
In fact, to tell the tale of Barker's scares.
Music in which we gladly lost ourselves,
Finding our tacets, rats, and herring too,
Unfazed by blood and buckets, crowded shelves;
Loving our new-found sense of derring do.
Look at us now, with engines roaring loud,
Offending some, inspiring most, we play:
Forever may we run, and always proud,
Justly arrived at this, our well earned day.
Opening, time to fully burst the pod:
Yes, for at last, we're Sweeney *Fucking* Todd!

Opening Night Gifts: Risko caricature drawing of all of us from the producers. We also received five dollars and a beer from our production stage manager Adam Hunter that was pretty genius. In rehearsal he told us that's what we'd get because "Who can't use five dollars and a beer?"—and we didn't believe him—until opening when we all got just that.

Celebrity Visitors: Paul Newman and Joanne Woodward sent a lovely note to the company, which we put on the board. We've also had plenty of *Sweeney Todd* alumni come to the show, such as Angela Lansbury, Sarah Rice, George Hearn, Victor Garber, Sal Mistretta, et al.

"Carols for a Cure" Carol: "Deck the Halls."

"Gypsy of the Year" Sketch: Alex Gemignani and I wrote and directed the "Gypsy" sketch. It was a take on how difficult it is to play the instruments and sing and act and move props all at the same time without messing up (which we inevitably do). We rewrote lyrics (and re-orchestrated) Sondheim's "You Could Drive A Person Crazy" and called it "Tourettes Todd" because especially during rehearsal there was plenty of swearing. We also poked fun at the 'little white coffins' many meanings.

"Easter Bonnet" Sketch: "Rhapsody in Blood" by Benjamin Magnuson, Manoel Felciano and Alexander Gemignani.

Who Has Done the Most Shows: Patti LuPone has been in "nineteen or twenty Broadway shows" (but she's 'not sure,' which is hilarious to me) and Dottie Stanley and Merwin Foard have done more than twenty-five Broadway shows between them.

Backstage Rituals: "It's Saturday night on Broadway" on the callboard from stage management.
Patti always goes through a litany from her chair saying "Good luck center stage…good luck stage left…good luck stage right…."
Everyone tunes at "places."
Everyone looks out of the rips in the curtain to see who's in the audience, and stage management always catches us and tells us not to.
There's vocal warmup at forty-five minutes to "places" onstage.
John Arbo always asks "Flies up? Ties down?" before the curtain goes up.
Ben Magnuson makes sure he goes around and says "Good show" to every cast member at "places."
Alex puts music jokes on the callboard every day. "It's _____ night/afternoon on Broadway, y'all" at curtain.
After Chris Beck puts Michael in the coffin at "places," they knock twice—Chris from the outsie and Michael from the inside. Michael then sticks his two fingers through the slats so that people can grab them "for luck."

The new 'coffin-table' show, "Half Hour With Adam Hunter" happens stage left.

Favorite Moment During Each Performance: There's always the deadly silence during Mano's "Pat-a-cake, pat-a-cake" and the Act II "Johanna" where the show seems to just settle for a second. The last note is exciting because it means we made it through again.

Favorite In-Theatre Gathering Place: Basement birthdays.

Favorite Off-Site Hangout: Upstairs at Orzo, Bar Centrale, Olympic Diner.

Favorite Snack Food: Krispy Kremes from producer Darren Bagert.

Mascot: Michael Cerveris' dog, Gibson.

Favorite Therapy: It's all about the Grether's Pastilles onstage. They're hidden behind the piano and get us through the show, since we can't leave the stage.

Memorable Ad-Libs: One night, before "The Contest," I threw my razor down and it bounced into the coffin. I kept trying to tell Mano to get it but he couldn't hear or didn't understand. It came time for the contest—and there was no razor. I realized there was nothing left to do but say to Mano and the rest of the audience, "My RAZOR-a is-a IN-a the coffin-a!" It did not get a laugh.
Someone sneezed in the audience during a silent moment in "Little Priest" and Michael said "Gesundheit." That didn't get a laugh either.

Cell Phone Rings: I recall a show where there were three cell phone incidents. But our biggest pet peeve is the behavior of some of the front row audience members. They're in full light and really close to us. Plus we all have a Pavlovian need to look in that area for a conductor (who isn't there) so any movement or noise from the front row makes us crazy. Our favorites so far have been people chewing ice, swishing drinks, eating M&Ms and crinkling the M&M bags, drinking beer (from the bottle), constantly chit-chatting, tape recording, picture taking, sleeping/snoring, smacky gum-chewing (out of time), constant hair twirling, two people making out, someone who practically draped himself and his program on the stage, rattling keys, plastic bags, and people eating peanuts, Twizzlers, potato chips, in tandem and the guy who *actually conducted* in the front row…poorly.

Memorable Stage Door Fan Encounters: There was the creepy "Hey Patti, you wanna get some pies?" guy. Alex was stalked by "The Tile Guy" who made all these crazy tiles/magnets et cetera, and gave them to Alex to try to sell to the company. They were endless, and the guy just kept dropping more and more off at the theatre. They also became progressively more disturbing in design until Alex finally asked him to stop.

Latest Audience Arrival: The worst offenders are on Tuesday when they think it is an 8 o'clock curtain. They pour in at 7:55 and seem incredulous that you could be nearing intermission already. They also seem to always be in the front

Sweeney Todd
Scrapbook

five rows! Sunday matinees at 2 p.m. (and not 3 p.m.) are a close second.

Fastest Costume Change: Putting on the lab coats can be nervewracking and a lot of them are musically timed and under three seconds.

Busiest Day at the Box Office: Day after opening, around $750,000 that day.

Heaviest/Hottest Costume: Diana DiMarzio actually wears the most layers and the least. She starts with at least six layers and then by the end of the show she's in one. If heavy instruments count, then John Arbo wins with the stand-up bass.

Who Wore the Least: Lauren Molina consistently, and Diana by the end of the show.

Catchphrases Only the Company Would Recognize: "Ya gotta want it."

"Possible tacet for buckets."

"Whooooooooop!"

"Busk it."

"From the top of the story…."

"Will Beadle Bailey be the judge?"

"Robert De Niro is here!"

Orchestra Member Who Played the Most Instruments: Mano and I tie with three (non-orchestra bells/percussion) instruments. Mano: clarinet, piano, violin. Me: flute, piano, accordion.

Orchestra Members Who Played the Most Consecutive Performances Without a Sub: Everyone but Patti, Ben and Alex is tied for first place.

In-House Parody Lyrics: Mano's Spanish ghetto rendition of "Not While I Am Round."

Beadle's "Ladies in their middle seventies."

Judge's "But first Sir, I think…a slave."

Joanna's "My cage has many smells, damask and dark. Nothing there sounds, not even my fart. Farts never will, you know, when they're captive. Teach me to take more laxatives! Ahhhhhh…."

Memorable Directorial Notes: "Less."

"Tell the story."

"That's another gin martini!"

"Is it feeling less like *Sweeney Todd*?"

Embarrassing Moments: When the drunk guy who was drinking beer from a bottle in the front row insisted on high-fiving Michael Cerveris during his bow. VERY embarrassing.

Everyone has had their own embarrassing moment of messing up lyrics, notes, squeaking, cracking, naffing, clamming in the show. Every show holds at least one moment of humiliation for every cast member, guaranteed. The trick is to get past it and keep moving forward. This whole process has been (and continues to be) one huge lesson in humility and managing embarrassing moments for all of us.

Company Legend: Stephen Sondheim.

Understudy Anecdote: During rehearsals: "If you think doing *Sweeney* with ten people is something, you should come by on Thursday and Friday and watch four try to do it!"

Nicknames: John "The Machine" Arbo

Michael "Mickey Raw Meats" Cerveris

1. Cast member Mark Jacoby arrives at the opening night party at Copacabana.
2. Patti LuPone and Michael Cerveris on opening night.
3. LuPone (C) with son Joshua (L) and husband Matt.

Donna Lynne "Black Box Bertha" Champlin
Diana "Dolly Licorice Stick" DiMarzio
"Sensitive Ben" Eakeley
Manoel "Raggs" Felciano
Merwin "No Chops" Foard
Alex "Knuckles" Gemignani
David "Spit Valve" Hess
Mark "Lips" Jacoby
Patti "Glock" LuPone
Benjamin "Benji the Jew" Magnuson
Stephen "IMac" McIntyre
Lauren "Lomo the Nymph" Molina
"Dottie Ruby Shoes" Stanley
Elisa "Sneezey" Winter
'Fiddler Jess'(-ica) Wright
Adam "Herb the Bookie" Hunter

Sweethearts Within the Company: Alex and me—massage marriage.

Diana and Newton—a marriage that defies description.

(There are no real romantic relationships within the company.)

Ghostly Encounters Backstage: We believe there are at least two ghosts at the Eugene O'Neill. One male and one female.

During previews, things would randomly fall from the upstage prop shelf—sometimes dangerous things like gardening shears—when no one was remotely near it.

Actors' hair gets tugged every once in a while, and they have heard their characters' names whispered in their ears onstage. There's a strong smell of lilacs sometimes downstage left. My whistle disappeared from my bloody lab coat pocket

(which never leaves the stage) and was found down in the basement in the "dead" rack of clothes. They only found it weeks later because they moved the rack and it fell to the ground.

Patti's dressing room has doors that open and close on their own. She also thought she had stepped backward onto her friend's foot, so she said, "Excuse me." Her friend said, "What for?" Patti turned around and her friend was a good two feet away from her.

Merwin Foard says: I set up the cot to take a nap between rehearsal and a show and asked out loud for a wake-up call. Sure enough, at 6:30, I was awakened by a slap on the bottom of my shoes that almost sent my head crashing up into the bottom of the counter that I had placed my cot under. No one was in the room but me!

Superstitions That Turned Out To Be True: The day before Patti called in sick a cast member said onstage during warm up "I'll bet that no one will be out until the Tonys." We knocked on wood, but it was too late. Then Alex was out the week after. We made that cast member go back onstage and reverse the curse by saying that "everyone would be out" by the Tonys and we haven't (knock wood) had anyone out since.

Coolest Things About Being in This Show: We get to play the score. Lots of young people in the audience. Working with Sondheim (who approves, thank God). Celebrities coming to the show. Fans outside the stage door. And…we're a critical "hit." That's all pretty cool and new for many of us.

Sweet Charity

First Preview: April 11, 2005. Opened: May 4, 2005.
Closed December 31, 2005 after 25 previews and 279 performances.

PLAYBILL

CAST

(in order of appearance)

Charity Hope Valentine	CHRISTINA APPLEGATE
Charlie	BOB GAYNOR
Policeman	TIMOTHY EDWARD SMITH
Nickie	JANINE LaMANNA
Helene	KEARRAN GIOVANNI
Herman	WAYNE KNIGHT
Ursula	SHANNON LEWIS
Vittorio Vidal	PAUL SCHOEFFLER
Frug Dancer	CORINNE McFADDEN
Waiter	TIMOTHY EDWARD SMITH
Manfred	TIMOTHY EDWARD SMITH
92nd Street Y Receptionist	TIMOTHY EDWARD SMITH
Woman at the 92nd Street Y	JOYCE CHITTICK
Oscar Lindquist	DENIS O'HARE
Daddy Johann Sebastian Brubeck	RHETT GEORGE
Daddy's All-Girl Rhythm Choir	JOYCE CHITTICK, KISHA HOWARD, MYLINDA HULL
Quartet	TODD ANDERSON, BOB GAYNOR, ERIC SCIOTTO, TIMOTHY EDWARD SMITH
Betsy	KISHA HOWARD
Carmen	MYLINDA HULL
Susanna	JOYCE CHITTICK
Alice	NINA LAFARGA

Continued on next page

♩ AL HIRSCHFELD THEATRE

A JUJAMCYN THEATRE
ROCCO LANDESMAN
PRESIDENT

PAUL LIBIN   **JACK VIERTEL**
PRODUCING DIRECTOR   **CREATIVE DIRECTOR**

Barry and Fran Weissler   Clear Channel Entertainment
IN ASSOCIATION WITH Edwin W. Schloss

PRESENT

Christina Applegate

AS

SWEET CHARITY

BOOK BY   MUSIC BY   LYRICS BY
Neil Simon   Cy Coleman   Dorothy Fields

Based on an original screenplay by Federico Fellini, Tullio Pinelli and Ennio Flaiano

STARRING

Denis O'Hare

Janine LaManna   Kearran Giovanni

WITH

Wayne Knight

as Herman

Shannon Lewis   Rhett George

AND

Paul Schoeffler

Corinne McFadden   Timothy Edward Smith
Todd Anderson   Alexis Carra   Joyce Chittick   Dylis Croman   Joey Dowling
Bob Gaynor   Manuel I. Herrera   Kisha Howard   Mylinda Hull   James Kinney
Keith Kühl   Nina Lafarga   Marielys Molina   Eric Sciotto   Seth Stewart

SCENIC DESIGN	COSTUME DESIGN	LIGHTING DESIGN
Scott Pask	William Ivey Long	Brian MacDevitt

SOUND DESIGN	HAIR DESIGN	MAKE-UP DESIGN
Peter Hylenski	Paul Huntley	Angelina Avallone

CASTING	ASSOCIATE DIRECTOR	ASSOCIATE CHOREOGRAPHERS
Jay Binder/Laura Stanczyk	Marc Bruni	Ted Banfalvi/Corinne McFadden

ORCHESTRATIONS	MUSIC DIRECTOR	ADDITIONAL MUSICAL & VOCAL ARRANGEMENTS	ADDITIONAL DANCE ARRANGEMENTS	MUSIC COORDINATOR
Don Sebesky	Don York	Michael Rafter	Jim Abbott	John Miller

GENERAL MANAGER	PRESS REPRESENTATIVE	PRODUCTION SUPERVISOR	PRODUCTION STAGE MANAGER
B.J. Holt	Barlow•Hartman	Arthur Siccardi	Marybeth Abel

EXECUTIVE PRODUCER	FOR CLEAR CHANNEL ENTERTAINMENT	ASSOCIATE PRODUCERS	IN ASSOCIATION WITH
Alecia Parker	Jennifer Costello	Daniel Posener Jay Binder	Hazel and Sam Feldman Allen Spivak Harvey Weinstein

CHOREOGRAPHY BY
Wayne Cilento

DIRECTED BY
Walter Bobbie

The producers wish to express their appreciation to Theatre Development Fund for its support of this production.
SWEET CHARITY IS LOVINGLY DEDICATED TO THE MEMORY OF CY COLEMAN.

10/1/05

The Ensemble performs Wayne Cilento's choreography for "Big Spender."

Photo by Paul Kolnik

Sweet Charity

MUSICAL NUMBERS

ACT ONE

Overture
"You Should See Yourself" ....Charity
"Big Spender" ....Nickie, Helene and The Company
"Charity's Soliloquy" ....Charity
"Rich Man's Frug" ....The Company
"If My Friends Could See Me Now" ....Charity
"Too Many Tomorrows" ....Vittorio
"There's Gotta Be Something Better Than This" ....Charity, Nickie and Helene
"I'm the Bravest Individual" ....Charity and Oscar

ACT TWO

"The Rhythm of Life" ....Charity, Oscar, Daddy,
Daddy's All-Girl Rhythm Choir and The Company
"A Good Impression" ....Oscar and The Quartet
"Baby, Dream Your Dream" ....Nickie and Helene
"Sweet Charity" ....Oscar and The Company
"Big Spender" (Reprise) ....The Company
"Where Am I Going?" ....Charity
"I'm a Brass Band" ....Charity and The Company
"I Love to Cry at Weddings" ....Herman and The Company
"I'm the Bravest Individual" (Reprise) ....Charity

ORCHESTRA

Orchestra conducted by Don York

Associate Conductor/Keyboards: John Samorian

Trumpets: Don Downs, Glenn Drewes

Trombones: Keith O'Quinn, Jeff Nelson

French Horn: Brad Gemeinhardt

Reeds: Chuck Wilson, Walt Weiskopf,
Tom Christensen, Roger Rosenberg

Guitar: Ed Hamilton

Bass: Bill Holcomb

Drums: David Ratajczak

Percussion: Charles Descarfino

Violins: Mineko Yajima, Cecelia Hobbs Gardner,
Jonathan Dinklage

Cello: Stephanie Cummins

Music Copyist: Kaye-Houston Music/
Anne Kaye
and Doug Houston

Music Coordinator: John Miller

Photo by Paul Kolnik

Christina Applegate performs "If My Friends Could See Me Now."

Cast Continued

Rosie ....DYLIS CROMAN
Fandango Girls ....DYLIS CROMAN,
JOEY DOWLING,
SHANNON LEWIS,
CORINNE McFADDEN,
MARIELYS MOLINA
The Company ....TODD ANDERSON,
JOYCE CHITTICK, DYLIS CROMAN,
JOEY DOWLING, BOB GAYNOR,
RHETT GEORGE, MANUEL I. HERRERA,
KISHA HOWARD, MYLINDA HULL,
KEITH KÜHL, NINA LAFARGA,
SHANNON LEWIS,
CORINNE McFADDEN,
MARIELYS MOLINA, ERIC SCIOTTO,
TIMOTHY EDWARD SMITH,
SETH STEWART

UNDERSTUDIES

For Charity Hope Valentine:
DYLIS CROMAN

For Oscar Lindquist:
TIMOTHY EDWARD SMITH,
BOB GAYNOR

For Nickie:
ALEXIS CARRA,
JOYCE CHITTICK

For Helene:
KISHA HOWARD

For Vittorio Vidal:
BOB GAYNOR,
ERIC SCIOTTO

For Herman:
MANUEL I. HERRERA,
TIMOTHY EDWARD SMITH

For Ursula:
JOEY DOWLING,
CORINNE McFADDEN

SWINGS:
ALEXIS CARRA, JAMES KINNEY

DANCE CAPTAIN:
CORINNE McFADDEN

TIME:
The 1960s
PLACE:
New York City

Sweet Charity

Christina Applegate
Charity

Denis O'Hare
Oscar

Paul Schoeffler
Vittorio

Janine LaManna
Nickie

Kearran Giovanni
Helene

Wayne Knight
Herman

Shannon Lewis
Ursula

Rhett George
Ensemble, Daddy

Todd Anderson
Ensemble

Alexis Carra
Swing, Assistant Dance Captain

Joyce Chittick
Ensemble

Dylis Croman
Ensemble

Joey Dowling
Ensemble

Bob Gaynor
Ensemble

Manuel I. Herrera
Ensemble

Kisha Howard
Ensemble

Mylinda Hull
Ensemble

Keith Kühl
Ensemble

Nina Lafarga
Ensemble

Corinne McFadden
Ensemble, Associate Choreographer, Dance Captain

Marielys Molina
Ensemble

Eric Sciotto
Ensemble

Timothy Edward Smith
Ensemble

Seth Stewart
Ensemble

Neil Simon
Book

Cy Coleman
Music

Dorothy Fields
Lyrics

Walter Bobbie
Director

Wayne Cilento
Choreographer

Scott Pask
Scenic Design

William Ivey Long
Costume Design

Brian MacDevitt
Lighting Design

Peter Hylenski
Sound Design

Paul Huntley
Hair Design

Don Sebesky
Orchestrator

Sweet Charity

Jim Abbott
Additional Dance Arrangements

John Miller
Music Coordinator

Marc Bruni
Associate Director

Ted Banfalvi
Associate Choreographer

Barry and Fran Weissler
Producers

Edwin W. Schloss
Producer

Allen Spivak
Associate Producer

Harvey Weinstein
Associate Producer

Rob Barlett
Herman

Gerrard Carter
Company

Kyra DaCosta
Helene

Anika Ellis
Helene/Daddy's All-Girl Rhythm Choir/ Fandango Girl/ Company

Tyler Hanes
Charlie/Company/ Quartet

Reginald Holden Jennings
Swing/ Dance Captain

Amy Nicole Krawcek
Alice/Company

Krisha Marcano
Carmen/Fandango Girl/Company/Swing

J. Elaine Marcos
Susanna/Daddy's All-Girl Rhythm Choir/ Woman at the 92nd Street Y/Company

Ernie Sabella
Herman

Marcus Choi
Company

Tyler Hanes
Company

J. Elaine Marcos
Susanna/Fandango Girl/Woman at the 92nd Street Y/ Company

Jonathan Ritter
Company

Ernie Sabella
Herman

LaQuet Sharnell
Betsy/Susanna/ Daddy's All-Girl Rhythm Choir/ Company

Nicole Snelson
Woman at the 92nd Street Y/Daddy's All-Girl Rhythm Choir/Company

Amanda Watkins
Carmen/Company/ Daddy's All-Girl Rhythm Choir

Sweet Charity

USHERS
Front Row (L-R): Michele Fleury, Mary Marzan, Tristan Blacer.
Second Row (L-R): Alberta McNamee, Julie Burnham, Lorraine Feeks, Jose Nunez.
Third Row (L-R): Henry Menendez, Theresa Lopez, Janice Rodriguez,
Amelis Tirado.
Back Row (L-R): Bart Ryan, Vladimir Belenky, Donald Royal.

STAGE MANAGEMENT
(L-R): David O'Brien (PSM), Beverly Jenkins (SM),
Stephen R. Gruse (ASM).

WARDROBE DEPARTMENT
Seated (L-R): Veneda Truesdale, Tina Clifton, Lisa Tucci (Supervisor), Sunny Vidrine.
Standing (L-R): Dana Calanan, Bruce Harrow, Losa Daniello and Paul Riner.

BOX OFFICE
(L-R): Gloria Diabo and Linda Canavan.

Sweet Charity

BACKSTAGE CREW
Front Row (L-R): Tina Marie Clifton (Wardrobe), Amanda Duffy (Wardrobe), Bruce Morrow (Wardrobe).
Second Row (L-R): Veneda Truesdale (Dresser), Lisa Tucci (Wardrobe Supervisor), Beverly Jenkins (Stage Manager),
Heather Richmond Wright (Hair Supervisor), Sunny Vidrine (Dresser), Jennifer Lerner (Asst. Production Electrician),
Billy Van De Bogart (Production Carpenter), Andy Trotto (Prop Man).
Third Row: (L-R): Francis Elers (Head Sound), David O'Brien (Production Stage Manager), Richie Fedeli (Asst. Carpenter),
Eric Norris (Asst. Production Electrician), Mike Maher (Carpenter).
Fourth Row: (L-R): Bonnie Runk (Asst. Sound), John Blixt (Electrician), Tom O'Malley (Electrician), Dan Coey (Production Electrician),
Ron Fucarino (Carpenter), Sal Sclafani (House Propertyman), Richard Fideli (Carpenter).
Fifth Row: (L-R) Paul Reiner (Dresser), Stephen R. Gruse (Stage Manager), Dennis Sheehan (Carpenter), Dan Coey (Production Electrician),
George Green Jr. (Production Prop Coordinator) and Joe Maher, Jr. (House Carpenter).

HAIR DEPARTMENT
(L-R): Heather Richmond Wright (Hair Supervisor), Amanda Duffy.

Not pictured: Nathaniel Hathaway (Assistant Hair Supervisor).

PROPS DEPARTMENT
(L-R): Dennis Sheehan, George Green Jr. (Production Prop Coordinator), Sal
Sclafani (House Propertyman) and Andy Trotto.

Sweet Charity

CARPENTRY DEPARTMENT
Seated (L-R): Richie Fedeli (Asst. Carpenter),
Billy Van De Bogart (Prod. Carpenter), Ron Fucarino.
Standing (L-R): Scott Dixon (Deck Automation), Mike Maher,
Gabe Harris (Automation Flyman), Joe Maher Jr. (House Carpenter).

ELECTRICS and SOUND DEPARTMENTS
Seated (L-R) Bonnie Runk (Asst. Sound), Tom O'Malley,
Dermot Lynch (House Electrician), Eric Norris (Asst. Production Electrician).
Standing (L-R): Francis Ehlers (Head Sound), John Blitx,
Dan Coey (Prod. Electrician), Jennifer Lerner (Asst. Production Electrician).

STAFF CREDITS

V.P. World Wide Marketing ....Scott Moore
Marketing Manager ....Ken Sperr
Company Manager.......................Hilary Hamilton
Stage Managers ....Beverly Jenkins, Stephen R. Gruse
Associate General Manager ....Michael Buchanan
Assistant Company Manager ....Jeff Klein
Assistant Dance Captain ....Alexis Carra
Associate Scenic Designer ....Orit Jacoby Carroll
Assistant Scenic Designers..................Lauren Alvarez,
Tal Goldin, Bryan Johnson
Associate Costume Designer ....Martha Bromelmeier
Assistant Costume Designer................Rachel Attridge
Associate Lighting Designer............Charlie Pennebaker
Assistant Lighting Designers...............Rachel Eichorn,
Jennifer Schriever
Moving Lights Programmer ....David Arch
Press Associates ....Dennis Crowley, Ryan Ratelle
Casting Associates........................Jack Bowdan CSA,
Mark Brandon, Sarah Prosser,
Megan Larche, Leah Alter
Associate Sound Designer ....Tony Smolenski
Production Carpenter ....William Van De Bogart
Automation Flyman ....Stephen Burns
Deck Automation ....Scott Dixon
Assistant Carpenter ....Richard Fedeli
Production Electrician ....James Fedigan
Head Electrician ....Daniel Coey
Followspot Operator ....Jennifer Lerner
Assistant Electrician ....Eric Norris
Sound Engineer ....Francis Elers
Assistant Sound Engineer ....Bonnie Runk
Production Prop Coordinator ....George Green, Jr.
Production Prop Assistant ....Angelo Torre
Production Prop Shopper ....Kathy Fabian
Wardrobe Supervisor ....Lisa Tucci
Assistant Wardrobe Supervisor ....Fran Curry
Ms. Applegate's Dresser ....Jane Rottenbach
Hair Supervisor ....Heather Richmond Wright
Assistant Hair Supervisor ....Nathaniel Hathaway

Notable Music Inc./
The Cy Coleman Office ....Terrie Curran, Mark York
Production Assistant ....Jennifer Marik
Accounting ....Rosenberg, Neuwirth & Kuchner/
Mark D'Ambrosi, Annemarie Aguanno
Legal Counsel ....Loeb & Loeb/
Seth Gelblum, Richard Garmise
Advertising ....SpotCo/Drew Hodges,
Jim Edwards, Tom Greenwald,
Amelia Heape, Jen McClelland, Vinny Sainato
Website/Internet Marketing ....Situation Marketing/
Damian Bazodona, Ian Bennett
Sponsorship ....Amy Willstatter's Bridge to Hollywood/
Broadway LLC
Artwork Photography ....Jill Greenberg
Production Photography ....Paul Kolnik
Merchandising ....SFX Merchandising
Insurance ....Stockbridge Risk Management,
DeWitt Stern
Banking ....JPMorgan Chase/Michelle Gibbons
Orthopedic Consultant ....Phillip Bauman, MD
Physical Therapy
Services ....Performing Arts Physical Therapy
Payroll Service ....Castellana Services, Inc.
Booking................................The Booking Group

National Artists Management Company

Howie Cherpakov, Jack DePalma, Bob Williams, Marian Albarracin, Erin Barlow, Brett England, Suzanne Evans, Emily Dimond, Michelle Coleman, Victor Ruiz, Peter Ohsiek.

Clear Channel Entertainment—Theatrical

Miles C. Wilkin, Scott Zeiger, David Ian,
Steve Winton, David Anderson, Lauren Reid,
Lynn Blandford, Bradley Broecker, Philip Brohn, Jennifer Costello, Jennifer DeLange, Joanna Hagan, Eric Joseph, Susan Krajsa, David Lazar, Hailey Lustig, Carl Pasbjerg, Debra Peltz, Denis Perry, Courtney Pierce, Dominic Roncace, Alison Spiriti, Dan Swartz.

CREDITS

Scenery built and painted by Hudson Scenic Studios. Lighting equipment from PRG Lighting. Sound equipment from PRG Audio. Costumes executed by Carelli Costumes, Inc.; Euro Co Costumes.(com); Jennifer Love Costumes; JenKing; Brad Musgrove; Scafati, Inc.; Schneeman Studio, Limited; and Timberlake Studios. Millinery by Rodney Gordon, Inc. Shoes by T.O. Dey Shoes and J.C. Theatrical. Band uniforms by Fruhauf Uniforms. Rehearsed at the New 42nd Street Studios. Throat lozenges provided by Ricola. Fitness equipment provided by Gym Source. Thank you to Equinox at Greenwich Avenue.

Special thanks to
GRAN CENTENARIO TEQUILA
for their generous support.

JUJAMCYN THEATERS

ROCCO LANDESMAN
President

PAUL LIBIN
Producing Director

JACK VIERTEL
Creative Director

JERRY ZAKS

DANIEL ADAMIAN
General Manager

JENNIFER HERSHEY
Director of Operations

MEREDITH VILLATORE
Chief Financial Officer

Staff for the Al Hirschfeld Theatre

Manager ....Carmel Gunther
Treasurer......................................Carmine La Mendola
Carpenter ....Joseph J. Maher, Jr.
Propertyman......................................Sal Sclafani
Electrician ....Dermot J. Lynch
Engineer ....Vladimir Belenky

Sweet Charity
SCRAPBOOK

Photos by Aubrey Reuben

1. (L-R): Christina Applegate and Kyra DaCosta autograph cast albums at FYE Rockefeller Center.
2. (L-R): Nathan Lane with Denis O'Hare at the Casting Society of America's 21st Annual New York Artios Awards at the American Airlines Theatre.
3. (L-R): Charlotte D'Amboise and Terrence Mann at the 2005 TDF/Astaire Awards at the American Airlines Theatre.
4. (L-R): Rhett George, Janine LaManna and Paul Schoeffler sign CDs.
5. Applegate at the 2005 Tony Awards.
6. (L-R): Corinne McFadden and Applegate show off their makeovers and unveil the show's partnership with Avon Shine Supreme Lip Glosses at Avon Salon and Spa Store.

Tarzan

First Preview: March 24, 2006. Opened: May 10, 2006.
Still running as of May 31, 2006.

PLAYBILL

CAST

(in order of appearance)

Kerchak	SHULER HENSLEY
Kala	MERLE DANDRIDGE
Young Tarzan	DANIEL MANCHE

(Tues., Fri., Sat. Mat., Sun. Eve.)
ALEX RUTHERFORD
(Mon., Wed., Sat. Eve., Sun. Mat.)

Terk	CHESTER GREGORY II
Tarzan	JOSH STRICKLAND
Jane Porter	JENN GAMBATESE
Professor Porter	TIM JEROME
Mr. Clayton	DONNIE KESHAWARZ
Snipes	HORACE V. ROGERS

Ensemble .... MARCUS
BELLAMY,
CELINA CARVAJAL,
DWAYNE CLARK, KEARRAN GIOVANNI,
MICHAEL HOLLICK,
KARA MADRID, KEVIN MASSEY,
ANASTACIA McCLESKEY,
RIKA OKAMOTO, MARLYN ORTIZ,
JOHN ELLIOTT OYZON,
ANDY PELLICK, STEFAN RAULSTON,
HORACE V. ROGERS,
SEAN SAMUELS, NIKI SCALERA

Continued on next page

RICHARD RODGERS THEATRE
UNDER THE DIRECTION OF JAMES M. NEDERLANDER AND JAMES L. NEDERLANDER

DISNEY THEATRICAL PRODUCTIONS
under the direction of
Thomas Schumacher

presents

Disney's
TARZAN

Music and Lyrics by
PHIL COLLINS
Book by
DAVID HENRY HWANG

with

JOSH STRICKLAND   JENN GAMBATESE
MERLE DANDRIDGE   CHESTER GREGORY II
TIM JEROME   DONNIE KESHAWARZ
DANIEL MANCHE   ALEX RUTHERFORD

and

SHULER HENSLEY

DARRIN BAKER MARCUS BELLAMY CELINA CARVAJAL DWAYNE CLARK VERONICA deSOYZA
KEARRAN GIOVANNI MICHAEL HOLLICK JOSHUA KOBAK KARA MADRID KEVIN MASSEY
ANASTACIA McCLESKEY RIKA OKAMOTO MARLYN ORTIZ WHITNEY OSENTOSKI JOHN ELLIOT OYZON
ANDY PELLICK ANGELA PHILLIPS STEFAN RAULSTON HORACE V. ROGERS SEAN SAMUELS
NICK SANCHEZ NIKI SCALERA NATALIE SILVERLIEB JD AUBREY SMITH RACHEL STERN

Based on the story *Tarzan of the Apes* by
EDGAR RICE BURROUGHS
and the Disney film *Tarzan®*
Screenplay by
TAB MURPHY, BOB TZUDIKER & NONI WHITE
Directed by
KEVIN LIMA & CHRIS BUCK

Scenic and Costume Design		Lighting Design
BOB CROWLEY		**NATASHA KATZ**

Sound Design	Hair Design	Make-Up Design
JOHN SHIVERS	**DAVID BRIAN BROWN**	**NAOMI DONNE**

Soundscape	Special Creatures	Fight Direction
LON BENDER	**IVO COVENEY**	**RICK SORDELET**

Vocal Arrangements	Dance Arrangements	Orchestrations
PAUL BOGAEV	**JIM ABBOTT**	**DOUG BESTERMAN**

Music Director	Music Coordinator	Casting
JIM ABBOTT	**MICHAEL KELLER**	**BERNARD TELSEY CASTING**

Production Supervisor	Technical Supervisor	Press Representative
CLIFFORD SCHWARTZ	**TOM SHANE BUSSEY**	**BONEAU/BRYAN-BROWN**

Associate Director	Associate Producer
JEFF LEE	**MARSHALL B. PURDY**

Aerial Design by
PICHÓN BALDINU
Music Produced by
PAUL BOGAEV
Choreography by
MERYL TANKARD
Direction by
BOB CROWLEY

TARZAN® owned by Edgar Rice Burroughs, Inc.

5/10/06

Jenn Gambatese
and Josh Strickland

Tarzan

MUSICAL NUMBERS

ACT I

"Two Worlds"	Voice of Tarzan, Ensemble
"You'll Be in My Heart"	Kala, Ensemble
"Jungle Funk"	Instrumental
"Who Better Than Me?"	Terk, Young Tarzan
"No Other Way"	Kerchak
"I Need to Know"	Young Tarzan
"Son of Man"	Terk, Tarzan, Ensemble
"Son of Man" (Reprise)	Terk, Tarzan, Ensemble
"Sure As Sun Turns to Moon"	Kala, Kerchak
"Waiting for This Moment"	Jane, Ensemble
"Different"	Tarzan

ACT II

"Trashin' the Camp"	Terk, Ensemble
"Like No Man I've Ever Seen"	Jane, Porter
"Strangers Like Me"	Tarzan, Jane, Ensemble
"For the First Time"	Jane, Tarzan
"Who Better Than Me?" (Reprise)	Terk, Tarzan
"Everything That I Am"	Voice of Young Tarzan, Tarzan, Kala, Ensemble
"You'll Be in My Heart" (Reprise)	Tarzan, Kala
"Sure As Sun Turns to Moon" (Reprise)	Kala
"Two Worlds" (Finale)	Ensemble

Instrumental score for "Two Worlds" and "Meeting the Family"
based on the original score by Mark Mancina, written for the Disney film TARZAN®.

Photo by Joan Marcus

Stefan Raulston and Andy Pellick with the Ensemble.

Cast Continued

SWINGS

VERONICA deSOYZA, JOSHUA KOBAK,
WHITNEY OSENTOSKI,
ANGELA PHILLIPS, NICK SANCHEZ,
NATALIE SILVERLIEB,
JD AUBREY SMITH, RACHEL STERN

Dance Captain .... MARLYN ORTIZ

STANDBYS AND UNDERSTUDIES

Standby for Kerchak and Porter:
DARRIN BAKER

Understudies for Tarzan:
JOSHUA KOBAK, KEVIN MASSEY
Jane:
CELINA CARVAJAL, NIKI SCALERA
Kerchak:
MICHAEL HOLLICK, HORACE V. ROGERS
Kala:
KEARRAN GIOVANNI, NATALIE SILVERLIEB
Terk:
DWAYNE CLARK, NICK SANCHEZ
Clayton:
MICHAEL HOLLICK, JOSHUA KOBAK
Porter:
MICHAEL HOLLICK

ORCHESTRA

Conductor: JIM ABBOTT
Associate Conductor: ETHAN POPP
Synthesizer Programmer: ANDREW BARRETT

Keyboard 1: JIM ABBOTT
Keyboard 2: ETHAN POPP
Keyboard 3: MARTYN AXE
Drums: GARY SELIGSON
Percussion: ROGER SQUITERO, JAVIER DIAZ
Bass: HUGH MASON
Guitar: JJ McGEEHAN
Cello: JEANNE LeBLANC
Flutes: ANDERS BOSTRÖM
Reeds: CHARLES PILLOW
Trumpet: ANTHONY KADLECK
Trombone: BRUCE EIDEM
French Horn: THERESA MacDONNELL

Music Coordinator: MICHAEL KELLER

Tarzan

Josh Strickland
Tarzan

Jenn Gambatese
Jane

Merle Dandridge
Kala

Shuler Hensley
Kerchak

Chester Gregory II
Terk

Timothy Jerome
Professor Porter

Donnie Keshawarz
Clayton

Daniel Manche
Young Tarzan

Alex Rutherford
Young Tarzan

Darrin Baker
*Standby for
Kerchak and Porter*

Marcus Bellamy
Ensemble

Celina Carvajal
Ensemble

Dwayne Clark
Ensemble

Veronica deSoyza
Swing

Kearran Giovanni
Ensemble

Michael Hollick
Ensemble

Joshua Kobak
Swing

Kara Madrid
Ensemble

Kevin Massey
Ensemble

Anastacia McCleskey
Ensemble

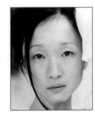
Rika Okamoto
Ensemble

Marlyn Ortiz
Ensemble

Whitney Osentoski
Swing

John Elliott Oyzon
Ensemble

Andy Pellick
Ensemble

Angela Phillips
*Swing/Assistant
Aerial Designer*

Stefan Raulston
Ensemble

Horace V. Rogers
Snipes/Ensemble

Sean Samuels
Ensemble

Nick Sanchez
Swing

Niki Scalera
Ensemble

Natalie Silverlieb
Swing

JD Aubrey Smith
Swing

Rachel Stern
Swing

Phil Collins
Music/Lyrics

Tarzan

David Henry Hwang
Book

Bob Crowley
*Director/Scenic and
Costume Design*

Meryl Tankard
Choreography

Natasha Katz
Lighting Design

John Shivers
Sound Design

David Brian Brown
Hair Design

Naomi Donne
Makeup Design

Lon Bender
Soundscape

Ivo Coveney
Special Creatures

Rick Sordelet
Fight Director

Paul Bogaev
*Music Producer/
Vocal Arrangements*

Jim Abbott
*Music Director/
Dance Arrangements*

Doug Besterman
Orchestrator

Michael Keller
Music Coordinator

Andrew Barrett
*Synthesizer
Programmer*

Bernard Telsey
Casting, C.S.A.
Casting

Jenn Gambatese as Jane and
Josh Strickland as Tarzan.

Tom Shane Bussey,
Glue
Technical Supervisor

Jeff Lee
Associate Director

Thomas Shumacher,
Director
Disney Theatrical
Productions
Producer

Photo by Joan Marcus

Tarzan

STAGE CREW

Front Row (L-R): Charlene Belmond (Hair), Valerie Gladstone (Hair), Margo Lawless (Dresser), Peggy Kurz (Assistant Wardrobe Supervisor), Mike Kearns (Winch Turner), Phil Lojo (Sound), Dave Brown (Automation), Steve Carver (House Electrician).

Second Row (L-R): Nanette Golia (Wardrobe Supervisor), Melanie McClintock (Dresser), Vivienne Crawford (Dresser), Gary Martori (Hair Supervisor), Angela Johnson (Makeup Supervisor), Thorvald Jacobson (Carpenter), Derek Healy (Electrician), Tommy Mahr (Carpenter), Denise Ozkar (Electrician), Eric Nahaczewski (Carpenter).

Third Row (L-R): Steve DeVerna, Jr. (Props), Linda Zimmerman (Dresser), Jay Gill (Dresser), Lisa Preston (Dresser), Jorge Vargas (Makeup), William Walters (Electrician), Scott DeVerna (Props), Ronald Knox (Carpenter), Angelo Grasso (Carpenter), Richard Force (Automation), Randy Zaibek (Light Board Operator), Dan Tramontozzi (Sound), Norman Ballard (Pyrotechnician).

Back Row (L-R): Steve DeVerna (House Props), Michael Fedigan (Deck Automation), Tommy McDonough (Carpenter), Will Carey (Carpenter), David Patridge (Sound Engineer), Kirk Aengenheyster (Carpenter), Greg Fedigan (Electrician), Kris Keene (Carpenter) and Brian Frankel (Electrician).

FRONT OF HOUSE STAFF, DISNEY MERCHANDISING TEAM AND PHYSICAL THERAPIST

Front Row (L-R): Hank Sanders, Robert Hays, Nicole Pasquale, Beth Frank, Dorothy Darby, Roseanne Kelly.

Middle Row (L-R): Rose Santiago, Ashley Pines, Stefanie Leigh, Jamie Sponcil, Lucy Horton, Barbara Rodell, Carmen Frank, Kenneth Klein.

Back Row (L-R): Jaime Hernandez Jr., Rafael Ortiz, Julia McDarris, Timothy Pettolina, Beverly Thornton, Joan Heller, Joe Melchiorre and Fred Santore.

Tarzan

BOX OFFICE
(L-R): Fred Santore, Jr., Fred Santore and Kenneth Klein.

COMPANY MANAGEMENT
(L-R): Eduardo Castro (Associate Company Manager) and
Randy Meyer (Company Manager).

STAGE MANAGEMENT
(L-R): Kenneth J. McGee, Robert M. Armitage, Clifford Schwartz,
Julia P. Jones and Tanya Gillette.

Photos by Ben Strothmann

STAFF FOR *TARZAN*®

Project Manager	LIZBETH CONE
Assistant to Associate Producer	Emily B. Powell
Show Accountant	Jodi Yeager

COMPANY MANAGER	RANDY MEYER
Associate Company Manager	Eduardo Castro

Assistant Choreographer	Leonora Stapleton
Assistant Aerial Designer	Angela Phillips

"Son of Man" Animated	
Sequence	Little Airplane Productions, Inc.

GENERAL PRESS REPRESENTATIVE
BONEAU/BRYAN-BROWN
Chris Boneau
Jim Byk   Matt Polk   Juliana Hannett

Production Stage Manager	Clifford Schwartz
Stage Manager	Frank Lombardi
Assistant Stage Managers	Julia P. Jones,
	Tanya Gillette,
	Robert M. Armitage
Dance Captain	Marlyn Ortiz
Assistant Dance Captain	Stefan Raulston
Fight Captain	Stefan Raulston

Production Assistants	Ryan J. Bell,
	Sara Bierenbaum

Associate Scenic Designer	Brian Webb
Scenic Design Associate	Rosalind Coombes
Assistant Scenic Designer	Frank McCullough
Associate Costume Designer	Mary Peterson
Assistant Costume Designer	Daryl Stone
Associate Lighting Designer	Yael Lubetzky
Assistant Lighting Designer	Aaron Spivey
Automated Lighting Programmer	Aland Henderson
Automated Lighting Tracker	Jesse Belsky
Assistant to Lighting Designer	Richard Swan
Associate Sound Designer	David Patridge
Assistant Sound Designer	Jeremy Lee
LCS Sound System Programmer	Garth Hemphill
"Son of Man" Visual Development	Kevin Harkey
Hand Lettering of	
Show Scrim	Harriet Rose Calligraphy & Design

Technical Supervisor	Tom Shane Bussey
Associate Technical Supervisor	Rich Cocchiara
Assistant Technical Supervisor	Matt Richman
Technical Production Assistant	Noelle Font
Production Carpenter	Jeff Goodman
Assistant Carpenter	Mike Kearns
Assistant Carpenter/Foy Operator	Richard Force

Scenic Automation	Dave Brown
Deck Automation	Michael Fedigan
Assistant Carpenter	Kirk Aengenheyster
Assistant Carpenter	Will Carey
Assistant Carpenter	Paul Curran
Assistant Carpenter	Thorvald Jacobson
Harness Construction	Dany Conde
Production Electrician	Jimmy Fedigan
Head Electrician/Light Board Operator	Randy Zaibek
Lead Follow Spot Operator	Andrew Dean
Moving Light Technician	Derek Healy
Pyrotechnician	Norman Ballard
Production Props	Denise Grillo
Assistant Props	Kevin Crawford
Props Shopper	Kate Foster
Production Sound	David Patridge
Sound Engineer	Phil Lojo
Atmospheric Effects	Chic Silber
Associate to Mr. Silber	Aaron Waitz
Wardrobe Supervisor	Nanette Golia
Assistant Wardrobe Supervisor	Margaret Kurz
Dressers	Vivienne Crawford, Jay Gill,
	Margo Lawless, Lisa Preston,
	Melanie McClintock, Linda Zimmerman
Hair Supervisor	Gary Martori
Assistant Hair Supervisor	Valerie Galdstone
Hairdresser	Charlene Belmond

Tarzan

Makeup Supervisor ....Angela Johnson
Assistant Makeup Supervisor ....Jorge Vargas

Music Copyist ....Russell Anixter, Donald Rice/
                            Anixter Rice Music Service
Synthesizer Programming ....Andrew Barrett
Synthesizer Programming Assistant ....Anders Boström
Electronic Drum Arrangements ....Gary Seligson
Rehearsal Drummer ....Gary Seligson
Rehearsal Pianist ....Ethan Popp
Music Production Assistant ....Brian Allan Hobbs

BERNARD TELSEY CASTING, C.S.A.
Bernie Telsey, Will Cantler, David Vaccari,
Bethany Knox, Craig Burns,
Tiffany Little Canfield, Stephanie Yankwitt,
Betsy Sherwood, Carrie Rosson, Justin Huff

DIALOGUE &
VOCAL COACH ....DEBORAH HECHT

Advertising ....Serino Coyne, Inc.
Production Photography ....Joan Marcus
Acoustic Consultant............Paul Scarbrough/a.'ku.stiks
Structural Engineering
Consultant ....Bill Gorlin, McLaren, P.C.
Technical Production Services ......Siam Productions, LLC
Production Travel ....Jill L. Citron
Payroll Manager ....Cathy Guerra, Johnson West
Children's Tutoring ....On Location Education/
                              Maryanne Keller
Physical Therapy ....Neuro Tour Physical Therapy, Inc./
                             Beth Frank, DPT
Medical Consultant ....Jordan Metzl, MD
Chaperone ....Robert Wilson
Assistant to Phil Collins ....Danny Gillen
Assistant to Bob Crowley ....Fred Hemminger
Press Assistant ....Matt Ross

TARZAN® owned by Edgar Rice Burroughs, Inc. and used by permission. TARZAN® cover artwork ©2006 Edgar Rice Burroughs, Inc. and Disney Enterprises, Inc. All rights reserved.

CREDITS
Scenery by Hudson Scenic Studio, Inc., Scenic Technologies, a division of Production Resource Group, LLC, New Windsor, NY; Dazian Fabrics; CMEANN Productions, Inc.; Stone Pro Rigging, Inc. Automation by Foy Inventerprise, Inc.; Hudson Scenic Studio, Inc., Show control and scenic motion control featuring Stage Command Systems® by Scenic Technologies, a division of Production Resource Group, LLC, New Windsor, NY. Lighting equipment by PRG Lighting. Sound equipment by Masque Sound. Costumes by Donna Langman Costumes; Tricorne, Inc.; DerDau; G! Willikers!; Pluma; Hochi Asiatico; Gene Mignola. Millinery provided by Rodney Gordon. Wigs provided by Ray Marston Wig Studio Ltd. Props by Paragon; Rabbit's Choice; Jauchem and Meeh; Randy Carfagno; ICBA, Inc.; John Creech Design & Production; Camille Casaretti, Inc.; Steve Johnson; Jerard Studios, Trashin' the Camp furniture fabric by Old World Weavers, division of Stark Carpet. Special effects equipment by Jauchem & Meeh, Inc. Firearms by Boland Production Supply, Inc. Soundscape by Soundelux. Atmospheric effects equipment provided by Sunshine Scenic Studios and Aztec

Stage Lighting. Acoustic drums by Pearl Drums. Rehearsal catering by Mojito Cuban Cuisine. Ricola natural herb cough drops courtesy of Ricola USA, Inc.

Makeup provided by M•A•C

TARZAN® rehearsed at Studio 2, Steiner Studios Brooklyn Navy Yard and New 42nd Street Studios.

SPECIAL THANKS
James M. Nederlander, James L. Nederlander, Nick Scandalios, Herschel Waxman, Jim Boese, David Perry of the Nederlander Organization and Ojala Producciones, S.A.

⋟N⋞
NEDERLANDER

Chairman ....James M. Nederlander
President ....James L. Nederlander

Executive Vice President
Nick Scandalios

Vice President	Senior Vice President
Corporate Development	Labor Relations
Charlene S. Nederlander	**Herschel Waxman**
Vice President	Chief Financial Officer
Jim Boese	**Freida Sawyer Belviso**

HOUSE STAFF FOR
THE RICHARD RODGERS THEATRE
House Manager ....Timothy Pettolina
Box Office Treasurer ....Fred Santore Jr.
Assistant Treasurer ....Daniel Nitopi
Electrician ....Steve Carver
Carpenter ....Kevin Camus
Propertymaster ....Steve DeVerna
Engineer ....Sean Quinn

DISNEY THEATRICAL PRODUCTIONS
President ....Thomas Schumacher
SVP & General Manager ....Alan Levey
SVP, Managing Director & CFO ....David Schrader

General Management
Senior Vice President, International ....Ron Kollen
Vice President, Operations ....Dana Amendola
Vice President, Labor Relations ....Allan Frost
Vice President, Theatrical Licensing ....Steve Fickinger
Director, Human Resources ....June Heindel
Director, Domestic Touring ....Michele Gold
Manager, Labor Relations ....Stephanie Cheek
Manager, Human Resources ....Cynthia Young
Manager, Information Systems ....Scott Benedict
Senior Computer Support Analyst ....Kevin A. McGuire

Production
Executive Music Producer ....Chris Montan
SVP, Creative Affairs ....Michele Steckler
Vice President, Creative Affairs ....Greg Gunter
VP, Physical Production ....John Tiggeloven
Manager, Physical Production ....Karl Chmielewski
Purchasing Manager.......................Joseph Doughney
Staff Associate Designer ....Dennis W. Moyes
Staff Associate Dramaturg ....Ken Cerniglia

Marketing
Vice President, Domestic Touring ....Jack Eldon
Vice President, New York ....Andrew Flatt
Manager, New York ....Michele Groner
Manager, New York ....Leslie Barrett
Website Manager ....Eric W. Kratzer
Assistant Manager, Communications ....Dana Torres

Sales
Vice President, Ticketing ....Jerome Kane
Manager, Group Sales ....Jacob Lloyd Kimbro
Assistant Manager, Group Sales...................Juil Kim
Group Sales Representative ....Jarrid Crespo

Business and Legal Affairs
Senior Vice President ....Jonathan Olson
Vice President ....Robbin Kelley
Director ....Harry S. Gold
Attorney ....Seth Stuhl
Paralegal/Contract Administration ....Colleen Lober

Finance
Director ....Joe McClafferty
Manager, Finance ....Justin Gee
Manager, Finance ....John Fajardo
Senior Business Planner ....Jason Fletcher
Production Accountants ....Barbara Toben,
                            Jodi Yaeger
Assistant Production Accountant ....Nikki Mitchell
Assistant Production Accountant ....Siu San Lee
Analyst ....Liz Jurist

Controllership
Director, Accounting ....Leena Mathew
Manager, Accounting ....Erica McShane
Senior Analysts ....Stephanie Badie,
                            Mila Danilevich,
                         Adrineh Ghoukassian
Analyst ....Ken Herrell

Administrative Staff
Dusty Bennett, Gregory Bonsignore, Jane Buchanan, Craig Buckley, Matthew Cronin, Cristi Finn, Cristina Fornaris, Dayle Gruet, Gregory Hanoian, Jonathan Hanson, Jay Hollenbeck, Connie Jasper, Kristine Lee, Kerry McGrath, Janine McGuire, Peter Ohsiek, Ryan Pears, Giovanna Primak, Roberta Risafi, Kisha Santiago, Lynne Schreur, David Scott.

BUENA VISTA THEATRICAL
MERCHANDISE, L.L.C.
Vice President ....Steven Downing
Merchandise Manager ....John F. Agati
Operations Manager ....Shawn Baker
Assistant Manager, Inventory ....Suzanne Jakel
Associate Buyer............................Violeta Burlaza
Retail Supervisor ....Mark Nathman
Merchandise Assistant ....Ed Pisapia

Disney Theatrical Productions • 1450 Broadway
New York, NY 10018

www.disneyonbroadway.com

Tarzan
SCRAPBOOK

1. (L-R): Composer Phil Collins and director Bob Crowley on opening night.
2. The principals take curtain calls on opening night.

Correspondent: Rachel Stern, Swing

Memorable Opening Night Note and Gifts: Phil Collins wrote us each a personal note expressing his deep feeling about our work on his show. Director/designer Bob Crowley gave us all beautiful tote bags and gave us each his sketches of our costumes based on his original designs.

Most Exciting Celebrity Visitors: Phil Collins is pretty exciting all by himself. When you're working with someone that brilliant, that's as exciting as it gets. We've also had visits from David Bowie and Alan Rickman.

Who Got the Gypsy Robe: Andy Pellick. If anyone can wear a gypsy robe it's that boy.

Which Actor Performed the Most Roles in This Show: The swings, of course, darling! Technically Kara Madrid has the most roles. She plays Tarzan's mother, then an ape, then a waterfall, then a flower, then an ape again, et cetera.

Special Backstage Rituals: Sometimes Merle Dandridge does a circle backstage before curtain.

Favorite Moment During Each Performance: When the apes appear to meet Jane and Porter. That's when all that beautiful, beautiful light is behind them, and it's really when two worlds become one family. It's huge and magical and I love it.

Favorite Off-Site Hangout: There's a world outside our theatre???

Favorite Snack Food: Anything but bananas!

Favorite Therapy: Beth, our physical therapist, who makes us all feel better. Spending so much time on our haunches, jumping up in the air

and flying—it's rockin' on the bod.

Favorite In-Theatre Gathering Place: That would be the penthouse, a.k.a. the Swing Room. It's a beautifully decorated studio with two sinks and a shower—and smashing view of the Church of Scientology across the street. We haven't seen John Travolta or Tom Cruise, but sometimes there are big limousines parked out front….

Memorable Ad-Lib: One night during previews Tarzan's torch didn't light. He was trying and trying and finally he turned to Terk and said, "C'mere man, try this…just *blow on it.*"

Latest Audience Arrival: People come late all the time and we don't even have a 7 P.M. show. It's so annoying! Once night about 60 people came in after the Prologue.

Busiest Day at the Box Office: They're all pretty busy.

Fastest Costume Change: Tarzan has about 30 seconds to put on his English suit. But we have great people backstage to help us.

Heaviest/Hottest Costumes: Heaviest has to be Jane's first dress, which opens into a gigantic spider web. It's all under there. Hottest has to be the spider costume. There are two people in there making the legs move, and it's like wearing two big fur coats.

Who Wore the Least: Tarzan.

Catchphrases Only the Company Would Recognize: "I need more tension in my a-hole!"

Best In-House Parody Lyrics: "Two worlds, one Tony nod."

Memorable Directorial Note: Bob is always

saying how "Extraordinary, extraordinary, extraordinary" we are.

Understudy Anecdote: Most of us swings have gone on, even before we opened. I can speak for the Swing Room when I say "It's a jungle in there." We pretty much have the coolest job ever.

Nicknames: Natalie is "Shanique Lipschitz." Sean is "Grace." Stacy has about a hundred nicknames. Our assistant choreographer, Leonora, is "Peaches" and she has her own theme song. I call Darrin Baker "Darrin Baker" always using both first and last names.

Embarrassing Moment: One night during the opening, one of the ape lines got caught in the silk that's supposed to come up later. It was very important to get the silk off that line. One of our climbers, who keep us safe when we're on those lines, tried to sneak out and untangle it. But that silk is very slippery. He wiped out and did a huge pratfall. Then, when he got up, down he went again. I never laughed that hard in my life. I won't say who it was, but we now call the show "*Thor-zan.*"

Superstitions That Turned Out To Be True: One of our young girls did say the title of The Scottish Play. We dragged her ass outside and made her spit. Hopefully it was quick enough not to do any serious damage, knock on wood.

Coolest Thing About Being in This Show: We have an incredible cast and we're so lucky that we love each other so much. But, come on! Flying is the coolest! I feel so bad that there are people in the world who will never know what it feels like to fly across a stage in a harness.

Photos by Aubrey Reuben

Three Days of Rain

First Preview: March 28, 2006. Opened: April 19, 2006.
Still running as of May 31, 2006.

PLAYBILL®

THREE DAYS OF RAIN

CAST

(in order of appearance)

ACT I

An unoccupied loft space in downtown Manhattan.
1995.

Walker ....PAUL RUDD
Nan ....JULIA ROBERTS
Pip ....BRADLEY COOPER

ACT II

The same space. 1960.

Theo ....BRADLEY COOPER
Lina....................................JULIA ROBERTS
Ned ....PAUL RUDD

UNDERSTUDIES

For Walker/Ned and Pip/Theo:
MICHAEL DEMPSEY

For Nan/Lina:
MICHELLE FEDERER

---

⑤ BERNARD B. JACOBS THEATRE

242 West 45th Street
A Shubert Organization Theatre

Gerald Schoenfeld, *Chairman*   Philip J. Smith, *President*

Robert E. Wankel, *Executive Vice President*

MARC PLATT   DAVID STONE   THE SHUBERT ORGANIZATION

present

JULIA ROBERTS   PAUL RUDD   BRADLEY COOPER

in

THREE DAYS OF RAIN

by

RICHARD GREENBERG

set and costume design	lighting design	original music and sound design
SANTO LOQUASTO	PAUL GALLO	DAVID VAN TIEGHEM

casting	rain	hair design	production stage manager
BERNARD TELSEY CASTING	JAUCHEM & MEEH	LYNDELL QUIYOU	WILLIAM JOSEPH BARNES

production management	press representative	general management
AURORA PRODUCTIONS	THE PUBLICITY OFFICE	STUART THOMPSON PRODUCTIONS/ JAMES TRINER

directed by

JOE MANTELLO

Originally produced in New York City by the Manhattan Theatre Club on October 21, 1997

Commissioned and first produced by South Coast Repertory

4/19/06

Paul Rudd and
Julia Roberts.

Photo by Joan Marcus

Three Days of Rain

Julia Roberts
Nan/Lina

Paul Rudd
Walker/Ned

Bradley Cooper
Pip/Theo

Michael Dempsey
*Understudy for
Walker/Ned and
Pip/Theo*

Michelle Federer
*Understudy for
Nan/Lina*

Richard Greenberg
Playwright

Joe Mantello
Director

Santo Loquasto
*Set and Costume
Design*

Paul Gallo
Lighting Design

Bernard Telsey
Casting, C.S.A.
Casting

Stuart Thompson,
Stuart Thompson
Productions
General Manager

Marc Platt
Producer

David Stone
Producer

Gerald Schoenfeld,
The Shubert
Organization
Producer

DOORMAN
Jerry Klein (Night Doorman)

STAGE MANAGEMENT
(L-R): Tim Semon (Stage Manager) and Billy Barnes
(Production Stage Manager).

GENERAL MANAGEMENT
James Triner
(Associate General Manager)

Photos by Ben Strothmann

Three Days of Rain

Photos by Ben Strothmann

FRONT OF HOUSE STAFF
Front Row (L-R): Roxanne Gayol (Usher), Sean Cutler (Ticket Taker), Martha Rodriguez (Usher), Rosa Pesante (Usher), Carrie Hart (Usher).
Middle Row (L-R): A. Pollock (Usher), John Minore (Director), Billy Mitchell (Manager), Patanne McEvoy (Usher), Daria Cherny (Usher).
Back Row (L-R): Al Peay (Usher), Paul Alonzo (Security), Eva Laskow (Chief Usher) and Anthony Tronchin (Usher).

STAGE CREW
Front Row (L-R): Michael Van Praagh (House Carpenter), Edward Ruggiero (House Flyman), Fred Ricci (Head House Propman), Daniel E. Carpio (House Propman), Michael LoBue (Production Electrician), Christopher Sloan (Production Sound Engineer).
Back Row (L-R): Freddy Mecionis (House Propman), Abe Morrison (Production Props) and Herbert Messing (House Electrician).

Three Days of Rain

WARDROBE AND HAIR DEPARTMENT
(L-R): Lyndell Quiyou (Hair Designer) and Barry Doss (Wardrobe).

BOX OFFICE
(L-R): Jose Hernandez (Asst. Treasurer) and Howard Fox (Treasurer).

STAFF FOR *THREE DAYS OF RAIN*

GENERAL MANAGEMENT
STUART THOMPSON PRODUCTIONS
Stuart Thompson   Caroline Prugh   James Triner

GENERAL PRESS REPRESENTATIVE
THE PUBLICITY OFFICE

Bob Fennell	Marc Thibodeau
Candi Adams	Michael S. Borowski

CASTING
BERNARD TELSEY CASTING, C.S.A.:
Bernie Telsey, Will Cantler, David Vaccari,
Bethany Knox, Craig Burns,
Tiffany Little Canfield, Stephanie Yankwitt,
Betsy Sherwood, Carrie Rosson, Justin Huff

PRODUCTION MANAGEMENT
AURORA PRODUCTIONS INC.

Gene O'Donovan	W. Benjamin Heller II
Bethany Weinstein	Hilary Austin

Production Stage Manager .... William Joseph Barnes
Stage Manager .... Timothy R. Semon
Assistant Director .... Michael Silverstone
Associate Set Designer .... Jenny Sawyers
Assistant Set Designer .... Wilson Chin
Assistant Costume Designer .... Matthew Pachtman
Associate Lighting Designer .... Paul Miller
Associate Sound Designer .... Jill BC Du Boff
Production Carpenter .... Donald "Buck" Roberts
Production Electrician .... Michael LoBue
Production Props .... Abraham Morrison
Production Sound .... Christopher Sloan
Wardrobe Supervisor .... Kristine Bellerud
Dresser .... Barry Doss

Production Assistant .... Maura Farver
General Management Assistant .... Megan Curran
Management Intern .... Jeremy Blocker
Production Intern .... Michelle Shannon
Press Assistant .... Matt Fasano
Banking .... JP Morgan Chase/Michelle Gibbons
Payroll .... Castellana Services, Inc./
Lance Castellana
Accountant .... Fried & Kowgios CPA's LLP/
Robert Fried, CPA
Controller .... Joseph S. Kubala
Insurance .... DeWitt Stern Group, Inc./
Jolyon F. Stern, Peter Shoemaker,
Anthony L. Pittari
Legal Counsel .... Schrek Rose Dapello & Adams LLP/
Nancy A. Rose
Advertising .... Serino Coyne, Inc./
Greg Corradetti, Ruth Rosenberg,
Joaquin Esteva, Hunter Robertson
Opening Night
Coordination .... Tobak Lawrence Company/
Joanna B. Koondel, Suzanne Tobak

Ms. Roberts' makeup designed by Richard Dean.

MARC PLATT PRODUCTIONS
President: Abby Wolf-Weiss
Adam Siegel, Lynda Brendish, Nicole Brown,
Jared LeBoff, Joey Levy, Chris Kuhl, Nik Mavinkurve

STONE PRODUCTIONS
Associate: Patrick Catullo

CREDITS
Scenery and scenic effects built and painted by
Showmotion, Inc., Norwalk, CT. Scenic paintings by Scenic
Art Studios, Inc. Lighting equipment from PRG Lighting.
Sound equipment from PRG Audio. Costumes by Euro Co.
Costumes, Inc. Dyeing by Dye-Namix and Gene Mignola
Inc. Military clothing provided by Kaufman's Army & Navy.
Furniture construction by Craig Grigg. Journals by Jeremy
Chernick. Plants by Modern Artificial. Rehearsed at the
Lawrence A. Wien Center for Dance and Theater.

MUSIC CREDITS
"Sakeena's Vision" (Wayne Shorter)
used by permission of EMI Unart Catalog, Inc.

 **THE SHUBERT ORGANIZATION, INC.**
Board of Directors

Gerald Schoenfeld	**Philip J. Smith**
Chairman	President
Wyche Fowler, Jr.	**John W. Kluge**
Lee J. Seidler	**Michael I. Sovern**

Stuart Subotnick

Robert E. Wankel
Executive Vice President

Peter Entin	**Elliot Greene**
Vice President -	Vice President -
Theatre Operations	Finance
David Andrews	**John Darby**
Vice President -	Vice President -
Shubert Ticketing Services	Facilities

House Manager .... William Mitchell

Three Days of Rain
SCRAPBOOK

Correspondents: Production Stage Manager William Barnes and Stage Manager Tim Semon.

Memorable Opening Night Note: "Careful, my dear, you mustn't get wet." From our friends at the *Wicked* national tour.

Opening Night Gifts: *Three Days of Rain* umbrellas, bright yellow rain hats (see our crew photo for stunning visual), beautifully bound copies of the script.

Most Exciting Celebrity Visitor: Mike Wallace. He came backstage but what he said is, unfortunately, unprintable.

Most Roles: Everyone played two roles. Though Michael Dempsey (understudy) had to learn the four men's roles!

Who Has Done the Most Shows: Billy Barnes.

Special Backstage Rituals: Playing a different "rain themed" song over the PA at the five minute call. These have included such hits as "Africa" by Toto, "Raindrops Keep Falling on My Head," "Don't Rain on My Parade," and the ever popular "Purple Rain."

Favorite Moment: When the cast gathers at "places," waiting to get the go-ahead from the house manager.

In-Theatre Gathering Place: Julia's dressing room.

Favorite Off-Site Hangout: Bar Centrale.

Favorite Snack Food: Wintergreen Lifesavers and cookies (all sorts).

Favorite Therapies: Ricola, massage, gossip.

Memorable Stage Door Fan Encounters: The hundreds who gathered after every show literally stopping traffic on 45th Street.

Busiest Day at the Box Office: Every day.

Who Wore the Wettest Costume: Bradley Cooper had to be thoroughly soaked offstage by his dresser, then had to slowly cross the stage in the pouring rain.

Who Wore the Least: Julia and Paul.

Catchphrase Only the Company Would Recognize: "We're gonna rock down to Electric Avenue."

Company In-Jokes: "It was crazy, that falafel."

Company Legends: The lovely Hazel, Phinneaus, Jack and Cassius.

Understudy Anecdote: Stage Manager to Michael Dempsey at 5:45 P.M.: "You're going on!"
Stage Manager to Michael Dempsey at 6:20 P.M.: "You're not going on!"

Nicknames: Mrs. Moder, Rudders, Coop, Barnsie, Sticky, Farvy.

Ghostly Encounters: EVERY NIGHT!

Coolest Thing About Being in This Show: The cast.

1. Julia Roberts at the opening night party at Cipriani.
2. Bradley Cooper at Cipriani.
3. Celia Weston and Paul Rudd join the party.
4. Director Joe Mantello and playwright Richard Greenberg on opening night.
5. Rudd, Roberts and Cooper take a curtain call on opening night.

The Threepenny Opera

First Preview: March 24, 2006. Opened: April 20, 2006.
Still running as of May 31, 2006.

PLAYBILL

CHARACTERS

(in order of appearance)

Jenny	CYNDI LAUPER
Smith	JOHN HERRERA
Walter/Betty	MAUREEN MOORE
Jimmy/Dolly	BROOKE SUNNY MORIBER
Rev. Kimball/Eunice	TERRY BURRELL
Robert	ROMAIN FRUGÉ
Vixen	DEBORAH LEW
Matthew	DAVID CALE
Macheath	ALAN CUMMING
Mr. Peachum	JIM DALE
Beggar/Beatrice	BRIAN BUTTERICK
Filch	CARLOS LEON
Mrs. Peachum	ANA GASTEYER
Polly Peachum	NELLIE McKAY
Jacob	ADAM ALEXI-MALLE
Eddie	KEVIN RENNARD
Tiger Brown	CHRISTOPHER INNVAR
Bruno/Molly	CHRISTOPHER KENNEY
Harry/Velma	LUCAS STEELE
Lucy Brown	BRIAN CHARLES ROONEY
Policemen and Beggars	MAUREEN MOORE,

BROOKE SUNNY MORIBER,
TERRY BURRELL, ROMAIN FRUGÉ,
DEBORAH LEW, BRIAN BUTTERICK,
CARLOS LEON, ADAM ALEXI-MALLE,
KEVIN RENNARD, CHRISTOPHER KENNEY,
LUCAS STEELE

Continued on next page

ROUNDABOUT THEATRE COMPANY

TODD HAIMES, Artistic Director
HAROLD WOLPERT, Managing Director
JULIA C. LEVY, Executive Director

Present

| Alan Cumming | Jim Dale | Ana Gasteyer | Cyndi Lauper | Nellie McKay |

in

The THREEPENNY OPERA

By Bertolt Brecht *and* Kurt Weill

In a New Translation by Wallace Shawn

Based on Elisabeth Hauptmann's German Translation of John Gay's *The Beggar's Opera*.

with

Christopher Innvar   Carlos Leon   Brian Charles Rooney

Adam Alexi-Malle   Terry Burrell   Brian Butterick   David Cale
Romain Frugé   John Herrera   Nehal Joshi   Christopher Kenney
Deborah Lew   Valisia Lekae Little   Maureen Moore
Brooke Sunny Moriber   Kevin Rennard   Lucas Steele

Set Design Derek McLane	*Costume Design* Isaac Mizrahi	*Lighting Design* Jason Lyons	*Sound Design* Ken Travis
Hair & Wig Design Paul Huntley	*Original Orchestrations* Kurt Weill	*Music Coordinator* John Miller	*Production Stage Manager* Peter Hanson

Casting Jim Carnahan, C.S.A.	*Technical Supervisor* Steve Beers	*General Manager* Sydney Beers

Press Representative Boneau/Bryan-Brown	*Director of Marketing* David B. Steffen	*Founding Director* Gene Feist	*Associate Artistic Director* Scott Ellis

Music Director Kevin Stites

Choreographed by Aszure Barton

Directed by Scott Elliott

Lead support provided by our Musical Theatre Fund partners;
The Kaplen Foundation, John and Gilda McGarry, Tom and Diane Tuft.

Major support for this production provided by The Blanche and Irving Laurie Foundation, the
National Endowment for the Arts, and the Eleanor Naylor Dana Charitable Trust.

4/20/06

(L-R):
Christopher Innvar,
Nellie McKay,
Alan Cumming

Photo by Joan Marcus

The Threepenny Opera

SCENES / MUSICAL NUMBERS

OVERTURE ....The Orchestra

PROLOGUE
"Song of the Extraordinary Crimes of Mac the Knife" ....Jenny and the Company

SCENE 1 – Wardrobe Department of Peachum's Begging Business
  "Peachum's Morning Hymn" ....Mr. Peachum
  "The 'Rather Than' Song" ....Mr. & Mrs. Peachum
SCENE 2 – An Empty Stable
  "Wedding Song" ....Matthew and the Gang
  "Pirate Jenny" ....Polly
  "The Army Song" ....Macheath, Tiger, Polly and the Gang
  "Wedding Song" reprise ....Matthew and the Gang
  "Love Song" ....Macheath and Polly
SCENE 3 – Peachum's Wardrobe Department
  "The 'No' Song" ....Polly
  "Certain Things Make Our Life Impossible" ....Mr. Peachum, Mrs. Peachum and Polly
SCENE 4 – The Stable
  "Goodbye" ....Macheath
  "Polly's Song" ....Polly

INTERMISSION

INTERLUDE – A Street
  "The Ballad of the Overwhelming Power of Sex" ....Mrs. Peachum
SCENE 5 – A Brothel in Turnbridge
  "The Ballad of the Pimp" ....Macheath and Jenny
SCENE 6 – The Prison of the Old Bailey
  "The Ballad of the Happy Life" ....Macheath
  "The Jealousy Duet" ....Lucy and Polly
  "How Do Humans Live?" ....Mac, Mrs. Peachum and Company
SCENE 7 – Peachum's Wardrobe Department
  "The Ballad of the Overwhelming Power of Sex" reprise ....Mrs. Peachum
  "The Song of Inadequacy of Human Striving" ....Mr. Peachum
  "The Song of Inadequacy of Human Striving" reprise ....Mr. Peachum
  "Solomon Song" ....Jenny
SCENE 8 – Lucy Brown's Bedroom, an Attic in the Old Bailey
  "Lucy's Aria" ....Lucy
SCENE 9 – The Death Cell
  "Cry from the Grave" ....Macheath
  "The Ballad in which Macheath Asks Everyone's Forgiveness" ....Macheath
  "Finale" ....Company

Cast Continued

SWINGS
NEHAL JOSHI, VALISIA LEKAE LITTLE

UNDERSTUDIES
For Mac:
ROMAIN FRUGÉ
For Jenny:
MAUREEN MOORE
For Polly:
BROOKE SUNNY MORIBER
For Mrs. Peachum:
TERRY BURRELL
For Mr. Peachum:
DAVID CALE
For Lucy:
LUCAS STEELE
For Filch:
ADAM ALEXI-MALLE
For Tiger:
JOHN HERRERA

Production Stage Manager: Peter Hanson
Stage Manager: Jon Krause

ORCHESTRA
Conductor – Kevin Stites
Associate Conductor – Paul Raiman

Reeds – Eddie Salkin, Roger Rosenberg
Trumpets – Tim Schadt, Matt Peterson
Tenor Trombone – Mike Christianson
Cello, Accordion – Charles duChateau
Guitar, Hawaiian Guitar, Banjo, Mandolin – Greg Utzig
Harmonium, Celeste, Piano – Paul Raiman
Percussion/Drums – Charles Descarfino
String Bass – Richard Sarpola

Music Coordinator – John Miller

Photo by Joan Marcus

(L-R): Jim Dale, Ana Gasteyer, Alan Cumming, Nellie McKay and Cyndi Lauper

The Threepenny Opera

Alan Cumming
Macheath

Jim Dale
Mr. Peachum

Ana Gasteyer
Mrs. Peachum

Cyndi Lauper
Jenny

Nellie McKay
Polly Peachum

Christopher Innvar
Tiger Brown

Carlos Leon
Filch

Brian Charles Rooney
Lucy Brown

Adam Alexi-Malle
Jacob

Terry Burrell
Rev. Kimball, Eunice

Brian Butterick
Beggar, Beatrice

David Cale
Matthew

Romain Frugé
Robert

John Herrera
Smith

Nehal Joshi
Swing

Christopher Kenney
Bruno, Molly

Deborah Lew
Vixen

Valisia Lekae Little
*Dance Captain/
Swing*

Maureen Moore
Walter, Betty

Brooke Sunny Moriber
Jimmy, Dolly

Kevin Rennard
Eddie

Lucas Steele
Harry, Velma

Bertolt Brecht
Book and Lyrics

Kurt Weill
Music

Wallace Shawn
New Translation

Scott Elliott
Director

Aszure Barton
Choreographer

Derek McLane
Set Design

Jason Lyons
Lighting Desiger

John Miller
Music Coordinator

Paul Huntley
Hair and Wig Design

Jon Krause
Stage Manager

Jim Carnahan
Casting

Gene Feist
*Founding Director,
Roundabout Theatre
Company*

Todd Haimes
*Artistic Director,
Roundabout Theatre
Company*

The Threepenny Opera

2005-2006 Awards

DRAMA DESK AWARD
Outstanding Featured Actor in a Musical
(Jim Dale)

OUTER CRITICS CIRCLE AWARD
Outstanding Featured Actor in a Musical
(Jim Dale)

THEATRE WORLD AWARD
Oustanding Broadway Debut
(Nellie McKay)

FRONT OF HOUSE STAFF AND CREW
Front Row (L-R): Jack Watanachaiyot (Associate House Manager), Allyn Bard Rathus, Larry Jennino, Nichole Larson (Company Manager), Lindsay Ericson (Production Assistant), Erin Delaney (Follow Spot Operator), LaConya Robinson (House Manager), Nicole Ramirez (House Staff).

Second Row (L-R): Mary Jeanette Harrington, Edward Wilson (Hair, Wig, and Makeup Supervisor), Susan Cook (Dresser), Nadine Hettel (Wardrobe Supervisor), Jean Scheller (Props Crew), Stella Varriale (House Staff), Kristina Olsen.

Third Row (L-R): Jennifer Kneeland (House Staff), Kimberly Mark Sirota (Dresser), Kate Longosky (House Staff), Dana McCaw (House Staff), Kimberly Butler (Dresser), Joe Hickey (Dresser), Douglas Lombardi, Sue Pelkofer (Deck Electrician), Josh Weitzman (House Head Electrician), Dorian Fuchs (Follow Spot Operator), Roger Rosenberg, Jonathan Martinez.

Back Row (L-R): Anthony Roman (House Staff), Nick Wheatley (House Staff), Kurt Kielmann (Day Worker), Dan Mendeloff (Props Crew), Billy Lombardi (Automation), Rob Mannsman, Al Steiner (Props Crew), John Wooding (Head Follow Spot Operator and Assistant Production Electrician) and Peter Hansen.

BOX OFFICE
(L-R): Krystin MacRitchie, Jaime Perlman (Box Office Treasurer) and Adam Owens.

ROUNDABOUT THEATRE COMPANY STAFF
ARTISTIC DIRECTOR .... TODD HAIMES
MANAGING DIRECTOR .... HAROLD WOLPERT
EXECUTIVE DIRECTOR .... JULIA C. LEVY
ASSOCIATE ARTISTIC DIRECTOR ... SCOTT ELLIS

ARTISTIC STAFF
DIRECTOR OF ARTISTIC DEVELOPMENT/
DIRECTOR OF CASTING .... Jim Carnahan
Artistic Consultant .... Robyn Goodman
Resident Director .... Michael Mayer
Associate Artists .... Scott Elliott, Doug Hughes,
Bill Irwin, Joe Mantello
Consulting Dramaturg .... Jerry Patch
Artistic Assistant .... Jill Rafson
Casting Director .... Mele Nagler
Casting Associate .... Carrie Gardner
Casting Assistant .... Kate Schwabe
Casting Assistant .... Stephen Kopel
Artistic Intern .... Rachel Balik

---

EDUCATION STAFF
EDUCATION DIRECTOR .. **Margie Salvante-McCann**

Director of Instruction and
Curriculum Development .... Renee Flemings
Education Program Associate .... Stacey L. Morris
Education Program Associate .... Carrie Soloman
Education Coordinator .... Jennifer DeBruin
Education Interns .... Allison Barcom, Molly Glenn
Education Dramaturg .... Ted Sod
Teaching Artists ....Phil Alexander, Tony Angelini, Cynthia
Babak, Victor Barbella,
Brigitte Barnett-Loftis, Caitlin Barton, Joe Basile,
LaTonya Borsay, Bonnie Brady, Lori Brown-Niang,
Michael Carnahan, Stella Cartaino, Joe Clancy,
Melissa Denton, Joe Doran, Katie Down,
Tony Freeman, Aaron Gass, Katie Gorum,
Sheri Graubert, Adam Gwon, Susan Hamburger,
Karla Hendrick, Lisa Renee Jordan, Alvin Keith,
Rebecca Lord, Robin Mates, Erin McCready,
Jordana Oberman, Andrew Ondrecjak, Laura Poe,
Nicole Press, Jennifer Rathbone, Chris Rummel,
Drew Sachs, Anna Saggese, Robert Signom,
David Sinkus, Derek Straat, Vickie Tanner,
Olivia Tsang, Jennifer Varbalow, Leese Walker,
Eric Wallach, Diana Whitten, Gail Winar

ADMINISTRATIVE STAFF
GENERAL MANAGER .... **Sydney Beers**
Associate Managing Director .... Greg Backstrom
General Manager, Steinberg Center .... Rebecca Habel
General Counsel .... Nancy Hirschmann
Human Resources Manager .... Stephen Deutsch
MIS Director .... Jeff Goodman
Facilities Manager .... Abraham David
Manager of Corporate and Party Rentals ..... Jetaun Dobbs
Office Manager .... Scott Kelly
Assistant to the General Manager .... Maggie Cantrick
Management Associate .... Tania Camargo
MIS Assistant .... Micah Kraybill
Receptionists .... Candice Alustiza, John Haynes,
Elisa Papa, Monica Sidorchuk
Messenger .... Robert Weisser
Management Intern .... Michelle Bergmann

FINANCE STAFF
CONTROLLER .... **Susan Neiman**
Assistant Controller .... John LaBarbera
Accounts Payable Administrator .... Frank Surdi
Customer Service Coordinator .... Trina Cox

The Threepenny Opera

Business Office Associate	David Solomon
Financial Associate	Yonit Kafka
Business Intern	Virginia Graham

DEVELOPMENT STAFF

DIRECTOR OF DEVELOPMENT ..... **Jeffory Lawson**

Director, Institutional Giving	Julie K. D'Andrea
Director, Individual Giving	Julia Lazarus
Director, Special Events	Steve Schaeffer
Manager, Donor Information Systems	Tina Mae Bishko
Capital Campaign Manager	Mark Truscinski
Manager, Friends of Roundabout	Jeff Collins
Institutional Giving Associate	Kristen Bolibruch
Special Projects Associate	Robert Weinstein
Patrons Services Liaison	Dawn Kusinski
Development Assistant	Chelsea Glickfield
Individual Giving Assistant	Dominic Yacobozzi
Special Events Assistant	Ginger Vallen
Development Assistant	Elissa Sussman
Special Events Intern	Casey Cipriani
Development Intern	Trey Gilpin

MARKETING STAFF

DIRECTOR OF MARKETING .... **David B. Steffen**

Marketing/Publications Manager	Margaret Casagrande
Assistant Marketing Director	Sunil Ayyagari
Marketing Assistant	Stefanie Schussel
Website Consultant	Keith Powell Beyland

**DIRECTOR OF TELESALES
SPECIAL PROMOTIONS** .... **Tony Baksa**

Telesales Manager	Anton Borissov
Telesales Office Coordinator	J.W. Griffin
Marketing Intern	Carla Borras

TICKET SERVICES STAFF

DIRECTOR OF SALES OPERATIONS . **Jim Seggelink**

Ticket Services Manager	Ellen Holt
Subscription Manager	Charlie Garbowski, Jr.
Box Office Managers	Edward P. Osborne, Jaime Perlman, Jessica Bowser
Group Sales Manager	Jeff Monteith
Assistant Box Office Managers	Paul Caspary, Steve Howe, Robert Morgan
Assistant Ticket Services Managers	Robert Kane, David Meglino, Ethan Ubell
Assistant Director of Sales Operations	Nancy Mulliner
Ticket Services	Solangel Bido, Jacob Burstein-Stan, William Campbell, David Carson, Andrew Clements, Johanna Comanzo, Nisha Dhruna, Adam Elsberry, Lindsay Ericson, Scott Falkowski, John Finning, Catherine Fitzpatrick, Amanda Genovese, Tova Heller, Dottie Kenul, Alexander LaFrance, Krystin MacRitchie, Mead Margulies, Chuck Migliaccio, Carlos Morris, Nicole Nicholson, Adam Owens, Shannon Paige, Thomas Protulipac, Jacki Rocha, Heather Siebert, Monté Smock, Lillian Soto, Greg Thorson, Pam Unger, Tiffany Wakely, Ryan Weible
Ticket Services Interns	Rachel Bauder, Elisa Mala

SERVICES

Counsel	Jeremy Nussbaum, Cowan, Liebowitz & Latman, P.C.
Counsel	Rosenberg & Estis
Counsel	Rubin and Feldman, P.C.
Counsel	Andrew Lance, Gibson, Dunn, & Crutcher, LLP
Counsel	Harry H. Weintraub, Glick and Weintraub, P.C.
Immigration Counsel	Mark D. Koestler and Theodore Ruthizer
House Physicians	Dr. Theodore Tyberg, Dr. Lawrence Katz
House Dentist	Neil Kanner, D.M.D.
Insurance	DeWitt Stern Group, Inc.
Accountant	Brody, Weiss, Zucarelli & Urbanek CPAs, P.C.
Advertising	Eliran Murphy Group/ Denise Ganjou, Katie Koch
Events Photography	Anita and Steve Shevett
Production Photographer	Joan Marcus
Theatre Displays	King Displays, Wayne Sapper

MANAGING DIRECTOR EMERITUS	ELLEN RICHARD

Roundabout Theatre Company
231 West 39th Street, New York, NY 10018
(212) 719-9393.

GENERAL PRESS REPRESENTATIVES
BONEAU / BRYAN-BROWN

Adrian Bryan-Brown	Matt Polk
Jessica Johnson	Shanna Marcus

CREDITS FOR *THE THREEPENNY OPERA*

GENERAL MANAGER	Sydney Beers
Company Manager	Nichole Larson
Asst. to the Company Manager	Allyn Bard Rathus
Production Stage Manager	Peter Hanson
Stage Manager	Jon Krause
Assistant Director	Marie Masters
Assistant Choreographer	William Briscoe
Associate Music Director/Rehearsal Pianist	Paul Raiman
Assistant Technical Supervisor	Elisa R. Kuhar
Assistant Set Designer	Shoko Kambara
Assistant Costume Designer	Courtney Logan
Second Assistant Costume Designer	David Withrow
Associate Lighting Designer	Jennifer Schriever
Assistant Lighting Designer	Carrie Wood
Assistant to Jason Lyons	Sandy Paul
Associate Sound Designer	Tony Smolenski
Assistant Musical Coordinator	Kelly M. Rach
Production Electrician	Josh Weitzman
Head Followspot Operator and Assistant Production Electrician	John Wooding
Moving Light Programmer	Victor Seastone
Conventional Light Programmer	Jessica Morton
Followspot Operators	Erin Delaney, Dorian Fuchs
Production Sound Mixer	Aaron Straus
Deck Sound	Greg Peeler
Deck Electrician	Sue Pelkofer
Wardrobe Supervisor	Nadine Hettel
Production Properties	Al Steiner
Props Crew	Al Steiner, Dan Mendeloff, Jean Scheller
Production Head Carpenter	Dan Hoffman
Head Flyman	Steve Jones
Automation	Billy Lombardi

Dressers	Kimberly Butler, Susan Cook, Joe Hickey, Kimberly Mark Sirota
Day Workers	Amanda Scott, Andrea Gonzalez, Kimberly Baird, Kurt Kielmann
Hair, Wig and Makeup Supervisor	Edward J. Wilson
Assistant Hair Stylist	Steven Kirkham
Production Assistants	Lindsay Ericson, Stephanie Cali
Music Copying	Emily Grishman Music Preparation/ Katharine Edmonds
Physical Therapy	Performing Arts Physical Therapy
Orthopedic Consultant	Phillip Bauman, MD
Scenery Constructed by	Showman Fabricators, Inc., NY
Computer Motion Control and Automation of Scenery by	Showman Fabricators, Inc.
Flying by	Foy
Props Built by	Gotham Scenic and Beyond Imagination
Soft Goods by	RoseBrand
LED Sign Provided by	Trans-lux Display Corporation
LED Sign Software	Steve Weiss from C-Scape
Sound Equipment by	Sound Associates
Shoes Made by	T.O. Dey
Hats by	Arnold Levine
Lighting Equipment from	PRG Lighting
Costumes Built by	Tricorne, Inc.
Makeup Provided by	M•A•C
Makeup Designer	Chantel Miller
Onstage Merchandising	George Fenmore/ More Merchandising Int'l
Stainless Steel Toilet Courtesy of	Bradley Corp.
Room Service Table by	Forbes Industries
Mobile Computer Courtesy of	Symbol Technologies, Inc.
Polyglass Plate Covers by	Carlisle Sanitary Maintenance Products
Acrylic Drinkware by	U.S. Acrylic, Inc.
Threepenny Opera Uses	Baldwin Pianos
Music Instruments by	Carroll Musical Instruments

SPECIAL THANKS

Trash and Vaudeville, Tripp NYC; Bra*Tenders for hosiery and undergarments; Dr. Arthur Fisher and Sal Martella of Progressive Prosthetics; Kenny Greenberg from Krypton Neon; Ricola USA for supplying the company with cough drops.

STUDIO 54 THEATRE STAFF

Theatre Manager	Tina Beck Carlson
House Manager	LaConya Robinson
Associate House Manager	Jack Watanachaiyot
Assistant House Manager	Jay Watanachaiyot
House Staff	Elicia Edwards, Jason Fernandez, Jen Kneeland, Kate Longosky, Latiffa Marcus, Nicole Marino, Jonathan Martinez, Dana McCaw, Nicole Ramirez, Anthony Roman, Nick Wheatley, Stella Varriale
House Head Electrician	Josh Weitzman
House Head Carpenter	Dan Hoffman
House Head Properties	Lawrence Jennino
Security	Gotham Security
Maintenance	Ralph Mohan, Maman Garba
Lobby Refreshments by	Sweet Concessions

The Threepenny Opera
SCRAPBOOK

Correspondent: Christopher Kenney, "Bruno" and "Molly."

Memorable Opening Night Letter: André Gregory sent us a letter telling us how brilliant the show is and how brilliant we all are in it. He had worked with Brecht and he said we'd gotten the whole idea of it exactly right.

Opening Night Gifts: Alan gave me a doll and a bottle of his cologne. We got T-shirts from Ana Gasteyer that say "Beggars, Thieves, Whores." Cyndi Lauper gave us a bag of stuff from the Pleasure Chest, including edible undies and a penis whistle. Jim Dale gave each person something personal; I got a DVD of *Kinky Boots*.

Most Exciting Celebrity Visitors and What They Said: Angela Lansbury, Joan Collins, Rosie O'Donnell and Marian Seldes all came back. Stephen Sondheim said he absolutely loved it.

Who Got the Gypsy Robe: Romain Frugé.

"Easter Bonnet" Sketch: We didn't present one, but we raised $6000 from the audience in four shows. I think we scared them!

Who Has Done the Most Shows in Their Career: Maureen Moore.

Backstage Rituals: Everybody does some really strange thing of their own. David Cale skips around the stage like an 8-year-old for 15 minutes. Cyndi does chin-ups.

Favorite On-Stage Moment: There is a scene where I play one of the prostitutes and Ana and Cyndi have a fight scene. I stand there thinking, Here I am on the stage of Studio 54, watching Ana Gasteyer and Cyndi Lauper, and there's the whole audience behind them. I have nothing to do but stand there, but I love that moment a lot. It's just one of those magical moments.

Favorite Off-Stage Moment: Nellie McKay is a prankster and quite a little gift giver. Each night when Jim Dale comes off the stage she has something ready for him, Sometimes it's something to eat like a veggie burger or a veggie dog (she's a strict vegetarian). Once she found an old clip of one of his performances and she set up a screen and video player and played it for him. And every night when we all march off the stage in a line after "Happy Life," she is standing there with a baked good

1. (L-R): Director Scott Elliott, cast members Ana Gasteyer, Jim Dale, Cyndi Lauper and Alan Cumming arrive at Studio 54 for opening night.
2. Jim Dale on opening night.
3. Ana Gasteyer in the lobby.
4. Cast member Christopher Innvar on opening night.
5. Special guest Rena Gill Brecht arrrives at Studio 54
6. (L-R): Cyndi Lauper and Alan Cumming.

Photos by Aubrey Reuben

The Threepenny Opera
SCRAPBOOK

or burgers cut in quarters, and hands them to us as we go by. And we all say "Thank you! Thank you!" It's incredibly generous and incredibly sweet. I find myself looking forward to it each day: "What will she have today?"

Favorite In-Theatre Gathering Places: First is the greenroom, which is really just a hallway. Alan Cumming's dressing room is probably the hot spot. You always know there's going to be some sort of party in there. Third is the Men's chorus dressing room. It's quite, quite festive.

Favorite Off-Site Hangout: We all love Vlada on 51st Street.

Favorite Snack Food: They keep huge tubs of pretzels and trail mix for us all the time.

Mascots: We love our visits from Alan Cumming's dog Honey and Jim Dale's dog Georgy Girl.

Favorite Therapy: We have physical therapy twice a week. Ana and Cyndi love that Entertainer's Secret throat spray. It's pump, pump, pump all the time, because they have to sing so much.

Memorable Ad-Libs: Cyndi Lauper's line is supposed to be, "So the guy says 'I'm not paying.'" One night she said, "So the guy says, 'I'm not coming.' Did I say 'coming'? I meant 'paying.'" That made us laugh hard.

One night, as Alan Cumming was finishing "Happy Life," Brian Charles Rooney missed his cue. After a moment, Alan said, "This is where Lucy Brown is supposed to enter." Another wait. "She should be here any moment." Another wait. "I'm sure she's just tied up." And it went on like that. Turns out, Brian had fallen asleep in his dressing room, which is way up in the tower on the third floor. You can imagine how it must have felt for Alan waiting that long. The audience was roaring and I remember Alan saying, "I don't think Lucy will ever forget this night!"

Memorable Stage Door Fan Encounter: In one scene John Herrara wears chaps, a leather vest and underwear—and nothing else. When he came out of the stage door one night, an 11-year-old boy said, "I really liked your outfit!" We almost died laughing.

Memorable Audience Encounter During a Show: Cyndi yells to Jim Dale and Ana Gasteyer, "You two aren't worth cleaning the men's toilet!" And two drunk suburban ladies shouted out, "Good one, Cyndi!"

Heaviest/Hottest Costume: Hattie Hathaway wears a long-sleeved Victorian jacket and long pants and a huge bustle. It's a lot of thick, heavy layers.

Who Wore the Least: At one point Alan Cumming is in his underwear. And then there's me when I have on just a corset and pumps.

Catchphrases Only the Company Would Recognize: "Boogie till your balls fall off!"

Orchestra Member Who Played the Most Instruments: Charles Descarfino plays nine: drum, tympani, orchestra bells, wood block, concert bass drum, tom-tom, field drum, triangle and tubular chimes.

Orchestra Members Who Played the Most Consecutive Performances Without a Sub: Paul Raiman and Charles duChateau.

Memorable Directorial Notes: Scott is always talking about teeth: "I want teeth! Show your teeth! Get your teeth into this production! The show should have teeth!"

Embarrassing Moments: Our stage manager one night told us, "I've never in my life given this note, but, please, *don't fart on stage.*"

Coolest Things About Being in This Show: I think the coolest thing is to do a show with so many amazing stars. Also cool is being asked to go out afterward with Alan and Cyndi. That's really exciting for me. I also love being in a controversial piece. Because I'm mainly a dancer, I always thought I'd wind up in a happy musical. This is the first show where I'm not dancing. It was cool when Scott Elliott called me on the phone and asked me to take part without an audition or anything. It's also cool to be in a piece that is so loved and loathed at the same time. And this cast is so tight! I asked Maureen Moore, "Is it always like this?" And she said "no" really fast, like before I'd even finished the sentence. I'm having the time of my life!

1. Nellie McKay displays her political causes on her chest on opening night.
2. Cyndi Lauper (L) and hostess Valerie Smaldone at a party adding her portrait for the Broadway Wall of Fame at Tony's Di Napoli restaurant.
3. Translator Wallace Shawn arrives at the cast party.
4. Designer Isaac Mizrahi meets the paparazzi outside Studio 54 on opening night.

A Touch of the Poet

First Preview: November 11, 2005. Opened: December 8, 2006.
Closed January 29, 2005 after 32 Previews and 50 Performances.

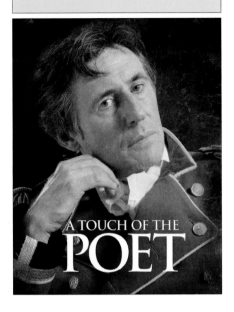

PLAYBILL

A TOUCH OF THE POET

CAST
(in order of appearance)

Mickey Maloy ....DANIEL STEWART SHERMAN
Jamie Cregan ....BYRON JENNINGS
Sara Melody ....EMILY BERGL
Nora Melody ....DEARBHLA MOLLOY
Cornelius Melody ....GABRIEL BYRNE
Dan Roche ....CIARAN O'REILLY
Paddy O'Dowd.............RANDALL NEWSOME
Deborah
  (Mrs. Henry Harford) ....KATHRYN MEISLE
Nicholas Gadsby ....JOHN HORTON

MUSICIAN
Uilleann pipes ....DAVID POWER

SCENES

Act I, Scene 1: Dining room of Melody's Tavern,
a few miles from Boston, 9 a.m., July 27, 1828
Scene 2: The same, later that morning

Act II, Scene 1: The same, that evening
Scene 2: The same, that night

UNDERSTUDIES

For Sara Melody: KRISTEN BUSH
For Cornelius Melody: COLIN LANE
For Roche and O'Dowd: KEVIN McHUGH
For Cregan and Maloy: RANDALL NEWSOME
For Nora and Deborah: ELIZABETH NORMENT

Production Stage Manager: PETER HANSON
Stage Manager: RACHEL S. McCUTCHEN

STUDIO 54

ROUNDABOUT THEATRE COMPANY

TODD HAIMES, Artistic Director
HAROLD WOLPERT, Managing Director
JULIA C. LEVY, Executive Director

Presents

Gabriel Byrne

in

Eugene O'Neill's

A TOUCH OF THE
POET

with

Dearbhla Molloy   Emily Bergl
John Horton   Byron Jennings   Kathryn Meisle
Randall Newsome   Ciaran O'Reilly   Daniel Stewart Sherman

Set & Costume Design by **Santo Loquasto**	Lighting Design by **Christopher Akerlind**	Original Music & Sound Design by **David Van Tieghem**
Hair & Wig Design by **Tom Watson**	Production Stage Manager **Peter Hanson**	Dialect Coach **Stephen Gabis**
Casting by **Jim Carnahan**, C.S.A.	Technical Supervisor **Steve Beers**	General Manager **Sydney Beers**
Founding Director **Gene Feist**	Associate Artistic Director **Scott Ellis**	Press Representative **Boneau/Bryan-Brown**	Director of Marketing **David B. Steffen**

Directed by

Doug Hughes

Lead support provided by our Play Production Fund partners:
Steven and Liz Goldstone, The Blanche & Irving Laurie Foundation, Mary and David Solomon

Roundabout Theatre Company is a member of the League of Resident Theatres. www.roundabouttheatre.org

12/8/05

Gabriel Byrne and Emily Bergl.

Photo by Joan Marcus

A Touch of the Poet

Gabriel Byrne
Cornelius Melody

Dearbhla Molloy
Nora Melody

Emily Bergl
Sara Melody

John Horton
Nicholas Gadsby

Byron Jennings
Jamie Cregan

Kathryn Meisle
Deborah

Randall Newsome
Paddy O'Dowd

Ciaran O'Reilly
Dan Roche

Daniel Stewart
Sherman
Mickey Maloy

Kristen Bush
u/s Sara Melody

Colin Lane
u/s Cornelius Melody

Kevin McHugh
*u/s Roche and
O'Dowd*

Elizabeth Norment
*u/s Nora Melody,
Deborah*

Eugene O'Neill
Playwright

Doug Hughes
Director

Santo Loquasto
*Set and Costume
Design*

Christopher Akerlind
Lighting Design

Tom Watson
Hair and Wig Design

Stephen Gabis
Dialect Coach

Rick Sordelet
Fight Direction

Jim Carnahan
Casting

Gene Feist
*Founding Director,
Roundabout Theatre
Company*

Todd Haimes
*Artistic Director,
Roundabout Theatre
Company*

2005-2006 AWARD

OUTER CRITICS CIRCLE AWARD
OUTSTANDING ACTOR IN A PLAY
(GABRIEL BYRNE)

ROUNDABOUT THEATRE COMPANY STAFF
ARTISTIC DIRECTOR .... **TODD HAIMES**
MANAGING DIRECTOR ...... **HAROLD WOLPERT**
EXECUTIVE DIRECTOR .... **JULIA C. LEVY**
ASSOCIATE
ARTISTIC DIRECTOR .... **SCOTT ELLIS**

ARTISTIC STAFF
Director of Artistic Development/
Director of Casting .... **Jim Carnahan**
Artistic Consultant .... Robyn Goodman
Resident Director .... Michael Mayer
Associate Artists .... Scott Elliott, Doug Hughes,
Bill Irwin, Joe Mantello
Consulting Dramaturg .... Jerry Patch
Artistic Assistant .... Jill Rafson

Casting Director .... Mele Nagler
Casting Associate .... Carrie Gardner
Casting Associate .... J.V. Mercanti
Casting Assistant .... Kate Schwabe
Casting Assistant .... Stephen Kopel
Artistic Intern .... Deborah Friedman

EDUCATION STAFF
EDUCATION DIRECTOR .... **Megan Kirkpatrick**
Director of Instruction and
Curriculum Development .... Renee Flemings
Education Program Associate .... Carrie Soloman
Education Program Associate .... Stacey L. Morris
Education Intern .... Amelia Stanley
Education Dramaturg .... Ted Sod
Teaching Artists .... Zakiyyah Alexander,

Phil Alexander, Cynthia Babak,
Victor Barbella, Brigitte Barnett-Loftis,
Caitlin Barton, Joe Basile,
LaTonya Borsay, Bonnie Brady,
Mike Carnahan, Joe Clancy,
Melissa Denton, Stephen DiMenna,
Joe Doran, Tony Freeman, Sheri Graubert,
Susan Hamburger, Karla Hendrick,
Jim Jack, Alvin Keith, Rebecca Lord,
Erin McCready, Andrew Ondrejcak,
Laura Poe, Nicole Press, Chris Rummel,
Drew Sachs, Anna Saggese, David Sinkus,
Vickie Tanner, Olivia Tsang,
Jennifer Varbalow, Leese Walker,
Eric Wallach, Diana Whitten,
Gail Winar, Kirche Zeile

A Touch of the Poet

ADMINISTRATIVE STAFF

GENERAL MANAGER ....**Sydney Beers**
Associate Managing Director ....Greg Backstrom
General Manager of the
Steinberg Center ....Don-Scott Cooper
General Counsel ....Nancy Hirschmann
Office Manager ....Scott Kelly
Human Resources Manager ....Stephen Deutsch
MIS Director ....Jeff Goodman
Manager of Corporate and Party Rentals ....Jetaun Dobbs
Facilities Manager ....Keith A. Smalls
Assistant to the General Manager ....Maggie Cantrick
Management Assistant ....Nicholas Caccavo
MIS Associate ....Lloyd Alvarez
MIS Assistant ....Micah Kraybill
Receptionists ....Candice Alustiza, Elisa Papa,
Monica Sidorchuk, John Haynes
Messenger ....Robert Weisser
Management Intern ....Tania Camargo

FINANCE STAFF

CONTROLLER ....**Susan Neiman**
Assistant Controller ....John LaBarbera
Accounts Payable Administrator ....Frank Surdi
Customer Service Coordinator ....Trina Cox
Business Office Associate ....David Solomon
Financial Associate ....Yonit Kafka

DEVELOPMENT STAFF

DIRECTOR OF DEVELOPMENT .....**Jeffory Lawson**
Director, Institutional Giving ....Julie K. D'Andrea
Director, Individual Giving ....Julia Lazarus
Director, Special Events ....Steve Schaeffer
Manager,
Donor Information Systems ....Tina Mae Bishko
Capital Campaign Manager ....Mark Truscinski
Manager, Friends of Roundabout ....Jeff Collins
Institutional Giving Associate ....Kristen Bolibruch
Assistant to
the Executive Director ....Robert Weinstein
Patrons Services Liaison ....Dawn Kusinski
Development Assistant ....Chelsea Glickfield
Individual Giving Assistant ....Dominic Yacobozzi
Special Events Assistant ....Ginger Vallen
Individual Giving Intern ....Alicia Hogan
Special Events Intern ....Katie Cush

MARKETING STAFF

DIRECTOR OF MARKETING ....**David B. Steffen**
Marketing Associate ....Sunil Ayyagari
Marketing Associate ....Rebecca Ballon
Website Consultant ....Keith Powell Beyland
Marketing Intern ....Ruth Fink
DIRECTOR OF TELESALES
SPECIAL PROMOTIONS ....**Tony Baksa**
Telesales Manager ....Anton Borissov
Telesales Office Coordinator ...................J.W. Griffin

TICKET SERVICES STAFF

DIRECTOR OF
SALES OPERATIONS ....**Jim Seggelink**
Ticket Services Manager ....Ellen Holt
Subscription Manager ....Charlie Garbowski
Box Office Managers ....Edward P. Osborne,
Jaime Perlman,
Jessica Bowser

Group Sales Manager ....Jeff Monteith
Assistant Box Office Managers ..Paul Caspary, Steve Howe,
Robert Morgan
Assistant Ticket Services Managers ....Robert Kane,
David Meglino,
Ethan Ubell
Ticket Services ....Solangel Bido,
Daniel Carlisle, Andrew Clements,
Nisha Dhruna, Adam Elsberry,
Lindsay Ericson, Scott Falkowski,
Catherine Fitzpatrick, Amanda Genovese,
Tova Heller, Dottie Kenul,
Bill Klemm, Alexander LaFrance,
Krystin MacRitchie, Mead Margulies,
Chuck Migliaccio, Carlos Morris,
Nicole Nicholson, Jillian Owdienko,
Adam Owens, Shannon Paige,
Thomas Protulipac, Amy Robinson,
Jacki Rocha, Heather Siebert,
Monté Smock, Lillian Soto,
Greg Thorson, Ryan Weible
Ticket Services Intern ....Lauren Cartelli

SERVICES

Counsel ....Jeremy Nussbaum,
Cowan, Liebowitz & Latman, P.C.
Counsel ....Rosenberg & Estis
Counsel ....Rubin and Feldman, P.C.
Counsel ....Andrew Lance,
Gibson, Dunn, & Crutcher, LLP
Counsel ....Harry H. Weintraub,
Glick and Weintraub, P.C.
Immigration Counsel ....Mark D. Koestler and
Theodore Ruthizer
House Physicians ....Dr. Theodore Tyberg,
Dr. Lawrence Katz
House Dentist ....Neil Kanner, D.M.D.
Insurance ....Dewitt Stern Group, Inc.
Accountant ....Brody, Weiss, Zucarelli &
Urbanek CPAs, P.C.
Advertising ....Eliran Murphy Group/
Denise Ganjou
Events Photography ....Anita and Steve Shevett
Production Photographer ....Joan Marcus
Theatre Displays ....King Displays, Wayne Sapper

MANAGING DIRECTOR
EMERITUS ....ELLEN RICHARD

Roundabout Theatre Company
231 West 39th Street, New York, NY 10018
(212) 719-9393.

GENERAL PRESS REPRESENTATIVES

BONEAU / BRYAN-BROWN
Adrian Bryan-Brown   Matt Polk
Jessica Johnson   Joe Perrotta

CREDITS FOR *A TOUCH OF THE POET*

GENERAL MANAGER ....Sydney Beers
Company Manager ....Nichole Larson
Production Stage Manager ....Peter Hanson
Stage Manager ....Rachel S. McCutchen
Associate Director ....Mark Schneider
Assistant Technical Supervisor ....Elisa Kuhar
Assistant Set Designer ....Rachel Nemec

Associate Costume Designer ....Mitchell Bloom
Assistant Lighting Designer ....Michael Spadaro
Associate Sound Designer ....Jill BC Du Boff
Consulting Dramaturg ....Robert Scanlan
Dialect Coach ....Stephen Gabis
Movement Consultant ....Barry McNabb
Makeup Design ....Angelina Avallone
Fight Director ....Rick Sordelet
Production Electrician ....Josh Weitzman
Assistant Production Electrician ....John Wooding
Production Sound Engineer ....Aaron Straus
Production Sound Mixer ....Greg Peeler
Wardrobe Supervisor ....Nadine Hettel
Production Properties ....Denise Grillo
Assistant Production Properties ....Kevin Crawford
Production Head Properties ....Lawrence Jennino
Production Head Carpenter ....Dan Hoffman
Props Running ....Erin Delaney
Dressers ....Joe Hickey, Kimberly Butler
Day Workers ....Amanda Scott,
Susan Cook
Hair Supervisor ....Daryl Terry
Production Assistant ....Lindsay Ericson
Scenery
Provided by ....Great Lakes Scenic Studios, Inc.
Costumes Built by ....Euro Co Costumes
Mr. Byrne's Boots by .............................T.O. Dey
Soft Goods Provided by ....Showman Fabricators, Inc.
Lighting Equipment
from ....PRG, Production Resource Group
Sound Equipment by ....One Dream Sound
Production Merchandising ....George Fenmore/
More Merchandising International
Pewterware Courtesy of ....Wilton Armetale
Candles by ....Colonial Candles of Cape Cod
Additional Set and
Hand Props Courtesy of ....George Fenmore, Inc.
Sound System
Design Consultant ....Lucas Indelicato
Special thanks to ....Robin Engelman

STUDIO 54 THEATRE STAFF

Theatre Manager ....Tina Beck Carlson
House Manager ....LaConya Robinson
Associate House Manager ....Jack Watanachaiyot
Assistant House Manager ....Jay Watanachaiyot
House Head Electrician ....Josh Weitzman
House Head Properties ....Lawrence Jennino
House Head Carpenter ....Dan Hoffman
Local One Apprentice ....Erin Delaney
House Staff ....Onercida Concepcion, Elicia Edwards,
Jason Fernandez, Jen Kneeland,
Kate Longosky, Latiffa Marcus,
Nicole Marino, Jonathan Martinez,
Dana McCaw, Nicole Ramirez,
Anthony Roman, Nick Wheatley,
Stella Varriale
Security ....Gotham Security
Maintenance ....Ralph Mohan, Maman Garba

Lobby Refreshments by Sweet Concessions

A Touch of the Poet
SCRAPBOOK

Cast photos by Aubrey Reuben

Marquee photo by Andrew Ku

Correspondent: Nichole Larson, Company Manager.

Memorable Opening Night Note: The cast of *Doubt* sent us a congratulatory fax full of nice comments like, "There are never enough Byrnes on Broadway."

Opening Night Gift: The Roundabout Theatre Company gave us a beautiful "family photo" of everyone on the production in a silver frame engraved with the play's title and the opening date. We also all got a copy of the show's poster.

Celebrity Visitors: We had a lot of famous folks, including Natasha Richardson and Liam Neeson, Julianne Moore, Kevin Pollak, Sam Mendes, Kate Winslet and Kevin Spacey.

Favorite Moment: I looked forward to the playing of the uilleann pipes. I have to say that I was against the idea of live uilleann pipe music at first. But I found that I loved the sound of it; it worked so well and was so perfect for the show.

Favorite In-Theatre Gathering Place: Whenever we had birthday cakes or other celebrations, they were mostly in the greenroom downstairs.

Favorite Off-Site Hangouts: We had two: Landmark Tavern and Matt's Grill.

Mascot: Emily Bergl had a stuffed tiger and Gabriel Byrne teased her about it so much, it wound up living in Gabriel's room.

Favorite Snack Foods: This cast had a big sweet tooth. A lot of the gang brought us snacks and treats, but Elizabeth Norment, Danny Sherman and Emily Bergl brought a different treat every day, usually some kind of doughnut, cookie or cake.

Favorite Therapies: Emer'gen-C, Ricola, Zicam and Airborne.

Record Number of Cell Phone Rings During a Performance: We had a lot in the first act, and the second act got so bad we finally instituted an after-intermission announcement. On the last Saturday matinee we had ten rings.

Memorable Fan Encounter: We had a group we called The Byrne Ladies who were there to see Gabriel but had absolutely no interest in the rest of the show. They sat in the front rows and when Gabriel left the stage in Act II, seven minutes before the end of the show, they would get up and leave without any regard for the other actors.

Sweethearts in the Company: I'm engaged to Lawrence Jennino, head of properties.

Coolest Thing About Being in This Show: The people I got to meet. It was a wonderful gang.

1. Curtain calls on opening night.
2. (L-R): Gabriel Byrne and director Doug Hughes arrive at the Millennium Broadway Hotel for the opening night party.
3. The marquee of Studio 54.
4. (L-R): Daniel Stewart Sherman and Byron Jennings arrive on opening night.
5. Emily Bergl at the cast party.

The 25th Annual Putnam County Spelling Bee

First Preview: April 15, 2005. Opened: May 2, 2005.
Still running as of May 31, 2006.

CAST

(in alphabetical order)

Mitch Mahoney ....DERRICK BASKIN
Marcy Park ....DEBORAH S. CRAIG
Leaf Coneybear ....JESSE TYLER FERGUSON
William Barfee.........................DAN FOGLER
Rona Lisa Peretti ....LISA HOWARD
Olive Ostrovsky ....CELIA KEENAN-BOLGER
Chip Tolentino ....JOSE LLANA
Douglas Panch ....JAY REISS
Logainne
Schwartzandgrubenierre ......SARAH SALTZBERG

UNDERSTUDIES

For William Barfee, Leaf Coneybear –
TODD BUONOPANE; for Mitch Mahoney –
TODD BUONOPANE, WILLIS WHITE; for Chip
Tolentino – WILLIS WHITE; for Douglas Panch –
TODD BUONOPANE, WILLIS WHITE; for Olive
Ostrovsky, Marcy Park – KATE WETHERHEAD,
LISA YUEN; for Rona Lisa Peretti – LISA YUEN;
for Logainne Schwartzandgrubenierre –
KATE WETHERHEAD

MUSICIANS

Conductor/Piano: Vadim Feichtner
Associate Conductor/Synthesizer: Carmel Dean
Reed: Rick Heckman
Cello: Amy Ralske
Drums/Percussion: Glenn Rhian
Music Coordinator: Michael Keller
Music Copying: Emily Grishman Music Preparation
Emily Grishman/Katharine Edmonds

CIRCLE IN THE SQUARE

UNDER THE DIRECTION OF
THEODORE MANN and PAUL LIBIN

David Stone   James L. Nederlander   Barbara Whitman   Patrick Catullo
Barrington Stage Company   Second Stage Theatre

Present

The 25th Annual Putnam County
SPELLING BEE

Music & Lyrics by
WILLIAM FINN

Book By
RACHEL SHEINKIN

Conceived by
REBECCA FELDMAN

Additional Material by
JAY REISS

With

DERRICK BASKIN, DEBORAH S. CRAIG, JESSE TYLER FERGUSON, DAN FOGLER,
LISA HOWARD, CELIA KEENAN-BOLGER, JOSE LLANA, JAY REISS, SARAH SALTZBERG
TODD BUONOPANE, KATE WETHERHEAD, WILLIS WHITE, LISA YUEN

Set Design by	Costume Design by	Lighting Design by	Sound Design by
BEOWULF BORITT	JENNIFER CAPRIO	NATASHA KATZ	DAN MOSES SCHREIER

Orchestrations by
MICHAEL STAROBIN

Music Director	Vocal Arrangements by	Music Coordinator
VADIM FEICHTNER	CARMEL DEAN	MICHAEL KELLER

Press	Casting
THE PUBLICITY OFFICE	TARA RUBIN CASTING

Production Stage Manager	Production Manager	General Management
ANDREA "SPOOK" TESTANI	KAI BROTHERS	321 THEATRICAL MANAGEMENT

Choreographed by
DAN KNECHTGES

Directed by
JAMES LAPINE

Based on C-R-E-P-U-S-C-U-L-E, an original play by THE FARM.
Original Broadway Cast Recording on GHOSTLIGHT RECORDS.

10/1/05

The pressure is on Jose Llana (center) as the rest of the cast watches.

Photo by Joan Marcus

The 25th Annual Putnam County Spelling Bee

Derrick Baskin
Mitch Mahoney

Deborah S. Craig
Marcy Park

Jesse Tyler Ferguson
Leaf Coneybear

Dan Fogler
William Barfee

Lisa Howard
Rona Lisa Peretti

Celia Keenan-Bolger
Olive Ostrovsky

Jose Llana
Chip Tolentino

Jay Reiss
Douglas Panch

Sarah Saltzberg
*Logainne
Schwartzandgrubenierre*

Todd Buonopane
*Understudy for
Barfee, Coneybear,
Mitch, Mr. Panch*

Kate Wetherhead
*Understudy for Olive,
Marcy and Logainne*

Willis White
*Understudy for
Mitch, Chip,
Mr. Panch*

Lisa Yuen
*Understudy for Olive,
Marcy, Ms. Peretti*

Todd Buonopane *(continued)*
William Finn
Music/Lyrics

Rachel Sheinkin
Book

Rebecca Feldman
Conceiver

James Lapine
Director

Dan Knechtges
Choreographer

Darren Katz
Resident Director

Beowulf Boritt
Set Designer

Jennifer Caprio
Costume Designer

Natasha Katz
Lighting Designer

Dan Moses Schreier
Sound Designer

Michael Starobin
Orchestrations

Vadim Feichtner
*Musical Director/
Dance Arrangements*

Carmel Dean
*Vocal Arranger/
Associate Conductor/
Synthesizer*

Michael Keller
Music Coordinator

Tara Rubin,
Tara Rubin Casting
Casting

Marcia Goldberg, Nancy Nagel Gibbs and
Nina Essman,
321 Theatrical Management
General Management

David Stone
Producer

James L. Nederlander
Producer

Barbara Whitman
Producer

The 25th Annual Putnam County Spelling Bee

TRANSFER STUDENTS 2005-2006

Josh Gad
William Barfee

Maurice Murphy
Understudy for Chip Tolentino and Douglas Panch

Sarah Stiles
Understudy for Olive Ostrovsky, Marcy Park and Logainne Schwartzandgrubenierre

Greg Stuhr
Douglas Panch

Law Tarello
Understudy for William Barfee

Lee Zarrett
Understudy for William Barfee and Leaf Coneybear

ORCHESTRA
Front Row (L-R):
Vadim Feichtner (Music Director),
Carmel Dean (Associate Music Director),
Rick Heckman (Reeds).

Back Row (L-R):
Randy Cohen (Associate Conductor, Sub),
and Dennis Arcano (Percussion, Sub).

HAIR AND WIG DESIGNER
Marty Kopulsky

MANAGEMENT
(L-R): Lisa Koch Rao (Company Manager), Kelly Hance (Stage Manager), Andrea "Spook" Testani (Production Stage Manager) and Jayna Neagle (Management Assistant).

Photos by Ben Strothmann

The 25th Annual Putnam County Spelling Bee

VOLUNTEER WRANGLERS
(L-R):
Keira Fromm and KJ Swanson.

STAGE CREW
Front Row (L-R):
Stephanie Vetter (Deck Sound),
Stewart Wagner (Head Electrician),
Robert Lindsay (Front-of-House Sound Engineer).

Second Row (L-R):
Billy Seelig (Flyman),
Susan Frankel (V.P. Finance for Theatre),
Robert Gordon (Head Carpenter),
and Owen Parmele (Prop Master).

FRONT OF HOUSE STAFF
Front Row (L-R):
Susan Frankel (V.P. Finance for Theatre),
Richard Berg (House Manager),
Tammy Cummisky (Directress),
Stephen Winterhalter (Merchandise Manager),
Whitney Kirk (Merchandiser).

Second Row (L-R):
Steve Chappell (Bar Manager),
Xavier Yaing (Usher),
Michael Trupia (Usher),
Anthony Martinez (Usher),
Laurel Brevoort (Usher).

Back Row (L-R):
Linda Rajotte (Usher),
Vinnie Palumbo (Usher),
Andrew Olver (Usher),
Sophie Koufakis (Usher)
and Margarita Caban (Usher)

The 25th Annual Putnam County Spelling Bee

Jesse Tyler
Ferguson

Photo by Joan Marcus

The 25th Annual Putnam County Spelling Bee
SCRAPBOOK

Photos by Aubrey Reuben

Correspondent: Todd Buonopane, "William Barfee"

Easter Bonnet Sketch: Sarah Saltzberg came up with the idea of two huskier guys doing a pas de deux to the *Brokeback Mountain* club-mix. She layered in Bush-isms from 2005. A fantastic dancer named Laurence Goldhuber danced with me (I got lifted for the first time ever!!) Our bonnet was a huge cowboy hat that said "Worst President Ever." We were a big hit.

"Carols for a Cure" Carol: "The 25th Annual Putnam County Spelling Bee Massacres 'The 12 Days of Christmas.'"

"Gypsy of the Year" Sketch: "John Doyle's *Spelling Bee*" by Jesse Tyler Ferguson and Vadim Feichtner.

Favorite In-Theatre Gathering Place: The greenroom. We have a great greenroom with all of our hand prints painted on the walls. No one starts getting ready till "fifteen minutes." We hang and talk as long as possible.

Favorite Off-Site Hangout: The Palm, Harmony View, and World Wide Plaza.

Favorite Snack Food: Whatever pastries Jose brings into the green room. Usually Starbucks treats or Dunkin Donuts.

Mascot: The Pandas from the dirty show.

Most Memorable Ad-Lib: "WHO DID IT?!" Dan Fogler said this upon entering and smelling the stinky one Jesse had just released.

Catchphrases Only the Company Would Recognize: "I'm just doing my *YOB*." "My eyes, my Christmas eyes!!"

Nicknames: Sarah S. is "Salty." Jose is "Josers." Celia is "Ceels." Jesse is "Kitty." Lisa Y. is "Coco." Derrick is "D." Maurice is "Mo." Josh is "Jason." Lisa H. is "Leelee." I am "Toddy" or "Toddles."

Sweethearts Within the Company: Tom Cruise and Katie Holmes. They joined the cast recently and are so damn cute. We are really rooting for them for the Best Replacement Tony!

Favorite/Craziest Volunteer Spellers:
1. Looney Tunes Jacket Guy.
2. Dusty Jacket Old Guy.
3. Young Mr. Patel, who got the farthest.

1. The cast attends a CD signing at Barnes & Noble/Lincoln Center.
2. Jose Llana at Stars in the Alley.
3. (L-R): Sarah Saltzberg, Lisa Howard and Derrick Baskin at Joe's Pub for fellow cast member Jesse Tyler Ferguson's cabaret show.
4. William Finn (R) surprises Jesse Tyler Ferguson with a hug.
5. Llana, Howard and Todd Buonopane perform their opening number a la *Sweeney Todd* at "Gypsy of the Year."
6. Fogler on the night he won a 2005 Tony Award.
7. Sara Ramirez (L, *Spamalot*) and Sarah Saltzberg (R) congratulate Ferguson after his show at Joe's Pub.

The Wedding Singer

First Preview: March 30, 2006. Opened: April 27, 2006.
Still running as of May 31, 2006.

CAST

(in order of appearance)

Robbie Hart ....STEPHEN LYNCH
Sammy ....MATTHEW SALDIVAR
George ....KEVIN CAHOON
Julia Sullivan ....LAURA BENANTI
Holly...................................AMY SPANGER
Glen Guglia ....RICHARD H. BLAKE
Rosie ....RITA GARDNER
Linda ....FELICIA FINLEY
Angie ....ADINAH ALEXANDER
Impersonators ....TRACEE BEAZER,
CARA COOPER,
PETER KAPETAN,
J. ELAINE MARCOS,
T. OLIVER REID,
CHRISTINA SIVRICH,
MATTHEW STOCKE
Ensemble ....ADINAH ALEXANDER,
MATT ALLEN, TRACEE BEAZER,
CARA COOPER,
ASHLEY AMBER HAASE,
NICOLETTE HART,
DAVID JOSEFSBERG,
PETER KAPETAN,
SPENCER LIFF,
J. ELAINE MARCOS,
T. OLIVER REID,
CHRISTINA SIVRICH,
MATTHEW STOCKE,
ERIC LAJUAN SUMMERS

Continued on next page

♩ AL HIRSCHFELD THEATRE

A JUJAMCYN THEATRE
ROCCO LANDESMAN
PRESIDENT

PAUL LIBIN   JACK VIERTEL
PRODUCING DIRECTOR   CREATIVE DIRECTOR

MARGO LION   NEW LINE CINEMA   THE ARACA GROUP
ROY FURMAN   DOUGLAS L. MEYER / JAMES D. STERN
RICK STEINER / THE STATON BELL OSHER MAYERSON GROUP   JAM THEATRICALS

in association with

JUJAMCYN THEATERS

and

JAY FURMAN   MICHAEL GILL   DR. LAWRENCE HOROWITZ   RHODA MAYERSON
MARISA SECHREST   GARY WINNICK   DANCAP PRODUCTIONS, INC.   ÉLAN V. McALLISTER / ALLAN S. GORDON / ADAM EPSTEIN

present

the WEDDING SINGER

music by
MATTHEW SKLAR
book by
CHAD BEGUELIN and TIM HERLIHY
lyrics by
CHAD BEGUELIN

BASED UPON THE NEW LINE CINEMA FILM
WRITTEN BY TIM HERLIHY

starring

STEPHEN LYNCH   LAURA BENANTI

RICHARD H. BLAKE   KEVIN CAHOON   FELICIA FINLEY
TINA MADDIGAN   MATTHEW SALDIVAR   AMY SPANGER

and

RITA GARDNER

ADINAH ALEXANDER   MATT ALLEN   TRACEE BEAZER   CARA COOPER
ASHLEY AMBER HAASE   NICOLETTE HART   ANGELIQUE ILO
DAVID JOSEFSBERG   PETER KAPETAN   KEVIN KERN   SPENCER LIFF
JOANNE MANNING   J. ELAINE MARCOS   MICHAEL McGURK   T. OLIVER REID
CHRISTINA SIVRICH   MATTHEW STOCKE   ERIC LAJUAN SUMMERS

scenic design   costume design   lighting design   sound design
SCOTT PASK   GREGORY GALE   BRIAN MacDEVITT   PETER HYLENSKI

casting by   hair design   make-up design
BERNARD TELSEY CASTING   DAVID BRIAN BROWN   JOE DULUDE II

orchestrations   incidental & dance music arranger   music director/conductor
IRWIN FISCH   DAVID CHASE   JAMES SAMPLINER

executive producer   production manager   associate choreographer   production stage manager
MARK KAUFMAN   JUNIPER STREET PRODUCTIONS   JOANN M. HUNTER   ROLT SMITH

press representative   marketing   music coordinator   general management
RICHARD KORNBERG   THE ARACA GROUP   JOHN MILLER   THE CHARLOTTE WILCOX
DON SUMMA   COMPANY

choreographed by
ROB ASHFORD

directed by
JOHN RANDO

The world premiere of "The Wedding Singer" was produced with The 5th Avenue Theatre in Seattle, Washington,
David Armstrong, Producing Artistic Director, Marilynn Sheldon, Managing Director.

Original Broadway Cast Recording on Sony Classical, a division of Sony BMG Masterworks,
an operating unit of Sony BMG Music Entertainment.

The producers wish to express their appreciation to Theatre Development Fund for its support of this production.

4/27/06

Stephen Lynch (center) and the ensemble perform "Casualty of Love.".

Photo by Joan Marcus

The Wedding Singer

SCENES AND MUSICAL NUMBERS

Ridgefield, NJ, 1985

ACT ONE

Scene 1: Reception Hall
"It's Your Wedding Day" .... Robbie and Company
"Someday" .... Julia
Scene 2: The Loading Dock
Scene 3: Robbie's Bedroom
"Someday" (Reprise) .... Robbie, Rosie
Scene 4: Reception Hall
"A Note From Linda" .... Linda
Scene 5: The Restaurant
"Pop" .... Holly, Julia, Angie and Company
Scene 6: Robbie's Bedroom
"Somebody Kill Me"* .... Robbie
"A Note From Grandma" .... Rosie
Scene 7: Reception Hall
"Casualty of Love" .... Robbie and Company
Scene 8: The Loading Dock
"Come Out of the Dumpster" .... Julia, Robbie
Scene 9: Reception Hall
"Today You Are a Man" .... Robbie, Sammy, George
"George's Prayer" .... George
Scene 10: The Mall
"Not That Kind of Thing" .... Robbie, Julia and Company
Scene 11: Holly's Closet/The Club
"Saturday Night in the City" .... Holly and Company

ACT TWO

Scene 1: Glen's Office
"All About the Green" .... Glen, Robbie and Company
Scene 2: Reception Hall
"Right in Front of Your Eyes" .... Holly, Sammy
Scene 3: Rosie's Porch
Scene 4: The Bar
"Single" .... Sammy, Robbie, George, Ricky, Bum and Men
Scene 5: Julia's Bedroom
"If I Told You" .... Robbie, Julia
Scene 6: Robbie's Bedroom
"Let Me Come Home" .... Linda
Scene 7: Reception Hall
"If I Told You" (Reprise) .... Robbie, Julia
"Move That Thang" .... Rosie, George
Scene 8: White House Wedding Chapel, Las Vegas
"Grow Old With You"* .... Robbie, Julia
Scene 9: Reception Hall
"It's Your Wedding Day" (Finale) .... The Company

* Written by Adam Sandler and Tim Herlihy

(L-R): Peter Kapetan, Eric Lajuan Summers, Matthew Saldivar and Kevin Cahoon perform "Single."

SWINGS
ANGELIQUE ILO, KEVIN KERN,
JOANNE MANNING, MICHAEL McGURK

Standby for Julia Sullivan:
TINA MADDIGAN

UNDERSTUDIES
For Robbie Hart:
MATTHEW STOCKE
For Holly:
CARA COOPER
For George, Glen Guglia:
KEVIN KERN
For Sammy:
DAVID JOSEFSBERG
For Linda:
NICOLETTE HART
For Rosie:
CHRISTINA SIVRICH

Dance Captains .... ANGELIQUE ILO,
MICHAEL McGURK

ORCHESTRA
Conductor: JAMES SAMPLINER

Associate Conductor: JOHN SAMORIAN

Guitars:
LARRY SALTZMAN, STEPHEN LYNCH,
JOHN PUTNAM, GARY SIEGER
Keyboards:
JAMES SAMPLINER, JOHN SAMORIAN,
JON WERKING
Bass:
IRIO O'FARRILL, MATTHEW SALDIVAR
Drums:
WARREN ODZE
Reeds:
CLIFFORD LYONS, JACK BASHKOW
Trumpet:
TREVOR NEUMANN
Percussion:
JAMES SAPORITO

Music Coordinator:
JOHN MILLER

Electronic Musical Instrument Programmer:
IRWIN FISCH

Music Copying:
EMILY GRISHMAN MUSIC PREPARATION/
EMILY GRISHMAN, KATHARINE EDMONDS

The Wedding Singer

Stephen Lynch
Robbie Hart

Laura Benanti
Julia Sullivan

Rita Gardner
Rosie

Richard H. Blake
Glen Guglia

Kevin Cahoon
George

Felicia Finley
Linda

Matthew Saldivar
Sammy

Amy Spanger
Holly

Tina Maddigan
*Standby
Julia Sullivan*

Adinah Alexander
Ensemble/Angie

Matt Allen
Ensemble

Tracee Beazer
*Ensemble,
Impersonator*

Cara Cooper
Ensemble

Ashley Amber Haase
Ensemble

Nicolette Hart
Ensemble

Angelique Ilo
*Dance Captain,
Swing*

David Josefsberg
Ensemble, David

Peter Kapetan
*Ensemble,
Impersonator*

Kevin Kern
Swing

Spencer Liff
Ensemble

Joanne Manning
Swing

J. Elaine Marcos
*Ensemble,
Impersonator*

Michael McGurk
Swing

T. Oliver Reid
*Ensemble,
Impersonator*

Christina Sivrich
*Ensemble,
Impersonator*

Matthew Stocke
*Ensemble,
Impersonator*

Eric Lajuan Summers
Ensemble

Matthew Sklar
Composer

Chad Beguelin
Book/Lyrics

Tim Herlihy
Book

John Rando
Director

Rob Ashford
Choreographer

Scott Pask
Scenic Design

Gregory Gale
Costume Design

Brian MacDevitt
Lighting Design

The Wedding Singer

Peter Hylenski
Sound Design

David Brian Brown
Wig/Hair Design

Joe Dulude II
Makeup Design

Bernard Telsey
Casting, C.S.A.
Casting

Richard Kornberg,
Richard Kornberg &
Associates
*Press
Representative*

Irwin Fisch
Orchestrator

James Sampliner
*Music Director/
Conductor*

John Miller
Music Coordinator

Anne McMills
*Assistant Lighting
Designer*

Eric Mack
*Merchandising
Manager*

JoAnn M. Hunter
*Associate
Choreographer*

Charlotte Wilcox,
The Charlotte Wilcox
Company
General Manager

Guy Kwan, John Paull III, Hillary Blanken,
Kevin Broomell, Ana Rose Greene,
Juniper Street Productions
Production Manager

Jen Bender
Assistant Director

Margo Lion
Producer

Mark Kaufman,
New Line Cinema
Producer

Roy Furman
Producer

Douglas L. Meyer
Producer

Rick Steiner
Producer

John and Bonnie
Osher
Producers

Dan Staton
Producer

Frederic H.
Mayerson
Producer

Rocco Landesman,
President
Jujamcyn Theaters
Producer

Michael Gill
Producer

Lawrence Horowitz,
M.D.
Producer

Rhoda Mayerson
Associate Producer

Marisa Sechrest
Producer

Elan V. McAllister
Producer

Allan S. Gordon
Producer

Adam Epstein
Producer

The Wedding Singer

Photo by Melissa Merlo

STAGE CREW
Kneeling (L-R): John Anderson (Carpenter), Andy Trotto (Props), Corina Frerotte (Props), Billy Vandebogart (Flyman)

Second Row (L-R): Ron Martin (Electrician), Dermot Lynch (House Electrician), John Blixt (Lead Spot), Aaron Straus (Deck Sound), Angelo Torre (Props), David Dignazio (Production Sound Engineer), Joe Maher (House Carpenter)

Third Row (L-R): Dan Ansbro (Spot Operator) and Tom Sherman (Carpenter)

Fourth Row (L-R): Eric Norris (Head Electrician), Ian Michaud (Automation Carpenter), Hank Hale (Head Carpenter) and Sal Sclafani (House Props)

NOT PICTURED: Eric 'Speed' Smith (Automation Flyman).

STAGE MANAGEMENT
(L-R):
Scott Rowen, Jamie Thoma, Janet Takami, Rolt Smith and Julie Baldauff.

Photo by Ben Strothmann

FRONT OF HOUSE STAFF
Front Row (L-R): Erica Jones, Fernando Colon, Julie Burnham, Henry Menendez, Mary Marzin, Donald L. Royal.

Middle Row (L-R): Hallie Miller, Tristan Blacer, Alberta McJamee, Kerri Gillen, Ralph Santos, Bart Ryan.

Back Row (L-R): Donald Morrell, Alexander Gotierrez, Lorraine Feeks, Mrs. Carmel Robinson (House Manager), Janice Rodriguez and Roberto Ellington.

Photo by Melissa Merlo

WARDROBE DEPARTMENT
Front Row (L-R): Jenny Barnes (Dresser), Julienne Schubert-Blechman (Dresser), Leslie Thompson (Dresser), Kay Gowenlock (Dresser).

Middle Row (L-R): Mary Ann Lewis-Oberpriller (Dresser), Tina Clifton (Dresser), Jason Heisey (Dresser).

Back Row (L-R): Chip White (Dresser), Tree Sarvay (Dresser), Alice Bee (Dresser), Danny Paul (Dresser) and Rick Kelly (Wardrobe Supervisor).

Photo by Melissa Merlo

The Wedding Singer

Staff for THE WEDDING SINGER

GENERAL MANAGEMENT
THE CHARLOTTE WILCOX COMPANY
Charlotte Wilcox
Matthew W. Krawiec   Emily Lawson
Steve Supeck   Margaret Wilcox   Beth Cochran

GENERAL PRESS REPRESENTATIVE
RICHARD KORNBERG & ASSOCIATES
Richard Kornberg   Don Summa
Carrie Friedman

MARKETING
THE ARACA GROUP
Clint Bond, Jr.   Kirsten Berkman   Drew Padrutt
John Wiseman

COMPANY MANAGER
Edward Nelson

ASSOCIATE COMPANY MANAGER
Beverly Edwards

CASTING
BERNARD TELSEY CASTING C.S.A.
Bernie Telsey, Will Cantler, David Vaccari,
Bethany Knox, Craig Burns,
Tiffany Little Canfield, Stephanie Yankwitt,
Betsy Sherwood, Carrie Rosson, Justin Huff

PRODUCTION MANAGEMENT
JUNIPER STREET PRODUCTIONS
Hillary Blanken   Guy Kwan
Kevin Broomell   Ana Rose Greene

PRODUCTION STAGE MANAGER	Rolt Smith
Stage Manager	Julie Baldauff
Assistant Stage Manager	Janet Takami
Dance Captain	Angelique Ilo
Assistant Dance Captain	Michael McGurk
Associate Choreographer	JoAnn M. Hunter
Assistant Director	Jen Bender
Associate Scenic Designer	Orit Jacoby Carroll
Assistant Scenic Designers	Lauren Alvarez, Edmund LeFevre
Assistant to the Scenic Designer	Jeff Hinchee
Associate Costume Designer	Brian Russman
Assistant Costume Designer	Janine Marie McCabe
Assistants to the Costume Designer	Rachel Attridge, Tracey Herman, David Withrow
Associate Lighting Designer	Charles Pennebaker
Assistant Lighting Designers	Rachel Eichorn, Anne McMills
Automated Lighting Programmer	Timothy F. Rogers
Assistant Sound Designer	T.J. McEvoy
Associate Hair/Wig Designer	Josh Marquette
Production Carpenter	Tony Menditto
Production Electrician	Dan Coey
Production Properties	Joseph P. Harris Jr.
Head Carpenter	Hank Hale
Assistant Carpenters	Ian Michaud, Tom Sherman, Eric Smith
Head Electrician	Eric Norris
Assistant Electrician	Ron Martin
Head Properties	Christopher Pantuso
Assistant Properties	Angelo Torre
Head Sound	David Dignazio
Assistant Sound	Tim Pritchard
Production Wardrobe Supervisor	Rick Kelly
Assistant Wardrobe Supervisor	Sarah Schaub
Dressers	Jenny Barnes, Gary Biangone, Tina Clifton, Jane Davis, Kay Gowenlock, Jason Heisey, Mary Lewis-Oberpriller, Danny Paul, Tree Sarvay, Leslie Thompson, Franc Weinperl, Chip White
Hair Supervisor	Carole Morales
Assistant Hair Supervisor	Tom Augustine
Hair Dressers	Wanda Gregory, Joel Hawkins, Jodi Jackson
Associate Producer/Margo Lion Ltd.	Lily Hung
Assistant to Executive Producer	Alexandra Loewy
Assistant to Margo Lion Ltd.	T. Rick Hayashi
Keyboard and Electronic Music Technician	Scott Reisett
Press Intern	Alyssa Hart
Assistants to the Araca Group	Maryana Geller, Aaron Schwartzbord
MIDI Consultants	Scott Riesett, Nick Vidar
Production Assistants	Scott Rowen, Sara Sahin, Jamie Rose Thoma, Sunneva Stapleton
SSDC Observer	Paul Stancato
Costume Intern	Mike Kale
Dialogue Coach	Deborah Hecht
Legal Counsel	Feitelson, Lasky, Aslan & Couture/ Jerold L. Couture
Accountants	Fried & Kowgios CPA's LLP/ Robert Fried, CPA
Controller	Sarah Galbraith
Advertising	Serino Coyne/ Greg Corradetti, Ruth Rosenberg, Andrea Prince, Natalie Serota
Group Sales	Show Tix
Merchandise	Araca Merch/ Anne MacLean, Philip McBride, Joey Boyles, Karen Davidov, Audra Ewing, Zach Lezberg, Julie Monahan, Bryan Pace, Peter Pergola
Website Design	Situation Marketing LLC/ Damian Bazadona
Production Photography	Joan Marcus
Additional Photography	Bruce Glikas
Banking	J.P. Morgan Chase
Payroll Service	Castellana Services, Inc.
Insurance Consultant	Stockbridge Risk Management/ Neil Goldstein
Theatre Displays	King Displays
Air Travel Services	Tzell Travel
Hotel and Ground Travel Services	Road Rebel

Souvenir merchandise designed and created by
Araca Merch, LLC
www.aracamerch.com or (212) 869-0070

CREDITS

Scenery fabricated and painted by Hudson Scenic Studio, Inc. Scenery fabrication by Scenic Technologies, a division of Production Resource Group, LLC, New Windsor, NY. Show control and scenic motion control featuring stage command systems® by Scenic Technologies, a division of Production Resource Group, LLC, New Windsor, NY. Scenic elements by Cigar Box Studios, Spoon Group, Seattle Opera. Scenic elements painted by Scenic Arts Studio. Water effect by Jauchem and Meeh Inc. Drapery by I. Weiss. Costumes constructed by Barbara Matera Ltd.; Euro Co Costumes; Jennifer Love Costumes; John Kristiansen NY Inc.; Vanson Leather; Timberlake Studios; Rawhides Custom Leatherwear; TRICORNE, INC.; and Western Costume Co. Custom boots and shoes by Fredrick Longtin Handmade Shoes; J.C. Theatrical & Custom Footwear; T.O. Dey Custom Shoes; Celebrity Dance Shoes; Elegance Dance Shoes; and Worldtone Dance Shoes. Custom veils and millinery by Rodney Gordon, Inc. Custom knitwear by C.C. Wei. Fabric painting by Hochi Asiatico. Custom jewelry by Martin Lopez and Larry Vrba. Sunglasses provided by Ray Ban. Custom Shirts by Sandy Perlmutter at Allmeier. Built props fabricated by Spoon Group. Floral arrangements by Portafiori Floral Design Studio. Tablecloth linens by Cloth Connection. Lighting equipment from PRG Lighting. Sound equipment from PRG Audio. Wigs by Ray Marston London. Throat lozenges provided by Ricola. Special thanks to Bra*Tenders for hosiery and undergarments.

Makeup provided by M·A·C

Gibson guitars, Epiphone guitars and Slingerland Drums provided by Gibson Musical Instruments. Musical equipment provided by Alto Music; Yamaha Corporation of America. Receptors provided by Muse Research. Amp simulators provided by Line 6 Electronics.

The Wedding Singer
rehearsed at the New 42nd Street Studios.

JUJAMCYN THEATERS

ROCCO LANDESMAN
President

PAUL LIBIN	**JACK VIERTEL**
Producing Director	Creative Director
JERRY ZAKS	**JORDAN ROTH**
Resident Director	Resident Producer
DANIEL ADAMIAN	**JENNIFER HERSHEY**
General Manager	Director of Operations

MEREDITH VILLATORE
Chief Financial Officer

Staff for the Al Hirschfeld Theatre

Manager	Carmel Gunther
Treasurer	Carmine La Mendola
Carpenter	Joseph J. Maher, Jr.
Propertyman	Sal Sclafani
Electrician	Dermot J. Lynch
Engineer	Vladimir Belenky

The Wedding Singer

SCRAPBOOK

Correspondent: Felicia Finley, "Linda"

Memorable Opening Night Note: Definitely J. Elaine Marcos' pamphlet called "The I-Melta-Da Fat OFF Workout" by Imelda Marcos (her character in the show)! Hilarious!

Opening Night Gifts: I LOVE the *Wedding Singer* warm-up jacket.

Who Got the Gypsy Robe? Big la da da moment! It was handed to Ashley Haase, but T. Oliver Reid ended up with it! Long story…

Actor Who Performed the Most Roles in This Show: I have one thing to say: "Our ensemble rocks it hard."

Special Backstage Ritual: I love our "1-2-3 Wedding Singer" moment as a company. It's truly amazing to see these amazing people unite before a show.

Favorite Moment During Each Performance (On Stage or Off): There are so many. Personally, I love walking up the stairs from the pit to do "Linda's Note"—always fun!

Favorite In-Theatre Gathering Place: I like the second floor!

Favorite Off-Site Hangout: Angus McIndoe, Vintage, Mercury Bar, Kodama.

Favorite Snack Food: Wine.

Mascot: My new dog—six months old, named "Jesse" for "Jesse's Girl." She's my heart.

Favorite Therapy: Massage.

Memorable Ad-Lib: "You know Robbie, let's do, you know…you know…the (I grunted here) thing." Wow. Really not anything understandable. Stephen repeated *exactly* what I said back to me and we fell apart off-stage. Funny moment.

Record Number of Cell Phone Rings During a Performance: None! Yeah!

Memorable Stage Door Fan Encounter: "Oh my God! I saw you as Amneris and now Amneris is stripping! Cool!"

Busiest Day at the Box Office: Love seeing lines around the block to Eighth Avenue. Such a great sight!

Who Wore the Heaviest/Hottest Costume: Easy. Tracee Beazer as Tina Turner.

Who Wore the Least: Me!

Company Legend: Rita Gardner!

Sweethearts Within the Company: Paul Stancato (Rob Ashford's SSDC Assistant) and Felicia Finley.

Embarrassing Moment: Being Linda.

Coolest Thing About Being in This Show: I love it with all my heart. There's *nothing* better than pure laughter!

1. Curtain call on opening night.
2. Felicia Finley at the opening night party at Crobar.
3. Librettist Tim Herlihy at Crobar.
4. Rita Gardner rehearses with Stephen Lynch at the New 42nd Street Studios.
5. Amy Spanger and lyricist Chad Beguelin at the opening night party.

Well

First Preview: March 10, 2006. Opened: March 30, 2006.
Closed May 14, 2006 after 23 Previews and 53 Performances.

PLAYBILL

WeLL

CAST
(in order of appearance)

Lisa ....LISA KRON
Ann ....JAYNE HOUDYSHELL
Nurse, and others ....JOHN HOFFMAN
Kay, and others .....SAIDAH ARRIKA EKULONA
Jim, and others ....DANIEL BREAKER
Joy, and others ....CHRISTINA KIRK

Stage Manager: ALLISON SOMMERS

STANDBYS
For Ms. Kron:
CINDY KATZ

For Ms. Houdyshell and Ms. Kirk:
RANDY DANSON

UNDERSTUDIES
For Ms. Ekulona:
DONNETTA LAVINIA GRAYS

For Mr. Breaker:
COLMAN DOMINGO

For Mr. Hoffman:
JOEL VAN LIEW

2005-2006 AWARD

THEATRE WORLD AWARD
Outstanding Broadway Debut
(Jayne Houdyshell)

---

⑤ LONGACRE THEATRE
220 West 48th Street
A Shubert Organization Theatre

Gerald Schoenfeld, *Chairman*   Philip J. Smith, *President*

Robert E. Wankel, *Executive Vice President*

ELIZABETH IRELAND McCANN   SCOTT RUDIN
BOYETT OSTAR PRODUCTIONS   TRUE LOVE PRODUCTIONS   TERRY ALLEN KRAMER
ROGER BERLIND   CAROLE SHORENSTEIN HAYS   JOHN DIAS
JOEY PARNES
EXECUTIVE PRODUCER
IN ASSOCIATION WITH
LARRY HIRSCHHORN
AND
THE PUBLIC THEATER AND THE AMERICAN CONSERVATORY THEATRE
PRESENT

WeLL
BY LISA KRON
STARRING
LISA KRON
WITH

DANIEL   SAIDAH ARRIKA   JOHN   CHRISTINA
BREAKER   EKULONA   HOFFMAN   KIRK
AND
JAYNE HOUDYSHELL

SCENIC DESIGN	COSTUME DESIGN	LIGHTING DESIGN	ORIGINAL MUSIC & SOUND DESIGN
TONY WALTON	MIRANDA HOFFMAN	CHRISTOPHER AKERLIND	JOHN GROMADA
HAIR & WIG DESIGN	PRODUCTION STAGE MANAGER		CASTING
TOM WATSON	SUSIE CORDON		JAY BINDER, CSA JACK BOWDAN, CSA
ASSOCIATE GENERAL MANAGER	PRESS REPRESENTATIVE		MARKETING
ELIZABETH M. BLITZER	BONEAU BRYAN-BROWN		TMG THE MARKETING GROUP

DIRECTED BY
LEIGH SILVERMAN

ORIGINAL NEW YORK PRODUCTION OF WELL WAS PRODUCED BY THE PUBLIC THEATER.
MARA MANUS, EXECUTIVE DIRECTOR; GEORGE C. WOLFE, PRODUCER
AND SUBSEQUENTLY BY THE AMERICAN CONSERVATORY THEATRE IN SAN FRANCISCO.
CAREY PERLOFF, ARTISTIC DIRECTOR; HEATHER KITCHEN, EXECUTIVE DIRECTOR

THE PRODUCERS WISH TO EXPRESS THEIR APPRECIATION TO THEATRE DEVELOPMENT FUND
FOR ITS SUPPORT OF THIS PRODUCTION.

3/30/06

Photo by Michal Daniel

(L-R): Lisa Kron and Jayne Houdyshell

Well

Lisa Kron
Playwright/Lisa

Jayne Houdyshell
Ann

Daniel Breaker
Jim, and others

Saidah Arrika Ekulona
Kay, and others

John Hoffman
Nurse, and others

Christina Kirk
Joy, and others

Randy Danson
Standby for Ann, Joy, and others

Colman Domingo
Understudy for Jim, and others

Donnetta Lavinia Grays
Understudy for Kay, and others

Cindy Katz
Standby for Lisa Kron

Joel Van Liew
Understudy for Nurse, and others

Leigh Silverman
Director

Tony Walton
Scenic Design

Miranda Hoffman
Costume Design

Christopher Akerlind
Lighting Design

John Gromada
Original Music and Sound Design

Tom Watson
Wig Design

Elizabeth Ireland McCann
Producer

Scott Rudin
Producer

Bob Boyett
Producer

Jeanne Donovan Fisher,
True Love Productions
Producer

Laurie Williams,
True Love Productions
Producer

Terry Allen Kramer
Producer

Roger Berlind
Producer

Carole Shorenstein Hays
Producer

John Dias
Producer

Joey Parnes
Executive Producer

Larry Hirschhorn
Associate Producer

Oskar Eustis,
*Artistic Director
Public Theater*

Mara Manus,
*Executive Director
Public Theater*

Carey Perloff,
*Artistic Director
American
Conservatory
Theater*

Bill Haber,
Boyett Ostar
Productions
Producer

Elizabeth M. Blitzer
*Associate
General Manager*

Marty Kopulsky
*Hair and Wig
Designer*

Jay Binder C.S.A.
Casting

Well

STAGE CREW
Kneeling: Ric Rogers (House Electrician).
Standing (L-R): Wayne Smith (Production Sound), John James (Hair Supervisor), Dave Olin Rogers (Wardrobe Supervisor), Francine Buryiak (Dresser), Julienne Schubert-Blechman (Dresser), Michael Smanko (Production Props Supervisor), John Lofgren (House Prop Head), Ed White (House Carpenter) and Joe Goldman (Stagehand).

FRONT OF HOUSE STAFF
Sitting: Russ Ramsey (Theatre Manager).
Standing (L-R): John Mallon (Usher), John Washman (Usher), Eileen Derann (Usher), Richard Guzman (Usher), Julie MacKenzie (Usher), Kathleen Spock (Usher), Brendan Wilhelm (Usher), Marian Mooney (Usher), Denise Eckels (Usher) and Rita Sussman (Infra-Red Headset Distributor).

Well

STAGE MANAGEMENT
(L-R): Elizabeth M. Blitzer (Associate General Manager/ Company Manager), Brian Rardin (Assistant Stage Manager), Susie Cordon (Production Stage Manager) and Allison Sommers (Stage Manager).

Photos by Ben Strothmann

BOX OFFICE
Patricia Kenary (Treasurer).

STAFF FOR *WELL*

GENERAL MANAGEMENT
JOEY PARNES
John Johnson   Christina Huschle

GENERAL PRESS REPRESENTATIVES
BONEAU/BRYAN-BROWN
Chris Boneau   Jackie Green
Susanne Tighe   Matt Ross

CASTING
JAY BINDER CASTING
Jay Binder CSA, Jack Bowdan CSA,
Mark Brandon, Megan Larche
Assistants: Rachel Shapiro, Diana Giattino

COMPANY MANAGER
ELIZABETH M. BLITZER

ASSISTANT PRODUCER
S.D. Wagner

PRODUCTION PHOTOGRAPHER
Joan Marcus

Production Stage Manager ....Susie Cordon
Stage Manager ....Allison Sommers
Dramaturg ....John Dias
Assistant to the Director ....Katherine Peter Kovner

Associate Set Designer ....Kelly Hanson
Associate Lighting Designer ....Michael Spadaro
Associate Costume Designer ....Brian J. Bustos
Associate Sound Designer ....Christopher Cronin
Assistant Sound Designer ....David S. Baker

Production Carpenter ....Larry Morley
Production Electrician ....Steve Cochrane
Production Props Supervisor ....Mike Smanko
Production Sound Operator ....Wayne Smith
Hair Supervisor ....John James
Wardrobe Supervisor ....Dave Olin Rogers
Dressers ....Francine Buryiak,
Julienne Schubert-Blechman
Production Assistant ....Marti McIntosh
Assistant to Lisa Kron ....Emily Campbell

Executive Assistant to Scott Rudin ....Michael Diliberti
Assistants to Mr. Boyett ....Diane Murphy, Tom Alberg,
Michael Mandell
Assistants to Mr. Haber ....Theresa Pisanelli,
Andrew Cleghorn
True Love Productions Associate ....Tom Cole
Assistant to Mr. Berlind ....Jeffrey Hillock
Literary Manager ....Gaydon Phillips
Advertising..SpotCo/
Drew Hodges, Jim Edwards,
John Lanasa, Kim Smarsh
Marketing ....TMG - The Marketing Group/
Tanya Grubich, Laura Matalon,
Trish Santini, Ronnie Seif,
Laura LaPonte, Meghan Zaneski
Website Design/
Online Marketing ....Situation Marketing LLC/
Damian Bazadona, Lisa Cecchini
Accounting ....Rosenberg, Neuwirth & Kuchner/
Mark A. D'Ambrosi, Patricia Pedersen
Banking ....JPMorgan Chase Bank/
Stephanie Dalton, Richard Callian,
Michele Gibbons
Insurance ....AON/Albert G. Ruben/
George Walden, Claudia Kaufman
Payroll ....Castellana Services Inc./
Lance Castellana
Legal ....Loeb & Loeb/
Seth Gelblum, Stephan Schick
Production Physician ....Dr. Barry Kohn, MD
Opening Night Coordinators ..Tobak Lawrence Company/
Suzanne Tobak, Michael P. Lawrence

CREDITS
Certain scenic effects built, painted, electrified and auto-mated by Showmotion, Inc., Norwalk, CT. Certain scenic effects by Centerline, Inc. Lighting equipment by PRG Lighting. Sound equipment by PRG Sound. Fly automa-tion, show control and breakaway effects by Showmotion, Inc., Norwalk, CT, using the AC2 computerized motion control system. Miss Kron's costumes executed by Tricorne, Inc. Costumes executed by Studio Rouge. Millinery by Lynne Mackey Studio. Flying by Foy. Custom dyeing and screen printing by Gene Mignola, Inc. Emergen-C vitamin C drink mix provided by Alacer Corp. Chair provided by La-Z-Boy Galleries, Clifton, Springfield and Woodbridge, New Jersey.

Rehearsed at the Roundabout Rehearsal Studio

www.wellonbroadway.com

SPECIAL THANKS FROM LISA & LEIGH
Special thanks to the following people and institutions who were instrumental in the development of *Well*: Kenajuan Bentley, Robert Blacker, Jocelyn Clarke, Martha Donaldson, Jill B.C. DuBoff, Greg Leaming, Allen Moyer, Lola Pashalinkski, A-men Rasheed, Charlotte Stoudt, Welker White, Baltimore Center Stage, Hartford Stage, Long Wharf Theatre, the NEA/TCG Playwrighting Fellowship Program and New York Theatre Workshop.

SPECIAL THANKS
Mary Harper, Lily Tomlin, Paul Rudnick, Janet Beroza, Connie Buck/Saks Fifth Avenue, Jason Fontenot, Ricola, U.S.A., Emergen-C.

THE SHUBERT ORGANIZATION, INC.
Board of Directors

Gerald Schoenfeld	**Philip J. Smith**
Chairman	President
Wyche Fowler, Jr.	**John W. Kluge**
Lee J. Seidler	**Michael I. Sovern**
Stuart Subotnick	

Robert E. Wankel
Executive Vice President

Peter Entin	**Elliot Greene**
Vice President -	Vice President -
Theatre Operations	Finance
David Andrews	**John Darby**
Vice President -	Vice President -
Shubert Ticketing Services	Facilities

House Manager ....Russ Ramsey

Well

SCRAPBOOK

Correspondent: Saidah Arrika Ekulona, "Kay and Others."

Memorable Opening Night Letter, Fax or Note: We got faxes from *Doubt* and a few other companies. One of the best things I got was a note from one of the producers, Larry Hirschhorn, who also has his own theatre company, Melting Pot Theatre, where I did my first show in New York back in 1997. Both of us are starting our Broadway careers with this production, so it was momentous and heartwarming to me.

Opening Night Gifts: We all got grabbers like the ones Lisa Kron uses in the show. The producers gave us each a silver pillbox with *Well* and the opening date inscribed on it.

Most Exciting Celebrity Visitors and What They Said: John Guare the playwright said "You are magnificent" and Tyne Daly thanked me for my work.

Which Actor Performed the Most Roles in This Show: I do. I play five: Kay, Mrs. Price, Lori Jones, Cynthia and myself.

Special Backstage Ritual: At "half hour" when it's Jayne Houdyshell's time to go on stage we all sing to her to let her know we love her. Among the songs we've sung: "You Light Up My Life," "Honey Honey" and "I Would Die for You" by Prince.

Favorite Moment During Each Performance (Onstage or Off): I like when I'm playing the bully, Lori Jones, and I get to drag Lisa across the stage.

Favorite In-Theatre Gathering Places: The hallway after we sing to Jayne, and Lisa's dressing room.

Favorite Off-Site Hangouts: We have a couple: Hurley's, Pigalle, Thalia, sometimes Angus McIndoe, sometimes Joe Allen's and, near the end of the run, Sombrero's (for their margaritas).

Mascot: Lisa's dog, Django.

Favorite Therapies: We've got a bunch: Ricola, Throat Coat Tea, Airborne and Zicam.

Memorable Ad-Lib: "You! You're tall!" I used this ad-lib two years ago and it got a laugh, so Lisa kept it in the show.

Memorable Stage Door Fan Encounter: We had a 12-year-old boy who came to town to visit his cousin and aunt, and when they asked him what show he wanted to see he picked us. He stayed afterward and had a lengthy conversation with Lisa and the rest of us, and it was obvious he was very intelligent. He got it all. He said he loved the show and it really affected him.

Memorable Audience Encounter: In the scene where I'm dragging Lisa across the stage she shouts to the audience to help her. One matinee, someone did! An audience member grabbed her arm and wouldn't let go until Lisa had to tell her to. It never happened before, and never happened since.

Catchphrases Only the Company Would Recognize: "See haw!"

Memorable Directorial Note: Leigh Silverman kept saying "It's comedy gold! It's comedy gold!"

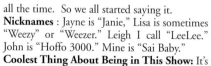

1. Jayne Houdyshell on opening night.
2. Author/star Lisa Kron (L) and director Leigh Silverman at the opening night party at the Hard Rock Cafe.
3. Cast member Saidah Arrika Ekulona on opening night.
4. Christina Kirk at the cast party.
5. Ann Kron, the playwright's mother and inspiration for the role of the mom in the play.

all the time. So we all started saying it.

Nicknames : Jayne is "Janie," Lisa is sometimes "Weezy" or "Weezer." Leigh I call "LeeLee." John is "Hoffo 3000." Mine is "Sai Baby."

Coolest Thing About Being in This Show: It's the show that has affected my life the most. It's all about love and it's as complicated and complex and easy and natural as love is.

Photos by Aubrey Reuben

Who's Afraid of Virginia Woolf?

First Preview: March 12, 2005. Opened: March 20, 2005.
Closed September 4, 2005 after 8 Previews and 177 Performances.

PLAYBILL

Edward Albee's
Who's Afraid
of Virginia Woolf?

CAST

(in order of appearance)

Martha . . . . .KATHLEEN TURNER

George . . . . .BILL IRWIN

Honey . . . . .MIREILLE ENOS

Nick . . . . .DAVID HARBOUR

THE SCENE

The living room of a house on the campus of a small

New England college, 1960.

ACT I: "Fun and Games"

ACT II: "Walpurgisnacht"

ACT III: "The Exorcism"

STANDBYS

For Ms. Turner: JENNIFER REGAN

For Mr. Irwin: CHRISTOPHER BURNS

For Ms. Enos: STINA NIELSEN

For Mr. Harbour: DAVID FURR

⊛ LONGACRE THEATRE

220 West 48th Street
A Shubert Organization Theatre
Gerald Schoenfeld, *Chairman*   Philip J. Smith, *President*

Robert E. Wankel, *Executive Vice President*

Elizabeth Ireland McCann   Daryl Roth   Terry Allen Kramer
Scott Rudin   Roger Berlind   James L. Nederlander   Nick Simunek

Joey Parnes   Executive Producer

present

Kathleen Turner   Bill Irwin

in

Edward Albee's Who's Afraid of Virginia Woolf?

with

Mireille Enos   David Harbour

| Scenic Design | Costume Design | Lighting Design | Sound Design |
| John Lee Beatty | Jane Greenwood | Peter Kaczorowski | Mark Bennett |

Production
Stage Manager
Susie Cordon

Casting
Jay Binder, CSA
Jack Bowdan, CSA/ Laura Stanczyk, CSA

Fight Director
Rick Sordelet

Associate General Manager
Elizabeth M. Blitzer

Press Representative
Shirley Herz Associates
Sam Rudy

Marketing
HHC Marketing

Directed By

Anthony Page

The producers wish to express their appreciation to
Theatre Development Fund for its support of this production.

LIVE BROADWAY

6/1/05

(L-R:) Bill Irwin Kathleen Turner play "Get the Guests" with Mireille Enos and David Harbour.

Photo by Carol Rosegg

Who's Afraid of Virginia Woolf?

Kathleen Turner
Martha

Bill Irwin
George

Mireille Enos
Honey

David Harbour
Nick

Jennifer Regan
Standby for Martha

Christopher Burns
Standby for George

Stina Nielsen
Standby for Honey

David Furr
Standby for Nick

Edward Albee
Playwright

Anthony Page
Director

John Lee Beatty
Scenic Designer

Jane Greenwood
Costume Designer

Peter Kaczorowski
Lighting Designer

Mark Bennett
Sound Designer

Rick Sordelet
Fight Director

Jay Binder, C.S.A.
Jay Binder Casting
Casting

Joey Parnes
Executive Producer

Elizabeth Ireland
McCann
Producer

Daryl Roth
Producer

Terry Allen Kramer
Producer

Scott Rudin
Producer

Roger Berlind
Producer

James L. Nederlander
Producer

Elizabeth M. Blitzer
*Associate General
Manager*

Susie Cordon
*Production Stage
Manager*

Allison Sommers
Stage Manager

Standbys
(L-R): Christopher Burns, Stina Nielsen, David Furr
and Jennifer Regan.

Photo by Ben Strothmann

The cast and crew of *Who's Afraid of Virginia Woolf?* on the stage
of the Longacre Theatre.

Photo by John Buryiak

Who's Afraid of Virginia Woolf?

Who's Afraid of Virginia Woolf?
SCRAPBOOK

1. Playwright Edward Albee and Kathleen Turner onstage at the Longacre Theatre.
2. Bill Irwin at "Broadway Barks 7!" in Shubert Alley.
3. Turner and Gary Beach at the *La Cage aux Folles* afterparty at Angus McIndoe restaurant the night of the 2005 Tony Awards.
4. Mireille Enos and David Harbour arrive at the 2005 Tony Awards.

Photos by Aubrey Reuben

Wicked

First Preview: October 8, 2003. Opened: October 30, 2003.
Still running as of May 31. 2006.

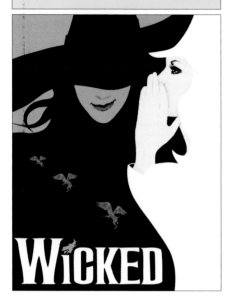

THE CAST

(in order of appearance)

Glinda .... MEGAN HILTY
Witch's Father .... SEAN McCOURT
Witch's Mother .... CRISTY CANDLER
Midwife .... JAN NEUBERGER
Elphaba .... SHOSHANA BEAN
Nessarose .... MICHELLE FEDERER
Boq .... JEFFREY KUHN
Madame Morrible .... RUE McCLANAHAN
Doctor Dillamond .... SEAN McCOURT
Fiyero .... DAVID AYERS
Ozian Official .... MICHAEL DeVRIES
The Wonderful Wizard of Oz .... BEN VEREEN
Chistery .... PHILLIP SPAETH
Monkeys, Students, Denizens of the Emerald City,
Palace Guards and Other Citizens of Oz ....
KEVIN AUBIN, JERAD BORTZ,
BEN CAMERON, CRISTY CANDLER,
MICHAEL DeVRIES, LORI ANN FERRERI,
ASMERET GHEBREMICHAEL,
LAUREN GIBBS, GAELEN GILLILAND,
ZACH HENSLER, DOMINIQUE KELLEY,
KENWAY HON WAI K. KUA,
BRANDI CHAVONNE MASSEY,
BRANDON MATTHIEUS, JAN NEUBERGER,
WALTER WINSTON ONEIL,
ROBB SAPP, MEGAN SIKORA,
PHILLIP SPAETH, MARTY THOMAS,
SHANNA VANDERWERKER
BRIANA YACAVONE

Continued on next page

GERSHWIN THEATRE

UNDER THE DIRECTION OF
JAMES M. NEDERLANDER AND JAMES L. NEDERLANDER

Marc Platt
Universal Pictures
The Araca Group and Jon B. Platt
David Stone
present

Shoshana Bean   Megan Hilty

WICKED

Music and Lyrics   Book
Stephen Schwartz   Winnie Holzman

Based on the novel by Gregory Maguire

Also Starring

Rue McClanahan

David Ayers

Michelle Federer   Jeffrey Kuhn   Sean McCourt

Adinah Alexander Clyde Alves Kevin Aubin Jerad Bortz Ben Cameron Cristy Candler
Michael DeVries Lori Ann Ferreri Anthony Galde Asmeret Ghebremichael Lauren Gibbs
Gaelen Gilliland Kristen Leigh Gorski Zach Hensler Dominique Kelley Kenway Hon Wai K. Kua
Brandi Chavonne Massey Brandon Matthieus Mark Myars Jan Neuberger Walter Winston ONeil
Robb Sapp Megan Sikora Phillip Spaeth Marty Thomas Shanna VanDerwerker Briana Yacavone

and

Ben Vereen
as the Wizard

Settings	Costumes	Lighting	Sound
Eugene Lee	Susan Hilferty	Kenneth Posner	Tony Meola
Projections	Wigs & Hair	Production Supervisor	Technical Supervisor
Elaine J. McCarthy	Tom Watson	Steven Beckler	Jake Bell
Music Arrangements	Music Director	Dance Arrangements	Music Coordinator
Alex Lacamoire & Stephen Oremus	Alex Lacamoire	James Lynn Abbott	Michael Keller
Associate Set Designer	Special Effects	Flying Sequences	Assistant Director
Edward Pierce	Chic Silber	Paul Rubin/ZFX, Inc.	Lisa Leguillou
Casting	Production Stage Manager	General Management	Press	Executive Producers
Bernard Telsey Casting	Thom Widmann	321 Theatrical Management	The Publicity Office	Marcia Goldberg & Nina Essman

Orchestrations
William David Brohn

Music Supervisor
Stephen Oremus

Musical Staging by
Wayne Cilento

Directed by
Joe Mantello

Grammy Award-winning Original Cast Recording on DECCA BROADWAY

LIVE BROADWAY

9/26/05

Eden Espinosa (L) as Elphaba gets pointers on how to be "Popular" from Kate Reinders as Glinda.

Photo by Joan Marcus

Wicked

MUSICAL NUMBERS

ACT I

"No One Mourns the Wicked"	Glinda and Citizens of Oz
"Dear Old Shiz"	Students
"The Wizard and I"	Morrible, Elphaba
"What Is This Feeling?"	Galinda, Elphaba and Students
"Something Bad"	Dr. Dillamond and Elphaba
"Dancing Through Life"	Fiyero, Galinda, Boq, Nessarose, Elphaba and Students
"Popular"	Galinda
"I'm Not That Girl"	Elphaba
"One Short Day"	Elphaba, Glinda and Denizens of the Emerald City
"A Sentimental Man"	The Wizard
"Defying Gravity"	Elphaba, Glinda, Guards and Citizens of Oz

ACT II

"No One Mourns the Wicked" (reprise)	Citizens of Oz
"Thank Goodness"	Glinda, Morrible and Citizens of Oz
"The Wicked Witch of the East"	Elphaba, Nessarose and Boq
"Wonderful"	The Wizard and Elphaba
"I'm Not That Girl" (reprise)	Glinda
"As Long As You're Mine"	Elphaba and Fiyero
"No Good Deed"	Elphaba
"March of the Witch Hunters"	Boq and Citizens of Oz
"For Good"	Glinda and Elphaba
"Finale"	All

ORCHESTRA

Conductor: Alex Lacamoire
Associate Conductor: David Evans
Concertmaster: Christian Hebel
Violin: Victor Schultz
Viola: Kevin Roy
Cello: Dan Miller
Harp: Laura Sherman
Lead Trumpet: Jon Owens
Trumpet: Tom Hoyt
Trombones: Dale Kirkland, Douglas Purviance
Flute: Helen Campo
Oboe: Tuck Lee
Clarinet/Soprano Sax: John Moses
Bassoon/Baritone Sax/Clarinets: John Campo
French Horns: Theo Primis, Chad Yarbrough
Drums: Gary Seligson
Bass: Konrad Adderley
Piano/Synthesizer: Adam Ben-David
Keyboards: Paul Loesel, David Evans
Guitars: Ric Molina, Greg Skaff
Percussion: Andy Jones

Music Coordinator: Michael Keller

(L-R): Eden Espinosa prepares to take flight in the Act I finale.

Photo by Joan Marcus

STANDBYS
For Glinda:
STACIE MORGAIN LEWIS

For Elphaba:
SAYCON SENGBLOH

UNDERSTUDIES
For Elphaba:
BRANDI CHAVONNE MASSEY

For Glinda:
MEGAN SIKORA

For Fiyero:
JERAD BORTZ,
BRANDON MATTHIEUS

For the Wizard:
SEAN McCOURT,
ANTHONY GALDE,
MICHAEL DeVRIES

For Dr. Dillamond:
MICHAEL DeVRIES,
ANTHONY GALDE

For Madame Morrible:
ADINAH ALEXANDER,
JAN NEUBERGER

For Boq:
CLYDE ALVES,
WALTER WINSTON ONEIL,
ROBB SAPP

For Nessarose:
CRISTY CANDLER,
STACIE MORGAIN LEWIS,
MEGAN SIKORA

For Chistery:
CLYDE ALVES,
KEVIN AUBIN,
MARK MYARS

For Witch's Father and Ozian Official:
JERAD BORTZ,
BEN CAMERON,
ANTHONY GALDE

SWINGS
ADINAH ALEXANDER, ANTHONY GALDE

DANCE CAPTAINS/SWINGS
CLYDE ALVES, KRISTEN LEIGH GORSKI,
MARK MYARS

Wicked

Shoshana Bean
Elphaba

Megan Hilty
Glinda

Ben Vereen
The Wizard

Rue McClanahan
Madame Morrible

David Ayers
Fiyero

Michelle Federer
Nessarose

Jeffrey Kuhn
Boq

Sean McCourt
*Witch's Father/
Doctor Dillamond*

Stacie Morgain Lewis
Standby for Glinda

Saycon Sengbloh
Standby for Elphaba

Adinah Alexander
Swing

Clyde Alves
*Swing; Assistant
Dance Captain*

Kevin Aubin
Ensemble

Jerad Bortz
Ensemble

Ben Cameron
Ensemble

Cristy Candler
Witch's Mother

Michael DeVries
Ozian Official

Lori Ann Ferreri
Ensemble

Anthony Galde
Swing

Asmeret
Ghebremichael
Ensemble

Lauren Gibbs
Ensemble

Gaelen Gilliland
Ensemble

Kristen Leigh Gorski
*Swing/
Dance Captain*

Zach Hensler
Ensemble

Dominique Kelley
Ensemble

Kenway Hon Wai K.
Kua
Ensemble

Brandi Chavonne
Massey
Ensemble

Brandon Matthieus
Ensemble

Mark Myars
*Swing/
Dance Captain*

Jan Neuberger
Midwife

Walter Winston
ONeil
Ensemble

Robb Sapp
Ensemble

Megan Sikora
Ensemble

Phillip Spaeth
Chistery

Marty Thomas
Ensemble

Wicked

Shanna
VanDerwerker
Ensemble

Briana Yacavone
Ensemble

Stephen Schwartz
Music and Lyrics

Winnie Holzman
Book

Joe Mantello
Director

Wayne Cilento
Musical Staging

Eugene Lee
Scenic Designer

Susan Hilferty
Costume Designer

Kenneth Posner
Lighting Designer

Tony Meola
Sound Designer

Tom Watson
*Wig and Hair
Designer*

Stephen Oremus
*Music Supervisor/
Music Arrangements*

William David Brohn
Orchestrations

Alex Lacamoire
*Music Director/
Music Arrangements*

James Lynn Abbott
Dance Arrangements

Michael Keller
Music Coordinator

Steven Beckler
*Production
Supervisor*

Chic Silber
Special Effects

Paul Rubin
*ZFX Flying Illusions
Flying Effects*

Bernard Telsey
Bernard Telsey
Casting, C.S.A.
Casting

Gregory Maguire
*Author of
Original Novel*

Marc Platt
Producer

Marcia Goldberg, Nancy Nagel Gibbs and
Nina Essman,
321 Theatrical Management
General Management

Jon B. Platt
Producer

David Stone
Producer

James M.
Nederlander
Producer

ALUMNI
2005-2006

Ioana Alfonso
Ensemble

James Brown III
Ensemble

Kathy Deitch
Ensemble

Melissa Fahn
Swing

Reed Kelly
Ensemble

Wicked

Clifton Oliver
Ensemble

Alexander Quiroga
Swing

Michael Seelbach
Ensemble

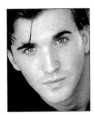
Charlie Sutton
Ensemble; Swing

Jennifer Waldman
Ensemble

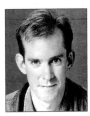
William Youmans
Doctor Dillamond

Katie Adams
Standby for Glinda

Eden Espinosa
Elphaba

Adam Fleming
Ensemble

David Garrison
The Wonderful Wizard of Oz

Rhett George
Ensemble

Jenna Leigh Green
Nessarose

Tiffany Haas
Witch's Mother Understudy

George Hearn
The Wonderful Wizard of Oz

Kisha Howard
Ensemble

Carol Kane
Madame Morrible

Reed Kelly
Ensemble

Jeremy Kocal
Ensemble

Corinne McFadden-Herrera
Ensemble

Clifton Oliver
Ensemble

Andrew Palermo
Ensemble

Eddie Pendergraft
Ensemble

Carson Reide
Ensemble; Witch's Mother

Kate Reinders
Glinda

Adam Sanford
Ensemble

Heather Spore
Ensemble

Eric Stretch
Swing

Charlie Sutton
Swing

Lorna Ventura
Ensemble; Swing

Jennifer Waldman
Ensemble

Katie Webber
Witch's Mother

Derrick Williams
Fiyero

Wicked

HAIR AND MAKEUP DEPARTMENT
(L-R): Jimmy Cortes (Makeup Supervisor),
Nora Martin (Assistant Hair Supervisor),
Beverly Belletieri (Hair Stylist), Al Annotto
(Hair Supervisor) and Jennifer Johnson
(Hair Stylist).

Photos by Ben Strothmann

CREW
First Row (L-R):
Mark Overton (Road Carpenter),
Nick Garcia (Props), Tim Shea (Carpenter),
Tom Gloven (Assistant House Electrician),
John Curvan (Sound), Valerie Gilmore
(Assistant Road Electrician),
Sandy Paradise (Vari Lite Technician)
Second Row (L-R):
John Riggins (House Carpenter),
Kevin Anderson (Props), Danny Viscardo
(Carpenter), Joe Pizzuto (Electrician),
Dennis Peters (Electrician), Pat Gilmore
(Road Electrician)
Third Row (L-R):
Mark Illo (House Propman),
Bill Breidenbach (Road Automation),
Jack Mulrain (Props), Ryan Conroy
(Carpenter), Rodney McKenna (Carpenter),
Jack Babin (Sound), Jordan Pankin (Sound)
and John Gordon (Props).

MANAGEMENT
Sitting: Susan Sampliner
(Company Manager)
Standing (L-R):
Jennifer Marik (Assistant Stage Manager),
Bob Brinkerhoff
(Associate Company Manager),
Jason Trubitt (Assistant Stage Manager),
Chris Jamros (Assistant Stage Manager)
and Thom Widmann
(Production Stage Manager.

Wicked

FRONT OF HOUSE STAFF
First Row (L-R):
Rick Kaye (House Manager),
Carmen Rodriguez (Usher), James Gunn
(Usher), Fran Bennett (Usher),
Kirth Crawford (Porter)
Second Row (L-R):
Brenda Denaris (Usher), Michelle Belmond
(Usher), Kathleen White (Usher),
Lorraine Lowrey (Ticket Taker),
Maria Szymanski (Usher), Joyce Pena
(Usher)
Third Row (L-R):
Jean Logan (Usher), Joe Ortenzio (Usher),
Mariana Casanova (Usher), Eileen Roig
(Usher), Siobhan Dunne (Usher),
Carlos Buelto (Porter) and Betty Friar
(Usher).

ORCHESTRA
Front Row (L-R):
Tuck Lee (Reed 2), David Evans
(Keyboard/Associate Conductor),
Robert Billig (Music Director/Conductor),
Misty Pereira (French Horn),
Janet Axelrod (Reed 1).
Second Row (L-R):
Pattee Cohen (Harp), Irina Karlin (Violin),
Barry Nudelman (Reed 4), Dale Kirkland
(Trombone), Theo Primis (French Horn),
John Moses (Reed 3), Kathy Cherbas
(Cello).
Third Row (L-R):
Joel Rudin (Viola), Chris Clark (Keyboard),
Mark McCarron (Guitar),
Paul Loesel (Keyboard)
and Matt Vander Ende (Drums).

Photos by Ben Strothmann

WARDROBE DEPARTMENT
Front Row (L-R):
Gayle Palmieri (Dresser) and
Barbara Rosenthal (Dresser).
Second Row (L-R):
Randy Witherspoon (Dresser), Artie Brown
(Dresser), Bobbye Sue Albrecht (Dresser),
Dianne Hylton (Dresser).
Third Row (L-R):
Kevin Hucke (Dresser), Kim Kaldenberg
(Dresser), Laurel Parrish (Dresser),
Jason Viarengo (Dresser), Trent Armstrong
(Assistant Wardrobe Supervisor).
Fourth Row:
Michael Michalski (Dresser).

Wicked

STAFF FOR WICKED

GENERAL MANAGEMENT
321 THEATRICAL MANAGEMENT
Nina Essman   Nancy Nagel Gibbs
Marcia Goldberg

GENERAL PRESS REPRESENTATIVE
THE PUBLICITY OFFICE
Bob Fennell   Marc Thibodeau
Michael S. Borowski   Candi Adams

CASTING
BERNARD TELSEY CASTING, C.S.A.:
Bernie Telsey, Will Cantler, David Vaccari,
Bethany Knox, Craig Burns,
Tiffany Little Canfield, Christine Dall,
Stephanie Yankwitt

TECHNICAL SUPERVISION
JAKE BELL PRODUCTION SERVICES LTD.

COMPANY MANAGER ....SUSAN SAMPLINER

Stage Manager ....Chris Jamros
Assistant Stage Managers ....Bess Marie Glorioso,
                    Andrew Neal, Jason Trubitt
Associate Company Manager...........Robert Brinkerhoff
Assistant Choreographer ....Corinne McFadden
Dance Captains ....Mark Myars, Kristen Leigh Gorski
Assistant Dance Captain ....Clyde Alves
Fight Captain ....Kristen Leigh Gorski
Assistant to Mr. Schwartz ....Michael Cole
Assistant Scenic Designer ....Nick Francone
Dressing/Properties ....Kristie Thompson
Scenic Assistant ....Christopher Domanski
Oz Map Design ....Francis Keeping
Draftsman ....Ted LeFevre
Set Model Construction ....Miranda Hardy
Associate Costume Designers ....Michael Sharpe,
                                  Ken Mooney
Assistant Costume Designers ....Maiko Matsushima,
                                  Amy Clark
Costume Coordinator ....Amanda Whidden
Associate Lighting Designer ....Karen Spahn
Associate Lighting Designer/
Automated Lights ....Warren Flynn
Assistant Lighting Designer ....Ben Stanton
Lighting Assistant...........................Jonathan Spencer
Associate Sound Designer ....Kai Harada
Sound Assistant ....Shannon Slaton
Projection Programmer ....Mark Gilmore
Assistant Projection Designers ....Jenny Lee,
         Michael Patterson, Jacob Daniel Pinholster
Projection Animators ....Gareth Smith, Ari Sachter Zeltzer
Special Effects Associate ....Aaron Waitz
Associate Hair Designer ....Charles LaPointe
Fight Director ....Tom Schall
Production Carpenter ....Rick Howard
Head Carpenter ....C. Mark Overton
Deck Automation Carpenter ....William Breidenbach
Assistant Carpenter ....Dan Janssen
Production Electrician ....Robert Fehribach
Head Electrician ....Pat Gilmore
Deck Electrician/Moving Light Operator ...David Karlson
Follow Spot Operator ....Valerie Gilmore
Production Properties ....George Wagner

Property Master ....Joe Schwarz
Assistant Property Master ....John Gentile
Production Sound Engineer ....Douglas Graves
Sound Engineer ....Jordan Pankin
Assistant Sound Engineer ....Jack Babin
Production Wardrobe Supervisor ....Alyce Gilbert
Assistant Wardrobe Supervisor ....Trent Armstrong
Dressers ....Bobbye Sue Albrecht, Artie Brown,
                  Kevin Hucke, Dianne Hylton,
         Kim Kaldenberg, Michael Michalski, Kathe Mull,
         Gayle Palmieri, Laurel Parrish, Barbara Rosenthal,
                  Jason Viarengo, Randy Witherspoon
Hair Supervisor ....Alfonso Annotto
Assistant Hair Supervisor ....Monica Costea
Hairdressers ....Nora Martin, Adenike Wright
Makeup Design ....Joseph Dulude II
Makeup Supervisor ....Jimmy Cortes
Music Preparation Supervisor ....Peter R. Miller,
                             Miller Music Service
Synthesizer Programming ....Andrew Barrett for
                        Lionella Productions, Ltd.
Rehearsal Pianists ....Randy Cohen, Ben Cohn,
                             Matthew Doebler
Rehearsal Drummer ....Gary Seligson
Music Intern ....Joshua Salzman
Assistant to the General Managers ....Rachel Marcus
Production Assistants .....Timothy R. Semon, David Zack
Marketing ....TMG - The Marketing Group/
                        Tanya Grubich, Laura Matalon,
                        Trish Santini, Lesley Alpert
Advertising ....Serino Coyne/
         Greg Corradetti, Joaquin Esteva, Ruth Rosenberg
Website/Internet Marketing ....Late August Design/
                        Jeff Prout, Jeff Bowen
Merchandising ....The Araca Group/
                  Clint Bond, Jr., Karen Davidov,
                  Julie Monahan, Edward Nelson,
         Daniel Pardes, James M. Pellechi, Jr.
Theatre Display ....King Displays
Group Sales ....Group Sales Box Office/
                  Stephanie Lee (800-223-7565)
Banking ....JP Morgan Chase Bank/
                             Michele Gibbons
Payroll ....Castellana Services, Inc.
Accountant ....Robert Fried, C.P.A.
Comptroller ....Lawrence Anderson
Insurance ....AON/Albert G. Ruben Insurance
Legal Counsel ....Loeb & Loeb/Seth Gelblum
Legal Counsel for Universal Pictures ....Keith Blau
Physical Therapy ........P.T. Plus, P.C./Marc Hunter-Hall
Onstage Merchandising..............George Fenmore, Inc.

Makeup provided by M.A.C Cosmetics

MARC PLATT PRODUCTIONS
President: Abby Wolf-Weiss
Adam Siegel, Nicole Brown, Greg Lessans, Joey Levy,
Jared Leboff, Josh Goldenberg, Nik Mavinkurve, Chris Kuhl

STONE PRODUCTIONS
Associate: Patrick Catullo

UNIVERSAL PICTURES
President & COO, Universal Studios, Inc.......Ron Meyer
Chairman....................................Stacey Snider
President of Marketing ....Adam Fogelson
Co-President of Marketing ....Eddie Egan

EVP, Business and Legal Affairs ....Jimmy Horowitz
VP, Business Development and
Strategic Planning ....Jonathan Fischer

For additional **WICKED** merchandise,
please visit www.wickedthemusical.com

CREDITS

Scenery built by F&D Scene Changes, Calgary, Canada. Show control and scenic motion control featuring Stage Command Systems© and scenery fabrication by Scenic Technologies, a division of Production Resource Group, New Windsor, NY. Lighting and certain special effects equipment from Fourth Phase and sound equipment from ProMix, both divisions of Production Resource Group LLC. Other special effects equipment by Sunshine Scenic Studios and Aztec Stage Lighting. Video projection system provided by Scharff Weisberg Inc. Projections by Vermilion Border Productions. Costumes by Euroco Costumes, Barbara Matera Ltd., Parsons-Meares Ltd., Scafati, TRICORNE New York City and Eric Winterling. Millinery by Rodney Gordon and Lynne Mackey. Shoes by T.O. Dey, Frederick Longtin, Pluma, LaDuca Shoes NYC, and J.C. Theatrical. Flatheads and monkey wings built by Michael Curry Design Inc. Masks created and made by Matthew W. Mungle; lifecasts by Todd Kleitsch. Fur by Fur & Furgery. Undergarments and hosiery by Bra*Tenders, Inc. Antique jewelry by Ilene Chazanof. Specialty jewelry and tiaras by Larry Vrba. Custom Oz accessories by LouLou Button. Custom screening by Gene Mignola. Certain props by John Creech Designs and Den Design Studio. Additional hand props courtesy of George Fenmore. Confetti supplied by Artistry in Motion. Puppets by Bob Flanagan. Musical instruments from Manny's and Carroll Musical Instrument Rentals. Drums and other percussion equipment from Pearl, Sabian, Remo, Pro-Mark and Black Swamp. Cough drops supplied by Ricola, Inc. Emer'gen'C provided by Alacer Corp. Rehearsed at the Lawrence A. Wien Center, 890 Broadway, and the Ford Center for the Performing Arts.

NEDERLANDER

Chairman ....**James M. Nederlander**
President ....**James L. Nederlander**

Executive Vice President
Nick Scandalios

Vice President	Senior Vice President
Corporate Development	Labor Relations
Charlene S. Nederlander	**Herschel Waxman**

| Vice President | Chief Financial Officer |
| **Jim Boese** | **Freida Sawyer Belviso** |

STAFF FOR THE GERSHWIN THEATRE

Manager ....Richard D. Kaye
Assoc. Manager ....Steven A. Ouellette
Treasurer ....John Campise
Assistant Treasurer ....Anthony Rossano
Carpenter ....John Riggins
Electrician ....Henry L. Brisen
Assistant Electrician ....Tommy Gloven
Property Master ....Mark Illo
Flyman ....Dennis Fox
Fly Automation Carpenter ....Michael J. Szymanski
Head Usher ....Martha McGuire Boniface

Wicked

SCRAPBOOK

1. Miss USA Chelsea Cooley (center, with sash) and contestants in the "Be Wicked" singing contest at the "Wicked Day" block party.
2. Megan Hilty and Shoshana Bean get into makeup.
3. Hilty and Bean at "Broadway on Broadway" event.
4. Rob Sapp and Adam Fleming backstage at the Gershwin Theatre.

Correspondent: Jason Viarengo, Star Dresser to The Wizard.

Record Breakers: On January 24, 2006, *Wicked* became the longest running show at the Gershwin Theater, surpassing the record previously held by the 1994 revival of *Show Boat* which ran for 959 performances.

On March 23, 2006, we celebrated our 1,000th performance!

The week of December 26, 2005 through January 1, 2006, we broke all Broadway box office records with $1,610,934 in ticket sales.

Fundraising: *Wicked* presented Broadway's Celebrity Benefit for Hurricane Relief on September 25, to help the victims of Hurricane Katrina. Audience members were treated to an evening of show-stopping performances by Bernadette Peters, Bill Irwin, Brian d'Arcy James, Susan Lucci, Bebe Neuwirth, Idina Menzel, Patrick Wilson, Ben Vereen, Liza Minnelli, and many more. The benefit raised over $200,000. On April 30, we had an Actors' Fund Performance.

Anniversary Parties and Gifts: There were quite a few memorable parties this past year. On May 31, 2005, the producers threw a party at Azalea for departing cast members Jennifer Laura Thompson (Glinda), Carole Shelley (Madame Morrible) and George Hearn (The Wizard).

On October 30, 2005 we celebrated our second anniversary on Broadway with *Wicked* Day. Hundreds of fans came to the Gershwin Theater to watch the final contestants in the singing contest, munch on popcorn and cotton candy and compete for prizes with some good old-fashioned carnival games. That evening after the show the producers invited the cast and crew of *Wicked* to celebrate across the street at The Palm Restaurant.

For Christmas the producers gave everyone on the show black fleece vests embroidered with the *Wicked* logo.

Wardrobe Supervisor Alyce Gilbert gave every *Wicked* company member freshly baked Greek Holiday bread from the Poseidon Bakery for Christmas and Easter.

On January 8, 2006 we all said farewell to Shoshana Bean (Elphaba), David Ayers (Fiyero), Michelle Federer (Nessarose) and Rue McClanahan (Madame Morrible). A party was held at the Grand Hyatt on 42nd street. As company members said good-bye they dined on sushi rolls, various cheeses and a dessert table which consisted of cookies, chocolate covered strawberries, and pastries dipped in freshly melted chocolate.

Celebrity Visitors: This year we had a variety of celebrity visitors backstage after the show: illusionist David Copperfield, TV talk show host Joan Lunden, Academy Award-winning actor Robert DeNiro, singer Cyndi Lauper, rocker Tommy Lee, actress Amy Irving, pop sensation Usher, Broadway's very own Bebe Neuwirth and Liza Minnelli, and "American Idol" winners

Wicked
Scrapbook

Carrie Underwood and Clay Aiken who has seen the show at least five times.

"Gypsy of the Year" Skit: "Team *Wicked*," which poked fun at National Cheerleading competitions. *Wicked* came in as first runner-up for our fundraising efforts. We raised a total of $221,298.

"Easter Bonnet" Skit: "*Wicked* on Ice" by Marty Thomas and Anthony Galde.

"Carols for a Cure" Carol: "We Are Lights" by Stephen Schwartz and Steve Young.

Backstage Rituals: Dresser Kevin Hucke created "The List of the Day" on the wipe board off-stage left. Every show Kevin posts a new topic in which company members are urged to share their thoughts. Past "List of the Day" topics have included: Casting *Wicked* with cartoon characters, Favorite Childhood Toys, and *Wicked* Olympic Events.

Memorable Ad-Lib: David Ayers who played Fiyero is supposed to say the line "I've been thinking about that lion cub and everything." Instead he said, "I've been thinking about *The Lion King* and everything."

In-Theatre Gathering Place: Every Sunday, brunch is held in the male ensemble dressing room. Cast member Anthony Galde organizes it and brings some of the food, which is bought with the collected money from the "Brunch Fund Jar." Some of the delicious treats Sunday brunch has to offer are bagels, chips & dip, baked goods, fresh fruit, Krispy Kreme Doughnuts, cheese & crackers, pizza, fruit juices and sometimes KFC or McDonald's cheeseburgers.

Off-site Hangout: On any day of the week cast members frequently can be seen after the show having a drink or bite to eat at nearby restaurants Sosa Borella or The Palm Restaurant. The Wizard, Ben Vereen sometimes enjoys having an after theatre meal at Azalea or Blue Chile.

Favorite Snack Foods: In the principal hallway there is a candy/snack jar that cast and crew are constantly dipping into. Some of its regular contents include M&M's, (all varieties) Hershey's Kisses, Gummi Worms and pretzels.

Mascot: The company mascot for the show is Chelsea (My Scene Barbie) who lives in the Male Ensemble Dressing Room. Chelsea wears glamourous costumes and she even has her very own Oz Dust Ballroom outfit.

Most Costume Changes: Male Ensemble members Clifton Oliver and Kenway Hon Wai K. Kua have the most costume changes in the show with 12 each. Female ensemble member Katie Webber has 10 and Heather Spore has 9.

Fastest Costume Change: Megan Hilty (Glinda) and Eden Espinosa (Elphaba) have the fastest costume change in the show. They have only 18 seconds to simultaneously change into their costumes for their Emerald City entrance.

Heaviest & Hottest Costume: It's worn by Michael DeVries. The costume known as the "The Ozian Gatekeeper" weighs over 40 lbs and is made mostly of wool.

1. Rue McClanahan, Ben Vereen and dresser Jason Viarengo.
2. Backstage at the Hurricane Katrina benefit: Idina Menzel, Jason Viarengo, hair supervisor Alfonso Annotto and dresser Joby Horrigan.
3. George Hearn and Carol Kane backstage getting into costume as the Wizard and Madame Morrible.

Photos Courtesy Jason Viarengo

The Woman in White

First Preview: October 28, 2005. Opened: November 17, 2005.
Closed February 19, 2006 after 25 Previews and 109 Performances.

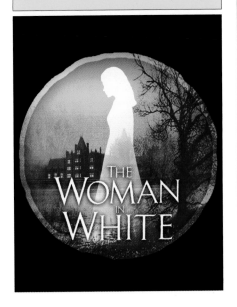

PLAYBILL®

CAST

(in order of appearance)

Walter Hartright	ADAM BRAZIER
Signalman	NORMAN LARGE
Anne Catherick	ANGELA CHRISTIAN
Marian Halcombe	MARIA FRIEDMAN
Mr. Fairlie	WALTER CHARLES
Mr. Fairlie's Servant	JOHN DEWAR
Laura Fairlie	JILL PAICE
A Village Girl	JUSTIS BOLDING
Sir Percival Glyde	RON BOHMER
Count Fosco	MICHAEL BALL
A Pawnbroker	NORMAN LARGE
A Con Man	RICHARD TODD ADAMS
The Warden	PATTY GOBLE
The Company	RICHARD TODD ADAMS,

JUSTIS BOLDING,
LISA BRESCIA, JOHN DEWAR,
COURTNEY GLASS,
PATTY GOBLE, NORMAN LARGE,
MICHAEL SHAWN LEWIS,
ELIZABETH LOYACANO,
DANIEL MARCUS, GREG MILLS,
ELENA SHADDOW, DANIEL TORRES

UNDERSTUDIES

For Walter Hartright:
MICHAEL SHAWN LEWIS, DANIEL TORRES

For Anne Catherick:
COURTNEY GLASS, ELIZABETH LOYACANO

Continued on next page

The Playbill Broadway Yearbook 2005-2006

⟜N⟞ **MARQUIS THEATRE**
UNDER THE DIRECTION OF JAMES M. NEDERLANDER AND JAMES L. NEDERLANDER

BOYETT OSTAR PRODUCTIONS   NEDERLANDER PRESENTATIONS, INC.   SONIA FRIEDMAN PRODUCTIONS, LTD.
THE REALLY USEFUL WHITE COMPANY, INC.
LAWRENCE HOROWITZ/JON AVNET   RALPH GUILD/BILL ROLLNICK
BERNIE ABRAMS/MICHAEL SPEYER   CLEAR CHANNEL ENTERTAINMENT/PIA

present

THE WOMAN IN WHITE

A NEW MUSICAL

Freely adapted from the classic novel by Wilkie Collins

Music by ANDREW LLOYD WEBBER

Lyrics by DAVID ZIPPEL   Book by CHARLOTTE JONES

with

MARIA FRIEDMAN

ANGELA CHRISTIAN   ADAM BRAZIER   JILL PAICE
RON BOHMER   WALTER CHARLES

and

MICHAEL BALL
as Count Fosco

with

RICHARD TODD ADAMS   JUSTIS BOLDING   LISA BRESCIA   LAURA DEKKERS   JOHN DEWAR   ROGER E. DEWITT
COURTNEY GLASS   PATTY GOBLE   LEAH HOROWITZ   NORMAN LARGE   MICHAEL SHAWN LEWIS
ELIZABETH LOYACANO   SEAN MACLAUGHLIN   DANIEL MARCUS   GREG MILLS   ELENA SHADDOW   DANIEL TORRES

Orchestrations by DAVID CULLEN
Orchestration Supervised by ANDREW LLOYD WEBBER
Musical Supervision by SIMON LEE

Movement Direction by WAYNE McGREGOR   Associate Musical Supervisor/Musical Director KRISTEN BLODGETTE
Technical Supervision by DAVID BENKEN   Projection Realisation and System Design MESMER–DICK STRAKER/SVEN ORTEL
Casting by JIM CARNAHAN, CSA   Music Coordinator DAVID LAI   Production Stage Manager RICK STEIGER
Marketing HHC MARKETING   Press Representative BARLOW•HARTMAN
General Management 101 PRODUCTIONS, LTD.   Associate Producers STAGE ENTERTAINMENT BV

Lighting Design by PAUL PYANT   Sound Design by MICK POTTER

Set, Costume and Video Design by WILLIAM DUDLEY

Directed by TREVOR NUNN

11/17/05

(L-R): Jill Paice, Maria Friedman, Angela Christian

Photo by Manuel Harlan

421

The Woman in White

MUSICAL NUMBERS

PROLOGUE
A railway cutting near Limmeridge, Cumberland, England

ACT ONE
Limmeridge, Cumberland
"I Hope You'll Like It Here"
"Perspective"
"Trying Not to Notice"
"I Believe My Heart"
"Lammastide"
"You See I Am No Ghost"
"A Gift for Living Well"
"The Holly and the Ivy"

Blackwater House, Hampshire
"All for Laura"
"The Document"
"Act I Finale"

ACT TWO
Blackwater House, Hampshire
"If I Could Only Dream This World Away"
"The Nightmare"
"All for Laura" reprise

London
"Evermore Without You"
"Lost Souls"
"You Can Get Away With Anything"
"The Seduction"

Cumberland

EPILOGUE
A railway cutting, near Limmeridge, Cumberland

Michael Ball, as Count Fosco, sings "A Gift for Living Well."

Photo by Paul Kolnik

The Woman in White

Maria Friedman
Marian Halcombe

Michael Ball
Count Fosco

Angela Christian
Anne Catherick

Adam Brazier
Walter Hartright

Jill Paice
Laura Fairlie

Ron Bohmer
Sir Percival Glyde

Walter Charles
Mr. Fairlie

Norman Large
Signalman/Ensemble

Richard Todd Adams
Ensemble

Justis Bolding
A Village Girl/ Ensemble

Lisa Brescia
Ensemble

Laura Dekkers
Swing

John Dewar
Ensemble

Roger E. DeWitt
Swing

Courtney Glass
Ensemble

Patty Goble
Ensemble

Leah Horowitz
Swing

Michael Shawn Lewis
Ensemble

Elizabeth Loyacano
Ensemble

Daniel Marcus
Ensemble

Sean MacLaughlin
Swing

Greg Mills
Ensemble

Elena Shaddow
Ensemble

Daniel Torres
Ensemble

Andrew Lloyd Webber
Composer

David Zippel
Lyrics

Charlotte Jones
Book

Trevor Nunn
Director

William Dudley
Set, Costume and Video Design

Paul Pyant
Lighting Designer

Wayne MacGregor
Movement Director

Mick Potter
Sound Designer

Simon Lee
Musical Supervision

David Cullen
Orchestrations

Kristen Blodgette
Associate Musical Supervision, Musical Director

The Woman in White

David Benken
Technical Supervisor

William Berloni
Theatrical Animals
Animal Trainer

David Lai
Musical Contractor

Jim Carnahan
Casting

Jon Avnet
Producer

Bob Boyett
Producer

Bill Haber,
Ostar Enterprises
Producer

Sonia Friedman
Producer

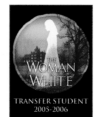

Jennifer Hope Wills
Ensemble

Photo by Ben Strothmann

Wardrobe, Hair and Make-up
(L-R):
Charlene Belmond, Vincent Schicchi,
Jeffrey A. Knaggs, Jay Woods,
Rodd Sovar, Franklin Hollenbeck, Eddie
Harrison, Dana Fucarino, Fran Curry,
Nancy Schaefer, Marisa Tchornobai,
Amber Isaac and Andrew Ross.

Photo by Manuel Harlan

Maria Friedman as
Marian Halcombe.

Adam Brazier as
Walter Hartright.

Photo by Manuel Harlan

The Woman in White

STAGE CREW

Front Row (L-R): Timothy Donovan (Assistant Electrician), Steven Ried (Carpenter), Ken Sheehan (Electrician).

Middle Row (L-R): Joe Valentino (House Head Carpenter), Jim Mayo (House Head Electrics), Craig Van Tassel (Production Sound Supervisor), Brian Collins (Electrician), Martin Van Beveren (Props), David M. Cohen (Assistant Props), Jerry L. Marshall (Production Props Supervisor), Michael L. Shep, Jr. (Production Automation).

Back Row (L-R): David Calhoun (House Manager), Chris Kurtz (Assistant Electricians), Rick Poulin (Electrician), Patrick Ainge (Head Electrician), Jersey (Electrician) and Robert Casey (Sound).

STAGE MANAGEMENT

Front: Lisa Dawn Cave.

Back Row (L-R): Rick Steiger, Kevin Bertolacci and Jennifer Marik.

FRONT OF HOUSE STAFF

Front Row (L-R): Ava Probst, Daisy Irizarry, Karen Garcia-Ortiz, Carol Reilly.

Middle Row (L-R): Phyllis Weinsaft, Elaine Healy, Charlie Spencer.

Back Row (L-R): John Clark, Jean Doty, Peter Shayne, Jim Lynch, Cecil Villar, Robert McCloskey, Stanley Seidman, Odalis Concepcion and Orlando Concepcion.

The Woman in White

The Woman in White
SCRAPBOOK

Photos by Aubrey Reuben

Correspondents: Jill Paice ("Laura") and the Cast.

Favorite Maria Friedman Quote: "I have two major problems! One: I have cancer! Two: I can't find my sock!"

Who Got the Gypsy Robe: Elena Shaddow.

Who Wore the Heaviest/Hottest Costume: Michael Ball as Count Fosco. His body temperature would increase by up to four degrees because of the fat suit.

Memorable Directorial Note: "We are steeped in the white hot crucible of creation." – Trevor Nunn.

Most Embarrassing Moment: We have chosen to award this honor to Norman Large. Upon making his final exit as the Signalman, Norman attempted to exit through a wall. The force of the impact sent him onto his back and he therefore dropped his lamp. The lamp split into several pieces and Norman, unable to regain his footing, had to crawl back onto the stage to attempt a meek recovery of the lamp. Finally managing to scoop up the pieces of the lamp, Norman had to push himself through the door to exit while still on his knees. He fell face-first onto the deck backstage and we are still laughing to this day.

Nickname: *Woman in White: The Broadway Experience.*

1. (L-R): Composer Andrew Lloyd Webber arrives at the cast party at Tavern on the Green with stars Maria Friedman and Michael Ball.
2. Angela Christian on opening night.
3. Ron Bohmer and Sandra Joseph at Tavern on the Green.
4. (L-R): Angela Christian, Maria Friedman and Michael Ball lead the cast in curtain calls on opening night at the Marquis Theatre.

Events

Stars in the Alley

June 1, 2005 in Shubert Alley

Photos by Aubrey Reuben

Performers from *All Shook Up, Spamalot, The Light in the Piazza, The 25th Annual Putnam County Spelling Bee* and nearly every other show on Broadway performed free in Shubert Alley as part of the 19th annual "Stars in the Alley" concert, presented by Continental Airlines and The League of American Theatres and Producers. Among stars who greeted fans were Roger Bart, Gary Beach, Carolee Carmello, Tim Curry, Christine Ebersole, Harvey Fierstein, Joanna Gleason, Cheyenne Jackson, Richard Kind, Andrea Martin, Kelli O'Hara, Elizabeth Parkinson, John Selya, J. Smith-Cameron, Bruce Vilanch, Tom Wopat and Ben Vereen. In addition to the song and dance, NYC Department of Education Chancellor Joel Klein was presented with the 2005 Star Award "for his support for Broadway theatre."

1. *Sweet Charity* co-stars Denis O'Hare and Christina Applegate.
2. Mary Bond Davis of *Hairspray.*
3. Shubert Organization Chairman Gerald Schoenfeld.
4. Ellen Marlow, Henry Hodges and Erin Dilly perform a number from their show, *Chitty Chitty Bang Bang.*
5. Adriane Lenox and Cherry Jones of *Doubt.*
6. Jesse Tyler Ferguson of *The 25th Annual Putnam County Spelling Bee.*

Broadway Under the Stars

June 13, 2005 in Bryant Park

The fourth annual "Broadway Under the Stars" concert saluted the leading men of Broadway and boasted performances by Brent Barrett, Mario Cantone, Michael Cerveris, Raúl Esparza, Dan Fogler, Hunter Foster, Victor Garber, Chester Gregory II, Cheyenne Jackson, Marc Kudisch, Brian Stokes Mitchell, Christopher Sieber and Tom Wopat as well as country music singer Billy Currington. The evening also included special appearances by *Sweet Charity*'s Christina Applegate and the Radio City Rockettes.

This year's event featured tunes by Broadway legends John Kander and the late Fred Ebb and Cy Coleman, both of whom passed away in 2004. Scott Wittman (*Hairspray*'s lyricist) directed the evening, which was viewed by more than 15,000 attendees in Bryant Park, and was later broadcast on CBS television.

Photos by Aubrey Reuben

1. The Rockettes get ready to perform.
2. Michael Cerveris (*Sweeney Todd*) with Brian Stokes Mitchell.
3. (L-R) Victor Garber joins *Chitty Chitty Bang Bang* stars Raúl Esparza and Marc Kudisch.
4. Angie Schworer (*The Producers*) and Rachelle Rak (*Dirty Rotten Scoundrels*).
5. Kudisch and Cheyenne Jackson (*All Shook Up*).

Broadway Show League Softball Championship

August 25, 2005 at Hecksher Ball Fields, Central Park

Broadway's best softball teams went head to head on August 25, with *Beauty and the Beast* upsetting three-time champs *The Producers* by the score of 13–3. The championship was a rematch for the two productions, who went head to head in 2004 as well, with *The Producers* pulling ahead that time.

Other squads in the 1:30 P.M. division were *Good Vibrations, The Lion King*, a combined *Steel Magnolia* and *Glass Menagerie* nine, and teams from Blueman Group, Atlantic Theatre Company and Lincoln Center Theater.

The sluggers from *All Shook Up* sewed up the 11:30 A.M. division (known as the John Effrat division for the League's founder). Undefeated in games against *Wicked, Fiddler on the Roof, Hairspray, Chitty Chitty Bang Bang*, Lab Gang, *Julius Caesar, Phantom of the Opera, Avenue Q, Dirty Rotten Scoundrels* and Manhattan Theatre Club, they lost 3–6 in a division playoff against *The Producers*.

On August 18, the Nederlander team won the 3:30 P.M. organizational division, beating Actors' Equity 17–13.

The Broadway Show League consists of 31 teams that play Thursday afternoon games in Central Park.

The 2005 show championship contenders:

Beauty and the Beast
Ryan Bentley: Left Field
Gabe Hernandez: 2nd Base
Nelson Vanquez: Short Stop
Juan Parra: Right Center Field
Wil Enriquez: 1st Base
Greg Collichio: 3rd Base
Steve Blanchard: Designated Hitter
Annie Moll: Right Field
John Sheppard: Captain/Manager
Melissa De Valle: Catcher

The Producers
Ryan McDonough: Center Field
Joe Muelle: Left Field
Tim McDonough, Jr.: Short Stop
Pat Sullivan: Right Center Field
Shawn McDonough: 2nd Base
Tom McDonough, Sr.: 3rd Base
Tim McDonough, Sr.: 1st Base
Cheryl Zimba: Right Field
Rocco Landesman: Pitcher
Dee Fox: Catcher

1. The championship team, from *Beauty and the Beast* with the scoreboard from the winning game.
2. The stars come out on opening day (L-R): Tom Wopat, Jeffrey Tambor, Jeff Goldblum, Christian Slater, Sara Ramirez, Gordon Clapp, Christopher Sieber, Sherie Rene Scott and (in front) Jenn Gambatese.
3. Commissioner Carlos Martinez.
4. Actress Paige Price on opening day.

Broadway on Broadway

September 18, 2005 in Times Square

The corner of Broadway and 44th Street came alive with the sounds of musicals old and new September 18 as the 14th annual "Broadway on Broadway" concert gave New Yorkers free samples of the offerings on Times Square stages. Hosted by Christina Applegate of *Sweet Charity* and John Lithgow of *Dirty Rotten Scoundrels*, the event drew an estimated 50,000 people to see selections from ongoing shows including *All Shook Up, Avenue Q, Beauty and the Beast, Dirty Rotten Scoundrels, Hairspray, Lennon, The Light in the Piazza, The Lion King, Mamma Mia!, The Producers* and *Wicked*, plus previews of upcoming musicals *The Color Purple, Sweeney Todd* and *In My Life*. Lithgow said, "'Broadway on Broadway' showcases the talent and energy which make up the Broadway community. I'm proud to be part of that community and I'm very excited to co-host this special concert. And spending a couple of hours side by side with Christina Applegate ain't so bad either."

1. (L-R): Dan Fogler, Lisa Howard, Jose Llana, Jesse Tyler Ferguson, Celia Keenan-Bolger, Jay Reiss, Derrick Baskin, Sarah Saltzberg and Deborah S. Craig of *The 25th Annual Putnam County Spelling Bee*.
2. Frenchie Davis of *Rent*.
3. The Goodtime Gals from *Sweet Charity*.
4. Raúl Esparza with chorus members Ellen Marlow and Libbie Jacobson from *Chitty Chitty Bang Bang*.
5. (L-R): LaChanze and Elisabeth Withers-Mendes of *The Color Purple*.

Broadway's Celebrity Benefit for Hurricane Relief

September 24, 2005 at the Gershwin Theatre

"Broadway's Celebrity Benefit for Hurricane Relief" raised money for victims of Hurricane Katrina with performances by dozens of stage and film actors, including Ben Vereen, Liza Minnelli, Susan Lucci, Rue McClanahan and Bernadette Peters. The one-night-only event, produced by the cast and creative team of *Wicked* at the Gershwin Theatre, raised more than $200,000 to benefit Second Harvest and Quilts for Kids, two organizations working directly with the survivors. Three quilts featuring the signatures of every performer in the show were auctioned at $6,000 apiece.

Among highlights: The cast of *The 25th Annual Putnam County Spelling Bee* performed a satirical interpretive dance that criticized the Bush administration's response to the disaster. Ben Vereen did an original take on the *Cats* anthem "Memory," which he recited as an introspective monologue. Bill Irwin relied on physical comedy to deliver Shakespeare's "Seven Ages of Man" speech in baggy clown pants. Julia Murney sang "It's Amazing the Things That Float," from Peter Mills' 1993 musical *The Flood*, about a refugee who must leave her home by boat.

Photos by Aubrey Reuben

1. Julia Murney, Idina Menzel and Joe Mantello gather backstage at the Gershwin Theatre.
2. Shuler Hensley flashes victory signs.
3. New Orleans native Bryan Batt (L) goes head to head with Ben Vereen.
4. Vereen, Denis O'Hare and Liza Minnelli take curtain calls.
5. Jack Klugman relaxes backstage.

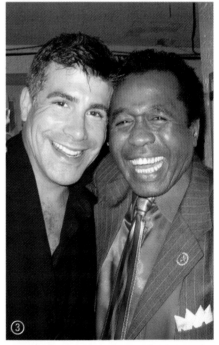

19th Annual Broadway Flea Market and Grand Auction

September 25, 2005 in Shubert Alley

Photos by Aubrey Reuben

The 19th annual Broadway Flea Market and Grand Auction raised $544,037 for Broadway Cares/Equity Fights AIDS, up from the previous year's $419,464. Fundraisers included a Celebrity Table, a Silent Auction, a Grand Auction and various booths manned by theatre folk. The United Scenic Artists booth raised the most this year: $23,865. *Wicked* raised $7,854, the most of any show. Among other highlights: *Dirty Rotten Scoundrels* sold autographed photos of star Norbert Leo Butz taken at his high school prom. Andy Karl, of the Off-Broadway show *Slut*, helped raise $1,000 by signing posters in which he is wearing only chili lights.

1. Producing Director of BC/EFA Michael Graziano.
2. Gregory Jbara (*Dirty Rotten Scoundrels*) and Sutton Foster (*The Drowsy Chaperone*).
3. Richard Thomas and Luba Mason.
4. (L-R): Jordan Gelber (*Avenue Q*), Steve Rosen (*Spamalot*) and Matthew Morrison (*A Naked Girl on the Appian Way*).
5. (L-R): Boyd Gaines and Michael McGrath (*Spamalot*) sign autographs.

Renaming the Virginia Theatre

October 16, 2005 at the new August Wilson Theatre

Broadway's Virginia Theatre at 245 West 52nd Street, formerly known as the Guild Theatre and the ANTA Playhouse and now owned by Jujamcyn Theatres, was renamed the August Wilson Theatre October 16, in honor of the two-time Pulitzer Prize-winning playwright, who died of liver cancer on October 2, 2005. In a career that spanned twenty years, Wilson saw eight parts of his 10-play cycle about the African-American experience in the 20th century reach Broadway. All eight were nominated for the Best Play Tony Award, with 1987's *Fences* taking the prize. *Fences* and *The Piano Lesson* also won Pulitzer Prizes. The rechristening was marked at the 1925-vintage theatre with an evening of readings and memories from many of the theatre folk who worked with Wilson over the years, including director Lloyd Richards and actor Charles S. Dutton. Guests of honor included Wilson's daughters, Azula Carmen Wilson and Sakina Ansari, and his widow, designer Constanza Romero.

1. (L-R): August Wilson's daughters Sakina Ansari and Azula Carmen Wilson with widow Constanza Romero outside the newly renamed August Wilson Theatre.
2. The new marquee is lit for the first time.
3. Actress Jamila Perry and director Lloyd Richards attend the post-dedication reception.
4. Actress Lillias White.
5. Actor Charles S. Dutton arrives at the theatre.
6. Director George C. Wolfe with Jujamcyn Creative Director Jack Viertel.

2005 Tony Honors

October 25, 2005 at Tavern on the Green

The 2005 Tony Honors for Excellence in the Theatre were bestowed on Peter Neufeld and the Theatre Communications Group at an October 25 ceremony at Tavern on the Green. A long-time general manager of Broadway shows, Neufeld now works at Broadway Cares/Equity Fights AIDS. The Theatre Communications Group, a service organization that promotes theatre nationwide, publishes dozens of theatre books each year, along with *American Theater* magazine.

Tony Honors are given each fall to "institutions, individuals and/or organizations that have demonstrated extraordinary achievement in theatre, but are not eligible in any of the established Tony Award categories." TCG was represented at the event by Executive Director Ben Cameron. The event was hosted by Cherry Jones. Presenters included Bill Irwin, Patti LuPone and other Broadway notables.

1. (L-R): Presenters Patti LuPone and Bill Irwin with host Cherry Jones at Tavern on the Green.
2. Honoree Peter Neufeld (R) and Ben Cameron, executive director of Theatre Communications Group.
3. Neufeld (center) with American Theatre Wing President Doug Leeds and Chairman Sondra Gilman.
4. Producer Roger Berlind with Jones.
5. Andrea McArdle and Kim Varhola, who serenaded Neufeld with numbers from *Annie, Chess, Crazy for You* and *Evita.*

Gypsy of the Year

December 5 and 6, 2005 at the Neil Simon Theatre

Monty Python's Spamalot earned top fundraising honors in the 17th Annual "Gypsy of the Year" competition, raking in $367,083 toward a $2,972,721.15 total for the event, which benefits Broadway Cares/Equity Fights AIDS. For the second year in a row, the sculpted dancers of *The Lion King* impressed the judges, winning the coveted award for best stage presentation, with "I Remember He Said…." Runner-up was "Chitty Chitty Bye Bye," a skit performed by the child actors of *Chitty Chitty Bang Bang.*

Collected by more than 50 Broadway, Off-Broadway and touring shows over the course of six weeks in nightly curtain-call appeals, the total was the second-highest ever, behind 2003's $3,359,533 but ahead of 2004's $2,754,632 total.

The two-day event was hosted by Brad Garrett and Lee Wilkof of *The Odd Couple.* Star performers included Cathy Rigby, Rosie O'Donnell, Patti LuPone, Michael Cerveris, Huey Lewis and Harvey Fierstein. Favorite satirical targets included the Tourette's Syndrome musical *In My Life* and the spare revival of *Sweeney Todd,* in which the performers double as the orchestra.

Fundraising runners-up among musicals were last year's winner *Wicked* ($221,298), *The Lion King* ($137,118), *Rent* ($130,793) and *Mamma Mia!* ($129,034). The top fundraising national tour was *Wicked* ($214,000), the top fundraising Off-Broadway show was *The Great American Trailer Park Musical* ($34,661), and the top fundraising Broadway play was *Doubt* ($105,715).

1. Winners Ray Mercer and Gabriel Croom of *The Lion King,* surrounded by runners-up from *Chitty Chitty Bang Bang.*
2. The cast of Off-Broadway's *The Great American Trailer Park Musical* make a joyful noise.
3. Cathy Rigby (L) gets tips on auditioning in *Peter Pan*'s sketch.
4. (L-R): Jesse Tyler Ferguson and Todd Buonopane perform the opening number of *The 25th Annual Putnam County Spelling Bee,* à la *Sweeney Todd.*
5. *Beauty and the Beast* cast member Meredith Inglesby performs in the sketch "Baby Mine."
6. Don Richard and Jennifer Cody reprise their *Urinetown* characters.

2005 Broadway Holiday Tree Lighting

December 7, 2005 in Father Duffy Square

1. Students from The Professional Performing Arts School sing in front of the Times Square holiday tree.
2. David Hyde Pierce and Chita Rivera (C, front) are surrounded by cast members from *Altar Boyz* at the Christmas Tree Lighting (L-R): Danny Calvert, James Royce Edwards, Dennis Moench, Jim Daly, Scott Porter, Carlos L. Encinas and Nick Sanchez.

Chita Rivera and David Hyde Pierce led a throng of theatregoers in the 2005 Broadway Holiday Tree lighting December 7 in Duffy Square at the north end of Times Square. The ceremony kicked off with a performance by the cast of the Off-Broadway musical *Altar Boyz*, singing "What Christmas Is...." by one of the musical's composers, Gary Adler. The Theatre Development Fund and The League of American Theatres and Producers presented a $5,000 gift to The New Victory Theater, New York's theatre for kids and families, which celebrated its tenth anniversary December 11, 2005. The event concluded with a performance by sixth grade students from The Professional Performing Arts School. Sponsored by Theatre Development Fund, The League of American Theatres and Producers and The Times Square Alliance, the annual ceremony was free and open to the public.

Broadway Bears IX

May 21, 2006 at B.B. King Blues Club & Grill

Broadway Bears IX, the annual fundraiser for Broadway Cares/Equity Fights AIDS that auctions a host of teddy bears dressed as famous Broadway characters, brought in $114,638 at the fundraiser, hosted by Broadway regular Bryan Batt. The annual event had been scheduled for Feb. 12 but was postponed due to a snowstorm. The bear that raised the most ($8,250) was the *Avenue Q* puppeteer bear, which was signed by original *Q* star John Tartaglia. Other top draws included *The Color Purple's* Sofia bear—signed by *Purple* star Felicia P. Fields and producer Oprah Winfrey—which brought in $5,500, and the *Spamalot's* King Arthur bear—signed by Tim Curry—which took in $4,800. A total of 40 bears were auctioned this year, representing such shows as *700 Sundays, Aida, Amadeus, The Boy From Oz, Carnival, Carrie, Cats, Chitty Chitty Bang Bang, Dirty Rotten Scoundrels, Doubt, Fiddler on the Roof, Funny Girl, Gypsy, Hairspray, Jersey Boys, Julius Caesar, La Cage aux Folles, The Light in the Piazza, Little Shop of Horrors, Movin' Out, The Odd Couple, The Phantom of the Opera, The Producers, Rent,* and *Sweet Charity.*

1. Tim Curry of *Spamalot*.
2. John Tartaglia of *Avenue Q*.

Theater Hall of Fame

January 30, 2006 at the Gershwin Theatre

The Theater Hall of Fame held its 35th induction ceremony January 30 in the rotunda of Broadway's Gershwin Theatre. The class of 2006—director/choreographer Graciela Daniele, scenic designer Ben Edwards, director Sir Peter Hall, costume designer William Ivey Long, playwright William Gibson, and actors Sada Thompson, John Lithgow and Dorothy Loudon—was chosen by the American Theatre Critics Association and the Hall's past honorees.

With columnist Liz Smith as emcee, individual tributes were made by Marian Seldes (to Daniele), Jack O'Brien (to Thompson and Lithgow) and Susan Stroman (to Long). Arthur Penn spoke on behalf of Gibson (*The Miracle Worker, Two for the Seesaw*) who was too frail to attend. Theatrical lawyer and producer Donald R. Seawell saluted Hall, who sent his thanks via letter from London. Edwards was remembered by his widow, the costume designer Jane Greenwood.

Agent Lioner Larner paid posthumous respects to Loudon. A Founders Award was presented by Zoe Caldwell to Seawell, who glanced at the golden list of names on the walls and quipped, "I think I've worked with all of them—except Edwin Booth."

1. (L-R): Honorees Graciela Daniele, William Ivey Long, Founders Award winner Donald R. Seawell, Sada Thompson and John Lithgow pose together at the Gershwin.
2. David Yazbek and Susan Stroman.
3. Jane Greenwood (L) and Zoe Caldwell.
4. Long (L) with Paul Rudnick.
5. (L-R): Seawell, Thompson and Lithgow.

Broadway Show Bowling League Championship

February 9, 2006 at Leisure Time Lanes

"Making Contact," the bowling team consisting of members who have stayed together from the closed show *Contact*, won first place in the semi-annual Broadway Show Bowling League Championship February 9 at the Leisure Time Lanes at Port Authority Bus Terminal.

League commissioner Scott Fagant said the League meets each Thursday to have fun and raise money for Broadway Cares/Equity Fights AIDS. Teams represent more than two dozen running and closed Broadway and Off-Broadway shows.

Season Ending February 9, 2006:

First Place: "Making Contact"
Second Place: "Lane Kings"
Third Place: "Sucks to Be Q"
Fourth Place: "Waste Management"
High Average - Female: Danielle Garner (152)
High Average - Male: Rodger Siegel (189)
High Game Scratch - Team: "Sucks to Be Q" (1000)
High Game Scratch - Female: Danielle Garner (203)
High Game Scratch - Male: Rodger Siegel (232)
Individual Points - Female: Cayte Thorpe (41.5)
Individual Points - Male: Robert Schneider (40)
Most Improved Team: "Dirty Laundry"
Most Improved Bowler - Female: Danielle Garner (+19 pins)
Most Improved Bowler - Male: Rodger Siegel (+68 pins)
Theron Montgomery Award: Jerry "Big Jer" Gallagher.

Season Ending August 29, 2005:

First Place: "Waste Management"
Second Place: "Making Contact"
Third Place: "Mickety Splits"
Fourth Place: "Lane Kings"
High Average - Female: Jenn Pesce (137)
High Average - Male: Tom Biglin (179)
High Game Scratch - Team: "Waste Management" (987)
High Game Scratch - Female: Cayte Thorpe (203)
High Game Scratch - Male: Tom Biglin (232) and Rodger Siegel (232)
Individual Points - Female: Fran Rubenstein (42)
Individual Points - Male: Rick Shulman (47)
Most Improved Team: "Mickety Splits"
Most Improved Bowler - Female: Joanne Decicco (+9 pins)
Most Improved Bowler - Male: Rodger Siegel (+19 pins)
Theron Montgomery Award: Mike Lesser

Photos by Ben Strothmann

First Place, season ending February 9, 2006 (L-R): Tree Sarvay, Jenn Pesce, Cayte Thorpe, Steve Bratton, Scott Fagant and Pete Mastronardi of "Making Contact."

First Place, season ending August 29, 2005 (L-R): Julio Lopez, Valerie A. Peterson and Jared DeBacker of "Waste Management."

(L-R): Steve McDonald, Amber Wedin, Jeff Schiller, Karyn Deandrade and Gary Adler of the "Sucks to Be Q" team.

(L-R): Doug Mestanza, Rodger Siegel and Alberto Vargas of "Holy Rollers."

(L-R): Christine Rudakewycz, Joanne Decicco, Joaquin Quintana, S.J. Runser and Chris Bruce.

Winner of the Theron Montgomery Award for February 2006: Jerry "Big Jer" Gallagher.

Nothin' Like a Dame

March 6, 2006 at the Imperial Theatre

The Imperial Theatre rang with song during the 11th annual "Nothin' Like a Dame" concert, which raised $300,000 for the Phyllis Newman Women's Health Initiative of the Actors' Fund of America.

Headliners included Shoshana Bean, Victoria Clark, Tyne Daly, Felicia Finley, Maria Friedman, Ruthie Henshall, Lauren Kennedy, Leslie Kritzer, Jill Paice and Angie Schworer. The girls of *Jersey Boys* and the women of *Sweeney Todd* performed as ensembles, and the younger generation was represented by Brynn Williams, Catherine Herlin and Jessica Feretti.

Kate Clinton auctioned off a diamond-studded Harry Winston wristwatch. Jennifer Ehle, Julianna Margulies and Cynthia Nixon read from the late Wendy Wasserstein's *Heidi Chronicles*, and the eponymous stars of *Jersey Boys* closed the show with "Big Girls Don't Cry" and the presentation of a $300,000 check from BC/EFA to Phyllis Newman, Bebe Neuwirth and producer Maria Di Dia. A reception followed at John's Pizzeria.

1. Ruthie Henshall and Angie Schworer
arrive at the reception.
2. Phyllis Newman (in white) and
the 2006 Dames take a bow.
3. (L-R): DeAnn Whalen, Rosemary Harris and
Laurie Canaan at John's.
4. Erica Piccininni and Andrew Brettler.
5. Maria Friedman arrives at the theatre.

Easter Bonnet

April 24 and 25, 2006 at the New Amsterdam Theatre

Proving there's more green about *Wicked* than its leading lady, the popular Broadway musical won the grand prize at the Broadway Cares/Equity Fights AIDS' 20th annual "Easter Bonnet" competition by raising $227,112 for the fight against the deadly disease.

The prize for best bonnet presentation went to *The Color Purple*, for the dance number "Lillies in the Field" in which dancers clad in purple welcomed a hat with purple and green streamers, which were taken up by the dancers like a maypole.

All told, $3,187,496 was raised by more than 50 participating shows in six weeks of post-show appeals from their respective stages, beating last year's $2,849,067.

This is the second highest total raised in the history of the Easter Bonnet competition. The record was set in 2004 (the Harvey Fierstein in *Hairspray* vs. Hugh Jackman in *Boy From Oz* year) when $3,435,000 was raised.

Special guests Julia Roberts (*Three Days of Rain*), Harry Connick, Jr. (*The Pajama Game*) and Ana Gasteyer (*The Threepenny Opera*) presented the awards at the New Amsterdam Theatre following two days of performances April 24 and 25.

The Broadway *play* that raised the most money: *Barefoot in the Park* — $76,694.

The national tour that raised the most: *Wicked*, the Shiz Company in Chicago— $206,044. Runner-up: *Mamma Mia!*— $155,000.

The Off-Broadway show that raised the most: *Altar Boyz* — $22,888.

Runners-up for fundraising: *The Color Purple* ($185,399), *The Phantom of the Opera* ($176,412), *Rent* ($149,736) and *The Lion King* ($146,805).

Runners-up for best bonnet and skit: *The Color Purple*, *Mamma Mia!* and *The Lion King*.

Special award for Best Designed and Constructed Bonnet: *Beauty and the Beast*

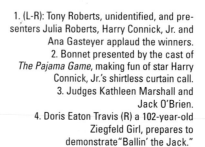

1. (L-R): Tony Roberts, unidentified, and presenters Julia Roberts, Harry Connick, Jr. and Ana Gasteyer applaud the winners.
2. Bonnet presented by the cast of *The Pajama Game*, making fun of star Harry Connick, Jr.'s shirtless curtain call.
3. Judges Kathleen Marshall and Jack O'Brien.
4. Doris Eaton Travis (R) a 102-year-old Ziegfeld Girl, prepares to demonstrate "Ballin' the Jack."

Other Theatre Awards

Covering the 2005-2006 Broadway Season

DRAMA DESK AWARDS

Outstanding Play: Alan Bennett, *The History Boys*
Outstanding Musical: *The Drowsy Chaperone*
Outstanding Revival of a Play: *Awake and Sing!*
Outstanding Revival of a Musical: *Sweeney Todd*
Outstanding Actor in a Play: Richard Griffiths, *The History Boys*
Outstanding Actress in a Play: Lois Smith, *The Trip to Bountiful* (OB)
Outstanding Actor in a Musical: John Lloyd Young, *Jersey Boys*
Outstanding Actresss in a Musical: Christine Ebersole, *Grey Gardens* (OB)
Outstanding Featured Actor in a Play: Samuel Barnett, *The History Boys*
Outstanding Featured Actress in a Play: Frances de la Tour, *The History Boys*
Outstanding Featured Actor in a Musical: Jim Dale, *The Threepenny Opera*
Outstanding Featured Actress in a Musical: Beth Leavel, *The Drowsy Chaperone*
Outstanding Director of a Play: Nicholas Hytner, *The History Boys*
Outstanding Director of a Musical: John Doyle, *Sweeney Todd*
Outstanding Choreography: Kathleen Marshall, *The Pajama Game*
Outstanding Music: Lisa Lambert and Greg Morrison, *The Drowsy Chaperone*
Oustanding Lyrics: Lisa Lambert and Greg Morrison, *The Drowsy Chaperone*
Outstanding Book of a Musical: Bob Martin and Don McKellar, *The Drowsy Chaperone*
Outstanding Orchestrations: Sarah Travis, *Sweeney Todd*
Outstanding Set Design of a Play: Michael Yeargan, *Awake and Sing!*
Outstanding Set Design of a Musical: David Gallo, *The Drowsy Chaperone*
Outstanding Costume Design: Gregg Barnes, *The Drowsy Chaperone*
Outstanding Lighting Design: Richard G. Jones, *Sweeney Todd*
Outstanding Sound Design: Steve Canyon Kennedy, *Jersey Boys*
Outstanding Solo Performance: Sir Antony Sher, *Primo*
Unique Theatrical Experience: *Christine Jorgensen Reveals* (OB)
Outstanding Ensemble Performances: The casts of *Stuff Happens* (Off-Broadway) and *Awake and Sing!*

NY DRAMA CRITICS' CIRCLE AWARDS

Best Play: Alan Bennett, *The History Boys*
Best American Play: No award
Best Musical: Lisa Lambert, Greg Morrison, Bob Martin and Don McKellar, *The Drowsy Chaperone*
Special Citations: John Doyle, Sarah Travis and the Company of *Sweeney Todd;* and Christine Ebersole for *Grey Gardens.*

THE PULITZER PRIZE FOR DRAMA

The Pulitzer committee voted to give no award for 2005-2006.

(L-R): Casey Nicholaw and Bob Martin of *The Drowsy Chaperone* accept Best Musical honors at the New York Drama Critics' Circle Awards.

OUTER CRITICS CIRCLE AWARDS

Outstanding Broadway Play: *The History Boys*
Outstanding Broadway Musical: *Jersey Boys*
Outstanding Off-Broadway Play: *Stuff Happens*
Outstanding Off-Broadway Musical: *Grey Gardens*
Outstanding New Score: *The Drowsy Chaperone*
Outstanding Revival of a Play: *Awake and Sing!*
Outstanding Revival of a Musical: *Sweeney Todd*
Outstanding Actor in a Play: Gabriel Byrne, *A Touch of the Poet*
Outstanding Actress in a Play: Lois Smith, *The Trip to Bountiful* (OB)
Outstanding Actor in a Musical: John Lloyd Young, *Jersey Boys*
Outstanding Actress in a Musical: Christine Ebersole, *Grey Gardens* (OB)
Outstanding Featured Actor in a Play: Richard Griffiths, *The History Boys*
Outstanding Featured Actress in a Play: Frances de la Tour, *The History Boys*
Outstanding Featured Actor in a Musical: Jim Dale, *The Threepenny Opera*
Outstanding Featured Actress in a Musical: Beth Leavel, *The Drowsy Chaperone*
Outstanding Solo Performance: Sir Antony Sher, *Primo*
Outstanding Direction of a Play: Nicholas Hytner, *The History Boys*
Outstanding Direction of a Musical: John Doyle, *Sweeney Todd*
Outstanding Choreography: Kathleen Marshall, *The Pajama Game*
Outstanding Set Design: David Gallo, *The Drowsy Chaperone*
Outstanding Costume Design: Gregg Barnes, *The Drowsy Chaperone*
Outstanding Lighting Design: Howell Binkley, *Jersey Boys*
John Gassner Award (presented for an American play, preferably by a new playwright): Danai Gurira and Nikkole Salter, *In the Continuum* (OB)

THE DRAMA LEAGUE AWARDS

Distinguished Production of a Play: *The History Boys*
Distinguished Production of a Musical: *Jersey Boys*

Distinguished Revival of a Play: *Awake and Sing!*
Distinguished Revival of a Musical: *Sweeney Todd*
Distinguished Performance Award: Christine Ebersole, *Grey Gardens*

THEATRE WORLD AWARDS

For outstanding Broadway or Off-Broadway debuts:
Harry Connick, Jr., *The Pajama Game*
Felicia P. Fields, *The Color Purple*
Maria Friedman, *The Woman in White*
Richard Griffiths, *The History Boys*
Mamie Gummer, *Mr. Marmalade* (OB)
Jayne Houdyshell, *Well*
Bob Martin, *The Drowsy Chaperone*
Ian McDiarmid, *Faith Healer*
Nellie McKay, *The Threepenny Opera*
David Wilmot, *The Lieutenant of Inishmore*
Elisabeth Withers-Mendes, *The Color Purple*
John Lloyd Young, *Jersey Boys*

A dapper Alan Cumming at the Drama League Awards.

THE CLARENCE DERWENT AWARDS

From Actors' Equity for "most promising female and male performers on the New York metropolitan scene":
Felicia P. Fields, *The Color Purple*
Jason Ritter, *Third* (OB)

THE RICHARD SEFF AWARDS

From Actors' Equity, to female and male character actors 50 years of age or older:
Jayne Houdyshell, *Well*
Jim Dale, *The Threepenny Opera.*

THE IRENE SHARAFF AWARDS

From the Theatre Development Fund, for outstanding theatrical design:
Robert L.B. Tobin Award for Lifetime Achievement: Franco Zeffirelli
Lifetime Achievement Award: Lester Polakov
Young Master Award: Emilio Sosa
Artisan Award: Martin Izquierdo
Posthumous Award: Lila De Nobili

TDF/FRED ASTAIRE AWARDS

Given to oustanding dancers and choreographers:
Best Male Dancer: Norbert Leo Butz
Best Female Dancer: No award.
Best Choreographer: No award.
Special Award: Charlotte d'Amboise

The Tony Awards

June 11, 2006 at Radio City Music Hall

The History Boys, Jersey Boys, Awake and Sing! and *The Pajama Game* won the major production categories of the 2006 Tony Awards.

The 60th annual awards, representing excellence in Broadway theatre for the 2005-06 season, were presented at Radio City Music Hall. In lieu of a single host, 60 presenters introduced portions of the show and handed out the awards.

Jersey Boys, the pop-hit-filled backstage tale of Frankie Valli and The Four Seasons snagged the Best Musical Tony Award, one design award and two acting nods.

The History Boys, Alan Bennett's comic and dramatic rumination on education, history and ambition, won six Tonys, the most of any show. Nicholas Hytner earned the Tony for Best Direction of a Play for his work with the ensemble of *History Boys*. The play freely shifts time and place, includes film sequences, a scene in French, a couple of cabaret numbers and soliloquies from its main characters.

Richard Griffiths, the British actor whose career has included classics, films and new works, was named Best Leading Actor in a Play for essaying Hector, an inspirational yet emotionally-closeted high school teacher in *The History Boys*. He created the role at the National Theatre in England (as did the entire company).

The one Tony for *The Color Purple* went to LaChanze, as Best Leading Actress in a Musical, for playing Celie in the musical inspired by the novel by Alice Walker.

Roundabout Theatre Company's production of *The Pajama Game*, which boasted a revised script and included songs not in the original run 50 years ago, won as Revival of a Musical. Lincoln Center Theater's mounting of Clifford Odets's Depression-era classic *Awake and Sing!* was named Best Revival of a Play. Here are all the nominees, with the winners listed in **bold**.

Best Play
The History Boys
The Lieutenant of Inishmore
Rabbit Hole
Shining City

Best Musical
The Color Purple
The Drowsy Chaperone
Jersey Boys
The Wedding Singer

1. Winners: John Lloyd Young of *Jersey Boys*, LaChanze of *The Color Purple*, Cynthia Nixon of *Rabbit Hole* and Richard Griffiths of *The History Boys*.
2. Alan Bennett, author of Best Play *The History Boys*.
3. Christian Hoff with his Tony for Best Featured Actor in a Musical for *Jersey Boys*.
4. Nominees Sutton Foster and Casey Nicholaw with winner Beth Leavel of *The Drowsy Chaperone* on the red carpet outside Radio City Music Hall.

Photos by Aubrey Reuben

Faculty

The Shubert Organization

Gerald Schoenfeld
Chairman

Philip J. Smith
President

Robert E. Wankel
Executive Vice President

Jujamcyn Theatres

Rocco Landesman
President

Paul Libin
Producing Director

Jack Viertel
Creative Director

Photos by Ben Strothmann

Photos courtesy Jujamcyn Theatres

Faculty

The Nederlander Organization

James M. Nederlander
Chairman

James L. Nederlander
President

NEDERLANDER STAFF
Front Row (L-R): Monica Blake, Alyce Cozzi, Lisa Lent, Angela Maisonet, Malera Musliwala.
Middle Row (L-R): Phyllis Buono, David Perry, Stephanie Vasquez, Rina Beallo, Julia Barr, Thuy Dang, Aaron Kelley, Rachel Jukofsky, Maria Fajardo, Blair Zwillman.
Back Row (L-R): Freddy Owen, Josh Salez, Ken Happel and Kevin Dunning.

Freida Belviso

Jim Boese

Susan Lee

Jack Meyer

Kathleen Raitt

GROUP SALES
(L-R): Aaron Kelley, Rachel Jukofsky, Brian Harasek.

Herschel Waxman

Faculty

Disney Theatrical Productions

(L-R): Alan Levey (SVP and General Manager) and Thomas Schumacher (President).

Rod Kollen
SVP, International

David Schrader
SVP, Managing Director and CFO

Todd Lacy
Lion King Associate Producer

Michele Steckler
SVP, Creative Affairs

Front Row (L-R): Laura Eichholz (*Lion King* Assistant Company Manager), Liz Jurist (Financial Analyst), Lynne Schreur (Marketing Coordinator), Nick Judge (Production Accountant), Violeta Burlaza (Associate Buyer), Suzanne Jakel (Assistant Inventory Manager).

Second Row (L-R): Kelli Palan (*Lion King* National Press Representative), Scott Hemerling (*Lion King* National Press Representative), Gregory Hanoian (Assistant, Tour Marketing), Cristina Fornaris (Creative Assistant), Ryan Pears (Marketing Assistant), Craig Buckley (Marketing Promotions Coordinator).

Third Row (L-R): Suyin Chan (Aubrey Lynch's Assistant), Aubrey Lynch (*Lion King* Associate Producer), Harry Gold (Director, Business and Legal Affairs), Dana Torres (Assistant Communications Manager), Emily Powel (Marshal Purdy's Assistant), Michael Height (*Lion King* Production Assistant), Jarrid Crespo (Group Sales Representative), Michele Groner (Marketing Manager).

Fourth Row (L-R): Marey Griffith (*Lion King* Production Dance Supervisor), Tara Engler (Todd Lacy's Assistant), Leslie Barrett (Marketing Manager), Kisha Santiago (General Management Coordinator), Matt Cronin (David Schrader's Assistant), Eric Kratzer (Web Producer).

Fifth Row (L-R): Dayle Gruet (Jonathan Olson's Assistant), Cristi Finn (Assistant HR and Labor Relations), Kerry McGrath (Production Assistant, House Seats), Juil Kim (Assistant Manager, Sales and Marketing), Kevin McGuire (Computer Support Analyst), Jonathan Olson (SVP Business and Legal Affairs), Dusty Bennett (Production Assistant).

Back Row (L-R): Janine McGuire (Receptionist), Lisa Mitchell (Operations Assistant), Seth Stuhl (Attorney), Jacob Kimbro (Group Sales Manager), Jerome Kane (VP Box Office Operations), Shawn Baker (Merchandising Operations Manager), Mark Nathman (Retail Supervisor), and Eddie Pisapia (Merchandise Assistant).

Portraits Courtesy of Disney Theatrical Productions

Photo by David Gewirtzman

Lincoln Center Theater

(L-R): André Bishop (Artistic Director) and Bernard Gersten (Executive Producer).

Photo by Ben Strothmann

Makeup Artists and Hair Stylists, IATSE Local 798

Ray Polgar, Broadway Business Representative

Photo by Ben Strothmann

Faculty

Roundabout Theatre Company

Harry Wolpert, Managing Director

Standing (L-R): Abraham David, Jetaun Dobbs, Rebecca Habel, Nancy Hirschmann, Maggie Cantrick, Tania Camargo.

Seated (L-R): Nicholas Caccavo, Sydney Beers and Greg Backstrom.

Photos by Ben Strothmann

Back Row (L-R): Robert Weinstein, Jill Rafson, Ginger Vallen, Chelsea Glickfield, Sarah Krasnow.
Middle Row (L-R): Sara Bensman, Mark Truscinski, Nicholas Stimler, Casey Cipriani, Arielle Kahaner, Elissa Sussman.
Front Row (L-R): Julia Lazarus, Jeffory Lawson and Steve Schaeffer.

Front Row (L-R): Trina Cox, Charlie Garbowski, David Carson.
Middle Row (L-R): Jacob Burstein-Stern, Pam Unger, Jim Seggelink, Ellen Holt, Nisha Dhruna.
Back Row (L-R): Robert Kane, Allison Ford, Lily Soto, Tova Heller and Jacki Rocha.

Standing (L-R): Carrie Gardner, Stephen Kopel, Kate Schwabe.
Seated (L-R): Mele Nagler and Jim Carnahan.

Standing (L-R): John Haynes, Robert Weisser, Elisa Papa, Scott Kelly, Jeff Goodman, Micah Kraybill, Nick Mustakas, Frank Surdi.
Seated (L-R): John LaBarbera, Susan Neiman, Carly DiFulvio and Yonit Kafka.

Back Row (L-R): Sunil Ayyagari, David Steffen.
Front Row (L-R): Margaret Casagrande and Stefanie Schussel.

(L-R): Jeremy Thomas, Allison Baucom, Renee Flemings, Jennifer DeBruin, George Keveson, Carrie Soloman.
Not Pictured: Margie Salvante-McCann, Education Director

Faculty

League of American Theatres and Producers

Gerald Schoenfeld
Chairman

Jed Bernstein
President

Back Row (L-R): Robert Davis, Neal Freeman, Jim Echikson, Erica Ryan.
Middle Row (L-R): Seth Popper, Karen Hauser, Britt Marden, Edward Forman, Ed Sandler, Roger Calderon, Jed Bernstein, Laura Fayans, David Carpenter, Melanie Seinfeld, Jennifier Stewart, Colin Gibson.
Front Row (L-R): Jazmine Estacio, Roxanne Rodriguez, Tahra Millan, Rachel Reiner and Joy Axelrad.

Not Pictured: Patricia Casterlin, Irving Cheskin, Robin Fox, Barbara Janowitz, Jean Kroeper, Jim Lochner, Ben Pesner, Harriet Slaughter, Jan Svendsen and Zenovia Varelis.

Live Nation

Front Row (L-R): Paul Dietz, Alison Spiriti, Jennifer Costello, David Anderson.
Back Row (L-R): Steve Winton, Susie Krajsa and Steve Winton.

Faculty

Manhattan Theatre Club

Front Row (L-R): Ryan Klink (Marketing Associate/Website Manager), Florie Seery (General Manager), Darren Robertson (HR/Payroll Manager), Lynne Meadow (Artistic Director), Barry Grove (Executive Director), Kristin Svenningsen (Casting Assistant), Sage Young (Patrons Liaison), Rey Pamatmat (Development Database Coordinator).

Second Row (L-R): Lauren Butler (Reception/Studio Manager), Aaron Leichter (Play Development Associate/Sloan Project Manager), Andrea Gorzell (Development Associate/Foundation and Government Relations), Paige Evans (Director of Artistic Development), Emily Bohanan (Telesales), Michael Bush (Director of Artistic Production), Amy Harris (Assistant Director of Education), Kacy O'Brien (Artistic Assistant), Jill Turner Lloyd (Director of Development).

Third Row (L-R): Holly Kinney (Business Manager), Rebekah Dewald (Subscriber Services Representative).

Fourth Row (L-R): Ryan McMahon (Production Manager), Lindsey Brooks (Associate General Manager), Nancy Piccione (Director of Casting), David Caparelliotis (Casting Director), Jeffrey Bledsoe (Director of Finance), Bonnie Pan (Assistant to the Executive Producer), Erin Moeller (Company Manager/NY City Center), Antonello Di Benedetto (Senior Development Associate, Individual Giving), Andrew Dumawal (Systems Analyst).

Fifth Row: Debra Waxman (Director of Marketing).

Sixth Row (L-R): Robert Allenberg (Director of Subscriber Services), Dale Edwards (Marketing Manager), Jessica Sadowski (Development Associate/Corporate Relations), Amy Gilkes Loe (Assistant to the Artistic Director), Mandy Greenfield (Director of Artistic Operations), Annie MacRae (Play Development Assistant), Liz Halakan (Development Associate/Planning and Projects), Denise Thomas (Senior Business Associate and HR Coordinator), Kayla Cagan (Education Assistant), Emily Shooltz (Literary Manager).

Back Row (L-R): Andrew Taylor (Associate Subscriber Services Manager), Mark Bowers (Subscriber Services Representative), Matthew Praet (Subscriber Services Representative), Ian McNaugher (Assistant Production Manager), Allison Gutstein (Director, Special Events), Casey Reitz (Director, Individual Giving), Tom Casazzone (Business Assistant), Karen Zornow Leiding (Director, Corporate Relations), Josh Jacobson (Director, Foundation and Government Relations) and Avishai Cohen (Manager of Systems Operation).

Faculty

American Theatre Wing

BOARD OF DIRECTORS and STAFF
Seated (L-R): Michael Price, Dasha Epstein, Sondra Gilman, Doug Leeds, Lucie Arnaz, Ron Konecky.
Standing (L-R): Howard Sherman, Robb Perry, Ted Chapin, William Craver, Jay Harris, Mallory Factor, David Brown, Matt Jarrett, Randy Ellen Lutterman and Stephen Abrams.

Not Pictured, Board: Marlene Hess, Henry Hewes, Anita Jaffe, Jeffrey Eric Jenkins, Jo Sullivan Loesser, Lloyd Richards, Jane Safer, Peter Schneider, Alan Siegel and Howard Stringer. Not Pictured, Staff: Raisa Ushomirskiy.

ATW Theatre Intern Group

COORDINATORS
(L-R): Sarah Rotker (Program Assistant) and Stephen Abrams (Program Manager).

Front Row (L-R): Oliver Wason, Aly Mifa Solot, Malissa O'Donnell, Raymond Wetmore, Michelle Lehrman, Danielle Toscano, Robin Steinthal, Jennifer Rosa, Holly Serber, Mara Jill Herman.
Second Row (L-R): Rebecca Bernstein, Allison Ford, Reva Minkoff, Jillian Goodman, Josh Schecter, Cara Chute, Arielle Kahaner, Shannon Marcotte, Carly DiFulvio, Casey Keeler, Zoë Block, Amy Schwartz, Nick Stimler.
Third Row (L-R): Jessie Pithik, Christy Denny, Rebecca Reaves, Daryl Eisenberg, Jeff Simno, Kristina Bramhall, Michael Coon, Rachel Reiss, Milan Rakic, Melinda Blake, Kerri Resnick, Ashley Pines.
Fourth Row (L-R): Alyssa Hart, Hailey Apter, Ruthie Wagh, Kristin Donnelly, Brent McCreary, Morgan Schreiber, Aaron Glick, Melanie Friedson, Evan Hay.
Back Row (L-R): Sarah Miller, Jessica Furr, Lindsay Kilgore, Beth Watson, Rebecca Schwartz and Paula Raymond.

Faculty

Tony Award Productions

Beth Blitzer

Elizabeth I. McCann

Joey Parnes

Emily Campbell

Kim Carpenter

Trini Huschle

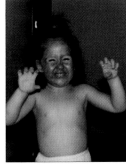

Kit Ingui

John Johnson

Sadie Keenan

Izzy Masucci

Gaydon Phillips

Diane Raillard

Stephen Sosnowski

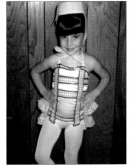

Sue Wagner

TonyAwards.com

(L-R): Ben Pesner and Andrew McGibbon.

Faculty

Producing Companies

RICHARD FRANKEL PRODUCTIONS and THE FRANKEL GROUP
Front Row (L-R): Rod Kaats, Laura Green, Marc Routh, Thomas Viertel, Richard Frankel, Jo Porter, Carter Anne McGowan, Joe Watson, Ronni Mandell, Mike Naumann.
Second Row (L-R): Maia Sutton, Roddy Pimentel, John Kivlen, Lori Steiger-Perry, Aliza Wassner, Jason Pelusio, Sammy Ledbetter, Jackie Newman, Marc Borsak, Liz Hines.
Third Row (L-R): Gena Chavez, Josh Saletnik, Brad Bauner, Allison Engallena, Stephanie Adamczyk, Melissa Marano, Katie Berkshire, Tracy Geltman, Seth Soloway.
Fourth Row (L-R): Lulu Zhang, Michael Sag, Leslie Pinney, John DiMeglio, Nicole O'Bleanis, Kim Sellon, Amy Clarke, Kirsten Rega, John Retsios.
Back Row (L-R): Tania Senewiratne, Heidi Schading, Heather Allen, Laura Thomas, Jeff Romley.
Not Pictured: Steven Baruch, Simma Levine, Simone Genatt, Maria Flotta, Adam Gentle, Grant Rice, Kathy Lowe, Myriah Perkins and Randy Rainbow.

BARRY AND FRAN WEISSLER

CAMERON MACKINTOSH

THE COOPER COMPANY
Sitting: Pamela Cooper (President).
Standing (L-R): Mink Chu (Managerial Assistant), Stephanie Adamczyk (Assistant), Jason Viarengo (Development Associate).

WAXMAN WILLIAMS ENTERTAINMENT
(L-R): Anita Waxman and Elizabeth Williams.

Faculty

Theatre Development Fund and TKTS

Front Row (L-R): Tina Kirsimae, Veronica Claypool, Lisa Carling, Tymand Staggs, Joy Cooper, Eric Sobel, Victoria Bailey, Catherine Lizima.
Second Row (L-R): Ann Matheison, Jane Pfeffer, Joe Cali, Greg Poplyk, Doug Smith, Costas Michalopoulos, Howard Marren, Christophe Mentor, Sal Polizzi, Eve Rodriguez.
Third Row (L-R): Robert Gore, Richard Price, Bill Costellano, Cheryl Schoonmaker, Fran Polino, David LeShay, Jonathan Post, Angel Blasini, Martha Bertram, Matthew Runion.
Back Row (L-R): Branden Huldeen, Lawrence Paone, Tony Heron, John Michael Diresta, Shari Tietlebaum, Michelle St. Hill, Amy Svoboda, Tom Westerman, William Holza, Angel Blasini, Joseph McLaughlin and William Roeder.

Local One (Stagehands)

OFFICERS
Seated (L-R): Michael Wekselblatt (Theatre Business Manager), Robert Score (Secretary), James J. Claffey, Jr. (President), Willie Walters (Vice President), Donald Kleinschmidt (Treasurer).
Standing (L-R): Edward McMahon (Television Business Manager), Robert Nimmo (Television Business Manager), Kevin McGarty (Theatre Business Manager), John M. Diaz, Sr. (Board of Trustees Chairman), William Ngai (Trustee) and Daniel Thorn (Trustee).

Faculty

Actors' Equity Association

Patrick Quinn
President

Alan Eisenberg
Executive Director

Photos by Ben Strothmann

NATIONAL COUNCIL
Front Row (L-R): Conard Fowkes (Secretary/Treasurer), Patrick Quinn (President), Mark Zimmerman (First Vice President).
Back Row (L-R): Ira Mont (Third Vice President), Arne Gundersen (Eastern Regional Vice President). Not Pictured: Jean-Paul Richard (Second Vice President).

Front Row (L-R): Kathy Mercado, Nancy Lynch, Rick Berg, Mark Kochanski, Kathryn Herrera, Nancy Fattorini.
Second Row: Zalina Hoosein.
Third Row (L-R): Mandy LeBlanc, Gisella Valenzuela, Diane Raimondi, Tatiana Kouloumbis, Sylvia Galloway, Beverly Sloan, Robin Thomsen, Ken Greenwood.
Fourth Row (L-R): Kristin Wolf, Lawrence Lorczak, Louise Fosey, Alison Hall, Tom Kaub, Russell Lehrer, Walt Kiskaddon.
Back Row (L-R): Catherine Jayne, Val LaVarco, William Adriance, Sylvina Persaud, Kevin Pinzon, Gary Dimon, Willie Boston, Joe Erdey, Julie Posner, Jamie Blankenship, Scott McNulty, Dwayne Upp, Barry Rosenberg, Nicole Compesi, Joel Solari and Nikki Lotito.

Front Row (L-R): Chris Lagalante, Helene Ross, Karlene Laemmie, Courtney Godan.
Back Row (L-R): J. P. Regit, Deborah Johnson, Altravise Smith, David Thorn and Alison Plotkin.

EXECUTIVE WING, 16th FLOOR GROUP
Front Row (L-R): Alan Eisenberg, Steve DiPaola, Marie Gottschall, Mary Lou Westerfield, Flora Stamatiades.
Second Row (L-R): Nicole Yanolatos, David Lotz, John Fasulo, Ann Fortuno, Diana Previtre, Amy Dolan-Fletcher.
Third Row (L-R): Tami Jean Lombardi, Chris Nee, Ellen Deutsch, Stuart Levy.
Back Row (L-R): Joe De Michele, Robert Fowler and Frank Horak.

Faculty

IATSE Local 306 Motion Picture Projectionists, Video Technicians and Allied Crafts (Ushers)

Front Row (L-R): Rita Russell, Mim Pollock, Barry Garfman, Hugo Capra.
Back Row (L-R): Susan Lehman, Ken Costigan, Dotty Rogan, Rosaire Lulu Caso, Arlene Reilly and Mike Terr.

United Scenic Artists, IATSE Local 829

(L-R): Carl Baldasso (Corresponding Secretary), Cecilia Friederichs (Financial Secretary), Michael McBride (Business Agent), Beverly Miller (President) and Joe Saint (Treasurer).

Faculty

Association of Theatrical Press Agents and Managers

Front Row (L-R): Bruce Cohen (President), Gordon G. Forbes (Secretary-Treasurer), David R. Calhoun (Vice President)
Back Row (L-R): Maria A. Somma (Board Member), Jim Baldassare (Board Member), David Gersten (Board Member), Lauri Wilson (Board Member), Mary Witte (Board Member), Doug Baker (Board Member), Shirley Herz (Board Member) and Mark Schweppe (Board Member).

Not pictured: Robert Nolan, Kevin McAnarney, Susan Elrod and Barbara Carroll.

Society of Stage Directors and Choreographers

Front Row (L-R): James Graves, Ron Shechtman (Counsel), Pamela Berlin (President), Barbara Hauptman (Executive Director), Kathryn Haapala (Deputy Executive Director).
Middle Row (L-R): Jen Flaxman, Tom Moore, Julie Arenal, Karen Azenberg (Executive Vice President), Edie Cowan, Gerald Freedman, Wendy C. Goldberg, Sheldon Epps, Tisa Chang, Sue Lawless (Secretary), Barbara Wolkoff, Renee Lasher, Michele Holmes.
Back Row (L-R): Ethan McSweeny, Sam Bellinger, Tracy Mendez, Dan Sullivan, Kathleen Marshall, David Warren, Mauro Melleno, John Dillon, Kim Rogers, Hope Clarke and Alisa Matlovsky.

Faculty

Treasurers & Ticket Sellers Union, IATSE Local 751

Photos by Ben Strothmann

Front Row (L-R): Kathy McBrearty, Joseph Scanapicco, Jr., Matthew Fearon.
Second Row (L-R): Patricia Quiles, Gene McElwain and Jim Sita.

Seated (L-R): Diane Heatherington, Robert Begin, Matthew Fearon, Joseph Scanapicco, Jr., Gene McElwain, Michael Loiacono, David Heveran.
Standing (L-R): Stanley Shaffer, Fred Santore, Jr., Peter Attanasio, Jr., Harry Jaffie, Karen Winer, John Nesbitt, Paul Posillico, Greer Bond and Noreen Morgan.

Theatrical Wardrobe Union, IATSE Local 764

Front Row (L-R): Nisa Pharms, Executive Board Trustee Shannon Koger, Executive Board Trustee Charles Catanese, Barbara Hladsky, Ginnie Weidmann,Tree Sarvay, Executive Board Trustee Patricia Sullivan.
Second Row (L-R): Gwyn Martin, Kate Gaudio, Ray Panelli, Vice President Kristin Gardner, Bobby Condon, Steve Epstein, Ann Comanar.
Third Row (L-R): Executive Board Trustee Shelly Friedman, J.C. Sheets, Rose Mary Taylor, Soomi Marano, Marilyn Knotts, Linda McAllister, Sergeant-At-Arms Terry LaVada.
Fourth Row (L-R): Judy Kahn, Dennis Birchall, Tim Hanlon, Martha Smith, David Ruble, President Patricia A. White.
Standing (L-R): Business Representative James Hurley, Vernon Ross, Executive Board Trustee Veneda Truesdale, Fund Administrator Mary Ferry, Business Representative Frank Gallagher, Staff member Michael Gemignani, Assistant Fund Administrator Carletta Pizzorno, Staff member Joan Boyce, Steve-John Losito, Staff member Chris Harris, Staff member Rosemary McGroarty and Secretary-Treasurer Jenna Krempel.

Faculty

Theatrical Teamsters, Local 817

EXECUTIVE BOARD
(Standing L-R): Kevin Keefe, Mike Hyde, Ed Iacobelli, T.J. O'Donnell, Jim Leavey and Frank Connolly, Jr. Seated: T.R. O'Donnell.

Photos by Ben Strothmann

STAFF
(L-R): Tina Gusmano, Christine Harkerss and Marge Marklin.

Service Employees International Union Local 32BJ

Photo by Ben Strothmann

EXECUTIVE OFFICERS
(L-R): Kevin Doyle (Executive Vice President), Héctor J. Figueroa (Secretary-Treasurer) and Michael P. Fishman (President).

International Union of Operating Engineers Local 30

Photo Courtesy Local 30

BUSINESS MANAGER
Jack Ahern

Faculty

Coalition of Broadway Unions and Guilds

Seated (L-R): Rebecca Frank, Ray Polgar, Pat White, Cecilia Friederichs.
Standing (L-R): Stacy Tillett, Tom Walsh, John Diaz, Miriam L. Pollock, Bruce Cohen, Barbara Hauptman, Mauro Melleno, Tony DePaulo, Gene McElwain, Ken Greenwood, Ira Mont and Alex Barreto.

Tobak-Lawrence Company

Suzanne Tobak

Michael Lawrence

Joanna B. Koondel

Richard Fromm

Faculty

Broadway Cares/Equity Fights AIDS

Front Row (L-R): Bobby McGuire, Jaime Bishton (holding picture of Chris Giarmo), Denise Roberts Hurlin, Chris Economakos, Frank Conway, Josh Blye.
Second Row (L-R): Peter Neufeld, Dennis Henriquez, Ed Garrison, Carol Ingram, Roy Palijaro, David Finch, Ariadne Villarreal.
Third Row (L-R): Trisha Doss, Jody O'Neil, Joe Norton, Tom Viola (Executive Director), Larry Cook (Director of Finance and Administration), Brian O'Donnell, Andy Halliday, Michael Graziano (Producing Director), Andy Smith, Kevin Burke, Jeff Perry, Rose James, Chris Kenney, Skip Lawing, Peter Borzotta.
Fourth Row (L-R): Scott Stevens, Nathan Hurlin, Charles Hamlen, Ngoc Ha Bui, Michael Kumor and Anthony LaTorella.

American Federation of Musicians, Local 802

Front Row (L-R): Jay Blumenthal (VP), David Lennon (President), Bill Dennison (VP).
Middle Row (L-R): Bobby Shankin, John Babich, Mary Whitaker, Mary Landolfi.
Back Row (L-R): John Bogert, Tino Gagliardi, Art Weiss and Jack Gale.

Not Pictured: Maura Giannini, Jay Schaffner and Jimmy Owens.

Faculty

Dramatists Guild

DRAMATISTS GUILD COUNCIL - STEERING COMMITTEE
Seated (L-R): Arthur Kopit, Jonathan Reynolds, John Weidman, Marsha Norman.
Standing (L-R): Ralph Sevush, David Henry Hwang, Carol Hall, Susan Birkenhead.

Not Pictured: David Auburn, Sheldon Harnick, Stephen Schwartz and Jeanine Tesori.

Seated (L-R): Gregory Bossler (Director of Publications), Joel Szulc (Managing Director), Susan Drury (Administrator Dramatists Guild Fund), John Minore (Executive Assistant), Tom Epstein (Director of Membership Services).

Standing (L-R): Doug Green (Webmaster/Director of MIS), Tari Stratton (Director of Education, Events & Outreach), Rebecca A. Frank (Director of Business Affairs), Ralph Sevush (Executive Director).

Faculty

Hudson Scenic Group

MEMBERS OF TPU LOCAL ONE
Front Row (L-R): Chuck Adomanis, Josh Braun, Roger Bardwell, Dave Rosenfeld, Phil Giller, Dom Godfrey, Jim Starr, John Sisilli, Shawn Larkin.
Second Row (L-R): Joselito Vasconez, Corina Frerotte, Katherine McCauley, David Steiner, Jerry Valenzuela, Russ Stevens, Don Cafaro, Gabriel Tepoxteco, Tony Goncalves, James Curry, Richard Chebetar, Zim Levine.
Third Row (L-R): Dean Kozelek, Jess Stevens, John Howie, Kevin Clifford, Marc Schmittroth, Christopher Pravata, Eric Czarnecki, Karl Schuberth, Diego Irizarry, Breffny Flynn, Nicole St. Clair.
Fourth Row (L-R): Jordan Gable, Jose Mauri, Carlos Ramos, Matthew Coviello, Alan Grudzinski, Kallica Hamment, Jeremy Palmer, Andrew Lanzarotta, Adam Cohan, Sean Farrugia, David Kidd, William Wells, Bill Mark, Rick George, Joshua Coakley, Ben Granucci, Elisio Rodriguez, John Tygert.
Fifth Row (L-R): George Sibbald, Bruce Kesner, Bart Coviello, Tony Tallarico, Matt Jones, Brian Griffin, Mike Fasulo, Kyle Weidner, Chad Hershey, David Berendes, Brian Chebetar.
Back Row (L-R): Joel Deryner, Mike Banta, David Lieber, Patrick Quinn, Ronald Walsh, Chris Labudde, Andrew Williamson and Matt Bell.

Photos by Ben Strothmann

MEMBERS OF LOCAL 829
Front Row (L-R): Patricia Bases, Carla Messina, Polly Holland, Louise Krozek, Clare Hein, Grace Brandt, Dana Heffern.
Second Row (L-R): Kristin Emery, Susan Blume, Kyle Higgins, Joyce Kubalak, Rise Abramson.
Third Row (L-R): Will Ball, Robert Braun, Mary Burt, Michael Lucas, Jane Thurn, Doug Sinclair, Reid Thompson, Amy Lyons.
Back Row (L-R): Boris Shulman, Lynn Nickels, Lynn Muniz, Jill Sternberg, Kathleen Coughlin, Carol Suchy, Richard Fuggetta, Leo Drondin, Vladimir Langransky and Jon Adam McGalliard.

ADMINISTRATIVE STAFF
Seated (L-R): Tom Sullivan, John Larkin, Neil A. Mazzella (President), Corky Boyd, Rick Mone.

Standing (L-R): David Howe, Yanique Berry, Barbara Bloomfield, Melissa McGhee, Joe Bellber, Mark O'Brien, Delia Washington, Mike Madravazakis, Carrie Silverstein, Daryl Haley, Sheri Snow and Sam Ellis.

Faculty

Boneau/Bryan-Brown

Chris Boneau

Adrian Bryan-Brown

Aaron Meier

Brandi Cornwell

Eric Louie

Heath Schwartz

Hector Hernandez

Jackie Green

Jessica Johnson

Jim Byk

Joe Perrotta

Juliana Hannett

Kevin Jones

Linnae Petruzzelli

Matt Polk

Matt Ross

Shanna Marcus

Susanne Tighe

Faculty

Barlow•Hartman Public Relations

John Barlow

Michael Hartman

Photos by Ben Strothmann

Leslie Baden

Carol Fineman

Bethany Larsen

Rick Miramontez

Ryan Ratelle

Andy Snyder

Gerilyn Shur

Wayne Wolfe

Springer Associates Public Relations

(L-R): Gary Springer and Joe Trentacosta

Faculty

The Pete Sanders Group

(L-R): Shane Marshall Brown, Katie Kirby, Glenna Freedman, Pete Sanders and Clifton Guterman.

Photos by Ben Strothmann

Richard Kornberg & Associates

Richard Kornberg

Don Summa

Carrie Friedman

Tom D'Ambrosio

Alyssa Hart

Jeffrey Richards Associates

Irene Gandy

The Publicity Office

Michael Borowski

Faculty

G. Anderson B. Aquart J. Aquino J. Cooper M. Barry D. Cox T. Coppola A. Cruz

A. Davis J. Disbrow S. Eckersley T. Francis A. Heape L. Hunter L. Johnson L. Kaiser

SpotCo Class of 2006

B. Berk J. Edwards T. Greenwald D. Hodges

R. Colb J. Lanasa R. Lederman M. Littell M. Masyga T. McCann J. McClelland

J. McNicholas P. Milano W. Mitchell G. Montalvo D. Preston M. Rheault A. Rothenberg

V. Sainato K. Smarsh D. Suyama D. Tandet E. Vicioso G. Wingfield

Text and page design by SpotCo

Faculty

Serino Coyne, Inc.

Nancy Coyne
Class Co-President

Class of 2005-2006

Matthew Serino
Class Co-President

Photos Courtesy Serino Coyne

Andy Apostolides

Sandy Block

Tom Callahan

Greg Corradetti

Angelo DeSimini

Scott Johnson

David Kane

Burt Kleeger

Roger Micone

Jim Miller

Thomas Mygatt

Ruth Rosenberg

Jim Russek

Sue Taylor

Ginger Witt

Faculty

Adam Neumann

Pamela Bush

Sean Keepers

Dave Kim

Betsy Gershaw

Jovan Villalba

DeWayne Snype

Jeff Matisoff

Katie Koch

Denise Ganjou

Clint White

Lynette Simmons

Martha Magnuson

emg-ltd.com

Jon Bierman

Davlynn Gundolff

Barbara Eliran

Lianne Ritchie

Brian Wertz

Ann Murphy

Elizabeth Findlay

Terry Newberry

Erika Creagh

Marshall Vickness

Steve Knight

Frank Verlizzo

Janice Brunell

Taryn O'Bra

Al Garcia

Patrick Flood

Suzanne Hereth

Heather Leibling

Lucy Lamela

Faculty

The Actors' Fund of America

Photos by Ben Strothmann

Seated (L-R): Icem Benamu, Stephanie Linwood Coleman, Patch Schwadron, Lucy Seligson, Liz Lawlor, Erica Chung, Josh Levine, Ryan Dietz.
Second Row (L-R): Debbie Schaum, Judy Fish, Belinda Sosa, Joe Benincasa, Sue Composto, Tamar Shapiro, Sara Meehan.
Third Row (L-R): Victor Mendoza, Jose Delgado, Gloria Jones, Dave Gusty, Billie Levinson, Wally Munro, Catherine Cooke, Ruth Shin.
Fourth Row (L-R): Melissa Haslam, Sylvian Underwood, Lorraine Chisholm, Lisa Naudus, Helene Kendler, Thomas Pileggi.
Fifth Row (L-R): Barbara Davis, Sam Smith, Charlene Morgan, Vicki Avila, Carol Wilson, Rick Martinez, Tim Pinckney, Israel Duran, Janet Pearl.
Back Row (L-R): Dr. Jim Spears, David Engelman, Jonathan Margolies, Keith McNutt and Bob Rosenthal.

Binder Casting

Front Row (L-R): Mark Brandon, Jay Binder C.S.A., Jack Bowdan C.S.A.

Back Row (L-R): Nikole Vallins, Megan Larche and Rachel Shapiro Cooper.

Faculty

Playbill / Manhattan

Philip S. Birsh
Publisher

Clifford S. Tinder
Senior Vice President/ Publisher, Classic Arts Division

MANHATTAN OFFICE
Front Row (L-R): Clifford S. Tinder, Ruthe Schnell, Terry Wilson, Ira Pekelnaya.
Second Row (L-R): Anderson Peguero, Lilian Richman, Jane F. Katz, Lavdi Sofia, Clara Tiburcio, Louis Botto, Andy Buck, Orlando Pabon, Esvard D'Haiti.
Third Row (L-R): Silvija Ozols, Oldyna Dynowska, Theresa Holder, Melissa Merlo, Natasha Williams, Joel Wyman, Jolie Schaffzin, Judy Samelson, Susan Ludlow, Irv Winick, Arturo Gonzalez.
Back Row (L-R): David Gewirtzman, Ari Ackerman, Bruce Stapleton, Amy Asch, Maude Popkin, Alex Near, Timothy Leinhart, Harry Haun and Robert Viagas.   Not pictured: Christina Foster, Kesler Thibert.

EDITORIAL
(L-R): Silvija Ozols, Louis Botto, Judy Samelson, Robert Viagas, Maude Popkin, Alex Near, Andy Buck and Clifford S. Tinder.

Not pictured: Harry Haun.

ADVERTISING
(L-R): Jane F. Katz, Clifford S. Tinder, Jolie Schaffzin, Glenn Asciutto, Susan Ludlow and Irv Winick.

Not pictured: Glenn Shaevitz, Erica Rubin and Ari Ackerman.

Faculty

Playbill / Miami

Arthur T. Birsh
Chairman

Joan Alleman
*Corporate Vice
President*

Leslie J. Feldman
*Publisher/
Southern Division*

Photos by Alex. Matschick

PUBLISHING AND ADVERTISING STAFF
Front Row (L-R): Sara Smith, Arthur T. Birsh, Leslie J. Feldman, Donald Roberts.
Back Row (L-R): Tom Green, Jeff Ross and Ed Gurien.

SOUTHERN PLAYBILL STAFF
First Row (L-R): Sara Smith, Mark Hamilton, Ruth Ingram, Laura Goldman, Maria Moreno, Maritza Lopez, Sally Coscia.
Second Row (L-R): Raquel Romero, Jeff Ross, Michelle Campos, Leslie J. Feldman, Arthur T. Birsh, Joan Alleman, Donald Roberts, Kevin Keegan.
Third Row (L-R): Tom Green, Silvia Cañadas, Christopher Diaz, Carolina Diaz, Milton McPherson, Eric Schrader, Lance Lenhardt, Ed Gurien and Baldemar Albornoz. (Photos taken at the Jackie Gleason Theatre in Miami Beach.)

ART STAFF
Front Row (L-R): Maria Moreno, Carolina Diaz, Joan Alleman (Vice President), Maritza Lopez, Silvia Cañadas.
Back Row (L-R): Lance Lenhardt, Christopher Diaz, Milton McPherson, Sally Coscia, Baldemar Albornoz.

PRODUCTION STAFF
Front Row (L-R): Raquel Romero, Laura Goldman, Linda Clark, Ruth Ingram.
Back Row (L-R): Mark C. Hamilton, Eric Schrader, Michelle Campos and Kevin Keegan.

Faculty

Playbill / Woodside

Photos by Ben Strothmann

PRODUCTION
(L-R): David Porrello, Sean Kenny,
Benjamin Hyacinthe and Patrick Cusanelli.

PRINTERS (DAY SHIFT)
Front Row (L-R): Clifford S. Tinder, Domingo
Pagan, Nancy Galarraga, Gilbert Gonzales,
Mary Roaid, Janet Moti, David Rodrigues,
Joe Luccania, Arnold Jaklitsch.
Back Row (L-R): Manny Guzman, Ray Sierra,
Louis Cusanelli, John Matthews,
Robert Cusanelli, Fabian Cordero, Scott Cipriano,
Larry Przetakiewicz, Ramdat Ramlall
and Wilfredo Lebron.

PRINTERS (NIGHT SHIFT)
(L-R): Clifford S. Tinder,
Robert Cusanelli,
Mike Rotundo,
James Ayala, Ken Gomez,
Frank Dunn, Tom McClenin,
Lennox Worrell,
Malik Greene, Gary Pope,
Elias Garcia and
Carlos Moyano.

Faculty

Playbill / Woodside

Photos by Ben Strothmann

PLAYBILL ONLINE
(L-R): Morgan Allen, Kenneth Jones, Ernio Hernandez, Ari Ackerman, Andrew Gans, Timothy Leinhart, Andrew Ku, Robert Simonson (Managing Editor) and David Gewirtzman.

ACCOUNTING (L-R): Lewis Cole, JoAnn D'Amato, John LoCascio, Theresa Bernstein, James Eastman and Beatriz Chitnis.

CLASSIC ARTS DIVISION PROGRAM EDITORS (L-R): Clifford S. Tinder (Publisher), Evan Dashevsky, Tom Nondorf, Claire Mangan, Scott Sepich and Kristy Bredin.

PLAYBILLARTS.COM STAFF (L-R): Ari Ackerman, Ben Mattison (Editor), Vivien Schweitzer, Timothy Leinhart, Andrew Ku and David Gewirtzman.

PROGRAM EDITORS (L-R): Pam Karr (Broadway) and Scott Hale (Off-Broadway).

Michael Buckley
Columnist

Harry Haun
Columnist

Steven Suskin
Columnist

Wayman Wong
Columnist

Faculty

Playbill / Yearbook Staff

Correspondents: Melissa Merlo and David Gewirtzman

Most Exciting Broadway Star Reaction: Without a doubt, Sara Ramirez (Original Lady of the Lake), from *Monty Python's Spamalot*. After seeing the yearbook, she grabbed Melissa's arm and starting jumping up and down while expressing how cool she thought it was. The cast of *The 25th Annual Putnam County Spelling Bee* were very receptive, but, alas, no jumping up and down.

Favorite Therapy: "Tasty Time," Mr. Softee, snacks, and our lunchtime picnics.

Favorite In-House Parody Lyrics: "A Real Nice Yearbook"
This is a real nice yearbook,
We've quite enjoyed this fling.
This year's small troupe has much less soup,
But production remained the king.
No courier
Did visit a page -
On wood, we give some knocks.
This is a real nice yearbook,
Now please insert a Shubert box.

Favorite Snack Food: Take Five Bar, Popcorn, Starbursts, Smarties, Tootsie Roll Pops, Nestle Crunch, Pretzels and many more. We call our stash "The Playbill Candy Store."

Mascots: The Carmen Miranda Hat, SpongeBob SquarePants and David's 2 Husky Dog Magnets.

How Many People Does It Take to Lift a Year-

(L-R): Ira Pekelnaya, Amy Asch, Robert Viagas, Melissa Merlo, Ben Strothmann and David Gewirtzman with the 2005 Yearbook. Not pictured: Kesler Thibert.

book: Punchline not available at press time.

Who Has the Smallest Handwriting: Amy.

Catchphrases Only the Staff Would Recognize: The Soup is canned. Production is king. "Should" is a dirty word.

Coolest Thing About This Job: Being able to meet and work with everyone in the Broadway community.

Aubrey Reuben

Playbill / Regional Advertising Salespersons

Kenneth R. Back
Sales Manager
Cincinnati

Betsy Gugick
Sales Manager
Dallas

Abigail Bocchetto
Sales
Houston

Elaine Bodker
Sales
St. Louis

Carol Brumm
Sales
St. Louis

Bob Caulfield
Sales
San Francisco

Margo Cooper
Sales Manager
St. Louis

Ron Friedman
Sales Manager
Columbus

Ira Kamens
Sales Manager
Philadelphia

Michel Manzo
Sales Manager
Philadelphia

Marilyn A. Miller
Sales Manager
Minneapolis

Judy Pletcher
Sales Manager
Washington, DC

John Rosenow
Sales Manager
Phoenix/Tucson

Kenneth Singer
Sales Manager
Houston

Not pictured: Megan Boles, Nancy Hardin, Maureen Umlauf and Dave Levin.

In Memoriam

May 2005 to May 2006

Louis H. Aborn
Don Adams
Tony Adams
Eddie Albert
Larry Alford
Jay Presson Allen
Paul Anderson
Keith Andes
Leon Askin
Doria Avila
Anne Bancroft
Jack Banning
Thomas Barbour
Tom Batten
Barbara Bel Geddes
Mary Hayley Bell
John Belluso
Joseph Bernard
Edward Bishop
Hubert Bland
Lloyd Bochner
James Booth
Joseph Bova
Jocelyn Brando
Barbara Brewster
Richard Bright
Donald Brooks
Oscar Brown, Jr.
Susan Browning
Gisela Caldwell
Hamilton Camp
Philip Campanella
J.D. Cannon
Al Carmines
Lawrence Carra
Jean Carson
David Case
Oleg Cassini
Clive Clerk
Alan Coleridge
Franklin Cover
Constance Cummings
Bob Denver
John Dorrin
Amanda Duff Dunne
Richard Eastham
Dana Elcar
Stephen Elliott
William Farner
Don Farnworth
Clifford Fearl
Cy Feuer
Geraldine Fitzgerald
Michael Fogarty
Johnny Ford
Phil Ford
Henderson Forsythe
Anthony Franciosa
Peark Frank
Lee Franklin
Elisabeth Fraser
Christopher Fry
Geoff Garland
Pietro Garinei

Michael Gibson
Priscilla Gillette
William Gleason
Frank Goodman
Frank Gorshin
Elaine Grollman
Mortimer Halpern
T. Edward Hambleton
Peter Hamilton
Blair Hammond
Lewis Harmon
Carl Harms
Skitch Henderson
Del Hinkley
Abe Hirschfeld
Joel Hirschhorn
Endesha Ida Mae Holland
Betty Lee Hunt
Evan Hunter
Mary Jackson
Luther James
Peter Johl
Justine Johnston
Dorothy Jordan
Roger Kachel
Andreas Katsulas
Virginia Kaye
Geoffrey Keen
Don Knotts
Karen Kristin
Frances Langford
Isidor Lateiner
Paula Laurence
Dai-Keong Lee
Ernest Lehman
Betty Leighton
Loretta Leversee
Richard Lewine
Al Lewis
Donald Linahan
Ann Loring
Sid Luft
Lillian Lux
June MacCloy
Susan MacNair
Jay Marshall
John McCabe
Barney McFadden
Darren McGavin
Charles McRae
Anne Meacham
Howard Miller
Constance Moore
Judson Morgan
Terence Morgan
Jeremiah Morris
Howard Morris
Alberta Nelson
Fayard Nicholas
David Nillo
Sheree North
Louise Nye
Fifi Oscard
Jean Parker

Rex Partington
Graham Payne
Brock Peters
Helen Phillips
Kenneth Porter
Ford Rainey
Charles Randall
Ron Randell
Lou Rawls
Dana Reeve
Mark Roberts
Patricia Roe
Maurice Rosenfield
Drusilla Ross
Gene Ross
Renee Roy
Kalman Ruttenstein
Gloria Willis Shenefield
John Seitz
Katharine Sergava
Raymond Serra
Diane Shalet
Palmer Shannon
Mildred Shay
Norman Shelly
Danny Simon
Jane Lawrence Smith
Lane Smith
Muriel Spark
John Spencer
Maureen Stapleton
Donald Stewart
Harold J. Stone
Paul Straney
Rod Strong
Enzo Stuarti
David Tabor
David Tebet
Lorna Thayer
Guy Thomajan
Frankie Thomas
Donald Tick
Geoffrey Toone
Ted Tulchin
Beverly Tyler
Michael Vale
Paul Valentine
Luther Vandross
Frederic B. Vogel
George D. Wallace
Herta Ware
Wendy Wasserstein
Arnold Weinstein
Louise Westergaard
Ronald Weyand
Alice White
Charles White
Taylor Williams
August Wilson
Shelley Winters
Robert Wise
Rose Teed Wohlstetter
Robert Wright
Richard Zobel

Index

Index

Index

Index

Index

Index

Index

Index

Index

Index

Index

Index

Index

Index

Index

Index

Index

Index

Index